The Concealment
of the State

CONTEMPORARY ANARCHIST STUDIES

A series edited by

Laurence Davis *National University of Ireland, Maynooth*
Uri Gordon *Arava Institute for Environmental Studies, Israel*
Nathan Jun *Midwestern State University, USA*
Alex Prichard *London School of Economics, UK*

Contemporary Anarchist Studies promotes the study of anarchism as a framework for understanding and acting on the most pressing problems of our times. The series publishes cutting-edge, socially engaged scholarship from around the world—bridging theory and practice, academic rigor and the insights of contemporary activism.

The topical scope of the series encompasses anarchist history and theory broadly construed; individual anarchist thinkers; anarchist-informed analysis of current issues and institutions; and anarchist or anarchist-inspired movements and practices. Contributions informed by anti-capitalist, feminist, ecological, indigenous, and non-Western or global South anarchist perspectives are particularly welcome. So, too, are manuscripts that promise to illuminate the relationships between the personal and the political aspects of transformative social change, local and global problems, and anarchism and other movements and ideologies. Above all, we wish to publish books that will help activist scholars and scholar activists think about how to challenge and build real alternatives to existing structures of oppression and injustice.

International Editorial Advisory Board:

Martha Ackelsberg, *Smith College*
John Clark, *Loyola University*
Jesse Cohn, *Purdue University*
Ronald Creagh, *Université Paul Valéry*
Marianne Enckell, *Centre International de Recherches sur l'Anarchisme*
Benjamin Franks, *University of Glasgow*
Judy Greenway, *University of East London*
Ruth Kinna, *Loughborough University*
Todd May, *Clemson University*
Salvo Vaccaro, *Università di Palermo*
Lucien van der Walt, *University of the Witwatersrand*
Charles Weigl, *AK Press*

The Concealment of the State

Jason Royce Lindsey

B L O O M S B U R Y

NEW YORK · LONDON · NEW DELHI · SYDNEY

Bloomsbury Academic

An imprint of Bloomsbury Publishing Plc

1385 Broadway	50 Bedford Square
New York	London
NY 10018	WC1B 3DP
USA	UK

www.bloomsbury.com

First published 2013

Library of Congress Cataloging-in-Publication Data
Lindsey, Jason Royce.
The concealment of the state : explaining and challenging the postmodern studies / Jason Royce Lindsey.
pages cm – (Contemporary anarchist studies)
Includes bibliographical references and index.
ISBN 978-1-4411-0206-5 (pbk.) – ISBN 978-1-4411-7245-7 (hardcover) 1. State, The.
2. Capitalism. 3. Anarchism. 4. Sovereignty. I. Title.
JC11.L55 2013
320.1–dc23
2013012217

ISBN: HB: 978-1-4411-7245-7
PB: 978-1-4411-0206-5
ePub: 978-1-4411-4123-1
ePDF: 978-1-4411-4856-8

Typeset by Integra Software Services Pvt. Ltd.
Printed and bound in the United States of America

For Holly

CONTENTS

ACKNOWLEDGMENTS

The main catalyst for *Concealment of the State* was my participation in the first annual conference of the Anarchist Studies Network (ASN) held at the University of Loughborough in 2008. After exchanging ideas with such an interesting group of peers, I began to devote much more time to some questions that are central to contemporary Anarchist Studies. How has political ideology changed following the end of the Cold War? What are the similarities and differences between our current period of global capitalism and that faced by the anarchists of the nineteenth and early twentieth centuries? How well does the anarchist critique fit contemporary nation states? Through the efforts of many people, including Ruth Kinna and Dave Berry at Loughborough University, the Anarchist Studies Network held its second "annual" conference there in 2012. My experience at the second ASN conference provided the inspiration to finish the manuscript. My thanks to the many organizers and participants.

I also learned about the proposed *Contemporary Anarchist Studies* book series through the ASN. Thanks to the series editors—Laurence Davis, Alex Prichard, Uri Gordon, and Nathan Jun—for their interest and constructive criticism. Alex Prichard is owed particular thanks for his guidance on how to put together a better book proposal. All were very supportive of my effort to contribute to the field of Anarchist Studies. Thanks are owed as well to my editor Ally Jane Grossan at Bloomsbury and to Marie-Claire Antoine for steering the proposal through its first steps. The final version of this book is better thanks to their input, though responsibility for errors and oversights rests with me.

I wrote the main draft of *Concealment of the State* while on a sabbatical from my home institution in Minnesota, St. Cloud State University. I also received a reduction in my teaching assignment the following year from the School of Public Affairs while finishing the book. This support for research time outside of the classroom was critical for completing the project. I owe special thanks to Dr Orn Bodvarsson, Dean of the School of Public Affairs, for his support. This support for research in contemporary Anarchist Studies shows that academic freedom, and the commitment to open inquiry, can still be found in US higher education. All of us in academia should work to make sure things stay that way through our professional organizations.

Some material presented in *Concealment of the State* appeared in three of my earlier publications. Two of these instances concern my discussion of coercion found in Chapter 4, "Engines of Oppression." An earlier description of the changing US military appears in my essay "America and the New Dynamics of War," *Peace Review*, vol. 19, no. 2, April 2007, pp. 255–60. An earlier discussion of the philosophical implications of non–lethal force technologies can be found in my article "Vattimo's Renunciation of Violence," *Ethical Theory and Moral Practice*, vol. 16, no. 1, February 2013, pp. 99–111. Some of the material discussing anarchist critiques of the state, presented in the conclusion, can also be found in my article "Functional Representation and Its Anarchist Origins," *Anarchist Studies*, vol. 18, no. 2, Autumn 2010, pp. 85–100. My thanks to all of the editors and publishers for permission to use excerpts from theses works here.

The most important collaborator for me to acknowledge is my wife, Holly Evers. It is thanks to her observations and criticisms that the arguments presented here became clearer. Several policy examples and political controversies that I use to illustrate my argument were also suggested by her. Holly's painstaking editing made my "final" manuscript much more comprehensible, for which my subsequent editors are no doubt grateful.

Jason Royce Lindsey
February 2013
Kharkiv, Ukraine

1

The concealment of the state

Our contemporary political discourse is dominated by the economic logic of capitalism. This growing monopoly over our political imaginations seems inevitable as the lessons of capitalism are applied to more and more areas of human life. This attempt to expand the use of economic "science" includes popular books that "explore the hidden side of everything," because "if morality represents how people would like the world to work, then economics shows how it actually does work."[1] The mechanics of the market are so familiar that many of us assume it is "natural," and we attempt to study it as we would study physics or chemistry. This iron-clad conception of reality also pushes for the privatization of traditional state services in the name of efficiency.

Thanks to this worldview, the inevitable political question that follows all government activity today is whether the market could provide the service or good more effectively. The story of how corporations have provided human beings with new methods for exploiting natural, financial, and human capital has become more familiar to us than the state's provision of public goods. Indeed, in the United States, the importance of the corporation has been enshrined by the Supreme Court's decision to expand the historical (and individual) "freedom of speech" protection to corporations engaged in political lobbying.[2] As a result of this intellectual trend, the state has been diminished in our political consciousness. Increasingly, the state is characterized as the less nimble, antiquated player in comparison to the dynamic free market.

However, states have not gone away, and, without them, the economic system we know would disappear. Much of the research investment underlying impressive new technologies, medical treatments, and the continued development of the fine arts is dependent upon state financial support. On a deeper level, the legal framework for corporations and the initial guarantee underpinning most transactions and agreements originate with the state's sovereignty. All of us routinely sign contracts and agreements ranging from consumer purchases to health insurance. In the most developed countries, we confidently agree to pay for services from faceless entities we know only as a brand. Yet, we feel comfortable engaging in such trust because we know that our legal systems are the ultimate arbiter of any potential disputes. In this sense, the state is the "unmoved mover" of our modern social world; the state's sovereignty is the first guarantee that anchors all others.

In addition, states are arguably the most important consumer in the market. Among the OECD states, government spending accounts on average for just over 19 percent of all economic activity.[3] The privatization of services is at its core, resulting in the transfer of taxpayer monies, collected by the state, to corporations and firms. The contracts for private companies to provide services ranging from garbage collection and education to policing and space travel are awarded by states and paid for by the public. What is the difference from public provision? The garbage collectors, space engineers, security guards, and their managers are technically not government employees, though the public is paying them one step removed. Indeed, the state's sovereignty underlies much of our daily consumer activity. The state regulates our work environment and may even pay our salary. However, the championing of contemporary economic thinking has slowly displaced our awareness of this fact.

Nonetheless, the state continues to play an enormous role in our lives. This has been a fact of human existence for centuries. States are arguably the most important of all human inventions since they mark a turning point in our evolution. Using the state, we harnessed the physical strength, intellectual creativity, and other talents of our populations for unprecedented economic growth and resource extraction. States provided society with the organization necessary to alleviate poverty, create educational institutions, and promote universal literacy. We have used the governing capacity of states to create a global market, as well as redistribute domestic resources. Of course, states have also exploited the scientific potential of societies to develop increasingly lethal military technologies. States also presided over industrial policies that have left us with permanent ecological damage. States brought a powerful new form of organization to human society, and we have used it for both good and ill, as with any other human invention.

Thinking about the state as a human invention can help us to better understand its overwhelming influence on history. However, the nation state differs from other inventions on one important point: it contains and is dependent on an enormous amount of human agency. It consists of institutions that are staffed by human beings who decide and implement the state's actions. The power these individuals wield through the state raises profoundly difficult moral questions. Why do they have the authority to act on behalf of others? What are the moral limits of the coercive power they exercise? How can human beings keep the state accountable, rather than falling into subservience to it?

These philosophical questions have accompanied the development of the state from its earliest inception. The results of this line of classical inquiry are various theories of political legitimacy. We can map this intellectual journey from the early, supernatural justifications of monarchical rule in Egypt and Mesopotamia, through the Greek's justifications and rankings of *poleis*, to contemporary theories about improving democracy. The increasing sophistication of these theories parallels the evolution of state structures. Yet, even in those political systems that strive for transparency and democratic accountability, the question of who is doing what, where, and why looms large. As nation states have taken on additional responsibilities, made use of increasingly sophisticated technology, and grown to govern millions of citizens, this thread of human agency becomes difficult to follow.

In contemporary times, another level of complexity further obscures the human agency of the state. The phenomenon labeled by the catchall term "globalization" has pushed accountability ever more toward the horizon. Today, when we attempt to unravel who owns some of our local businesses, we are confronted with chains of capital that are transnational. When we demand accountability or action from our local state authorities, they often patiently explain to us how the free market works. Citizens worried about a local impact, such as the zoning of a new superstore, the environmental consequences of development, or the threat to local employment due to outsourcing, are told that little can be done. Free trade agreements that allow capital to flow across borders and rules of private investment that trump the commons hinder action on local community concerns.

What is the primary motivation for states to participate in this system of global capitalism? Isn't it paradoxical for nation states to jealously assert their sovereignty vis-à-vis other states while allowing global capitalism to whittle away their authority? In the case of democratic political systems, it seems illogical for the state to allow democratic control to wither locally for the sake of foreign capital. Why do contemporary nation states participate in an economic system that undermines their sovereignty?

It is in fact the state's goal of maintaining sovereignty that forces very different political regimes from around the planet to pursue globalization. Power in the international system is intertwined with economic competitiveness. Only states with a highly productive economy can develop the technology that lies behind modern military might. Only states with large economies influence multinational meetings like the G20. Thus, the state's *raison d'être*, its sovereignty, compels it to participate in the global economy, even though that participation is at odds with the immediate interests of much of the population.

For example, political groups advocating increased taxes to fund community assistance, education, or health care provisions are warned that this is either impossible or unrealistic since it would undermine the national economy's competitiveness. How can the state take the risk of investing in such concerns if other states ignore them? Instead, the state must channel its efforts into fostering immediate economic growth or risk falling behind those powers that do. This competition leads the state to demand many sacrifices from its population. The power of the state could be harnessed to provide additional social benefits, but it would be at a cost to economic performance. This stark choice creates a political dilemma for contemporary nation states.

Globalization rewards states that integrate into the international economic regime. However, the citizenry of these states demand a set of conflicting responses. Some economic elites support this vision of autonomous markets. For this interest group, the continued existence of sovereign states is an ongoing interference into the "natural" activity of global markets; the state is too sovereign. From another quarter, much of the citizenry demands policies that run counter to the free-market orthodoxy of globalization. For this interest group, the sovereign state is failing to mitigate the problems created by globalization; the state is not sovereign enough.

States augment their power, and thus their capacities to exercise coercion and guarantee their sovereignty, through economic success. Yet, contemporary economic health is linked with integration into a global capitalist economy that appears to ignore sovereign borders. How can the state maintain its usefulness if its sovereignty is eroded? If states are no longer sovereign, then why should we support them? On the other hand, how can a contemporary state guarantee its sovereignty in the world other than by joining the economic competition of globalization? This paradox explains the contemporary difficulty of legitimizing state power within a context of globalizing capitalism.

The ideological solution for contemporary states is to maintain their sovereign agency while insisting that they have given much of it up to the new rules of global capitalism. Today, the state claims that its creation, the market, has become even more autonomous than in the past and stands as an alternate entity to the state. The state can then retreat behind the screen of the "free" market to answer both camps in contemporary society. For the winners of globalization, the state appears to get out of the way of market innovation and productivity. For the citizenry alarmed at globalization's outcomes, the state claims to be powerless against the inevitable. Contemporary states put forward this position despite the fact that they provide the regulatory infrastructure the market relies upon and the sovereign guarantee necessary to underpin all other agreements, including transnational free trade agreements. States will also violate all the usual "rules" and intervene into the market when necessary to prevent its collapse.

However, state sovereignty, by its very nature, is a competition with other states. This competition requires participation in the global economy in a race to stay ahead of other states. The importance of this fact, and the bearing it has on the continued existence of the state, trumps popular concerns with globalization's effects. Thus, there is a common interest in maintaining the useful fiction of an inevitable and autonomous global capitalism. For many economic elites, this belief reinforces their class interests. For political elites, this ideology is important because of the power it confers on the state. For many inside and outside of our ruling elite, this ideology reflects a certainty that seems so obvious it is unquestioned.

Nonetheless, there is an obvious contradiction in this ideology. The state cannot strengthen its sovereignty by participating in a regime that undermines it. Yet, contemporary states that are well integrated into the global economic system seem to be the most powerful of all. This paradox dissolves once we realize that states have turned to the ideology of concealing their agency. This concealment relies in part on the diversion of political demands into the closed ideological system of free-market orthodoxy.

The politics of concealment

Increasingly, politicians and policy makers from across the political spectrum insist that the market is an immovable force that constrains their ability to act. To maintain this facade, contemporary states have bifurcated their functions into two broad areas: the deep and shallow state. The shallow state has been freed from much of the policy formulation and implementation that is truly constrained by the needs of state sovereignty. Instead, this important function now rests with the less visible deep state. By compartmentalizing many responsibilities to the deep state, the shallow state can proclaim the limitations of state action imposed by the market, despite the implausible contradictions of this claim.

Although this ideological turn allows contemporary states to dissolve the immediate tensions of globalization, it is also transforming traditional political dynamics. By bifurcating politics into a deep and shallow state, contemporary states hide their ability to act, but at a cost. Political actors in the shallow state are left to visibly debate policies, which, from the outset, have been closely circumscribed by the actions of the deep state. This shift of responsibility allows politicians in the shallow state to pursue votes with popular, or populist, policies that ignore increasingly hard economic and ecological constraints. To some extent, politicians must engage with their constituents (and with each other) in this circumscribed, populist arena because so many issues of substance have been removed from their sphere of influence.

While the state has traditionally had to maintain secrecy in some areas (e.g. defense, intelligence, or the all-pervasive category of "security"), we now see a shift of even mundane policy decisions to less visible agencies in the deep state. Examples include budget recommendations, environmental regulations, consumer and workplace safety, scientific investment, transportation planning, and educational policies. Thus, elected officials can grandstand on what issues are left in this hollowed out, shallow arena of politics. With substantive (and often unpopular) policy made and implemented in the deep state, we see the remains of politics in the shallows. Here the focus is increasingly on national identity, cultural controversy, consumer frustrations, and symbolic acts of solidarity with constituents. Politicians in the shallow state have come to rely on the quiet competence of the deep state and have little incentive to engage publicly with the difficult policy choices facing society.

This book maps the ideological and functional logic that makes this behavior seem "natural" to the human actors who are, collectively, the state. As I show in the subsequent chapters, political actors within both the deep and shallow state, despite still having sharp disputes on many topics, have come to accept the concealment of the state as a background assumption to contemporary politics. I do not argue that this acceptance is necessarily a conscious one for most political actors and state functionaries. Instead, this behavior can be thought of as agents within the state following an "institutional logic" that colors their perception and frames the choice of actions available to policy makers.[4]

For example, under the pressures of global capitalism, many states have reduced their services to achieve macroeconomic stability. Consider the remarkable responses of governments to economic crisis in 2008 and 2009. In the United States and many other countries, rather than an expansion of welfare services, most state assistance was directed toward large financial organizations. Although many commentators criticized these "bail outs," fierce criticism was also directed at practically any state assistance to the citizenry in the aftermath of the crisis. Stimulus spending by governments, modest extensions of unemployment insurance, and assistance to local levels of government were routinely attacked in the popular media. Thus, the startling twist in the political fallout from the crisis is that this criticism came from those sections of the population that state assistance was supposed to help.

This phenomenon shows the extent to which states have found a useful ideological logic in the concealment of the state. The removal or reduction of services to the population has become associated with responsible economic management. As a result, we see in European countries, ranging in size from Great Britain to Latvia, the possibility of securing popular support by pledging austerity.[5] In the United States, we see a popular movement, the Tea Party, demanding that candidates implement pro-business austerity measures to reduce deficit spending. The economic crisis of 2008 also provoked the authoritarian (and notionally still communist) government of China to protest over interference in the free market from the currency policies of the United States. Whether supposedly left or right wing, authoritarian or democratic, a common ideology is beginning to cut across our traditional political divisions.

What about those cases where the citizenry still makes demands of the state? In the aftermath of the great recession of 2008, we have seen governments in Greece insist that they must implement austerity, despite massive protests in 2012, because of "economic reality." In Italy that same year, a technocratic, caretaker government was hailed as a positive development since it would remove politics from responsible economic management. Thus, decisions about taxing, spending, and what to cut from public budgets were safely removed from politics in these Western democracies.

In all of these cases, the foundation for this political orientation (which claims to be a reality outside of and above politics) is the widespread acceptance that the state should only provide a minimal level of benefits and services to its population. The rest of what the citizenry needs is to be fulfilled through their individual agency within a market as free as possible from government interference. In turn, citizens accepting this view see the state retreating from their lives as social benefits are withdrawn. Privatization of various services leaves more and more citizens with market relationships rather than political ones. This pattern satisfies the ideological imperative to rely on markets rather than the "heavy hand of government." Of course, there are still political rituals such as voting and some remaining vestiges of local participation, especially in federal political systems. Yet, to many individual citizens, the state has retreated from the horizon of their daily perception.

Evidence for this trend can be seen in its duplication around the world. As in the past, the ideological norms of the developed states are transmitted to developing societies through cultural, economic, and political connections. Thus, some supporting evidence for my argument is the parallel movement we find in the developing countries. Those states have taken up this same behavior, but with some delay. The same processes of influence, cajoling, seduction, and coercion that originally pushed societies into adopting the nation state are now pushing them to adopt the contemporary ideology of the most developed, postmodern states.

The other cache of evidence is in the ideological reactions we see to incidents that expose the state's ability to act. When faced with great risk, society falls back to an earlier position of looking to the state. However, this sudden surfacing of the state provokes convoluted political responses in a desperate effort to bridge an ideology that denies the state can act with urgent, practical needs. In the case of the United States, we see the odd political maneuvers that have followed in the aftermath of the threat of terrorism and natural disaster.

For example, in the aftermath of the terrorist attacks on September 11, 2001, there was the startling call by President Bush for patriots to continue shopping. By fulfilling their duty as consumers, that is maintaining their market relationships, the citizenry could keep America strong. How else should the citizenry be mobilized in response to such an event? Yet, this call for citizens to remain active in the free market accompanied startling state actions, ranging from the invasion of Afghanistan to extraordinary rendition and the "enhanced interrogation" of suspects. Thus, American citizens were told to show their patriotism and fulfill their longing to help by going about their important daily business of market transactions. In contrast, the decisive, sharp end of the state was deployed without conscription, without a formal declaration of war, or other traditional *political* actions that call attention to the power of the state.

Or, in another striking example from the United States in 2005, the country witnessed the complete breakdown of civilization in New Orleans after hurricane Katrina decimated the city. At first, government reaction seemed to show only an inexplicable inertia. This initial paralysis was quickly followed by odd commentaries that asked why poorer residents, living in one of the areas of deep poverty in the United States, had not saved themselves by evacuating. In other words, why did citizens think that their government would save them from natural disaster? Why would they think the state has the power to do so? Isn't it unrealistic to expect the state to protect all of its citizens in this way? On the other hand, the authorities eventually took action to assist the city's beleaguered residents. This belated intervention took place against another set of commentaries: is the United States still a powerful, developed country given that the government cannot muster an adequate response to a natural disaster?

In this sense, the concealment of the state allows for paradox. The state can assert that it has no agency to employ when it is able to shift burdens onto the population within the market sphere. However, if this denial of agency begins to be perceived as weakness, the state can unleash coercion with less political cost or oversight. Thus, we have the paradox of supposedly globalized and less sovereign states that, nonetheless, possess unprecedented instruments of coercion and surveillance.

More globally, we see this phenomenon tied to the political fallout from an increasing awareness of universal environmental risks. Many individuals voice concern about the environment in global public opinion polling. However, in a classic "free rider" problem, citizens around the world also voice frustration at the fact that, acting alone, they cannot do anything about it.[6] Even if the individual tries to make a difference, their effort seems hopeless in the face of transnational problems like climate change. The failure of collective action in this policy area may also be driving some individuals to take more extreme, direct action. As I discuss below, the deep state has begun to prepare for environmental challenges despite arguments in the shallows over whether a problem even exists.

An interpretation of politics as broad as mine should raise some immediate skeptical questions. Perhaps the most obvious counterfactual to my argument is this: if this is a new hegemonic ideology, then when did it start? The contention of this work is that its origins lie at the end of the

Cold War. While many studies (including ones that claimed to be autopsies) were applied to the former Soviet Union, few have stopped to consider how deeply the end of this conflict affected the United States and the "developed" world.[7] Yet, the end of the Cold War was also the end of many political certainties for the West. In this sense, the concealment of the state is an ideological reaction to the new political, social, and economic challenges that states face in our post–Cold War world.

The collapse of communist regimes discredited statist economic systems and removed a rival example from the mental map of the world. During the Cold War, state involvement in the economy and daily life in the West could always be contrasted to the extremes of the Eastern Bloc. Now in the twenty-first century, even modest interventions into the economy of the United States are labeled totalitarian, communist, or socialist by partisan opponents. Perhaps one could argue that there has always been a tendency to such inflated and alarmist rhetoric in the political systems of the West, especially in the United States. However, the discrediting of state socialism has led to a general skepticism of the state having a role in any area of everyday life. As I discuss in a later chapter, this skepticism is now so profound that it has led to efforts to conceal the state's role in exercising coercion and, in the most traditional state role of all, national defense.

In addition, the end of the Cold War cleared the way ideologically for the triumph of neoliberal capitalism as the new global status quo. The tension between the benefits to the state's capabilities from the globalization of capitalism and the backlash among the population from globalization's fallout creates a fundamental contradiction. One logical response would be for politicians to clearly make the case for globalization or, at least, argue that its benefits outweigh its shortcomings. However, this response carries the risk of rejection by the population. Such a rejection would be incompatible with the state's need to participate in this system. Instead, by concealing the ability of the state to act, policy makers can make globalization and its effects on the population seem inevitable. This ideological maneuver limits political debate to "responsible" discourse about when and where we should mitigate the effects of global capitalism.

Aside from its impact upon contemporary politics, the concealment of the state also has a wider cultural impact. In turn, this cultural influence feeds back into the political system. As the state's positive importance becomes more hidden, the citizenry of the most developed countries begins to think of politics and government only as an interference. Suburbanization has probably fed this tendency, at least in the United States and other developed countries. In such communities, the illusion of a modern self-sufficiency easily takes hold. As commuters do not rely on public transport and withdraw into their private homes, the idea that they do not need government becomes common. They see themselves as maintaining their homes, their private transportation, and their private schools, and become unaware of the deeper infrastructure they depend upon. This includes the state's maintenance of a legal framework that supports the ownership of private property and that requires safety in the products they consume.

By exposing this behavior and giving it easily comprehensible labels, I hope that popular political activity from below can challenge it more effectively. Otherwise, our political systems are likely to become increasingly opaque despite our traditional forms of participation like voting, grassroots interest group organization, unionization of the workplace, and, at the end of the day, demonstrations or strikes. These forms of political activity were progressive in the nineteenth and twentieth centuries. However, it is difficult to imagine how they can pressure the state in the future, when, from the outset, the state denies that it has the ability to meet our demands.

Ideology and the state

My core argument is that the concealment of the state is a recent ideological turn. Unfortunately, ideology is often seen as a slippery foundation for the scientific study of politics. In recent decades, the methodology of rational choice has become a dominant approach in political science. This turn toward rational choice is popular since it promises political science a firmer foundation for its studies, one akin to the core assumptions of economics.[8] Thus, an attempt at linking broad political realities to ideological motivations is, from the outset, open to criticism from political science methodologies that attempt to distill politics to clearer, value-free analysis. On the other hand, adopting methodologies that exclude concerns of value such as justice, equality, or freedom seems doomed to fall into a pattern of economic rather than *political* analysis. The political salience of these ideals is not what any of those values ultimately are. Few contemporary philosophers hold out any hope for settling such perennial questions. What is important for politics is what individuals think those values are.

There is an alternative, influential methodology in political science that is more akin to the perspective adopted here. Generally described as "new institutionalism," this approach looks more broadly at institutional constraints and the way structure influences policy. While still assuming that individuals are behaving rationally, this approach attempts to place that behavior within a realistic social and political context. While individuals are indeed probably pursuing interests and policies they consider rational, they do so within an environment that influences what they consider to be possible, plausible, and the best, or morally correct, course of action.

Hall and Rosemary have provided a typology of the "new institutionalism" that has influenced political science over the last two decades.[9] Among these frameworks is historical institutionalism, which includes a cultural approach. As the authors explain,

From this perspective, institutions provide moral or cognitive templates for interpretation and action. The individual is seen as an entity deeply embedded in a world of institutions, composed of symbols, scripts, and routines, which provide filters for interpretation of both the situation and oneself, out of which a course of action is constructed. Not only do institutions provide strategically useful information, they also affect the very identities, self-images and preferences of the actors.[10]

Thus, the concept of ideology becomes more concrete when we firmly link it to the historical development of specific institutions. In addition, the policy choices made by these institutions can serve as further evidence for the worldviews of the actors serving within them.

The use of such a methodology is critically important for understanding the contemporary state. The state is a collection of human agents organized into various institutions. The perceptual framework of these human beings shapes the choices they make, their convictions about the use or misuse of power, and their belief in what is best for society. From the perspective of historical institutionalism, change is created from the conflict of views and interests that human beings pursue within these institutions.[11] What is striking about our contemporary times is the similar ideological outlook of political elites across differing societies.

Nonetheless, whenever one turns to a discussion of ideology, the ground is in many ways less firm. In sociological theory, we can find the concept stretched across a broad range of human activity. For example, Mann in his classic study of social power describes the rise of world religions as the triumph of ideological power.[12] Further back in the sociological canon, we have Weber's example of linking the development of capitalism with the Protestant work ethic.[13] Thus, ideology can quickly become a very expansive concept. In this sense, ideology can become the explanation for more and more areas of social life. There is also a risk when studying ideology to dismiss human action as driven by irrational cultural factors.

In contrast, my use of the concept of ideology is focused more narrowly on the political. Using ideology for more narrowly defined political analysis carries risks too. In this more restricted view, ideology can easily become a simplistic explanation of class politics. In his classic formulation, Marx argued that an ideology performs two very important functions. One is that it takes something historically contingent, for Marx this was the capitalist market, and transforms it into an everlasting universal. Second, an effective ideology explains the order of things so that everyone theoretically benefits, not just the class in charge. From this perspective, ideology becomes a simple product of class antagonisms.

However, the current behavior of the state extends beyond a simplistic explanation of class behavior. There is also more to it than the relationship between the market and the state, discussed so frequently by a range of scholars and activists. This includes sophisticated studies of the so-called "power elite."[14] Arguably the most developed criticisms of the state in this category examine the United States.[15] In some cases the analysis of this elite relies on traditional Marxist categories of class. However, the inspiration for this school of thought is the idea that Marx's definition of a ruling class has become hopelessly antiquated. In Mills' classic study, he attempted to expand the definition of the ruling elite to include those that direct culture as well as politics and capital. He argued that

> The power elite are not solitary rulers. Advisers and consultants, spokesmen and opinion-makers are often the captains of their higher thought and decision. Immediately below the elite are the professional politicians of the middle levels of power, in the Congress and in the pressure groups, as well as among the new and old upper classes of town and city and region. Mingling with them, in curious ways which we shall explore, are those professional celebrities who live by being continually displayed but are never, so long as they remain celebrities, displayed enough. If such celebrities are not at the head of any dominating hierarchy, they do often have the power to distract the attention of the public or afford sensations to the masses, or, more directly, to gain the ear of those who do occupy positions of direct power.[16]

Thus, elite studies have attempted to broaden our understanding of who rules to fit our contemporary times.

Yet, even these broader studies tend to explain elite membership and elite behavior in terms of concrete benefits. Although it is difficult to deny that wealthy individuals benefit from current political and economic orthodoxy (i.e. that there is a relevant separation between market and state), there is also a deeper conviction present. For these individuals, the "reality" of the market is an obvious refutation of political interference. This argument resonates so strongly in current society that we find it enthusiastically proclaimed by many individuals who are clearly not in the class that sits atop globalization. For many individuals, the market is the home of their aspirations despite the odds they face.

Furthermore, a second group has an interest that is often absent in the usual critique of class interests or the hidden relationships of the state and market. To individuals serving in the institutions and agencies of the state, maintaining the power of the state is important for the common good. From their perspective, society needs the organizational power that the state provides. Without this force, how can one right wrongs in society and protect the vulnerable? The ideal of a career in "public service" is based upon this very basic idea that the state exists for the benefit of society. From this perspective, the state must constantly enhance its capabilities for maintaining sovereignty to continue its beneficial role.

Thus, my discussion of ideology has a more focused target than broader sociological studies, but at the same time, it is not a narrow discussion of class politics. There are cultural implications from this ideological turn, which I explore in a later chapter. However, even when examining the cultural fallout from this set of ideas, my concern remains focused on its political implications. My argument is an attempt to explain how a particular political development has become both so prevalent and unquestioned. It is in this sense that my study is one of ideology.

Does the state still exist?

The concealment of the state is not confined to conscious efforts to assist in ideological obfuscation. Critics of the state, including some currents within contemporary anarchist thinking, question whether the state even exists, or, more accurately, whether it is useful to think about the state as a separate, concrete institution. For example, Richard J.F. Day's reflections on the work of Foucault and Lefort lead him to argue that activist politics needs to move on beyond making demands of the state.[17] From this perspective, the state has metastasized into society. Now that the state's mechanisms of discipline are everywhere, the state is in effect nowhere.

Thus, the state as a separate, comprehensible institution is gone, and Foucault is right in criticizing anyone who still thinks that a revolution must behead the king. On the other hand, Foucault himself states,

> I don't want to say that the state isn't important; what I want to say is that relations of power, and hence the analysis that must be made of them, necessarily extend beyond the limits of the state in two senses. First of all, because the state, for all the omnipotence of its apparatuses, is far from being able to occupy the whole field of actual power relations; and further, because the state can only operate on the basis of other, already-existing power relations.[18]

In this sense, Foucault does not dismiss the state, but wants to expand our understanding of power. For Foucault, this is essential to grasping the creative aspects of power beyond the repressive power we associate with the state.

Thanks to Foucault's insight, this broader perspective on power, and its expansion across social space, underlies many observations about contemporary society. For example, in the burgeoning field of surveillance studies, the current consensus is that surveillance, and its social effects, must be approached as the study of something more than state action. Although the state does engage in surveillance and deploys cutting-edge technology for this purpose, individuals encounter surveillance pervasively throughout society in the most developed countries. Thus, the recent trend in surveillance studies is to explore the "assemblages" of surveillance found in the market as well as the state's activities.[19] The main thrust of this line of inquiry is that aside from the surveillance activities of the state, we increasingly find individuals being tracked in the developed world through credit reports and various market tools. Arguably, the disciplining effects of surveillance outside of the state have a profound effect on the behavior of individuals in the developed world compared to state surveillance directed toward traditional concerns of security and military affairs.[20]

I suggest an additional complication with our reading of this situation; there is agency and design to the contemporary state's declining visibility. The state is still an important institution, but this fact has become more difficult to see thanks to ideological camouflage. Rather than arguing that the market is doing the disciplining of the state, rendering the state somewhat obsolete, we should consider the possibility that there is no independent, free market. From this perspective, the state has not metastasized into society and become less relevant. Instead, the state has greatly expanded its control of society by employing surveillance and discipline at a distance. This sleight of hand allows the state to creep into (or to use the terminology of Jurgen Habermas, "colonize") more and more areas of life. Nonetheless, the state remains an organized institution behind this colonized front.

For example, drawing again upon research in surveillance studies, why has surveillance of individuals thrived? In the United States, the state has decided to allow credit bureaus to co-opt the social security number of citizens to aid surveillance. Various mechanisms for tracking individuals online for marketing purposes are cleared by state agencies for deployment. The US government opened up the GPS system, initially designed and deployed for military purposes, for commercial exploitation. These efforts have now led to the ability of law enforcement to subpoena and track individuals through their cell phones. Thus, it is obviously true that a comprehensive understanding of surveillance today requires scholars to examine market and commercial activities as well as state actions. Nonetheless, the linchpin for these efforts and the approval for operating these commercial forms of surveillance always lead back to the state and its decisions.

If we delve deeper into the intellectual history of anarchism, then we often find claims that the state does not really exist. Rather than an independent institution, we are told that the state is a false category serving one or more different purposes. In some interpretations, the state is an idea for obfuscating the power of the ruling class. In other descriptions, the state's purpose is reifying the rule of some human beings over others. Or, more abstractly, the state is seen as a fictional, ideological entity that embodies economic power (which is the *real* source of power).

However, this line of argument often blends together two things: the state and metaphysical claims of who or what inhabits it. For example, the idea of the nation or country is often blended together in the literature with the state. Anarchist literature can easily compare arguments about the political legitimacy of European states (whether based on the divine right of kings, nationalism, or other traditions) to theological arguments.

For Bakunin, the concept of state sovereignty is an obvious parallel to the role of God, the unmoved mover, in various theologies. In both cases, we find metaphysical claims that are often irrational. Yet, behind these irrational claims, the state is still a real force in the world. As Bakunin noted,

> The state is force, and for it, first of all, is the right of force, the triumphant argument of the needle-gun, of the *chassepot*. But man is so singularly constituted that this argument, wholly eloquent as it may appear, is not sufficient in the long run. Some moral sanction or other is absolutely necessary to enforce his respect.[21]

Nations are much like God in this sense. One chooses to believe in them or not. The state though is a much more real entity. Anyone who fails to pay his taxes can find out how real the state is when it comes to collect. There is also a very sharp end to contemporary states when we look at their coercive abilities. Thus, we should distinguish between describing the institutions that are the state, staffed by "real" human beings, and the metaphysical ideas, including ones about nations, countries, and supernatural beings, that legitimate these institutions.

On the other hand, skepticism about using the state as a category of analysis does emphasize an important point. The success of the state's colonization of much that we regard as "social" is beyond dispute. However, this does not mean that the state, which is everywhere, is now nowhere. Instead, this looming presence of the state in more and more areas of life creates the contradictions that have lead to the ideology of concealment. The increase in our dependence on the state, and its ever-growing invincibility, undermines many of the ideas that have legitimated it in the past. Thus, we see a turn toward a new ideology, one that attempts to conceal the ubiquitous state. Denying the usefulness of the state as a category of analysis risks aiding this concealment.

A postmodern state?

Rather than denying that the state exists, or that it matters, we should instead look at states as they are. Just as the state has, through previous centuries, undergone many changes, so too the contemporary state differs from the past. For want of a better term, we can describe contemporary states as postmodern. Unfortunately, the term "postmodern" has become overused to the point of almost losing any meaning. Nonetheless, it can serve as a marker for us if we are attempting to distinguish the current nation state from its past iterations.

The term "postmodernism" was coined to try and express the idea that our contemporary situation differs from that of other recent history. In other words, we live in a different context than the recent past. So, too, the context within which contemporary states operate seems fundamentally different from the modern period. Today states must compete within the globalized form of contemporary capitalism to maintain their sovereignty. Thus, contemporary states face a paradoxical situation with global capitalism: it empowers them as well as imposing constraints. Does this mean that the state is postmodern?

The context of globalized capitalism also appears to be one of enormous risk. Increasingly, we face potential global disasters from climate change to the proliferation of nuclear weapons. Yet, our political institutions are organized into nation states with sovereign borders. Transnational risks and policy problems are inherently endemic to such a system. Furthermore, though we are economically interconnected with individuals on the other side of the world, we vote alongside neighbors we barely know.

Both of these observations are closely intertwined with the cultural context of contemporary states. In a recent analysis of this phenomenon and contemporary politics, Paul James notices something similar. Attempting to describe the "postmodern nation," James points out that today

> ...the state is most often viewed either as a baleful institution to be minimized or deregulated or as a necessary, if intrusive, organ of public administration, as a provider of essential services for the vulnerable.[22]

This indeed is the common picture we have of the contemporary nation state. Yet, as James notes further,

> The image of the nation state as an aging Leviathan, more comfortable lumbering amidst the inglorious structures of the past, is belied by the alacrity with which "it" has taken up various administrative techniques such as electronic information storage and other forms of disembodied surveillance.[23]

The quotes around "it," in the above statement, are intended by James as a qualifier. For him, as for so many other theorists, the state is a complicated agglomeration of institutions, individuals, and practices, making it difficult to define. Nonetheless, as these observations by James point out, the state has not gone away.

Thus, we should still be concerned with the state. However, the state we are attempting to understand is different than its earlier, modern form. Or at least, we can say that the problems, international context, and needs of the contemporary state are no longer modern, despite its politics remaining stubbornly modern in form. In this sense, the behavior of the state that I describe in subsequent chapters is an attempt to bridge the continued practice of a modern politics by states confronting the postmodern condition.

Of course, terms like the "postmodern condition" have become suspect to many of us because of weak scholarship. However, the idea and description of the postmodern condition is a useful one so long as we remain clear about what we mean. Lyotard explains the broad cultural atmosphere, historical moment, intellectual perspective, and social context that is the postmodern as "the condition of knowledge in the most highly developed societies."[24] This condition is one of a crisis of legitimation because of the skepticism with which we regard all narratives. From this foundational crack running through contemporary knowledge, profound consequences follow.

The state, too, is affected by this cultural shift. Postmodernism is a challenge to our modern theories of political legitimacy. As Lyotard and other serious scholars of this unfolding moment in intellectual history point out, the most solid characteristic of the postmodern condition is a profound skepticism toward any metanarratives. These narratives include claims of nationalism, religious affirmation, and even the civic myths that underpin our identities as citizens of the state. How does one justify the state's absolute authority in an age where absolutist arguments are viewed with cynicism?

The best example of this quandary is the current efforts in political theory to justify citizenship as a positive category. Skeptics, influenced by the postmodern deconstruction of identity, have questioned how one can morally justify borders. For example, Joseph Carens argues that in today's world, citizenship in the most developed nations is an inherited privilege.[25] The moral luck of one's birthplace has profound consequences. Some of us will experience the educational and health care systems of the developed nations, while others are condemned to grinding poverty. Carens draws the parallel between this luck at birth and the past consequences of being born to privilege or servitude in the feudal age. What moral grounds can justify us excluding individuals who want to come and join our wealthier society? Aren't we just trying to defend our privileged existence?

This problem of political philosophy underpins the current obsession with identity politics. How can we define citizenship in an age skeptical of narratives? On what basis do we decide who belongs? What narrative of identity in our postmodern universe can withstand deconstructive criticism?

Other theorists, such as Benjamin Barber and Richard Dagger, have argued that we can anchor citizenship in the value of democracy.[26] The argument is that we must have citizens to establish functioning democracies. From this perspective too, boundaries are necessary to enable meaningful democratic participation. How can I influence the decisions affecting my neighborhood or county, unless voting is limited to local residents? If instead, I only vote as a global citizen, then how can I meaningfully influence policy that affects my small corner of the world?

Democracy is also the suggested answer for who belongs. Noted theorist Jurgen Habermas argues that we can establish citizenship as an identity solely through legal, constitutional means. Habermas' conception of "constitutional patriotism" suggests that we can create an identity that will hold up the corrosive deconstruction of postmodernism if we remove the past residues of nationalism and other narratives from it.[27]

However, these suggested answers to the dilemma of political legitimacy in our postmodern world cut against the grain of contemporary states. As discussed earlier, globalization has pushed states into an increasingly paradoxical competition. To maintain their sovereignty, they must participate. To provide the guarantees to other states necessary for this system of global capitalism (most starkly free trade agreements), nation states cannot risk too much democratic control of this infrastructure. Thus, the suggestion of theorists like Habermas for more democracy runs headlong into the state's growing reliance on technocratic management.

Similarly, focusing on the need for local boundary drawing, so that citizens can democratically influence local policies, runs counter to the state's needs. Globalization is about reducing barriers to capital. Strengthening local control risks democratic support for "protectionism." At the same time, returning to our modern narratives of political identity runs counter to the needs of contemporary states. Although much of the population in the developed world might be comfortable with such a *revanchist* turn, the state cannot pursue such a turn as real policy. Narratives of nationalism may be used in elections and political marketing; however, our political and economic elites cannot maintain such ideas with a straight face when conducting business across the borders (political and cultural) of global capitalism.

Thus, we have the paradoxes that make up the postmodern state. In our contemporary situation, states lack a description of citizenship that can satisfy postmodern skepticism toward grand narratives of identity. The suggested solution of our contemporary philosophers is to replace these old stories of nationalism and cultural identities (which postmodern deconstruction shows to be hollow) with more transparent democratic procedures. However, that solution poses great risk to the state because the demos might vote to opt out of or restrict global capitalism. Such a turn would make the state less competitive and undermine its strength in the international system.

The solution to this dilemma has become the ideology of concealing the state. While our political systems continue to use institutions, procedures, and rhetoric that is relentlessly modern, the postmodern state conceals itself. Although many of the forms of modern politics are still with us, like elections, lobbying, demonstrations, and local participation, these forms seem more and more antiquated. The rapid changes in communications technology and our popular culture surrounding these changes make politics seem like a backwater of stagnated practices and ideas.

For these various reasons, the postmodern state is an institution that attempts to conceal its agency. By denying it has the power to act, the postmodern state makes the continuing development of globalized capitalism seem inevitable. The postmodern state also claims that the market it has created is now an autonomous entity. This claim allows the state to avoid responding to democratic demands to modify the rules and outcomes of the market. Finally, by concealing its agency, the postmodern state can continue to neglect the ossifying modern political system it inherits from the past. Arguably, the urgency for action in this last area is diffused if we come to believe it does not matter much anyway, especially in comparison to the reality of the market.

With a topic as broad as this, where do we begin? A good starting point is the bifurcation of the contemporary state into a shallow and deep set of institutions. This separation is arguably the central mechanism for the concealment of the state. In many ways, this bifurcation of the state's institutions is also reliant on the idea of a separate free market, autonomous from the state. It can also be argued that this is not a new political development but rather the outcome of a long historical trend. Nonetheless, as I argue in the next chapter, the deep and shallow state has become so important to contemporary politics that one can also argue that it is a defining characteristic of the postmodern state.

Notes

1 Here, I am referring to the enormously popular book: Steven D. Levitt and Stephen J. Dubner, *Freakonomics: A Rogue Economist Explores the Hidden Side of Everything* (New York: Harper Collins, 2006). This quote is from p. 11 of their book. For a scholarly critique of viewing economics this way, see Ben Fine and Dimitris Milonakis, *From Economics Imperialism to Freakonomics: The Shifting Boundaries between Economics and other Social Sciences* (New York: Routledge, 2009).

2 See: *Citizens United v. Federal Election Commission*, 558 U.S. 50 (2010).

3 This statistic can be found at www.oecd.org, and in early 2012 this site contained accurate figures through 2007. We can assume the average will be quite different with data from 2008 forward, reflecting the stimulus efforts of some governments, and the austerity cuts by others, during the great recession.

4 Excellent studies on the impact of institutional logic include James C. Scott, *Seeing Like a State: How Certain Schemes to Improve the Human Condition Have Failed* (New Haven, CT: Yale University Press, 1999), or Graham Allison's classic *Essence of Decision: Explaining the Cuban Missile Crisis* (New York: Little Brown, 1971).

5 Consider the pledges and program of the British Conservative–Liberal coalition that took power in 2010, or the re-election success of the Latvian government of Prime Minister Dombrovskis in October 2010 by pledging to stay the course on an extreme austerity package.

6 The classic description of the "free rider" problem comes from Mancur Olson's *The Logic of Collective Action* (Cambridge, MA: Harvard University Press, 1965).

7 For example, Jack Matlock's *Autopsy on an Empire* (New York: Random House, 1995), or David Remnick's, *Lenin's Tomb* (New York: Random House, 1993).

8 For an overview of the debate in political science about this approach, see Donald P. Green and Ian Shapiro, *Pathologies of Rational Choice: A Critique of Applications in Political Science* (New Haven, CT: Yale University Press, 1994) and the closely related volume, Jeffrey Friedman ed., *The Rational Choice Controversy* (New Haven, CT: Yale University Press, 1995).

9 Peter A. Hall and Rosemary C.R. Taylor, "Political Science and the Three New Institutionalisms," *Political Studies*, no. XLIV, 1996, pp. 936–57.

10 Hall and Taylor, "Political Science," p. 939.

11 For a good discussion of the role of conflict, see B. Guy Peters, Jon Pierre, and Desmond S. King, "The Politics of Path Dependency: Political Conflict in Historical Institutionalism," *The Journal of Politics*, vol. 67, no. 4, November 2005, pp. 1275–300.

12 For a summary of this expansive discussion, see Michael Mann, *The Sources of Social Power*. vol. I (Cambridge: Cambridge University Press, 1986), pp. 363–71.

13 Max Weber, *The Protestant Ethic and the Spirit of Capitalism*, trans Peter Baehr and Gordon G. Wells (New York: Penguin Books, 2002).

14 This is the title of C. Wright Mills' classic study. See C. Wright Mills, *The Power Elite* (Oxford: Oxford University Press, 1956, 2000).

15 Including the popular textbook by Michael Parenti, *Democracy for the Few* (9th edition, Boston, MA: Wadsworth, 2010).

16 Mills, *The Power Elite*, p. 4.

17 Richard J. F. Day, *Gramsci Is Dead: Anarchist Currents in the New Social Movements* (London: Pluto Press, 2005).

18 Michel Foucault, "Truth and Power," in *Essential Works of Foucault 1954–1984*, vol. 3, ed. James D. Faubion (New York: The New Press, 1994), pp. 122–3.

19 For a discussion of the logic behind this approach, see Sean P. Hier, "Probing the Surveillant Assemblage: On the Dialectics of Surveillance Practices as Processes of Social Control," *Surveillance and Society*, vol. 1, no. 3, 2003, pp. 399–411.

20 David Lyon, *Surveillance as Social Sorting* (New York: Routledge, 2003).

21 Mikhail Bakunin, *God and the State* (New York: Dover Publications, 1970), p. 83.

22 Paul James, *Globalism, Nationalism, Tribalism: Bringing Theory Back In* (London: Sage Publications, 2006), p. 257.

23 James, *Globalism, Nationalism, Tribalism*, p. 257.

24 Jean-Francois Lyotard, *The Postmodern Condition: A Report on Knowledge* (Minneapolis, MN: The University of Minnesota Press, 1993), p. xxiii.

25 Joseph H. Carens, "Aliens and Citizens: The Case for Open Borders," in *Theorizing Citizenship*, ed. Ronald Beiner (Albany, NY: State University of New York Press, 1995), pp. 229–53.

26 See Benjamin Barber, *Strong Democracy: Participatory Politics for a New Age* (Berkeley, CA: University of California Press, 1984), and Richard Dagger, *Civic Virtues: Rights, Citizenship, and Republican Liberalism* (New York: Oxford University Press, 1997).

27 Jurgen Habermas, "Citizenship and National Identity: Some Reflections on the Future of Europe," in *Theorizing Citizenship*, ed. Ronald Beiner (Albany, NY: State University of New York Press, 1995), pp. 255–81.

2

Deep and shallow state

In the run-up to national elections in 2012, two US House Representatives publicly announced their skepticism about a number of scientific issues. Rep. Paul Broun told an audience of constituents that evolution, the Big Bang theory, and embryology are "lies straight from the pit of hell."[1] He also explained that he had reviewed scientific evidence showing that the earth is only around 9,000 years old. Two months before, his colleague Rep. Todd Akin said in a television interview that he favored more regulations on abortion since women's bodies will naturally abort a pregnancy caused by what he called "legitimate rape."[2] These statements were especially interesting given that both congressmen are members of the US House Committee on Science, Space, and Technology.

These two incidents illustrate an increasingly common pattern in US politics. While an array of conservative politicians deny the existence of evolution to appease the religious right, the US federal budget still quietly contains millions of dollars in research support to critical areas of biomedical research. Investment in areas of science, which some elected officials claim to reject or doubt, is seen as necessary to maintain the competitive edge of the United States in the worldwide race for new cures and breakthroughs. Thus, we see politicians in the United States attacking the science being done in the "private sector" and often threatening to cut off public funding for grants that support such science. Yet, these threatened cutoffs and new regulations never occur except at the margins of overall research and development. This puzzling political behavior is a small example of the postmodern state's larger ideological dynamics. The dominant ideology of postmodern states is to conceal their agency.

What motivates this ideological reaction? In his analysis of the emerging "risk society," Beck argues that increasingly what matters to all of society are decisions made in areas that were traditionally considered nonpolitical.[3] This traditionally nonpolitical area includes private-sector industrial and technological development. However, as Beck stresses, the risks attached to these decisions are now much more universal. Beck claims that

> The promotion and protection of "scientific progress" and of "the freedom of science" become the greasy pole on which the primary responsibility for political arrangements slips from the democratic political system into the context of economic and techno-scientific politics, which is not democratically legitimated. A revolution under the cloak of normality occurs, which escapes from possibilities of intervention but must all the same be justified and enforced against a public that is becoming critical.[4]

The state needs these continued developments in technology and science to maintain its competitiveness and thus its sovereignty. Yet, the pursuit of scientific breakthroughs, such as bioengineering new organisms, genetically modified crops, or research into mind-altering pharmaceuticals, raises the risk of a technologically fueled catastrophe.[5]

The tensions and contradictions of this position call forth an ideological response. In the case of scientific risks, the state claims that these innovations occur in a global marketplace that is difficult for the state to regulate. In this manner, the state avoids a larger debate and public pressure to weigh the risks of research into creating new life-forms and mind-controlling pharmaceuticals. However, this response is not limited to concerns about risky science, but has become the postmodern state's default response when challenged in many policy areas that it deems too important for politics. The claim that the state's hands are tied is increasingly heard whenever citizens voice complaints. This ideological response is especially useful for the state in the broad realm of economic policy.

We see in many developed states a rising populist backlash to the forces of globalized capitalism. This growing tide of popular outrage ranges from worries about local jobs moving abroad to the insecurities triggered by immigration. Across the EU, the new cross-border labor market has triggered grievances about employment. But the most telling example of this backlash can be seen in the reaction to austerity imposed in EU countries like Greece following the great recession of 2008. In Greece, the government has had to make substantial concessions to other EU states and creditors to stave off a financial meltdown. The crowds in the streets of Athens and the defection of parliamentarians from establishment parties attest to the broad, popular hostility to the arrangements that have been made. Yet, the Greek government has patiently explained again and again that there is no alternative to Greece making such concessions while remaining part of the global economic system. The alternative, reintroducing the drachma and exiting the euro, is presented as the worst option for the country. However, many Greeks disagree and have begun to ask about the cost to the population of the remaining part of the "system."

Arguably, the state's denial of being able to act only inflames the pent-up demands of this backlash to globalization. As the Greek parliament continued to vote for austerity, the crowds on the streets became more frustrated and violent. We have also seen more extremist reactions to continued globalization across the developing world. For example, in the United States populist militias have offered to police the country's border with Mexico. The United States has also seen an explosion of local initiatives to make English the official language in municipalities. Areas in northern Europe like Denmark and the Netherlands, long famous for their progressive social attitudes, have seen the rise of anti-immigration parties. Perhaps even more worrying has been the growth of links between various groups, such as elements of the American Tea Party and the English Defence League, which claim to be part of an international, "anti-Islamification" front.[6] In these more extreme cases, the attempt to find scapegoats for the complicated problems of globalization smacks of desperation. If the state insists that global economic integration is out of its hands, then this political acquiescence risks inviting more desperate, confused, and extreme responses.

We can see the ideological reaction of hiding the state's agency most clearly in the complete denial anti-globalization protests face. The groups protesting at meetings of the G20, WTO, or the Davos forum represent a broad range of complaints linked to global capitalism. Yet, because they are attempting to voice the complaints of the multitude, it is easy for supporters of global capitalism to characterize the protests as inchoate. The continued integration of the world's economies is presented as a given, only resisted by the deluded or confused. The fact that it is necessary for the world's states to meet at the highest "summit" level to coordinate and advance this integration is blithely ignored. If this integration is so natural and unstoppable, then why must sovereign states agree to it by treaty?

The concealment of the state's agency works well in this case because it is indeed difficult for anti-globalization forces to point to one agent responsible for the many ills they seek to address. If the broad movement attempts to assert the local against the global, then it falls into the trap of denying international solidarity with other wronged groups. The other political advantage concealment enjoys is the gulf between the two groups mentioned here. On the one hand, we see anti-immigration populist movements voicing their discontent, and on the other we have a leftist anti-global capitalism movement. The obvious ideological distance between these two strands of resistance makes it easy for the state to dismiss both camps as impractical or extremist. Instead, we are told that the trends of "globalization" are irresistible.

In this sense, the concealment of the state benefits from leaving globalization as an amorphous description of our contemporary situation. Attempts to deconstruct globalization into positive and negative elements are drowned out by the overarching claim that it is a process beyond the control of nation states. Even our humanitarian concerns with providing freedom of movement are folded into the larger ideological claim that this can only be accomplished with unfettered global capitalism. As a result, the political message of the anti-global capitalism movement is inevitably too nuanced in the ideological contest against "globalization's" narrative. Instead, the received idea of our time becomes that we must accept the good and bad of globalization.

In all of these cases, the state is faced with a populist revolt over the outcomes of continued global economic integration. This same system that provides many rewards to economic elites also punishes those workers, students, small business owners, and the growing number of unemployed who lag behind. However, can any state, by the logic of state competition and the maintenance of sovereignty, afford to disengage from this process? In the case of Greece, many economic institutions (including large banks) claimed that the country's economy would immediately contract by 30 percent or more if it left the euro, leading to economic chaos.[7] From this perspective, the concealment of the state satisfies an immediate ideological need. By hiding the agency of the state, politicians can argue that their hands are tied and the demands of the citizenry are simply impossible to meet. Thus, their state's continued participation in global capitalism is stated as unchangeable fact regardless of what the population may want.

The relative success of this ideological sleight of hand rests upon the compartmentalization of the state into a shallow and deep component. If we look at the state from this dualistic perspective, then the mechanism for concealing the state's power is easier to see. The public sees a shallow state interacting with an autonomous market. This shallow state insists that it has little control over this autonomous, global market. What the public does not see is a deeper state that maintains this market and even decides *what the market is*.

Thanks to this bifurcation of the state, politicians in the shallows can adopt extreme ideological positions in public, knowing that the deep state will quietly maintain critical policy areas regardless of popular opinion. Indeed, we increasingly witness politicians making contradictory or outright irrational statements as they grandstand on the ideological, populist, and cultural issues left to the shallow state. This explains how a state and economy like that of the United States, constantly developing new technology and advancing science, can also have national politicians who publicly reject rational science. Public policy has been increasingly shifted to the deep state, leaving elected officials free to grandstand on increasingly symbolic, rather than substantive, issues.

Thinking about a deeper state is not an entirely new form of political analysis by any means. Some policy areas have historically been concealed such as intelligence and defense. Both are of obvious importance to maintaining the sovereignty of the state in the international arena. For clear functional reasons, we expect states to conceal much of their defense preparations and clandestine intelligence activities. Thus, the institutions of "national security" have often been thought of as a "deeper" state. But contemporary states have pushed more policy areas into the deep state than in the past. The deep state now includes very mundane policies and regulations.

There is no better place to start with policy examples of this dynamic than the current ecological crisis. In the United States, we see a number of politicians arguing that there is no such thing as climate change. Indeed, one elected state attorney general attempted to file fraud charges in the state of Virginia against an academic researching this area with state funding.[8] Yet, we find, at the same time, the US Department of Defense describing the need to prepare for the ramifications of climate change in its Quadrennial Defense Review. Similarly, the US Securities and Exchange Commission has advised corporations that best practice should now include disclosure to investors about the company's exposure to risks from climate change.[9]

Aside from global threats, many politicians in the United States continue to debate the merits of any environmental regulations. This includes some presidential candidates in the Republican primaries saying that they would close down the US Environmental Protection Agency (EPA). Yet, we see the deep state stepping up its efforts at enforcement in this area. This includes the fact that the EPA now posts a most wanted list similar to the FBI. The existence of this list came to wider public attention following the extradition of a wanted individual who had fled abroad.[10] Thus, we see the dynamic of the deep state providing the regulations, policies, and legal infrastructure that public officials in the shallows argue is unnecessary.

Such examples are not limited to the United States. In Canada, a conservative government, whose members have at times displayed skepticism about global warming, has provided additional funding to patrol the arctic (as it melts and opens new sea lanes). Indeed, a host of very different states has joined in on this arctic rush: Russia, the United States, Canada, Denmark, and Norway, despite their varying levels of acceptance or denial on climate change.[11] In the UK, we find various committees advising the government on the need to move railways infrastructure away from the eroding coastline.[12] Thus, while politicians in the shallow state debate the reality of "global warming" or the more neutral "climate change," the deep state in many countries is quietly preparing for it.

Examples of the state concealing its agency in the areas of scientific, environmental, and broad economic policy are initially suggestive. However, there is further evidence to support these observations from two main areas that I describe below. First, there is the sheer number of policy examples that illustrate the political dynamic operating between the deep and shallow state. As we examine the breadth of these examples, the pattern of the deep state taking on more and more responsibility for public policy becomes clear. Second, although it is easier to observe these characteristics in some states compared to others, the recurrence of this behavior in a range of nation states, supposedly governed by very different political regimes, further proves the existence and potency of this ideological turn. To better understand this political dynamic, we should begin by examining the part of the postmodern state that is the most visible, the shallows.

The shallow state

The shallow state consists of the state's visible institutions, agencies, and practices that interact with the population. Obviously, this interaction includes elections or whatever forms of politics the state permits. For many, this visible, front end of the state is what they think of as "government." This popular conception of the state is not surprising since visible institutions of government give the larger intangible aspects of the state a concrete form. In this sense, we can say that the shallows represent the state to most citizens.

At its most extreme, this representation of the state can be vested in one individual. In authoritarian political systems, the focus of "politics" in the shallows usually becomes one strongman (though in our contemporary world they typically style themselves "presidents"). In more transparent democratic systems, the individual officeholder (a president or a prime minister) can embody the state but is seen competing with others in the politics of the shallows. Democratic political systems also include visible institutions of government like legislatures and provincial or local functionaries that are driven into the background under authoritarian rule. Finally, democratic systems also stage the largest spectacle to be found in the shallows, elections, on a regular cycle too.

Beyond this representation of the state by officeholders and institutions, the citizenry experiences the shallow state primarily as a source of resource extraction, regulation, and public benefits. Individuals may think they have little connection to the state, until tax season. Then, they are confronted with the fact that they are paying into the state for the services and benefits it renders. This creates a difficult dynamic in the most developed countries where the citizenry is becoming less aware of the infrastructure that it uses every day, but is painfully aware that they are taxed. On the other hand, benefits awarded to some individuals may be highly visible, such as social welfare provisions. Much of the daily turbulence of politics centers on the citizenry's perceptions of who is contributing to the upkeep of the state, how much they are contributing, and who is reaping the benefits.

This area can also be the sharp end of the state for individuals.[13] In the United States and other federal systems, individual citizens are often ignorant of their local government structures, and how to participate within them, until they are confronted with an unpleasant reality: perhaps the zoning of their neighborhood is being changed to allow high rises, the authorities plan on opening a prison nearby, or there is a sudden change in property taxes and values. The sudden shock of these very concrete policy outcomes renews the citizen's awareness of the power and role of local government.

Beyond these concrete manifestations of the state, most citizens lack a broader comprehension of the state's totality. Instead, elected officials who appear on television and everyday news reporting are the point of contact for many citizens' political consciousness.[14] Other ideas of the state are primarily ideological, including feelings of patriotism or nationalism.[15] This tendency is a continuation of a long-observed trend in modern societies. Studies of political psychology have noted the tendency for citizens to think of their state concretely as tax and spending policies or as specific institutions and politicians. When asked about the state more broadly, citizens tend to discuss vague conceptions of the nation.

Recent political science research conducted in many of the world's democracies underlines the weak connections individuals have to the state in the shallows. For example, in the United States, citizens show a great deal of ignorance about the basic structure and function of their government when surveyed by social scientists.[16] This general level of ignorance appears to be fertile ground for questionable campaign practices like push polling or outrageously misleading campaign advertising by direct mail and less visible media outlets. Political science research shows that the better informed citizens are, the more difficult it is to manipulate them.[17] On a deeper level, research in political psychology indicates that lower levels of political knowledge correlate with individuals having incoherent worldviews.[18] The concern for more practical politics is that these confused, larger understandings of the world transfer over into weak understandings of public policy choices.

The overall trend that emerges in the shallows is a growing lack of accountability. There are multiple reasons for this decline, aside from the decline in the public's political knowledge. For example, contemporary political science research has attempted to untangle the complicated relationship between modern media and the public's understanding of policy issues. This recent research includes concerns with the increasing consumption of entertainment rather than news.[19] Another important factor in declining accountability seems to be the dominance of cultural issues in contemporary politics. Many of the intense issues associated with political polarization in the United States focus on symbolic and "values" topics rather than more substantive policy challenges. These trends combine to form a public that seems less informed on many complicated topics, but is often energized about broad social issues. In the United States, recent examples have included same-sex marriage, the role of religion in public schools, and the use of English as an "official" language. In Great Britain and the Netherlands, we find highly charged debates about immigration and national identity. In Japan, there have been highly controversial arguments about national identity and coming to terms with the nation's past.

These are important issues in many ways; however, they are also far removed from the nuts and bolts of economic, environmental, educational, and science policy. Politicians engaging with citizens in these broad, hot-button topic areas do not have to reveal much about their support for more substantive policy actions. In many ways, the behavior of politicians in the shallows increasingly resembles that of an irresponsible minority. This phenomenon is familiar to observers of parliamentary systems. After a parliamentary election that is quite decisive (and leaves a smaller party locked out of policy making by a majority), the minority group has little incentive to assist with policy formation. Instead, the minority group, denied policy portfolios and whose votes are not needed to pass legislation, logically focuses on attacking the majority government. There is little constraint on these attacks, since their only purpose is short-term political gains as opposed to actual policy formation.

For example, during the primary season of the US presidential campaign of 2012, one candidate announced that she would bring back "$2 gasoline" for all Americans. As commentator Thomas Friedman noted in response the next day, such a statement ignores not only the environmental challenges such an outcome would hold, but also the very practical market constraints on oil as countries like China and India industrialize.[20] In some ways, this behavior seems like the very traditional one of unfulfilled campaign promises. However, the exploitation of weaknesses in public knowledge also appears to be undergoing a fundamental change.

If we think about the behavior of politicians in the shallow state, then we see the opportunity these low levels of public knowledge enable. Inflammatory statements and misleading characterizations thrive within such an environment. The more complex the policy question, the greater the ability of politicians to exploit this gap. Thus, in the United States recent debates on the most complicated topics, such as health care reform, the debt ceiling, structural deficits, and fiscal stimulus efforts, have produced the most heated rhetoric. It is very surprising to see presidential candidates using campaign rallies to denounce the "treasonous" behavior of a Federal Reserve chairman (in regard to the fiscal stimulus effort of quantitative easing).[21] On the other hand, more traditional hot-button topics for American politics, such as continuing the wars in Afghanistan and Iraq or the provision of welfare services, seem to have disappeared into the deep state. What many politicians appear to prefer are simple, inflated pronouncements over very complicated and subtle policies that few in the public understand.

There is an understandable political logic to this behavior, given the evidence of various political science studies. For example, in a study of natural disaster preparedness in the United States, political scientists found that voters overwhelmingly gave credit for post-disaster assistance to the incumbent presidential political party, but absolutely none to politicians engaged in pre-disaster planning and preparedness.[22] Thus, the policy authors of disaster assistance received no credit, but the president who happened to distribute aid afterward did. In some cases, US presidents received credit for distributing assistance even though they had earlier opposed creating the programs that became so essential in the aftermath of disaster. With examples such as this, few politicians in the shallows have an incentive to work on the complex problems that come due in the future.

The modern political phenomena of the twenty-four-hour media cycle and instant polling appear to have only intensified this tendency.[23] Individual politicians can obtain almost instant feedback on their recent actions, provided the public sees it. Thus, the time frame of elected officials has shortened much like the overall cycle of information in today's world. What is easily measured is short-term feedback over highly visible public pronouncements. On the other hand, credit for hard work on complicated, long-term policy problems is unlikely to register with voters.

Thus, the shallows serve as the "front end" of the state. The shallow state provides an interface between the population and the larger collective entity of the state. This interface includes both signals from the population, which can range from voting to demonstrations, and signals from the state. The signals from the state can include rewards, incentives, and punishments. These activities are important for the state's day-to-day existence. In this sense, they are important for the survival of the state and its maintenance of sovereignty. Even symbolic actions can in the long run contribute to the maintenance of a polity. For example, Anderson in his classic study emphasizes the importance of creating a psychological context or imagined link across a community for it to function as a polity.[24]

However, the connection between sovereignty and these daily interactions or symbolic references is at a distance compared to the activities of the deep state. For example, the mundane task of tax collection has a larger impact on state capabilities. Individual citizens encounter this routine activity often on a daily or at least weekly basis. Does the citizen pay VAT or sales tax on every transaction? Is there a weekly income tax deduction from the citizen's paycheck? Or, is doing one's taxes an annual ritual? While not very dramatic, this microlevel activity eventually adds up to empowering the state with financial resources.

The key difference in the bifurcation of the postmodern state is the visibility of the shallows compared to its deep counterpart. In a long-studied tension between the need to maintain accountability versus the ability of the state to maintain its long-term sovereignty, the bureaucracy is a necessary source of institutional knowledge, experience, and continuity. In this less visible part of government we find the deep state. Increasingly, politicians in the shallow state are passing the difficult work of deciding and implementing policy to this less visible area. In democratic systems, the advantage of this behavior for elected politicians is the escape from the responsibility of making difficult choices. As Michael M. Ting demonstrates in a detailed study, there is often a logical, political advantage for legislatures to abdicate spending authority to the bureaucracy.[25] Doing so saves professional politicians the difficulty of putting together the necessary votes if they suspect the bureaucracy is likely to make decisions similar enough to the legislator's own preferences.

Another advantage for politicians in democratic systems is the better fit of short term and symbolic policy with electoral politics. In a study of policy responsiveness by state governments in the United States, Lax and Phillips found that "states effectively translate majority opinion into policy about half the time," even when those majorities are quite large.[26] In addition, the policy that is made by state governments tends to be more ideologically conservative or liberal (in the American sense) than the opinion of median voters. This implies a sort of overcorrection by state politicians where they are relying more on ideological cues than on finer-grain public opinion. In this sense, it is much easier for politicians to rely on such thumbnail sketches of their electorate's policy preferences than to invest the time and effort necessary to gauge their constituents' opinions on specific policy choices. Nonetheless, this is not a bad strategy for politicians in the shallows. There is growing evidence that voters tend to prioritize their ideological or symbolic preferences over more practical concerns.[27] This tendency only serves to reinforce the behavior of politicians in the shallows. Like the older example of the irresponsible minority in parliamentary politics, contemporary politicians in the shallow state can pander to popular prejudice with fewer and fewer repercussions.

However, drawing on so many examples from the United States points to another complication with studying this ideology. The bifurcation of the state is more visible in some political systems, less so in others. For example, in his recent analysis of contemporary China, Richard McGregor explains that despite popular perceptions of wholesale reform, the Chinese Communist Party still directs large segments of the economy from behind the scenes. Thus,

> The Party's removal of itself from the many areas of life and work of its citizens into which it once crudely and cruelly intruded has been as strategic as it has been enlightened. As intoxicating as these changes have been for the Chinese people, the retreat has also paradoxically empowered the authorities. The Party has been able to maintain its own secret political life, directing the state from behind the scenes, while capturing the benefits and the kudos delivered by a liberalized economy and a richer society at the same time.[28]

Thus, in an authoritarian system like contemporary China, the presence of a deeper state, setting policy from behind the facade of a free market, is much easier to grasp. As McGregor explains in meticulous detail, many companies in China are still "state enterprises" despite being listed on overseas stock exchanges. In these cases, the CEO of the firm is still a Communist party member, with a notional civil service rank in the formal government bureaucracy.

In a democratic political system with a robust civil society and a longer history of capitalism, the presence of a deep and shallow state is much harder to conceptualize. However, we can consider another interesting example from the United States. An investigative series from the *New York Times* revealed that the large American corporation General Electric paid no taxes in 2010. In fact, the company received over $3 billion from the government to add to its profits that year of 14.2 billion.[29] In essence, the United States, supposedly a system with a very free, autonomous market, subsidizes some of its largest corporations through its tax policies. Although a step removed from the subsidies or money injected into a state company in China, in both cases we find the deep state quietly subsidizing large corporations that compete in the global "free market." Yet, in which case is the state's concealment deeper?

The fact that similar political behavior is increasingly common to both democratic and authoritarian regimes suggests its importance within the context of contemporary politics. Indeed, the political science subfield of comparative politics argues that when we find a similar institution (or in this case, similar state behaviors) cutting across differences of culture, place, and regime, this commonality is serving an important purpose. If we consider the two examples of corporate governance mentioned earlier, then we can begin to see how this bifurcation of the state enables concealment in both democratic and authoritarian regimes.

In the case of Chinese companies, it is difficult for overseas investors, or even many local Chinese businessmen, to associate large telecommunications firms with the government. Although many are aware of the party membership held by directors of state companies, it remains conceptually difficult for many of us to associate these organizations with what we think of as the state. Similarly, despite receiving government subsidies, it is difficult for citizens in the United States to associate a firm like General Electric with concrete institutions of government like the US Congress or the presidency.

For this reason, we need to think about what constitutes the broader state. There is more to the state than the highly visible institutions and officeholders of the shallows. On the other hand, this other part of the state seems to be more than just the less visible bureaucracy. As opposed to the shallow front end of the state, there is a deeper state. As we shall see, defining what constitutes the deep state is very challenging.

The deep state

Unfortunately, a quick Internet search reveals that discussion of the deep state is most commonly found in two domains. First, it has been a perennially popular idea in Turkish politics. There, the deep state is thought of as an informal establishment, centered on the military, which dominates politics from behind the scenes.[30] Over time, this idea has spread to the popular analysis of other political systems across the Middle East, Russia, and beyond. In the case of Turkey, the deep state (supposedly consisting of the country's military leadership and fellow traveling elites) is often assigned responsibility for policy outcomes with little supporting evidence. Nonetheless, the supposed existence of this behind-the-scenes cabal is convenient for politicians across the country's political spectrum.

For secular-leaning liberal politicians in Turkey, it remains a source of comfort. In this version, the potential of intervention by the deep state acts to confine the cultural politics of religious conservatives within "responsible limits." On the other hand, from the conservative side of politics, the threat of the deep state has been used to justify the reforms pushed through in recent years by Prime Minister Erdogan's AK (Justice and Development) Party.[31] These reforms are democratic in that they roll back some of the mechanisms used in the past by the secular military leadership to constrain the actions of the country's politicians. On the other hand, those reforms appear to secularists as the first step toward more conservative social policies. From either perspective in contemporary Turkish politics, it is difficult to discern how much of a factor the deep state really is as opposed to a useful fiction. Similarly, the application of this idea to other political systems is of questionable utility.

Even worse, the idea of a deep state also thrives on the Internet among the conspiracy minded.[32] As with all conspiracy theories, these observations attempt to simplify the complexity of the world by projecting responsibility for events onto a concrete agent. For example, a common conspiracy explanation for globalization is an all-powerful UN (despite all the contrary evidence of that organization's decline). Or, we often see conspiracies claim that there is actually a double game going on with cataclysmic events rather than facing the reality of a state's failure. In the United States, the classic example is the conspiracy theory claiming that the government allowed the attack on Pearl Harbor in 1941 to provide a pretext for entering the war. Apparently, many find this idea easier to believe than accepting the simpler explanation that the United States could fail to defend itself. This phenomenon seems to have repeated itself in recent years with the vast growth of conspiracy theories surrounding the 9/11 attacks.[33] Again, for many individuals, it is easier to accept the idea that their government allowed this to happen, rather than the simpler explanation of the US failure to defend itself and the vulnerability that comes with this truth. Instead, grossly elaborate scenarios are suggested to link events with a particular agent, whether that is a secretive government agency or an unbelievably effective United Nations.

Thus, there is a risk of turning to the deep state as an answer to everything, rather than as an aid to careful political analysis. Once it is asserted that a layer of the state is concealed, it can become a projection of our fears and anger about politics. This difficulty is compounded by the simple fact that the deep state's activity is opaque. In the Turkish political system, the deep state reference appears to have worn out its utility as it can now be used and abused by all sides in the country's politics. For the conspiracy-minded lurking online, the idea of a deep state becomes a convenient site of agency responsible for all of the complications of politics. To avoid the errors of logic found in either of these examples, a clearer definition of the deep state and its political role is needed. We need to look at specific policy examples to gauge the utility of this idea for explaining the behavior of contemporary nation states.

In the area of policy study, the idea of a deep state is routinely used to try and understand the national security establishment of the most developed countries, especially the United States. For example, in Peter Gill's attempt to "develop a systemic framework for the comparative analysis of security intelligence agencies," he discusses the utility of a dual or multilayer state perspective.[34] As Gill points out, this perspective is important to avoid the pitfalls of imagining the state as a unified, rational actor. In the case of intelligence and security concerns, it is particularly obvious that some parts of the state do not know what is happening elsewhere.

From the perspective of such security studies, we can ask, how deep is the deep state? Consider that in November 2010, President Obama, in an attempt to reduce confusion and improve transparency, issued an executive order on the proper classification of sensitive material. A new designation, "Controlled Unclassified Information (CUI)," was introduced to replace more than 120 designations that the bureaucracy had invented.[35] These designations illustrate two points. First, that information is power, especially in the policy process of a modern nation state, and thus there is a need to control it. Second, claiming that all of this empowering information is classified or top secret, because of its importance to national security, is simply implausible. Thus, new gradations of information must be invented. The classification of information also provides an idea of the scope of the deep state. In the midst of the WikiLeaks scandal, it emerged that the employee who passed on classified information to the site possessed a clearance of "secret." In turn, apparently more than 900,000 individuals currently hold that same level of clearance across the US government.[36]

Thus, in policy studies, the one area of the deep state that does draw attention is intelligence and security. Various warnings over the years of the rise of the "national security" state were common during the Cold War.[37] Further iterations of this concern then emerged under the threat of global terrorism. Since sovereignty is closely linked to the state's coercive capabilities, defense, intelligence, and the ever-expanding "security" have traditionally been in the shadows. The instrumental ends of warfare and intelligence gathering require secrecy. Thus, as long as there are nation states dedicated to maintaining their sovereignty, we can expect the deep state to always have this coercive core.

However, the remarkable change in the post–Cold War environment has been the scope of state activity that has followed clandestine intelligence into the shadows. For example, in an attempt to explain both recent political successes and setbacks in reforming US social policy, Suzanne Mettler has turned to the idea of a "submerged state."[38] Mettler describes the submerged state as:

> a conglomeration of federal social policies that incentivize and subsidize activities engaged in by private actors and individuals. These feature a variety of tools, including social benefits in the form of tax breaks for individuals and families; the regulation and tax-free nature of benefits provided by private employers, including health care benefits in the form of insurance; and the government-sponsored enterprises and third-party organizations that receive federal subsidies in exchange for carrying out public policy goals, such as the banks and lending associations that have administered student loans.[39]

Mettler's analysis draws on earlier conceptions of welfare provisions in the United States constituting a shadow state.[40] According to Mettler, the fact that social policy in the United States is administered by this elusive, submerged state has two important consequences.

First, its complexity and scattered connections make reforming it extremely challenging for both the executive branch and Congress. Tinkering with policy changes in one area often produces unexpected consequences elsewhere and at times engenders political resistance from unexpected quarters. For politicians worried about popularity and their next election, there is little incentive to take on such a task. Second, the complicated arrangements surrounding the implementation of social policy obscures its impact from average citizens. In a study of public opinion about social welfare policies in the United States, political scientists found that the public was not only uninformed, but misinformed.[41] The difference means that they often believed with great certainty erroneous facts about this area of public policy. These false beliefs included extremely inaccurate assumptions of how much the US government spends on such policies and how many citizens receive benefits.

This potent combination of complicated policy and poor public knowledge about it discourages involvement by political actors in the shallow state. In turn, this lack of visibility creates a growing unaccountability in the policy area of social welfare. The deep (or in Mettler's analysis, "submerged") state is increasingly relied on by frustrated or unmotivated officials to make and maintain social policy. Given its inaccessibility, the public is ill informed on the subject. This feeds into the deep state having a free hand to make policy since there is little call for accountability. In addition, given the complex obscurity of this policy area, elected officials can hope to win few votes by engaging with it. Thus, in a policy area far removed from intelligence gathering or defense, we find policy determined by the less visible, deep state.

At the same time, the complex interactions of the public policy process discredit a simple description of the deep state. We can view a human invention that is as vast and complicated as the state in many ways. In some cases, there is greater utility in imagining even more elaborate models of the state, depending on the level of analysis pursued. Close analysis of particular policy areas reveals the involvement of many actors including elected officials, bureaucrats, and individuals in the "private sector." This complex interaction has spawned a new "paradigm" in policy studies and public administration. The shorthand for this new approach is "governance rather than government."[42] In other words, public policy is formed in part by actors outside of government institutions. To many observers this shift is a positive development. Rather than traditional government regulation, the idea of contemporary governance is to allow society more access to policy making so that it is driven from below.

However, a number of studies have pointed out that despite the promise of opening up policy "beyond the state," to actors in the private sector and at the community level, the messy chaos of governance rather than government can also undermine democratic accountability.[43] This outcome is due to the often bewildering array of government institutions, nongovernmental organizations, private-sector leaders, and professional lobbyists, engaged with highly specific policy issues. Paradoxically, this expansive inclusion of focused participants only serves to obscure the ultimate agency of the state. Once the consultations, open forums, feedback sessions, and so forth end, it is still the state acting and implementing policy. But following this link to the state through all of the noise becomes extremely difficult.

Thus, the deep state should not be thought of as a list of secretive organizations hidden away by government. Instead, the deep and shallow state dynamic is very fluid within contemporary states. We can argue that, in a perverse way, the addition of nongovernmental actors to the policy process can transform such organizations into part of the deep state. Given this challenge, what criteria can we use to identify the "deep" state? If the contemporary state often includes so many nongovernmental actors in the policy process, then is it even possible to identify such a category of the state?

It is if we focus on the concept of sovereignty. It is here, at the bedrock of the state, its *raison d'être* that the state's active efforts become visible. How? First, the state must continue to be the human organization that regulates all others. In this sense, the deep state must maintain the oversight functions that subordinate all other human organization to it. Aside from our traditional understanding of "security" agencies and functions, this oversight includes a vast array of legal infrastructure. The maintenance of sovereignty can involve other agencies concerned with planning, health care, or even education. Given that states are increasingly competitive in their efforts at socioeconomic development, even the health of the population can be seen as important to the continued sovereignty of a state. Similarly, education that makes the workforce competitive in global capitalism can begin to acquire a national security complexion.[44]

The second aspect of sovereignty that the deep state must support is perpetuity. Why can a state like the UK offer bonds with a maturity of thirty years? How can states guarantee leases of land for 100 years or pledge in treaties to maintain a position forever? Or consider that on October 3, 2010, the Federal Republic of Germany made the last reparations payment set by the Versailles treaty of 1919.[45] Why? Because the FRG is the successor to the other German states before it. Because the state will exist forever, it can make promises and provide assurances that no other human organization can. Even powerful market corporations cannot assert this level of guarantee since they are ultimately regulated by the state, but also because the free-market ideology they draw upon assumes many companies will, and must, fail.

Due to these imperatives, the deep state possesses a logic that is more objective than the political fashions we see in the shallows. This also explains the attempt at times by various politicians to link their policy concerns to national security. To secure itself, the state must rely on the resources of the deep end both to scrutinize its contemporary position and to maintain or improve that position into the future. These twin needs are absolute since nothing from within the state's infrastructure can trump the importance of preserving the state. Thus, we should think of the deep state less as a set of concrete institutions and more as a functional logic that pervades the state.

How then should we define the deep state? The deep state is best understood as the parts of the state most vital to the *praxis* of maintaining sovereignty. "Praxis" is a broad and perhaps overused philosophical term. Nonetheless, it is useful in this context. At its simplest, praxis is the process of turning an idea into reality. But attached to this idea of process, praxis also refers to the embodiment of this idea in the world. The praxis of maintaining state sovereignty requires the concrete creation of many institutions, bureaucracies, and officeholders. In turn, these institutions create legislation and policies to maintain state sovereignty.

However, a list of all state institutions does not identify the deep state. Instead, the deep state is a shifting set of institutions and officeholders that are most closely connected to the core objective of maintaining the sovereignty of the state. The preservation of the state overrules other imperatives within the state, including, when necessary, the political rules of the shallow state.

This dynamic means that even with a simple, dualistic separation of the state into two categories, there are many areas of the state that are difficult to classify. For example, what about a state's legal system? In the developed democracies, court activities are exceedingly well documented and by law accessible through public records. Even in more authoritarian regimes, courts make some pretense of following published rules and allowing access to their decisions. At the same time, courts are important for the state's maintenance of sovereignty since they provide oversight for agreements and contracts through all levels of society. Should an institution like the judiciary be considered part of the deep state?

In a recent study, Richard Hasen found that the US Supreme Court has gained power at the expense of Congress over the last two decades.[46] This power stems from the fact that Congress has been polarized into inactivity. It rarely takes action to override the Court's findings. Instead, increasingly partisan, ideological debates in Congress have led to a vacuum in not only interpreting but also adjusting and fine-tuning the complex federal laws and regulations that do manage to pass the legislature. The downside to this outcome is that important decisions on policy implementation are shifting to a less accountable, and by comparison, less visible branch of government. In the United States, it is not plausible to categorize the Supreme Court as an institution of the deep state. However, given the current political divisions in the United States, we do see this less accountable branch of government filling the vacuum from a gridlocked legislature. In this sense, the logic of the deep state is present in recent Supreme Court behavior.

Thus, the other important question with defining the deep state is visibility. Typically, the deep state is made up of institutions and agencies that are usually headed by an unelected official, and thus only indirectly accountable to the electorate. Here, we can think of all of the directors and heads of agencies appointed throughout the state bureaucracy. Obviously, some of these positions are much more important for the deep state's mission of maintaining sovereignty than others. In addition, the activity of the agency is either not a matter of public record or if it is then it is very difficult to access. But at the same time, the failures of the shallow state can also push more visible branches of government, like the judiciary in the United States, into the functional role of the deep state.

The battle over accountability and implementation of public policy is an old topic in the study of state bureaucracies. In the literature studying the American political system, there has long been concern about "iron triangles" or "issue networks" made up of the bureaucracy, members of Congress, and lobbyists who capture control of policy making, to the exclusion of the public.[47] In studies of British politics, there has long been a worry about the "mandarins" of Whitehall determining public policy with little oversight from parliament. In these older policy studies, the key difference between state institutions like the legislature, the courts, and the bureaucracy is their relative visibility. Legal decisions are generally intended to be public knowledge, because this is part of their function, to lay down rules that guide private and public activities. Similarly, the legislative acts of a parliament by their function are intended for larger public consumption. In contrast, the bureaucracy performs its functions with little or no visibility. Thus, a more traditional policy studies approach would suggest that defining the deep state is an issue of transparency in government.

However, these older studies are predicated on the idea of identifying various interests present in the policy process. For example, classic studies of iron triangles attempted to expose the monopoly that interest groups could acquire in specific policy areas, with little public oversight. Similarly, classic studies of bureaucratic influence worried that the agenda of an unelected bureaucracy could reign unchecked by elected officials. The interests conceived of in these studies tend to be very concrete ones: for example, interest groups concerned with making more money in the marketplace through changes to regulations, and bureaucrats influencing policy so that their department receives a larger budget allocation or avoids tasks the bureaucrats do not want to pursue.

In contrast, the functional logic of the deep state is a more elusive motivation. Consider, for example, the question of whether the actions of the state are a conscious attempt at concealment. Clearly, this is the case in some circumstances. In intelligence gathering and other areas connected to the state's security, secrecy is a functional requirement. Thus, conscious efforts to conceal the state's activities are expected here. Another sort of functional logic can be found where the state attempts to publicly tie its own hands. The best example of this conscious restraint is by granting "independence" to a central bank. This independence from politics makes promises of the central bank, and the setting of interest rates, more credible to the market. Thus, the fiction that this administrative arrangement places a central bank outside of state control (despite the influence the state retains over it) is a very conscious decision to conceal the state's agency.

On the other hand, if the concealment of the state has emerged as an ideological norm, then arguably many policy decisions that enable this concealment are not, strictly speaking, conscious ones. For example, attempts at privatization or outsourcing motivated by the state's budget concerns may very well have consequences for government transparency and accountability that state actors failed to consider. Also, given how complicated the state is in many places, concealment can be a by-product of otherwise innocuous rule changes in the bureaucracy. The objective of decision makers within different state agencies and institutions is never unitary. Various actors within the state have differing agendas, sometimes very modest ones. Therefore, we must look closely at policy decisions before we can conclude that they represent a conscious attempt at concealing the state.

Nor is activity by the deep state necessarily secretive by design. The complexity of modern policy across integrated, developed societies is obviously complex in ways unforeseen even two decades ago. With globalized capitalism outside its borders and complex, diverse societies within, contemporary developed states must act on a range of problems beyond the scope of legislative oversight. Thus, the bureaucracy often acts within extremely broad boundaries set by elected officials. In a study from the United States, the relatively innocuous Food and Drug Administration was found to act autonomously in the absence of congressional scrutiny. When prodded by legislators, the agency did respond to congressional concerns.[48] Yet the sheer complexity of the day-to-day decisions made by this agency ensures that it is often left alone by the shallow state.

However, the deep state's most important role in concealing the postmodern state is arguably its oversight of a theoretically autonomous, free market. The deep state's maintenance of the market enables the more public shallow state to claim that this area is beyond its control. In this sense, the deep state is a paradox. Many observers worry about the hidden activities of intelligence and defense agencies. Yet, the dynamic of the deep and shallow state has its most corrosive effects on accountability and transparency here. Although classification and state secrets have been part of the state since the early modern period, the ideology of the free market has created new possibilities for concealing the postmodern state's agency. What is deeper than the classified and secret parts of the state? The answer is the part of the state hidden in plain sight.

Hiding behind the market

When a firm merges with another or buys out a rival in the marketplace, the description is often of a "takeover." Yet, when the state privatizes services by awarding a contract to a firm, the assumption is that the firm continues to be independent in the free market. Describing a firm as taken over by the state would imply an unusual level of interference. Nonetheless, the distinctions are a matter of degree. A number of private firms depend on taxpayer money from the state for their existence. Why are they not considered part of the state?

Arguably, the key difference with privatization is that a change in ownership alters incentives. In turn, these new incentives push the organization to strive for greater efficiency to maximize profit. However, an exhaustive study of privatization in the UK by Vickers and Yarrow concluded that

> The efficiency implications of these changes in incentives depend very much on the competitive and regulatory environment in which a given firm operates. Indeed, it can be argued that the degree of market product

competition and the effectiveness of regulatory policy typically have rather larger effects on performance than ownership *per se*.[49]

This is an important point given that the public is often assured that privatized services will match rigid guidelines set by the state. Such regulations obviously place some limits on what a private firm can do differently from a public one.

If this is the case, then again the question becomes, why these private firms are not part of the state? Their employees provide a good or service to the public or in the public's interest. The contracts the firms receive are awarded by the state with guidelines or performance targets set by the state. Often the public is required to use the firm's service because the state has designated only one firm or a small number of them as acceptable providers. To ensure their good performance, the state theoretically holds a great incentive over these firms; their contracts could be awarded to a competitor. However, it is often the case that these "private" firms become monopolies once this connection to public funds is established.

Firms that survive primarily through receiving taxpayer money cover a large area of the economy. In the United States, a number of firms specialize in providing garbage collection to municipalities and local governments. Other firms in the United States have specialized in setting up and running "charter" schools. These are essentially nonofficial public schools that the state allows to function free of the interference and costs of teachers organized within the national teachers' unions. Other companies manage and provide basic utilities. In all cases, the contracts awarded to such firms are decided by the state, with specific rules and targets. The employees are receiving taxpayer funds and often have a local monopoly for the service they provide.

Why are they not part of the state? Theoretically, the state could decide not to renew their contract and find a new provider in the competitive marketplace. This is plausible in some cases such as the new, hot field of companies providing education services. It is much less plausible when we consider a "private" electric utility. If it loses a contract, will it then be withdrawing its generating stations from the local grid? Is it still the case that the mere difference of notional ownership can transform the internal incentives and efficiencies of these firms?

Nor is this pattern confined to routine matters such as garbage collection and utilities. In a startling case from the UK, we find the state outsourcing or privatizing a core function of the state: policing. As the UK prepared to host the 2012 Summer Olympics in London, details emerged about the role of private security services, such as the firm G4S, in providing security for the games.[50] One of the political controversies surrounding the Olympics is always the cost to the host city. The government argued that security costs would be reduced by outsourcing security to firms that could quickly gear up for the large event as opposed to regular police and security forces attempting to do so.

Nonetheless, this private firm is using taxpayer money to pay security guards to provide policing in all but name at the event. The distinction between "security" and "policing" seemed very thin in the context of the Olympic Games. The government assured critics that these "private security" forces were completely integrated into the larger protection effort, including military backup in the event of the worst. Again, what distinction remains then between these contractors and all of the other forces they are integrated with? In the end, the private firm was unable to hire enough security guards for the many venues of the London games. This led to the British government deploying 18,000 soldiers to supplement the "private" contractor. Why were publicly funded security guards working side by side with British soldiers still considered a private force?

Arguably, the most dramatic example of the state using the market is with the privatization of prisons. Here, the hollowness of claiming that state action taking place in the market is somehow not of the state is most apparent. Individuals are incarcerated in buildings and conditions that are supposed to match explicit government criteria.[51] Land for the prison is often obtained for the firm through government assistance. Guards and staff at private prisons are supposed to abide by the same standards as "official" guards and wardens. The application of discipline and coercion to prisoners is supposed to match state rules on the use of force. These operations are paid for with taxpayer money. The prisoners are sentenced to these facilities by state courts. Yet, through the magic of the market, these are private rather than state prisons. What is the difference? Private prisons are supposedly more cost-efficient, though scholarship indicates "that other institutional characteristics—such as the facility's economy of scale, age, and security level—were the strongest predictors of a prison's daily per diem cost."[52] Perhaps the wages of private guards are lower than "official" state-employed guards. The legacy costs of pensions and health service are perhaps less because private guards are not unionized. But most importantly, the state can claim that rather than expanding itself with yet another prison, it is instead somehow cutting back the state by outsourcing this need to the cheaper, more efficient, and nimble market. Otherwise, the state must admit that it is expanding.

Beyond these examples taking place on planet Earth, the state has increasingly "outsourced" more spectacular services. In the United States, NASA has awarded a contract for cargo missions to the International Space Station to a private firm. The argument was that this market-based firm could provide an alternative to the retired shuttle program more quickly and efficiently than NASA's traditional pipeline for such projects. And indeed, the firm Space X has delivered on its contract sending a cargo flight to the ISS in June 2012. However, why is this an example of an autonomous market doing something better than the state? The firm was created and worked very hard on one goal, to win the contract NASA offered. The firm's payment comes from public money. NASA set the targets and rules for the contract. In this sense, our example seems to be less about the state getting smaller, rather than it acquiring a new firm. The US Congress could have approved a program to shut down the unsafe American space shuttle program and create a whole new, safer delivery system to resupply the ISS from scratch. However, the announcement to retire the old, costly NASA program, and then contract out to entrepreneurs for a new, cheaper, and more efficient system sounds better politically.

Occasionally, the paradoxes of this situation undermine its ideological camouflage. In a startling example from the United States, a court case is looming over the privatization of collecting legal fines in several states. In an effort to cut costs, a number of local and state governments contracted collection agencies to collect fines ranging from parking tickets to those levied by the criminal courts. The legal conundrum that had arisen is that these supposedly private agencies have been given the power to increase these fines with late penalties and other fees beyond what the courts established. In some cases, they have also requested that delinquent payers be incarcerated for not paying. In the United States, these actions raise a number of complicated constitutional questions about jurisdiction and legal authority since it is giving power to a private agency to order someone arrested. One judge in the US state of Alabama commented that the drive for this privatization was supported by state legislators, some of whom suggested that state courts should be "self-financing" through collecting such fees rather than depend on the state budget![53]

In this sense, the state can be interchangeable with the market in the other direction. For example, in the United States, a minor scandal emerged around the issue of prisons bidding for government contracts against the private sector.[54] In the UK, it emerged that individuals were being forced to participate in a work-training scheme that the government arranged with a number of private employers. Thus, employees at large retailers in Britain and a few other firms find themselves working next to people who are receiving only welfare support rather than the minimum wage. So, the state can order people to work within the supposedly autonomous marketplace. Of course, in the UK case, the government could only do so with the cooperation of the private firms choosing to participate in the program.[55]

The state is capable of even more dramatic incursions into the market. During the global financial crisis of 2008, a number of states took over or nationalized banks that were "too big to fail." Other banks were ordered to merge or to sell off some of their units. A number of central banks intervened in the markets with measures to ease the availability of credit or in some cases, to prop up government debt.

Such takeovers, interventions, and nationalizations are presented as a response to crisis. Political rhetoric justifies such emergency measures and assures citizens that they are temporary. The state claims that it will quickly get itself out of the car business (in the case of the United States taking over General Motors) or the banking business (in the case of the UK National Rock). The blatant and visible action of the state in these cases is incompatible with the ideology of concealment unless it emphasizes the idea that the state is temporarily intervening in the autonomous market.

The state itself decides what entities are market- or state-controlled. The state also sets the parameters for market activity. So, just as the state can claim that it has privatized operations or outsourced services to the market, it can also reclaim parts of the market or change its rules of engagement. So what is the market? It is what the state says it is. What is the distinction between a private firm and state agencies? Does it depend on the quantity of business devoted to government contracts? What about the "official" oversight of the firm or agency's activities? Are the employees officially working for the state (typically with more rules, salary, benefits, and protections) or not? These weak distinctions between what is private and public mean that the state sets the boundaries of the market.

Thus, the idea of an autonomous market allows the state to further conceal its agency in plain sight. Despite the ideological rhetoric of privatization "downsizing" or "rolling back" the state, the actual outcome is the expansion of the state. Rather than engaging in a political fight to expand the government workforce, or increase public services, the state acquires outside firms (with employees, equipment, etc.) while simultaneously claiming to cut costs. And indeed costs are often lowered through this maneuver as these new employees are paid less than official government workers (though the offset is that the managers of these firms seem to be better paid than official government supervisors). This shell game of having official government employees and agencies versus off-the-books contractors allows the state to claim it is following the indisputable logic of the market and trimming the size of the state. The state can then quietly expand or shift resources to new projects.

On the other hand, the state can also choose not to act by insisting on the inviolability of the market. Recurring examples of this state behavior are seen in cases that involve the maintenance of the commons. For example, in a case from the United States, residents in Michigan became embroiled in legal action against the Nestle Corporation over water. In this case, Nestle is accused by residents of pumping out so much water for a bottling plant that it has reduced the flow through local aquifers. In essence, various local citizen groups claim that this corporation, after buying a small parcel of land, is extracting local water from broader regional sources, bottling it, and selling it for a profit. This action is pulling water from a much larger area, but legal efforts against the company have floundered over the corporation's assertion of its property rights. The state initially indicated to residents that there was little it could do, given the free market and rights of property owners. Yet, it was the state that enabled the corporation's actions by providing tax incentives and assistance in obtaining the land it built on.[56]

In his recent study of water policies from around the world, Christopher Fishman points to a similar example in Fiji. The free market has created a profitable business there. Local water is bottled and shipped all over the world. Yet, half of Fiji's population lacks access to a reliable water supply.[57] Is the state of Fiji truly powerless to harness this same know-how for the sake of its citizenry? Or, does such a paradox illustrate the priorities of the state? The government of Fiji can argue that it lacks the resources to provide potable water to the population, while licensing and taxing a global bottled water brand that is operating within the boundaries of an autonomous, free market.

In these examples, the state fails to act on the concerns of the public to protect public resources or the common use of resources. The private interests of the market are asserted and the state indicates its hands are tied. With a bit of digging and careful research, we find the state has enabled the behavior via tax incentives, land acquisition assistance, and other policies that it now says it is impotent to stop.

We can consider another interesting case from the United States. In congressional hearings in 2010 about the failures of for-profit colleges, a key point that emerged was the institutions' reliance on guaranteed government loans to students. Their supporters attempted to argue that these institutions represented a more nimble form of higher education that could quickly adapt to student needs and market demands. Nonetheless, the congressional hearings showed that the profits of these institutions were completely reliant on the student loans and financial aid the state provided to students. So, in the case of for-profit, market competitive education in the United States, the federal government provides students the grants and loans for tuition.

A parallel development emerged in America's K-12 education policies. In 2010 and 2011, an increasing number of primary and high schools began offering their students the option of online classes. Previously, online courses were the domain of higher education but they have become increasingly attractive to school districts facing budget cuts. However, a few states began to require students to take a set number of their high school classes online. This latter decision is especially interesting given the extensive lobbying for such provisions by private companies that provide online content to public schools.[58] In effect, such measures have taxpayer money going to private companies and conceal the state shifting toward support for cheaper instruction.

We can also find state concealment in the very mundane policy area of pensions. In many countries, but especially in the United States, UK, and some EU states, parts of the pension system have shifted to the open market. The argument is that better returns could be had from investing parts of pension funds in the market. This shift was framed as utilizing the greater efficiency of the marketplace. However, closer analysis reveals that these pension funds are primarily purchasers of government debt. As *the Economist* pointed out in a recent article,

> An example of this tangled relationship can be seen in the efforts of individual American states to deal with budget shortfalls. Some states are launching special bond issues to get the funds needed to finance their pension contributions. And who are likely to be significant buyers of those bonds? State pension funds.[59]

Once again the move toward privatization simply obscures the source of funding for this area of social policy. Across the United States, many public employees are no longer provided with pension programs. Instead, they are required to invest part of their salary in stocks, bonds, and other assets through management companies such as TIAA-CREF or banks like Wells Fargo, in lieu of a pension. In some programs the local, state, or federal government matches these contributions. Yet, what is the significant difference between the old-style pension system and mandatory investments by workers (deducted from their paychecks by the state) into heavily regulated retirement funds?

In another policy area that seems mundane or even arcane, we find state action creating new economic realities. Consider the insurance market in the United States. In an attempt to improve their local economies, several US states have made fundamental changes to laws regulating the insurance industry. As a result, states such as Vermont now allow insurance companies to create shell holdings in which they deposit steep company losses, making the parent company's ledger much healthier.[60] Thanks to this state intervention, private corporations are suddenly able to pay dividends again and hire more employees. Once again, despite the myths of an autonomous market, the state has changed the so-called "realities" and disciplinary "constraints" of the market.

In all of these examples, we see that the deep state is buttressing a theoretically autonomous market. However, even a modest effort reveals that these "free market" areas are parasitic upon the legal infrastructure of the state and often receive their funding from the state. We see for-profit companies in education paid by students and school districts, whose funding originates with the federal government. Stock markets receive large inflows of capital from institutional investors managing 401(k) programs, mandated for government employees.

Occasionally, the neat ideological division of free market and the state is ruptured by scandal. These moments can be useful for highlighting the inconsistencies and contradictions that are papered over by the ideological claim that the market is a freestanding entity. In the UK, the recent and ongoing scandal over phone hacking by subsidiaries of the News Corporation revealed the tight networks between the media and elements of the state. Despite the ideology of a self-regulating market, this scandal revealed the illegality that can occur when the state and free-market institutions collaborate behind the scenes. In this instance, the British government has launched an exhaustive investigation into allegations of police being bribed by reporters for information and breaches of privacy by reporters. The fact that some accused members of the press had close access to elected officials further complicated the issue. How can the press remain a watchdog for government accountability if it is so dependent on access to the state? If the market truly provides a bulwark against the state, then why is there such a need for clear rules about contact between members of the shallow and deep state with the media?

The recent trial of Iceland's former prime minister Geir Haarde is another prime example. The Icelandic state resorted to criminal charges against the former prime minister following the banking collapse there. In essence, the state attempted to charge its former head of government with a form of criminal negligence in failing to maintain and oversee the market.[61] In moments such as this, the bifurcation of the state and the ideal of a free market are suddenly thrust back into the public's consciousness. If markets are self-regulating and autonomous, and the state is increasingly losing sovereignty over them, then how can a former head of government face criminal charges for regulation of his country's financial system?

Concealment of our dependency

Another, almost universal motive drives the ideology of concealment. In contemporary societies, we have become highly dependent on the state. In the developed world, the state maintains the socioeconomic system that provides us with much day-to-day comfort. In the developing world, the state has become the force that promises to deliver a quality of life similar to the most developed states. However, within our current culture of global capitalism, this stark dependence on the state raises troublesome misgivings.

If the state is a driving force for the development and maintenance of the economy, then how do we define the private sector? In the policy examples discussed earlier, privatization merely turns into a distancing of implementation from the state, but nonetheless, an implementation reliant upon taxpayer support. In addition, debates in the shallow state often conceal a consensus and quiet policy development and implementation by the deep state. What links these two forms of state behavior together?

The parallel thread between these examples is the need to reconcile our absolute dependency on the modern state with our myths about freedom, equality, and the independence of the individual. If we recognize that the outcomes of our socioeconomic system are not the result of an impartial, invisible hand of the marketplace, then we are forced to confront the unpleasant truth. The state structures the rewards, incentives, and punishments of our present system. Yet, many of us prefer to consider ourselves as largely autonomous agents standing or falling on our talents and effort. Instead, in the developed world, our comfortable lives depend on state policies. Conversely, this also means that the inequalities in our societies are due largely to state policies. For those of us living in the developing world, the progress, or lack of progress, in our lives can be traced to state policies.

The other unpleasant truth connected to the deep state's increasing co-optation of policy is that our survival depends on the state. While debates on the coming ecological crisis play out in the shallows, the deep state attempts to take the actions necessary for the survival of our societies. In the past, existential threats to our social order came from the threat of war by other states. Today, we face profound risks from environmental damage, industrial accidents, and weapons of mass destruction. These dangers drive us even more into the arms of the state. What human institution besides the state is powerful enough to protect us from these dangers? Concealing the state shields us from recognizing this dependency.

This dependency on the state for continued survival strikes at the core of much conventional wisdom about economic development and the role of the individual. Much of the world has worked out some sort of accommodation with the status quo of global capitalism. However, this ideological concordance is tied to several underlying assumptions. One is that the private market is somehow autonomous from politics and thus allows individuals to succeed on the merit of their talents and industriousness. Another is that the present model of economic development faces no real limitations on growth. Thus, each generation hopes to be more successful than the previous one and all remain confident that their standard of living will improve indefinitely.

The worldview embodied in this understanding is currently under siege. The looming ecological crisis undercuts the assumption that growth based on our inherited model of capitalism is unlimited. Instead, the realities of shortages in nonrenewable resources and the risks to sustaining a vast global population are impinging on the consciousness of many. Catastrophic risks, such as climate change and the degradation of our food supplies, are irresolvable through the mantra of more competition and freer markets. For example, more competition seems unlikely to stop overfishing. Similarly, less regulation seems unlikely to control experiments with genetically modified crops. Rather, there is an increased need for the state to protect common resources, regulate growth, and to coordinate these policies with other sovereign states.

To acknowledge this need, and the fact that our survival now hinges on political actions, undermines a lot of comfortable assumptions. Individuals are not free to rise as far as they can in the economy, unless their activity is compatible with state policies on manageable growth. The invisible hand of the market will not lead to fair, equal outcomes, but, if unrestrained, will cause pernicious results. Many of us will face a future of, at least, a more modest standard of living as resources are depleted. Our fate, now more than ever, rests in the hands of our governments. The individual has less control over his own destiny, and must accept this to survive in a depleted, overcrowded world.

This reality is troubling and fits poorly with the theories of political legitimacy we have inherited. In the most developed countries, our various constitutional theories begin with core assumptions about individual freedom. By extension, it is this individual freedom that enables us to place limits on authority from an autonomous vantage point outside of state control. To recognize instead our dependency on the state means that we must also confront the weakness of constitutional constraints on the postmodern state.

If we turn to examine theories about the state, then we find that the ideology of concealing the state avoids confronting two difficulties. First, the history of state formation demystifies the origin of contemporary governments. Contemporary nation states evolved to meet the specific social and political problems of their time. Concealing the state avoids an obvious question: if nation states had to evolve in the past when confronted with broad challenges, then isn't our contemporary situation a good candidate for another period of rethinking the state? By denying its current role in global capitalism, the postmodern state avoids the question of whether or not contemporary failures show it is time to replace it.

Second, if we examine theories of political legitimacy that have evolved alongside state institutions, then we find an unresolved, recurrent problem. As the anarchist tradition shows, state sovereignty is closely linked to coercion. Justifying the state's use of coercion has long been a challenge to theories of political legitimacy. For contemporary states, the challenge of justifying their coercive powers is even more problematic, given the almost invincible technologies of coercion and surveillance that are available to the most developed nations. Given this unresolved tension from the past, it is simply easier for the state to conceal its ability in this area.

This last point raises another question, though. Nation states have existed for quite some time and have weathered earlier crises. If contemporary states are turning to a newer ideology to resolve their political contradictions, then surely this recent turn is displacing a previous ideological consensus? If the current response to crisis is a shift in ideology, then surely history can provide us with previous examples of this dynamic? For this reason, we should look at past theories of the state. These theories have evolved alongside the state's institutions in an attempt to legitimize the state's claims to sovereignty. As we shall see, the greatest challenge for these theories has always been to legitimate the state's use of coercion against its subjects and, more recently, its citizens. The overwhelming power of contemporary states is easier to conceal than justify.

Notes

1   Matt Williams, "Republican Congressman Paul Broun Dismisses Evolution and Other Theories," *The Guardian*, October 6, 2012. Available at: http://www.guardian.co.uk/world/2012/oct/06/republican-congressman-paul-broun-evolution-video

2   John Eligon and Michael Schwirtz, "Senate Candidate Provokes Ire with 'Legitimate Rape' Comment," *The New York Times*, August 20, 2012, p. A13.

3   Ulrich Beck, *Risk Society: Towards a New Modernity* (London: Sage Publications, 1992).

4   Beck, *Risk Society*, p. 186.

5   Francis Fukuyama provides a philosophical and political exploration of this theme in his *Our Posthuman Future: Consequences of the Biotechnology Revolution* (New York: Picador, 2003).

6   Mark Townsend, "English Defence League Forges Links with America's Tea Party," *The Observer*, October 9, 2010. Available at: http://www.guardian.co.uk/uk/2010/oct/10/english-defence-league-tea-party?INTCMP=SRCH

7   Nelson D. Schwartz, "U.S. Companies Brace for an Exit from the Euro by Greece," *The New York Times*, September 3, 2012, p. A1.

8   John Collins Rudolph, "A Climate Skeptic with a Bully Pulpit in Virginia Finds an Ear in Congress," *The New York Times*, February 23, 2011, p. A 15.

9   This decision by the SEC was widely reported in the media; the original press release can be found on the SEC website. Available at: http://www.sec.gov/news/press/2010/2010-15.htm

10 Leslie Kaufman, "Woman Wanted by E.P.A. is Arrested," *The New York Times*, November 2, 2010, p. A17.

11 Scott G. Borgerson, "Arctic Meltdown: The Economic and Security Implications of Global Warming," *Foreign Affairs*, vol. 87, no. 2, March/April 2008, pp. 63–77.

12 Severin Carrell, "Network Rail Study to Assess Impact of Climate Change," *The Guardian*, July 1, 2010. Available at: http://www.guardian.co.uk/environment/2010/jul/01/network-rail-study-climate-change?INTCMP=SRCH

13 Law enforcement visibly polices in the shallows. This police function includes the maintenance of the criminal justice system and everyday local ordinances. In addition, we find at this level of the state the political science phenomenon of NIMBY (not-in-my-backyard) issues. For a good summary of research on NIMBY issues, see Carissa Schively, "Understanding the NIMBY and LULU Phenomena: Reassessing Our Knowledge Base and Informing Future Research," *Journal of Planning Literature*, vol. 21, no. 3, 2007, pp. 255–66.

14 For an example of recent research on this topic, see Kathleen M. McGraw and Thomas M. Dolan, "Personifying the State: Consequences for Attitude Formation," *Political Psychology*, vol. 28, no. 3, 2007, pp. 299–327.

15 For an example of the complexities surrounding this point, see Markus Kemmelmeier and David G. Winter, "Sowing Patriotism, But Reaping Nationalism? Consequences of Exposure to the American Flag," *Political Psychology*, vol. 29, no. 6, 2008, pp. 859–79.

16 For a good summary of the US case, see William A. Galston, "Political Knowledge, Political Engagement, and Civic Education," *Annual Review of Political Science*, vol. 4, June 2001, pp. 217–34.

17 For a good study on this topic in the United States, see Michael X. Delli Carpini and Scott Keeter, *What Americans Know About Politics and Why It Matters* (New Haven, CT: Yale University Press, 1996).

18 Kristy E. H. Michaud, Juliet E. Carlisle, and Eric Smith, "The Relationship Between Cultural Values and Political Ideology, and the Role of Political Knowledge," *Political Psychology*, vol. 30, no. 1, 2009, pp. 27–42.

19 For an example, see Markus Prior, "News vs. Entertainment: How Increasing Media Choice Widens Gaps in Political Knowledge and Turnout," *American Journal of Political Science*, vol. 49, no. 3, 2005, pp. 577–92.

20 The campaign statement was made by Rep. Michelle Bachmann. Friedman's critical commentary can be viewed at: http://www.cnn.com/video/#/video/politics/2011/08/21/rs.friedman.politics.cnn?hpt=hp_t2

21 The reference is to a campaign talk by Governor Rick Perry in August 2011. See Ashley Parker, "A Day After Fed Uproar, Perry Tones It Down," *The New York Times*, August 18, 2011, p. A12.

22 Andrew Healy and Neil Malhotra, "Myopic Voters and Natural Disaster Policy," *American Political Science Review*, vol. 103, no. 3, 2009, pp. 387–406.

23 For a good discussion, see Howard Rosenberg and Charles S. Feldman, *No Time to Think: The Menace of Media Speed and the 24-hour News Cycle* (New York: Continuum, 2008).

24 Benedict Anderson, *Imagined Communities: Reflections on the Origin and Spread of Nationalism* (London: Verso, 1991).

25 Michael M. Ting, "Legislatures, Bureaucracies, and Distributive Spending," *American Political Science Review*, vol. 106, no. 2, May 2012, pp. 367–85.

26 Jeffrey R. Lax and Justin H. Phillips, "The Democratic Deficit in the States," *American Journal of Political Science*, vol. 56, no. 1, January 2012, pp. 148–66.

27 Richard R. Lau and Caroline Heldman, "Self-Interest, Symbolic Attitudes, and Support for Public Policy: A Multilevel Analysis," *Political Psychology*, vol. 30, no. 4, August 2009, pp. 513–37. This article builds on earlier research by Lau in David O. Sears, Richard R. Lau, Tom R. Tyler, Harris M. Allen, "Self-Interest vs. Symbolic Politics in Policy Attitudes and Presidential Voting," *American Political Science Review*, vol. 74, 1980, pp. 670–84.

28 Richard McGregor, *The Party: The Secret World of China's Communist Rulers* (New York: Harper Collins, 2010), p. 27.

29 David Kocieniewski, "But Nobody Pays That: G.E.'s Strategies Let It Avoid Taxes Altogether," *The New York Times*, March 25, 2011, p. A1.

30 For a good description and some historical context, see Merve Kavakci, "Turkey's Test with Its Deep State," *Mediterranean Quarterly*, vol. 20, no. 4, 2009, pp. 83–97.

31 Dexter Filkins, "Letter from Turkey: The Deep State," *The New Yorker*, March 12, 2012. Available at: www.newyorker.com/reporting/2012/03/12/120312_a_fact_filkins

32 Peter Dale Scott's description of the "deep politics" of the United States has inspired many followers. For example, one can visit the online forum www.deeppoliticsforum.com. Scott's most recent book is *American War Machine: Deep Politics, the CIA Global Drug Connection, and the Road to Afghanistan* (New York: Rowman and Littlefield, 2010).

33 For a summary of these conspiracy theories and rumors about the 9/11 attacks, see "9/11 Conspiracy Theories: How They've Evolved," *BBC News Magazine*, 28 August 2011. Available at: http://www.bbc.co.uk/news/magazine-14665953

34 Peter Gill, *Policing Politics: Security, Intelligence, and the Liberal Democratic State* (London: Frank Cass & Co. Ltd., 1994), pp. 75–9.

35 Charlie Savage, "A Simpler Label for Not-So-Secret Information," *The New York Times*, November 5, 2010, p. A23.

36 For a concise discussion, see "Briefing: WikiLeaks," *The Economist*, December 4, 2010, pp. 33–5.

37 For a recent study, see Michael J. Hogan, *A Cross of Iron: Harry S. Truman and the Origins of the National Security State, 1945–1954* (Cambridge: Cambridge University Press, 2000).

38 Suzanne Mettler, "Reconstituting the Submerged State: The Challenges of Social Policy Reform in the Obama Era," *Perspectives on Politics*, vol. 8, no. 3, September 2010, pp. 803–24.

39 Mettler, "Reconstituting the Submerged State," p. 804.

40 For example, see Christopher Howard, *The Hidden Welfare State: Tax Expenditures and Social Policy in the United States* (Princeton, NJ: Princeton University Press, 1994); and Marie Gottshcalk, *The Shadow Welfare State: Labor, Business, and the Politics of Health Care in the United States* (Ithaca, NY: Cornell University Press, 2000).

41 James H. Kuklinski, Paul J. Quirk, Jennifer Jerit, David Schweider, and Robert F. Rich, "Misinformation and the Currency of Democratic Citizenship," *The Journal of Politics*, vol. 62, no. 3 August 2000, pp. 790–816.

42 For a good overview of this development, see Donald F. Kettl, "The Transformation of Governance: Globalization, Devolution, and the Role of Government," *Public Administration Review*, vol. 60, no. 6, 2002, pp. 488–97; and Andrew Jordan, Rüdiger KW Wurzel, and Anthony Zito, "The Rise of 'New' Policy Instruments in Comparative Perspective: Has Governance Eclipsed Government?" *Political Studies*, vol. 53, no. 3, 2005, pp. 477–96.

43 For a good theoretical overview of this paradox, see Erik Swyngedouw, "Governance Innovation and the Citizen: The Janus Face of Governance-beyond-the-State," *Urban Studies*, vol. 42, no. 11, October 2005, pp. 1991–2006. In contrast, for a microlevel case study, see Ross Beveridge, "Consultants, Depoliticization and Arena-Shifting in the Policy Process: Privatizing Water in Berlin," *Policy Sciences*, vol. 45, no. 1, March 2012, pp. 47–68.

44 Consider the themes of President Obama's 2011 State of the Union speech. He warned of another "Sputnik moment" where the United States must invest heavily in education and infrastructure to foster economic innovation. Apparently, in any policy area the safest political ground is to make your issue one of national security.

45 Isabelle de Pommereau, "Germany Finishes Paying WWI Reparations, Ending Century of 'Guilt,' " *The Christian Science Monitor*, October 4, 2010. Available at: http://www.csmonitor.com/World/Europe/2010/1004/Germany-finishes-paying-WWI-reparations-ending-century-of-guilt

46 Richard L. Hasen, "End of the Dialogue? Political Polarization, the Supreme Court, and Congress (August 14, 2012)," *UC Irvine School of Law Research Paper* No. 2012–65. Available at SSRN: http://ssrn.com/abstract=2130190. This academic study was publicized by Adam Liptak, "Sidebar: In Congress's Paralysis, a Mightier Supreme Court," *The New York Times*, August 21, 2012, p. A10.

47 For a review of the literature, see Grant A. Jordan, "Iron Triangles, Woolly Corporatism and Elastic Nets: Images of the Policy Process," *Journal of Public Policy*, vol. 1, no. 1, February 1981, pp. 95–123; and Paul A. Sabatier, "Toward Better Theories of the Policy Process," *PS: Political Science and Politics*, vol. 24, no. 2, 1991, pp. 147–56.

48 Charles R. Shipan, "Regulatory Regimes, Agency Action, and the Conditional Nature of Congressional Influence," *American Political Science Review*, vol. 98, no. 3, 2004, pp. 467–80.

49 John Vickers and George Yarrow, *Privatization: An Economic Analysis*, vol. 18 (Cambridge, MA: MIT press, 1988), p. 3.

50 Robert Booth and Nick Hopkins, "London 2012: Depth of G4S Security Crisis Revealed," *The Guardian*, July 12, 2012. Available at: http://www.guardian.co.uk/sport/2012/jul/12/london-2012-g4s-security-crisis

51 Richard Harding, "Private Prisons," *Crime and Justice*, vol. 28, 2001, pp. 265–346.

52 Travis C. Pratt and Jeff Maahs, "Are Private Prisons More Cost-Effective than Public Prisons? A Meta-Analysis of Evaluation Research Studies," *Crime & Delinquency*, vol. 45, no. 3, 1999, pp. 358–71.

53 Ethan Bronner, "Poor Land in Jail as Companies Add Huge Fees for Probation," *The New York Times*, July 3, 2012, p. A1.

54 Diane Cardwell, "Private Businesses Fight Federal Prisons for Contracts," *The New York Times*, March 15, 2012, p. B1.

55 Negative publicity surrounding the program caused British companies to begin withdrawing their support. See Nicholas Watt, Patrick Wintour, and Shiv Malik, "Government U-Turn on Work Scheme," *The Guardian*, February 29, 2012. Available at: http://www.guardian.co.uk/politics/2012/feb/29/government-work-experience-scheme-uturn?INTCMP=SRCH

56 *Flow* (2007). This political and legal battle led to the creation of a number of citizens' initiatives in Michigan, such as Michigan Citizens for Water Conservation. See http://www.savemiwater.org/ and Stop Nestle Waters and http://stopnestlewaters.org/communities/mecosta-county-mi

57 Charles Fishman, *The Big Thirst: The Secret Life and Turbulent Future of Water* (New York: The Free Press, 2011), pp. 138–9.

58 Trip Gabriel, "Rise in Online Classes Flares Debate about Quality," *The New York Times*, April 6, 2011, p. A1.

59 "Buttonwood: In Debt to Grandpa," *The Economist*, January 29, 2011, p. 73.

60 See Mary Williams Walsh and Louise Story, "Seeking Business, States Loosen Insurance Rules," *The New York Times*, May 9, 2011, p. A1.

61 For a summary, see Michael Stothard, "Former Icelandic PM Guilty of Negligence," *The Financial Times*, April 23, 2012. Available at: http://www.ft.com/cms/s/0/f774d980-8d50-11e1-b8b2-00144feab49a.html#axzz1uNzRpGXi

3

Theories of the state

My argument is that the ideology of concealment is necessary to satisfy the political contradictions of postmodern states. The previous chapters imply that we are witnessing a radical ideological shift. However, another consideration is whether the ideology of concealment is that radical a change. From a broader perspective, the contemporary ideology of concealing the state can also be interpreted as the latest turn in the intellectual history that accompanies state development.

At various points in history, the state has been forced to innovate. This motivation has come most often from the competition between states. Indeed, one thing all theories of the state share, ranging from anarchist literature to contemporary scholarship in political science, is that war drove state formation in early modern Europe. The competition between states in the context of Europe drove innovation to raise and organize the finances, manpower, and materials needed for warfare.

Much closer to our own time, states were forced to innovate again due to domestic changes. The most obvious example can be seen in the vast canon of literature exploring the state's response to industrialization and the social changes unleashed by capitalism. This response includes the creation of modern welfare states in the West. These regimes choose to use state power to ameliorate some of the social tensions generated by capitalism. In Russia, and then the developing world, we also see an alternate reaction. In this case, the state attempts to build an entirely different, anti-capitalist order. Across this range of extremes, we find the state responding to the difficult domestic problems arising from the broad social changes triggered by capitalist development.

In turn, these transformations generated accompanying parallel theories about the state, including attempts to legitimate its power. For nation states in Europe during the modern period, nationalism became a dominant justification for states engaged in warfare. Nationalism was used by both states struggling to assert their independence in Europe during the nineteenth century and Imperial powers asserting their claims to colonization. Later, as many of these European states transformed into liberal welfare states, various forms of social contract theory and constitutionalism became the legitimating theory of the state's power.

The Soviet model of state communism developed a very different ideology to justify its political and economic system. Rather than an appeal to nationalism, the Soviet model attempted to create an elaborate ideology of state socialism. At various stages in Soviet history, this ideology shifted between claims to universal leadership based on class struggle and a latent Russian nationalism. Ultimately, the nationalism of the various regions constituting the Soviet Union would outlive the Soviet state. The entire region, including Russia itself, now runs the gamut of contemporary regimes. We find the Baltic states joining the European Union's liberal democracies on the one hand, and varying degrees of capitalist, but authoritarian systems on the other.

From this perspective, an important source of support for my argument is its fit with a larger pattern of history. As state institutions have transformed, in response to various demands (whether international competition with other states or domestic pressure), new ideologies have struggled to justify the state's power. If today's postmodern state possesses previously undreamed of instruments of coercion, and requires an unprecedented level of discipline from its population for successful economic competition, then concealment as an ideology becomes less surprising and more politically logical. The ideology of concealing the state reflects the challenge of continuing this long tradition in the face of states with unprecedented power.

To gain a better understanding of this latest ideological turn, we should examine two narratives that describe the state. The first of these narratives is provided by a scholarly consensus on the formation and evolution of the nation state. According to this view, the origin of states can be traced to constellations of social, cultural, and technological factors interacting with political innovation. The context provided by this history further illuminates the current ideology of concealing the state's agency. As in the past, the contemporary ideology of the state attempts to legitimate the state's actions. This need for legitimacy is especially pressing in policy areas that states consider absolutely necessary to protect their sovereignty.

The second narrative describing the state comes from the tradition of the radical left and focuses upon both the unintended consequences of the state and its intentional pernicious use. Historically, we find a set of criticisms from this tradition that shadow the various theories of political legitimacy justifying the state. Again and again, this tradition has challenged claims that the state is acting in the best interest of the population. In some cases, this criticism has claimed that the state is simply an institution designed to benefit a ruling class at the expense of everyone else.

However, an even deeper set of anarchist criticisms from within this second critical tradition question how an institution like the state, which claims to possess sovereignty and a monopoly for the legitimate use of violence, could ever be beneficial to human beings. The main points of this critique still resonate since, despite our increasingly sophisticated theories of political legitimacy, the state contains the same contradictions that inspired the anarchist critique of the nineteenth century.

The first and foremost of these contradictions is state sovereignty. Sovereignty provides an initial guarantee for contracts and agreements across society. In this sense, the state is the unmoved mover that underpins the increasingly complex business arrangements of contemporary societies. Our ability to pay for items with the swipe of a card or by entering electronic information online relies on complex infrastructure guaranteed by the state. Cards, account numbers, and user names are taken to represent real individuals because of the state's policing of identity theft. The assumption that items on the shelf in the first world will work once we get them home comes from the consumer warranties the state requires. The confidence that business partners on the other side of the world will deliver on a contract comes from the knowledge that the state's courts will arbitrate disputes and enforce agreements. The more powerful the state, the more confident we are of these transactions in the marketplace.

However, this enforcement power ultimately rests on physical coercion. My certainty that business partners will deliver on their end of the bargain, because we have a contract, is based on the power of the state. Although it is possible to describe the constraints placed on all parties to a contract as emanating from "the law," ultimately it is the state's coercive power that limits the freedom of contracting parties. From the anarchist perspective, theories of political legitimacy can be deconstructed as efforts to conceal this kernel of violence that is the real foundation for the state. The sanctions the state applies are so certain and absolute because they ultimately can be backed by violence to the individual resisting them.

In addition, the anarchist tradition provides a moral critique that sheds further light on the attractiveness of the ideology of concealment. For the anarchists of the nineteenth century, the state's attempt to underpin all social cooperation with the guarantee of sovereignty was leading to an unprecedented dependency on the state. They saw the state expanding into more and more areas of life through regulations, policing, and new social policies. Increasingly, it would be the state providing education, pensions, workplace regulations, and even oversight of the family.

While this process delivered some short-term gains to different classes in society, it also pointed to a future of decaying, alternate social institutions. What need is there for unions, cultural associations, educational funds, and other civic organizations if the resources of the state are used to provide the social goods these groups were formed for? The anarchists feared a future that would see our utter dependence on the state for any sort of social policy initiatives. In such a future, the anarchists asked, what sort of "citizens" would any of us really be? How could citizens maintain critical oversight of something they were so utterly reliant upon?

On the one hand, if we consider the use of the state through history, then it is difficult to argue that it is inherently pernicious. Indeed, states have at times promoted progressive social policies. It is also difficult to imagine challenging many contemporary social injustices without using state structures.[1] Furthermore, the late twentieth and early twenty-first centuries have presented us with frightening examples of failed states. On the other hand, the twentieth century also provides examples of the state evolving into totalitarian dictatorships. Thus, the highly effective set of institutions that make up the nation state hold both great promise and risk. This dilemma is a constant presence that looms over the various theories of political legitimacy that have evolved in step with the nation state.

Attempts to legitimate contemporary states now face a final difficulty. Today, we are witnessing similar policies implemented by regimes that are (theoretically) radically different from one another. The examples of this behavior abound. We see surveillance technologies aggressively deployed by a democracy like the UK and an authoritarian state like China.[2] We see the world's champion of free-market principles, the United States, nationalizing financial and automobile companies in response to crisis, as well as similar actions in Russia's authoritarian system. And in almost every political system the most heated politics surround cultural issues instead of policy.[3] What explanation of political legitimacy can satisfy us while also explaining the fact that distinct political regimes are adopting similar policies?

Authoritarian behavior by democratic regimes seems paradoxical given the widespread optimism that surrounded "globalization" after the Cold War. Most political observers expected that tighter integration into a global regime of free markets would lead to greater democratization and less conflict. A recent comprehensive study of post–Cold War authoritarian regimes found that the incentive of access to global capitalism discourages authoritarian elites from blatant coercion.[4] Instead, authoritarian regimes have begun to use a mix of tools including managed elections to shore up their power. This sort of finding from political science is more in keeping with the idea that the spread of an international regime of global capitalism, including the norms it inherited from its Western origins, puts beneficial limits on state power.

If we view the issue from the perspective of an authoritarian political system, then the advantages of global capitalism to the elites of such a system are not just personal enrichment. To survive in the competition of the international system, those regimes must have economic power to support their sovereignty. Poor states in the international system have little leverage in their relations to others. A poor economy is also a weak foundation for military forces and an internal coercive apparatus. In an authoritarian system, the state operates domestically with low levels of legitimacy, thus it must rely on higher levels of coercion to maintain its sovereignty. The contemporary technology of coercion is expensive, thus authoritarian governments need global markets.

Yet, the stress of globalization is not creating a one-way convergence toward a model of liberal, free-market democracy. Indeed scholars such as Wolin have gone as far as arguing that this stress is creating an "inverted totalitarianism" in formerly democratic regimes.[5] By this term, Wolin means a regime that, although it claims to be formally democratic, is instead dominated by corporate interests and reliant upon a depoliticized and apathetic citizenry. While this assertion is clearly debatable, the fact that global capitalism creates a new context surrounding all functioning political systems is not.

If we view the issue of globalization from the perspective of a democratic political system, then we see a challenge here. In a democratic system, the state operates domestically with higher levels of legitimacy at home, and relies much less on coercion to maintain its sovereignty. However, domestic criticism in such a system often asserts local democratic values in opposition to this larger, global economic system that extends beyond its borders. In cases of conflict between these two values, the state is put in the position of asserting the need of global capitalism against its own citizenry's wishes.

In both cases, the rewards for participating in the system of global capitalism, including the economic power it provides, outweigh domestic concerns. In authoritarian regimes, more domestic dissent is tolerated for the sake of continued access to global markets. In democratic regimes, violations of popular sovereignty and democratic ideals are committed by the state for the sake of remaining competitive in this global economic system. The mutual competition between states, regardless of their political complexion, pushes all into the system of global capitalism.

This common policy outcome, on a global scale, marks an important break with the past. The formation and evolution of states reflected different paths taken in response to policy problems within particular political environments. Today, states are facing a set of similar challenges around the world. At the same time, the need for states to continue competing with one another within the context of global capitalism has reduced the range of responses available to them. Therefore, all regimes are facing a dwindling set of options. Increasingly, the common ideological solution that resolves the worst of these contradictions is for states to conceal their agency.

From this broad perspective, the ideology of concealing the state is just the latest turn in a very long process linking the state's evolution to a parallel, unfolding history of political thought. Yet, for the argument made here to be credible, two points need to be established. First, that contemporary state behavior is a logical extension of past attempts by the state to innovate in the face of challenges. Second, that the contemporary ideology of concealing the state's agency attempts to answer criticisms of the state's legitimacy in a new way. This mission of the contemporary ideology is broadly similar to that of past political philosophies. However, what is changed in both cases is the specific set of challenges faced by contemporary states, and the intellectual solution to justifying, or in this case *concealing*, current state behavior.

Formation and evolution of the state

The literature exploring the evolution of the nation state is vast. This breadth is inevitable since states were formed through different means, in different places, and at different times. For example, Charles Tilly has developed two models of state formation based on whether the state wanted to expand commerce or increase resource extraction tied to agriculture.[6] Other authors have distinguished between a West European variant of state formation and an Eastern one.[7] This last line of scholarship generally focuses on the "peasant question" and the state's responses to it. Similarly, Barrington Moore attempted to show outcomes of dictatorship or democracy depending on whether the path of state formation was rooted in patterns of agriculture or trade.[8]

In addition, we have a canon that explores the method by which the developed Western world imposed the technology of the state onto developing societies. Both through the process of creating an international system that relies on the nation state as its building block and through the violent (in some cases less violent) episodes of "decolonization," the West has pushed, pulled, encouraged, or forced the societies of the world into the mold of the modern nation state.[9] Almost always, the imposition of the Western state model in these societies came at the expense of destroying or displacing alternate local forms of social organization.

In turn, a large body of scholarship explores how well or poorly this model of the state fits the context of regions outside of Europe. For example, in Africa the process of state-building had to occur within a different geographic context than Europe. African states faced the difficult task of integrating territories with vaster environmental and ethnic diversity than in Europe. In addition, African states have attempted to consolidate themselves in an international system that puts more constraints on states going to war, for the sake of changing territorial boundaries, compared to the earlier experience of Europe.[10]

More recent scholarship has focused on the state's role in shaping domestic political systems, as well as the limitations of the nation state in today's international environment.[11] In the former case, political scientists assert that the institutional structures of the state profoundly shape even the political culture of a country. In the latter case, political scientists assert that these state institutions are declining in influence due to the growing influence of international politics. There is also an ongoing argument in political science about how much explanatory power studies of the state yield compared to studies of other political actors like parties and interest groups. Yet other political scientists argue that the study of domestic political culture or the constraints of the international economic system are more likely to tell us something relevant about contemporary politics.[12] Thus, even the relevance of focusing on the state as an object of useful study has generated a significant literature in political science.

Any author adding more commentary to this vast literature should do so with trepidation. Fortunately, from this expansive literature a few points of consensus emerge, at least for the case of states that evolved in Europe and its settler societies. First, the formation and consolidation of modern state structures is connected to the war-making function.[13] In some accounts this becomes very reductionist, citing the introduction of firearms and other technologies. Rather than specialized knights with their elaborate training and expensive armaments, states begin to draft the peasant into standing armies. These standing armies required a whole infrastructure to conscript, train, and maintain full-time soldiers. In turn, the constant expense of this state activity forces the state to modernize the collection of revenue. Arguably, these institutional changes have a deep impact on culture as well. The success and power of states that adopt this new model, especially France, forced rivals on the continent to adopt the same design for the sake of survival or deterrence.[14]

An example of these trends coming together is in the well-documented history of officer training. In France and Britain, the need for a better-educated officer to operate the sophisticated technology of the artillery and navy, respectively, leads to new military schools. The success of these new military techniques in Europe forces other societies to adopt them as well.[15] In turn, these breakthroughs in military training raise the question of what else can be accomplished with better-educated soldiers. This need for continued military development has the unforeseen consequences of breaking the old aristocratic monopoly on military command and leads to some early calls for national and public education.

Second, the theoretical empowerment of the state emerges as a legacy of religious and civil warfare. On the continent, the legacy of the Reformation and the Thirty Years' War forced the political philosophers of the age to innovate. The solution that many propose in various guises is sovereignty. In the case of territories further to the East, the solution is partition along religious lines with a sovereign ruler. Inside France, where partition is not a solution, given that the Protestant Huguenots are concentrated in urban centers and Catholics in the countryside, Jean Bodin offered a slightly different interpretation of sovereignty. Here, sovereignty becomes connected to territory and a king who stands above the divisions within the society. A subject of the French king lives in France, regardless of his individual religious affiliation. Therefore, Bodin's theoretical support for an absolutist sovereign paradoxically allows for more diversity in the society among the sovereign's subjects.[16]

In Britain, the civil war leads Thomas Hobbes to a similar paradox. His answer too is the creation of an invincible, sovereign state. The advantage of sovereignty here is that it creates a perpetual guarantor for the law (and order) society needs. Hobbes argued that this guarantor function must be perpetual if the state assumes the role of the unmoved mover that can guarantee all other contracts in the society. Thus, in his masterwork, *Leviathan*, Hobbes proposed a one-time social contract that creates a perpetual sovereign. This powerful state paradoxically provides more freedom for the individual since it provides the neutral judge needed to uphold contracts, provide law and order, and guarantee the property of individuals.

Third, the state moving into the industrial and later postindustrial periods of economic development acquires an important mediating role in the social tensions created by capitalist development. Obviously, one of the greatest ideological debates in human history is where and to what extent the state should regulate the market economy. Nonetheless, careful comparative research by political scientists documents very clearly the role of the state in addressing human concerns with the outcomes of capitalism, though with varying degrees of effectiveness in each case.[17] In the West, nation states adjust the legacy of their earlier social contracts to include economic and social guarantees beyond the legal rights discussed by Hobbes, Locke, and others.

Thus, despite the vast literature available on state development, there is an overall theme that is consistent. In Europe and its settler societies, the nation state develops as a reaction to three major challenges. The state needed to improve its ability to wage war for self-defense. In reaction, states became more centralized and justified their power largely through appeals to nationalism or religious affiliation. Later, to incorporate religious diversity, the state needed a new relationship to its subjects. This led, paradoxically, to new forms of absolutist theory where a sovereign state stands over an entire territory and everyone residing in it. More recently, the state faced a new challenge with the social tensions unleashed by capitalism. For the liberal welfare states of the West, the sovereign had to adjust the "old" social contract to include new social protections. In Russia and states following its path in the developing world, the alternative to Western capitalist society becomes the construction of a totalitarian state. The absolute absolutism of these totalitarian examples of state socialism attempts to impose a different social order to that found in the capitalist West.

The solution in all three of these diverse cases was for the state to reinforce its sovereignty. Through the use of sovereignty, the state could guarantee the society from outside attack by consolidating all of its resources (material and manpower) into one centralized army. As Foucault has shown, this process leads to the refinement of disciplines that wring even more productivity and effectiveness from this manpower and material.[18] By the twentieth century we see this process leading to total war. The states in the West, and eventually Japan, can harness their entire productive capacity for war making. The two world wars become the proof that war has shifted to an all-pervasive, society-wide endeavor.

Sovereignty also allowed the state to expand its borders and include a larger and more religiously diverse population. From the religious complications of Bodin's time, states slowly acquired the theoretical explanation for why they should be sovereign over various peoples. As the territorial breadth of states included a greater breadth of people, sovereignty became linked to the idea of a separate political identity that could be universal. In this sense, universal, political citizenship is the analogue of sovereignty. The religious affiliation of the individual becomes secondary to his earthly membership in society. God becomes more distant in comparison with one's relationship to the Leviathan state.

The guarantee of sovereign authority also provided the legal infrastructure that aided capitalist development. Increasingly complex contracts and chains of transactions were possible, thanks to the legal foundation provided by an ultimate sovereign. Later, market interventions by the sovereign state allowed it to mitigate some of the tensions inherent in capitalist society. The harsh conditions of Manchester-style industrialization eventually gave way to state-enforced labor codes, market regulation, and welfare provisions.

In an extreme reaction to the tensions of early capitalism, the Russian empire was transformed through the Soviet experience into a totalitarian, state socialist alternative. In this case the state becomes arguably even more sovereign than in the West, given the imposition of state direction not only over the economy but all aspects of society. Under Soviet rule, the state closely supervised the arts, the sciences, sport, and any conceivable form of social organization in its quest for ideological conformity.

These earlier European states became, in turn, the model for state formation across the planet. This includes not only the imperialism and colonialism of the Western nation states but also the Soviet Union's domination of its satellite allies during the Cold War. The nation states we know today evolved as a response to several historical challenges that emerged in Europe. The solution to these specific problems, the nation state, was then transposed onto other societies through the process of war, colonization, imperialism, and cultural influence.

The utility and contingency of the state

Given their common histories and origins, it is interesting to think about the uses made of the state. In the eighteenth century, Liberals used the state to finish off the privileges of the old feudal order in much of Europe. The ideological arguments advanced in this conflict eventually assisted struggles for suffrage and the expansion of individual rights. In the nineteenth century, the state became active in the formation of the new capitalist market. The disruptions caused by the transition from agrarian to market society led to the twentieth-century state acting as a bulwark against market failures and the social tensions it triggers.[19] Thus, it is difficult to argue that the state has always had a pernicious impact on human beings. In some cases, the state has responded to alleviate human suffering.

However, we also see in the totalitarian dictatorships of the twentieth century the use of the state to terrorize societies. This last point, the possibility of state-organized terror, is linked to the fact that the state is not just a set of institutions and agencies. For states to function well, they must also operate in the world of ideas. At their core, states depend on the citizenry believing it has some sort of common identity.[20] For many contemporary philosophers, one explanation for totalitarianism in the twentieth century is that it was an attempt to use the state to impose an ideology upon society despite the concerns, interests, objections, or resistance of that community. Rather than recast the state's ideology, violence is used to attack the real-world constraints and human beings that have gotten in the way of utopia.[21]

These nightmare examples of totalitarianism from the twentieth century are most commonly interpreted as showing the need for keeping the state accountable through the institutions and practices of representative democracy. Indeed, since the state has been used for many ends, it seems difficult to argue that it is inherently detrimental to human beings. If one considers the religious warfare after the Reformation, the refinement of Bodin's sovereignty becomes an attractive solution to the problem of political identity. The war capabilities the state develops can in some instances be credited with deterring external aggression. Also, the social contract theories supporting the state forced it to eventually intervene in the most egregious cases of tension triggered by capitalist development. In our own historical period, the effects of failed states in the international system point to the usefulness of states. If one examines conditions in failed states like Somalia or Congo, then Hobbes' call for a strong state to guarantee order looks less objectionable.[22] Thus, the state appears to be, at least, a necessary evil when we consider life without it.

Furthermore, the necessity of the state only seems to be reinforced by the challenges of our contemporary situation. Contemporary nation states are tasked with managing an extremely complex array of social, economic, and technological policies. The state has gained enormous power through this management. At the same time, the development of these capacities has created a vast risk of catastrophe.

Governments around the world must weigh choices on economic development that are fraught with long-term risks to the environment and often short-term risks to social stability in areas like employment. Even the most noninterventionist, market-oriented states must consider education policy if they are to remain economically competitive. States must regulate specific technologies like nuclear power and genetic engineering to avoid the potentially catastrophic risks tied to them; nation states have also entered into treaty obligations with one another to regulate these specific areas of danger. Finally, aside from the risks of economic and technological development, contemporary nation states face the risks of ideologically based terrorism practiced on a scale that surpasses past episodes of political violence.

The state seems to be essential for the well-being of humans given these realities confronting contemporary society. Nonetheless, there is a tradition that argues that the state is inherently harmful to human society, no matter how well designed its institutions. Anarchist arguments against the state touch on several areas. But their overall point is that the state is ultimately harmful to human interests. As I explain later, some of these criticisms are an interesting complement to the academic consensus on the state discussed earlier. Although the anarchist tradition is rooted most firmly in the nineteenth century, its criticisms of the state take on more urgency in the aftermath of twentieth-century totalitarianism.

The development of the state provided the means to address challenges posed by new forms of warfare, political identity in growing societies, and the tensions of capitalist industrialization, but the haunting question has always been: at what cost? What paths were not taken on the way to developing the nation state that could solve these same problems?

Setting aside even older philosophical treatments,[23] radical criticism of the state takes a decisive turn with Rousseau. In his discourses on "the Arts and Sciences" and "the Origins of Inequality," Rousseau rejected the enlightenment view of historical progress. Instead, Rousseau is an early voice posing a positive category of nature to the scientific and technological progress of his time. This vein of criticism also leads him to eventually invert the social contract of theorists like Hobbes and Locke. Rather than a social contract to exit the state of nature and create a new legitimate political order, Rousseau tried to imagine a social contract to escape the sick, artificial order of his time and return to a free, natural society.

Rousseau's philosophical efforts are popularly associated with his subsequent influence on the French Revolution. However, this importance for intellectual history tends to obscure the radical implications of Rousseau's criticism of political legitimacy. By contrasting his own time with a natural ideal, Rousseau amplifies a classic but underarticulated idea: that the state is an artificial construction. Rousseau puts this bluntly in the first discourse:

> While governments and laws provide for the safety and well-being of assembled men, the sciences, letters, and arts, less despotic and perhaps more powerful, spread garlands of flowers over the iron chains with

which men are burdened, stifle in them the sense of that original liberty for which they seemed to have been born, make them love their slavery, and turn them into what is called civilized peoples.[24]

This basic point sets in motion a whole chain of related questions. First, if the state is artifice, a product of human agency, then isn't it open to further change by us? Second, if the state is not natural, then what purpose should it serve?

For Rousseau, the state in France was created to accomplish certain ends, first and foremost the protection of property. From this initial purpose, Rousseau traces the subsequent development of the current social order. In the second discourse, he asserts,

The first person, who, having fenced off a plot of ground, took it into his head to say this is mine and found people simple enough to believe him, was the true founder of civil society.[25]

The subsequent attempts by Liberal social contract theorists, Conservative Monarchists, or the church to explain this institution by other means are simply camouflage for its real purpose—protecting the property of the wealthy. In this sense, they are an example of the "garlands of flowers" Rousseau criticizes in his first discourse. Living in an age before theories of trickle-down economics, Rousseau dismissed any plausible justification for this role out of hand.

Another important point that emerges from Rousseau is his criticism of representation. For Rousseau, the only way to return toward natural freedom is to have direct democracy. In his *Social Contract*, Rousseau questions the believability of an elected official serving as my substitute after an election.[26] While Locke argued that representatives are simply delegates for those of us unable to devote ourselves full time to government, Rousseau argued that representatives are only accountable the day of an election. How could a representative know every constituent's true interest on every policy topic? Even if I voted for a representative at an election, because he campaigned on certain policy preferences, how would that representative know if I changed my mind afterward when confronted with new information? This concern with direct, immediate participation in governing leads Rousseau to call for independent, small-scale communities.[27]

This impulse also lies behind Rousseau's assertion that he approved of the *corvée* (a levy of labor) more than taxation.[28] In the former, the citizen would know exactly what his contribution was and where it went. Indeed, the logic of Rousseau's point is appealing. How many of us would gain a better understanding of welfare policy and social conditions if we volunteered to help with public assistance rather than writing a check at tax season? If we are worried about public education where we live, then shouldn't we attempt to gain direct experience with local schools before we criticize the way they are funded and managed?

Echoes of Rousseau's criticism of the state appear throughout other radical traditions. For example, Rousseau's assertion that the purpose of the state was primarily to protect property, and thus serves as the origins of inequality, reemerges in Marx as the assertion that the state is the executive committee of the ruling class. Just as Rousseau dismissed various theories of political legitimacy as window dressing to justify the state maintaining inequality, so too Marx argues that:

> all struggles within the state, the struggle between democracy, aristocracy, and monarchy, the struggle for the franchise, etc., etc., are merely the illusory forms in which the real struggles of the different classes are fought out among one another...[29]

Thus, the state becomes an entity used for the protection of property and interests of a ruling class.

However, more than others, the anarchist tradition points to nagging questions about the state that have never gone away. This radical tradition's criticism of the state encompasses more than the focus on inequality and class interest found in the current of socialist ideas extending back through Marx to Rousseau. Although many anarchists would agree with the fact that the state defends inequalities that benefit the ruling class, the anarchist analysis of the state also questions the plausibility of the state's ultimate monopoly on authority and the moral consequences of society relying on the state.

For example, on the point of the state serving as the final sovereign authority for society, Bakunin long ago voiced a pertinent question. How can one institution, the state, be an expert in all areas? How is it possible for the state to judge all questions within society?

> Does it follow that I reject all authority? Far from me such a thought. In the matter of boots, I refer to the authority of the bootmaker; concerning houses, canals, or railroads, I consult that of the architect or engineer.[30]

For Bakunin, authority derives from rational recognition of areas of expertise. What is irrational to Bakunin is the idea that an individual invested with political authority is now an expert over all areas of life. Regardless of how an individual comes to political power, he is still an individual. Obviously, all individuals have strengths and weaknesses. No individual is a master of all the arts and sciences. Thus, no matter how we refine our democratic procedures, the idea of sovereign authority elevates human beings to an unnatural role.

In many ways, this skepticism of political authority is an echo of Plato's classical question: how does one train to be a politician? Other experts train in specific fields, medicine for a doctor, physics for an engineer, and the law for a lawyer. Yet, what is the required training to become a ruler over others? Historically, one answer has been warfare, such as Machiavelli's description of a prince. But in a modern state, with all of the policy areas now under its influence, what possible training could equip someone to be an expert in governing? Kropotkin vividly expresses his skepticism on this point:

> Is it not indeed absurd to take a certain number of men from out [of] the mass, and to entrust them with the management of all public affairs, saying to them, "Attend to these matters, we exonerate ourselves from the task by laying it upon you: it is for you to make laws on all manner of subjects—armaments and mad dogs, observatories and chimneys, instruction and street-sweeping, since you are the chosen ones whom the people has voted capable of doing everything!"[31]

With this skepticism toward political authority, Kropotkin echoes Rousseau's older skepticism of representation over direct participation. Since no individual can be an expert in everything, shouldn't we have as many people as possible not just voting, but governing?

Yet the idea of everyone governing in a modern nation state seems utopian. Thus, modern, liberal democratic states turned to the idea of representative government. The logic of this solution follows that of Locke's social contract. Since I cannot devote myself full time to government business, I do the next best thing by deputizing someone to represent me. From the anarchist perspective, though, this solution only seems to replicate the issue of expertise. How could a representative ever know my true needs, preferences, and aspirations? Referring to the view of a hypothetical representative, Kropotkin posits the following:

> I am unacquainted with most of the questions upon which I shall be called on to legislate. I shall either have to work to some extent in the dark, which will not be to your advantage, or I shall appeal to you and summon meetings in which you will yourselves seek to come to an understanding on the questions at issue, in which case my office will be unnecessary.[32]

In other words, no one could be a better expert in an area of immediate interest than myself. Why do I need to go through a set of representatives to reach agreements with others?

Of course, Kropotkin writing in the nineteenth century could scarcely imagine the complexity of current societies and their legal frameworks. Arguably, the advantage a representative has over common citizens is that he may draw on large resources to get to the bottom of issues. Modern representatives in government have staffs, a budget, and in many countries, the ability to issue subpoenas. Thus, the representative brings in experts to explain policy options and then chooses the one he thinks is best.

This idea is embodied in the common-law tradition of juries. Twelve jurors drawn at random from the community are not expected to be legal experts. Instead, they are expected to exhibit through their deliberations what Aristotle called "the wisdom of the multitude." Although none are experts in the law, all of the jurors can draw upon their respective education and experience. This pooling of ability gives them a collective strength lacking if we examine each individual in turn. From this perspective, the common-law tradition presumes that a jury can make a correct decision in a case if all of the facts and legal procedures are clearly presented to them by experts (in this case lawyers for both sides and a judge).

To dismiss the criticisms of the anarchists, many observers have used a similar argument. When Kropotkin, Bakunin, or other critics question the omniscient competence of the state, the counterargument is that they perform Plato's classical sleight of hand. That is, they take an individual and ridicule the idea of any one person ruling competently in all areas. Instead, the philosophical defense of the state's omniscience is usually a variation of Aristotle's "wisdom of the multitude." The state is not one individual, but instead a pooling of the expertise and abilities of many individuals. One individual cannot perform competently in all areas, but representatives supported by an expert bureaucracy can. In this sense, representatives are like a jury. Each has his or her limitations; their selection may even be somewhat random, but taken together and provided with expert guidance, the jury as a collective can reach a competent decision.

Deeper challenges

However, the anarchist criticism runs philosophically deeper than these dueling analogies indicate. A jury is deciding a question of fact. Similarly, we can imagine a democratically elected representative, provided with expert advice, choosing between policies if the issue was merely one of fact. But political decisions are often more than a choice of facts. Instead, political authorities must choose between different policies on the basis of philosophical convictions. Should the state invest more in education or lower taxes for greater economic growth? When, if ever, should the state go to war? These sorts of questions extend beyond analysis of factual information.

For Rousseau, even the best procedures to elect representatives would only guarantee that the elected official implemented the general will at that moment. Once an election passes, how could an official claim, for example two years later, that he still knew how his constituents would want him to vote on any issue? We can imagine a situation where even the most dedicated representative cannot know this. For example, imagine a member of the US House of Representatives, or an MP from the British House of Commons, or even a representative from a local city council holding a number of meetings to ask his constituents how they wish for him to vote on a specific upcoming bill. Imagine further that these constituents answer with a resounding positive vote for the legislation. The representative then attends his meeting of the House, Parliament, or city council prepared to cast a supporting vote as his constituents instructed him to do a week or more ago.

However, during that session, our imaginary representative listens to a lengthy debate that includes updated information. During the course of this debate the representative finds himself shifting his own opinion as he listens to an impassioned debate. At this point in our imaginary example, would the representative not wonder if his constituents would also change their minds if they were present? Doesn't it seem illogical for the representative to cast a vote from instructions he received previously before engaging in the actual debate on legislation? It is in this sense that Rousseau argues true representation is an impossibility. Even the most dedicated representative can only hope to know what his constituents wanted at a particular moment in the past.

Furthermore, as we increase the stakes involved in such decisions, the moral authority of political office seems to inversely decline. Delegating authority to a professional politician to decide some mundane matters might seem plausible. Locke argued in his idea of the social contract that individuals needed to delegate the business of government to others, so that they are free to tend to their private interests. However, would it ever be rational to cede authority to someone else to decide on war or peace? For Bakunin it is highly irrational to cede the power of life and death (a monopoly on coercion) to someone else. Why would I ever admit that someone has a right to kill me or order me to kill someone else?

This also brings us to the other complication between deciding a question on facts versus philosophical beliefs. If my beliefs clash with the course taken by my representatives, then why should I acquiesce? The answer from Locke and most social contract theory, arguably up through the twentieth-century political philosophers John Rawls and Jurgen Habermas, is a procedural one. If we structure the competition of ideas and political positions fairly, then the outcome of this clash should be fair. Or, at least, it is a pragmatic way to structure politics to avoid violence.

From the anarchist perspective, this question invites an analysis of degrees. Perhaps I would easily acquiesce to the majority on many policy points. Giving in to the majority is easier the less concerned I am with an issue. On the other hand, politics is also about a clash of values. The more important the value to me, the harder it will be for me to admit political defeat. Arguably, I should do so in many cases for the greater good of social peace, tolerance, or out of concern and empathy for others.

Yet, there is always a limit. In Locke's social contract, his concern with this point leads him to conclude that one always has the right to "appeal to heaven." By this euphemism, Locke means a right to rebel if one is convinced that the government is tyrannical. Even in Hobbes' seemingly iron-clad contract, the sovereign must still have police since he cannot expect an individual accused of violating the sovereign to surrender voluntarily. Thus, in the social contract theories we associate with contemporary constitutional regimes, there is an idea of limits to authority and justified resistance or rebellion.

Arguably, the most sophisticated version of social contract theory available to us is that of the late twentieth-century theorist John Rawls. This modern version of the social contract replaces Hobbes and Locke's speculative state of nature with a hypothetical "original position."[33] This original position is described by Rawls as a thought experiment where individuals have all of their rational capacities, but no knowledge of their status in society. In Rawls, the social contract's limits seem even grayer since it would be irrational for us in this original position to choose anything other than a set of arrangements that benefit the least well-off in society. Rawls attributes this rational conclusion to the fact that since any of us in the original position could find ourselves in this least well-off position, we will want to minimize poverty and other misfortunes. For Rawls, then, the requirements of the social contract demand that the state provide many of the social welfare provisions we associate with modern, developed states. In this sense, Rawls places even broader limits on state authority than in the older social contract theory of Locke. Now individual rights include a broad basket of minimum welfare guarantees that the state must provide.

Among sophisticated theories of political legitimacy, there are always limits to state authority. Social contract theories are the most explicit in their call for limits to state power. However, it is difficult to imagine any theories of the state that lack such claims. Even extreme supporters of state power find themselves beholden to some sort of limits. For example, in Carl Schmitt's notorious work on sovereignty, *Political Theology* (published in Weimar Germany), the discussion is that of the state's power during the exception, or in other words, crisis and emergencies.[34] Schmitt attempts to construct an extreme definition of sovereignty claiming that it truly lies with the part of the state (or the individual) that can decide to suspend the rule of law. Schmitt argues that "All tendencies of modern constitutional development point toward eliminating the sovereign in this sense."[35] However, Schmitt questions the realistic limits of constitutionalism, arguing that "...whether the extreme exception can be banished from the world is not a juristic question."[36] Instead, Schmitt argues that the true limits of the state are grounded in the needs of an emergency situation, and the state's need to do what is necessary to survive. Thus, even a theorist of dictatorship like Schmitt implies that the state requires some sort of justification, such as an emergency due to social disorder, to fully exercise its sovereign power.

Other highly charged nationalist or communist ideological claims about the legitimacy of the state rely, almost always, on a claim of necessity. In other words, the vast power being turned over to the state is a necessary evil for the sake of a higher cause. Though such claims support extreme totalitarian states, the "ends" that they claim to seek are used to justify dictatorial "means." Thus, in a philosophical sense (though not one of much use to those trapped under such a regime), even totalitarian theories of state legitimacy contain the germ of a limit to state authority. The vast power of the state still must be linked, however tangentially, to the ideological goal of communism, fascist superiority, or extreme nationalism.

When the ideology supporting totalitarian regimes crumbles, the political system collapses. We have seen such events again and again in the wave of regime change that swept across Eastern Europe at the end of the Cold War. In some historical cases, the totalitarian regime can go on for a while in a twilight period that rests on almost pure coercion.[37] Yet, even in contemporary times with sophisticated mechanisms of coercion, pure force remains a very ineffective prop for political rule. In this sense, sovereignty is always problematic for theories of political legitimacy. Even extreme supporters of the state, and apologists for dictatorship, find that they need a justification for the absolute authority the state claims.

Perhaps Schmitt, as an open theorist of dictatorship, is less afraid to grapple with an unpleasant truth. Sovereignty is ultimately about force, and theories of political legitimacy attempt to justify this monopoly of violence. However, with the exception of the anarchist tradition, the necessity of the state's ability to use violence, however selectively, is never questioned. Here, we see why for many anarchists like Bakunin the state seems akin to a belief in God. The state serves as an unmoved mover, a final authority that is always correct. This infallibility of the state serves as a linchpin to everything else, much as God's ultimate authority is the keystone for various theologies. We cannot really question the omnipotence of God within various theologies, but theology attempts to explain how this is for the best.

One answer that is often repeated to the anarchist challenge of legitimating political authority is constitutionalism. Yet, given the amount of scholarship now available on creating constitutions, constitutionalism is not an easy refutation of the anarchist position.[38] Elites usually draft constitutions with little input from society, often in secrecy, and then submit their efforts to a plebiscitary referendum for legitimacy. Indeed, the elites typically drafting a constitution rely upon their social status, fame, or moral authority to justify their actions.

Despite these elitist origins, the contemporary political philosopher Jurgen Habermas argues that we can still view constitution making as an example of democratic action if we interpret a constitutional convention as "the founding act in an ongoing process of constitution making that continues across generations."[39] In other words, we can view constitution making as an act that enables participation to occur. Thus, despite their elitist origins, constitutions are co-original with democratic participation since constitutions, with their rules and institutions, make future democratic activity possible.

However, from an anarchist perspective this view of constitution making ignores an important point. Politics introduces a moral dimension that requires some judgments and understanding of the original motivation behind constitutional arrangements. Central to Habermas' broader philosophy is the idea that reason is integral to human communication because I wish to convince or explain to others some goal.

However, we can think of many other interactions, common to the human condition, which rely on subterfuge and efforts at obfuscation rather than transparency. Consider the examples of seduction, "white lies" to avoid hurting others, and the ancient art of selling in the marketplace. In all of these cases, how we morally judge an individual's efforts turns on the question of his initial motivations. A "white lie" is often acceptable to us if we learn that it shielded another from unnecessary emotional pain, some exaggeration is expected in the market place, and moral judgments on seduction are as old as human literature. Therefore, judgments about communication rest in part on the motivations behind it. The communication used to construct a constitution is potentially undermined by the motivations of those behind it.

This point is especially relevant given the scale of constitution making. The number of individuals affected by this activity is much larger than some of the examples of smaller-scale social interactions mentioned above. Given this impact when designing political rules that individuals must submit themselves to, the pragmatic acceptance of constitutional origins found in Habermas' and others' commentaries is difficult to accept. How can the rules created by elites, often for vary narrow political ends, be accepted as justifying state sovereignty? Even if this original act leads to positive reforms later in history, how does this original act justify the ultimate authority of the state?

Furthermore, another insight from the anarchist tradition turns on the issue of motivation and its link to the morality of action. In other words, even if I act correctly, there is a difference between me doing so of my own volition rather than from fear of punishment. From this perspective Bakunin explains:

> And even when the State enjoins something good, it undoes and spoils it precisely because the latter comes in the form of a command, and because every command provokes and arouses the legitimate revolt of freedom; and also because, from the point of view of true morality, of human and not divine morality, the good which is done by command from above ceases to be good and thereby becomes evil. Liberty, morality, and the humane dignity of man consist precisely in that man does good

not because he is ordered to do so, but because he conceives it, wants it, and loves it.[40]

Thus, when I act out of fear of the state, I behave as a believer does from fear of God's punishment. Are my actions then that of a moral, rational individual? From the anarchist perspective, this instead makes my behavior akin to an ignorant servant or slave, motivated by fear.

Closely related to this point is the anarchist concern of dependency. The existence of the state lulls society into accepting that it is dependent on it. As Kropotkin explains,

> The absorption of all social functions by the state necessarily favoured the development of an unbridled, narrow-minded individualism. In proportion as the obligations toward the state grew in numbers the citizens were evidently relieved from their obligations towards each other.[41]

From this perspective, the state's role and dominance becomes self-fulfilling. In a more recent study of the contemporary state and its contradictions, Jens Bartelson argues that "we simply seem to lack the intellectual resources necessary to conceive of a political order beyond or without the state, since the state has been present for long enough for the concept to confine our political imagination."[42] Thus, our dependence on the state cripples our ability to imagine alternatives to social organization.

For Bakunin and other anarchists, improving the process of choosing our representatives does not resolve these issues. Once an individual delegates authority to someone else, they are no longer equal. While we might imagine some individual trustee relationships in society that seem plausibly acceptable (parents to children, expert assistance in some area), this model falls apart once we invest the trustee with lethal, coercive power over other adults, based on philosophical convictions, rather than facts.

Of course, Bakunin's run-in with the authority of Russian and Prussian autocracy colored his view of the state. For Bakunin the state attempting to serve in its role as the unmoved mover was the blundering, overreaching empire of the nineteenth century. This perception of the state is reflected in the enthusiasm of the nineteenth-century anarchists for science as a foil to the ignorant state of their time. Starting with Proudhon, this current of scientific opposition to the state carries on through much of the radical left including Marx's development of scientific socialism.

However, for the anarchists the realization that the state could co-opt science was also present early on. Kropotkin and others became alarmed at the ability of the state to apply scientific method to coercion, both in domestic policing and in its military efforts against other states.[43] The concerns of nineteenth- and twentieth-century anarchists in this area included permanent, standing armies and the vast files that police agencies were beginning to accrue. As technology enhances the coercive power of the state, the anarchist fear has been of a dwindling space for social and individual independence.

Thus, the anarchists were pioneers in pointing to the latent dangers of technocracy. On the one hand, rule by experts would seem more logical to the anarchist critique of authority than other options. Long ago, Jeremy Bentham hoped to reduce the politics of his time to arithmetic through his philosophy of utilitarianism. Bentham argued that by accepting the goal of pursuing "the greatest good for the greatest number," social policy could be reduced to a science of calculating costs and benefits.[44] To this end, Bentham devoted himself to the attempt to quantify human happiness so that it could be measurably compared to the costs of obtaining it.

Despite this effort at a science of politics, Bentham returned to a position not that far removed from Plato's speculations of *Republic*. Bentham argued that utilitarianism would require the training of "sympathetic observers" to put a number to human happiness and thus make his political calculus possible. Similarly, Plato argued that only the philosophers of his time, with their training in dialectics, would be able to rule correctly, thanks to this expertise.

Yet, in the end rule by expertise falls to the same criticism the anarchists raise against the procedural attempt to legitimize state authority. How could one area provide the expertise needed for all of society? What possible training or education can plausibly prepare an individual for such high office? On the other hand, if we adopt Aristotle's idea of the wisdom of the multitude, how do we explain a small number of individuals making choices that extend beyond facts into competing moral positions?

State, markets, and political legitimacy

The nation state emerged as a solution to specific problems faced by political elites in the early modern period. After this initial stage of formation, the state was further adapted to resolve subsequent problems such as the tensions created by capitalist industrialization. In the twentieth century the state was also reorganized into more extreme forms, including totalitarian variants to support increasingly complex political ideologies. Thus, the state has been used for varying ends, some progressive and others pernicious.

This long path of state development is shadowed by the arguments used to explain and justify the state. At various stages in the state's development, these efforts have been more or less successful depending on the use of the state. In the nineteenth century, liberal states offered a progressive development in many policy areas that fit well with ideas of constitutionalism. Later, the social tensions unleashed by nineteenth-century capitalism eroded the legitimacy of the liberal state. In the twentieth century, totalitarianism destroyed trust in the state with its use of state-directed terror. In our own time, the examples of failed twenty-first-century states in parts of the world show many may simply crave any government that provides basic social order.

From this broader, historical perspective, the concealment of the state is not necessarily a radical turn. Instead, we can view this ideology as simply the latest in a long line of arguments that attempt to justify the state. What does make this latest ideological turn different is the fact that the difficulties of justifying the contemporary state are so acute. In fact, the contradictions of the postmodern state are so pronounced that an ideology of concealing the state becomes the best solution.

What is so difficult about legitimating current states? In part the problem is the latest iteration of the point anarchists made long ago. The state's goal of sovereignty is so closely tied to the coercive function that it undermines the credibility of this human innovation. Thus, the state has evolved with various ideological tools to try and justify this connection. What these various theories of political legitimacy all have in common is their ability to obscure the fact that the state relies on human agency.

For the state to fulfill its domestic function, the ultimate guarantor of all other agreements within a society, it must maintain its sovereignty. For the state to fulfill its international function, the management of relations between societies by speaking with one voice for an entire society, it must maintain its sovereignty. But sovereignty is more than a concept of international law. To maintain it, states must engage in the practice of coercion.

As I discuss in Chapter 4, the coercive capabilities of contemporary states have created a new ideological need. Instruments of coercion and surveillance have grown exponentially in the late twentieth and early twenty-first centuries. The technologies now available to the state are so troubling; they effectively puncture our remaining myths about privacy and the limits of effective coercion. This development is another aspect of contemporary politics well served by the ideology of concealing the state.

And for this reason, the ideology that legitimates contemporary states is one of outright concealment. This phenomenon of obscuring the state exploits an area of the anarchist tradition that seems weak: the state's intertwining with markets. We should not be too surprised by weakness in this area of anarchist thought. After all, a long-running debate in contemporary political science is over the link between democracy and the markets.[45] This debate has become even more complex as the process of "globalization" has forced other states to integrate into the international economic system.[46]

For Kropotkin and other anarchists, the idea of markets was antithetical to democracy since the market requires a sovereign state, with vast coercive power, to make it a reality. Kropotkin, among many others, called for replacing the market and the state with a new federative system of cooperation. The vision was to replace the domineering unmoved mover of the state with institutions of a more human scale. Kropotkin attempts to sketch how this future can be organized in his *Fields, Factories, and Workshops*. Smaller-scale economic activity would remove the need for the Leviathan state.

However, anarchist thought on how to replace the market, or to restructure labor and work, fails to take into account the ability of the state to recede into the background behind the market. Consider the attempt Kropotkin makes to untangle the state from other concepts in his *The State: Its Historic Role*. On the one hand, Kropotkin warns against the mistake of "the German school, which enjoys confusing state with society."[47] On the other hand, Kropotkin also cautions against confusing the state with "government." As he explains,

> The state idea means something quite different from the idea of government. It not only includes the existence of a power situated above society, but also of a territorial concentration as well as the concentration of many functions of the life of societies in the hands of a few. It carries with it some new relationships between members of society, which did not exist before the establishment of the state. A whole mechanism of legislation and of policing has to be developed in order to subject some classes to the domination of others.[48]

Thus, Kropotkin implies here that "the market" is indeed a fiction of the state.

Following Kropotkin as quoted above, we could argue that the market, with its labor and class relations, is part of the state. On the other hand, does that not return us to the fallacy of the German school he describes, conflating aspects of society with the state? Should we turn to an analysis of a true or "real" society that is still present despite the distortions of the state and its pseudo-autonomous free market? In his historical analysis of the state, Kropotkin shows that there have been forms of society prior to the creation of the state and thus, we can return to a community that does not have a state.

What is missing, though, from any of these options is an analysis of how the state can convincingly alienate this part of itself from the public and, yet, at other times suddenly assert its role. In times of market crisis, the state steps forward to reinforce the market. The paramount examples of this dynamic are the Great Depression of the 1930s and the financial crisis of 2008–2009. But aside from these moments of state support and intervention, the dynamic of the twentieth century, which accelerated toward its end, has been for the state to use the market as cover for its withdrawal. Behind the screen of the market, increasingly dominant in daily life, the state can choose where and when to act much more selectively than in the recent past.

How then do we explain the market's relationship to the state? Is the public's perception of the market simply an ideological illusion? This implies that the market is simply part of the state. However, this runs the risk of making the mistake Kropotkin fears and denying that there is anything happening outside of the state: conflating state and society. Despite the state's dominance, regulations, and maintenance, the "market" still seems to contain elements of individual initiative and cooperation. On the other hand, if we attempt to abstract out the state from the market, or a true part of society, then we seem to risk focusing on what Kropotkin warns is "government" rather than the state.

By exploiting this difficult terrain between state, society, and the market, and through the use of the deep and shallow state dynamic described in the previous chapter, the state can choose to conceal itself. As we shall see, the state can even hide its coercive abilities. If we examine the instruments of coercion and surveillance available to contemporary states, then this motivation for concealment becomes clear. The postmodern state's coercive power is so great that it undermines the conventional theories that have legitimated the state's power in the past.

Notes

1   The need for state involvement in the interest of social justice is an important point in Nancy Fraser's debate with Axel Honneth over "redistribution vs. recognition." See Nancy Fraser and Axel Honneth, *Redistribution or Recognition?* (New York: Verso, 2003).

2   In fact, the UK's government-appointed surveillance commissioner warned that "Britain may be in breach of its own human rights laws." See Rob Hastings, "New HD CCTV Puts Human Rights at Risk," *The Independent*, October 3, 2012. Available at: www.independent.co.uk/news/uk/crime/new-hd-cctv-puts-human-rights-at-risk-8194844.html#

3   Arguably, this is most pronounced in the United States and is supported by findings from recent political science. See Richard R. Lau and Caroline Heldman, "Self-Interest, Symbolic Attitudes, and Support for Public Policy: A Multilevel Analysis," *Political Psychology*, vol. 30, no. 4, August 2009, pp. 513–37. Lau also refers to earlier evidence of this trend. David O. Sears, Richard R. Lau, Tom R. Tyler, Harris M. Allen, "Self-Interest vs. Symbolic Politics in Policy Attitudes and Presidential Voting," *American Political Science Review*, vol. 74, 1980, pp. 670–84.

4   Steven Levitsky and Lucan A. Way, *Competitive Authoritarianism: Hybrid Regimes after the Cold War* (Cambridge: Cambridge University Press, 2010).

5   Sheldon S. Wolin, *Democracy Incorporated: Managed Democracy and the Specter of Inverted Totalitarianism* (Princeton, NJ: Princeton University Press, 2008).

6   Charles Tilly, *Coercion, Capital, and European States, AD 990–1990* (Cambridge, MA: Blackwell, 1990). Tilly is also editor of the classic, massive study, Charles Tilly ed., *The Formation of National States in Western Europe* (Princeton, NJ: Princeton University Press, 1975).

7   For example, Perry Anderson, *Lineages of the Absolutist State* (London: NJB, 1974).

8   Barrington Moore, *Social Origins of Dictatorship and Democracy; Lord and Peasant in the Making of the Modern World* (Boston, MA: Beacon Press, 1966).

9   Contemporary examples of studies in this area include Jeffrey Herbst, *States and Power in Africa* (Princeton, NJ: Princeton University Press, 2000). Atul Kohli, *State Directed Development: Political Power and Industrialization in the Global Periphery* (Cambridge: Cambridge University Press, 2004). Fernando Lopez-Alves, *State Formation and Democracy in Latin America, 1810–1900* (Durham: Duke University Press, 2000).

10 See Cameron G. Thies, "National Design and State Building in Sub-Saharan Africa," *World Politics*, vol. 61, no. 4, October 2009, pp. 623–69.

11 For example, Peter B. Evans, Dietrich Rueschemeyer, and Theda Skocpol, *Bringing the State Back In* (Cambridge: Cambridge University Press, 1985), or Stephen D. Krasner, Sovereignty: Organized Hypocrisy (Princeton, NJ: Princeton University Press, 1999).

12 For a good review of this literature, see Tuong Vu, "Studying the State through State Formation," *World Politics*, vol. 62, no. 1, January 2010, pp. 148–75.

13 For a concise overview, see Michael Mann, *The Sources of Social Power: A History of Power from the Beginning to AD 1760* (Cambridge: Cambridge University Press, 1986), pp. 453–58.

14 For an interesting counterexample of a society that does not follow this trend, see Gregory Hanlon, *The Twilight of a Military Tradition: Italian Aristocrats and European Conflicts, 1560–1800* (London: University College of London Press, 1998).

15 David B. Ralston, *Importing the European Army: The Introduction of European Military Techniques into the Extra European World, 1600–1914* (Chicago, IL: The University of Chicago Press, 1990).

16 The best study of Bodin on sovereignty remains Julian H. Franklin, *Jean Bodin and the Rise of Absolutist Theory* (reissue edition, Cambridge: Cambridge University Press, 2009).

17 For recent examples of research on the state's role in modern and contemporary welfare state economies, see Maritn and Thelen, "The State and Coordinated Capitalism: Contributions of the Public Sector to Social Solidarity in Postindustrial Societies," *World Politics*, vol. 60, no. 1, October 2007, pp. 1–36. David Bradley, Evelyne Huber, and Stephanie Moller, "Distribution and Redistribution in Postindustrial Democracies," *World Politics*, vol. 55, no. 2, January 2003, pp. 193–228.

18 Michel Foucault, *Discipline and Punish*, trans. Alan Sheridan (New York: Vintage Books, 1995).

19 The development of the state's role in managing the downsides of the market was famously described midcentury in Karl Polyani, *The Great Transformation* (New York, Farrar and Rinehart, Inc., 1944).

20 Benedict Anderson, *Imagined Communities: Reflections on the Origin and Spread of Nationalism* (New York: Verso, 1983).

21 Alain Badiou, *Ethics: An Essay on Understanding Evil* (New York: Verso, 2001).

22 For a good description of the Congo case, see Jason Stearns, *Dancing in the Glory of Monsters: The Collapse of Congo and the Great War of Africa* (New York: Public Affairs, 2011).

23 For example, one thinks of Karl Popper's alarmist efforts to trace radical opposition to the state and link totalitarianism to Western foundations starting with Plato, Karl Popper, *The Open Society and Its Enemies* (Princeton, NJ: Princeton University Press, 1971).

24 Jean Jacques Rousseau, *The First and Second Discourses*, ed. Roger D. Masters (New York: St. Martin's Press, 1964), p. 36.

25 Rousseau, *The First and Second Discourses*, p. 141.

26 Jean Jacques Rousseau, *The Social Contract*, ed. Roger Masters (New York: St. Martin's Press, 1978), p. 102.

27 Rousseau, *The Social Contract*, pp. 103–4.

28 Rousseau, *The Social Contract*, p. 102.

29 Karl Marx, *The German Ideology*, in *The Marx-Engels Reader*, ed. Robert C. Tucker (New York: Norton and Company, 2nd edition, 1978), pp. 160–1.

30 Michael Bakunin, *God and the State*, ed. Paul Avrich (New York: Dover Publications, 1970), p. 32.

31 Petr Kropotkin, *The Place of Anarchism in Socialistic Evolution*, trans. Enry Glasse (London: William Reeves, 1886). Address delivered in Paris, translated by H. Glasse. First appeared in *Le Révolté*, 28 March–9 May; London: William Reeves. I have used the electronic version available at http://dwardmac.pitzer.edu/Anarchist_Archives/kropotkin/place_1.html

32 Kropotkin, *The Place of Anarchism*.

33 John Rawls, *Theory of Justice* (Cambridge, MA: Harvard University Press, 1971).

34 Carl Schmitt, *Political Theology: Four Chapters on the Concept of Sovereignty*, trans. George Schwab (Chicago, IL: University of Chicago Press, 2005).

35 Schmitt, *Political Theology*, p. 7.

36 Schmitt, *Political Theology*, p. 7.

37 Ian Kershaw explores the limits of coercion during the dying days of Hitler's National Socialist regime in his *The End: The Defiance and Destruction of Hitler's Germany, 1944–1945* (New York: Penguin Books, 2011).

38 For recent examples of scholarship on the politics of drafting constitutions, see Edward Schneier, *Crafting Constitutional Democracies: The Politics of*

Institutional Design (Lanham, MD: Rowman and Littlefield Press, 2006) or Andrew Reynolds ed., *The Architecture of Democracy* (Oxford: Oxford University Press, 2002). On the topic of transitional justice, see Jon Elster, *Closing the Books: Transitional Justice in Historical Perspective* (Cambridge: Cambridge University Press, 2004).

39 See p. 768 of Jurgen Habermas, "Constitutional Democracy: A Paradoxical Union of Contradictory Principles?"*Political Theory*, vol. 29, no. 6, 2001, pp. 766–81.

40 Mikhail Bakunin, "The Immorality of the State," in *The Political Philosophy of Bakunin*, ed. G.P. Maximoff (New York: The Free Press, 1953). Available at: http://dwardmac.pitzer.edu/Anarchist_Archives/bakunin/bakuninimmorality.html

41 Petr Kropotkin, *Mutual Aid* (London: William Heinemann, 1910), p. 227.

42 Jens Bartelson, *The Critique of the State* (Cambridge: Cambridge University Press, 2001), pp. 1–2.

43 A very thorough examination of the police methods that confronted the anarchists of the nineteenth century is provided by Alex Butterworth, *The World that Never Was: A True Story of Dreamers, Schemers, Anarchists, and Secret Agents* (New York: Pantheon, 2010).

44 Jeremy Bentham, *A Fragment on Government*, series eds Geuss and Skinner, *Cambridge Texts in the History of Political Thought* (Cambridge; Cambridge University Press, 1988).

45 For a good cross section of this debate, see Adam Przeworski, *Democracy and the Market* (Cambridge: Cambridge University Press, 1991); Amy Chua, *World on Fire* (New York: Knopf Doubleday, 2004).

46 For a discussion of the pressures on states to integrate into this system in the late twentieth century and the first decade of the twenty-first century, see Beth A. Simmons, Frank Dobbin, and Geoffrey Garrett, *The Global Diffusion of Markets and Democracy* (Cambridge: Cambridge University Press, 2008).

47 Petr Kropotkin, "The State: Its Historic Role," in *Selected Writings on Anarchism and Revolution*, ed. Martin A. Miller (Cambridge, MA: The M.I.T. Press, 1970), p. 212.

48 Kropotkin, "The State: Its Historic Role," p. 213.

4

Engines of oppression

There is an additional policy area that has driven contemporary states to adopt the ideology of concealment. As political observers have pointed out for centuries, coercion is a key function of the state. The state supplies the ultimate sanction over all other institutions and organizations in a society. Thus, it becomes the unmoved mover guaranteeing all other promises. The state's coercive power is the instrument that underpins its sovereignty externally and internally. In the international arena, the state's coercive capability is a deterrent to other states. Within a state's borders, the logic of the state's "monopoly of the legitimate use of physical force"[1] is that found in Thomas Hobbes: covenants without the sword are meaningless. Yet, in our contemporary time, the state has begun to conceal this role as well.

While the state's monopoly on the use of force has always been a challenge to theories of political legitimacy, the postmodern state has begun to conceal even basic police functions. Why is this a contemporary ideological need? Because, aside from challenges by other nation states, the instruments available to the nation state of today have leapt beyond any plausible opposition. Concealment of the state's coercive power reflects the need to paper over the huge gulf between the capabilities of private citizens to physically protect themselves and maintain an expectation of privacy and the state's invincible instruments of coercion and surveillance.

The technological and organizational changes found in modern military formations and police agencies represent not only quantitative improvements but also a disturbing qualitative change. In the following chapter, I discuss three different trends that support this assertion. The increasing sophistication of surveillance, including our consumer behavior in the "free market," means we face not just a reduction of privacy, but perhaps no longer have it all. The use of new military technologies like drone aircraft makes it much easier for countries, including those with democratic regimes, to wage war with less accountability. Finally, the new technologies of nonlethal force point to a future where states can ignore even the largest protests.

Throughout history, theories of political legitimacy have attempted to reconcile the coercive power of the state with morality. The state's monopoly on violence has always challenged philosophical justification ranging from arguments about the need for order to more subtle theories of "just war." The difficulty of reconciling moral authority with violence now faces an even greater challenge given the absolute coercive power available to the state. This situation leads the state to engage in unusual efforts to conceal its ability. Without this concealment, our collective myths about individual liberty and autonomy would suffer a significant blow.

Yet, the competition in the international state system forces states to develop and refine their instruments of coercion. Just as unilateral disarmament was unthinkable during the Cold War era, so too today, states must pursue new military technology like robotics lest they fall behind others. In addition to the conventional threats of war between states, there is an increasing arms race inside of states for surveillance and policing technologies that can guarantee the state's sovereignty within its borders. Arguably, the state must show other states in the international system that its "homeland" is secure before it can make credible claims to sovereignty. A secure homeland is also a place of secure financial transactions, enforceable business contracts, and lower risks of fraud. Thus, the growing complexity of market transactions has accelerated the need for internal surveillance in order to maintain business confidence.

It is important to consider the concealment of coercion separately since it is tied so closely to the state's core function of maintaining sovereignty. In this sense, the political dynamics surrounding the ideology of concealing the state should be clearer relative to this core area of state activity. Because of the links between coercion and violence, this particular area of state power has always posed the greatest challenge to theories of political legitimacy. Thus, the need for the state to now move to a strategy of concealment in this area also shows us the degree of challenge the contemporary state faces when seeking legitimacy.

Today, the state has acquired technologies that virtually eliminate privacy, ensure that enemies fight only replaceable machines rather than living soldiers, and provide non–lethal force options. The possibilities that these technologies create for controlling the population are very frightening. We can only imagine what would have happened had the totalitarian regimes of the twentieth century possessed such capabilities. The engines of oppression now available to the state have undermined past theories of legitimacy to such an extent that the state must resort to an ideology of concealment.

Historical dynamics

One of the most popular galleries in New York's Metropolitan Museum of Art is "Arms and Armor." This section is dominated in its center by a display of four complete knight's suits of armor arranged as if mounted for battle (or perhaps more romantically, a tournament). The original purpose of the medieval suits of armor and weapons in that gallery is softened by their antiquity. Nonetheless, these antiques are illustrative of an important dynamic in history. In the past, there have been periodic stages of state development where its coercive capabilities outstrip any conceivable opposing force aside from other states. Such monopolies on force, not just *de jure* but *de facto*, remained in place until new technological developments, or new forms of social organization, broke this dominance. The knight that we can romanticize today was once a state-of-the art engine of oppression.

Indeed, the best example of this dynamic is the feudal period, marked by the great gulf between the average person and its soldiery.[2] Armored knights engaged in a type of warfare that was highly specialized and required enormous up-front investment. No common person could hope to challenge them on the battlefield until their obsolescence, thanks to new technology like Swiss pikes and, eventually, firearms. The other state-of-the art technology from the feudal period was fortification. The enormous investment required for increasingly sophisticated castles illustrates again the great gulf between individuals and rulers. Thus, an age that knew great disparity between the types of armed force that a state (albeit a weak one) could organize and that available to the commons was also an age of despotism. No mass uprising or communal resistance could hope to challenge the might of armored knights until technology and social change (like urbanization) provided new possibilities.

We then see a period in the sixteenth century and late seventeenth century where commoners, though often led by nobles, were able to disrupt the state. For example, in the principalities of Germany there were the great peasant uprisings inspired in part by new religious ideas.[3] In Britain, we see the English Civil Wars toppling the Monarchy and its Cavaliers, thanks in part to the more modern forces of Cromwell's Roundheads. This period marks a transitional stage where the (often-crude) use of new firearms and cannon were disruptive to the received military strategy of the day.

However, the absolutist state that emerged later in Europe was able, through increased capacities like revenue collection, to reassert its distance. If we think about the problem of political philosophy that Hobbes faces in his masterwork, *Leviathan*, it was to logically call for the reestablishment of centralized state power after the English Civil Wars. Why should subjects support the restoration of a monarch after the freedom of the civil war period? For Hobbes, the obvious answer was that this freedom had become the war of all against all, and thus, we are paradoxically safer, and freer, under an absolute law-giving state.

In France, we find a very different political context. Why could the absolutist Sun King hold court at the open and unfortified Versailles? Because his absolutist, centralized state reduced the fortresses of the nobility and disbanded any rival military organization. The idea of a French noble raising an army that can challenge the King's standing forces becomes an anachronism under Louis XIV. It is not until Louis the XVI that new forms of resistance from an urban population with firearms could threaten the monarchy.

Closer to us in time, the twentieth century gives us the phenomenon of total war and weapons of mass destruction. However, it is also a period marked by revolution and the success of guerrilla warfare. The success of guerrilla tactics is reflected in the resources devoted to the perfection of counterinsurgency doctrine by the major powers. It is also reflected in the varying degrees of failure dealt to the military organizations engaged in such fighting. One can argue that the success of the guerrilla in the twentieth century depends in part on new international norms that oppose excessive civilian deaths. Yet, this same complicating factor, the rules of warfare for the age, has often placed some limits on the technical possibilities of state violence.[4] As the twentieth century shows, however, states have also often ignored the rules in the pursuit of total war.

From this broad historical perspective, what should we make of our contemporary situation and the armed forces of our states, especially in the developed North (or West, or whatever we want to call wealthier states)? Today, we see engines of war that are once again far beyond the capabilities of ordinary citizens. Indeed, many of these technologies are far beyond the capacity of most other nation states. Instead of being driven by metallurgy and the disciplining or reorganization of people, they are now driven by the investments in and refinements of advanced technology.

Consider that, increasingly, the most developed nations deploy robots on the battlefield. Their opponents are thus forced to engage at a great distance. The current trend points to a future where less developed nations or insurgencies send out armed combatants to engage with machines. In the case of Afghanistan, the United States has developed an entire operational infrastructure for using unmanned drone aircraft. This use of unmanned machines also reduces the visibility of coercion to its home audience. Rather than the disruption to daily life of a soldier deployed far from home, the military is able to send a machine to the battlefield. In the case of the use of drone aircraft in Afghanistan by the United States, it emerged that many of the operators piloting the machines did so in shifts at an Air Force base in the US state of Ohio. This has raised the concern that operators of drone aircraft engage in killing at a much greater psychological distance than traditional soldiering.[5] Rather than traditional combat, these operators reported to work, controlled the aircraft for a few hours, sometimes discharging weapons, and then commuted home at the end of their shift.[6]

Nonetheless, the United States has remained embroiled in the Afghanistan war for years. From this perspective, one can argue that the guerrilla or "insurgent" still has a lot of fight left in him. What is remarkable, though, is that the United States has maintained forces in Afghanistan for so long with so little political cost at home. It is on this point that we see the largest impact of shifting the fight from living soldiers to machines. The wear and loss of drone aircraft is invisible to the public compared to the suffering of soldiers. As mechanization replaces soldiers, states that can afford this technology go to war with less political cost.

Besides this deployment of technology, the most advanced nation states have developed all-volunteer armies. The use of such structures greatly reduces the visibility of coercion to the domestic population. Rather than conscripting a broad range of individuals from society for the military, volunteers are largely drawn from particular classes and regions. In the United States, Secretary of Defense Robert Gates expressed concern about this trend in 2010. He noted that for many Americans, the wars in Afghanistan and Iraq were a distant reality, because a smaller number of career soldiers carried the burden of multiple deployments. Gates also commented on the evidence showing that these volunteers tended to come from similar educational and class backgrounds. Finally, Gates noted that the recruitment of volunteers had fallen into such a regional dichotomy that US military bases were now concentrated in the US Southeast, Southwest, and West. Alternatively, the fewest number of installations are in the Northeast of the country.[7]

What is emerging is a military structure that the United States can deploy with less domestic political cost to the American government.[8] The consequences of this change are profound for the United States and the world. As Secretary Gates noted in his speech, one of the key trends within this troubling change is the increasing compartmentalization of the military from the rest of American society. Many observers, especially abroad, are puzzled by the small amount of political protest in the United States over the war in Iraq. What this point of view fails to see are the changes that have occurred within the US armed forces and American society since the 1970s. The critical difference is that, unlike the past, today's military practically constitutes a separate social class within American society. As an all-volunteer body, with many life long members, deployment of this professional military force does not create domestic political opposition like the 1960s conscript army that was sent to Vietnam.

Instead, the modern American military relies on a core of full-time military personnel who have chosen the service as a career. Many Americans choose the military career path in an effort to move up in society from poorer backgrounds. Studies of military recruitment consistently show that the service's most significant appeal to young people is its educational benefits. Individuals enlisting in the military after high school earn college tuition credits for each year they serve. While feelings of patriotism are also important to military recruitment, studies consistently show that the military's chief attraction is the social mobility it enables. For example, surveys show that high school students with college-educated parents and higher grades in school are less likely to enlist. However, traditionally poorer ethnic minorities, specifically African Americans and Hispanics, are more likely to enlist than their white peers. Thus, military service often provides a path to college and social advancement for individuals with less affluent origins in American society.[9]

Although this professional, volunteer force is ethnically diverse, it remains concentrated in specific, cohesive communities. This slice of the American population lives on or near military installations across the United States and learns to expect deployment as a possibility. Divisions within this community do exist, such as that between higher-level officers from the prestigious American military academies and lower-ranking soldiers. However, the neighborhoods near military bases across the United States are some of the most racially integrated in the country. This social cohesion sets these communities apart from others across the Unites States.[10] In surveys of opinion, military personnel drawn from similar backgrounds in American society and with similar career paths show significant attitudinal differences from civilians. From this perspective, US military personnel live in tight-knit communities that are supportive of soldiers and families, but are also disconnected from the average American's daily life.[11]

On this point, it is noticeable that the major source of resentment toward the wars in Iraq and Afghanistan has been from the National Guard and Reserve members' families. These reservists traditionally support full-time soldiers as needed during emergencies. However, the Iraq conflict has seen many National Guard units deployed for 12 or more months at a time, depending on the unit and its specialization. This group is drawn from a much more inclusive cross section of the citizenry compared to the compartmentalized career soldiers. As a result, deployment of the National Guard has been one of the more politically difficult aspects of the war for both Republican and Democratic presidential administrations.

Further deployments of reserve units would be necessary if the professional army were not also supported by so-called "contract soldiers" serving with US forces in Iraq.[12] Contract soldiers are employees of private American companies under contract with the US Department of Defense. Currently, these contract soldiers are one of the largest contingents of coalition troops in Iraq and are almost equal in size to the British contribution. These mercenary forces perform a broad range of functions that used to be the exclusive responsibility of US troops. The most elastic of these duties, security, allows contract soldiers to fill critical gaps in the overstretched volunteer army. Given this group's monetary motive for being in Iraq, it is not plausible to expect any political pressure from the public over casualties in this group. Indeed, the casualties from the contract forces are largely invisible since the media does not give them the same attention as other battlefield deaths.

Besides these structural changes to the military's composition, improvements in weaponry and battlefield medicine have held American casualties in Iraq to a minimum. Compared to the Vietnam conflict, fewer American soldiers die on the battlefield. Compared to an even larger number of wars, the recent conflicts in Afghanistan and Iraq show that while soldiers are still grievously wounded, the lethality of those injuries has declined remarkably.[13] Improvements that cost the United States less lives on the battlefield make the overall likelihood of using force more likely. This tragic paradox stems from the simple political calculation that force is easier to apply the lower its cost in American lives. Thus, fewer casualties increase the likelihood of some lives being lost because all deployments are politically cheaper.

This decline in American military deaths through better battlefield medicine also corresponds to an increased effectiveness on the battlefield. With improvements in military weaponry and technology, fewer soldiers can cover larger areas of occupation. Thus, American military forces can occupy a country the size of Iraq, at least tenuously, with a relatively small force of about 160,000 troops. The result of these two trends is fewer forces deployed and fewer casualties from that smaller force.

Another irony of this situation is that improvements in battlefield medicine and weapons technology that save the life of the common American soldier also increase the odds of collateral damage affecting foreign civilians. For example, reliance on cruise missiles and air strikes reduces American military deaths, but this is offset by the likelihood of injuring innocent bystanders. Estimates of Iraqi civilian deaths range in the tens of thousands. Yet, large numbers of Iraqi civilian deaths have so far failed to make a strong impression on the American public. Obviously, the moral logic of distinguishing between the two groups is tragically nearsighted. Even by conservative estimates, the total number of Iraqi civilian deaths since the American-led invasion began is far beyond the number of US military casualties. Besides the immediate suffering these deaths represent for the people of Iraq, this violence has triggered an exodus of the country's middle class and best educated. Thus, Iraq will continue to feel the consequences of this population loss for decades to come.

Nonetheless, American politicians know that what is significant in domestic politics are American military casualties, not the innocents caught in the fray a world away from their constituents. So, as the political costs for using military force come down through fewer battlefield deaths and the deployment of smaller, compartmentalized forces, it is easier for this and future American administrations to use force.

Further technological developments are likely to continue this political trend. For example, recent reports in the news media and scholarly sources reveal that the US Department of Defense is investing heavily in robotics research.[14] This priority is supported by an enthusiastic US Congress, which has consistently increased funding in this area over the last few years. The military already uses robots to help with bomb disposal and other dangerous tasks. Most impressive to date has been the increased use of robotic aircraft, drones, for aerial reconnaissance and remotely controlled air strikes.

Besides robotics, reports of even more bizarre military research, with far-reaching ethical consequences and questions, have appeared in the American and British media. The research arm of the Department of Defense, the Defense Advanced Research Projects Agency (DARPA), has been experimenting with the remote control of animals. Apparently, one of their largest experiments has involved using sharks for naval reconnaissance. The sharks have electronics implanted in them allowing an operator to steer them toward a chosen target. DARPA has pioneered this line of research because using a living organism, like a shark, saves much time and cost over developing a machine to do the same task (i.e. swim like a shark). The research is attempting to ascertain the feasibility of using sharks and other modified animals for dangerous reconnaissance missions.[15] Similarly, a more mundane but equally bizarre area of research is the possible use of smaller animals such as insects for both spying and small amounts of electrical power generation.[16]

The instrumental logic driving these developments in technology and capability raises a fundamental question for a democratic state. If robots, machines, and modified animals make up an increasingly significant element of US fighting forces, then what will happen to the politics of military action?

One obvious point is that the use of machines and other substitutes for human soldiers reduces the political pressure on policy makers. The public's tolerance for casualties is an important calculation when a democracy goes to war. With the increased use of machines, this political pressure can be reduced. Therefore, current trends within the American military establishment may make it much easier for politicians to support future wars. This possibility represents a challenge to long-held assumptions about democracies and war.

In political philosophy, theorists have long assumed that one of the responsibilities of democratic citizens is defense of the state. Modern political scientists, who have been concerned with the public's lack of interest in foreign policy, knew that voters would at least pay attention on issues of war and peace. This traditional assumption is often cited as an important advantage of democracy. Many argue that democratic governments are more pacific since citizen armies will only support wars that are vital for self-defense. Yet, this traditional assumption, already debatable, is made even less plausible by career, volunteer armies and technologies that reduce the human cost to the home front.

Coercion and the market

The state's concealment of coercion is also aided by popular belief in an independent "free" market. For example, in the United States, arguably a country with the greatest freedom of speech protections available, we see the market aiding state surveillance. It is particularly interesting to consider the case of US telecommunications companies, an area of the economy that is considered world leading. In the fall of 2010, it emerged that private companies were having difficulty quickly responding to government requests for wiretapping surveillance.[17] All of the firms involved quickly agreed to make necessary changes so that wiretaps could be easily "switched on" when requested. Implementation of this feature required close technical collaboration. In fact, officials explained to *The New York Times* that telecommunications companies were never fined for failing to comply with wiretap requests, because this would be disruptive to the close collaboration between their engineers and government technicians. Thus, quiet state action hides behind the myth that free markets, with many private companies providing services, act as a bulwark to state encroachment.

A well-publicized dispute between the Canadian firm RIM and the governments of India and the United Arab Emirates also shows that private companies are rarely bulwarks against the state. In this case, the two governments demanded that RIM turnover encryption "keys" that would allow their security agencies to monitor communications. As the dispute was resolved, by RIM turning over this information to the two states, it emerged that what these governments wanted was the same access that RIM had already provided to governments like the United States and most of Western Europe.[18]

In a similar case following rioting in London in 2011, private companies met with British officials to discuss allowing police forces greater access to various social media. The looters and rioters (in some cases) appeared to organize events and share information through social networking services like Twitter. This voluntary meeting with representatives from Facebook, Twitter, and RIM appeared to be a retreat by the government from earlier calls for legislation in this area. However, the paradox of voluntary cooperation from these companies, conducted in a closed-door meeting, is that the government's surveillance demands have now been met in a less transparent way than legislation would have demanded.[19] This behind-the-scenes agreement with private enterprise also allowed the British government to avoid unpleasant comparisons to authoritarian regimes, like China and Iran, which have also sought such controls. Thus, rather than serving as a bulwark against state intrusiveness, we often find private enterprise enabling the state.

Surveillance links between the state and free-market enterprises are not especially new. In the United States, private industry has co-opted the individual social security number because it is the most reliable form of identification. Now individuals routinely give this number to private companies for access to services and lines of credit. Arguably, this activity has reduced privacy in the United States faster than any government action. A stolen social security number has devastating consequences for individuals.

The media is filled with stories of individuals who suffer this loss spending years "trying to get their life back."

A similar pattern is emerging in Britain with national identity cards. Although there are objections being raised by traditional civil liberties groups to the introduction of identity cards, another objection is that many private companies will piggyback onto the larger official database.[20] The assumption is that various consumer services will begin to use this form of identification. Hence, consumer demand for increasingly sophisticated services, ones that require a company to firmly establish with whom they are dealing, will make this identity scheme increasingly pervasive. Indeed, the British government has speculated that the scheme's costs may be partially covered by charging private financial companies for access to the registry. It is easy to foresee how this new registry will be used to tie individuals with good credit to financing for various status objects and increasingly more intricate, at a distance, services. This will drive the expansion of the original government project to more and more corners of daily life.

The contemporary state's outsourcing of coercion is even more surprising. The best example in this case is the reliance of the United States on private military contractors to provide manpower in Iraq and Afghanistan. However, the creative fiction of hiring "independent contractors" enables the US military to avoid the public scrutiny, and political fallout, of conscription. In the United States, this has become a standard operating procedure for the country's armed forces. Along with the enlisted volunteers, various contractors are hired in roles ranging from logistical support to combat.[21] The latter role typically occurs under the euphemism of "security" work. Overall, there has been a pervasive privatization of armed forces.

Other states have also increasingly outsourced coercion. In Australia, the government has privatized the detention of illegal immigrants. This privatization has come with a long list of abuses and failures by the private companies involved.[22] A similar trend toward privatization of prisons can be seen in the United States. In a recent case in Florida, a state judge blocked the looming privatization of twenty-nine state prisons. This instance of the courts blocking privatization was interesting because the judge complained that state legislators hid the legislation for this action within the "hidden recesses" of a budget bill.[23] Thus, market obfuscation can empower the state. Yet, this obfuscation undermines the argument, heard across the spectrum of political rhetoric and academic discourse, that the free market helps to check the power of the state.

The myth of the free market provides another ideological analogue in the United States. The right to bear arms is often defended on the political right as an ultimate check against tyranny. Indeed, many argue that the widespread legal ownership of firearms is proof of the freedom embodied in the American republic. Of course, this ideological position aids the concealment of true coercion. It is absurd to think that the light weapons citizens may legally own is a counterweight to the vast instruments of coercion possessed by modern, developed states. In the United States, citizens, providing they follow the rules, may legally own semiautomatic assault rifles. However, these are only a threat to other citizens. The contemporary state found in the United States possesses an arsenal that is a galaxy away from that which even the wealthiest and most unscrupulous individual could plausibly obtain. Thus, the argument that the right to bear arms is an ultimate check on state power serves the ideology of concealing the state. This myth obscures the truly invincible nature of contemporary state power.

Privatization of coercion and surveillance increases the concealment of the state as accountability is a step removed from government. We can consider the extraordinary case that emerged in the UK during the winter of 2011. The case against a group of so-called environmental extremists, accused of planning to occupy a privately run power plant, collapsed when it emerged that an undercover police spy had been embedded in various environmental groups for seven years. In court, the role of this individual became a central question as it began to look as though he were an agent provocateur and had clearly breached ethical guidelines.

Yet, even more amazing was the discovery of the agent's organization in Britain. The National Public Order Intelligence Unit is neither a branch of Scotland Yard nor the London Metropolitan Police. Instead, its functions were privatized to a limited company run by the Association of Chief Police Officers (ACPO).[24] This organization, which operates as a private limited company, had become controversial in 2009 when it emerged that it was under government contract to produce lists of "domestic extremists" for use by the nation's police forces. After receiving bad publicity for putting clearly innocuous, peaceful but perhaps politically active citizens on this list (for which there was no mechanism of appeal and apparently no method to obtain for public scrutiny), the contract was revoked. In 2011, following this further scandal involving ACPO, the government promised a thorough review of the contract.

This is an example of the state concealing itself behind privatization. Once the scandal broke in Britain's national press, the state announced an investigation into the bad behavior of this nongovernmental contractor. Of course, it is still the taxpayer's money being used to spy on citizens. But privatization, justified for the sake of efficiency, makes this activity less accountable to the public and provides a stalking horse for the state. Bad behavior, or shall we say, behavior that would embarrass a democratic state with rule of law, is subcontracted in the name of efficiency. However, if this unpleasant surveillance operation then comes to light, the state can claim ignorance of the methods used, and promise a review. The punishment will obviously be to revoke the lucrative contract issued to the agency by the state.

An even deeper question of accountability emerges from a trend in the United States. In the face of continuing budget cuts, as local and state governments refuse to increase taxes or fees, many police departments have resorted to unpaid volunteers.[25] Although unarmed, these unpaid volunteers are being used to make up for shortfalls in police personnel in a variety of roles. The goal of such programs is to free regular police to handle the most dangerous crimes, while leaving volunteers to follow up on more routine investigatory procedures. However, one must wonder at the unpaid volunteers' motivations. There is also an unresolved question of oversight of such volunteers. If a police officer is found in violation of rules in the field, then he risks a formal review process and sanctions. Unless their behavior is found criminally corrupt, it is unclear what sanctions could be applied to unpaid volunteers other than asking them to stop donating their time.

Surveillance and the market

Arguably, the best example of the market obfuscating the role of the state is in the domain of surveillance. A dynamic of particular importance in developed countries is that products and services, which incorporate surveillance technologies, have become status objects. Increasingly, it is routine for consumers to sign away access to private data in return for "free" communications services. The most sought-after smart phones and tablet computers come now with the convenient features made possible by constant GPS tracking technology. Yet, most scholarly treatments of privacy compare the right to privacy to large policy issues that raise questions of community welfare. The comparison of trade-offs between privacy and security is most common. However, there are other examples too like the trade-offs between public health and the privacy of medical records.[26]

Although an important dimension of the problem, these discussions of privacy can also obscure some of the social dynamics surrounding surveillance technologies. For example, some scholars are concerned that the consistent framing of the debate between surveillance and privacy as one of trade-offs obscures the political issues surrounding the deployment of surveillance technology.[27] The risk is that that when we look at surveillance this way, we lose sight of which economic interests, such as specific firms, benefit from and thus lobby government for additional surveillance.

Therefore, to gain some perspective on this other dynamic connected to surveillance, we should look at privacy differently. We should think about surveillance and privacy as a question of maintaining a collective good. This perspective is harder to find in treatments of the subject.[28] Analyzing the threat to privacy as a problem of collective action, similar to that of environmental degradation, highlights the feedback between politics and cultural forces that is missing from current discussions of privacy rights and trade-offs.

For example, Kieran O'Hara has argued that the growing social practice of publishing private photos and information on Facebook and other social networking sites could lead to changes in expectation within courts of law over reasonable expectations of privacy.[29] Thus, in a broad look at the growing loss of privacy due to consumer technologies, O'Hara has called privacy a public, rather than an exclusively private, good.[30]

At first glance, discussing privacy as a collective good may appear counterintuitive. A plausible concern is that if we move away from a rights idea of privacy, then we may risk devaluing the overall status of privacy. However, the nature of privacy as a right, and theorizing about its complexity, is a common discussion in political and social theory. For example, in a classic article on the topic, Judith Jarvis Thomson argued that privacy, while important to individual well-being, is philosophically derived from other first principle rights (such as individual liberty, freedom of association, or the right of controlling one's body).[31] Thomson argues that in many cases, what appears to be an argument about privacy can, on closer analysis, be reconstructed as an argument about property rights including ownership of our bodies and nonpublic space.

On the other hand, Jeffrey H. Reiman has objected to Thomson's thesis arguing that it risks whittling away at privacy through smaller arguments about where ownership and property rights end. Instead, Reiman introduces an argument containing a perspective closer to that of privacy as a collective good. He argues that:

> Privacy is a social practice. It involves a complex of behaviors that stretches from refraining from asking questions about what is none of one's business to refraining from looking into open windows one passes on the street, from refraining from entering a closed door without knocking to refraining from knocking down a locked door without a warrant.[32]

Thus, Reiman calls privacy a "complex social ritual" that often involves close contextual analysis when we are making judgments about it. Why do we engage in it? Because Reiman argues it is what confirms to us our individuality.

This example from the field of political theory shows that there is room within discussions of privacy for a collective perspective. The advantage of looking at privacy as a collective good is that an individual's access to privacy can be severely eroded by the choices of others in the marketplace. Thus, claims that the state is not eroding privacy are disingenuous on this point. The state is allowing privacy to disappear by allowing this activity to exist in the "free market."

There are many examples of consumer behavior undermining public goods. For example, we are all aware of the problem of environmental damage due to consumer choices. The best contemporary examples are consumers choosing inefficient, gas-guzzling SUVs or the growing difficulty of handling the waste generated by our disposable products. In a pattern similar to the aforementioned, our short-term consumer choices of convenience and status are outweighing the long-term collective good of privacy. Just as the status acquired from our large inefficient automobiles wrecks the environment, so too is our rush to be early adopters of new consumer gadgets, always connected to our ever-growing global communications network, which in turn erodes privacy. Thus, on the surface, the loss of privacy due to new consumer technologies seems similar to other collective action problems such as the environment.

In both cases, consumer choices focused on short-term results eventually lead to larger, pernicious changes. However, one key difference is that our environmental resources and thresholds are fixed in a way that privacy is not. We can imagine privacy as a resource, but one that is much more flexible and subject to altering perceptions over time. A casual look at the breadth of available historical, philosophical, and legal scholarship on the topic makes this clear.[33] Thus, attempts to define a threshold of damage or proof of erosion are much more difficult here than with environmental concerns.

Similarly, identifying state neglect in this area becomes more difficult than in the environmental case. Many commentators devote significant attention to the risks of state surveillance and the subsequent risk of creating "Big Brother." What is much more difficult to criticize is the state's role in market activity that erodes privacy. For example, many individuals are aware that choosing a large polluting automobile has a negative environmental impact. However, it is much more difficult to show that consumer demands (including individual subscriptions) for services that track one's mobile phone position reduce everyone's privacy. The common belief is that it is up to the individual to weigh the trade-offs between the benefits of new services and ceding some level of privacy. As a consequence, the state neglects to protect the commons, including our collective level of privacy.

Furthermore, in the case of environmental damage due to large cars and oversized homes in the United States, there are less harmful options available such as smaller, more fuel-efficient cars and homes. In the case of privacy and surveillance technology, there is no small car option. Instead, the technology being sold inherently reduces this good through the service it provides. The only alternative to this service and convenience is to do without. Thus a more parallel example from environmental concerns would be the waste generated by bottled water in recent years. In the developed world, clean tap water is widely available. So the product of bottled water is marketed as one of convenience and status (most bottled waters claim to be of better taste, health, unique sources, etc.). The best alternative to bottled water's long-term environmental hazards is to avoid the product all together.

Many surveillance technologies are now tied in with required social practices or, at least, social expectations. For example, mobile phones are now not only a convenience but a "necessity." The argument is that possession of a cell phone provides one with a safety net in daily life. In response to consumer perceptions that some elderly users were uncomfortable with the technology, and that many children were not prepared for an open link to the outside world, the industry has responded with a simplified phone. In addition to being very simple to operate, this class of phone will only dial out to numbers pre-programmed into it. It will also only receive calls from pre-programmed numbers.[34] The fact that our culture adjusts to these changes is apparent to anyone who has recently attempted to find the once-common, now close to extinction, public pay phone.

Another familiar example is the use of credit cards for air travel, car rentals, and hotel rooms. Initially, individuals used credit cards for their convenience when traveling. Yet, anyone attempting to pay cash for these services will gain first hand experience of the pressure to adopt these new "standards." What was once a convenience is now considered the only legitimate method of obtaining these services. Attempts to opt out and use cash for travel arrangements are likely to cause suspicion and perhaps even trigger surveillance. For example, anyone attempting to purchase an airline ticket in the United States or EU using cash is investigated by state security services.

In addition, the security and convenience of widely accepted credit cards has led us to accepting the constant monitoring of our transactions. Thus, our consumer demands for safety have led most lenders to develop constant scrutiny of our financial activity for suspicious activity. For example, a sudden trip overseas or even using your card in a new neighborhood can trigger a red flag. Anyone who has in recent years broken their usual profile or pattern of behavior is familiar with a sudden phone call from their credit card's security office or even the cancellation of their credit card. While this "service" provided by various financial institutions can be marketed as meeting a demand from customers for security, its usefulness for state surveillance is intrinsic.

Here again, the comparison to environmental concerns and consumer choices is highly relevant. Arguably, the best inroads against wasteful environmental choices have been the development of marketable alternatives. For example, marketing has created a certain status associated with owning a hybrid automobile rather than a large SUV, or the shift in more exclusive restaurants back to tap water rather than polluting, branded bottled waters.

In the case of surveillance requirements and technologies within the market, we do not find such options. Instead, the only way we can access many daily services is through participation in these surveillance practices. As two justices of the US Supreme Court recently noted, the idea of individuals giving up privacy voluntarily (by turning over information to a third party with disclosure) is increasingly questionable.[35] The justices pointed out that many consumers instead are likely to have a reasonable expectation of privacy when using services like cell phones (despite the phone company having a list of all of the numbers they call and the user's physical location) or toll payment devices in their car (which record the date and time of one's travel).

The state ultimately benefits from the collection of this vast amount of information. Although it can hide behind the argument that it is individual choice made in a free market full of data, realistically, many of us have little choice but to participate. If we wish to travel, then we must surrender personal details. If we wish to communicate using recent technologies, then we must surrender more personal details. When the state now focuses on one of us, it can (in democratic systems) take out a warrant to obtain this treasure trove from "private" companies. Thus, the idea of an independent market enables the state to conceal its growing ability to maintain surveillance over everyone in ways never possible before.

The nonlethal future of coercion

What is the future of concealing coercion? Currently, a number of governments are developing nonlethal weapons. The stated goal of developing such weapons is to provide police and military forces with a more humane use-of-force option. As one observer has pointed out, the US military began serious research into such devices after its intervention into Somalia in the 1990s.[36] Since that time research and discussion of the usefulness of such devices has continued in the US military establishment and subsequently spread internationally.

This expansion of interest has spawned a growing policy and strategy literature about nonlethal technologies. The majority of this literature focuses on two main areas. One is the possibility nonlethal options present to first-world military forces when conducting peacekeeping and humanitarian missions or interventions. Another is growing commentary over the criteria and testing necessary to deem a weapon non- or less than lethal.[37]

In addition to more practical and immediate questions surrounding the ethical use of such devices, the development of non–lethal force technologies also challenges many traditional assumptions of political theory. One of these core assumptions is the relationship between violence and power. Consider Hannah Arendt's classic distinction between power and violence:

> one of the most obvious distinctions between power and violence is that power always stands in need of numbers, whereas violence can manage without them because it relies on instruments.... The extreme form of power is all against one, the extreme form of violence is one against all. And this latter is never possible without instruments.[38]

Yet, we are seeing today radical technological change in the "instruments" that states can now deploy. How will these new technological instruments change this dynamic of power and violence?

Consider the great upheavals of the late 1980s in Eastern Europe. In the case of East Germany and Czechoslovakia, hundreds of thousands demonstrated in the streets for change. The regimes had only two choices. They could use deadly force and disperse these protests by raking the streets with gunfire and stay in power, but with nothing left except coercion. If they did not shoot, it would be a signal of the regime's abdication. China in 1989 was the exception that proved the rule; there the authorities faced throngs but were willing to shoot and remain in power. However, even in that case we see that the party had to adjust its line in the wake of this ultimatum. The party survives, but with economic concessions that have fueled rapid social change.

What if these regimes had possessed the technology to break up 100,000 demonstrators without using lethal force? What difference would this technology have made back in 1989 when the bankrupt communist regimes of Eastern Europe were told by thousands of people that their time had passed? Could such instruments provide an escape for the state from the logic of power and violence that Arendt describes? One of the unexplored implications of nonlethal force is that it allows contemporary states to wriggle out of this dilemma. Thousands or tens of thousands of us may mass in future, but the state can force us to disperse in a more humane way, removing this moral ultimatum.

In 2010, there was a curious standoff in Stuttgart, Germany, between a broad group of residents and the federal government over plans for redevelopment. The issue was over plans to demolish the city's 100-year-old train station to make way for a new high-speed rail project. The plan included clearing hundreds of trees from a nearby park much beloved by residents. The local population argued that they never fully understood what the redevelopment involved until the demolition had begun. They resorted to direct demonstrations to stop it.

The resort to direct action was necessary, according to resident leaders, because they were told the plans and development were too far along to stop. Once again, the state argued that its hands were tied. The standoff took a critical turn in the last week of September 2010. Riot police using water cannon ultimately broke up demonstrators attempting to protect the trees. The pictures of wounded demonstrators embarrassed the national government. These pictures triggered a march of 25,000 Stuttgart residents whose cry was "shame" on the government for such heavy-handed tactics.[39] This led to the chancellor herself intervening and calling for a halt to the project. Wounding citizens of the Federal Republic for protecting trees was clearly a step too far in support of train station redevelopment.

Similarly, the attempt by the French government to increase the minimum retirement age from 60 to 62 was met with massive protests in the fall of

2010. A growing strike led to an increase in transportation disruptions, and that in turn began to trigger shortages in fuel, food, and other goods in France. By October 19, police estimates had close to half a million French citizens demonstrating throughout the country.[40] The police acted with great restraint in the face of this resistance. Indeed, could the state justify using force against demonstrators over the issue of raising the retirement age by two years? Is it defensible to employ force against the citizenry in the name of pension reforms?

In the future though, the use of coercion by the police can be concealed in such situations. Of course, we have many historical examples of new technologies leading to less-than-benevolent outcomes. In her work referred earlier, Arendt emphasizes that violence requires instruments and how these instruments are applied is up to the human imagination. From this perspective, one could argue that the new nonlethal technologies are quantitative improvements on older crowd-control technologies like tear gas and water cannons.

In contrast, the technologies now being developed by a number of nation states not only are quantitative improvements but also signal a qualitative change. This qualitative change is linked to another core assumption of political theory that these technologies challenge: the proportionality of force.

As Michael Walzer discusses in his classic study of the morality of war, a key idea of just applications of force is that coercion should be proportionate to the threat. In the case of deterrence, just use of force would suggest that enough coercion is applied to deter the act.[41] From the perspective of military and police research, there is an argument that nonlethal technologies expand the spectrum of responses available to soldiers and police so that a more proportionate level of force can be applied to a situation. This is especially the case in situations of asymmetric conflict where the military faces combatants hidden among civilians.[42] On the other hand, some observers have commented on the challenge these technologies present to traditional theories of just war.[43] This challenge includes the fact that by disrupting traditional ideas of proportionality and discrimination on the battlefield, nonlethal weapons may lead to more civilians being affected by a conflict.[44]

There is a pressing domestic political concern in states developing a nonlethal capacity. Here, we need to consider the purpose of these new machines. In the United States, the Active Denial System (ADS) technology is a microwave that creates a burning sensation at a considerable distance. In Israel, the technology behind the "skunk" is an odor foul enough to trigger physical flight. These devices cause an individual otherwise committed to holding his or her ground to flee. Is this the technology needed to break up a riot or looting? Are individuals in a riot committed to standing and holding ground in the face of police force and current crowd-control methods?

Instead, the new nonlethal technologies currently under development are instruments capable of forcing even the most committed individuals to break and run due to uncontrollable physical reactions. These technologies are designed beyond what is needed to break up an atomistic, rioting crowd. Instead, they hold the possibility of dispersing crowds pulled together because of higher ideological causes or political grievances. Rather than riot control, nonlethal force on this scale represents a new instrument of social control. It provides the state with a way to break up mass crowds that are drawn together for a purpose and highly motivated to stand their ground. On this point, there are an increasing number of alarmist newspaper and more popular journalistic articles warning about the future limits of protest and civil disobedience.

Possible judgments about the proportionality of this coercion are disrupted because nonlethal technologies of social control can conceal the use of coercion. What lasting effects are there from the US microwave device, or Israel's "skunk"? None, and that is precisely the point of these devices. There will be no visible body count on the streets or casualties showing up in hospital. Arguably, one can say that these technologies do not entirely obscure the deployment of coercion. People will still know that the crowd-control machines were deployed. Yet, how are we to judge the proportionality of this much less visible form of coercion? To what extent can we argue that a disproportionate amount of coercion has been used when there is no obvious physical harm left behind?

If these devices are being developed for larger-scale social control, then the evaluation of harm and proportionality must turn to the intent of the state deploying this coercion and the individuals being controlled. Rappert observes in his study of nonlethal weapons that the deployment of such technology by police against civilians becomes highly contextual:

Here, questions about the legitimacy of force tie in with assumptions about the identity of those taking part in "public order" events and about their motivations.[45]

Thus, in the absence of obvious physical harm we will need to develop a different rubric for evaluating the proportionality of nonlethal coercion that includes some measure of intent.

If these concerns seem overblown then perhaps an example of this logic from another theater is in order. On a smaller social scale, we can see the moral implication of nonlethal force on display in the use of conducted energy devices (CEDs). The best-known manufacturer of such devices is Taser International. In fact the brand is so well known it has entered popular speech with a verb "tasing." The website for Taser International provides links to various publications, both scientific and legal, in an effort to show that the products are indeed nonlethal and are an alternative to firearms.

The widespread availability of this device to police departments has allowed police a more acceptable first use of force option. In the past when confronted with the choice of using deadly force or more traditional methods of physical coercion, police were more likely to err on the side of restraint. Now, the quick resort to "tasing" individuals and the frequency with which these devices are being used is documented by organizations like Amnesty International.[46]

There is also growing commentary in the UK about the resulting change to policing there. Famous for not carrying deadly weapons, the recent decision to arm thousands of police in the UK with tasers has caused some observers to speculate about whether this signifies a more profound shift in social relations between police and public. Thus, with the nonlethal technology of tasers, we already see that coercion is more likely to be used and that it is difficult to gauge the proportionality of this coercion.

Concealing invincibility

The future refinement of technologies like nonlethal force and the continued privatization of police and armed forces are improving the state's ability to conceal its use of coercion. As democratic accountability declines and the might of the state becomes practically invincible, the ideological pressure for concealing the state grows. The state faces similar pressure in other areas of policy, but none touches on the state's core function of maintaining sovereignty like coercion. At the same time, justifying the state's monopoly on coercion has always been the most challenging area of theories of political legitimacy. As the coercive power of the state grows exponentially, this tension has driven the state to the ideological solution of concealment.

Arguably, there is an even deeper reason for the state's concealment. Sovereignty is a goal that can never truly be satisfied. In her broad discussion about war and violence, Butler describes the impossibility of the "sovereign subject."[47] She laments that violence is "justified" or "legitimated"

> even though its primary purpose is to secure an impossible effect of mastery, inviolability, and impermeability through destructive means.[48]

In other words, the goal of sovereignty, whether for an individual subject or for a nation state, is never ending. To remain the unmoved mover, capable of guarantees and contracts that recede into the future, the state must constantly expand and refine its efforts to remain in control.

Wendt and Duvall have gone to extraordinary lengths in an analysis of sovereignty to think about its limits.[49] They argue that for the contemporary state, power flows primarily from the deployment of specialized knowledges for the regularization of populations, rather than from the ability to kill. But when such regimes of governmentality are threatened, the traditional face of the state, its sovereign power, comes to the fore,[50]

Many of us enable this ideological obfuscation through our own behavior. Thinking about the vast power wielded by the contemporary state is unsettling.

In the developed world many of us have grown used to relying on passwords to unlock our computer files, credit card monitoring to protect us from identity theft, and home surveillance systems to guard our property. However, there is an important difference beneath our day-to-day experiences of security. Our computer passwords, identity theft insurance, and home security systems are all efforts to protect our private property and us, as individuals, from other citizens. In contrast, the state has the tools and the authority to do whatever it likes to us. None of the tools available to the private citizen can defeat the powerful instruments and unlimited resources of the state. Events that reveal this stark difference and expose the older sovereign face of the state, with its link to coercion and violence, are unsettling.

Yet, how could any of us survive without this protection? Our longing for the security of our property and ourselves logically leads us to shelter beneath the state. The risks posed by other states also lead us to form and maintain the military power of our own. This paradoxical relationship is clearly described by Butler,

> To be protected from violence by the nation state is to be exposed to the violence wielded by the nation state, so to rely on the nation state for protection from violence is precisely to exchange one potential violence for another.[51]

In many ways, the iron-clad logic of Hobbes' Leviathan is still with us. We surrender ourselves to the state to escape from all the risks we face without it.

Another unpleasant fact is that individuals can benefit from immediate increases in "governmentality." This somewhat loose example of academic jargon refers to the increase in the ability of the state to govern society. Thus, as the infrastructure of the state improves, it can dramatically increase or reinforce the state's ability to regulate society. In this sense, the vast security and surveillance of the state enables many things to happen.

For example, consider the project in India to register its entire population into a new identity database. Many privacy advocates fear the long-term consequences of registering every individual's fingerprints and retina pattern with the government. At the same time, many anti-poverty organizations have long sought a new method of providing the poor in India with a reliable form of identification.[52] With this reliable identification, poorer Indians, often in rural locations, will be able to access government services and obtain credit that was impossible before. The Indian government also expects that it will allow for greater mobility within the country, enabling workers to migrate away from home villages (and the local government registry there), without losing access to government services. Thus, the Leviathan state does in some ways empower individuals within its borders. In India, a piece of identification recognized anywhere opens up many new possibilities.

Yet, there is an important difference between our contemporary Leviathans and Hobbes'. In Hobbes' world, there was still the idea that the individual remained free wherever the law is silent. Hobbes could never imagine the size and comprehensiveness of modern governments. The reach of contemporary economic regulation and the depth of surveillance that citizens tolerate (from the "private sector" and the state) are obviously beyond the scope of what any observer could imagine from even a few decades ago, much less Hobbes' time. Explaining why any entity should have this absolute power becomes more difficult as that power becomes invincible. Thus, our contemporary ideological turn is to attempt to conceal the state even here, in its traditional domain of sovereignty and coercion.

The engines of oppression available to the contemporary state have advanced quantitatively to the point that a qualitative change has occurred. The unsettling invincibility of developed states' arsenals and surveillance technologies are a challenge to traditional methods of legitimating state sovereignty. By concealing these facts behind the fiction of an autonomous market and the myth of individual choice (and possible individual resistance), we continue to enjoy the shelter of state protection while denying this disturbing trend.

Returning to an earlier theme of this chapter, there have been other periods in history where a huge gulf existed between the military capabilities of the state and the individual. As discussed earlier, the medieval period saw an overwhelming difference between a peasantry and mounted knights. Despite periodic bursts of violence in the countryside and more organized uprisings, the peasantry was no match for the coercive powers of the state. We too live in an age where the state's military capabilities have qualitatively leaped beyond the plausible opposition of society. This raises an interesting question, are we similar in any other ways to the peasants of the past?

Notes

1   Of course this is a reference to Max Weber's famous definition of the state. "A compulsory political organization with continuous operations (*politischer Anstaltsbetrieb*) will be called a 'state' insofar as its administrative staff

successfully upholds the claim to the *monopoly* of the *legitimate* use of physical force in the enforcement of its order." Max Weber, *Economy and Society*, eds. Guenther Roth and Claus Wittich (Berkeley, CA: University of California Press, 1978), p. 54.

2 For a concise overview, see Michael Mann, *The Sources of Social Power: A History of Power from the Beginning to AD 1760* (Cambridge: Cambridge University Press, 1986), pp. 391–4.

3 Although these peasant uprisings have often been commented on by more radical theorists, and sometimes forced to fit Marxist class analysis, the millenarian element and religious commitment of those involved deserves more attention than it often receives. For a good discussion of this point, see Alberto Toscano, *Fanaticism: On the Uses of an Idea* (New York: Verso Press, 2010), pp. 68–92.

4 For a wide-ranging discussion, see Michael Walzer, *Just and Unjust Wars* (New York: Basic Books, 1977).

5 John Sifton, "Drones, A Troubling History," *The Nation*, vol. 294, no. 9, February 27, 2012, pp. 11–15.

6 Mark Mazzetti, "The Drone Zone," *The New York Times Sunday Magazine*, July 8, 2012, p. MM32.

7 Speech by Secretary Robert Gates at Duke University, September 29, 2010. Available at: http://www.defense.gov/transcripts/transcript.aspx?transcriptid=4691

8 See my earlier discussion in Jason Royce Lindsey, "America and the New Dynamics of War," *Peace Review*, vol. 19, no. 2, April 2007, pp. 255–60.

9 Eighmey, John, "Why Do Youth Enlist: Identification of Underlying Themes," *Armed Forces and Society*, vol. 32, no. 2, 2006, pp. 307–28.

10 David R. Segal and Mady Wechsler Segal, "America's Military Population," *Population Bulletin*, vol. 59, no. 4, December 2004.

11 Ole R. Holsti, "A Widening Gap between the U.S. Military and Civilian Society? Some Evidence, 1976–1996," *International Security*, vol. 23, no. 3 (winter, 1998–1999), pp. 5–42.

12 The pioneering study of this new development is P. W. Singer, *Corporate Warriors: The Rise of the Privatized Military Industry* (Ithaca, NY: Cornell University Press, 2003).

13 Atul Gawande, "Casualties of War—Military Care for the Wounded from Iraq and Afghanistan," *New England Journal of Medicine*, vol. 351, no. 24, 2004, pp. 2471–5.

14 For scholarly studies, see George A. Bekey, *Autonomous Robots: From Biological Inspiration to Implementation and Control* (Cambridge, MA: MIT Press, 2005); and Alex Roland and Philip Shiman, *Strategic Computing: DARPA and the Quest for Machine Intelligence* (Cambridge, MA: MIT Press, 2002).

15 See Susan Brown, "Stealth Sharks to Patrol the High Seas," *The New Scientist*, no. 2541, March 1, 2006, p. 30; and satirically, Tom Engelhardt,

"Shark and Awe," *Salon*, March 10, 2006. Available at: http://www.salon. com/opinion/feature/2006/03/10/sharks/ Nonetheless, this odd line of research is derived from serious science. See, for example, Shaohua Xua, Sanjiv K. Talwar, Emerson S. Hawley, Lei Li, John K. Chapin, "A Multi-Channel Telemetry System for Brain Microstimulation in Freely Roaming Animals," *Journal of Neuroscience Methods*, vol. 133, nos. 1–2, February 2004, pp. 57–63.

16   James Gorman, "The Snails of War," *The New York Times*, March 20, 2012. Available at: http://www.nytimes.com/2012/03/21/science/the-snails-of-war-and-other-robotics-experiments.html?_r=1

17   For a good press description of the issue, see Charlie Savage, "Officials Push to Bolster Law on Wiretapping," *The New York Times*, October 18, 2010, p. A1. Also, Charlie Savage, "US Tries to Make It Easier to Wiretap the Internet," *The New York Times*, September 27, 2010, p. A1.

18   Amol Sharma, "RIM Facility Helps India in Surveillance Efforts," *The Wall Street Journal*, October 28, 2011. Available at: http://online.wsj.com/article/SB 10001424052970204505304577001592335138870.html

19   Ravi Somaiya, "In Britain, A Meeting on Limiting Social Media," *The New York Times*, August 26, 2011, p. A4.

20   For the language of the proposed act, see *The Guardian*. Available at: http://www.guardian.co.uk/commentisfree/libertycentral/2009/jan/15/identity-cards-act

21   P. W. Singer, *Corporate Warriors: The Rise of the Privatized Military Industry* (Ithaca, NY: Cornell University Press, 2007).

22   Nina Bernstein, "Companies Use Immigration Crackdown to Turn a Profit," *The New York Times*, September 29, 2011, p. A1.

23   Lizette Alvarez "Florida Prison Privatization Plan Hits Roadblock," *The New York Times*, October 1, 2011, p. A15.

24   See: George Monibot, "Eco-terrorism: the Non-Existent Threat We Spend Millions Policing," *The Guardian*, January 18, 2011, p. 27. Available at: http://www.guardian.co.uk/uk/2009/oct/25/police-domestic-extremists-database, and www.dailymail.co.uk/debate/article-1347832/Whos-policing-undercover-police.html

25   Jesse McKinley, "Police Departments Turn to Volunteers," *The New York Times*, March 2, 2011, p. A13.

26   Amitai Etzioni, *The Limits of Privacy* (New York: Basic Books, 1999).

27   Torin Monahan ed., *Surveillance and Security: Technological Politics and Power in Everyday Life* (New York: Routledge, 2006).

28   For examples, see Christian Parenti, *The Soft Cage: Surveillance in America from Slavery to the War on Terror* (New York: Basic Books, 2003); and Felix Stalder, "Privacy Is Not the Antidote to Surveillance," *Surveillance & Society*, vol. 1, no. 1, 120–4.

29   Zoe Kleinman, "How Online Life Distorts Privacy for All," *BBC News*, January 8, 2010. Available at: http://news.bbc.co.uk/2/hi/technology/8446649. stm

30 Kieron O'Hara and Nigel Shadbolt, *The Spy in the Coffee Machine* (Oxford: Oneworld, 2008).

31 Judith Jarvis Thomson, "The Right to Privacy," *Philosophy and Public Affairs*, vol. 4, no. 4 Summer 1975, pp. 295–314.

32 Jeffrey H. Reiman, "Privacy, Intimacy, and Personhood," *Philosophy and Public Affairs*, vol. 6, no. 1, Autumn, 1976, pp. 26–44.

33 For examples, see Barrington Moore ed., *Privacy: Studies in Social and Cultural History* (New York: M.E. Sharpe, 1984); and Alan F. Westin, *Privacy and Freedom* (New York: Atheneum, 1967); or Westin's more recent, Alan F. Westin, "Social and Political Dimensions of Privacy," *Journal of Social Issues*, vol. 59, no. 2, 2003, pp. 431–53.

34 The most well-known brand of this sort of phone in the United States marketed for children is called "Firefly." Available at: http://www.fireflymobile. com. The most popular service for the elderly is called jitterbug. See http:// www.jitterbug.com

35 See the remarks of Justices Alito and Sotomoyar reported in Adam Liptak, "Justices Say GPS Tracker Violated Privacy Rights," *The New York Times*, January 24, 2012, p. A1.

36 F. M. Lorenz, "Non Lethal Force: The Slippery Slope to War," *Parameters*, Autumn 1996, pp. 52–62.

37 Nick Lewler, "Non-Lethal Weapons: Operational and Policy Developments," *The Lancet*, vol. 362, no. 1, 2003, pp. 20–21.

38 Hannah Arendt, *On Violence* (New York: Harcourt, Brace & World, 1970), pp. 41–2.

39 For a good news summary of the episode, see Michael Slackman, "Germany Halts Demolition of Train Station," *The New York Times*, October 6, 2010, p. A11.

40 For a good news summary of the demonstration in France, see Alan Cowell, "In France, Labor Strikes Head for Showdown," *The New York Times*, October 19, 2010, p. A6.

41 Michael Walzer, *Just and Unjust Wars* (New York: Basic Books, 1977), pp. 119–20, 129–30, and 152–9.

42 Michael L. Gross, "The Second Lebanon War: The Question of Proportionality and the Prospect of Non-Lethal Warfare," *Journal of Military Ethics*, vol. 7, no. 1, 2008, pp. 1–22.

43 David Fidler, "Non-Lethal Weapons and International Law: Three Perspectives on the Future," in *The Future of Non Lethal Weapons: Technologies, Operations, Ethics, and Law*, ed. Nick Lewer (London: Frank Cass, 2002), pp. 26–38.

44 Christian Enemark, "Non-Lethal Weapons and the Occupation of Iraq: Technology, Ethics, and Law," *Cambridge Review of International Affairs*, vol. 21, no. 2, June 2008, pp. 199–215.

45 Brian Rappert, *Non-Lethal Weapons as Legitimizing Forces?* (London: Frank Cass, 2003), p. 130.

46 See Amnesty International, "USA: Excessive and Lethal Force? Amnesty International's Concerns about Deaths and Ill-treatment Involving Police Use of Tasers," AI index: AMR 51/139/2004 or "Canada: Excessive and Lethal Force? Amnesty International's Concerns about Deaths and Ill-treatment Involving Police Use of Tasers," AI Index: AMR 20/02/2004.

47 Judith Butler, *Frames of War: When Is Life Grievable* (New York: Verson, 2009).

48 Butler, *Frames of War*, p. 178.

49 Alexander Wendt and Raymond Duvall, "Sovereignty and the UFO," *Political Theory*, vol. 36, no. 4, pp. 607–33.

50 Wendt and Duvall, "Sovereignty and the UFO,", p. 612.

51 Butler, *Frames of War*, p. 26.

52 See Lydia Polgreen, "Scanning 2.4 Billion Eyes, India Tries to Connect Poor to Growth," *The New York Times*, September 2, 2011, p. A1.

5

A postindustrial peasantry?

The contemporary state possesses practically invincible instruments of coercion and surveillance. The state's weapons and machines are enormously expensive and their operation requires specialized training. In this sense, the possibility for individuals to resist the state resembles the condition of the peasantry of an earlier age. For the peasant living in medieval Europe, it was almost inconceivable to challenge armored knights or besiege a fortified castle. Such weapons and fortifications represented an unimaginable (for the peasant) investment of wealth, specialized training, and more than anything else time spent on their development rather than agricultural labor.

Later, the peasants of the early modern period did rebel, sometimes with temporary success. Their inspiration ranged from local injustices to new forms of religious fervor. However, all of the peasant uprisings from this period share a similar fate: they were eventually crushed by the superior organization of the state. Kropotkin vividly describes the outcome of the sixteenth-century German Peasants' War:

> And it was only by the stake, the wheel, and the gibbet, by the massacre of a hundred thousand peasants, in a few years, that royal or imperial power, allied to the papal or reformed church—Luther encouraging the massacre of the peasants with more virulence than the pope—that put an end to those uprisings which had for a period threatened the consolidation of the nascent states.[1]

The power gap between the German princes and their peasants was not as great as in the medieval period, but still decisive nonetheless.

Today, the citizens of the most developed, postmodern states inhabit an eerily similar context. Instead of armored knights and fortified castles, drone aircraft, vast intelligence agencies, and professional standing armies loom over the contemporary citizen. As with earlier periods of history, these coercive instruments represent a level of investment far beyond what any individuals could possess. The idea that individuals could somehow resist such powerful states is not credible. The power gap between individuals and contemporary states instead resembles a much earlier age. This observation raises an interesting question. If we resemble the early modern peasantry in this aspect of our relationship to the state, then what other parallels are there?

The usefulness of an analogy

Comparing contemporary individuals to the pre- and early modern peasantry may seem facetious. We currently live in societies with increasingly complex economic interactions linked by accelerating technology. The literacy levels of contemporary societies are a world away from that found in even the most developed countries prior to the late nineteenth century. Both the physical and social mobility offered by today's global economy are beyond what was available in even the early to mid-twentieth century. Thus, the idea of peasant cultural characteristics surviving or being replicated in the contemporary developed states seems like an inflammatory slogan rather than a reasoned critique.

Furthermore, it risks distracting us from thinking about the "real" peasants of our time in the developing world. Peasants are still engaged in subsistence agriculture in many parts of the world. We should also remind ourselves of the "peasant-like" conditions endured by immigrant labor living at the margins of the richest societies ever known. In this sense, comparing the living conditions of individuals in the most developed countries to peasants seems grotesque.

However, what we are considering is the possibility of a *postindustrial* peasant, living in postmodern states. Other observers have proposed this characterization because of the contradictions posed by postindustrial economies. For example, Leicht and Fitzgerald have used the idea for a broad analysis of the situation faced by the middle class in the United States.[2] Particularly striking to them are the high levels of debt US middle-class consumers take on, evoking memories of the always-indebted peasantry of early modern Europe. As they explain,

> Stagnant incomes, rising taxes, the pocketing of productivity gains by the corporate elite, a surplus of available credit, globalization, privatization, and labor market changes have altered what it means to be part of the American middle class. This combination of factors has produced a "post-industrial peasant"—someone who is so in debt that those to whom they owe money (and the employers and economic elites who provide the investment and consumption capital for the system) control them.[3]

Leicht and Fitzgerald attribute continuation of this situation, in part, to the dominance of neoliberalism and supply-side economics in the United States. However, they are also critics of the culture associated with modern consumerism.

While structural questions such as the organization of labor are important for the analysis presented here, to a large extent, the possibility of a postindustrial peasantry is a cultural question. We know that the living conditions of individuals in the developed world are much better than those found in poorer countries. Stark statistics on child mortality and life expectancy suffice to show that the conditions we are looking at in the most developed countries are an order of magnitude better for human thriving compared to poorer societies. Nonetheless, this fact does not rule out the possibility that cultural similarities between the two examples exist.

Like the peasantry in an earlier age, citizens in many contemporary political systems feel little connection to the state and believe they are self-reliant. In public opinion surveys, individuals in the United States overwhelmingly identify themselves as middle class despite huge differences in wealth. Hostility toward welfare is another common finding of public opinion surveys in the United States. Despite the fact that a majority of individuals receive some sort of benefit ranging from farm subsidies, student loans, and mortgage guarantee programs to traditional welfare benefits, many citizens insist that they are self-reliant.

The most extreme outcomes of this pattern in the United States have been the rise of the gated community and incorporated suburbs that maintain separate police, schools, and other services. The appeal of such neighborhoods is that they provide better and more efficient services than traditional, local government. An echo of this desire for "self-sufficiency" can be found in the archaeological evidence of medieval peasant households. The long-term trend of that era was for peasant homes to become more elaborate (with the introduction of subdivided rooms) and attempts to enclose a private lot.[4] In both cases, the desire for independence is reflected in these attempts to build a freestanding home.

Of course, today's perception of independence and self-reliance in the American suburbs is highly ironic given that it is enabled by the state. In the United States, the state-backed mortgage lenders Freddie Mac and Sallie Mae (though quasi-independent) have funded the vast majority of mortgages across the country. Without government support from these two institutions, few individuals in the United States could have obtained financing for their suburban homes. Thus, the concealment of the state here carries a great deal of irony. Many suburban homeowners, skeptical about state services, would never have obtained their property without the vast infrastructure and state subsidies the US government provided. However, consciousness of this close dependency on the state is rare. Instead, the concealment of the state allows individuals to ignore the question of why state subsidies are increasingly necessary for citizens to be able to afford homes.

For different reasons, the world of the early modern peasant was also very far removed from the state. The key demand of the peasantry across cultures has been ownership of the land, and thus, an end to rents. For the peasantry the idea of ownership of land on which they did all of the work was always an alien, imposed law. Thus, the state was an impediment, a force supporting the landowner's claims. What was missing from the peasant's conception of the state was an understanding of what the state could be doing for the peasant. The possibility of influencing the state, or using it to redistribute the land, remained an almost religious hope.

In both cases, the state is something far removed from daily consciousness. Even in cases where the state provides some sort of assistance, there is little awareness of this link to authority. Instead, the state is viewed as a probable impediment. For the early modern peasantry, the state upholds the artificial claims of landlords to the fields the peasant maintains. If only the rents could end, then the peasant would be free. For the postmodern citizen, the state is suspected of always playing the role of a taxing, regulating, interference. Thus, if you can afford it, a gated community with private services is a better solution. If only the state would get out of the way, then people could keep their hard-earned money and pursue their interests in the market.

The idea of using the state, or changing its direction for the benefit of the peasantry, seems less realistic to contemporary citizens as well. For the early modern peasant, the hope that the situation would change was an almost mystical one. For example, in the Russian empire, generations of peasants hoped that the Tsar would one day grant the mythical "black reparation" giving the land to the peasants. The firm belief of many was that the divine Tsar would already have done so if not for the false council and corruption of his advisers.

Contemporary citizens are obviously much more sophisticated, yet what are their hopes for public policy? Increasingly fewer individuals belong to political parties in the West. In Great Britain, the numbers are particularly striking, "from respective figures of around three million and one million 50 years ago, Conservative and Labour membership is down to around 177,000 and 194,000; the Lib Dems are at 50,000, down from 100,000 20 years ago."[5] The increasing expense of elections in the United States, and the huge amounts of money used to influence them, appears to be fueling cynicism about government there. In Spain and Greece, vast demonstrations opposing austerity policies have occurred. When these austerity policies are nonetheless implemented, most Greeks and Spaniards logically conclude that they have little influence over public policy. Why should such disaffected citizens hope for much at all from their distant governments?

Thus, the idea of describing contemporary citizens as a postindustrial peasantry is not far-fetched if our concern is examining individuals' relationship with the state. In this way, the comparison of contemporary citizens to a peasantry serves a useful purpose. The analogy provides some insight into the current cultural dynamics that form the wider context for the ideology of concealing the state. This is an important source of support for the ideology's success since contemporary culture works against the creation of any political challenges to the state's concealment. For many citizens, the state is a remote entity that is perceived either as not having much influence on their "real life" problems or as a distant regime that fails to listen to everyday people's complaints.

Cultural similarities

A key characteristic of any peasant society is the lack of mobility.[6] Depending on the society (and historical period) under consideration, this can mean either social mobility or an actual lack of physical mobility. However, the two are closely connected since individuals who are unable to move cannot seek out opportunities elsewhere.[7] With peasant communities of the past and present, financial burdens and complex agreements tied the peasant to the site of his agricultural work. The web of debt the peasant enters keeps him rooted to this spot despite the possibility of better opportunities elsewhere.

How different is this from the fate of many current working-class people in the developed world who cannot afford to move? In the wake of the financial crisis of 2008, many mortgage holders found their complex financial arrangements now holding them hostage to a particular place. For many their home was no longer worth what they borrowed, or they simply could not sell a home in a market flooded with repossessed (and thus marked down in price) properties. In a complex postindustrial economy, success depends in large part on one's participation in an increasingly national, indeed global, labor market. Following the great recession of 2008, the inability to move, due to high levels of housing debt, has crippled the flexible postindustrial labor market in many developed countries. The nimble, ever-changing employment scene associated with the most developed countries demands a high level of individual mobility. Job seekers that cannot keep up are quickly left behind.

On a deeper level, there is evidence for declining social mobility in the most developed countries. Compared to even a generation ago, fewer individuals are likely to leave the class they are born into. Although various measures show that economic growth worldwide has increased overall incomes, the gap between the richest and poorest has also grown. This increase in extremes began in 1980 following a period from the 1930s in which the income gap closed worldwide.[8] In the most developed countries, part of the explanation for this change has been the loss of manufacturing jobs. This form of work provided an important career track for the middle class in the twentieth century. Now in our postindustrial economies intergenerational social mobility has declined.[9]

Another surprising parallel to the peasant past can be found in the sophistication of contemporary marketing and advertising. In the peasant world of early modern Europe, one's social status was visibly obvious through dress, food, and credit the peasant received, or not, from local merchants. In our world, past purchases and even the things we look at on the Internet can affect what sort of offers we receive and whether some companies bother to advertise to us at all.[10] As the sophistication of this technology increases, we may find that the sorts of services we can easily access are predetermined by this filtering. Thus, in a technological parallel to the past, it is increasingly difficult to pass ourselves off above our station in the consumer hierarchy; we simply don't have access to the same goods and services.

Furthermore, contemporary and historical experience contradicts the assumption that a peasant population is incompatible with a modern industrial, or postindustrial, economy. In the case of Russia in the nineteenth century, we see industrialization adapting to the conditions of a peasant workforce.[11] Obviously, too, we find populations in the developing world today who can be described as peasants despite the effects of contemporary global capitalism. The existence of more modern economic organization and technology does not eliminate the possibility of individuals living in conditions of unredeemable debt, low or nonexistent mobility, and convoluted agreements over labor that characterize peasantry.

For example, some observers have pointed to the intriguing similarities between contemporary society and feudalism raised by the technology that makes our society so advanced. David Carr has raised the point that many social network companies and Internet content sites derive much of their value from the contributions users provide for free.[12] Yet, these contributors, much like peasants of an earlier age, only obtain the use of "space" given to them. Few of us own part of Facebook or Twitter, yet we are allowed to use the services for free in return for the content we provide, while the owners reap profits. Specifically, the profits for these services lie in advertising to a large audience, drawn by the content we all create.

Interestingly, in opposition to this monetization of Internet activity we find the open-source software movement. This call for creating alternative, noncommercial computing resources is oddly similar to the calls for empowering labor in an earlier age. In both cases, the call is to give away the tools and resources needed for productive labor through cooperative ventures rather than for profit ones.

Nor is education an absolute, objective remedy for peasant-like conditions. Increasingly in the United States, there is concern over an impending student debt "crisis." Some commentators worry that this area of finance is as unsustainable as the real estate bubble that collapsed in the United States beginning in 2008.[13] In an effort to provide guaranteed access to this credit, the US government has created increasingly draconian rules regarding this financing. Federal legislation prevents student loan debt from being forgiven by individuals taking personal bankruptcy. Individuals failing to pay back their student loans can have their wages garnered and be ordered to turn over financial information so that an amount to be paid from each paycheck is determined. Such modern arrangements to provide access to higher education include a level of oversight and absolute, unredeemable debt that seems more akin to the one-sided arrangements of a peasantry.

The experience of daily social interaction in contemporary societies also bears remarkable similarities to the peasant's world. The peasantry of the past was connected, intensely, to a local community.[14] Inside that world, privacy was rare to absent under the surveillance of all. It was also a sphere in which information, and rumor, spread very quickly though locally.

Many of us use communications technologies that are beyond the imagination of early modern peasants. However, with this technology we lose much of our privacy and it empowers the spread of wild rumors and conspiracy theories. Social networks like Facebook and micro-blogging services like Twitter lead many of us to reveal our daily lives in depth to a large, though virtual, audience. Although we may live at a greater physical distance from others, we can instantly relay gossip to thousands of people at once.

Another intriguing parallel in this area is the rising problem of cyber bullying or cyber stalking. Although communication technologies enable us to link with more people, they can also empower local feuds and antagonisms. In the world of the early modern peasant, we know that the intense emotions of those isolated communities led at times to shunning and even the vilification of individuals as witches. For the individual in this isolated environment, it became impossible to escape from this relentless persecution. This experience is eerily similar to the isolation and intense persecution many individuals describe in our contemporary cyber communities by victims of bullying.

These pernicious side-effects of modern communications are very disheartening. It is considered a truism today that the world is more interconnected and that an individual can travel anywhere via the Internet. We are told the world is flat, that the world is a village, or another similar metaphor. The rise of network societies and communication technologies was hailed at the beginning of this century as the foil of authoritarian regimes and a way to put power back into the hands of the individual, allowing free association.[15] The often-expressed hope was for a new era of enlightenment as individuals engaged in communication across not just political boundaries but life worlds.

However, this same technology provides new ways for individuals to segregate themselves and create their own boundaries. As one early critic pointed out,

> Even as our media technology becomes increasingly global, seamless, and interconnected, it is also individualizable, atomising, privatised and commercialised.... Though the Internet and e-mail are changing what we understand to be communication and social interaction, replacing passive television viewing with networked dialogue, there is nothing automatically democratic about this kind of interactivity.[16]

Pariser has warned that some of this segregation is happening without our awareness, thanks to targeted Internet advertising.[17] The most insidious form of this filtering to Pariser includes increasingly customized Internet search results so that we are seeing less and less of the total information, and by extension a narrower breadth of views, available online.[18]

The more commonplace form of this new boundary drawing is familiar to all of us who go online and consciously choose which media we will consume. How many of us still make an effort to listen to voices strongly opposed to our own beliefs? Increasingly, we choose narrower seams of information about our world and have less conversation with individuals outside of our cultural subgroups. Perhaps one of the most complicated of these new, chosen boundaries is religious belief.

In many of the most developed countries, those individuals committed to fervent religious ideals seemed to be a dwindling minority, concentrated in the lower class.[19] The largest successes for most missionary organizations are concentrated in the developing world, especially among the poorest and most marginalized. Of course, for many individuals in the contemporary world, religious inclinations have become very fragmented. Yet the extent to which intense superstitions and beliefs can still take hold of individuals in the most developed countries is striking.

Consider the fervor with which some Americans in 2011 took up the cause of Harold Camping, a radio host and entrepreneur who predicted that the "rapture" would occur on May 21, 2011.[20] These fervent but odd religious associations are reminiscent of peasant characteristics described by Fossier. In his analysis of daily peasant life in the medieval period, Fossier explains that "peasant worship was irregular, their knowledge and understanding of dogma scanty in the extreme."[21] Thus, the peasantry in this earlier period lacked more thoughtful, theological knowledge, but also had a fervent faith that led to "feverish outbursts of millenariasm."[22]

Ironically, the advanced communications technology and ease of publishing in today's world also enables individuals to segregate themselves. Again, religion is an interesting and complex case. In the United States, the evangelical denominations have, to a surprising degree, established parallel institutions and cultural content that is disconnected from the broader arts and sciences.[23] This subculture spans institutions, including universities, and content like bestselling books and curriculum for home schooling. Thus, despite growing interconnectedness, we also find increasingly independent subcultures in contemporary society as well.

Popular conspiracy theories and other end of the world prophecies, which often trivialize or completely ignore scientific realities, reflect a tendency that hearkens back to the pre- and early modern peasantry. Such theories and cult-like beliefs seem to be a projection, as they were in the past, of collective hopes and fears. Interesting examples include the various conspiracy theories in the United States that questioned President Obama's place of birth or the events of September 11, 2001. In these two cases, the fear of otherness directed at President Obama from a nativist, conservative leaning strain of politics and in the latter, ongoing suspicions of "big government" from more extreme libertarian outlooks coalesced into ornate conspiracy theories.

The transmission of these odd ideas across an educated society illustrates the ability of individuals, in our always-connected world, to use contemporary social networking and communications technology to delineate new borders. Despite the advocacy of philosophers like J. S. Mill and other advocates of free speech, the freedom of speech and instant availability of information found in much of the world does not lead to a coherent set of rational conclusions. Instead, we find societies drifting and subdividing into different cultural segments that can ignore one another. This outcome resembles the isolation of the homogeneous peasant villages of an earlier time, despite the fact that individuals are not as spatially segregated.

In contemporary culture, we see a widespread fetishization of technology. Devices are routinely adopted and updated by individuals not because of any intrinsic utility but because they are status objects. The rush to be a first adopter is related to status seeking rather than to exploiting the new possibilities of technology. By adopting the latest consumer device before others, many of us are trying to prove something about who we are. What is this something? It is the status that comes from being connected. Like other consumer-driven status symbols, it is constantly fleeting as the market rushes to create new status objects for us to buy. In his commentary on the meaning of gizmos and gadgets, Baudrillard observes that

> In a world dominated by communications and information, the sight of energy at work has become a rarity.[24]

Indeed it has, so how do we prove that we are working and that this work is important? We do so by being connected all the time. In daily life, we see individuals striving to show their importance by being tracked, connected, and "on." They are needed at all times and situations. This subtext is clearer if one examines the marketing behind such devices and services.

For example, Blackberry tells us that its phone, the Storm, "makes a great impression as you travel across town or to almost any corner of the world."[25] Google's latitude service allows for users with GPS on their phones to "see where your friends are right now."[26] Facebook provides us with a handy widget so that we can tell everyone what we are doing "right now." Another example that has elicited more commentary is Twitter. This popular service allows individuals to send constant updates about what they are doing moment to moment. On the other hand, cultural critics have noticed that it also seems to be a popular cry for attention.[27]

The odd tribal allegiances to brands that we see in contemporary society appear to be at their most potent here. How often do we see individuals camping out now to be the first in line for a new electronic product? Are these items scarce? Only initially, thus conferring the status sought upon the early adopter. This behavior reflects an apparent desperation to distinguish ourselves within the cacophony of consumer noise. Yet, rather than distinguishing our individuality, this behavior settles for standing out as a member of a somewhat smaller, yet fleeting subgroup. As soon as one item gains cachet with consumers, another arrives to replace it.[28]

We can consider cultural writing on the current generation of young people. Many of them express the opinion that technology gives them access to information in a transformative way. Yet, they do not seem able to explain how this transformation should translate into their education or into the workplace. Something is happening with technology and access to information, but it is unclear what practical difference this makes in their lives.

Thus, in many ways, the relationship individuals have to the technology around them is magical.[29] Objects seem empowering and important. However, these status objects are created and work through scientific principles that the general public is ignorant of. Ironically, we find much vocal, though at times incoherent or contradictory, opposition to scientific findings (evolution, global warming, etc.) while individuals rapidly embrace the technological artifacts and medical procedures this world of science provides.

While this modern peasantry objects to the science behind such improvements, the state quietly funds the research. In a pattern similar to the enlightenment of the past, the sovereign worries too much about falling behind the competition. Thus, the peasantry is reassured that various functionaries in government share their less rational worldviews, while the state quietly funds a scientific race against the rest of the world for future breakthroughs.

Thus, describing contemporary citizens in the most developed countries as a postindustrial peasantry is plausible if we consider two broad cultural patterns. First, individuals in these societies, despite their modern and postmodern comforts, are increasingly captive to a never-ending cycle of debt. Like peasants everywhere, they have little hope of ever becoming economically independent. Debt also limits their mobility and is increasingly part and parcel with the pursuit of higher education.

Second, despite our access to technology, contemporary communities seem to be returning to a past of fragmented worldviews. We could use communication technology to reach out to people very different from us. Instead, most use this capability to associate with others "like us." We can drop out of larger national cultures and embed ourselves within narrower subcultures. For most of us, our relationship to this technology is magical. We see the devices and services as transformational, but have not articulated quite how or why. Nonetheless, association with this technology confers status, so we rush to be seen with it. We are moving backward toward a time of vulnerable individuals living in fragmented cultural communities with little privacy.

Finally, the combination of debt, credit instruments, and technology is creating a daily environment similar to the peasant's past. Access to goods and services (and even our ability to "pass" as someone realistically in the market for such things) is increasingly predetermined by our highly visible credit histories. This contemporary equivalent of sumptuary laws may even be determining which goods and services we see and know about in the first place.

Peasants and politics

The common thread to all of these developments is that our worldview is becoming narrower and our social mobility reduced. Aside from technology and esoteric beliefs, individuals also segregate themselves through more traditional market activities. The starkest example of this behavior is in the dynamic of suburbanization so prevalent in the most developed countries, and now spreading to the developing world. In an earlier age, the peasantry was separated by both cultural and physical boundaries from the upper classes. Today, we see a combination of these factors coming together to sort the population by income and the "private market" in housing.

Indeed, some political analysts looking at the United States attribute increasingly homogeneous communities, including electoral districts, to the mobility individuals enjoyed there before the market crash of 2008.[30] According to this commentary, the ease with which individuals could move in the United States did not lead to increasingly diverse communities. Instead, individuals tended to segregate themselves into communities with similar cultural, economic, and political outlooks. We see this behavior reflected in the political system with the ever-rising number of noncompetitive political districts of the United States.

In contrast, a number of political scientists, such as Abrams and Fiorina, challenge this claim that individuals in the United States are sorting themselves spatially, with concomitant political effects.[31] After reviewing various survey data, they conclude that

> neighborhoods are not important centers of contemporary American life. Americans today do not know their neighbors very well, do not talk to their neighbors very much, and talk to their neighbors about politics even less. And they do not see themselves swimming in a sea of like minded people who have intimidated or cast out anyone who believed otherwise; they are aware that their neighbors differ politically.[32]

However, Abrams and Fiorina also point to survey evidence that shows fewer Americans know who their neighbors are. In addition, when they do talk to their neighbors they rarely discuss politics. What is interesting about this last point is that many Americans still think they know whether they differ from their neighbors politically despite not talking about politics.[33] Though they may often be wrong, they think that they know their neighbors' political affiliation from other indicators.

What sorts of indicators tell us an individual's political affiliation? Cultural commentary indicates that brands of consumer products are one possible source. Increasingly, the choices individuals make in the marketplace, such as buying a hybrid car rather than a gas-guzzling SUV, are seen as a tell for their political sympathies. In an eerie parallel to the very visible economic sorting described earlier, many now think they can determine a fellow citizen's politics just by looking at them. Thus, the question of geographic sorting may be moot. Either way, citizens are increasingly not talking about politics with their neighbors. Yet, despite this lack of political speech, they think they know where their neighbors stand politically. The classic idea of politics as speech is subsumed by a cultural politics.

Nor is this trend limited to the United States. In quasi-authoritarian systems like Russia, there is a similar political stratification occurring. President Putin has attempted to paint opposition to his regime as the symptom of a Westernized urban class. In Ukraine, opponents of the Orange Revolution described its supporters as cappuccino revolutionaries, invoking the stereotype of the urban, laptop-carrying, and hence Westernized coffeehouse patron. In China, the recently fallen politician Bo Xilai attempted to inject an odd-class politics into his program by promoting "red culture."[34] This nostalgic movement for China's more communist past made Bo Xilai popular with many who resent China's growing economic inequalities. Yet, rather than openly addressing this politically volatile topic, the nostalgia of the "red culture" movement provided a largely symbolic commentary and outlet for these concerns.

It is at this point, where culture feeds back into politics, that we see the long-term consequences of this situation. Politics is taking a cultural turn within very different political systems. In some cases, like the United

States, the same political institutions are present, but behavior seems to be changing. Does this simply reflect the evolution of a vibrant culture and society? Or, does this shift signal an attempt to get by or make do with a shallower politics, one where I know my opponents just by looking at them? Are we changing our politics because of some deep shift in our culture? Or, are we trying to continue practicing politics in a cultural context that is inhospitable to political participation?

On this last point, much of the "culture war" in the United States seems to be a substitute for the state. There is much dissatisfaction in the population, but who is to blame? With the state increasingly less visible, the venom directed at "Liberal Democrats" or "Right Wing Republicans" seems to be a search for the guilty. Here there is an eerie similarity to the peasants of old attempting to take back control of their lives by finding the guilty witch or other scapegoat. In this sense, the deepening culturalization of politics in the shallows may reflect a search by a postindustrial peasantry for the real culprits, since the state has removed itself as a suspect.

Does our current culture in the most developed countries pose an additional hurdle for challenging the ideology of concealing the state? In an earlier chapter, I described the dynamics between the deep and shallow state and how this aids concealment of the state's agency. Do we also face a set of cultural dynamics that reinforce these political maneuvers of state institutions?

Arguably, criticism of contemporary mass culture, and the preferences of most people, simply reflects an elitist strain of thought. From an anti-elitist perspective, one could argue that having more of the population behave like a postindustrial peasantry reflects progress in eroding antiquated social and class divisions. After all, from what possible foundation can one criticize these cultural trends other than one rooted in the false consciousness of asserting that some cultures (or aspects of culture) are higher and better than others? If politics seems shallower today, then maybe this reflects the progress we have made toward exposing the long-standing hollowness of our political systems.

However, the political salience of these cultural observations becomes apparent when we turn to a classic question. What does a citizen need to know, so that he can participate in a democracy? Perhaps for some of us this seems weak. From the anarchist tradition one could just as easily ask, what does a citizen need to know to be co-opted into a liberal democracy? However, from this more radical perspective, the question becomes even harder. What does an individual need to know to challenge their political system effectively? It is on this point, the political challenge presented by a postindustrial peasantry, that the previously presented criticism moves beyond elitist prejudices.

In various forms, what a citizen needs to know is an old question often used against participation. The claim for many centuries was that the common person could not participate responsibly in government due to their ignorance about public affairs. For example, Edmund Burke worried that the expansion of suffrage in Britain would lead to the manipulation of ignorant voters by unscrupulous political entrepreneurs. For Burke, the dangers of expanding participation too quickly were all too apparent in the excesses of the French Revolution.

Despite the misgivings of Burke and others, revolution and reform expanded suffrage during the eighteenth and nineteenth centuries across Western Europe and its settler societies. Eventually, the twentieth century saw some of the great promise of these changes reach minorities and women. Thus, the question, then, of whether the citizenry is capable of participating in a democracy appears to have been answered decisively long ago.

Yet, contemporary surveys of the public in the United States have shown widespread ignorance on a variety of topics: foreign affairs, political knowledge, historical knowledge, science, and basic health. Comparisons with other nations show different strengths and weaknesses across the developed world. The United States has become notorious for particularly striking examples, such as the widespread rejection of evolution and other basic scientific knowledge. As these policy areas increasingly come together in very complicated ways, the positions advocated by politicians seeking popularity in the shallow state can be strikingly disconnected from practical constraints.

The response from the left and progressive areas of political commentary in the West has been worry over the "dumbing down" of the citizenry. Within various countries, the literature often focuses on specific manifestations of the problem. For example, in the United States, Barbara Ehrenreich has written on the popular belief and faith in positive thinking.[35] A more scholarly dissection of America's self-help industry and obsessions is provided by Micki McGee.[36] In both of these examples, the authors follow a similar vein of thought. The cultural behaviors they document are linked to individuals attempting to cope with the vicissitudes of a complex economy, and an increasingly complex society beyond our control. Yet, much of the American myth rests on the belief that we are autonomous individuals, capable of forming a life of our own choosing. Thus, for the left, cultural degradation is linked to the tensions between our belief in individual autonomy and the reality of the pressures of global capitalism.

Drawing links between political activity and cultural patterns is of course fraught with difficulty. For example, Connolly in his attempts to unravel the links in American politics between the evangelical, Christian right, and the Republican Party quickly encounters this difficulty.

Does, say a corporate-Republican elite manipulate the evangelical wing of this assemblage, leading it to subordinate its economic interests to spurious appeals to faith? Or are leading parties to this coalition linked above all by economic interests, with evangelical and corporate leaders together manipulating their followers? Or, alternatively, do the two groups share a general doctrine or creed, which defines common interests and allegiances? My sense is that none of these explanations, nor others like them adequately fills the bill.[37]

These complications lead Connolly to pose a more complicated model of resonance rather than cause and effect. His difficulty with drawing firm links between two closely allied forces in US politics, one a party and the other a cultural movement and its institutions, illustrates the complexity of connecting culture and politics.

Nonetheless, if we focus on political participation, then this line of thinking returns us to an older, but also more solid, debate. Burke and many political theorists worried about the capabilities of the common citizen. More broadly, philosophers such as J. S. Mill also worried about the negative effects of a broader, popular culture. In Mill's case, he worried that the public opinion of Victorian England weighed down upon the most creative and independent individuals of his day. In the twentieth century, Ortega Y. Gasset voiced these worries within a continental European conservatism.[38] More recent worries about popular culture and its corrosive effects are found cutting across the traditional fault lines of left- and right-wing political commentary. In the United States, right-leaning intellectuals like Alan Bloom have fretted over similar concerns. For the right, cultural degradation is often tied to perceptions of a decline in cultural standards linked to the erosion of social institutions like the church or the family. From the left in the United States, there is criticism of a populist, anti-intellectualism associated with the right.

Such criticisms, then and now, often veer into elitism. On the other hand, they do raise the question of what minimum levels of education and civic awareness are necessary for democratic institutions to function. For example, James Mill and Burke argued that "common" individuals could serve in local-level institutions like juries. From this experience, they argued that citizens would gain familiarity with the law and governing institutions. More conservative thinkers also saw participation in juries as a means of forcing citizens to think more broadly about the social good or "national interest" as compared to their narrower individual interests.[39]

It is difficult to imagine where individuals in the most developed societies are acquiring this experience today, other than juries. Declining rates of participation in political activity, aside from voting, show little progress from this earlier elitist suggestion of how to train the citizenry. Recent studies that show declining levels of "social capital" reinforce this disturbing idea.[40] As Putnam explains succinctly,

Whereas physical capital refers to physical objects and human capital refers to properties of individuals, social capital refers to connections among individuals—social networks and the norms of reciprocity and trustworthiness that arise from them.[41]

Thus, if individuals are increasingly segregating themselves into separate subcultures, then where do they learn about their broader political community?

We can phrase this issue even more provocatively. What additional means of civic education are available to citizens today compared to the nineteenth century? Jury duty is still a possibility. Public education in many countries is now universal and typically provides some form of civic education. However, because of the contentiousness of school curricula, efforts at civic education are usually lukewarm. This holds true even for countries where schools are important agents of political socialization. In a study of civic education in Great Britain, Derricott describes the weak nature of the national curriculum. This noncontroversial approach to civic education consists of courses in "political literacy." On closer examination, political literacy is primarily a passive discussion of issues such as voting.[42] This blandness was intended to avoid the political controversy of more substantial political discussions. Not surprisingly, a large-scale study of civic education in sixteen countries found that while students understood the basic mechanics of democracy like voting, they had a much weaker understanding of other forms of political participation.[43] The authors' explanation for this finding is that:

> Although some schools attempt to foster discussion of issues, there are constraints on teachers against making statements that might be interpreted as politically partisan.[44]

Thus, evidence from large studies of civic education in democracies show that teaching students about relatively noncontroversial political values is usually ineffective at improving students' political knowledge and subsequent interest in political participation.

Similarly, political philosophers for at least three centuries have agonized over the question of how a common person could ever be informed enough to participate in questions of foreign affairs or weighty issues like war and peace. With the rapid rise of the phenomenon of globalization, we should expect this to be an ever-more pressing question. Much of the literature on globalization envisions the possibility of greater participation by individuals around the world as globalization creates connections between the international and the local. The use of new communications technology by various peoples in their efforts to bring down authoritarian regimes is often trumpeted as an example of globalization changing politics.

However, it is difficult to see where these new chances for democracy are becoming institutionalized. Common to all political commentaries is the assumption that individuals will be participating in state institutions.

In examples of people bringing down authoritarian regimes, like the Arab Spring of 2011, the goal of these movements has been to recapture the state. Thus, the core objective of such movements is to take the state back from someone else. In the most straightforward cases, this someone else is the strongman dominating an authoritarian regime.

The pessimistic voices to these events typically worry about whether the country in question is ready for democracy. Often these arguments have been phrased in the terms of "realism" about political development versus the needs of international security. Thus, the elitist thrust of such arguments has often been how to transform the citizenry so that they can participate in such institutions, rather than asking how to change institutions to meet the needs of citizens. Ironically, this seems to be the same debate from the early modern and modern period. On one side the question becomes, how can the people take the state back from the elites? On the other side, are the people ready or capable of running the state themselves? Thus, even when a popular uprising retakes the state from an authoritarian leader, we still find skepticism about democracy.

Leaving aside the long battle over this in Western intellectual history, our contemporary context presupposes some different rules. In democratic, developed states, the assumption is that all adult individuals should participate in governance. This assumption has expanded to include significant participation in national politics as well as local representation. The well-institutionalized political systems of the developed North and West have settled, long ago, on the structures for this political activity. Nonetheless, a fundamental contradiction remains. If individuals are participating less effectively within these structures, then what needs to change? Is the issue one of failing civic education? Or, is the explanation one of failing political structures?

In either case, less effective participation empowers the concealment of the state. If individuals do not effectively participate within the shallow state, then the ideology of concealing the state faces few conventional challenges. If our contemporary political institutions are failing to address urgent policy problems, then the deep state, under the pressure of maintaining sovereignty, will attempt to fill this vacuum.

For example, in the United States in recent years, there has been a large increase in homeschooled students. Although there are many reasons for parents to choose this option, the overwhelming majority of these students come from deeply religious, usually evangelical Christian, families. A growing body of evidence indicates that the parochial education these students receive is hostile to various scientific concepts. Religious hostility to evolution is the most prominent concern of these families with various lesser objections a distant second.

Given the guarantees of religious freedom in the United States, and the civil liberties protections expected in the society, there is little the state can do about this trend. And to a large degree, most citizens in the United States are skeptical of state interference in this area. On the other hand, this behavior places the state in quite a bind. Increasingly, societies are facing pressing ecological and technological risks. If significant portions of the population turn their backs on science, then the state, for pressing functional reasons including the need to protect its sovereignty, will have to rely on the experts it does have at hand.

It is in this area of contemporary science that the tension between technocracy and the practice or ideal of democracy is most visible. However, can we expect states to sacrifice scientific progress, and by extension their competitiveness in global capitalism, based on the population's varying belief systems? Or, should we expect the state to do what it has come to rely on, redefine the scientific challenges as an area of "national security" and subsequently, an area to be managed by the deep state?

A postindustrial peasantry?

If this comparison between today's citizenry and the peasantry of the past is apt, then what outcomes should we expect? Should we expect to see similar political effects to the past if the situations of both groups parallel one another? In the modern period, the peasantry in Europe was excluded from politics. In much of the world and for the vast part of humanity, participation prior to the nineteenth century was limited to periodic bursts of political upheaval. Examples include both world-shaking events like the French Revolution and smaller *jacqueries*. Eventually, the European peasant made the long journey of becoming a voting citizen.

However, even this process can be viewed as something other than political. The great peasant uprisings in Germany during the sixteenth century and the more radical groups such as the "Diggers" and "Ranters" during Britain's seventeenth-century revolution and Civil Wars were inspired in large part by cultural change. The religious shock of the Protestant Reformation set in motion the ideas that inspired these earlier peasants to rebel.[45] In both cases, the state eventually triumphed over the peasants with its superior organization. As Christopher Hill has argued, the "Glorious Revolution" in England was almost superseded by a much more radical revolution that was stopped by Cromwell's new state and army.[46]

Arguably, the peasantry had to come to the city before gaining political access. In cases like Britain, there was no smallholders party for the countryside's poorer residents. Instead, the new working class finds representation in the new and urban Labour Party. These developments emphasize the deep process of cultural and social change necessary for the peasantry of an earlier age to become political participants. In contrast, what economic development or cultural changes would politicize (or perhaps more accurately, repoliticize) today's postindustrial peasantry?

The continuing trend of suburbanization suggests that we will not see the public living closer together in the most developed countries, at least not anytime soon. Continued ecological stress may make this lifestyle, with its long commutes to work and heating/cooling expenses for large freestanding homes, increasingly expensive. Arguably, this separation of communities into self-contained spaces works against improving the social capital needed for more robust political participation. Would a countermigration back to city centers act as a catalyst for new political activism?

Perhaps the question of urbanization and social space is less relevant today, thanks to new communication technologies. Yet, as discussed earlier, these technologies appear to fragment the public as much as they can bring it together. The overall impact of these new technologies is still ongoing, but early signs are that social networking, blogging, and the ubiquitous presence of smart phones have largely been co-opted by marketing and conventional political campaigns. Thus, rather than opening up new avenues for political activism, these technologies are becoming another channel for the conventional electoral messages of well-established parties and groups.

In contrast to many hopes, the question of globalization does not appear to be radically transforming politics either. Contemporary examples of democratic struggle in the context of globalization have restarted the long-standing trope in political theory of two possibilities. The first is the progressive campaign and idea that the people need to take the state back from elites. Examples here include various "take back the state" movements in the developed world including the recent Occupy protests. A more recent theoretical twist to this type of political activism is the argument that corporations have captured the state. This line of political engagement ignores the ideology of concealing the state. Instead, it continues to insist on a distinction between the public state (which should be used for progressive ends) and private corporations attempting to "take over" this public state.

The second is a "realistic" concern with whether the people are ready or capable of such responsibility. Typically this line of political elitism is directed at politics in the developing countries. For example, in the immediate aftermath of the Arab Spring we find evidence of this commentary. Two decades earlier, similar "realistic concerns" were voiced about democratic upheavals in Eastern Europe. The political transitions of Spain, Portugal, and Greece were also received with such doubts decades ago.

Can the people take back the state? Are the people capable of democracy? Both of these questions are false choices. They suppose two political outcomes that have arguably never been fulfilled. Which state in human history has actually been administered by "the people" versus various elites? When has a democracy ever been safely introduced after careful analysis of whether the citizenry was ready for it? Obviously, these questions ignore the reality of our common historical experience. At best we can ask to what degree the population held the state accountable in a specific period of time.

Since the nineteenth century, the anarchist tradition has argued that society's reliance on the state has pernicious effects. From this perspective, the state's organizing role is a hindrance to social cooperation. Rather than resolving problems in society through free, individual collaboration, the state becomes a crutch that grows ever larger as we abandon more and more initiatives to it. Our contemporary situation, with the state's agency increasingly concealed, compounds this moral dilemma. Not only are we ever-more dependent on the state, but this dependence has reached such a pitch that we not only deny it, we do not even recognize it.

In the nineteenth century, the anarchist concern was with the ability of the state to move into more and more areas of social policy. This expansion came with the cost of innervating alternative forms of social organization and cooperation. State oversight of workplace conditions immediately removed one motivation for union participation. Public education supported by the state undermined the efforts of worker organized education. Arguably, this trend has now taken on an additional dimension of complexity. Not only are we more dependent on the state today, but many of us prefer to ignore this fact as well. If we are pressed to think about policy innovation, then we immediately turn to the one alternative the ideology of concealing the state recognizes, the market.

For example, the United States has seen its rankings in international standards of education plummet. The response has often been attempts to spend more per pupil in public education or spend money differently. More recently, budget cuts have undermined many public schools, leading to calls for unleashing market innovation. As in other cases described in this book, market innovation translates into shifting taxpayer money into less accountable areas of private enterprise. In this example, we find private companies rushing to offer consulting services for establishing charter schools, turnaround services for failing schools, packaged curriculum content to replace current offerings, or offers to run entire school systems on a contract basis.

We can compare this contemporary trend of "privatizing" public education with the innovative approaches of the nineteenth and early twentieth centuries. There we see an explosion of innovation such as Montessori and Waldorf, as well as ideas driven by the needs of various religious communities. The pedagogy of these new schools often reflects Godwin's call for experiential and noncoercive learning.[47] Arguably, the Sudbury school model represents the most coercive-free product of this movement. In contrast, today we find across the United States Colleges of Higher Education that are geared to producing teachers for an increasingly standardized public school system. The alternative to this failing state system are various "market solutions" where the concealed state funds similarly trained, or less trained, individuals engaged in similar efforts, but contracted as "experts."

This pattern of undermining and innervating institutions is deflected in part by relying on the political ideologies of another age. We have come to live inside vast nation states interconnected with one another through global capitalism. Our older ideologies of representative democracy seem increasingly inapplicable to these contemporary Leviathans. The classical ideals of independence and liberty seem increasingly implausible given the degree of social organization that contemporary capitalism requires.

Faced with this situation, the concealment of the state allows our political systems to continue drawing upon the symbols and ideals of representative democracy. We continue to vote in regular elections, despite the fact that increasingly obscure organized interests provide massive funding to political campaigns. In the popular mind, and among quite a number of our elites, our political debates are organized into the categories of the nineteenth century. For example, we find supposed left and right positions on the usefulness of the market, the role of religion in public life, and the size of government. Concealing the state, and its growth beyond the boundaries of such debates, allows this political culture to survive.

In addition, the risk of catastrophe faced by all societies has deepened our dependence on the state's coercive and regulatory powers. Concealing the state allows us as individuals to carry on believing in our autonomy and that progress in life comes solely from our abilities and efforts. Many of us are rabidly committed to lifestyles, beliefs, and cultural interests that obscure our dependence on the state. The intensity of our commitments seems to increase with the risk of exposing these activities and comfortable ideas in one of two ways. We fear seeing them as either dependent on or undermined by the state.

The ideology of concealment relieves these tensions, but at a cost. Just as the anarchists in an earlier critique of the state warned that reliance on the state has pernicious social outcomes, so too the concealment of the state leads to corrosive consequences within contemporary culture. The long-term effect of concealing the state is that individuals are beginning to resemble a disconnected peasantry rather than a politically active citizenry.

This trajectory seems self-fulfilling. If the state's agency is increasingly concealed from the population, then we can expect that the state is receding from the citizenry's consciousness. The state becomes an increasingly remote entity from individual, daily experience. Another source of strength for the ideology of concealing the state is the dynamic of the state's withdrawal followed by the adjustment of our contemporary culture to this fact. In this sense, the comparison of today's population to the disconnected peasantry of the early modern period is more plausible than we would wish.

Regardless of one's ultimate political preferences, all of these scenarios suggest that the outcome most likely to draw a postindustrial peasantry back together into a stronger citizenry is crisis. We have seen crisis bring down a number of authoritarian regimes. As argued earlier in this work, crisis can also bring out authoritarian behavior from more democratic regimes. Political history shows that crisis is the time when the largest political changes occur for both good and ill, much like the state itself.

If waiting for a crisis is an unappealing idea, then is there another option for challenging the state? The contemporary ideology of concealing the state presents a formidable challenge. If many of us today are living in conditions that resemble the structural challenges of an earlier peasantry, then what should we do to expose the state's agency? Furthermore, once we expose the agency of the state, how can we change what is done with the enormous power of contemporary, postmodern states?

To address these questions, we need to think about political activities that expose the hidden agency of the state. We also need to think about how to challenge the state's use of this agency. The suggestive idea of a postindustrial peasantry shows the need for new political tactics to address the cultural dimension of concealing the state. Arguably, this is a key need missing from the arsenal of modern political tactics. What sort of politics can supply this missing need?

Notes

1   P.A. Kropotkin, "The State: Its Historic Role," in *Selected Writings on Anarchism and Revolution*, ed. Martin A. Miller (Cambridge, MA: MIT Press, 1970), p. 243.

2   Kevin Leicht and Scott Fitzgerald, *Postindustrial Peasants: The Illusion of Middle-Class Prosperity* (New York: Worth Publishers, 2006).

3   Leicht and Fitzgerald, *Postindustrial Peasants*, p. 11.

4   Robert Fossier, *Peasant Life in the Medieval West*, trans. Juliet Vale (New York: Basil Blackwell Inc., 1988), pp. 72–5.

5   John Harris, "Time to Put the Party Back into the Conference Season," *The Guardian*, October 8, 2012. Available at: http://www.guardian.co.uk/politics/2012/oct/08/put-party-back-conference-season?INTCMP=SRCH

6   This is a key factor in Blum's evaluation of the position (and level of exploitation) of peasants in the Russian empire at various points in the region's social history. See his classic study Jerome Blum, *Lord and Peasant in Russia: From the Ninth to the Nineteenth Century* (Princeton, NJ: Princeton University Press, 1961).

7   For a brief description of this phenomenon in the United States, see Sean Coughlan, "Downward Mobility Haunts US Education," *BBC News*, December 3, 2012. Available at: http://www.bbc.co.uk/news/business-20154358

8   The Economist, "For Richer, for Poorer," Special Report on the World Economy, *The Economist*, October 13, 2012, p. 9.

9   *The Economist*, "For Richer, for Poorer," p.10.

10 For a good overview of this phenomenon and an introduction to his larger book on the subject, see Joseph Turow, "A Guide to the Digital Advertising Industry That Is Watching Your Every Click," *The Atlantic*, February 7, 2012. Available at: http://www.theatlantic.com/technology/archive/2012/02/a-guide-to-the-digital-advertising-industry-thats-watching-your-every-click/252667/

11 Turow, "A Guide to the Digital Advertising Industry," pp. 308–25 and 615–16.

12 David Carr, "At Media Companies, A Nation of Serfs," *The New York Times*, February 14, 2011, p. B1.

13 "Student Loans in America, The Next Big Credit Bubble?" *The Economist*, October 29–November 4, 2011.

14 For a description of this intensity within the confines of such small societies, and the possible negative outcomes, see Robin Briggs, *Witches and Neighbors: The Social and Cultural Context of European Witchcraft* (New York: Viking, 1996), pp. 157–61.

15 Consider Francis Fukuyama's argument about the dystopia of Orwell's *1984* misreading the democratic possibilities of new communication technologies and media in his "A Tale of Two Dystopias," in *Our Posthuman Future: Consequences of the Biotechnology Revolution* (New York: Picador, 2003). Or the larger perspective on this point provided by Manuel Castells, *The Rise of the Network Society (The Information Age: Economy, Society, and Culture)*, vol.1 (2nd edition, Malden, MA: Wiley Blackwell, 2000).

16 Beth Simone Noveck, "Transparent Space: Law, Technology and Deliberative Democracy in the Information Society," *Cultural Values*, vol. 3, no. 4, 1999, p. 474.

17 Eli Pariser, *The Filter Bubble: What the Internet Is Hiding from You* (New York: Penguin Press 2011).

18 Evgeny Morozov discusses this particular aspect of Pariser's book in his review for *The New York Times*. See Evgeny Morozov, "Your Own Facts," *The New York Times Book Review*, June 12, 2011, p. BR20.

19 For discussion of the many variables that influence religiosity, see Loek Halman and Veerle Draulans. "How Secular Is Europe?" *The British Journal of Sociology*, vol. 57, no. 2, 2006, pp. 263–88; and Edward L. Glaeser and Bruce I. Sacerdote, "Education and Religion," *Journal of Human Capital*, vol. 2, no. 2, Summer 2008, pp. 188–215.

20 For a description of how seriously some took this prediction, see Ashley Parker, "Make My Bed? But You Say the World's Ending?" *The New York Times*, May 19, 2011, p. A1. For a description of the aftermath of May 21, 2011, passing as usual for the group, see David Batty, "Apocalypse Not Now: The Rapture Fails to Materialise," *The Guardian*, May 21, 2011. Available at: http://www.guardian.co.uk/world/2011/may/21/apocalypse-not-now-rapture-fails-materialise

21 Fossier, *Peasant Life*, p. 40.

22 Fossier, *Peasant Life*, p. 43.

23 Randall J. Stephens and Karl W. Giberson, *The Anointed: Evangelical Truth in a Secular Age* (Cambridge, MA: Harvard University Press, 2011).

24 Jean Baudrillard, *The System of Objects* (New York: Verso, 1996), p. 118.

25 See the various marketing materials and slogans at: http://www.blackberry.com/

26 http://www.google.com/latitude/intro.html

27 Virginia Heffernan, "Let Them Eat Tweets," *The New York Times*, April 19, 2009, p. MM22.

28 Nicole Perlroth, "The Blackberry as Black Sheep," *The New York Times*, October 16, 2012, p. B1.

29 Consider the frequency with which "magical" appears in marketing materials of late. Often, we read about a new "magical" device.

30 Bill Bishop, *The Big Sort: Why the Clustering of Like Minded America Is Tearing Us Apart* (New York: Houghton Mifflin Company, 2008).

31 Samuel J. Abrams and Morris P. Fiorina, " 'The Big Sort' That Wasn't: A Skeptical Reexamination," *Political Science and Politics*, vol. 45, no. 2, April 2012, pp. 203–10.

32 Abrams and Fiorina, "The Big Sort," p. 208.

33 Abrams and Fiorina, "The Big Sort," p. 207.

34 For a discussion, see Mark Leonard, "What the Rise and Fall of Bo Xilai Tells Us about China's Future," *The Daily Telegraph*, March 18, 2012. Available at: http://www.telegraph.co.uk/news/worldnews/asia/china/9150391/What-the-rise-and-fall-of-Bo-Xilai-tells-us-about-Chinas-future.html

35 Barbara Ehrenreich, *Bright Sided: How Positive Thinking Is Undermining America* (New York: Picador, 2010).

36 Micki McGee, *Self Help, Inc.: Makeover Culture in American Life* (Oxford: Oxford University Press, 2005).

37 William E. Connolly, *Capitalism and Christianity, American Style* (Durham: Duke University Press, 2008), p. 39.

38 Ortega Y. Gasset, *The Revolt of the Masses* (New York: W.W. Norton & Company, 1994).

39 Albert W. Dzur, "Democracy's 'Free School': Tocqueville and Lieber on the Value of the Jury," *Political Theory*, vol. 38, no. 5, October 2010, pp. 603–30.

40 Perhaps the best-known work in this area is Robert Putnam, *Bowling Alone: The Collapse and Revival of the American Community* (New York: Simon and Schuster, 2001).

41 Putnam, *Bowling Alone*, p. 19.

42 John J. Cogan and Ray Derricott, *Citizenship for the 21st Century: An International Perspective on Education* (New York: Kogan Page Ltd., 1998), pp. 24–7.

43 See: J. Amadeo, J. Torney-Purta, R. Lehman, V. Husfeldt, and R. Nikolova, *Civic Knowledge and Engagement* (Amsterdam: IEA, 2002), p. 81.

44 Amadeo, Torney-Purta, Lehman, Husfeldt, and Nikolova, *Civic Knowledge and Engagement*, p. 89.

45 For a discussion of this in England's case, see Lawrence Stone, *The Causes of the English Revolution, 1529–1642* (New York: Routledge, 2002). The literature on the German Peasants' War is vast. However, a good example of linking the conflict to religious ideas can be found in James M. Stayer, *The German Peasant's War and Anabaptist Community of Goods* (Montreal: McGill-Queen's University Press, 1994).

46 Christopher Hill, *The World Turned Upside Down: Radical Ideas during the English Revolution* (New York: Penguin Books, 1984).

47 For a concise introduction to Godwin's thinking on education, see William Godwin, "The Evils of National Education" and "Education through Desire," in *The Anarchist Reader*, ed. George Woodcock (Atlantic Highlands, NJ: Harvester Press, 1977), pp. 267–73.

6

Conclusion

We all possess a significant motivation for acquiescing to the concealment of the state. Concealing the state frees us from admitting the unpleasant truth: in today's world we are utterly dependent on the state. We prefer the comfortable illusion that we are autonomous individuals pursuing our plans in a free market. If we hold fast to that idea, then our distance from policy makers and dwindling political influence doesn't seem so important. Instead, many of us like to believe that there is an economic reality detached from politics. This belief frees us from the responsibility of political action, and we can prioritize our private life concentrating on careers, family, and other projects without guilt.

Yet, the environment within which we pursue these individual goals is shaped by the state in both a positive and negative sense. After all, the state can empower us. This influence includes the state's investments in infrastructure that allow for economic growth, educational policies that benefit many, and retirement guarantees for our long-term planning. This positive area of state involvement is what we stand to lose first as the state's agency is concealed, leaving us with what the marketplace will sell. However, we know that the state can change the parameters of the marketplace. The state can intervene in our daily lives and provide guarantees and support that radically alter our quality of life.

On the other hand, the negative influence of the state consists of its failures. Concealing the state allows us to ignore the state's increasingly frantic efforts to control risk. Our world faces ecological limits that mean the status quo of global capitalism is unsustainable. The growing possibility of catastrophe, whether from an industrial or technological accident (we can think of GM food nightmares, artificial organisms, nuclear power plant accidents, or terrorism with weapons of mass destruction), forces us into the arms of the state. We are dependent on the decisions of the state as never before. The concealment of the state papers over this grim reality.

Aside from these common motivations and distractions, elites in our societies are also strongly attached to the ideology of concealing the state. Many politicians, so visible in the shallow state, have an immediate interest to continue this concealment. With the current dominance of free-market ideology across the world, it is easier to appeal to voters by accepting this trend rather than challenging it. In those policy areas where the state's self-preservation is itself at risk, the visible policy makers know they can rely on the deep state to quietly implement difficult policies. In complex policy areas that attract less public attention, political elites have little incentive to risk their careers. Thus, there is a clear political logic behind the ideological conformity we find among governing elites.

Yet, this reliance on the deep state is less a strategy and more of a delaying tactic. An important question is at what point will shifting policy to the deep state completely hollow out political meaning in the shallows? In many states, the increasing tendency of politics to devolve into lifestyle, consumer, and de facto entertainment questions points the way. This erosion of political content undermines the efficacy of political participation. Our ability to hold the state accountable is at risk as it denies having the capacity to act on our concerns.

The danger for democracy within this context has received a growing level of scrutiny from political scientists and political philosophers. For example, Jeffrey Edward Green has argued that the idea of participation within democracy should be recast as one of spectator rather than participant.[1] His point is that it is increasingly unrealistic to hold on to the classical idea of a citizen as an active participant within the deliberations of our vast, complex nation states. Instead, Green argues that we should rethink the role of citizen as one who critically observes the deliberations of those elites who are actively participating in governance. This leads Green to advocate for elevating the virtue of candor within contemporary democracies to the place formerly held by direct citizen participation.

In a narrower study of the American presidency, legal theorists Posner and Vermeule reach a similar conclusion.[2] They argue that the executive in the American system (and presumably most political systems) has become completely dominant despite constitutional checks on executive authority. To a large extent, Posner and Vermeule see this development as irresistible given the challenges faced by modern "administrative" states. However, they argue that the presidency in the United States is still constrained by public opinion and the constant scrutiny that Green discussed in his broader study of contemporary democracy.

What is striking about both of these studies is their apologetic themes for the contemporary state. Both Green's broad study and Posner and Vermeule's analysis of the American presidency concede that classical theories of democracy and popular participation no longer match reality. Yet, rather than criticizing contemporary institutions from this foundation, they argue that new realistic theories of democratic participation are required. In Green's case, he attempts to revive the idea of plebiscitary democracy in a positive form. For Posner and Vermeule, the power of the modern executive becomes acceptable because it still faces the constraints of popular opinion expressed in polling and elections.

In contrast, a number of political theorists have developed more critical, activist arguments about contemporary democracy. For example, Nadia Urbinati has argued that the classical ideal of democratic representation is unrealistic but she has also attempted to develop a critical replacement.[3] In an earlier stage of her argument, Urbinati compared two major philosophical views on representation from John Locke and Edmund Burke.[4] In Locke's social contract theory, my representative was a delegate, a stand-in for myself so that I do not have to devote myself full time to government business. On the other hand, Urbinati points out that few of us would be willing to represent Burke's contrasting view of a "trustee" representative. Burke famously argued that a representative must be willing to tell his constituents "no" and overrule their wishes for their own good. However, the shortcomings of these classical views of representation have led Urbinati to reformulate democratic representation as an idea of advocacy. Urbinati has in mind the role of other expert advocates in contemporary society such as lawyers, teachers, social workers, or medical professionals. While we must rely on these advocates' expertise to make our case for us, Urbinati argues these roles are not as paternalistic as Burke suggested, or as unrealistic as Locke's delegates.

Thus, a great deal of contemporary scholarship in political theory, political science, and more activist social criticism senses that there is something wrong with our current understanding and practice of democracy. However, most of this commentary is oriented toward returning the state to accountability. From the argument of preceding chapters, this goal of accountability is made ever more difficult by the ideology of concealing the state. How can citizens regain and keep any oversight of a concealed state? Furthermore, what sort of common strategies can we pursue in confronting this ideology given the fact that it has become dominant across widely varying political systems? This last point is especially challenging. The larger the number of political systems adopting the ideology of concealment, the more this state of affairs seems "natural" rather than ideological.

On the other hand, despite the growing trend of concealing the state, not all states are equal in both a literal and moral sense. Just as some states are more powerful in the world, so too some are better for human flourishing. At times in this text my description of the concealment of the state implies that all regimes are fundamentally the same ideologically. However, it is easy to see on pragmatic grounds the relative advantages and disadvantages of different states. We can compare the broad free speech protections and very open media of the United States to the self-censorship and state manipulation currently present in the authoritarian regimes of Russia or China. Many of us admire the better social justice available in Scandinavia from the governments there. Few of us would willingly opt for the authoritarian regimes found in many places. The fact that not all states are the same should be seen as a source of inspiration.

If there are such differences in the quality of life under various states, then this shows that there is the possibility of improvement. The fact that authoritarian regimes have been overthrown by popular action proves that significant political change is possible in today's world. The difficulty we face for reform or improvement obviously depends on the starting point. As we have seen most recently in the Arab-speaking world, and two decades earlier in Eastern Europe, facing down authoritarian regimes often calls for great risk and sacrifice. In some cases, the regime is so bankrupt that it must be displaced in entirety. On the other hand, those of us fortunate enough to be living under open and democratic regimes face a more subtle set of challenges within highly developed and pluralistic political systems. Regardless of which type of state we live under, there are two broad challenges for contemporary political action: revealing and challenging the state.

Revealing the state

Arguably, the best way to challenge the ideology of concealment is to expose the agency of the state. If the state can deny from the outset that it has the ability to act on our concerns, then it is difficult to imagine how any new theory of democratic accountability can influence it. Regardless of our tactics, the concealed state can stonewall us by insisting that there is nothing it can do. Thus, the most important challenge to the ideology of concealing the state is to expose the state's unused, or misdirected, power.

However, a source of strength for concealing the state is the increasing "transparency" found elsewhere in our contemporary society and culture. In the sphere of consumption, individuals are increasingly accustomed to instant feedback, user reviews, and the constant scrutiny a world of users can bring to bear upon private companies and services. In addition, the rise of social media has created the appearance of a constant flow of information about everyone in real time. All of this activity gives the impression of much transparency in our daily lives. The distraction of our consumer activities, and perhaps the self-satisfaction we derive from being smart consumers, is an obstacle to tuning into state activity.

These cultural changes also seem to be eroding our older distinctions of private and public spheres. This erosion implies that our sense of a separate, civic area of life is becoming lost in the collision of our private acts of consumption with public interaction. Some commentators have expressed concern that the growing popularity of social media like Facebook may lead to future legal decisions where the reasonable expectation of privacy is much reduced.[5] Similarly, Lyon has expressed concern about the cultural changes that make increased surveillance more socially acceptable. He is concerned that the increasing acceptance of voyeurism in our popular culture

> …helps to explain further why companies and governments seem to have so little trouble selling and installing surveillance technologies.[6]

With all of this noise, it is easier for the state to recede into the background. Our daily life seems increasingly transparent compared to the past. Since it is so difficult to keep anything private in today's interconnected world, we assume that the state and politics must also be increasingly transparent.

Thus, an ironic outcome of our current communications technology is that the state is harder to see than ever. The increasing universe of information available to us seems a likely resource to expose the state, but its sheer volume undermines the efficacy of this information. Rather than greater transparency, this wilderness of information from traditional and new sources enables the state's concealment. For example, a recent report by the US Federal Communications Commission expressed alarm over the decline in local reporting.[7] The study found that despite the abundance of new media outlets, the decline of local newspapers is leaving a vacuum at the local level in the United States. The report warns that this loss of oversight at the local level risks leaving citizens in the dark about local government activities. Citizens may feel that they have more choice than ever for information and news, but in many political systems, much of this information has become centralized in its focus, despite its fragmentary delivery. Any one of us can blog online about local government and community affairs. However, who will listen to us among all of the choices out there and why should they respect our particular opinion?

This point is the central difficulty with making use of new technologies to reveal the state. Despite the cacophony of voices we find in this new landscape, recent examples of technology and social media have led some observers to conclude that we are entering a new era of radical transparency. The best example of this trend is the media coverage and commentary surrounding the WikiLeaks case. In one commentary on the WikiLeaks case, Umberto Eco suggested that we have entered an age where the citizen can now turn the tables and spy upon the state.[8] The plausibility of Eco's claim seems to be enhanced by the reaction of many web activists who supported the activities of WikiLeaks by hosting its servers, and by the retaliation of online hackers to the pressure placed on WikiLeaks.

Despite this high-profile case, it is difficult to imagine that these sorts of efforts can lead to larger political transformations. Already the state is attempting to adapt to these new forms of communication technology. A prime example of these efforts was the recently revealed US program of placing propaganda on social media through the use of false Facebook and Twitter identities.[9] The rapid pace at which marketing has taken over social media also suggests we should be skeptical. The new tactics for commercial companies in the social media age include the interesting examples of companies paying individuals to start up "buzz" about products and write positive reviews.[10]

How do we know whether to trust this information we see online? Initially it seemed that simply the scale of feedback encountered online, such as a very large number of posted, anonymous reviews about a product, could insure that, despite some planted fakes, an overall clear picture would emerge. Now with the increasingly sophisticated tactics of advertising, relying on simple rules of scale do not ensure reliable information.[11] Without the voice of trusted media sources, it seems that all of the information coming from our new technology risks becoming more unreliable noise. Thus, despite the excitement surrounding new communications technology and less hierarchical means of organizing the media, a critical piece of resolving this problem is the role of intermediaries.

A growing body of political science research points to the need for strong intermediaries to enable effective democratic participation. For example, in an exhaustive study of accountability in Italy, political scientists found that even criminal charges failed to dislodge incumbent representatives, unless local media were effective at communicating the situation to voters.[12] The need for intermediaries in a political system emerges once we move beyond small-scale interaction. This is an important point because, as was discussed at the beginning of this book, critics of the state since Rousseau's time have contended that scaling down to direct democratic participation is the best way to check the power of the state. A similar vein of argument can be found in contemporary political theory. Philosophers like John Rawls and Jurgen Habermas have attempted to elucidate the procedures needed to insure that outcomes are democratic by focusing on smaller scale interactions. One consistent challenge to the project of such theorists hearkens back to Rousseau and the anarchists. How can the positive forms, procedures, and outcomes of small-scale interaction ever be scaled up to the complexity of a contemporary state?

For example, consider Habermas' extremely well-developed theory of discourse ethics.[13] Despite the complexity and subtlety of his work, the main point of Habermas' philosophy is easy to grasp in a small-scale interaction between individuals. If I present a paper at an academic conference, then I enter a discourse with others. Habermas argues that in such a setting all of us participating in this event entered with assumptions of mutual intelligibility. In other words, we would not rationally engage in this activity if we did not expect some sort of end result. Hence, there is some form of reason present in our efforts to communicate with one another. Furthermore, this is not just instrumental thinking, participating for the sake of some outcome. We also have a prior, deeper commitment to reasonable intelligibility. If we did not, then we would not have a basis for interacting with each other.

However, even in a small-scale interaction questions can emerge. Why did I travel to and participate in the conference? Was it because I wanted to debate an important issue with others and get to the bottom of it? Did I go because I felt a conference appearance would help my quest for tenure? Did I want an excuse to visit a different city, while drawing upon departmental funding? Habermas argues that this initial motivation for joining the conversation does not matter. Regardless of why I attended, participation would be based on some common procedures and debate about my paper would be on "reasonable" grounds. I may have hidden motivations and be engaged in some double game, but the rules of the discourse will produce a reasonable end despite that.

This idea seems plausible in a small-scale interaction like a conference. However, it seems much less plausible when we apply it to larger forms of political activity. The difficulty is the qualitative difference that emerges when we apply communicative action to broader issues on a social scale compared to smaller individual interactions. Politics introduces an important moral dimension that requires some judgments about the original motivation of discourse participants. Central to Habermas' overall argument is the idea that reason is integral to human communication because I wish to convince or explain to others some goal.

But as stated earlier in this work, we can find many examples of human interaction that rely on subterfuge. Most cultures accept some form of white lies in personal relationships and a degree of exaggeration in the marketplace. Our judgment about the use of dishonesty in these situations is influenced by the motivation of the individual. A white lie to avoid unnecessary hurt among friends is very different from commercially motivated fraud. Politics is an even better example of the disconnect between the motives, speech, and actions of individuals. Yet, politics also differs from other examples of human deception because the stakes are so much higher.

For some guidance on this issue, we can turn to classic political philosophy. A point that has deep roots in this tradition is the difference between the way things are and the way they seem to be. In the case of Machiavelli, he urges a prince to take advantage of this dichotomy. It enables a prince to maintain the facade of being good, and reaping the advantages of such an appearance, while doing what needs to be done. More generally, the classical idea of remembering this distinction enables one to look critically at the motivations of political actors. This cynical position enables us to expose hidden motives and influence.

Consider Thucydides' description, in *The Peloponnesian War*, of Diodotus' speech for leniency toward Mytilene before the assembly at Athens. As one commentator points out, "the intellectual attitude of both Cleon and Diodotus is determined by their immediate purposes, and their speeches are essentially dishonest."[14] If Diodotus appeals to the Athenians on the grounds of justice, then they will assume that he has instrumental motives. On the other hand, we know that the Athenians are concerned about the justice of their previous decision to harshly punish the Mytilenes. In the end, Diodotus argues for leniency on the cold grounds of political expediency. He argues that leniency now toward democratic elements in Mytilene may encourage rebellious elements in other cities to defect or surrender to Athens later. Ironically, he must lie to the assembly to get it to do the right thing. He conceals his concern for justice within an argument of power politics. As another commentator points out,

> In our conclusions about the causes of this Athenian decision, we must weigh the subtle force of this style of argument—with this specific audience—in addition to its context.[15]

Thus, to understand what happened in this political discourse at Athens, it is important to weigh the stature of the individual speaking and how he presents his argument.

How has this historical example been handed down to us? Would I know if the individual is participating in a double game? In Thucydides' example, Diodotus misleads the assembly with the rhetoric of political expediency so that they make a humane decision. We know about this classic double game of discourse, not because of the assembly exposing it among themselves, but thanks to the authority of the author, Thucydides. He applied analysis to this situation and reveals the facts to us. Did the members of the assembly recognize all of this? Did they reveal the hidden motives in their midst? Perhaps they did, but used Diodotus' argument as political cover while really voting their conscience.

This ancient example of politics may seem odd to think about when discussing contemporary concerns. Nonetheless, it illustrates the problem Habermas' discourse ethics has when weighing the normative content of politics. His theory's foundation in the pragmatism of communicating to solve common problems is difficult to scale up. It is easy to imagine individuals working together on a common, well-defined problem. It becomes much more difficult to accept when we move to broader, high stakes politics. In the latter case, the motivation of individuals does have a moral bearing on the questions we consider. Yet, who can expose these motivations other than intermediaries like an authoritative commentator?

If this is the case for a society on the scale of ancient Athens, then we can expect more complications in our contemporary setting. In our experience of contemporary democracy, it takes someone with stature to engage effectively with the state. An individual citizen's voice, regardless of how rational, cannot expose double games like a media authority of national stature. We are dependent upon *The New York Times* or a similar voice of authority to weigh in. Other possible voices are respected commentators and critics. In addition, we increasingly see celebrities adopting political causes. In all cases, we are dependent on voices with stature. This intermediary's stature may be highly imaginary, such as celebrity support of political causes, but the voice of such intermediaries is necessary for a discourse to reach and engage citizens.

How do these intermediaries acquire such stature? There seem to be two routes. The first and obvious is a long track record in exposing the hidden motivations and double games of political participants. Here we can think of established media that are recognized for their independence and past efforts. If one doubts their importance, then the easy example is to look at the lengths to which authoritarian and totalitarian regimes go to silence such critics.

Under authoritarian regimes, any media willing to speak the truth can become an important intermediary quite suddenly. The wealth of documentary evidence available from the former totalitarian regimes in Eastern Europe shows that even one individual voice can undermine a tightly closed, ideological regime. What is much more difficult to imagine, and establish, is how such truth-telling intermediaries can emerge within developed, postmodern states. This conundrum brings us to the other option for establishing an intermediary's legitimacy.

This second route is to comment on politics from an area of clear autonomy. The best example is the arts. Recently, political theorist Benjamin Barber has devoted some effort to exploring why the arts are important for a democracy.[16] Barber argues that the fine arts form an important interest-free space that escapes our contemporary consumer culture. From this more autonomous area, the arts can critique society, and government, with a voice that is much more authoritative than political or popular commentary.

However, it is difficult to imagine how either of these routes toward becoming an intermediary could be a strategic decision. The occurrences in life that drive an artist, or the many incidents that establish the track record of an authoritative voice in journalism, are impossible to create as a political response to the immediate. Nonetheless, it is hard to imagine how the state can be exposed politically without using an intermediary. How could just any discourse, like all of the chatter we find in our current communications media, perform this task without establishing itself as an authority of some sort?

In the example of discourse on a small scale that I discussed earlier, the setting was presenting a paper at a conference. At the end of a presentation, the audience will reach its own conclusions about the merits of the paper. The idea of needing to reach mutual understanding and intelligibility among such a small group of actors, regardless of individual motives, seems plausible. Whatever reason I had for coming to a conference and giving a paper, the audience will judge the paper on reasonable grounds. So, even if my individual motivations are of a baser sort, they will be transcended by the activity of discourse. A similar logic applies to much of our activity in social media and across the Internet.

What is less clear is how these simpler discourses could be built up into something as complicated as the politics we find in democratic societies. Consider a simpler example such as misleading research in medicine compared to political theory. On an abstract level, we may argue that concealing contrary results or misleading others in our findings is the same academic transgression in either field. Nevertheless, the consequences of dishonesty in medical research are much more harmful to others. In the realm of political theory, only my reputation and the squandering of other experts' time are at risk.

In the example of medical research, the motivations of actors matter more because the stakes are so high. So the relative weight of effort and performance matters depending on the field. Similarly, it is important to know what motives a politician has for advocating war or peace. In the case of war, we are deciding the morality of taking human lives. The motives of individuals debating such a topic matter in a way the motives of those debating an academic paper do not. Thus, the ability to recognize double games and hidden motives is morally necessary when we engage in politics at this level.

Furthermore, continued participation in political discourse requires motivation. If the individual's real motivation (an emotional attachment) is disguised, then how much commitment does he have toward democratic participation? How do we know if others are participating authentically in the discourse? Over time, will the requirements of a double game undermine the individual's commitment to participating in democratic institutions? Will this harm the legitimacy of democratic institutions?

After all, the use of double games reduces communication based on practical reason to an instrumental strategy. Couldn't an individual engage in a double game of reaching conclusions for emotional reasons, then dress up his arguments in a rational disguise like the ancient Diodotus? Perhaps to Habermas this does not matter. As long as the individual uses practical reason in public discourse, others will be convinced, or not, on the grounds of practical reason rather than the emotional commitment concealed underneath. Thus, the individual's internal motivation could be detached from her external activity.

Nonetheless, I suspect that Habermas would admit that it is important to discover the motives individuals have for advocating war, peace, or even more mundane political topics. Yet, is it through discourse over time that we uncover these hidden interests? Habermas often refers in his work to the tension between participant and observer perspectives. For Habermas this point is important because discourse ethics rests on the thin foundation of reason motivating the participants. Thus, Habermas asks,

> How can we appropriate naïve, everyday ethical knowledge in a critical fashion without at the same time destroying it through theoretical objectification? How can ethical knowledge become reflective from the perspective of the participants themselves?[17]

Unfortunately, it is precisely the jaded "observer" perspective of intermediaries that is required to expose the moral dimension of discourse participants' motivations.

Habermas' theory is often interpreted as a philosophical argument that advocates civil society as a means of keeping the state accountable. Concerns with keeping the state accountable have driven much scholarly discussion of civil society in recent years.[18] However, reliance on civil society is not a guarantee of democracy or democratic outcomes. Movements from below can also be destructive calls for nationalism or other political programs that Habermas would criticize.[19] Much of the civil society scholarship is also weak on explaining how this area avoids co-optation in contemporary postmodern states. Instead, the available scholarship tends to focus on the use of civil society against authoritarian regimes or its reemergence with the collapse of totalitarian regimes.[20]

The situation within postmodern states is very different. As discussed, the challenge within these political systems is not asserting the right to speak or publish. There is a world of tools available for such activity, and a free online forum waiting for political speech. Instead, the challenge within the postmodern state is raising a critical voice above all of the background noise. For this reason, we need to think about the role of critical intermediaries that expose the state's agency.

Does the idea of using intermediaries to challenge the state seem paradoxical? After all, the suggestion implies that one needs a different set of authorities to challenge state authorities. Such a program does not sound very new or different than the scrum of traditional politics. Nor does it sound like a tactic at home within the anarchist tradition.

On the other hand, we have had a recent example of an intermediary emerging from obscurity and challenging the state with the WikiLeaks case.[21] After the disclosure of a large trove of classified US diplomatic cables began, various officials from the United States and other governments reacted with a sort of hysteria. Secretary of State Clinton claimed the leaks represented an attack on democracy, and several American officials quickly attempted to outdo each other in their calls for severity. Unsubstantiated claims that WikiLeaks has blood on its hands from these actions have been referred to in calls for prosecution. These extreme reactions showed the extent to which the WikiLeaks disclosures struck at the concealment of the state.

Furthermore, this example of an intermediary revealing the state shows the moral difference that emerges when the stakes under consideration are higher. Many officials and political commentators argued that the exposure of "private" diplomatic activity undermined its effectiveness. The comparisons they used were to individuals having private details made embarrassingly public. But the governments of nation states are not individuals. Nor are officials acting as diplomats (and filing cables filled with advice and suggestions) mere individuals swapping private opinions. The diplomatic activities of these states have repercussions for millions of citizens. Unlike an assumption of privacy for individuals, we should expect government activity to err on the side of openness.

Furthermore, in the democracies, we expect individuals to be able to make an informed choice when voting. If we learn that our governments and elected officials have in fact been engaged in a double game—that is, reassuring us in public while quietly engaging in very different calculations— then how can one plausibly claim with a straight face that this is the same as private information becoming public? Should citizens not know what their government is "really" thinking, planning, and doing? Should citizens' knowledge of their government be confined to a need-to-know basis?

In the WikiLeaks case, involving diplomatic cables, there may be a Machiavellian argument for secrecy in effective diplomacy. However, the US and other government's reactions to the case are very telling of how widely accepted the ideology of concealing the state has become. After all, how is WikiLeaks different from traditional journalism? Exposing the state's real opinion, planning, options, and concerns is not the same as outing the foibles of a person. The stakes for citizens are extremely high with the policies pursued by contemporary states. The potential for catastrophic results from bad policies is pressing. Every citizen has a stake in the activity documented in the cables.

The revelations from WikiLeaks point to a much larger, uncomfortable question. What is the moral argument for a democracy keeping its citizens in the dark? I am not referring to the age-old argument about keeping things on a need-to-know basis on a particular issue, or in one clearly sensitive policy area like counterterrorism. In the case of the State Department, one can try to argue that secrecy and double-dealing is the nature of diplomacy. Maybe, but what would we learn if we could see what our government really says and thinks in its additional fourteen cabinet departments and scores of agencies with thousands of public officials?

The real philosophical question is the morality of systematically saying one thing in public while doing something else across the entire spectrum of policy areas. On this last point it is interesting to note that the authoritarian governments named and shamed in the WikiLeaks cables seem much less concerned than the democracies. The WikiLeaks case is interesting because it serves as an example of an intermediary suddenly emerging and credibly exposing the agency of the state.

The idea that intermediaries need some sort of authority or stature to expose the state seems counterintuitive to the anarchist tradition. However, the idea of intermediaries returns us to the deeper philosophical question of the anarchist tradition, the problem of representation and the possibility of a "real" authority of politics. For many anarchists the question of challenging the state is not one of abandoning politics, or any form of authority. Instead, the issue is challenging the false form of politics and authority the state perpetuates. From this perspective, the call for intermediaries to expose the state may be less counterintuitive to the anarchist tradition than it sounds.

Intermediaries, representation, and anarchism

Even as unimpeachable a voice of the anarchist tradition as Bakunin says that there are some forms of legitimate authority. For example, consider Bakunin's response to the question of authority: "Does it follow that I reject all authority? Far from me such a thought. In the matter of boots, I refer to the authority of the bootmaker; concerning houses, canals, or railroads, I consult that of the architect or engineer."[22] The authority of such specialists is limited by reason. As Bakunin explains further,

> I bow before the authority of special men because it is imposed upon me by my own reason. I am conscious of my inability to grasp, in all its details and positive developments, any very large portion of human knowledge … Thence results, for science as well as for industry, the necessity of the division and association of labor.[23]

This insight into where *real* authority lies is at the heart of the anarchist and syndicalist traditions.

When combined with the subject of political representation, this perspective on authority undermines most traditions familiar to political theory. From a broad anarchist or syndicalist perspective on the realities of authority and power, traditional politics within state institutions is a ruse that avoids the *real* struggle of class in the economic arena. The political arena is used to inhibit the working class from fighting the class struggle within the economic sphere, where they have potential power to organize. The foundational assumption of this line of thought is, of course, the kind of membership that we believe to be most salient for politics. A good example of the alternatives is provided in Jennings' account of the syndicalist critique of political parties. As he explains in his history of syndicalism in France,

> The class based nature of the *syndicat* was deemed to be in marked contrast to the pattern of support and membership of all political parties. What distinguished the political party (including those of the Left) was precisely that it grouped people according to opinions and not interests…[24]

Thus, for syndicalists the *syndicat* was superior to the political party because it understood the significance of class allegiance. Similarly, *syndicat* industrial action and worker-centered activities were superior to traditional politics within the parameters allowed by the state. This logic informs the syndicalist call for industrial rather than political action. Arguably, this perspective also applies to what many political theorists would consider the cultural activities of the *syndicats*. Even social activities and organization could have a role to play in this struggle if those activities contributed to the education of the working class.

From this anarchist and syndicalist perspective, real politics is likely to take place outside of state institutions on economic and cultural fronts. In an early attempt to describe the ideas of syndicalism to a general audience, Bertrand Russell explained in *Roads to Freedom* that syndicalism "aims at substituting industrial for political action, and at using trade union organization for purposes for which orthodox socialism would look to parliament."[25] Indeed, this is the logical strategy to pursue since, from the syndicalist perspective, parliament is a distraction: How could a state institution based on an idea of territorial representation and class co-operation possibly be effective other than as a diversion from real politics?

In contrast to continental syndicalism, the more institutionally minded proposals of the Guild Socialists in Great Britain provide us with a slightly different perspective. Here the focus is how to institutionalize real representation within a broadened political sphere. As G. D. H. Cole explains,

> the Guild Socialist conception of democracy, which it assumes to be good, involves an active and not merely a passive citizenship on the part of the members. Moreover, and this perhaps the most vital and significant assumption of all, it regards this democratic principle as applying, not only or mainly to some special sphere of social action known as, "politics," but to any and every form of social action, in especial, to industrial and economic fully as much to political affairs.[26]

To this end, some varieties of guild socialism eventually proposed the creation of an alternative institution to parliament based on functional representation. Bertrand Russell explains the idea:

> Guild socialists regard the state as consisting of the community in their capacity as consumers, while the Guilds will represent them in their capacity as producers; thus Parliament and the Guild Congress will be two coequal powers representing consumers and producers respectively.[27]

Thus, the Guild socialists in Great Britain differed from Continental syndicalists in their attempt to take functional representation inside the state's political institutions. This move would convert (or restore) the political sphere into a functioning place of *real* politics. According to G. D. H. Cole, the plan opened the possibility for the state to truly wither away as the functional representation of society replaced the "debris of a decayed system."[28] This change would happen gradually as traditional politics was replaced with the real political action required by class or functional interest.

Real politics seems to lie closer to the economic functions individuals perform and to the interests they hold in everyday life. Hence, we find the argument that contemporary political concerns are connected to more concretely defined interests such as our economic role, our environmental needs, or the needs of our cultural or ethnic membership. Second, both perspectives appear to blur the boundaries between the political and the cultural. In the case of contemporary political theorists, we see this trend in the growing focus on identity politics, while in the syndicalist tradition, it is more closely associated with educational, consciousness-raising efforts such as the cultural initiatives of the *syndicats*.

Recently, political theorists from the post-foundational (or sometimes still labeled "postmodern") camp have attempted to distinguish between "the political" and "politics."[29] As Oliver Marchart points out in a recent study of this school of contemporary theory, this distinction has radical implications since it opens up a broader range of cultural, economic, and social questions outside of mainstream politics. This turn toward identifying a broader range of issues as political bears a striking resemblance to earlier anarchist and syndicalist efforts to define a *real politics* as opposed to the political institutions of the state.

Just as the anarchist tradition posed the idea of a real politics to the sham of mainstream political activity, perhaps so should we think about Bakunin's idea of *real authority*. In this sense, the intermediaries who can expose the concealed, postmodern state are authorities in Bakunin's sense. Of course, for Bakunin there should always be an element of individual judgment. We should consult several boot makers or engineers and choose for ourselves which one convinces us with their skill and expertise.[30] So, too, a broad range of intermediaries is needed. We can then make choices between these voices and support those that expose the state.

Thinking about intermediaries this way also provides an important flexibility. In the case of differing political regimes, we can expect to find a variety of sources for this real authority. In the twentieth century under totalitarian regimes, even high art could acquire a political meaning within the highly charged ideological context of those societies. Under twenty-first century authoritarian regimes, anyone brave enough to speak out will immediately acquire the sort of stature that this simple act alone cannot expect under a freer democratic government. In this latter case, an intermediary would have to be a person who speaks out about the truth of power, but in a way that distinguishes them from the cacophony of other voices citizens hear.

The role of an intermediary is not that of simply being another expert. Instead, it is a highly fluid role that various individuals can acquire within the political context of the state. The tools that the intermediary draws on to expose the truth about power and the state may be highly symbolic acts, satirical commentary, civil disobedience, or academic prose. What remains true in each case is that an individual who acquires this real authority can, perhaps only briefly before the political context shifts again, use it to expose the state.

Challenging the state to act

On that last point, perhaps we can look at the search for a real politics as an effort to challenge the state to act. In this sense, asserting a real politics becomes the effort to force the state to use its agency to address the policy problems it ignores. The idea of forcing the state to act does not fit well with the anarchist tradition. After all, for the anarchists the question is not how to improve the state, but the best means of replacing it. However, our postmodern situation may require the use of the state to address problems that the anarchist tradition did not imagine. Many of the catastrophic risks discussed earlier, like the looming threat of ecological disaster, may require us to harness the power of states to take urgent action. In addition, as Iris Young has pointed out, in the face of powerful, private economic power, democracy seems dependent on state power. Contemporary civil society is unlikely to defeat injustice alone without state assistance.[31]

On the other hand, there are many policy areas where using our agency from below can become a challenge to the state. This tactic of self-organization outside of the state is much closer to the anarchist tradition. But the ideology of concealment complicates the use of this more traditional tactic. The difficulty is in organizing action so that we expose the state's neglect in an area of policy, or challenge the state's claims of sovereignty by doing better than the state. The risk is always that the state co-opts our efforts and thus adds the policy concern to the list of issues it can ignore. So, we need to do it better than the state (and publicize the fact to shame the state), but not aid the state's concealment by allowing it to withdraw from yet another area of need.

How do we challenge the dominance of the contemporary state? Some observers think that individuals acting as consumers can have an impact. This idea lies behind claims that all of the consumer information and feedback now available online can be used for activist purposes. In a sense, this idea holds out the promise of bypassing the state in areas of environmental regulation or work conditions and instead applying direct pressure on industry. However, despite the appealing logic of this idea, scholarly evidence is mixed. Early research indicated that such boycotts of activist pressure are much more dependent on capturing the media's attention rather than actually forcing corporations to act due to market pressure.[32] More recent scholarship has pointed to the difficulties of using consumer power in the first world to influence conditions in the developing world.[33] In the past, boycotts of a particular business were effective. But in the future, with chains of capital so difficult to follow, and with businesses present all over the world, economic action would seem to require an ever-greater degree of international organization to be effective.

The other difficulty with using consumer activism is that it easily plays into the ideology of concealing the state. Consider the recent example of a call for mass action by bank withdrawal in Europe.[34] The celebrity advocate (French soccer player Eric Cantona) for this idea proposed that a bank run triggered by mass withdrawals coordinated on the same day would have a greater effect than any mass demonstration on the streets. Although Mr Cantona's call appealed to some activists, it failed to trigger any mass event. While the idea of organized consumer action for political ends remains an intriguing one, would even a successful action like this challenge the state? What is the policy or action that the protesters wish to see changed?

The weak regulatory framework that these banks exploited is a product of the state. If one organized a successful boycott of a large bank, then does it follow that the state will change this framework? Does bringing down a bank put pressure on the state? The ideology of concealing the state will argue in such a situation that consumers are directing their ire at a private economic enterprise rather than the state. Crippling such an organization leads to job losses for other citizens, not state officials.

On the other hand, consumer activism directed toward a whole segment of the economy could force the state's hand. However, we should expect such an outcome only in cases where the state fears a loss of economic competitiveness. This suggests that consumer activism would have to be organized on a scale that we have not seen. The marketplace in the most developed states mitigates against this as well with its bewildering diversity of products and services. Contemporary capitalism has created extremely complex chains of ownership within developed economies. The vastness of contemporary corporations makes it difficult for a consumer to determine which company or firm is ultimately behind a product.

If the point of challenging the concealment of the state is to expose its agency, then a more promising possibility is to expose the state's action (or lack of action) through counter organization. The logic behind this strategy is straightforward. If we fear becoming dependent on the state for our survival, then we should try to organize solutions outside of the state. One of the ideological motives for the concealment of the state is that none of us want to admit this dependence. By organizing outside of the state we can reduce this dependence and remove one of the principal motivations for the ideology of concealing the state.

Again, there is a fundamental challenge to any organizational effort. By providing a service, or helping others outside of state structures, are we merely enabling the state's retreat? Consider the use made by conservative political parties of such efforts. In the case of the United States, President Bush Senior appealed for a "thousand points of light," that is a new grassroots voluntarism to fill the gaps left by budget cuts and trickle-down economics. Similarly, his son, George W. Bush, started his presidency with a call for "faith based" organizations to shoulder this burden rather than the state. More recently, Prime Minister Cameron in the UK has talked about the need for a "Big Society" and a smaller state in the face of looming austerity budgets. What does the call for voluntarism from these ideological sources demonstrate?

If we wish to revive the ideal of individual independence and liberty, then we need to work toward solutions on restraining growth, ecological improvement, and social justice that reduce our dependence on the state. We need to do this for ourselves to remove the inevitability of the state. On the other hand, the state pursuing the ideology of concealment would be only too happy to shift the burden of other responsibilities back upon society. The social work of NGO's funded by charitable contributions can be a useful shell game for the state. Claiming to reduce the tax burden, the state can instead hold hostage the conscious of the citizenry.

From this perspective, we need to think about grassroots organization in areas that expose the state rather than enabling its concealment. We need to avoid making the concealment of the state easier. Thus, we face a difficult challenge in structuring our efforts and assistance to others in a way that highlights the choices the state makes rather than covering for it.

Because of this dilemma, some activists have wrestled with the difficult question of tactics from an anarchist perspective. For example, Day has advocated the use of "Temporary Autonomous Zones" (TAZs) as an effective tactic.[35] Day turns to this tactic, originally envisioned and described by Hakim Bey because, if politics today is not about capturing the state, then what should it be about? The TAZ is a consciousness-raising tactic in that a space (either real physical space, an activity of some sort, or an imaginary space) is temporarily organized from below. The fact that these places are temporary in itself makes a point when challenging the state, which strives for permanent sovereignty. Day and others stress the transformative, education effects these experiences have on participants. For a brief period of time, a way to organize human activity outside of the state is enjoyed by participants. This suggests the possibilities that exist for a politics that is outside of the state.

This line of anarchist thought points to a possible tool to combat the declining social capital we see in the most advanced postindustrial societies.

If individuals are increasingly segregating themselves economically, through the housing market, and technologically, by social networking with like-minded others, then there is a clear need to bring people back together. This fits with the longstanding anarchist idea of consciousness raising through experience.

The recent experiences of the Occupy Wall Street movement seem to confirm this view. On the one hand, the movement seemed to rely on media attention, much like consumer activism, to get its message out. The fact that the movement relied most on the tactic of occupation also seemed to limit its broader effectiveness. One critical observer notes that Occupy was able to gain such notoriety because of its centralized location in the media focal point of Manhattan.[36]

Nonetheless, the early evidence we have from these events is that the more lasting impact of the movement on participants was their experience with self-organization.[37] For the participants in the Occupy movement, the experience of maintaining the various Occupy sites as a community was very empowering. The various Occupy encampments required individuals to cooperate effectively to feed, shelter, and care for the common community. The key difficulty became transforming this small-scale experience into something much broader.

There is a parallel here to the earlier discussion of exposing the state's agency. As discussed above, it is difficult to imagine exposing the state's agency without some sort of intermediaries. Arguably, we face a similar problem when challenging the agency of the postmodern state. Scaling up the community action of something like Occupy so that it has a longer-lasting political impact is difficult to imagine without some form of authority emerging. The Occupy movement's attempt to be leaderless and outside of mainstream politics, from fear of co-optation, also made it very difficult to sustain or expand.[38] Yet, it is also difficult to imagine Occupy continuing to have an impact without engaging in politics.

If we are no longer operating within the state, then are our activities still politics? For many in the anarchist tradition, breaking free of the state means escaping from politics and its limitations. In classical Marxism, the nonpolitical "administration of things" is what Marx foresaw once the state withered away. Yet, political scientists would expect conflict in human society even if we live together differently than today. We know from the anthropological record that all human societies, or at least those beyond a simple complexity, had some form of politics—that is, if we understand politics as a set of practices that enable human beings to settle their differences without violence.

The lesson from the recent examples of WikiLeaks and Occupy Wall Street is that it is indeed possible to expose and challenge the contemporary postmodern state. However, it may be ineffective to try and argue that these are examples of change coming from outside of politics or without authority.

Instead, they seem to be examples of what the anarchist tradition would consider *real* authorities emerging to expose the state's agency in the case of WikiLeaks. Rather than being outside of politics, Occupy can be better understood as an example of a successful politics. Occupy points toward a politics that is capable of bursting through the noise and fundamentally challenging the ideology of concealing the state.

What is difficult to conceptualize is how to create and sustain such intermediaries and real political movements within our contemporary society. In many ways, the examples of WikiLeaks and Occupy struck even informed observers as having come from nowhere. How can we produce similar efforts in a more deliberate manner? Furthermore, can such breakthroughs be turned into something more sustainable?

The delusion of violent resistance and so-called direct action

In December 2011, security employees at Deutsche Bank intercepted a letter bomb sent to the bank's chief executive. Initially, suspicion fell upon fellow travelers of the Occupy Wall Street movement. However, this attempted act of violence was immediately denounced by the German branch of the OWS movement and a subsequent letter from the Italian-based, self-proclaimed, Informal Anarchist Federation claimed responsibility.[39] This group had claimed responsibility for a series of letter bombs sent to foreign embassies the previous December. The next day a letter bomb exploded in the offices of Italy's tax collection service, wounding an employee there.[40] These incidents seemed very similar to actions claimed in 2010 by a Greek anarchist group that called itself the "Conspiracy of Fire Nuclei."[41]

What can this sort of violence possibly accomplish? Nothing. Political change through conspiratorial violence is a delusion. As discussed in an earlier chapter, the forces of coercion and powers of surveillance available to contemporary states are virtually invincible. Spectacular acts of terrorism, or pathetic attempts at terrorism (which nonetheless manage to maim employees opening the mail), cannot change a contemporary, developed postmodern state. These actions may redirect the state's coercive power toward the source of the disruption, but the idea that randomly killing individuals, or even attempting to target famous individuals will ever lead to substantive political change within a stable, contemporary state is a chimera. The only thing that comes from this violence is further claims that our reliance on the state for safety and security is inevitable.

Aside from the practical futility of such actions, meaning they cannot obtain their object, there is also a moral failure. By committing violence for a political objective, one is not challenging the state. Instead, political violence can be read as simply an attempt to replace the current state with another. Claims that a political program justifies violent action are a mirror image of the state's claims to its use of violence being legitimated by various theories of political legitimacy. Kropotkin pointed this parallel out in a 1920 letter to Vladimir Lenin. Condemning recent acts by Lenin's Bolshevik government, including the taking of hostages, Kropotkin warned that the Revolution was turning back into a state.

> With all of its serious deficiencies (and I, as you know, see them well), the October Revolution brought about enormous progress…. Why, then, push the revolution on a path leading to its destruction, primarily because of defects which are not at all inherent in socialism or communism, but represent the survival of the old order and old disturbances, of an unlimited, omnivorous authority?[42]

Thus, Kropotkin considered Bolshevik violence as the revolution lapsing back into the behavior of a state.

A similar argument can be heard a generation earlier in a letter from Proudhon to Marx. Writing in 1846, Proudhon admonishes Marx on the risks of establishing a new form of dogmatism. He then makes the following comment on the idea of direct action:

> I have also some observations to make on this phrase of your letter: *at the moment of action*. Perhaps you still retain the opinion that no reform is at present possible without a *coup de main*, without what was formerly called a revolution and is really nothing but a shock. That opinion, which I understand, which I excuse, and would willingly discuss, having myself shared it for a long time, my most recent studies have made me abandon completely. I believe we have no need of it in order to succeed; and that consequently we should not put forward revolutionary action as a means of social reform, because that pretended means would simply be an appeal to force, to arbitrariness, in brief, a contradiction[43]

Thus, from an anarchist perspective, political violence can be read as a moral failure. It is in fact a return to the claim that states have always made, that a theory of politics can somehow legitimate force.

Of course, violent resistance can be successful in changing odious regimes. Organized resistance from below can topple authoritarian states like Gaddafi's in Libya. Consistent resistance from grassroots, organized demonstrators brought down the sclerotic regime of Mubarak in Egypt. However, these are not examples of states on the cutting edge of development: ideological or economic. Violent resistance can still topple a modern, authoritarian state. In these cases the state is not concealed. Instead, the state is a very real force in the lives of citizens, and embodied in the personality of a strong man.

Within this context, resistance to a clearly defined opponent can be made concrete.

The other disadvantage modern authoritarian systems struggle with, when challenged by organized resistance, is that the regime's interdependence with the market is also easy to personalize. If we look at the Arab Spring in Egypt or Tunisia, one point of the demonstrators was that the ruler's family and assorted cronies enjoyed dominant positions across the economy. Thus, when challenging a modern authoritarian political system from below, resistance can point to a concrete set of individuals, easily identifiable by their bloodlines and clan ties, dominating the economy as unfairly as they do the state.

Therefore, violent resistance may succeed against modern, authoritarian states because of the difficulty of concealing the state under those conditions. Modern authoritarian regimes are heavily reliant on state intervention and it is easy for opposition to rally people against such a visible opponent. In addition, the claim of the resistance in these cases is not a complicated appeal to some ideological commitments. Instead, resistance to modern authoritarianism is based on the appeal to end concrete, human suffering at the hands of a very visible regime.

In contrast, this form of resistance has no moral legitimacy or political efficacy within a postmodern state practicing the ideology of concealment. If we imagine this context for a moment, then who is the opponent of the resistance? There is no authoritarian strong man in the most developed nation states. In the United States and other democratic systems, there is a rotating cast of politicians spread across visible institutions. In more advanced authoritarian regimes like China, there is a party and its *apparatchiks* spread across visible and hidden institutions. What is not present is a leader that can become the enemy for a movement from below. Attempts to cast politicians from the democratic systems in this role can only create laughable propaganda. Attempts to cast the party in China for this role run aground in their inability to give a face to the remote bureaucracy of that system.

Can we identify a similar set of individuals in a postmodern state? In the recent case of the Occupy Wall Street movement, the slogan of the 1 percent quickly caught on. However, could anyone in the United States or Western Europe concretely identify this 1 percent? Is it easy to link the same personalities from the political system to the heights of the economy? Furthermore, who among us, living within such political systems can show that we are not incriminated in some way? The Occupy Wall Street protesters were often seen using the technological tools produced by the system they were protesting.

The complexity of the postmodern state will always frustrate attempts at personifying the contemporary integration of states and global markets, because we are all complicit in many ways. Most of us continue to participate in the economic system of advanced, global capitalism despite our political convictions. Many of us continue to use products and services that are less sustainable despite our ecological fears. As Zizek points out, we often aggressively insist on some smaller practices (recycling, buying local, etc.) in a way that makes us feel better, without really resolving these larger problems.[44] This dilemma is the challenge we face when confronting the postmodern state.

Thus, what would be the rational target of so-called direct action in a postmodern state? Ourselves because of the complicity we show when behaving like consumers in the market? The rotating cast of politicians in the shallow state who have delegated much of their agency to the deep state? The compartmentalized bureaucrats of the deep state who struggle to maintain some semblance of a national interest in increasingly complicated policy environments?

Aside from the moral failure of political violence, Violence marks the failure of politics. When a society has failed to resolve its differences through other social mechanisms, violence is the result. Thus, anarchism in a postmodern state should focus on establishing a real politics within the society. Violence means giving up on politics and claiming a source of absolute authority as difficult to legitimate as any state's.

Some final questions

Increasingly, we all face threats from political violence (i.e. international terrorism), environmental degradation, and economic disruption that ignore borders. Our societies are increasingly diversified through international flows of immigration. Culturally, we live in a time of unprecedented collision between varying worldviews. Amidst this new dynamism, should we be surprised that nation states seem paradoxical? We remain citizens of states with borders dividing us "politically" despite our increasing economic and cultural integration. The resulting deficit in legitimacy for these nation states leads to the contemporary ideology of concealment.

Nation states are struggling to make themselves relevant and acceptable to populations that are caught in a precarious middle. We are increasingly connected to each other through a brutal, uncaring market mechanism whose ruthless efficiency has become part of the competition between nation states. When we turn to our political institutions for relief from the burdens of this inhuman market, we are told that nothing can be done. The state claims to lack the agency to control the market. Yet, many things are being done by the state out of sight, including the maintenance of this supposedly autonomous global market.

How long can the state's current ideology of concealment reconcile these tensions? The answer depends in part on how we, the citizens of the various nation states, choose to confront this ideology. This chapter provides some initial suggestions on exposing and confronting the ideology of concealment. So far, I have suggested that we need to find new intermediaries with *real* authority who can expose the state. In addition, we need activism that challenges the state by doing things better than it can, without falling into the trap of monetizing our activity in the market. Finally, for those of us living in postmodern states, I have attempted to point out both the moral failure and the utter futility of political violence.

We can speculate further on the future of the postmodern state by asking some pointed questions about our current situation. In a sense, these questions are more theoretical than practical. However, challenging a dominant ideology requires countertheory. This means that we need to think about the bigger questions related to the concealment of the state.

First and foremost, if states are concealing their ability to act, so that some questions are removed from political contestation, then what is contemporary democracy? From a classical perspective, political organizations have often placed some questions and policies out of bounds by agreement. The rights enshrined in constitutions are in a sense agreements to set some areas of life beyond politics. Yet, with the concealment of the state, we are now seeing traditional political questions about economic management and social policy quietly removed from the public arena.

Does this mean that we are all heading for an authoritarian form of "managed democracy"? The importance of this question can also be seen in the way that concealment short-circuits so many mainstream ideas about keeping the state accountable. In much of the political science literature on democracy, the focus is on accountability and transparency. The ideology of concealing the state thwarts the best-intended policy efforts with its definition, from the outset, of what can realistically be done. The fact that an increasing number of states (with supposedly very different political regimes) are adopting the same policies should be of greater concern to us than it is.

Second, if states are invested in global capitalism because of their mutual competition, then is there a way to reduce this struggle? Would a reform of international relations remove our dependence on the life support of global markets? Is it then possible for citizens within democracies to decide for greater investment in social services rather than cutting budgets to be competitive? An attractive dream is to imagine how competitive such societies might be in the future after recasting their social arrangements in favor of more humane, internal investment in people rather than focusing on competition in global markets.

With the strategy of concealment, the shallow state increasingly focuses on cultural politics and symbolic actions. This is an unfortunate turn since it means that, at precisely the moment societies everywhere are being transformed by unprecedented levels of global migration, politicians are attempting to popularize their commitments to specific cultural traditions. Thus, we see the rise of right-wing political parties calling for the maintenance of "national identities" or "true nature of societies" around the world. This dynamic has emerged in many democracies including those traditionally seen as very progressive and tolerant. What political outcomes can we expect from such deep internal contradictions?

If we cut through the ideology of concealing the state, then what are we left with? We see that a technology for organizing society is reaching its limits. There is an urgent need for more effective political participation. Yet, individuals face an uphill fight today over, what were in the past, very common political issues. As citizens find that representative government is less responsive, and that even local governance claims to be powerless over an increasingly large area of daily life, what will they conclude? As voices are not heard or ignored, the citizenry must resort to more confrontational tactics outside the norm of our current political institutions. However, as the Occupy movement showed, even successful political confrontation raises the question of what comes next.

What are our first steps out of this situation? First, we need to expose the deep state and its agency. As discussed above, intermediaries are needed to authoritatively expose the state. These intermediaries are also necessary to provide the expertise that can expose the complex activities of the deep state. The challenge here is for such intermediaries to show that they are a *real* authority in the anarchist sense discussed above. This suggests that we should look for new, disruptive voices rising from the more open media our contemporary technology provides. We should also look to that second route of establishing autonomous authority, the arts, for voices and actions that expose the state. These new intermediaries can (one hopes) expose the state's concealed agency effectively to the public because they are free from the political biases that undermine older channels of political commentary.

Second, our politics needs to highlight the ability to organize and get things done without the state. Such activities undermine the ideology of concealing the state because they teach us that our current dependency on the state is not a dead end. However, there are two potential pitfalls here. One is that the state, concealing its agency, may be all too happy to claim that its support in critical policy areas is no longer necessary, thanks to volunteer and charitable action. The second risk is that by turning away from the state, we fall into its ideological alter ego, the market. Thus, we need to create organizations that resist the co-optation of both the state and market. The first of these needs means that charitable organization needs to assist others while asking how much more could be done if the state applies its resources. The second of these needs means that charitable organization should reject the limitation that it must be self-supporting.

More concretely, both of these requirements suggest that organization from below should be iconoclastic. The rules of the market, with its conformity to "professional behavior" and business norms, should be rejected. Instead, an important alternative could be provided to the public imagination if public goods can be provided by radically different forms of human self-organization. Are there ways to provide education to working families that do not look like traditional schools, or in our contemporary setting, for-profit charter schools? Can we imagine charities that break down the walls of client and provider in a new institutional form? In other words, can we imagine organizations powered by human agency that do not look like those of the state or the market?

Third, we should, as citizens of various political systems step forward and demand that the state *does* act in policy areas that we prioritize. Such a call seems contrary to the anarchist tradition drawn on in many places throughout this work. However, this call for pressuring the state to act satisfies two important, contemporary needs. The looming ecological threats of our time require the decisive, coordinating action that nations states have provided historically. The challenge though is for all of us to push our respective states to coordinate policy action on a planetary scale to avert universal disaster. Acting in concert is not what states are good at. Even with their current consensus on global capitalism, we see nation states still angling for the competitive advantage, or particular interest that allows them to "win." Breaking this habit, and harnessing the power of the state to stave off ecocide, will require mass action by citizens across borders.

In turn, an effort to use the state effectively in policy areas like ecology can challenge the ideology of concealing the state. Tackling our current environmental crisis should show the citizens of the world that relying on markets does not produce optimum outcomes, but can instead lead to mutual degradation. If we can harness the power of the state to protect our ecological commons, by constraining market forces, then we could perhaps revitalize popular consciousness of the state's agency.

By reviving our consciousness of the power of the state, we may also be working toward its obsolescence. Nation states have provided human beings with enormous power to coordinate, and thus exploit, the potential of society. Now that we live in a period where that exploitation has reached a dangerous pitch, through ecological ruin and technological risk, perhaps we will reconsider the utility of this invention. Such speculation may seem outlandish as we still live in a world of borders and states. Nonetheless, we need to accept that our old/modern politics, with its modern forms and institutions, is failing to fit our postmodern situation. We must try to re-imagine politics in this contemporary condition, and perhaps postmodern states are not part of that future.

Notes

1   Jeffrey Edward Green, *The Eyes of the People: Democracy in an Age of Spectatorship* (Oxford: Oxford University Press, 2010).

2   Eric A. Posner and Adrian Vermeule, *The Executive Unbound: After the Madisonian Republic* (Oxford: Oxford University Press, 2011). For a highly

critical review of this book, see Harvery Mansfield, "The Executive Unbound," *The New York Times Sunday Book Review*, March 13, 2011, p. BR12.

3 Nadia Urbinati, *Representative Democracy: Principles and Genealogy* (Chicago, IL: University of Chicago Press, 2008).

4 Nadia Urbinati, "Representation as Advocacy: A Study of Democratic Deliberation," *Political Theory*, vol. 28, no. 6, December 2000, pp. 758–86.

5 Haley Plourde-Cole, "Back to Katz: Reasonable Expectation of Privacy in the Facebook Age," *Fordham Urban Law Journal*, vol. 38, 2010. Available at: http://ssrn.com/abstract=1703748

6 David Lyon, "9/11, Synopticon, and Scopophilia: Watching and Being Watched," in *The New Politics of Surveillance Visibility*, eds Haggerty and Ericson (Toronto, ON: University of Toronto Press, 2006), pp. 35–54.

7 Joelle Tessler, "FCC Report Finds Major Shortage in Local Reporting," *The Associated Press*, June 9, 2011.

8 Unmberto Eco, "Hackers vengeurs et espions en diligence," *Liberation*, December 2, 2010. Available at: http://www.liberation.fr/monde/01092305696-hackers-vengeurs-et-espions-en-diligence

9 Nick Fielding and Ian Cobain, "Revealed: US Spy Operation that Manipulates Social Media," *The Guardian*, March 17, 2011. Available at: http://www.guardian.co.uk/technology/2011/mar/17/us-spy-operation-social-networks

10 For an interesting case study and how-to in this area, see Rick Ferguson, "Word of Mouth and Viral Marketing: Taking the Temperature of the Hottest Trends in Marketing," *Journal of Consumer Marketing*, vol. 25, no. 3, 2008, pp. 179–82.

11 For small, but telling examples, see David Streitfeld, "In a Race to Out Rave, 5 Star Web Reviews for 5$," *The New York Times*, August 20, 2011, p. A1; or David Streitfeld, "The Best Book Reviews Money Can Buy," *The New York Times*, August 25, 2012, p. BU1.

12 Eric C. C. Chang, Miriam A. Golden, and Seth J. Hill, "Legislative Malfeasance and Political Accountability," *World Politics*, vol. 62, no. 2, April 2010, pp. 177–220.

13 For a good introduction to Habermas' discourse ethics, see William Rehg, *Insight and Solidarity: The Discourse Ethics of Jürgen Habermas*, vol. 1. (Berkeley, CA: University of California Press, 1997).

14 Henry R. Immerwahr, "Pathology of Power and the Speeches in Thucydides," in *The Speeches in Thucydides*, ed. Philip A. Stadter (Chapel Hill, NC: University of North Carolina Press, 1973), p. 29.

15 Marc Cogan, *The Human Thing: The Speeches and Principles of Thucydides' History* (Chicago, IL: University of Chicago Press, 1981), p. 210.

16 Benjamin Barber, "The Museum and the Mall," Keynote Address to the Annual Conference of the Association of Performing Arts Presenters [APAP] in New York, January 7, 2011. Available at: http://www.benjaminbarber.comTHE_MUSEUM_AND_THE_MALL_APAP_Jan2011_Benjamin_Barber.pdf

However, Barber has been interested in the links between politics and art for much of his career. For an earlier example of his thinking, see Benjamin Barber, "Rousseau and Brecht: Political Virtue and the Tragic Imagination," *The Artist and Political Vision*, ed. Barber and McGrath (New Brunswick: Transaction Press, 1983), pp. 1–86.

17   Jurgen Habermas, *Justification and Application*, trans. Ciara P. Cronin (Cambridge, MA: MIT Press, 1993), pp. 22–3.

18   For examples, see Adam B. Seligman, *The Idea of Civil Society* (New York: Simon and Schuster, 1992); Jean L. Cohen and Andrew Arato, *Civil Society and Political Theory* (Cambridge, MA: MIT Press, 1994).

19   For an interesting discussion of this point, see S. Chambers and J. Kopstein, "Bad Civil Society," *Political Theory*, vol. 29, no. 6, 2001, pp. 837–65.

20   See, for example, Ernest Gellner, *Conditions of Liberty: Civil Society and Its Rivals* (London: Hamish Hamilton, 1994).

21   For useful press archives of this case, see *the Guardian*'s online at: http://www. guardian.co.uk/world/the-us-embassy-cables or *The New York Times* online at: http://www.nytimes.com/interactive/world/statessecrets.html?hp

22   Michael Bakunin, *God and the State*, ed. Paul Avrich (New York: Dover Publications, 1970), p. 32.

23   Bakunin, *God and the State*, p. 33.

24   Jeremy Jennings, *Syndicalism in France: A Study of Ideas* (New York: St. Martin's Press, 1990), p. 31.

25   Bertrand Russell, *Roads to Freedom: Socialism, Anarchism, and Syndicalism* (first published 1918, New York: Barnes and Noble, 1965), p. 54.

26   G. D. H. Cole, *Guild Socialism Re-Stated* (London: Leonard Parsons Ltd., 1920), p. 12.

27   Russell, *Roads to Freedom*, p. 65.

28   Cole, *Guild Socialism Re-Stated*, p. 188. See his discussion in the chapter "Evolution and Revolution," pp. 174–88.

29   Oliver Marchart, *Post Foundational Political Thought: Political Difference in Nancy, Lefort, Badiou, and Laclau* (Edinburgh: Edinburgh University Press, 2007).

30   For a good description of Bakunin's take on such authority, see Peter Marshall, *Demanding the Impossible: A History of Anarchism* (Oakland, CA: PM Press, 2010), pp. 293–5.

31   Iris Young, *Inclusion and Democracy* (Oxford: Oxford University Press, 2000), pp. 156–86.

32   Monroe Friedman, "On Promoting a Sustainable Future through Consumer Activism," *Journal of Social Issues*, vol. 51, no. 4, 1995, pp. 197–215.

33   Matthew Hilton, *Prosperity for All: Consumer Activism in an Era of Globalization* (Ithaca, NY: Cornell University Press, 2009).

34   This story was covered in many European newspapers. For two very concise articles in English on the original call for action and its failure, see Kim

Willsher, "Eric Cantona's Call for Bank Protest Sparks Online Campaign," *The Observer*, November 20, 2010, p. 3; and Angelique Chrisafis, "Eric Cantona Protest Fails to Put Boot into Banks," *The Guardian*, December 8, 2010, p. 24.

35 Richard J. F. Day, *Gramsci is Dead: Anarchist Currents in the Newest Social Movements* (London: Pluto Press, 2005).

36 Alasdair Roberts, "Why the Occupy Movement Failed," *Public Administration Review*, vol. 72, no. 5, September/October 2012, pp. 754–62.

37 For commentary on this point and a broader description of the movement and events surrounding it, see Todd Gitlin, *Occupy Nation* (New York: Harper Collins, 2012).

38 Gitlin, *Occupy Nation*, pp. 140–57.

39 Nicholas Kulish, "Letter Bomb Sent to German Bank Chief," *The New York Times*, December 9, 2011, p. A15.

40 Rachel Donadio, "Letter Bomb Explodes in Italian Tax Office," *The New York Times*, December 9, 2011.

41 BBC News, "Greece Bombs: Nine Suspected Anarchists in Athens Trial," BBC News, January 17, 2011. Available at: http://www.bbc.co.uk/news/world-europe-12204741

42 P. A. Kropotkin, *Selected Writings on Anarchism and Revolution*, ed. Martin A. Miller (Cambridge, MA: MIT Press, 1970), p. 339.

43 Pierre-Joseph Proudhon, "To Karl Marx, 1846," *Correspondence, 1874–1875*. Available at: http://dwardmac.pitzer.edu/Anarchist_Archives/proudhon/letters/proudhontomarx.html

44 Slavoj Zizek, *Living in the End Times* (London: Verso, 2011).

BIBLIOGRAPHY

Chapter 1

Allison, Graham, *Essence of Decision: Explaining the Cuban Missile Crisis* (New York: Little Brown, 1971).

Bakunin, Mikhail, *God and the State* (New York: Dover Publications, 1970).

Barber, Benjamin, *Strong Democracy: Participatory Politics for a New Age* (Berkeley, CA: University of California Press, 1984).

Carens, Joseph H., "Aliens and Citizens: The Case for Open Borders," in *Theorizing Citizenship*, ed. Beiner, Ronald (Albany, NY: State University of New York Press, 1995), pp. 229–53.

Dagger, Richard, *Civic Virtues: Rights, Citizenship, and Republican Liberalism* (New York: Oxford University Press, 1997).

Day, Richard J. F., *Gramsci is Dead: Anarchist Currents in the New Social Movements* (London: Pluto Press, 2005).

Fine, Ben and Milonakis, Dimitris, *From Economics Imperialism to Freakonomics: The Shifting Boundaries between Economics and Other Social Sciences* (New York: Routledge, 2009).

Foucault, Michel, "Truth and Power" in *Essential Works of Foucault, 1954–1984*, vol. 3 ed. Faubion, James D. (New York: The New Press, 1994).

Friedman, Jeffrey, ed., *The Rational Choice Controversy* (New Haven, CT: Yale University Press, 1995).

Green, Donald P. and Shapiro, Ian, *Pathologies of Rational Choice: A Critique of Applications in Political Science* (New Haven, CT: Yale University Press, 1994).

Habermas, Jurgen, "Citizenship and National Identity: Some Reflections on the Future of Europe," in *Theorizing Citizenship*, ed. Beiner, Ronald (Albany, NY: State University of New York Press, 1995), pp. 255–81.

Hall, Peter A. and Taylor, Rosemary C. R., "Political Science and the Three New Institutionalisms," *Political Studies*, no. XLIV, 1996, pp. 936–57.

Hier, Sean P., "Probing the Surveillant Assemblage: On the Dialectics of Surveillance Practices as Processes of Social Control," *Surveillance and Society*, vol. 1, no. 3, 2003, pp. 399–411.

James, Paul, *Globalism, Nationalism, Tribalism: Bringing Theory Back In* (London: Sage Publications, 2006).

Levitt, Steven D. and Dubner, Stephen J., *Freakonomics: A Rogue Economist Explores the Hidden Side of Everything* (New York: Harper Collins, 2006).

Lyon, David, *Surveillance as Social Sorting* (New York: Routledge, 2003).

Lyotard, James-Francois, *The Postmodern Condition: A Report on Knowledge* (Minneapolis, MN: University of Minnesota Press, 1993).

Mann, Michael, *The Sources of Social Power*, vol. I (Cambridge: Cambridge University Press, 1986).

Matlock, Jack F., Jr., *Autopsy on an Empire* (New York: Random House, 1995).

Mills, C. Wright, *The Power Elite* (Oxford: Oxford University Press, 1956, 2000).

Olson, Mancur, *The Logic of Collective Action* (Cambridge, MA: Harvard University Press, 1965).

Parenti, Michael, *Democracy for the Few* (9th edition, Boston, MA: Wadsworth, 2010).

Peters, B. Guy, Pierre, Jon, and King, Desmond S., "The Politics of Path Dependency: Political Conflict in Historical Institutionalism," *The Journal of Politics*, vol. 67, no. 4, November 2005, pp. 1275–300.

Remnick, David, *Lenin's Tomb* (New York: Random House, 1993).

Scott, James C., *Seeing Like a State: How Certain Schemes to Improve the Human Condition Have Failed* (New Haven, CT: Yale University Press, 1999).

Weber, Max, *The Protestant Ethic and the Spirit of Capitalism*, trans. P. Baehr and C. Wells (New York: Penguin Books, 2002).

Chapter 2

Anderson, Benedict, *Imagined Communities: Reflections on the Origin and Spread of Nationalism* (London: Verso, 1991).

Beck, Ulrich, *Risk Society: Towards a New Modernity* (London: Sage Publications, 1992).

Beveridge, Ross, "Consultants, Depoliticization and Arena-Shifting in the Policy Process: Privatizing Water in Berlin," *Policy Sciences*, vol. 45, no. 1, March 2012, pp. 47–68.

Borgerson, Scott G., "Arctic Meltdown: The Economic and Security Implications of Global Warming," *Foreign Affairs*, vol. 87, no. 2, March/April 2008, pp. 63–77.

Carpini, Michael X. Delli and Keeter, Scott, *What Americans Know about Politics and Why It Matters* (New Haven, CT: Yale University Press, 1996).

Fishman, Charles, *The Big Thirst: The Secret Life and Turbulent Future of Water* (New York: The Free Press, 2011).

Fukuyama, Francis, *Our Posthuman Future: Consequences of the Biotechnology Revolution* (New York: Picador, 2003).

Galston, William A., "Political Knowledge, Political Engagement, and Civic Education," *Annual Review of Political Science*, vol. 4, June 2001, pp. 217–34.

Gill, Peter, *Policing Politics: Security, Intelligence, and the Liberal Democratic State* (London: Frank Cass & Co. Ltd., 1994).

Gottshcalk, Marie, *The Shadow Welfare State: Labor, Business, and the Politics of Health Care in the United States* (Ithaca, NY: Cornell University Press, 2000).

Harding, Richard, "Private Prisons," *Crime and Justice*, vol. 28, 2001, pp. 265–346.

Hasen, Richard L., "End of the Dialogue? Political Polarization, the Supreme Court, and Congress (August 14, 2012)," UC Irvine School of Law Research Paper No. 2012-65. Available at: http://ssrn.com/abstract=2130190

Healy, Andrew and Malhotra, Neil, "Myopic Voters and Natural Disaster Policy," *American Political Science Review*, vol. 103, no. 3, 2009, pp. 387–406.

Hogan, Michael J., *A Cross of Iron: Harry S. Truman and the Origins of the National Security State, 1945–1954* (Cambridge: Cambridge University Press, 2000).

Howard, Christopher, *The Hidden Welfare State: Tax Expenditures and Social Policy in the United States* (Princeton, NJ: Princeton University Press, 1994).

Jordan, Andrew, Wurzel, Rüdiger K. W., and Zito, Anthony. "The Rise of 'New' Policy Instruments in Comparative Perspective: Has Governance Eclipsed Government?" *Political Studies*, vol. 53, no. 3, 2005, pp. 477–96.

Jordan, Grant A., "Iron Triangles, Woolly Corporatism and Elastic Nets: Images of the Policy Process," *Journal of Public Policy*, vol. 1, no. 1, February 1981, pp. 95–123.

Kavakci, Merve, "Turkey's Test with Its Deep State," *Mediterranean Quarterly*, vol. 20, no. 4, 2009, pp. 83–97.

Kemmelmeier, Markus and Winter, David G., "Sowing Patriotism, But Reaping Nationalism? Consequences of Exposure to the American Flag," *Political Psychology*, vol. 29, no. 6, 2008, pp. 859–79.

Kettl, Donald F., "The Transformation of Governance: Globalization, Devolution, and the Role of Government," *Public Administration Review*, vol. 60, no. 6 2002, pp. 488–97.

Kocieniewski, David, "But Nobody Pays That: G.E.'s Strategies Let It Avoid Taxes Altogether," *The New York Times*, 25 March 2011, p. A1.

Kuklinski, James H., Quirk, Paul J., Jerit, Jennifer, Schweider, David, and Rich, Robert F., "Misinformation and the Currency of Democratic Citizenship," *The Journal of Politics*, vol. 62, no. 3, August 2000, pp. 790–816.

Lau, Richard R. and Heldman, Caroline, "Self-Interest, Symbolic Attitudes, and Support for Public Policy: A Multilevel Analysis," *Political Psychology*, vol. 30, no. 4, August 2009, pp. 513–37.

Lax, Jeffrey R. and Phillips, Justin H., "The Democratic Deficit in the States," *American Journal of Political Science*, vol. 56, no. 1, January 2012, pp. 148–66.

McGraw, Kathleen M. and Dolan, Thomas M., "Personifying the State: Consequences for Attitude Formation," *Political Psychology*, vol. 28, no. 3, 2007, pp. 299–327.

McGregor, Richard, *The Party: The Secret World of China's Communist Rulers* (New York: Harper Collins, 2010).

Mettler, Suzanne, "Reconstituting the Submerged State: The Challenges of Social Policy Reform in the Obama Era," *Perspectives on Politics*, vol. 8, no. 3, September 2010, pp. 803–24.

Michaud, Kristy E. H., Carlisle, Juliet E., and Smith, Eric, "The Relationship Between Cultural Values and Political Ideology, and the Role of Political Knowledge," *Political Psychology*, vol. 30, no. 1, 2009, pp. 27–42.

Pratt, Travis C. and Maahs, Jeff, "Are Private Prisons More Cost-Effective than Public Prisons? A Meta-Analysis of Evaluation Research Studies," *Crime & Delinquency*, vol. 45, no. 3, 1999, pp. 358–71.

Prior, Markus, "News vs. Entertainment: How Increasing Media Choice Widens Gaps in Political Knowledge and Turnout," *American Journal of Political Science*, vol. 49, no. 3, 2005, pp. 577–92.

Rosenberg, Howard and Feldman, Charles S., *No Time to Think: The Menace of Media Speed and the 24-hour News Cycle* (New York: Continuum, 2008).

Sabatier, Paul A., "Toward Better Theories of the Policy Process," *PS: Political Science and Politics*, vol. 24, no. 2, 1991, pp. 147–56.

Schively, Carissa, "Understanding the NIMBY and LULU Phenomena: Reassessing Our Knowledge Base and Informing Future Research," *Journal of Planning Literature*, vol. 21, no. 3, 2007, pp. 255–66.

Sears, David O., Lau, Richard R., Tyler, Tom R., and Allen, Harris M., "Self-Interest vs. Symbolic Politics in Policy Attitudes and Presidential Voting," *American Political Science Review*, vol. 74, 1980, pp. 670–84.

Shipan, Charles R., "Regulatory Regimes, Agency Action, and the Conditional Nature of Congressional Influence," *American Political Science Review*, vol. 98, no. 3, 2004, pp. 467–80.

Swyngedouw, Erik, "Governance Innovation and the Citizen: The Janus Face of Governance-beyond-the-State," *Urban Studies*, vol. 42, no. 11, October 2005, pp. 1991–2006.

Ting, Michael M., "Legislatures, Bureaucracies, and Distributive Spending," *American Political Science Review*, vol. 106, no. 2, May 2012, pp. 367–85.

Vickers, John and Yarrow, George, *Privatization: An Economic Analysis*, vol. 18 (Cambridge, MA: MIT press, 1988).

Chapter 3

Anderson, Benedict, *Imagined Communities: Reflections on the Origin and Spread of Nationalism* (New York: Verso, 1983).

Anderson, Perry, *Lineages of the Absolutist State* (London: NJB, 1974).

Badiou, Alain, *Ethics: An Essay on Understanding Evil* (New York: Verso, 2001).

Bakunin, Michael, *The Political Philosophy of Bakunin*, ed. Maximoff, G. P. (New York: The Free Press, 1953).

Bakunin, Michael, *God and the State*, ed. Avrich, Paul (New York: Dover Publications, 1970).

Bartelson, Jens, *The Critique of the State* (Cambridge: Cambridge University Press, 2001).

Bentham, Jeremy, *A Fragment on Government*, series eds. Geuss R. and Skinner, Q., *Cambridge Texts in the History of Political Thought* (Cambridge; Cambridge University Press, 1988).

Bradley, D., Huber, E., and Moller, S., "Distribution and Redistribution in Postindustrial Democracies," *World Politics*, vol. 55, no. 2, January 2003, pp. 193–228.

Butterworth, Alex, *The World That Never Was: A True Story of Dreamers, Schemers, Anarchists, and Secret Agents* (New York: Pantheon, 2010).

Chua, Amy, *World on Fire* (New York: Knopf Doubleday, 2004).

Elster, Jon, *Closing the Books: Transitional Justice in Historical Perspective* (Cambridge: Cambridge University Press, 2004).

Evans, Peter B., Rueschemeyer, Dietrich, and Skocpol, Theda, *Bringing the State Back In* (Cambridge: Cambridge University Press, 1985).

Foucault, Michel, *Discipline and Punish*, trans. Alan Sheridan (New York: Vintage Books, 1995).

Franklin, Julian H., *Jean Bodin and the Rise of Absolutist Theory* (Cambridge: Cambridge University Press, reissue edition, 2009).

Fraser, Nancy and Honneth, Axel, *Redistribution or Recognition?* (New York: Verso, 2003).

Habermas, Jurgen, "Constitutional Democracy: A Paradoxical Union of Contradictory Principles?" *Political Theory*, vol. 29, no. 6, 2001, pp. 766–81.

Hanlon, Gregory, *The Twilight of a Military Tradition: Italian Aristocrats and European Conflicts, 1560–1800* (London: University College of London Press, 1998).

Herbst, Jeffrey, *States and Power in Africa* (Princeton, NJ: Princeton University Press, 2000).

Kershaw, Ian, *The End: The Defiance and Destruction of Hitler's Germany, 1944–1945* (New York: Penguin Books, 2011).

Kohli, Atul, *State Directed Development: Political Power and Industrialization in the Global Periphery* (Cambridge: Cambridge University Press, 2004).

Krasner, Stephen D., *Sovereignty: Organized Hypocrisy* (Princeton, NJ: Princeton University Press, 1999).

Kropotkin, Petr, *The Place of Anarchism in Socialistic Evolution*, trans. Enry Glasse (London: William Reeves, 1886).

Kropotkin, Petr, *Fields, Factories, and Workshops* (New York: G.P. Putnam's Sons, 1909).

Kropotkin, Petr, *Mutual Aid* (London: William Heinemann, 1910).

Kropotkin, Petr, "The State: Its Historic Role," in *Selected Writings on Anarchism and Revolution*, ed. Miller, Martin A. (Cambridge, MA: MIT Press, 1970), pp. 210–64.

Levitsky, Steven, and Way, Lucan A., *Competitive Authoritarianism: Hybrid Regimes After the Cold War* (Cambridge: Cambridge University Press, 2010).

Lopez-Alves, Fernando, *State Formation and Democracy in Latin America, 1810–1900* (Durham: Duke University Press, 2000).

Mann, Michael, *The Sources of Social Power: A History of Power from the Beginning to AD 1760* (Cambridge: Cambridge University Press, 1986).

Maritn, Cathie Jo and Thelen, Kathleen, "The State and Coordinated Capitalism: Contributions of the Public Sector to Social Solidarity in Postindustrial Societies," *World Politics*, vol. 60, no. 1, October 2007, pp. 1–36.

Marx, Karl, "The German Ideology," in *The Marx-Engels Reader*, ed. Tucker, Robert C. (2nd edition, New York: Norton and Company, 1978), pp. 160–1.

Moore, Barrington, *Social Origins of Dictatorship and Democracy; Lord and Peasant in the Making of the Modern World* (Boston, MA: Beacon Press, 1966).

Polyani, Karl, *The Great Transformation* (New York: Farrar and Rinehart, Inc., 1944).

Popper, Karl, *The Open Society and Its Enemies* (Princeton, NJ: Princeton University Press, 1971).

Przeworski, Adam, *Democracy and the Market* (Cambridge: Cambridge University Press, 1991).

Ralston, David B., *Importing the European Army: The Introduction of European Military Techniques into the Extra European World, 1600–1914* (Chicago, IL: The University of Chicago Press, 1990).

Rawls, John, *Theory of Justice* (Cambridge, MA: Harvard University Press, 1971).

Reynolds, Andrew, ed., *The Architecture of Democracy* (Oxford: Oxford University Press, 2002).

Rousseau, Jean Jacques, *The First and Second Discourses*, ed. Masters, Roger D. (New York: St. Martin's Press, 1964).

Rosseau, Jean Jacques, *The Social Contract*, ed. Masters, Roger (New York: St. Martin's Press, 1978).

Schmitt, Carl, *Political Theology: Four Chapters on the Concept of Sovereignty*, trans. George Schwab (Chicago, IL: University of Chicago Press, 2005).

Schneier, Edward, *Crafting Constitutional Democracies: The Politics of Institutional Design* (Lanham, MD: Rowman and Littlefield Press, 2006).

Simmons, Beth A., Dobbin, Frank, and Garrett, Geoffrey, *The Global Diffusion of Markets and Democracy* (Cambridge: Cambridge University Press, 2008).

Stearns, Jason, *Dancing in the Glory of Monsters: The Collapse of Congo and the Great War of Africa* (New York: Public Affairs 2011).

Thies, Cameron G., "National Design and State Building in Sub-Saharan Africa," *World Politics*, vol. 61, no. 4 (October 2009), pp. 623–69.

Tilly, Charles, *Coercion, Capital, and European States, AD 990–1990* (Cambridge, MA: Blackwell, 1990).

Tilly, Charles, ed. *The Formation of National States in Western Europe* (Princeton, NJ: Princeton University Press, 1975).

Vu, Tuong, "Studying the State through State Formation," *World Politics*, vol. 62, no. 1, January 2010, pp. 148–75.

Wolin, Sheldon S., *Democracy Incorporated: Managed Democracy and the Specter of Inverted Totalitarianism* (Princeton, NJ: Princeton University Press, 2008).

Chapter 4

Alvarez, Lizette "Florida Prison Privatization Plan Hits Roadblock," *The New York Times*, 1 October 2011, p. A15.

Amnesty International, "USA: Excessive and Lethal Force? Amnesty International's Concerns about Deaths and Ill-treatment involving Tasers," AI Index: AMR 51/139/2004.

Amnesty International, "Canada: Excessive and Lethal Force? Amnesty International's Concerns about Deaths and Ill-treatment involving Police Use of Tasers," AI Index: AMR 20/02/2004.

Arendt, Hannah, *On Violence* (New York: Harcourt, Brace & World, 1970).

Bekey, George A., *Autonomous Robots: From Biological Inspiration to Implementation and Control* (Cambridge, MA: MIT Press, 2005).

Bernstein, Nina, "Companies Use Immigration Crackdown to Turn a Profit," *The New York Times*, 29 September 2011, p. A1.

Butler, Judith, *Frames of War: When is Life Grievable?* (New York: Verson, 2009).

Eighmey, John, "Why Do Youth Enlist: Identification of Underlying Themes," *Armed Forces and Society*, vol. 32, no. 2, 2006, pp. 307–28.

Enemark, Christian, "Non-Lethal Weapons and the Occupation of Iraq: Technology, Ethics, and Law," *Cambridge Review of International Affairs*, vol. 21, no. 2, June 2008, pp. 199–215.

Etzioni, Amitai, *The Limits of Privacy* (New York: Basic Books, 1999).

Fidler, David, "Non-Lethal Weapons and International Law: Three Perspectives on the Future," in *The Future of Non-Lethal Weapons: Technologies, Operations, Ethics, and Law*, ed. Lewer, Nick (London: Frank Cass, 2002), pp. 26–38.

Fotion, Nick, "Proportionality," in *Moral Constraints on War*, eds. Coppieters and Fotion (Lanham, MD: Lexington Books, 2008), pp. 125–37.

Gawande, Atul, "Casualties of War—Military Care for the Wounded from Iraq and Afghanistan," *New England Journal of Medicine*, vol. 351, no. 24, 2004, pp. 2471–5.

Gross, Michael L., "The Second Lebanon War: The Question of Proportionality and the Prospect of Non-Lethal Warfare," *Journal of Military Ethics*, vol. 7, no. 1, 2008, pp. 1–22.

Holsti, Ole R., "A Widening Gap between the US Military and Civilian Society? Some Evidence, 1976–1996," *International Security*, vol. 23, no. 3, winter, 1998–1999, pp. 5–42.

Kleinman, Zoe, "How Online Life Distorts Privacy for All," *BBC News*, 8 January 2010. Available at: http://news.bbc.co.uk/2/hi/technology/8446649.stm

Lewer, Nick, "Non-Lethal Weapons: Operational and Policy Developments," *The Lancet*, vol. 362, no. 1, 2003, pp. 20–1.

Lorenz, F. M., "Non Lethal Force: The Slippery Slope to War?" *Parameters*, Autumn 1996, pp. 52–62.

Mann, Michael, *The Sources of Social Power: A History of Power from the Beginning to AD 1760* (Cambridge: Cambridge University Press, 1986).

Mazzetti, Mark, "The Drone Zone," *The New York Times Sunday Magazine*, 8 July 2012, p. MM32.

McKinley, Jesse, "Police Departments Turn to Volunteers," *The New York Times*, 2 March 2011, p. A13.

Monahan, Torin, ed. *Surveillance and Security: Technological Politics and Power in Everyday Life* (New York: Routledge, 2006).

Moore, Barrington, ed. *Privacy: Studies in Social and Cultural History* (New York: M.E. Sharpe, 1984).

O'Hara, Kieron and Shadbolt, Nigel, *The Spy in the Coffee Machine* (Oxford: Oneworld, 2008).

Parenti, Christian, *The Soft Cage: Surveillance in America from Slavery to the War on Terror* (New York: Basic Books, 2003).

Rappert, Brian, *Non-Lethal Weapons as Legitimizing Forces?* (London: Frank Cass, 2003).

Reiman, Jeffrey H., "Privacy, Intimacy, and Personhood," *Philosophy and Public Affairs*, vol. 6, no. 1, Autumn, 1976, pp. 26–44.

Roland, Alex and Shiman, Philip, *Strategic Computing: DARPA and the Quest for Machine Intelligence* (Cambridge, MA: MIT Press, 2002).

Segal, David R. and Segal Mady Wechsler, "America's Military Population," *Population Bulletin*, vol. 59, no. 4, December 2004.

Sifton, John, "Drones, A Troubling History," *The Nation*, vol. 294, no. 9, 27 February 2012, pp. 11–15.

Singer, P. W., *Corporate Warriors: The Rise of the Privatized Military Industry* (Ithaca, NY: Cornell University Press, 2007).

Stalder, Felix, "Privacy is Not the Antidote to Surveillance," *Surveillance & Society*, vol. 1, no. 1, 120–4.

Thomson, Judith Jarvis, "The Right to Privacy," *Philosophy and Public Affairs*, vol. 4, no. 4, Summer 1975, pp. 295–314.

Walzer, Michael, *Just and Unjust Wars* (New York: Basic Books, 1977).

Weber, Max, *Economy and Society*, eds. Roth, Guenther and Wittich, Claus (Berkeley, CA: University of California Press, 1978).

Wendt, Alexander and Duvall, Raymond, "Sovereignty and the UFO," *Political Theory*, vol. 36, no. 4, 2008, pp. 607–33.

Westin, Alan F., *Privacy and Freedom* (New York: Atheneum, 1967).

Westin, Alan F., "Social and Political Dimensions of Privacy," *Journal of Social Issues*, vol. 59, no. 2, 2003, pp. 431–53.

Chapter 5

Abrams, Samuel J. and Fiorina, Morris P., " 'The Big Sort' That Wasn't: A Skeptical Reexamination," *Political Science and Politics*, vol. 45, no. 2, April 2012, pp. 203–10.

Amadeo, J., Torney-Purta, J., Lehman, R., Husfeldt, V., and Nikolova, R., *Civic Knowledge and Engagement* (Amsterdam: IEA, 2002), p. 81.

Baudrillard, Jean, *The System of Objects* (New York: Verso, 1996).

Bendix, Reinhard, *Kings or People: Power and the Mandate to Rule* (Berkeley, CA: University of California Press, 1978).

Bishop, Bill, *The Big Sort: Why the Clustering of Like Minded America is Tearing Us Apart* (New York: Houghton Mifflin Company, 2008).

Blum, Jerome, *Lord and Peasant in Russia: From the Ninth to the Nineteenth Century* (Princeton, NJ: Princeton University Press, 1961).

Briggs, Robin, *Witches and Neighbors: The Social and Cultural Context of European Witchcraft* (New York: Viking, 1996).

Carr, David, "At Media Companies, A Nation of Serfs," *The New York Times*, 14 February 2011, p. B1.

Castells, Manuel, *The Rise of the Network Society (The Information Age: Economy, Society, and Culture)*, vol. 1 (2nd edition, Malden, MA: Wiley Blackwell, 2000).

Cogan, John J. and Derricott, Ray, ed., *Citizenship for the 21st Century: An International Perspective on Education* (New York: Kogan Page Ltd., 1998), pp. 24–7.

Connolly, William E., *Capitalism and Christianity, American Style* (Durham: Duke University Press, 2008).

Dzur, Albert W., "Democracy's 'Free School': Tocqueville and Lieber on the Value of the Jury," *Political Theory*, vol. 38, no. 5, October 2010, pp. 603–30.

The Economist, "Student Loans in America, The Next Big Credit Bubble?" *The Economist*, 29 October 29–4 November 2011.

Ehrenreich, Barbara, *Bright Sided: How Positive Thinking is Undermining America* (New York: Picador, 2010).

Frassier, Robert, *Peasant Life in the Medieval West*, trans. Juliet Vale (New York: Basil Blackwell, Inc., 1988).

Fukuyama, Francis, *Our Posthuman Future: Consequences of the Biotechnology Revolution* (New York: Picador, 2003).

Gasset, Ortega Y., *The Revolt of the Masses* (New York: W.W. Norton & Company, 1994).

Glaeser, Edward L. and Sacerdote, Bruce I., "Education and Religion," *Journal of Human Capital*, vol. 2, no. 2, Summer 2008, pp. 188–215.

Godwin, William, "The Evils of National Education" and "Education through Desire," in *The Anarchist Reader*, ed. Woodcock, George (Atlantic Highlands, NJ: Harvester Press/Humanities Press, 1977), pp. 267–73.

Halman, Loek and Draulans, Veerle, "How Secular is Europe?" *The British Journal of Sociology*, vol. 57, no. 2, 2006, pp. 263–88.

Heffernan, Virginia, "Let Them Eat Tweets," *The New York Times*, 19 April 2009, p. MM22.

Hill, Christopher, *The World Turned Upside Down: Radical Ideas during the English Revolution* (New York: Penguin Books, 1984).

Kropotkin, P. A., "The State: Its Historic Role," in *Selected Writings on Anarchism and Revolution*, ed. Miller, Martin A. (Cambridge, MA: MIT Press, 1970).

Leicht, Kevin and Fitzgerald, Scott, *Postindustrial Peasants: The Illusion of Middle-Class Prosperity* (New York: Worth Publishers, 2006).

Le Goff, Jacques, *Medieval Civilization, 400–1500* (New York: Barnes and Noble Books, 2000).

McGee, *Self Help, Inc.: Makeover Culture in American Life* (Oxford: Oxford University Press, 2005).

Morozov, Evgeny, "Your Own Facts," *The New York Times Book Review*, 12 June 2011, p. BR20.

Noveck, Beth Simone, "Transparent Space: Law, Technology and Deliberative Democracy in the Information Society," *Cultural Values*, vol. 3, no. 4, 1999, pp. 472–91.

Pariser, Eli, *The Filter Bubble: What the Internet is Hiding from You* (New York: Penguin Press, 2011).

Putnam, Robert, *Bowling Alone: The Collapse and Revival of the American Community* (New York: Simon and Schuster, 2001).

Schulze, Hagen, *States, Nations, and Nationalism* (Cambridge, MA: Blackwell Press, 1996).

Stephens, Randall J. and Giberson, Karl W., *The Anointed: Evangelical Truth in a Secular Age* (Cambridge, MA: Harvard University Press, 2011).

Stayer, James M., *The German Peasant's War and Anabaptist Community of Goods* (Montreal, QC: McGill-Queen's University Press, 1994).

Stone, Lawrence, *The Causes of the English Revolution, 1529–1642* (New York: Routledge, 2002).

Treasure, Geoffrey, *The Making of Modern Europe, 1648–1780* (New York: Routledge, 2003).

Turow, Joseph, "A Guide to the Digital Advertising Industry that is Watching Your Every Click," *The Atlantic*, 7 February 2012. Available at: http://www.theatlantic.com/technology/archive/2012/02/a-guide-to-the-digital-advertising-industry-thats-watching-your-every-click/252667/

Chapter 6

Bakunin, Michael, *God and the State*, ed. Avrich, Paul (New York: Dover Publications, 1970).

Barber, Benjamin, "The Museum and the Mall," Keynote Address to the Annual Conference of the Association of Performing Arts Presenters [APAP] in New York, 7 January 2011. Available at: http://www.benjaminbarber.com/THE_MUSEUM_AND_THE_MALL_APAP_Jan2011_Benjamin_Barber.pdf

Barber, Benjamin, "Rousseau and Brecht: Political Virtue and the Tragic Imagination," *The Artist and Political Vision*, eds. Barber, B. and McGrath, M. (New Brunswick, NJ: Transaction Press, 1983), pp. 1–86.

Chambers, S. and Kopstein, J., "Bad Civil Society," *Political Theory*, vol. 29, no. 6 (2001), pp. 837–65.

Chang, Eric C. C., Golden, Miriam A., and Hill, Seth J., "Legislative Malfeasance and Political Accountability," *World Politics*, vol. 62, no. 2, April 2010, pp. 177–220.

Cogan, Marc, *The Human Thing: The Speeches and Principles of Thucydides' History* (Chicago, IL: University of Chicago Press, 1981).

Cohen, Jean L. and Arato, Andrew, *Civil Society and Political Theory* (Cambridge, MA: MIT Press, 1994).

Cole, G. D. H., *Guild Socialism Re-Stated* (London: Leonard Parsons Ltd., 1920).

Day, Richard J. F., *Gramsci is Dead: Anarchist Currents in the New Social Movements* (London: Pluto Press, 2005).

Ferguson, Rick, "Word of Mouth and Viral Marketing: Taking the Temperature of the Hottest Trends in Marketing," *Journal of Consumer Marketing*, vol. 25, no. 3, 2008, pp. 179–82.

Friedman, Monroe, "On Promoting a Sustainable Future through Consumer Activism," *Journal of Social Issues*, vol. 51, no. 4, 1995, pp. 197–215.

Gellner, Ernest, *Conditions of Liberty: Civil Society and Its Rivals* (London: Hamish Hamilton, 1994).

Gitlin, Todd, *Occupy Nation* (New York: Harper Collins, 2012).

Green, Jeffrey Edward, *The Eyes of the People: Democracy in an Age of Spectatorship* (Oxford: Oxford University Press, 2010).

Habermas, Jurgen, *Justification and Application*, trans. Ciara P. Cronin (Cambridge, MA: MIT Press, 1993).

Hilton, Matthew, *Prosperity for All: Consumer Activism in an Era of Globalization* (Ithaca, NY: Cornell University Press, 2009).

Immerwahr, Henry R., "Pathology of Power and the Speeches in Thucydides," in *The Speeches in Thucydides*, ed. Stadter, Philip A. (Chapel Hill, NC: University of North Carolina Press, 1973).

Jennings, Jeremy, *Syndicalism in France: A Study of Ideas* (New York: St. Martin's Press, 1990).

Kropotkin, P. A., *Selected Writings on Anarchism and Revolution*, ed. Miller, Martin A. (Cambridge, MA: MIT Press, 1970).

Marchart, Oliver, *Post Foundational Political Thought: Political Difference in Nancy, Lefort, Badiou, and Laclau* (Edinburgh: Edinburgh University Press, 2007).

Marshall, Peter, *Demanding the Impossible: A History of Anarchism* (Oakland, CA: PM Press 2010).

Plourde-Cole, Haley, "Back to Katz: Reasonable Expectation of Privacy in the Facebook Age," *Fordham Urban Law Journal*, vol. 38, 2010. Available at: http://ssrn.com/abstract=1703748

Posner, Eric A. and Vermeule, Adrian, *The Executive Unbound: After the Madisonian Republic* (Oxford: Oxford University Press, 2011).

Proudhon, Pierre-Joseph, "To Karl Marx, 1846," *Correspondence, 1874–1875*. Available at: http://dwardmac.pitzer.edu/Anarchist_Archives/proudhon/letters/proudhontomarx.html

Rehg, William, *Insight and Solidarity: The Discourse Ethics of Jürgen Habermas*, vol. 1 (Berkeley, CA: University of California Press, 1997).

Roberts, Alasdair, "Why the Occupy Movement Failed," *Public Administration Review*, vol. 72, no. 5, September/October 2012, pp. 754–62.

Russell, Bertrand, *Roads to Freedom: Socialism, Anarchism, and Syndicalism* (first published 1918, New York: Barnes and Noble, 1965).

Seligman, Adam B., *The Idea of Civil Society* (New York: Simon and Schuster, 1992).

Urbinati, Nadia, "Representation as Advocacy: A Study of Democratic Deliberation," *Political Theory*, vol. 28, no. 6, December 2000, pp. 758–86.

Urbinati, Nadia, *Representative Democracy: Principles and Genealogy* (Chicago, IL: University of Chicago Press, 2008).

Young, Iris, *Inclusion and Democracy* (Oxford: Oxford University Press, 2000), pp. 156–86.

Zizek, Slavoj, *Living in the End Times* (London: Verso, 2011).

INDEX

war
  changing nature of 86–92
  and state formation 63–5
Weber, Max 11
WikiLeaks 35, 141, 147–8, 155–6

Wolin, Sheldon 61

Yarrow, George 41
Young, Iris 152

Zizek, Slavoj 158–9

Y

Mandy Lee

Other books by Mandy Lee:

The *You Don't Know Me* Trilogy
You Don't Know Me - B0103IR52O
True Colours - B01CROPPUG
Shut Your Eyes - B06X3XGPG6

The X, Y, Z Trilogy
X - B081FD4HZY

Acknowledgements

Dedicated to my lovely fans:

Sarah Hayward and
Yvonne Eason

Preface

X, Y, Z is a trilogy about three brothers: Max, Sebastian and Zach. Each book is a standalone in its own right, and the trilogy as a whole works backwards in time. By the end of X, you'll know exactly who ends up with who, but there will still be mysteries, twists and surprises along the way.

So why am I working backwards in time?

Firstly, I just wanted to do something a little different. It's a challenge mapping out a trilogy like this, dropping in little hints of things to come in the next instalment.

Secondly, most readers of romance books – including me – love their happy endings. We become so invested in the hero and heroine that we need them to get together. And let's be honest, it's never really a surprise when they do. So, I'm working on the premise that it makes no difference that you know who couples up. It's the journey that counts, not the destination!

Finally, readers often ask for more about minor characters. In this trilogy, the 'more' is built in. As you read the trilogy, you'll find out more about all three brothers, and other characters too.

I really hope you enjoy reading X, Y and Z. Happy reading!

Mandy Lee

Chapter One

My stomach rumbles, reminding me of the need to eat before closing time. With a distinct lack of enthusiasm, I survey the contents of the cake cabinet, taking in a dried-out scone, two desiccated flapjacks and a thoroughly underwhelming slice of millionaire's shortbread. It's all way past edible – and really ought to be consigned to the bin – but Wallace would never hear of it. 'Waste not, want not,' he'd say. 'That's my mantra for success... unless the health inspector shows his ugly face.'

'Success?' I mutter. 'Pull the other one.'

I glance round at the scuffed floor and battered walls, home to a motley collection of untrustworthy chairs and rickety tables, only one of which is currently occupied: by a loved-up couple who've been here for an hour now, winding me up with their sickly-sweet assignation. The Phoenix Café isn't a place for their kind. It belongs to the lost and lonely, the misfits and outcasts. And this ridiculous pair, who fit none of those categories, should really have the decency to take their little bubble of happiness elsewhere.

The very second I form the thought – as if they've miraculously managed to read my mind – Romeo and Juliet finally get to their feet and head for the exit.

'Thank God,' I mutter.

The doorbell tinkles in their wake.

And again, as the door swings back open.

A momentary pinch of anxiety disappears when I realise my new regular's back for the fourth night in a row. Sporting a long grey coat, shirt and tie, black trousers and a pair of black brogues, he could easily be mistaken for an elderly businessman. But on closer inspection, the shoes are scuffed, the shirt a little discoloured at the collar, and the trousers fraying at the hem.

'Hal.' I greet my fellow lost soul with a broad smile. 'Nice to see you again.'

He frowns.

'Mary,' I remind him. The usual lie.

'Mary.' A flicker of recognition sparks in his eyes. 'Of course. Mary.' He approaches the counter. 'Quiet in here tonight.'

'It's always quiet. Don't know why the boss keeps it open.'

Another lie. It's all down to an unhealthy dose of denial, fuelled by a deepening love affair with the local off-licence and a total lack

1

of interest in accounts and business plans. The writing's on the wall for The Phoenix, but Wallace won't acknowledge a word of it. Even though it's been months since the old customers were lured away by a brand-new café on the nearby hospital grounds, he's still convinced they'll be back.

'Fancy a tea?'

Hal sways a little. 'Always.'

'Are you okay?'

'I'm fine.'

'You don't look it. Tell you what. Take a seat and I'll make a pot.'

He wafts a hand towards the front bay. 'Usual place?'

'Where else?'

While Hal takes a seat and busies himself with gazing out of the window, I load up a tray with a stainless-steel teapot, a couple of mugs and a plate of cheap biscuits. And then, leaning back against the counter and waiting for the urn to boil, I wonder about my mysterious companion's identity. But try as I might, I just can't work out why a man like this – well-spoken, with a distinct air of wealth to match – would be haunting the streets of Bermondsey.

'Here we go.' With the tea made, I carry the tray over to the window and settle in under the sickly-green glow of a neon phoenix. 'When was the last time you ate, Hal?' Knowing we're about to plough back through exactly the same conversation we had last night, and the two nights before, I pour the tea and add milk.

'Not sure.'

'You've got to keep your energy up.' I nudge the plate of biscuits towards him. 'Go on. Take one.'

Hands shaking a little more than last night, he wiggles his fingers over the plate, opts for a digestive, dunks it twice and takes a bite.

'Tell me something,' he says. 'Why do you work here?'

'Why?' I laugh. 'Because it's a job.'

'But you can't earn that much.'

'Enough to pay the rent.' In a crappy little shared house, owned by the couple from Hell.

'You deserve better.'

'There's nothing wrong with being a waitress.'

'No, but...'

'And work's hard to come by.' Especially when the only sort of work you can take is cash in hand, no questions asked. I spoon a couple of sugars into his mug, and stir.

'I suppose so,' he muses. 'But this can't be the sort of work you want to do.'

2

'Definitely not.'

'Tell me then. What would you do, if you had the choice?'

'I don't know. I'd maybe work in an office.'

'An office?' One overgrown eyebrow shifts upwards. 'My brother has offices. Lots of them. I could ask him...' He drifts into silence, eyes losing focus.

'Hal? Are you alright?'

'Alright? Oh, yes.' He finishes off the digestive. 'What time do you finish?'

A complete change of topic, but I'm used to the drifting concentration. 'Are you asking me out?'

'Of course not.' His eyes twinkle. 'Come on. Tell me. What time?'

'Eleven.'

'That late? I do hope you're not walking home alone. It's dangerous out there.'

'It is.' More dangerous than he knows. But as long as I carry on living in the shadows, I'll be safe enough.

'You're not from round here.'

'No.' I smile, amazed he's remembered something from our previous chats. 'I'm not.'

'So, where do you hail from?'

I take a slow sip of tea, and then another. Judging by previous experience, if I dither long enough, he'll soon forget the question – and that's the aim. After all, I daren't risk offering up a speck of truth, not even in the presence of an old man with a leaky memory. And seeing as I'm sick to death of pretence, it's the best option.

'Have another biscuit.' I nod to the plate. Time to distract.

'If I must.' He helps himself to a ginger nut, dunks it three times, and takes a bite.

'Any luck today?'

Chewing quickly, he shakes his head. 'I looked everywhere. The High Street, the market, all the shops. I even asked at the hospital.'

'And?'

'Nothing. No one's even heard of her.' As if it's suddenly unpalatable, he stares at the remains of the biscuit. 'I can't understand. I thought she might be here tonight. Perhaps she was?' His eyes return to mine. 'Long blonde hair, just like yours.'

'I'm sorry, Hal. I haven't seen her.' And I doubt I ever will.

'Maybe if I stay a while. She's probably still on shift. She's a nurse, you know.'

I know. He tells me every night.

'At the hospital... along the road.' He finishes off the ginger nut and squints up at the glowing, plastic phoenix in the window. 'That's new.'

'It's been here over twenty years.' A fairly accurate estimate, judging by the rusty screws, the amount of grime on the off-white electric cable dangling from the bird's backside, and – most tellingly – the tiny inscription etched into one of its feet: Julie luvs Daz. 1997.

'Twenty?' His brows crease.

'That one's been here longer.' I gesture to the tiled wall opposite the counter, where an image of a phoenix plays out in shades of red, blue, and cream. With outstretched wings, engulfed in flames, it seems to be crying out in pain, or anger... or both.

'Oh, yes. I've seen that one.' He gives it an appreciative glance. 'A Victorian beauty. I do love a phoenix. You know the story, don't you?'

I nod, because I've listened to it three times now; and I'm pretty sure I'm about to hear it again.

'When the Phoenix dies, it's consumed by fire.' He reaches up and touches a neon flame. 'A new Phoenix rises from the ashes of its predecessor. It's a myth, of course.'

'Of course.'

'And like most myths, it has something to teach us. The phoenix reminds us we can rise again from destruction. It's a symbol of hope, you see.' He looks out at the dark street. 'And that's human nature, isn't it? The instinct to keep going, to rise again from mistakes and disaster, to dream of better days.'

I'm sorely tempted to inform Hal that it's not always possible to rise again from mistakes and disaster, but that would be pointless. Instead, I put down my mug and brush a finger over my right wrist.

'What is that?' he asks.

'Nothing.'

'A tattoo?'

A single letter, swirling and curling like a snake.

'It's a Y.' He leans in. 'What does it stand for? Is it your name?'

'My name's Mary,' I remind him.

'So, if it's not your name...'

I trot out the usual explanation. 'An old boyfriend. Yves. He was French.'

'French, eh? Ooh la la.'

'I shouldn't have had it done.' At the age of seventeen, I should never have given in to a reckless whim. But then again, back then,

4

there was no way I could have foreseen the future. And now, seven years later, there's no point in dwelling on the past. 'Why don't you tell me about Cynthia?' I ask. It's another story I've heard before, but I don't mind hearing it again. Anything to avoid talking about myself.

'Cynthia?' He smiles. 'Such a beautiful lady, inside and out. Just like you. And caring too. A wonderful woman. I met her at the hospital, you know.'

His eyes flick to the window. It's time for a prompt.

'What were you doing there?'

'A little argument with a Morris Minor. Just a few bumps and bruises. A nice case of...' He touches his forehead.

'Concussion?'

'That's the one. Should have been more careful. But then again, if I had been careful, I'd never have met her.' He leans forward. 'We got on like a house on fire. Two peas in a pod. We had a connection, so when they discharged me, I asked her out.'

'And she said yes?'

'Of course she did. In my day, I'll have you know, I was considered quite a catch.'

'I can believe it.'

And I can. Because the years might have taken their toll on Hal, leaving the usual ravages of time in their wake, but in spite of the pearly-white hair, the thinning skin and faded irises, it's still obvious he was a handsome man in his day.

'We used to meet here. Sat in this very window. She liked watching people.' He surveys the scene. 'I took her dancing, to the theatre, the cinema.' His eyes brighten. 'We went to see *Half a Sixpence*. She loved that film. And then...' He falls silent.

Knowing we've arrived at the tragedy, I'm about to try a little more distraction when he speaks again.

'We were supposed to meet here one night, but she didn't show up. I waited for hours.' He picks up his mug. 'The next day, I tried her lodgings. She'd cleared out her things and gone. I asked at the hospital, but they wouldn't tell me anything. I thought perhaps she'd found a better place to live, and she'd come back.' He peers out of the window, fully alert now, as if she might walk past at any minute. 'I was going to ask her to marry me.'

Watching the mug wobble in his hands, I realise the time has come to break the cardinal rule. I might have sworn to keep the world at arm's length, but this man's in trouble, and with no sign of friends or family, I see no other choice.

MANDY LEE

'Hal?' I venture. 'What year is it?' I already have a pretty good idea why he's searching for a woman he last met decades ago, but I'd still like confirmation.

'Don't you know?'

'Not really. I lose track.'

'Oh, I wouldn't worry about it. It doesn't matter.'

And there it is. He doesn't have a clue. Which means my suspicions are correct. He's probably suffering from some sort of dementia, and I can't let him wander off again.

'You're not from round here either, are you?' I ask, fishing for information.

'Goodness, no.'

'Where's home, then?'

He points to the window. 'That way, I think.'

'North or south of the river?'

He shrugs.

'Are you going home tonight?'

'No need. I'm staying in the hotel.' He pulls a key card from his pocket. 'Room 114. It's just around the corner.' He turns the card in his fingers, and I catch a name. The British Inn. 'Used to stay there when I came to see Cynthia. It's got a different name now, I think.' He gazes out of the window again, eyes empty of everything but despair. 'She's not coming... is she?'

'I don't think so, Hal.' I let the blow sink in before pressing on. 'Perhaps you should go home.'

'Perhaps you're right.'

'I could get you a taxi, but I'll need an address.'

For a moment or two, he simply stares at me. 'My memory's not what it used to be. That's age for you.'

It's a damn sight more than that. 'Maybe just the road?'

'Road?' He puts an index finger to his thin lips. 'Right. Give me a moment.'

Patiently sipping at my tea, I do as he asks. I've drunk at least half the mug before I prompt again. 'Thought of one yet?'

'One what?'

'The name of the road?'

'What road?'

'The road you live on.'

'Why do you want that?'

'So I can get you a taxi.'

'Whatever for? I'm staying in a hotel.'

6

It's not his fault. I understand that. Facts and ideas seem to fly in and out of his brain like startled birds. But I still need to wait at least a minute before I'm calm enough to try again.

'Hal.'

'What?' Raising his mug to his lips, he spills tea over the rim. 'Oh, dear. Look at that. Butter fingers.' A split second later, butter fingers and mug somehow part company, leaving a puddle of tea spreading across the tabletop, and a mess of broken crockery on the floor.

In an instant, I'm on my feet, pulling the table away from Hal. After checking he's untouched, I set about mopping up the mess with a handful of serviettes.

'I'm so sorry,' he says.

'It's okay.'

'I don't know what happened. I feel rather strange.'

Abandoning the soggy serviettes in a pile, I move closer and put the back of my hand to his forehead. No temperature, but he's as pale as death. 'In what way do you feel strange?'

'A little weak.'

'We should get you to a doctor.'

'No need for that.'

'Yes, there is.'

'I'll be fine.'

'For God's sake,' I huff. 'You're ill. My grandma was just like you.'

'How so?'

Resilient, independent, determined to cope on her own. She always had to be harangued into getting help.

'Pig-headed,' I tell him. 'Wait here. I'll be back in a minute.'

Keeping a close eye on him, I clear up, switch off the urn and coffee machine, and quickly grab my coat, work keys and backpack. By this time of night, my boss will be drunk as a lord, even more unreasonable than usual, and totally unwilling to let me help a vulnerable, old man in need of medical attention.

'Come on, then.' I urge Hal to his feet.

'Where are we going?'

'For a nice little walk to the hospital.'

'But I've already been there.'

'And now, you're going again.'

'But...'

'Save your breath, Hal.' Throwing the backpack over my shoulder, I take him by the arm. 'You're on a hiding to nothing. I can be just as pig-headed as you.'

7

Chapter Two

A faltering walk along the High Street brings us to the hospital where, thanks to Hal almost passing out on arrival at A&E, he's quickly assessed and taken through to Majors. After some initial bustle, with a nurse carrying out tests and a young, over-worked doctor peppering Hal with questions, the old man falls asleep.

Within minutes, I've visited the toilet, helped myself to a free cup of water, and exhausted all interest in people-watching. It's then, with nothing else to do, that I dig through Hal's pockets. I'm hoping to find a clue to his identity, but they offer up nothing more than a pen, a serviette from The Phoenix, a beautiful, silver ring in a little black box, and a hotel key card. Resolving to search his hotel room, I slip the card into my bag, return everything else to the pockets, and slump into a chair at his side.

It's just after two in the morning when a second doctor appears, saline bag in one hand, and a file in the other. Older than the first, she's also clearly more senior.

'Right. Let's see.' She draws the curtain round the cubicle.

I sit up straight. 'Is he okay?'

'All the tests aren't back yet.' She puts down the bag and consults the file. 'But he's dehydrated, and I'm guessing he's got a urine infection. That's probably why he's been so confused.'

'It's more than that, though?' I have no idea why this random stranger has become so important to me, but I seem to be determined to get him the right treatment.

'Probably. From what you've told us, it's entirely possible he's suffering from dementia. We'll admit him, get him on a drip and fill him with antibiotics if necessary. After that, we'll be able to properly assess him. You're not family, I understand.'

'No.'

She flips a page. 'We don't seem to have any contact details.'

'He wasn't in the mood to share.' In fact, during a long and extremely frustrating interchange with a nurse, he clamped his lips shut at every request for information. 'Want me to try?'

'If you wouldn't mind.'

'I'll give it a go.' After all, I'm the only recognisable face in a strange world, and trust goes a long way. But given my earlier efforts, I rather suspect he'll take 'pig-headed' to an entirely new level.

'You can stay with him until he's transferred to a ward. Should be a while yet.'

'Which ward?'

She consults her notes again. 'Thirteen.'

'Lucky for some.'

It's a pathetic attempt at humour. I'm not surprised it goes unappreciated. Without so much as a smile, the doctor sets about inserting a cannula into the back of Hal's hand and attaching the drip. When she's satisfied that everything's in order, she makes herself scarce, leaving me to settle back in the chair and resign myself to the mind-numbing boredom of a hospital wait.

'Poor boy,' Hal mutters, no more than a minute later.

I lean forward and put a hand on his arm.

'It was all my fault.'

'It's okay,' I whisper, hardly knowing what else to say. I've no idea what he's talking about. 'It's not your fault.'

His eyelids flutter, then rise. He blinks, glances round the room, and finally concentrates on me. 'Do I know you?'

'Mary. From the Phoenix.'

'Ah. I do know you. My beautiful, blue-eyed friend.' His brow creases. 'But I don't know this place. Where am I?'

'In hospital.'

'Hospital?' He begins to push himself up. 'Which hospital?'

'The Royal, in Bermondsey.' I place a hand on his chest and urge him back down. 'But she's not here. I've already asked about Cynthia.' Anything to get him to relax.

'She never is here.' He tries to raise himself again. 'I'd better get going then.'

'You're going nowhere.' I press his chest. 'You're ill.'

'I'm never ill.'

'You are now. You're dehydrated.'

'Me?'

'You've not been drinking enough. You're on a drip.' I motion to the bag.

'A drip? What are they putting into me?'

'Saline, I think.'

'Salt water?'

'It's good for you.'

'What rubbish.' His head flops back onto the pillow. 'How long do I have to stay like this?'

'Not sure.' It's time to deliver the news, not that he'll retain it for very long. 'They're admitting you.'

9

'Ridiculous.'

'It's not ridiculous.'

He rolls his eyes.

'Look at me, Hal.' If he's determined to behave like a child, then I'll just have to treat him like one. 'Look at me.' I'm amazed when he does. 'They think you've got an infection, and that sort of thing needs treatment. You can't just go wandering off. It'll only get worse. Do you understand?'

'I haven't …'

'Hal.' Bloody hell, I sound like a strict schoolteacher. 'Do. You. Understand?'

He screws up his nose. 'Yes.'

'So, you're going to just lie here.'

'If I have to.'

'And do as you're told.'

With a barely restrained growl, he glares up at the ceiling.

'Hal?'

'Yes, yes. Alright. I'll be a good boy.' Smothering all signs of irritation, he pats my hand. 'I'm sure they'll let me out in no time.' Finally. A hint of reason.

'I'm sure they will,' I agree, resolving to make the most of it. 'But they'll need to know who's picking you up.'

'Nobody needs to pick me up. I can find my own way around. I'm not a child.'

'I know.' I give his forearm a gentle squeeze. 'But they'll want to know you're safe.'

'I am safe.'

He's digging in his heels again. Maybe it's time for Plan B. A touch of emotional blackmail.

'Oh, Lord.' I shake my head. 'I won't sleep a wink until I know you've got someone coming. If I could just get in touch with someone, anyone.' I sigh, dramatically. 'You must have a family, Hal.' And if he does, then they'll be worrying themselves to death over where he is.

'Of course I have a family.' His expression clouds, and I'm convinced he's about to tell me to sod off when he speaks again. 'I have a brother, for what it's worth. And then there are the boys.'

Excellent. Now, this is progress.

'I don't suppose you've got an address,' I try, without much hope of success.

He shakes his head.

'How about a phone number?' I glance at his overcoat. It's currently draped over the back of the other visitor's chair. 'A mobile? You must have a mobile. Back at the hotel, perhaps'

'What would I do with one of those things?'

'Phone people.' I grin. 'Store numbers... so you don't need to remember them.'

He pats my hand again. 'I'll get one.'

'Good idea. But in the meantime, how am I supposed to get you back to your family?'

'I'll do that myself.'

As if. Knowing he's about as likely to take himself home as he is to buy a mobile, I swallow back a growl of my own. Prizing information from this man is about as easy as swimming through treacle.

'I know. Why don't you tell me your surname?'

'I never tell people my surname.'

'Why not?'

He laughs. 'Best to keep things like that quiet.'

There's no point asking him to explain. It's bound to result in nothing but gobbledegook. Instead, I lean in and double down. 'If you tell me your surname, I might be able to help.'

'I don't need any help.'

'Okay.' I think for a moment, then try again. 'How about your brother's name?'

'Same as mine.' His eyes twinkle. 'Surname, that is. We've got different first names.'

'Hal, you can trust me, you know.'

'Can I?'

'If you give me your brother's name – his full name – I could track him down.'

'You're not getting a surname.'

'He's probably worried about you.'

'I doubt that very much. Whatever decency he had, he lost it years ago. Anyway, he's got enough on his plate, what with the boys losing their mother. Terrible business.' He thinks for a moment. 'Maybe I should go to them?'

'Maybe, you should.' Yet again, I have no idea what he's going on about, but I certainly spot an opportunity. 'I tell you what. Give me an address and I'll call a taxi.' I won't, of course. But I'm getting tired now, and more than a little desperate. 'Just a road, perhaps.'

'A road? Let me think.'

11

And yes, we've been here before. If I do as he says, I'll get sweet nothing in return. I'm on the proverbial hiding to nothing, and I might as well give up for now. If he takes another nap, perhaps I'll catch him off-guard when he wakes.

'I think you need to rest.'

'Do I?'

'Yes.' I rub his arm again. 'Try to get some sleep.'

'Do I have a choice?'

'No.'

With a loud tut, he closes his eyes, and the next few minutes pass in silence. I'm still focussing on his chest, trying to work out if he has fallen asleep, when he speaks again.

'You're very good to me. You've got a kind heart, young lady.'

'Thank you.'

'There's not enough kindness in this world.'

'You really do need to sleep.'

'I'll sleep when I'm dead.' He opens his eyes and smiles. 'Bring me my coat. I've got a little something for you.' He notes my hesitation. 'Come along, now. Indulge an old man.'

I get up again, retrieve the coat and offer it to him.

'No. You get it. I'm too tired. It's in the pocket.'

'Okay.' I dig through the first pocket, pulling out the serviette and pen. 'How lovely, Hal. You do know how to spoil a woman.'

'Not that. The other one.'

With no small amount of trepidation, I dump the serviette and pen on the bed, slip my hand into the second pocket, and produce the little black box. Surely, he can't mean to give me the ring.

'It was for Cynthia. She was a nurse, you know. I've probably told you that already. I repeat myself. It's age. Gets you here.' He touches his head. 'Anyway, I was going to ask her to marry me. Never got round to it. So, I've no use for the bloody thing anymore.' He pauses. 'I want you to have it.'

'Me?'

'You,' he says, utterly serious now.

'But...' I need to make light of things, distract him from a thoroughly inappropriate idea. 'I do hope you're not asking me to marry you.'

He laughs. 'Dear girl, if only I were a few years younger.' He taps the box. 'Open it. Go on.'

I can tell he's not about to back off, which is why I open the box for a second time.

'Isn't that something?' he asks.

12

'It certainly is.'

And clearly a cut above. Encircled by smaller, perfectly matched stones, a single diamond sits as the centrepiece; and several more embellish the silver band to each side.

'Platinum,' Hal explains. 'I'm still working on the exact provenance, but it's said to have belonged to Coco Chanel. A woman who looked to the future, not the past. Maybe I should take a leaf from her book.'

'Maybe I should too.' Turning the ring, I watch the stones wink and glimmer under the light. 'It's lovely.'

'And it's yours.'

'No. Hal, I can't.' There's no way I can accept his gift. I thrust the box back at him.

'Yes, you can.' He holds up a hand. 'It's mine. I can do what I like with it.'

'But you can't give it to me.'

He tuts. 'What did I just say? Anyone would think you were the one who couldn't remember a thing.'

'Yes, but...' This is mad. Off-the-scale bonkers. 'You should give it to someone in your family, not a complete stranger.'

'You're not a complete stranger.'

'You've known me for four days.'

'Oh, that doesn't matter.' He waves a hand. 'I'm going to tell you a little secret now.' He raises an eyebrow. 'I've always had the ability to see a person's heart, right from the very moment I meet them. It's a gift, you know.'

'I wish I had it.' Don't I just? A gift like that would have prevented no end of trouble.

'And I see your heart,' he goes on. 'You're a good person. No doubt about it. And because you're a good person, you deserve something wonderful in your life.'

I'd like to tell him that's not the way the world works. Instead, I hold out the open box. 'I don't deserve this. Keep it for your family. The boys.'

'The boys need love, not baubles.'

'But this is wrong.'

'What's wrong about making an old man happy?'

'Hal...'

'Sell it.'

'No.'

'You'll get a good price.'

'No.'

He laughs again. 'Ungrateful wench.'

'How dare you call me a wench?' Laughing along with him, I reach out and smooth his hair. And now, I'm thinking of the grandfather I knew from nothing more than photographs and old tales. He had that same kindly twinkle in his eyes. 'I'm very grateful, Hal. But it's not right for me to accept this. I'm going to put it back in your pocket.'

'Don't you dare. That ring's worth a lot of money.'

'Exactly.'

'And this place is full of thieves and scoundrels. Just look at him.' He nods to the glass partition. Just beyond it, there's no one else but the young, over-worked doctor. 'A desperate vagrant, most likely.'

'He works here.'

'Anyone can steal a uniform. You'd think he'd comb his hair.'

'He might have messy hair, but he is a doctor.'

'That's what you think.'

'That's what I know. And he was very patient with you earlier.'

'Was he?'

'Trust me.'

'I do trust you. That's why I want you to take the ring.' Clearly calculating his next move, he purses his lips. 'If you leave it with me, I'll get no sleep. I'll be too worried, and then I really will be ill.'

'For goodness' sake...'

'You'll have the poor health of an old man on your conscience.'

'I don't have a conscience.'

'I'll give it to her then.'

Again, I follow his gaze out to the hub. The doctor's been joined by a scrawny middle-aged woman. I have no idea whether she's a patient or a relative, but she's clearly had a few too many.

'You wouldn't.'

'I would,' he counters. 'And she'd definitely accept it.' And sell it. And fritter away the proceeds. 'You can always bring it back tomorrow.'

'Can I?'

'Yes.'

We spend the next few seconds eyeballing each other, both of us summoning as much determination as we can. The trouble is, unlike Hal, I'm far too tired to keep it up for long.

'Fine,' I grumble, taking the only course I can. Picking up the pen and napkin, I scribble the name and address of the café on it, and my fake name underneath. 'This is me. I'll look after the ring for you. When you want it back ...'

'I won't want it back.'

'When you want it back,' I repeat, 'you'll know where to find me.' I shove the napkin and pen into his coat pocket, deposit the coat on the chair, and return to his side. 'I'll be back tomorrow, and I'm bringing this with me.' I wave the box.

'Good. Now I can rest. And you can go home.'

'I will.' I sit down again. 'When you're asleep.'

'I'll sleep when I'm...'

'Shut your eyes.'

'Bossy lady.'

With a disgruntled huff, he lowers his eyelids. It doesn't take long for his breathing to deepen and his features to relax. Within minutes, he's gently snoring.

I yawn, lean back in the chair, and stretch out my legs.

I could leave now, I tell myself.

But I make no move...

Because after a year in the wilderness, there's something comforting about this brittle, temporary connection.

And I intend to enjoy it for as long as possible.

Chapter Three

It's the only thing that links me to the past: a single, tattered photograph.

Oma on the left, grey-haired and proud. Mum on the right, beautiful still, but clearly in the grips of illness. And me – the girl in the middle – a beaming, happy ten-year-old, blissfully ignorant of times to come.

Remembering that tight web of love, I touch the faces, one by one.

And before I know it, I'm sinking into the doldrums, wondering how life managed to come to this.

'Should have seen it coming.'

But I didn't.

Because I was blinded by innocence. Because I made a stupid mistake that left me trapped in a limbo-land; cut off from the past and incapable of moving forward. As usual, the misery of it all resurrects a conversation from other miserable times.

'You cannot think like this. You'll never be happy again? Was für ein unsinn.'

'But it's true, Oma. She's dead, and it's never going to be the same.'

'Yes, your mother is gone, but think, girl. Where will all this self-pity get you?' I can almost feel the tap on the back of my hand. 'Nowhere. That is the answer. Remember, I've been through far worse, and I survived. There is only one thing you need, and that is hope. One day the sun will rise, and you will smile again.'

I'm roused by a grim reminder of my current reality: a sudden crash, followed by a screeching female voice.

'You've burnt it, you fucking prick!'

I hear a muffled shout, the clatter of a plate thrown at a wall: the tell-tale signs that Baz and Kath are at it again, locking horns over anything and everything, with Baz coming out the worse for wear, as he usually does. Frustration's boiling over, and I'm not surprised. It's the unavoidable result of sharing their tiny home with two unwanted lodgers. With an endless stream of insults ringing in my ears, I heave myself out of bed and twitch back the curtains.

'Great.'

A slab of grey, and the distinct threat of rain. Springtime's certainly struggling to get itself going this year. But at least my plans for the day are all based indoors. Eager to get going, for once, I snatch up my towel and wash bag, and take myself to the bathroom for a quick shower.

The usual stomach-churning sight greets my eyes: smears of toothpaste and blood in the sink; a smattering of short, dark hairs, probably left by the strange man who inhabits the box room at the back.

'Yuk.'

I swill away the mess and brush my teeth. A few seconds later, with my pyjamas dumped on the floor, I'm standing in the bathtub, listening to a strange spluttering sound, trying to ignore the mouldy grout, and willing a half-hearted spray of water to warm up. I've barely begun to shampoo my hair when there's a ferocious banging at the door.

'Won't be long,' I shout.

'Better not be,' Baz shouts back.

I finish washing my hair and give myself a scrub, upping the pace to avoid a confrontation. If Kath hears a row, there'll be all hell to pay, with Baz firmly in the line of fire. And I don't want that. He might be decidedly rough around the edges – and in possession of the world's most uncooperative bowels – but underneath all that filth and crumpled clothing, he's a halfway decent man. Within a minute, I'm out of the shower and towelling myself down.

'Come on,' Baz growls. 'I need a pony.'

'You need a pony every time I'm in here,' I call back. 'Two minutes.'

It takes less than that to finish drying off, wrap my hair in the towel, slip back into my pyjamas and gather the toiletries. But it's still not good enough for Baz. As soon as I open the door, he pushes straight past me.

'It's come to something when a man can't shit on his own toilet.'

The bathroom door slams shut, and I bite back the urge to remind my landlord that he takes a dump on his own toilet at least twice a day, and I pay rent – which should entitle me to use the less-than-wonderful facilities whenever they're free. But he's already had enough grief for one morning. Instead, I withdraw to my room, take a long, despondent look around, and wonder why I pay rent at all.

Roughly ten feet by ten, it's more of a cell than a room, and barely big enough for its contents. A single bed takes up most of the space. It's accompanied by a disintegrating chest of drawers and a fake pine wardrobe, the doors to which have swung open again – as they do on an irritatingly regular basis. After selecting today's outfit, I leave them where they are and get on with the business of assuming the armour. Five minutes later, I'm examining the result in a full-length mirror screwed to the wall.

Plain and forgettable.

It's the look I've been working on over the past few months. And today's choice – an oversized grey sweatshirt matched with a pair of jeans – is no exception. To add to the effect, because the aim is to attract zero attention, I'm also wearing no make-up whatsoever, and my long, blonde hair is pulled into a tight ponytail. More than once I've considered chopping it all off, but always stopped short, almost sensing Oma at my shoulder, delivering her usual advice. 'Never hide, my little one. Be proud of yourself.'

'But I have to hide,' I insist, donning the final touches: a dowdy brown anorak, a dull-green woollen hat, and a pair of cheap, black trainers.

With the disguise complete, I shove my work keys into my jeans pocket, grab my rucksack, make sure the key card and ring box are safely stowed inside, and head out of the door.

***

Walk with your head down, eyes trained on the ground. Move as if you have a destination, even when you don't. Look up occasionally, but only when absolutely necessary. These are my rules. Never to be broken.

And I follow them now, checking my surroundings even less than usual because I know exactly where I'm going. Walking fast, and managing to dodge every single passer-by along the way, I reach the hotel less than ten minutes after leaving the house, pausing for no more than a few seconds in the doorway before I enter the lobby. Determined to brazen it out and pass myself off as a guest, I look at no one as I make my way to the lift. Another few seconds see me safely installed, taking a short ride to the first floor, where I gamble on finding Room 114.

I stumble across it almost immediately.

Feeling every inch the thief, I pass the key card over the door mechanism and enter a bland, rather tatty space. With the bed freshly made, apart from a leather hold-all sitting under the window, there's no sign of an inhabitant. After a quick search of the bathroom, the drawers and the wardrobe – which yields nothing – I place the hold-all on the bed, and rummage through the contents.

18

There's a change of clothes, a set of pyjamas, and a toiletries bag. It's all clearly expensive stuff, and needs to be returned to Hal. Zipping up the bag, I check the room one last time.

It's then that I notice a photograph on the nearest bedside table. It's of a man, possibly in his fifties, standing behind three boys. As soon as I pick up the photo, I realise the man is a younger version of Hal – minus the wrinkles and the grey hair. I have no idea who the boys are, but I'm pretty sure they're an important connection to his past. Which is why I stow the photograph in a coat pocket, fully intending to talk to him about it later. Adding a small, unopened packet of biscuits I'm sure no one will miss, I grab the holdall and beat a hasty retreat.

It's another short walk to the hospital, but that's where simplicity ends. Finding Ward 13 is like navigating a path through a cryptic maze. With one eye on a series of fiendishly complicated signs, I thread my way through an endless set of corridors, digging ever deeper into the belly of the hospital. I'm beginning to think I'm being led on a merry dance, when I finally reach my target. Relieved, I readjust the rucksack, swap Hal's holdall from one hand to the other, and push through a set of double doors.

Hit by a rush of warm air, I'm soon hovering in front of a reception desk that's manned by two nurses – one male, one female – both of whom seem to be engrossed in a computer screen. Edging towards the desk, I cough quietly.

The female nurse notes my presence. Steely-eyed, intimidating, and completely in charge, she's the very epitome of an old-fashioned matron. 'Can I help you?'

'I'm looking for Hal.' Wondering if I've taken a wrong turn, misread one of those fiendishly complicated signs and ended up in entirely the wrong place, I waver. 'In his seventies. Admitted last night.'

'Hal?' She studies the computer screen. 'Surname?'

'I... don't know.'

'You don't know?' Her eyes meet mine, and they're brimming with suspicion.

It's enough to kick off an attack of the nerves. An explanation is in order.

'I brought him in last night. I work in a café, down the road. He came in for a cup of tea, and biscuits. He's done it for a few nights now. But last night he wasn't very well.' I'm babbling, and I know it... because both nurses are staring at me now, as if I'm a total lunatic. 'So, I brought him here. I mean, to A&E. And I thought I'd come and visit today, because he couldn't remember where he lived, and he wasn't saying much about family...'

'Hang on a minute.' The female nurse focusses back on the screen and shifts the mouse. 'Do you mean Harry?'

'Harry?' I blink in confusion. 'I suppose so.' Because Hal's short for Harry, isn't it?

'Here he is.'

'Oh, thank God.' Ridiculously pleased that I am in the right place, I laugh. 'Can I see him?'

'No.'

Oh, here we go. You're not related, so you're not getting access.

'But there's nobody else ...'

'He's gone.'

'Gone?' Nerves give way to shock. 'Please don't tell me he's dead.'

'No, not dead. He was picked up a couple of hours ago.'

'Picked up?' How on earth did that happen? 'Who picked him up?'

'You were here, Ashley. Who picked him up?'

The male nurse leans over and peers at the screen. 'A relative.' He suppresses a grin. 'Caused quite a stir, actually. Tall, dark and handsome as sin. Bit of a dish.'

'Dish?' Dispensing with the shock, I flip straight to irritation. 'What on earth does that matter? Let's not get distracted, shall we?' Watching Ashley's eyes narrow to dangerous slits, I give him a sweet smile, and resolve to dial it down. After all, I'm still in need of information. 'Was it his son?' I ask. Not that Hal's ever mentioned a son.

'Not sure.' Ashley shrugs. 'It was some sort of relative, though. He'd been looking for Harry for a few days. Had people going round all the hospitals with photos. Someone on the early shift recognised him.'

Which is brilliant, but I've still got a holdall to deal with. 'I don't suppose you could give me an address...'

'Not allowed,' the intimidating matron-type intervenes. 'Data protection.'

'Of course.' I heave the holdall onto the desk. 'It's just that I've got Hal's belongings. Sorry to be a pain. I know you're busy.'

'We are.'

'But I don't know where Hal's gone, so I'll just have to leave this here.' I tap the bag. 'I'm sure you'll be good enough to return it to him.'

20

'Oh, are you now?' Like a steadily inflating balloon, her chest begins to expand.

'I'll do it,' Ashley trills, springing to his feet and grabbing the bag. 'Don't you worry. We'll have an address on record somewhere.'

'Thank you.'

My thoughts settle back on the ring. Still tucked away in the depths of my rucksack. And this is probably the precise moment I should hand it over, drawing a firm line under my dealings with Hal.

But do I hand it over?

I consider one nurse, and then the other. In all likelihood, they're perfectly decent people. Just a tad overworked. Maybe so overworked, they might forget to trace Hal's whereabouts and reunite him with his belongings. Which is no big problem when it comes to a pair of pyjamas, a change of clothing and a toiletries bag.

But a diamond ring?

I watch as the bag's dumped in a corner, and make my decision.

Trust no one.

It's a mantra I've lived by for the last few months. And as far as I can see, it's also the best way forward now. After all, I promised to keep the ring safe. And Hal's got my note. Leaving the little black box exactly where it is, I take my leave.

Chapter Four

It's only just midday, and a little chilly, but at least the rain's holding back for the time being.

As soon as I escape the hospital, I head north. I've almost reached the outskirts of Southwark when I veer right, taking a familiar route to the south bank of The Thames. Minutes later, I'm sitting on my favourite bench next to the river, half-hidden by a clump of trees, keeping one eye on the passers-by while I dig into my pocket for those illicit biscuits.

'Oh.' My fingers touch the photograph.

I pull it out, studying it closely while I nibble at two completely tasteless digestives, and before long, I'm wondering if these are the boys Hal talked about, his nephews, the ones who lost their mother.

'Must be,' I murmur. Because it would certainly explain the resemblance between them all.

The boy in the middle must be six or seven: the two flanking him, in their early teens. At a guess, I'd say the photograph's about twenty years old, meaning the boys would be in their twenties or thirties by now.

So, maybe one of them is the 'dish' who rescued Hal from Ward 13. But which one? The boy on the right, looking across with a hint of distrust? The one on the left, grinning back in a self-satisfied sort of way? Or the youngest boy, stuck in the middle, gazing straight into the camera with an innocent smile? Whichever one it is – if it is any of them – I can only hope he makes sense of that serviette.

Biscuits finished, it's time to move again. With the photograph safely stored in my backpack, I stand up and check on my surroundings. Since the walkway's wide at this point, and there's hardly anyone else around, I can almost believe I'm safe. Which is why I wander a little further along the river, allowing myself the rare luxury of taking in the scenery. It's only when I catch sight of a clock that I come crashing back to reality.

'Shit.'

In ten minutes, I should be starting my shift at the Phoenix, but it's going to take at least half an hour to walk back, even at a brisk pace. Knowing I'm in trouble, I make a panicked start, virtually yomping through the streets of Bermondsey, and almost getting run over in the process. I'm pretty much exhausted by the time I burst into the café.

'Sorry I'm late, Chet.' I glance round at the empty tables.

'Half an hour late.' My co-worker scowls. 'I'm letting Wallace know. That's my pay. Not yours.' Without waiting for an answer, he storms off, leaving me to get on with my shift.

As usual, I begin with a quick clean at the front, hunting down every last crumb and coffee stain until the counter's pristine. After giving the coffee machine a thorough going-over, I check the till for change. And then, I pause, stomach rumbling, and decide to grab something to eat while there's no one here. Retreating to what's laughingly called the kitchen, I help myself to a couple of rounds of flimsy white bread, spread them with margarine, and cut myself a few slices of bright orange cheese. I've just taken the first bite of my sandwich when I'm interrupted by a lazy, indolent voice.

'Stealing from me again?'

Mouth full, I turn slowly to find I've been joined by the boss. A sad excuse for a human being. With greasy hair, a treble chin, and constantly moist lips, he reminds me of something that belongs in the ocean – The Antarctic, to be specific – because he's certainly amassed enough blubber.

I chew quickly, and swallow. 'Wallace.' I smile, silently pleased I haven't inadvertently called him Walrus: my private nickname for the man.

'Didn't expect to see me tonight, did you?' His beady little eyes rove up and down my body, making me feel distinctly queasy.

'No. I...' I motion to the doorway. 'I'd better get out there.'

'Why?' He moves towards me, belly oozing over of the top of his jeans. 'There's no punters. You might as well finish your dinner.' He waves a hand at my sandwich.

I put it down on the tabletop. 'Later, maybe.' My appetite's taken a hike. Wallace always has that effect on me. Avoiding eye contact, I study the floor.

'You'll lose those curves if you don't eat.'

My attention snaps back to him.

'And I love those curves.' He takes another step towards me.

'Pack it in. You're out of line.'

'Sorry, darling.' He holds up both hands. 'I keep forgetting. Got to be PC these days.' With a wink, he brushes past. 'Chet called.'

'He did?' I swivel round.

'Told me you were late today.'

'It was an accident. I lost track of time.'

'Sure about that?'

'Of course.'

'And that's what happened last night, is it?' Opening the fridge, he leans down to eye the contents.

'Last night?'

'I swung by... about half nine.'

I can't help a quiet laugh. 'The pubs were still open, Wallace. You must be ill.' Either that, or he'd run out of funds and needed to raid the till.

'Don't get cheeky.' He straightens up and slams the door. 'I swung by to do a little stock check. Imagine my surprise when I found this place shut up for the night.'

'Oh.'

'Oh,' he mimics, launching into a slimy grin, all brown teeth and glistening tongue. 'Where was you, babe?'

I steel myself to tell the truth. He's not going to like it. 'A customer wasn't well.'

'And?'

'I had to take him to hospital.'

'You didn't have to take him anywhere.'

'He's an old man. He wasn't well.'

'And you're suddenly the Good Samaritan?'

'I couldn't just leave him. The café was empty. I shut up half an hour early. That's all. It's no big deal.'

He slams a palm on the table top. 'You don't get to decide that.'

'I...'

'Who's the boss around here?'

I don't answer.

'I said... who's the boss?'

'You.'

'Yeah, me. So, it wasn't your decision to make.'

'Half an hour...'

'Time,' he growls, 'is profit.'

I stare at him, dumbfounded. Where the Phoenix is concerned, I'm pretty sure time is anything but profit. 'Why don't you just knock it off my wages?'

'Knock it off your wages? Is that your answer to everything?' He picks up the discarded sandwich, squeezes it into a ball and tosses it to the floor. 'Tell you what. I'll do more than knock it off your wages.'

'Wallace.' Sensing a turn for the worse, I hold up my hand, palm upwards in supplication. I may not like The Walrus, but he's the only employer I've come across who's happy to go down the cash-in-hand route, no questions asked.

'You're taking the piss, lady.'

'I'm sorry.'

'Too late. Hand over the keys.'

'I'll make up the time.'

'You'll get the fuck out.'

'Wallace, please.'

'You're sacked.'

'But I need this job.'

'You should have thought about that before ...'

He doesn't finish his sentence, but from the look in his eyes, I know exactly what's going through his mind. I should have thought about that before I rejected all those pathetic advances, or bit back at his filthy innuendos, or made it perfectly clear I wasn't amused by his throwback, sexist attitude.

'I'll take my wages then.' I raise my chin.

'No, you won't.'

'But you owe me...'

'Cash flow problems, darling.' The gruesome teeth make a reappearance. 'Come back next week.'

'When?'

He shrugs.

'My rent's due.'

'Not my problem.' He holds out a hand. 'Keys.'

I pull them from my pocket, and drop them.

'Go on then,' he sneers. 'Off you trot.'

'Screw you.'

He laughs at me, hard-eyed. 'Now, if you'd done that, darling, you wouldn't be in this pickle.'

***

With the first few drops of rain touching my face, I've barely made it fifty metres down the road when the full implications of the last few minutes hit me. I've just lost my only source of income. Which wouldn't be such a huge problem if the rent weren't due tomorrow. It's not Baz I'm worried about. I can easily manage him. But if I don't come up with the money, Kath's sure to have me out on my ear.

'Calm down,' I whisper, reeling to a halt. 'Just think.'

I might be up to my eyeballs in shit, but there's no way I can give up. It's just not in the genes.

'Right...'

MANDY LEE

First thing tomorrow, I'll start pounding the streets in search of a new job. Wallace can't be the only heartless, conniving, underhand business owner in London. There must be others willing to pay below the minimum wage, cash-in-hand. I've been lucky before and I'll be lucky again. Something's bound to come up. But first things first. Shaking the backpack from my shoulder, I dig out my battered purse and look inside, only to find I'm in possession of nothing more than a five-pound note and a few bits of change. With a resigned sigh, I unzip the central section of the purse and check my bank card's still there.

It is.

Dropping the purse back into the bag, I make my decision. It's the last thing I want to do, and possibly the last thing I should do. But it might, at least, buy me a few days' grace.

I set off again, moving quickly now, determined to fulfil my mission before I chicken out. Occasionally, I check out a passing stranger, or look up to cross a side street, but for the most part my eyes remain fixed on the pavement. An hour or so later, I'm hovering outside a bank, frozen stiff by a sudden onslaught of second thoughts.

'Don't be silly,' I instruct myself. 'Get it done.'

Mindful of CCTV, I pull my hood up before taking out the card and closing in on the cash machine. A distinctly unsteady hand slips the card into the slot. Cold fingers key in the PIN. A paltry balance flashes up on the screen. Forty-two pounds. Not as much as I thought, and barely worth the effort. Tapping in forty pounds, I listen to a quiet whirring, and snatch away the cash and card as soon as they appear. And that's when it enters my mind: the chilling realisation that even with my face obscured, the CCTV footage makes no difference whatsoever. The fact is, I've just planted my footprint in the ether, which is more than enough to summon up the demon.

But this is no time to dither.

I turn away and head back towards Baz and Kath's, telling myself that he couldn't possibly know what I've done, that he's moved on, that I'm panicking over nothing. And then I remind myself I'm a couple of miles from home, that he'd be lucky to trace me from here. But no amount of logic can purge the growing paranoia, or stop the tightening in my chest and sickness in my stomach.

I need to get a grip.

And that's why I pause, steadying myself against a shop front, and recall some more of Oma's much-needed wisdom.

'Fear doesn't need to be your enemy, my girl. Put it on a leash and make it work for you.'

She'd drum those words into me whenever I faced an unnerving situation. And I let her too, because she knew what she was talking about.

'If Oma could do it, so can I.'

Gritting my teeth, I push away from the shop and continue to walk, willing my pulse and heartbeat back under control. By the time I return to the house, I'm totally drained. Shutting out the night, I pause in the hallway to check the clock. It's just past nine, and my charming landlord and his delightful wife are in full flow: television blaring, the stench of cigarette smoke oozing through the house, Kath's raucous laugh scratching at the walls.

Bowl in hand, Baz emerges from the kitchen. 'Want to try my nuts?'

'I'm alright, thank you.'

He thrusts the bowl at me. 'Go on. They're tasty.'

'I'm not hungry.'

'You're missing out.' He winks, lowers the bowl, and becomes serious. 'Rent tomorrow. Don't forget.'

As if I need a reminder. I think of the money in my purse. Half a week's rent. I could hand it over now and buy myself three or four days to land another job. But even if I do, I won't get paid straight away. And with no more sneaky sandwiches at the Phoenix, I'll need to buy food. It all seems completely hopeless. Still, it's worth angling for a little help.

'I wanted to talk to you about that, Baz.'

'Oh, yeah?'

'It's just that...' Here goes nothing. 'Any chance of an extension?'

'A what?'

'I've got a bit of a cash flow problem. Well, actually it's my boss who's got the cash flow problem.'

'I need it though.' He wipes his mouth with the back of his hand. 'Can't have Kath going off on one.'

'Just three days. That's all.'

He scrutinises me for a few seconds. 'Alright. I'll sub you for three days, but that's it.'

A problem I'll have to confront in due course. 'Thank you, Baz.' I start up the stairs, grateful to still have a roof over my head. 'You're a complete star.'

'Dunno about that,' he calls after me. 'Must be getting fucking soft.'

MANDY LEE

I can't get to my bedroom quickly enough.

As soon as the door's closed behind me, I retrieve the purse and ring box from my backpack, slump onto the bed and lay out my funds. Forty-seven pounds and eighty-five pence. Hardly worth the risk.

'Idiot.'

My attention wanders to the little black box. I flick it open, remove the ring and admire its beauty. I could pawn it. And I'm certainly tempted, even though I'd get nowhere near its true value. The proceeds might just cover a week or two of rent, which would give me time to get things back on track. But then again, if I did pawn it, I'd never be able to get it back. It's a realisation that halts temptation in its tracks. Because I'm the one who landed myself in this mess, and there's no way I'm about to rip off an old man to dig myself out of it.

There has to be another way.

Chapter Five

The need for work dictates routine for the next three days. After leaving the house extra early, and avoiding Baz and Kath in the process, I walk for miles: as far west as Chelsea, as far east as Canary Wharf. Searching north and south of the river, I call into practically every shop, café and restaurant along the way. But there's no sign of a job – at least nothing cash-in-hand – and I'm not surprised. Every single time I step through a doorway, the panic and desperation must be glaringly obvious. Coming hand-in-hand with a seemingly inexplicable determination to stay off-grid, it's enough to put off any prospective employer.

At the end of the first two days, I return to the house as late as possible, retreat to my bedroom and count out the funds. But without the café's resources to fall back on, they're dwindling at a worrying pace. By the end of the third day, I've run out of time, energy and ideas. Which is why, after a fruitless visit to Brick Lane, I'm back in Bermondsey, standing across the road from the Phoenix Café.

Straining to see past the glow of the neon bird, I spend at least ten minutes mentally preparing myself for what comes next. At last, when I'm finally good and ready, I dart across the road and shove open the door. Hit by a blast of warm air, I blink a few times, adjusting my vision to the bright light. And then, he comes into focus. Standing behind the counter, clearly in the middle of counting up today's takings, Wallace registers my arrival.

'Evening.'

I falter.

'Got a problem, Treacle? Expecting someone else?'

'I thought Chet...' Is that a fake smile? Or is he actually pleased to see me?

'Can't work lates.'

'Oh.' I glance back at the door.

'Don't tell me you're going.'

'I...'

'I've missed you.'

'Really?'

'Really.' He gathers up a selection of notes and thrusts them into his jacket pocket. 'I've had to work every sodding night since you left.'

'Since you sacked me,' I correct him. I might be confused over the warm welcome, but I'm not about to let him twist the facts.

'You did shut up shop an hour early.'

He's still smiling, which means he is pleased to see me. I have no idea whether it's because he's seen the error of his ways, or he's been at the bottle again. But either way, I'm not above taking advantage of the situation. Edging forwards, I stop at the counter.

'You'll wear yourself out, Wallace. Why not give me my job back? Then you can spend more time with Jack Daniels.'

'Might think about that.' He gives his belly a lazy scratch. 'Maybe I was a bit harsh.'

'Maybe...' And all that walking and worrying might have been for nothing.

'Fancy a cuppa?'

'Wouldn't say no.'

'Take a seat. I'll bring it to you.'

I hesitate.

'Go on,' he urges. 'Make yourself at home.'

I can barely believe he's about to reinstate me. And this 'nice' Wallace just isn't the Wallace I know. Nevertheless, concerns aside, there's a possibility of work and money in the offing, and I'd be a fool to scupper the chance. Choosing a table close to the door – just in case I need to make a quick escape – I hang my coat over the back of a chair, sit down and wait patiently while Wallace prepares the drinks. Obviously taking his time, he leaves the bags to soak in their mugs and picks up his mobile.

'You're stewing it, Wallace.'

'Just gotta reply to a couple of texts.' He frowns at the screen. 'Anyway, it's a free brew. You should be grateful whichever way it comes.' Messages sent, he slips the mobile into his pocket and finishes the tea.

A couple of minutes later, he finally emerges from behind the counter, wielding a tray with all the necessary accompaniments. 'Got you a scone.' He slips the tray onto the table and takes a seat. 'Don't say I don't treat you right.'

I inspect the scone, and then the mugs. 'You could stand a teaspoon up in this.'

'Puts hairs on your chest.'

I help myself to the mug nearest to me, and sip at the tea. Too strong for my liking, but it's the first hot drink I've had all day. 'So,' I venture. 'About the job?'

'What about it?'

'Can I have it back?'

'I'm still thinking about it.' He slurps at his own drink. 'Is that all came here for? Your job?'

'No.' I shift in my seat. There's no point lying. He obviously knows the truth. 'I came for my wages.'

'Ain't got no cash on me at the minute.'

'You've got some in your pocket.'

'No spare cash. I need this little lot.'

'But I'm desperate, Wallace.'

'Yeah, I'd noticed.' He picks up the scone. 'Go on. I bet you're hungry.'

I am. But not hungry enough to break my teeth on a lump of concrete. 'It's probably stale.'

'Probably.' He drops the scone back onto the plate. 'Beggars can't be choosers. Go on. It won't kill you.'

'I don't need a scone, Wallace. I need money.'

'Rent due?'

'Yes.'

'Still staying in that shithole round the corner?'

'Yes.' He knows exactly where I live. Something I'm not exactly comfortable with, but it's none of my doing. Just after I started at the Phoenix, he followed me home one night, got caught in the act, and then tried to wriggle out of it by claiming he was concerned for my safety. 'So I need what you owe me.'

'I've already explained, darling. Nothing doing. Not tonight. I could help you out in another way if you like.'

'How?'

It takes him forever to come up with an answer. 'I could speak to your landlord.'

Great. That's the sum total of his help? 'What difference would that make?'

'Well...' He prods the scone. 'I could tell him you've still got a job.' He raises an eyebrow. 'Which you might have. And then I could tell him I've got a bit of a cash-flow situation at the minute. And then... I could tell him you'll be getting your wages soon enough.'

I frown at Wallace, and then the scone. 'You'd actually do that?'

'Why not?'

'So, I can have my job back?'

'If you're nice to me.' He licks his lips.

31

I fight back a wince. 'Wallace, I am being nice to you.' And it's killing me. 'You know I can do the job. And you obviously need someone. Just take me on again.'

'I still need to think about it.'

'What's there to think about?'

'I need to know there'll be no more silly incidents.'

'I promise.'

'And no more helping yourself to food.'

'I won't.' Although I will. There's no other way to keep going.

'Mmm...' He raises his mug, takes another mouthful of tea, and seems to drift into thought.

'So what do you say?' I ask.

A text arrives. 'Give me a minute.' He pulls out his mobile and reads the message.

'Who's that?'

'Just the missus. Can't wait for me to get home.'

'Really?'

Having met 'the missus' on numerous occasions, and having witnessed, first-hand, her clear disdain for The Walrus, I find that hard to believe. I'm about to say as much when his phone rings. He silences it, sends another text, and glances out of the window.

And suddenly, it's obvious.

He's waiting for someone.

I put down my mug. 'I'll come back tomorrow.'

'No.'

An over-hasty response, which means he's desperate for me to stay. My thoughts sharpen, and I think of the napkin. Perhaps Hal's family have been in touch. But if they have, why the need for all the subterfuge?

'Has someone been looking for me?'

'Weird question.'

'Try answering it.'

He takes another slurp of tea. 'Who'd be looking for you?'

'I don't know. Maybe someone offering a reward?'

He hesitates. 'Nobody's been asking, Treacle.'

An obvious lie.

Meaning there's only one explanation for Wallace's strange behaviour. That stupid cash withdrawal did exactly the sort of damage I feared it would. The devil gained his first clue. And now, he's tracked me down.

Survival instincts shift into gear. I get to my feet. 'Thanks for the tea.'

'No. Hey, where you going? Sit back down. I'll get you another.'

I grab my backpack. 'Don't bother. I've had enough.'

'Wait.' Standing up, he reaches into his pocket. 'I'll give you the cash.'

A last-ditch attempt to stop me leaving. There's definitely someone on the way. And it's probably the last person I want to see.

'I don't need your money, Wallace. I've got to go.'

***

Under the harsh light of the bare bulb, I pack in a frenzy, hastily shoving clothes into my backpack with no real thought for what I'll need. Grateful, at least, that I won't have to think about my period for another three weeks, I add a half-full box of tampons. A hairbrush, toothbrush and toothpaste follow. Once the backpack's full, I snatch my precious photograph from the bedside table and thrust it deep into a side pocket. It's joined by Hal's photograph, and the ring box. Less than ten minutes after reaching the house – and with absolutely no idea where I'm going next – I'm back downstairs, tugging open the front door.

A slurred voice stops me in my tracks.

'Leaving me? Without paying your rent?'

I turn. 'No, I'm just off to...'

Baz eyes the backpack. 'You're doing a runner.'

'Honestly. No.'

'I should hope not.' He closes in, bringing the stench of whiskey with him. 'Three days you've stayed here, rent-free.'

'I'm not doing a runner.'

'So, what's this then?' He flicks the backpack.

'Laundry.'

'Is it fuck? I give you extra time, and this is all the thanks I get?'

'Honestly, I'm going to the laundrette.' I can hear the tremor in my own voice. 'I'll be back later. And I'll get the money while I'm out.'

'Will you?'

'Yes. I'll pay you...'

He leans forward, placing a hand on the door. 'It's Kath's bingo night, you know.'

'And?'

'Forget the laundry. Come and join me on the settee. I'll break out the nuts.'

33

That does it. On more than one occasion, he's strayed a little too close to my boundaries, but this is a step too far. One minute I'm staring into a pair of half-focussed eyes. The next, I've let Baz know exactly what I think of his nuts... by ramming a knee straight into them. Leaving him to keel over in agony, I make my escape, breaking into a run as soon as I hit the pavement.

By the time I come to a halt, I'm completely out of breath, but far enough away from Baz and Wallace to finally take a rest. I'm still wrestling my lungs back under control when I get the strangest feeling. An unearthly chill in my veins. A ghostly tickle at the back of my neck. Nothing more than paranoia, I'm sure, but I still check in all directions, registering a handful of gloomy figures before I move on again.

Deciding it's time to swap safety in numbers for a quiet hiding place, I leave the lights of the High Street behind and scurry off down a gloomy side road, only slowing the pace when I'm sure there's no one following in my wake. It's then, with raindrops pricking at my skin, that I finally take a few moments to assess the situation. With just over twenty-five pounds in my backpack, and no chance of a hotel room for the night, I'll need to find somewhere safe to bed down. And quickly too, if I don't want to end up soaking wet. Wandering from one backstreet to another, I finally stumble across a suitable doorway. Throwing my backpack into one corner, and taking a seat in the other, I draw up my legs and watch the rain begin to gather in force. It's not long before the cold and damp begin to permeate my bones.

'Idiot,' I say to no one in particular. 'No job, no home, and now you're on the streets.' With a shaking hand, I wipe away a tear. 'Stop it,' I order myself, because I have no right to self-pity. After all, I'm the one who broke the cardinal rule and let the mistakes snowball.

'Alright, darling?'

A man's voice drags me back to the moment. I look up at a dark silhouette, and decide it's best to say nothing.

'Talking to yourself. First sign of madness.' The silhouette moves closer. 'Fancy some company?'

'Leave me alone.'

'But this is my spot.'

'It's a doorway. It doesn't belong to anyone.' I wrap my arms around my knees, hoping he'll go away. But he doesn't.

'Been on the streets long?'

'First night.' Great. Another mistake. Now, he knows I'm a novice.

The silhouette moves again. The outline of a face comes into view, then fades back into darkness. A second backpack lands on the concrete. Complete with a rolled-up sleeping bag, it's much bigger than mine... and dirtier too.

'You've got a lot to learn then, love.' There's a barely audible click, the brief flickering of a flame, a pinprick of russet-orange. 'Want one?'

'I don't smoke.'

'Don't blame you.' He takes a drag on his cigarette. 'Here's your first lesson on life in the gutter. The streets are a nasty place, full of nasty bastards, and everything belongs to someone. This delightful little abode, for example, belongs to me.'

I get it. He's telling me to leave. But I'm fed up with being pushed around. 'I don't see your name on it.'

'Second lesson.' He takes another drag. 'Mind your tongue. You never know who you're dealing with.'

I stiffen at the threat. There's only one thing worse than being pushed around, and that's being attacked. I'm on the verge of struggling to my feet when he speaks again.

'Lucky for you, I'm a reasonable sort of bloke. In fact, I'm more than willing to share my bedroom with the right person.'

He flicks away the cigarette and crouches down. Preparing myself for the worst, I stiffen again. But he simply unrolls his sleeping bag, sets up his backpack as a makeshift pillow, and sits down. Stretching out his legs, he produces a small bottle from his coat pocket.

'Want some?'

'What is it?'

'Vodka.'

'No, thanks.'

I can see his face clearly now. It's almost skeletal.

'Everyone turns to this in the end.' He unscrews the top and takes a swig. 'Either this ... or smack.'

'Not me.'

'Not yet.' He laughs quietly. His chest rattles. 'But you will. Believe me. It takes the edge off, see. Numbs the body and freezes the mind.' He takes another swig. 'How'd you end up here then?'

I see no point in sharing my story. Why waste the time? No one can help.

'What was it?' he pushes. 'Family problems?'

'Yes,' I lie.

'Take my advice. Whatever you're running away from, it can't be as bad as this.'

'I don't need your advice.'

'A naïve little girl like you needs all the advice she can get.'

'I'm not a little girl...'

'Girl, woman, whatever. You won't last a day out here because you don't know shit.' He coughs. Phlegm shifts. His chest rattles again. 'It's dog-eat-dog on the streets. There's people out here who won't think twice about taking advantage of a clueless little rookie. They'll lie to you, nick your stuff, relieve you of your cash – if you've got any. And that's if they're in a good mood.'

I shiver. 'And why should I trust you?'

'Never said you should.' With a chuckle, he screws the top back onto the bottle and slips it into his pocket. 'Gonna be a cold one. And you ain't got a sleeping bag. Tell you what, I'll share mine with you. We'll make a little bed right here.' He pats the concrete. 'Snuggle up, exchange some body heat... if you know what I mean.'

Yes, I do know what he means, and it turns my stomach. No matter how cold I get, that's never going to be an option. 'I'd rather not, thank you.'

'Sorry, darling. I think you've got the wrong end of the stick.'

'How?'

'My bedroom. My rules. And you don't get a choice.'

'I always get a choice.'

I struggle to my feet, grab my backpack and stumble off down the road. It's not long before the tears surge back to life, and this time there's no stopping them. Courtesy of a few brutal words from a stranger, they're born of pure desperation. I'm in massive trouble here. And I'm not entirely sure I'll get through it.

On automatic pilot now, I arrive back at the High Street. Head down, and determined to remain invisible, I keep walking. But I can't keep this up all night. Already worn out, soaked through, and with hunger gnawing at my stomach like a rat, if I don't find somewhere to settle soon, I'll end up collapsing on the pavement.

I'm about to try another side street when the gaudy lights of an off-licence lure my attention. Dithering outside, I gaze at a tacky display: straw baskets, filled with bottles of gin, vodka, whiskey, wine and rum. I fixate on a bottle of gin.

'Numb the body and freeze the mind,' I murmur.

And step inside.

***

36

A few minutes later, I've acquired the gin, stored it in the backpack, and found exactly what I need: a lonely bench guarding the locked entrance to a park. Set back a little from the road and protected by a wall to the rear, it's the perfect place for a pity party. So perfect, in fact, that I waste no time in taking a seat, positioning the rucksack next to me and retrieving the bottle.

'Here goes nothing.'

The first swig leaves me wincing at the bitter tang of juniper, but it doesn't stop the mission. Sweet oblivion can't come quickly enough.

Another mouthful... and another... and another...

Within half an hour, the alcohol takes effect, banishing the cold, relaxing muscles, and coaxing a small smile to my lips. A short while later, my vision begins to blur, the smile morphs into an idiotic grin, and the world becomes a joke only I can understand. It hardly seems to matter when fear slips into a deep coma, and I enter the realms of the reckless.

Deciding I'd like a quick look at a super-expensive ring, I take the box out of the side pocket and flick it open.

'Very nice,' I slur. 'Should really put it somewhere safe.'

After all, I'm on the streets now, rubbing shoulders with people who'll take everything from me, given half a chance. And while they're welcome to every last piece of my crap, they're getting nowhere near Hal's precious memories. Slipping the half-empty bottle into the backpack, I stagger to my feet and sway a little.

'Jeez.' Everyone's going to know I'm pissed as a fart, but I really don't care. I've got more important matters on my mind. 'Need to hide the ring.'

I swerve along the pavement, clutching the box for dear life and getting increasingly drunk by the second. Disjointed images flash in front of my eyes – a lamp post, a bin, a dog-walker, a kerb – until I'm finally standing still, staring up at the silhouette of a building.

A determined squint brings it into focus.

'A church.' Squat. Victorian. Brick-built and surrounded by a low stone wall. There's a bell tower to the right; a graveyard to the left.

The next thing I know, I'm wandering between headstones: some almost upright; others leaning precariously to one side. It's almost impossible to decipher the swirling inscriptions in the dark, but as soon as I stumble to the front of the graveyard, where a nearby streetlamp aids the search, I find the perfect candidate for the job.

Matthew Longhorn, born 1803, died 1852.

MANDY LEE

'Matthew.' My father's first name. One of the few things I know about him. At least it's something to help me remember where I've hidden the ring.

Circling round to the back of the stone, I dump the backpack on the ground, drop to my knees and claw at the earth, eventually gouging out a hole big enough to bury the box. As soon as it disappears beneath the mud, I sit back on my haunches and survey my work.

'Rest in peace,' I whisper, grabbing the gin and taking a few slugs. I'm almost three-quarters of the way through the bottle now, and sorely tempted to lie down right here, and sleep in the dirt. 'Where I belong... with the dead.'

But before I can give in to temptation, something brushes against my leg: a timely reminder that a vermin-infested graveyard is no place to bed down on a cold, rainy night. I stagger to my feet, sling the backpack over my shoulder and head back out onto the High Street, without the slightest idea where I'm going. The last few mouthfuls of gin haven't kicked in yet. But when they do, I'm liable to pass out on the spot, which is bound to attract the attention of the police. Desperate to avoid any attention at all, I lurch to a halt and lean against a lamp post.

Taking a few deep gulps of air, I squint along the street... and freeze.

I may be drunk as a lord, but I can make out the figure of a man about thirty feet away. With his hood up and head slightly bowed, his face is indistinguishable. But there's still something vaguely familiar about his physique; something that hits me straight in the stomach.

As quickly as my idiotic feet will carry me, I take off again. A couple of checks over my shoulder tell me he's also on the move, matching his pace to mine. Determined to confirm whether it actually is him, and not some innocent stranger, I swivel round.

And stop breathing.

Because he's loitering again, pretending to examine the contents of a shop window.

And it's him.

Definitely him.

He's found me... just when I'm at my weakest, my most vulnerable, my least guarded.

'No.'

Even through an alcoholic haze, a resulting panic takes hold, prompting my pulse to race and my lungs to tighten. It's a miracle I manage to turn away and break into a run. But the miracle doesn't last long. At just the wrong moment, the gin switches up a gear. And the world begins to tumble.

'I can't,' I gasp. 'I can't, I can't, I can't.'

He'll keep following me until I'm too tired to run any more. And then, he'll make his move. Maybe that's why I veer off into a dark alleyway. Maybe I know the game's over.

I drop the rucksack and lean back against a wall.

Drunk. Exhausted. Shaking. Totally aware that he's approaching me now.

Slowly. Deliberately.

When his features finally emerge from the shadows, my breathing falters.

I hear a familiar voice. It's gritty. Northern.

'Did you think you could run forever?'

No. I didn't. Not really. Not deep down. 'Get on with it.'

'Okay, then.' There's a silence. 'Die, you fucking bitch.'

Time to embrace the end. I just hope it comes quickly.

I close my eyes, let darkness envelop me... and sink into unconsciousness.

Chapter Six

I dream of Oma: so real, I could reach out and touch her. She's in the kitchen, busying herself with an ancient, dog-eared recipe book.

'He found me,' I tell her.

'I know.'

Of course. Oma knows everything, which is reason enough to ask the obvious question.

'Am I dead?'

'Maybe.' She licks an index finger, flicks a page. 'And maybe not.' At last, she makes eye contact.

'Time to give up then?'

'No.' The book snaps shut, and her next words hardly come as a surprise. After all, they're the very same words she drilled into me when Mum died. 'Never give up, my little one. No matter what life throws at you.'

I'd like to inform her that life's recently thrown a little too much in my direction, and that I'm heartily sick of the struggles, but I get no chance. The next thing I know, the scene disintegrates, and I'm dragged back across that brittle path between sleep and consciousness. I open my eyes, spend a few moments wallowing in complete confusion, then register the tiny shards of light dancing in the air above my head. They're waif-like, serene, almost heavenly; and I could gaze at them forever.

'What the...' The dancing spirits to come into focus. 'A chandelier?'

With a groan, I sit up, holding my head for a few seconds before I'm ready to survey my surroundings. One strange sight follows another: gold brocade curtains that wouldn't look amiss in a millionaire's mansion; a series of landscape paintings gracing creamy walls; an intricately carved mahogany chest of drawers; matching bedside tables topped with antique lamps. To my right, there's a mirrored wardrobe; to the left, an open door, leading to what looks like a lavish en-suite. A plush red sofa separates it from another door – this one closed. Finally, I concentrate on the massive bed I seem to have spent a night in, cossetted by an array of silky gold and russet covers. Absolutely everything about this place screams luxury. It's a thousand miles away from my grotty bedsit; a million miles from a dank doorway.

'I am dead.'

I must be. There's no other explanation for it.

Squeezing my eyelids shut, I call up the evidence. A hotchpotch of swirling memories. A bench on a rainy street. The tart hit of gin. Mud in a churchyard. Dark alleyways. And then – in the briefest of flashbacks – his face, that voice.

Did you think you could run forever?

On the verge of panic, I throw back the covers and shuffle to the side of the bed, only to find myself staring at a spotlessly clean marble floor and a plastic bucket. And that's when logic finally clicks into place. I can't be dead. For three good reasons. Firstly, I'm fairly sure there's no such thing as panic in the afterlife. Secondly, I'm perfectly certain there are no hangovers in the great hereafter. And thirdly, I'm absolutely convinced no one ever throws up – especially not into a plastic bucket – when they're dead.

So...

I'm alive.

Most definitely alive.

But where am I? And who am I with?

My heart stutters to a temporary halt... and then begins to thunder.

'Shit.'

Homing in on the closed door, I come to the only possible conclusion. After finally tracking me down, he must have decided that vengeance is best served on a fully sentient victim.

'Shit, shit, shit.'

My heart thunders again, this time so hard I'm convinced I'm about to vomit. Because he must be out there now – at the other side of that door – waiting patiently to make his move.

'Calm down, woman.'

I clutch at the bed covers and try to think things through. But it's no easy task, not with a swirling stomach, a mallet cracking the inside of my skull, and a brain that seems intent on entertaining every single hideous way I might be about to meet my end.

'Just think.' Willing my thoughts to behave, I scan the room again.

If he is sobering me up prior to finishing me off, then why on earth go to the trouble of doing it in such opulent surroundings? It makes no sense whatsoever... unless he's playing mind games, lulling me into a false sense of security before going in for a nasty, drawn-out kill. It's a distinct possibility, but one that's difficult to believe, largely because this kind of luxury is way out of his league.

MANDY LEE

I'm on the cusp of slipping back into total confusion when the door clicks open.

I hold my breath, watching as someone enters and approaches the bed. Wearing a tight-fitting red dress and an aura of complete self-confidence, she's the sort of woman who turns heads and stalls conversations. Like a complete idiot, I can do nothing but gawp. Which isn't surprising, seeing as every last detail – from the pale skin and mint-green irises, to the crimson lips and liquorice-black bob – demands my full attention. A modern-day Mata Hari, elegant, inscrutable, and dangerous, I can only imagine the effect she has on men. But I know the exact effect she has on me. Immediately, I draw back and pull the covers to my neck.

'No need to be afraid.'

Really? Are you sure? That's what I'd like to ask, but my mouth seems to have seized up.

'I expect you've got quite a hangover.' Reaching the side of the bed, she places a glass of water and a box of painkillers on the table.

Instinctively, I reach for the glass, then recoil. The water can wait. Because a raging hangover's the least of my troubles. I need to get a handle on this situation. And quickly too. 'Where am I?'

'You'll find out soon enough.' She takes a moment to examine me. 'You're filthy. Take a shower and get dressed. You'll find clean clothes in the wardrobe. Make yourself presentable. You've got half an hour.'

That's it? That's all I get? 'Half an hour before what?'

There's no reply. Within seconds, she's gone.

Battling back a rush of nausea, I spring out of bed, stagger to the door and grab the knob.

'Shit.' I'm locked in.

I turn back to the room and catch sight of the painkillers. A small act of kindness, I tell myself; and one that wouldn't even cross a certain person's mind.

All well and good, a voice grumbles at the back of my head. But if it's not him holding you here – and it really doesn't seem to be – then who the hell is? And why? And where, exactly, is here?

It's not something I can think about with a semi-imploding brain – which is why I head straight to the table and help myself to a couple of pills. A few seconds later, I'm standing at the window, curtains drawn, trying to make sense of a glorious view. Beyond a balcony, there's a vast, beautifully tended lawn, a glimmering lake, acres of rolling woodland in the distance. From here, it looks like paradise. But it also looks like the middle of nowhere, which doesn't bode well.

'Oh god,' I breathe, suddenly gripped by a new idea. 'He's sold me.' To some super-twisted, ultra-wealthy weirdo. And now I'm being kept as a sex slave. 'No, don't be daft.' I give myself a good, mental slap. 'Stop panicking. Just wait.' For the facts, whatever they might be. And in the meantime, I tell myself, follow Mata Hari's advice and spruce yourself up. After all, it's always a good idea to face your fate with a modicum of self-respect.

With that in mind, I make my way to the bathroom, faltering just inside the threshold at the sight of a huge, sunken bath set into an alcove, and a walk-in shower the size of a box room. Nudging myself back into action, I take a few steps forward, admiring the pristine marbled floor and walls, a pair of vases filled with fresh white roses, a silver bowl overflowing with expensive toiletries. Shampoo and shower cream selected, I pull off the t-shirt and realise it's not mine. And then, registering the fact that I'm not currently wearing a bra or knickers, I step into the shower and switch it on.

Ten minutes later, purged of all filth and wrapped in a luxuriously soft towel, I'm back in the bedroom. A quick rummage through the drawers produces a brush and hair dryer. After sorting my hair, I go in search of the promised clothes, finding nothing in the drawers, not even underwear. But the wardrobe contains a handful of short, skimpy dresses – all black. With no other option, I slip one on, face the full-length mirror ... and freeze at the sight of someone I haven't seen for a long time. I'm wearing no make-up and no jewellery, but in a figure-hugging dress, with my cleavage on full show and my long blonde locks tumbling over my shoulders, I look like the woman I used to be: a woman who felt comfortable in her own femininity, and never once baulked at displaying her charms.

Behind me, the door opens again.

I watch in the mirror as Mata Hari re-enters the room. 'Where are my clothes?' Wishing I could shrink into oblivion, I wrap my arms around myself.

'In the bin.'

'Why?'

'Because they were covered in vomit.'

Fair enough, but... 'I had more clothes in my backpack.'

'I binned those too. And the backpack.'

My hackles rise. 'But that was my stuff.'

'It'll be replaced.'

'Will it?'

'Obviously. And don't worry. I didn't throw away the photos.'

'You didn't?'

'Of course not.'

I scowl into those cat-like eyes.

'By the way, you're wearing one of my old dresses. Vera Wang. You're welcome.' I just about catch the all-too-brief, but totally unmistakable tinge of sarcasm. It's the first breach in that self-contained veneer.

'I'm not too keen on Vera Wang,' I tell her. The truth is I don't care a fig about labels. Whoever designed this dress, the stupid thing's making me feel distinctly nervous. I'm in desperate need of something a little less showy. 'I'd prefer jeans. I could wear them with that t-shirt.' I point to a crumpled heap of material on the bed.

'I don't own jeans.'

'How about a hairband, then? I like to put my hair up.'

'Because you like to avoid attention.'

'What?' How the hell did she work that out?

'And with your looks, it's obviously no mean feat.' She takes a step closer. 'I dare say you're about to attract a little attention now. So, I'll give you some advice, woman to woman.' Her eyes narrow, just a little. 'Be very careful how you use it.'

Her words are enough to set me on edge. And just at the wrong moment too. Completely unbalanced, I follow her out into a wide hallway, vaguely registering yet more polished marble flooring and plain cream walls. Moments later, I'm standing in what seems to be the main living space, taking in a kitchen-diner to the right, an open fireplace to the left, two huge sofas, a bookcase, and various pieces of occasional furniture. In front of me, a set of bi-folds reach from one side of the room to the other, framing a well-tended rooftop garden, and a stretch of pure blue sky beyond.

'Your guest,' Mata Hari announces.

'Thank you.'

I can only assume I've been followed down the corridor, because the voice comes from behind me. Rich and velvety, it's laced with a slightly upper-class accent. And when the owner comes into view, I'm floored by an onslaught to the senses. Caused by a mop of thick, dark hair, a pair of chocolate-brown eyes I could drink in for hours, and a firm, clean-shaven chin framing the sort of lips that invariably turn a woman's limbs to jelly, it leaves me completely mesmerised.

And as if that isn't enough to contend with, a quick check also confirms that the newcomer seems to be tall, lean and broad-shouldered. And chiselled to perfection, judging by the way those jeans and that black jersey top are clinging to him. No wonder I'm bowled over by a floodtide of naughty chemicals. No wonder I can't help drawing in one sharp breath after another while he studies me as closely as I'm studying him.

'You can leave us now,' he says.

With a graceful nod, his accomplice turns on her designer heels and virtually glides down the corridor.

I wait until she's gone before I confront the Adonis in front of me. 'What's going on?'

'Nothing to worry about. You're perfectly safe.'

'So I've been told.' The floodtide withdraws, but leaves a low, incessant buzz of electricity in its wake. A symptom of pure physical attraction, embedding itself into every fibre of my being, it's the sort of thing I can do without right now. Because I really shouldn't be attracted to a complete stranger, especially when there's a distinct possibility he's a psychopathic weirdo who collects women like other people collect stamps. 'But that doesn't answer my question.'

'No, it doesn't.' He waves a hand at one of the sofas. 'Please. Take a seat.'

With all the poise of a new-born gazelle, I do as I'm asked, watching in awe as he moves to the opposite sofa and settles himself into place. Crossing his legs, he sets about studying me again, which renders me completely embarrassed, and more than a little turned on. It's a miracle I remember I'm wearing a ridiculously short dress, with no knickers, and bring my knees together.

'Well?' I dare to make eye contact. Now the initial shock and surprise are wearing off, the smaller details come into focus. He seems a little tired, a little drawn.

'Well?' he repeats.

'Are you going to tell me who you are?'

'I don't think so.'

'Why not?'

'Because.' He smiles.

And good grief, he's got the loveliest smile. It softens his lips and sets off a delicious fluttering between my legs.

'Okay.' I will myself to remain calm. 'Maybe you could tell me where I am?'

'Somewhere.'

'Any chance you could be more specific?'

'None at all.'

'Why not?'

'Because.'

'Okay. How about you tell me why I'm here?'

'Not yet.'

'Not yet?' A tiny growl escapes my lips. This man might be God's gift to womankind, but he's already promising to be one of the most exasperating human beings I've ever encountered. 'Alright, perhaps you might like to inform me why I was locked in a bedroom?'

'To stop you getting out.'

'Jesus.' Another growl, slightly louder this time. 'Are you going to tell me anything?'

'All in good time.'

His eyes sweep over my entire body. And suddenly, I'm wondering what those lips would feel like on my skin. On the verge of simpering, I remind myself that while I'm pinging between lust and irritation, this totally calm, completely self-assured man is toying with me, something like a cat with a defenceless mouse.

'Perhaps it's best if we begin with my questions.' Oh, yes. He's the one in control, and he knows it.

'Go on, then,' I urge, because I'm desperate to get a handle on this mad situation.

'What's your name?'

I lean forward, blind-sided. 'You don't know?'

'Should I?'

Yes. If my personal nemesis is involved. 'You really don't know?'

'Of course not. That why I'm asking.'

A surge of relief washes through me. If this man doesn't know my name, then it's confirmation he's nothing to do with Crawley. It's one hideous possibility crossed off the list, but I've still gone from drunk and destitute to waking up in the lap of luxury, which makes no sense at all. I need to keep pushing.

'Why do you want to know my name?'

'Just interested.'

'I'm not buying that.' I get to my feet. 'And anyway, I don't see why I should give you my name when you won't give me yours.'

'I don't think you're in any position to bargain.' He arches an eyebrow.

'Fair enough.' I'll try the usual. 'Mary.'

'Wrong answer.'

'It's the only answer.'

'Mary, Mary, quite contrary.'

'Oh, shut up.'

It all happens so fast. Rising from the sofa, he closes the gap between us. And I'm gawping at his chest, wondering exactly when those long fingers closed around my right wrist, infesting my body with tiny prickles of energy.

'Come on, Mystery Woman. What harm can it do?' He squeezes gently. 'Just give me your real name.'

The prickles surge, and with no input whatsoever from my brain, my mouth decides to run amok. 'None of your business.'

'Not Mary, then.'

A glimmer of triumph flickers in his eyes, and I silently curse myself. Thanks to the hangover from Hell, and an unwanted touch of something I can only call idiocy, I've just given myself away.

'I'd say it probably begins with a Y,' he muses.

I move my left hand over the tattoo.

'Too late. I've already seen it.'

'It's nothing.'

'What does it stand for?'

'Nothing.'

'So, you're in the habit of having random letters tattooed on your body?'

'It's an old boyfriend's name. Yves. He was French.'

'Bollocks.' He runs a finger across my forearm.

And I grit my teeth, because there are more prickles now: thousands of the bloody things, all dancing and prancing and homing in on my core.

'It's too feminine.' He lowers his voice to a husky whisper. 'This is a girly tattoo for a girly name. What is it? Yvonne? Yvette?'

'It's nothing to do with my name.'

'So what is your name?'

'We're going round in circles.'

'I know. Feeling dizzy yet?'

Yes. I am feeling dizzy. And it's all down to those strong fingers and that gorgeous face. It's torture. Nothing more, nothing less. And I need to fight it.

'Just give up on the name,' I growl. 'I'm not in the mood to share.'

'Why not?'

'Because.' Aha! A dose of your own medicine.

'Then we have a problem.'

I'm about to ask him why we have a problem when he grips my left wrist and pulls back.

'What are you doing?'

'What does it look like?'

Examining my arms. That's what it looks like.

'I don't have any more tattoos.'

'I'm not looking for more tattoos.'

'Then what are you looking for?'

'Tracks.'

It takes a few seconds for the word to sink in. And when it does, I bristle with indignation.

'You think I'm a junkie?'

Examination over, he releases me and makes his way to the kitchen. 'Not sure.'

'But what makes you think that?' Even though I'm still bristling, I can't help admiring his pert backside and his sexy walk. Which only serves to make me bristle some more. 'Come on. What makes you think I'm a drug addict?'

'You were found on the streets.'

'Not everybody on the streets does drugs.'

'You can't be too careful.' He fiddles with a coffee machine.

'I don't do any drugs at all. Never have. Never will. It disgusts me.'

'You don't inject.' He flicks a switch. 'That's all I know.'

'I don't do anything. If I did, I'd be desperate for a fix by now.'

Folding his arms, he leans back against a counter. 'And what about alcohol?'

'What about it?'

'You were pissed as a fart last night.'

'Is that any surprise? I'd lost my job, my home, everything. I just fancied a bit of oblivion, thank you very much.' I gesture to the luxurious surroundings. 'Not that you'd ever understand.'

'You might be surprised.'

'I doubt it.' I raise my chin. 'I've had enough. Just give me my stuff – or replace my stuff – and I'll be on my way.'

'No.'

'What do you mean no?'

'Exactly what I say.'

'So...' I shake my head. 'You're holding me prisoner?'

'Not exactly. You'll be free to go when you've given me what I want.'

'Which is?' Here we go. A sexual favour or two. 'I'm not a prostitute.' Oh, Jesus. Did I really just blurt that out? Judging by the twinkle in his eyes, I'd say I did. 'I'm not. Okay? I'm just not.'

All traces of humour disappear. He watches me from under hooded lids. And I'm straight back to the idea that I've been kidnapped by a sex fiend. But if that is the case, then why don't I feel the slightest hint of fear?

'Just to put your mind at rest,' he says quietly. 'I don't use prostitutes – not that you look like one – and I don't force myself on women. And where you're concerned, I'm not in the least bit interested in sex. Are we clear?'

'Clear?' I squeak, relieved by his first two points and slightly disappointed by the third. 'Yes. I suppose so.'

'Good. So, take a seat, calm down, and I might just fill you in on my terms.'

'Might,' I grumble, flinging myself back onto the sofa.

'Coffee or tea?' he asks.

'Pardon?'

'Coffee or tea?'

'Coffee, please,' I smile, playing along with the social niceties. 'White. No sugar.' I might be struggling to understand a bizarre situation, but I'm still desperate for a drink.

While he fiddles with mugs and waits for the machine to perform its magic, I give my surroundings another once-over, get on with the business of calming down, and silently resolve to keep the attraction on a very short leash.

'Here.' A mug appears in front of my face.

I take it, watching as he settles himself back onto the opposite sofa, takes a few sips of his own coffee, and says nothing.

'So, these terms,' I begin.

'What about them?'

'Why don't you fill me in?'

'I'd love to.' His eyes flash.

And I'm reduced to a mess, resolution shattered by a handful of words and one distinctly mischievous suggestion. Determined to hide the resulting blush, I lift the mug to my mouth.

'But we'll get to that when I'm ready.' He leans back into the cushions and hits me with another curveball. 'First things first. Who was that man last night?'

The mug comes to a halt, mid-air, and begins to jitter. 'What man?'

'You don't remember?'

'No.' Best to keep this close to my chest.

'You were being attacked.' He pauses. 'We reached you just in time.'

Blinking back an image of a snarling face, I lean forward and gingerly place my untouched coffee on the floor.

'Who was he?'

'Nobody.'

'Try again.'

I look up. 'A mugger.'

'Sure about that?'

'Yes.'

'I don't know.' His expression softens. 'Perhaps you're in trouble.'

'And perhaps I'm not.'

'If you tell me your name, I might be able to help.'

'Why would you want to help?'

'I have my reasons.'

Which I'm pretty sure he's not about to share. Not that they're of any relevance, seeing as I'm way beyond salvation.

'What happened to him?' I ask.

'Who?'

'The mugger.'

'You're interested?'

I bite my lip, and decide to double down. 'Just tell me. What happened?'

'My people scared him off.'

'Your people?'

Dismissing my question with a shrug, he reaches behind one of the cushions and produces a photograph. 'Nice picture.'

'Oh, for God's sake. I'm sick of flip-flopping around. Can't we just get down to the terms?'

'First things first.'

'Of course.' Because he's determined to wear me out.

'Who are they?' He turns the photo.

In an instant, I'm consumed by a rush of adrenalin. Knocking all remnants of fatigue from my body, it launches me to my feet. 'Give that to me.' I hold out a hand.

'I'm guessing you're the girl in the middle. Who are the others? Mother? Grandmother?'

'I said, give it to me.' He's gone too far now, and I'm furious. 'What gives you the right to dig into my life? Who the hell do you think you are?'

Apparently intrigued by my response, he holds out the photograph. I snatch it from him, throw myself back onto the sofa and focus in on those three happy faces, hoping they'll bring me some strength. Instead, they only manage to summon up tears.

'Please,' I beg. 'Just tell me why I'm here.'

'Because I had you tracked down.'

'What?' Completely thrown for a third time, I meet his gaze. 'Why?'

'Why do you think?'

He waits patiently while I dig through a sludge of clues. So, he's tracked me down, but he doesn't know about Crawley or who I really am, which can only mean...

'Oh, thank God.' The relief's complete, but why didn't I think of it before? That hastily scribbled note on the back of a napkin? 'You know Hal.'

'Hal?' An eyebrow quirks, and he makes a connection. 'That's what they used to call him. I know him as Harry.'

'Harry. Right.' I rub a hand over my face. 'So...' What was it the nurse said? 'You're the gorgeous man who picked him up.' Immediately, I wince.

'I'm flattered.'

'I didn't say that. Someone else did.' Carefully, I place the photo on the cushion next to me.

'But you clearly agree.'

And now, he's teasing me. Jesus. I hope I'm not blushing again.

'Why couldn't you just tell me that in the first place?'

'I have my reasons.'

'Of course.' Leaning back against the cushions, I spend the next few seconds studying my mysterious companion. Whoever he is and whatever he wants, I now know one thing for certain. He's connected to Hal, which means he's likely in possession of a modicum of decency. And that gives me something to work with. Bit by bit, the balance of control is swinging my way, and I'm about to do all I can to make it swing some more.

'How is he?'

'Who?'

'Hal.'

'Fine.'

'That's all you're going to say?'

'For now.'

Not good enough. I'm about to demand more detail when he hits me with a salient question.

'Where's the ring?'

'Oh...' I should have known. It was all too good to be true. Rescued by a gorgeous, uber-sexy man who also happens to be a cold-hearted, grasping relative. He's gone and given himself away. 'That's what you want.'

'It wasn't in your belongings.'

'You shouldn't have gone through my stuff.'

'Celine went through your stuff.'

'Celine?' I can't help laughing at his slip-up. 'I take it you mean Mata Hari?'

Clearly irritated with himself, he grimaces. 'Yes. Mata Hari. She also undressed you and got you into bed.'

'That was nice of her.'

'No mean feat, given the state you were in.' He notes my confusion. 'Throwing up all over one of my lodges? Screaming the place down?'

'I did that?' Yet again, I'm stunned. I have absolutely no memory of it.

'That's why I had you brought up here.'

I shrug.

'Marble floors,' he explains. 'Not to mention, excellent soundproofing. Had to lock your door to stop you causing more havoc.' He holds up a hand. 'But don't worry, we checked on you throughout the night.'

'Oh.' I glance out of the window, and realise I've just been handed another clue. 'You talked about lodges. What is this place?'

'Wouldn't you like to know?'

'That's why I'm asking.'

'I know, but back to the ring.'

'You really are obsessed with it.'

'My precious.' He grins.

And that fluttering kicks off again between my legs. Time to put Mystery Man in his place.

'Worth a lot of money, is it?' I take another look around the room. 'I'm willing to bet this luxurious lifestyle takes some upkeep.' Oh, yes. Definitely a grasping relative. 'You must be struggling to keep up appearances.'

'I don't need money.' Suddenly, he's serious, and more than a little intimidating. 'Where is it?'

'Wouldn't you like to know?' That'll have to do. In actual fact, I don't really remember. And even if I did, I wouldn't tell him.

'Don't mess with me, Mystery Woman.'

'Don't mess with me, Mystery Man.'

52

'I hope you didn't pawn it.'

'Why would I do that? I gave Hal a note...'

'So, where is it?'

'The note?'

'The ring.'

'Give me a minute.' I close my eyes, and the image of a churchyard flashes back into my mind.

Shit. I buried it, didn't I?

What a stupid thing to do.

A stupid thing that leaves me with no alternative. I'll just have to go back to Bermondsey, retrace my drunken steps, and somehow find that church. But seeing as my 'host' seems to trust me as much as I trust him, I'm pretty sure he won't let me do it alone. In fact, I'm pretty sure he'll drag me down there, only to take possession of the ring and abandon me to my fate in a deserted graveyard. Shuddering at the thought, I conjure up Oma's mantra.

'Never give up, my little one. No matter what life throws at you.'

It's enough to resuscitate those dying survival instincts. Time to be ruthless, to buy myself a few days... and come up with a plan for staying alive.

Eyelids rise. 'Take me to see Hal and I'll let you know where it is.'

'And why should I let you see him?'

'To make sure he's alright.'

'No can do.'

'Why not?'

'Because.'

'Oh, for God's sake.' I slam a palm against the sofa. 'Just explain yourself. And use sentences, if you don't mind.'

'Okay.' Without any further argument, he actually does as he's told, laying out the facts in a slow, unhurried manner. 'You were very kind to Harry – and thank you for that – but I've been advised to be very careful about what I divulge to you. I apologise for the secrecy, but I'm afraid it's necessary. The fact is, I don't know who you are, what you are... or what you're caught up in.'

'You think I'd blackmail you?'

'I have no idea. Which is also why I'm letting you nowhere near Harry. Because I'd also like to protect him, if you don't mind.' He snakes an arm across the back of the sofa. 'Now, this is what I do know about you. You've clearly fallen on hard times and might be in some sort of trouble. You stashed that ring somewhere. And now you know it's valuable, you might just think it's worth a lot more than any reward I'd be willing to offer, which might lead you to decide to keep it for yourself. And that's something I can't allow. So, to conclude, you need to tell me exactly where the ring is. And when it's in my possession, I'll think about letting you go.'

Think about? 'No can do.'

'Why not?'

'Because I want to see Hal. I want to see for myself that he's alright. I want to make sure the ring gets into his hands, not yours.'

'It will get into his hands.'

'I don't believe you.'

'Then we've got a stand-off.'

Exactly what I've been angling for. But just to check... 'So, until I give you the ring, you're keeping me prisoner?'

'I wouldn't put it that way.'

'How else would you put it?' I fake a huff. 'Never mind. I can handle a few days in the lap of luxury.'

'A few days is all I need.'

'If you think I'm going to crack, you can think again.'

'Oh, I'll crack you, Mystery Woman... one way or another.'

A dangerous smile materialises on his lips. It sends a wonderful frisson right through me.

'Right.' Suddenly brusque, he gets up. 'I've got things to do. Time to get you back to your room.'

'No.' Springing to my feet, I dart to the back of the sofa.

'Do I really have to lay my hands on you again?'

'You're not locking me up. I've not even drunk my coffee.'

'I'll have a whole tray-full of drinks delivered to your room.'

'I don't want to go to my room.'

'Fine.' He prowls after me.

'What are you doing?'

'Whatever's necessary.' Closing the gap between us, he lifts me with ease and throws me over his shoulder.

I gasp... and gasp again when a strong arm wraps around my thighs. It's a raw, visceral contact that threatens to rob me of all logical thought, but I still manage a pathetic complaint.

'Put me down!'

'Don't waste your breath,' he laughs.

'But my photo. Give me my photo.'

'I'll look after it for you.'

With no further ado, he marches me back to my room and drops me onto the bed.

'You're a pig.' I sit up. 'Do you know that?'

'Yes, thank you.'

54

'And this is mad.'

Getting ready to make his exit, he grabs hold of the door handle. Those deep brown eyes glimmer with something I can't quite put a finger on. 'Not as mad as you think.'

He smiles knowingly.

And then, he's gone.

Chapter Seven

I watch the door swing shut, listen to the scrape of the key, and lie back.

'What the hell?' I ask the chandelier.

In response, it does nothing more than glitter and gleam in the morning light.

'Okay...'

Deciding it's time to rake back through what I know so far about a batshit crazy situation, I begin with the indisputable facts. Whatever else he might be, my mysterious captor is definitely a relative of Hal's; super-protective of the old man, and wary enough of me to keep his family identity under wraps. And now, for the not so indisputable. He's wealthy in his own right (if he's to be believed), determined to reunite a priceless ring with its true owner, and vaguely interested in helping me out with my difficulties. All of which would be perfectly fine (if he is to be believed), if it weren't for the further indisputable fact that he thinks it's acceptable to keep a woman under lock and key.

'And what sort of man does that?'

Only one possibility comes to mind. A ruthless man. The sort of man who wouldn't know a conscience if it smacked him in the face. And therein lies the problem, because no matter how I look at it, I just can't seem to accept my own answer. And that's because after spending barely half an hour in this particular man's company, I'm already feeling completely secure in it – even if it does come with a totally unwanted side-order of insane, sexual attraction.

'Oh, give up,' I mutter, rolling onto my side and shutting out the light.

Within seconds, I'm replaying the last few minutes in my head, desperately trying to pin down every last smile on those sensuous lips, and each little twinkle in his eyes. And then, I'm wondering if those smiles and twinkles actually mean anything, because if they do – and if the attraction works both ways – then he might be more inclined to drag out this situation.

I'm back to reliving the meeting for what must be the sixth or seventh time when exhaustion finally gets the better of me. I have no idea how long I spend in a deep, dreamless sleep, but the next thing I know I'm jolted awake by a slam. Instinctively, I heave myself up from the bed, scurry over to the door and press my ear to the keyhole.

'I got what you wanted,' Celine's calls.

There's a muffled answer.

'For God's sake, Sebastian. Not again!'

Another muffled reply.

'It's eleven in the morning. You need to stop this before it gets out of hand.'

I can't help grinning now, because I'm picking up information left, right and centre. These people must be the most incompetent kidnappers ever. And from the way they're bickering, possibly in a relationship: something I should have considered before, because it would certainly explain Celine's icy demeanour towards me. I strain to hear the next interchange, but it's impossible to make out a single word. I'm about to lope off back to the bed when I'm startled by the sound of my captor raising his voice.

'Stop! I can deal with that shit myself.'

'Of course you can.'

'Enough.'

'Get a grip.'

My eyes widen, and I almost giggle. If they are a couple, then it's Baz and Kath all over again, but this time accompanied by all the bells and whistles of serious wealth.

'Oh well,' I tell myself, 'I suppose money really can't buy you happiness.'

I hear the clacking of heels, and spring back.

The key turns in the lock. The door flies open.

'More clothes.' Without making eye contact, Celine slings a couple of bags onto the floor and beats a hasty retreat.

The door slams shut. The key turns again.

And I decide I might as well get settled in.

After swigging back a few glasses of water in the bathroom – because those promised drinks still haven't arrived – I return to the bedroom, empty the bags onto the bed, and wrestle back a twinge of disappointment. Two pairs of jeans and three pairs of jogging bottoms. A selection of t-shirts and sweatshirts, all grey. A set of flowery granny pants. Two bras: one white and one black. Two pairs of black trainers and a pack of socks. It's all brand new. And Celine's certainly honoured my preferences, procuring the dullest range of clothing I've ever seen. But I can't help wondering if there's another motive behind her choices: if it's all guaranteed to stop me deploying my wiles.

'Shame,' I mutter.

Because somewhere between waking up and emptying the bags, I seem to have resolved to try them out on the delectable Sebastian, even if he is in a relationship with Celine. It's a mercenary plan, born of a passing thought and fuelled by the need to survive. But seeing as my captor's own actions are morally questionable, I'm absolutely fine with it.

I put away the clothes and gravitate towards Celine's dresses, taking the first that comes to hand: another short, black number, this time in silk. After donning the black bra and a pair of knickers, I squeeze into the dress and examine myself in the mirror. It's far shorter than anything I've ever worn, figure hugging to a ridiculous degree, and it certainly does the job. With my hair tumbling down over my shoulders and my cleavage accentuated, I'm locked and loaded in the most feminine way possible.

'Ready.' To exploit any possible attraction and gain the upper hand. 'Let's do it.'

Without warning, the door swings open behind me.

Caught off guard, I swivel round to face my nemesis. And that's when my evil machinations hit their first hurdle. Immediately, with all thoughts of playing the arch seductress flying out of my brain, I'm more concerned about his effect on me, than my effect on him. In the face of the perfect masculine form, my heartbeat quickens, my lungs seem to shrivel, and there's a sudden, tortuous warmth between my thighs. Without saying a word, he turns and walks away, leaving the door wide open, and my body in complete chaos.

'Bugger.'

Reminding myself there's a job to do, I follow him out into the lounge and come to a halt by a sofa. I watch him saunter over to the marble-topped counter separating the kitchen from the rest of the room. He takes a seat on a stool, touches the side of a tumbler half-filled with amber fluid, and seems to lose himself in thought. A quick check on the kitchen clock brings the pieces of the puzzle into place. It's almost quarter to twelve, way too early for a cheeky drink, but not too early to launch my attack.

Giving it all the audacity I can, I amble over to the counter. 'You can stop locking me in now. I've decided not to cause havoc.'

'Is that so?' He doesn't look up.

'Yes.'

'And what if you decide to murder me in my bed?'

'Do I look like a murderer?'

'Difficult to tell.'

'But you can tell I'm not a prostitute.'

Finally, he makes eye contact. 'Definitely not a prostitute.'

In between willing my body to behave, I wonder why I'm actually offended now. I suppose it's because I'm trying to be all sexy and alluring, and apparently not doing a very good job of it.

'But when it comes to murderers,' he goes on. 'I've no idea what they look like. By the way, are the new clothes to your taste?'

'Yes, thank you.' Not that I'm wearing any of them. I just hope he doesn't know what was in those bags. If he does, then he'll also know I'm pushing my luck. Time to change the subject. 'Celine didn't seem to be in a good mood. She was a bit ... abrupt.'

'I apologise on her behalf.'

'Oh.' I hesitate.

Because, for some unknown reason, my conscience seems to have woken up. And now it's reminding me, in no uncertain terms, that moving in on another woman's man is never the done thing. There are no two ways about it. Before I get down to any serious flirting, I need to ascertain the lie of the land.

'Are you okay?'

His voice sends a shiver right to my core; not a good thing at a time like this. I can't have him undermining me with raw, effortless sex appeal when I'm trying to gather intelligence. Speaking of which, I'd better get on with it.

'Yes,' I half-squeak. This isn't going to be easy. Feigning nonchalance, I glance round the room. 'I was just wondering about you and Celine. Are you two ...' I wave a hand, think about finishing the sentence, and fail spectacularly.

He picks up the glass. 'Are we what?'

'You know.'

'Ah.' Biting back a smile, he takes a sip of whiskey. 'No. We're not a couple.'

'Oh.' Which means the floozy-fest is on.

'And you're interested because?'

'Dynamics. I... I just thought she might be jealous.'

'Why would she be jealous?'

'Oh, you know what women are like.'

'Not really. It's been a while since I got close to one.'

'Oh.'

His eyes glimmer. 'And I'm not gay, if that's what you're thinking.'

'No.' I laugh. 'Didn't even cross my mind. Not that it's any of my business.' And now, I'm blushing again, because it did cross my mind, and he knows it. 'Glad we've got that sorted though.' I run a finger across the marble top. 'Right. Anyway.' Bloody hell, I'm making a total pig's ear of this. Come on, woman. Get a grip. 'So ...' I straighten up. Having determined he's not attached, it's time to go on the offensive. Cleavage on full display, I summon my inner temptress. 'Maybe we could discuss what's going on?'

'You know what's going on.' As if they're a pair of misbehaving puppies, he gives my breasts a disapproving look, then raises the glass again.

'Oh come on, Sebastian. I don't know everything.'

The glass comes to a halt, and I'm rewarded with a smouldering frown. 'You know my name?'

'Yes.'

'How do you know my name?'

I put my hands on my hips. 'The outer walls might be soundproofed, but you can hear plenty through a keyhole. Like, for example, your argument with Celine.'

He slams down the glass.

'Turns out neither of you are any good at subterfuge.'

'Maybe not.' The frown morphs into something like a glare. 'So, now you know my name, how about you tell me yours?'

'Not a chance.'

'Fair's fair.'

'Not in this case.'

Eyes locked, we spend a good ten seconds indulging in a silent staring contest before I decide to speak again.

'I'd give up if I were you. I'm much better at keeping secrets.'

'I bet you are.' He chews at his bottom lip. 'Go on then, Mystery Woman. Tell me what else you heard through that keyhole.'

If I do as he says, it's bound to put a swift end to the planned seduction. But then again, seeing as my efforts seem to be going nowhere fast, I might as well change tack. After all, the ultimate goal is control, and there are more ways to skin the proverbial cat.

'I heard that you were doing something you really shouldn't do at eleven o'clock in the morning.'

He makes a fist with his right hand, and glances at the whiskey. 'And that's important?'

'Could be.'

'Why?'

'Because.'

'Okay.' He sits back. 'Seeing as you're so interested. The fact is I was taking afternoon tea... at eleven o'clock in the morning.' He cocks his head. 'A terrible faux pas.'

'Very funny.' A sense of humour. I like it. But there's no way he's throwing me off course. 'If you ask me, there's only one thing that worries people when you do it too early in the day. And it's nothing to do with tiny sandwiches and a pot of Earl Grey.'

'It's a good job no one's asking you then.'

A brief, insincere smile disappears behind a well-practised poker face. He's getting tetchy now – I can hear it in his voice – but I'm not backing off. In fact, I'm about to ratchet it up a gear.

'Could it be you're a lush, Sebastian?'

'Don't be ridiculous.'

'But you did look a bit rough earlier... a bit hung-over, in fact.'

'And that's coming from you, Miss Several-Sheets-to-the-Wind?'

'What I did last night was a one-off.'

'Really?'

'Yes.' I can't even remember the last time I drank myself into oblivion. 'But this clearly isn't.' I point at the glass. '"Not again." That's what Celine said. It's quite a recent thing, isn't it? If you were already a raging alcoholic, she wouldn't have sounded quite so upset. So, what is the matter? What's eating you?'

'Nothing.'

'"I can deal with that shit myself."'

'Can you now?'

'That's what you said.'

He stares at me, mouth clamped shut.

'To Celine,' I push, spotting the tiniest twitch of a jaw muscle.

'And?'

'Were you talking about me?'

'No.'

'Drinking?'

'Of course not.'

'Then it's something else.'

That does it. He gets to his feet, swipes up the glass and hurls it into the sink. Job done. Mystery captor thoroughly unbalanced... and pretty furious too. I should be nervous. After all, I have no idea what this man's capable of. But I'm not, because curiosity has got me firmly in its grips.

'Again,' he half growls, 'why are you so interested?'

'Just nosey.'

'Downright intrusive.' He prowls round the counter, homing in on me like a military-grade drone.

I take a step back. 'Celine's obviously worried, and I'd love to know why.'

'I don't see how it's any of your business.'

'Perhaps it's the whole 'kidnapping a woman' thing?'

'You have not been kidnapped.'

'I mean, you're bound to worry if your friend suddenly takes to abduction.'

'You have not been abducted.'

'Unless you've done it before, which you definitely haven't.'

He stops, barely inches away. 'There's a first time for everything.'

A shiver dances down my spine.

'But it's not just the whole 'kidnapping a woman' thing.'

'I told you...'

'Because whatever's driven you to the bottle, it definitely started before I turned up.'

Without warning, he grabs my right arm.

'Enough.' He looks at his hand, loosens the grip.

I've definitely won control. The trouble is, I haven't got a clue what to do with it. Perhaps that's why I opt for another push.

'I thought kidnappers were supposed to be scary. All mean and hard and cruel.'

'That's not me.'

'I know it's not.'

'What am I then?'

'Not sure.' Do I make a suggestion? To hell with it. 'A complete mess?'

He looks up, slowly. And although I can't make out exactly what I'm seeing in his eyes, I'm pretty sure there's an undertone of hurt.

Abruptly, he releases my arm... and walks away.

***

I follow him down the corridor, dithering a few feet behind while he prowls to the far end and disappears to the left. A few seconds later, a door slams, leaving me to home in on where I lost sight of him: an archway housing a set of marble steps. With my heart thudding in my chest, I climb the steps, arriving at a closed mahogany door. I hesitate, finally seeing sense.

After prodding him to breaking point, I should probably leave him alone.

62

'And do what?' I mutter, retreating down the steps.

The answer comes quickly... when I find the Devil himself waiting for me at the bottom, complete with a little work for my foolishly idle hands. 'After all,' I imagine him saying, 'while Sebastian's occupied upstairs, what's the harm in a good old snooping session?'

No harm at all, I decide. And immediately get on with the task.

It doesn't take long to ascertain the basics of the hallway. As well as the staircase at the end, there are four doors in total – two on each side. I try the door opposite mine, discovering it's unlocked, and enter another spacious bedroom. Decorated in a similar style to the one I'm currently inhabiting, it's furnished with a bed the size of Wales, a couple of sturdy chests of drawers, an armchair and a pair of matching bedside tables. The bed covers are rumpled to within an inch of their life, the bedside lamp still on, and there's a half-empty glass of water right next to it. All of which leads me to the conclusion that this must be Sebastian's room, and only serves to double the intrigue.

I spend a few moments studying a picture above the bed – a beautiful watercolour of an old-fashioned boathouse – and then I search for more clues. But there are no other pictures, and certainly no photographs on display. With nothing else to examine, my attention wanders to the mirrored doors of a built-in wardrobe. Moments later, with one of the doors wide open, I'm surveying a range of jeans, t-shirts, shirts, and a handful of suits. And then, I'm on my knees, riffling through a huge selection of trainers and shoes: all high-end, and most likely super expensive. I'm leaning right in when I discover a black cardboard box at the back. Flicking open the lid, I suck in a tiny gasp of air... because I'm staring at a pair of silver handcuffs, and a key.

'Bloody hell.' He's into kink.

At that precise moment, I lose my balance and topple into the footwear. And my new-found sense of derring-do shrivels into inexistence. Realising that Sebastian could return downstairs at any minute, and find me head-down, arse-up in his wardrobe, I struggle onto my hands and knees, carefully reposition the box, reverse out into the bedroom, and slide the door shut.

Back in the living area, I satisfy myself with studying the view, although it's little more than a rooftop veranda, a selection of luxury garden furniture and numerous oversized potted plants. Because of a stone balustrade, I can see nothing else apart from the sky. And I really don't know why I bother trying the bi-folds – they're obviously locked.

Giving up on the outside, I switch my attention to the living room. All very luxurious – and beautifully designed – but strangely impersonal. It's not long before I realise why. There are landscapes aplenty, but not a single photograph. Wondering if he's purposefully hidden his life from view, I scan the room again, searching for drawers. But I find them gracing nothing more than a bulky sideboard opposite the window. Moving quickly now, I make my way over to it and try each drawer in succession, but they just won't budge.

'Bollocks.' A complete waste of time.

There's only one more thing to investigate. And while it won't give up any of Sebastian's secrets, it's sure to keep me occupied for the time being.

Heading over to the kitchen, I run my hands across the sleek marble counter, then quickly get down to business, checking out the hob and oven, rummaging through numerous drawers and cupboards, and discovering just about every gadget, dry ingredient and condiment known to man. Finally, I investigate the built-in fridge, almost launching into gleeful dance when I'm greeted by a wide range of top-quality, fresh produce. Faced with an Aladdin's Cave like this, what happens next is completely inevitable.

Five minutes later, I've not only decided on a dish; I've also gathered all the ingredients on the counter. Bacon lardons sit next to a pack of diced steak. Behind them, mushrooms, onions, and all the necessary extras wait patiently for the show. After cracking a bottle of red wine, I settle down to work – frying, seasoning, tasting, seasoning again – building layers of flavour until they're deep and rich and heavenly. And before long, I'm drifting away in a trance-like state, forgetting the world and all its woes. It's something I've experienced a thousand times before: the alchemy of cooking; a wonderful, comforting magic I've seriously missed.

***

'What's going on?' His voice stirs me from the reverie.

'What does it look like?' I bring the casserole dish from the oven to the counter and remove the lid with a flourish. 'Thought you might be hungry after all that brooding. Peace offering.'

He peers into the dish. 'Do I need a peace offering?'

'I think I upset you earlier.' I check the time. Almost two hours since he skulked off. At least, he seems to have calmed down since then, but I'm not about to risk a repeat performance. No prodding, I tell myself. No pushing, no digging, and definitely no insults.

'You didn't upset me.'

'But I called you a...'

'Complete mess.'

His face melts into a smile. And with immediate effect, the buzz is back. Emanating from somewhere deep inside my core, it threatens to transform me into a gibbering idiot.

'What the...' As quickly as it appeared, the smile disintegrates. He reaches for the open wine bottle. 'Don't tell me you used this.'

'You can't make beef bourguignon without red wine.'

'Point taken.' He grimaces. 'However, you don't make a beef bourguignon with a 2007 Sassicaia.'

'Why not?'

'Because you've already used about a hundred pounds' worth.'

'Bum.'

'Bum, indeed.' He puts down the bottle. 'I was seriously looking forward to this.'

'Oh, God. I'm so sorry.'

The smile returns. 'Never mind. You weren't to know.' He heads for a cupboard, selects a couple of glasses and half fills one with what I now know is stupidly expensive wine. 'We might as well enjoy the rest.' He offers it to me. 'I believe the sun's now past the yard arm.'

'No thanks.'

'Not even at a hundred and fifty pounds a glass?'

'Not even that.'

'Your loss.' With a shrug, he sits at the counter, takes a mouthful of wine, and watches me plate up the bourguignon. 'By the way,' he says. 'I'm not an alcoholic.'

'But according to Celine, you are drinking too much.' Silently, I curse my mouth for running away with itself. This is no way to avoid more upset.

'You know what?' He levels his gaze on mine. 'Just because I'm keeping you locked up in my home, it doesn't give you the right to poke your nose into my affairs.'

I push the casserole dish to one side. 'And if you keep someone locked up in your home, you can't exactly claim the high ground.' Bringing a pan of creamy mash over to the counter, I place a spoonful onto the side of a plate and flatten it into a smear. Now, that's a mistake. Quickly, I slap a healthy dollop over the top, then add another to the second plate.

'Fair enough.'

'And anyway, you should be warned. I get bored easily. I need something to keep me busy.' Finally, I add the fresh vegetables, scattering them all over the place.

'So, you've taken to playing Miss Marple?'

'I wouldn't have to play Miss Marple if I knew who you were.' I nudge his plate towards him, along with a knife and fork.

'You know enough.'

'Oh, yes. Silly me.' I take a seat. 'You're Sebastian So-and-So, relative of Hal So-and-So. Owner of a hotel, perhaps. Abductor of strange women.'

'Very strange women.' Taking his first mouthful of bourguignon, he chews thoughtfully, cocks his head, then helps himself to another.

Safe in the knowledge he's enjoying his food, I tuck into my mine. The presentation might be an abomination, but in terms of taste, it's the best bourguignon I've ever made.

And it certainly hits the mark with Sebastian. He doesn't speak again until he's cleared the entire plate. 'Fuck me.' He drops his fork.

Resisting the urge to try a cheeky 'Maybe later', my face flushes with heat.

'Where did you learn to cook like this?'

'Just picked it up.'

'But this is ridiculously good.'

'I've practised a lot.'

'A hell of a lot. You cook like an angel.'

'Can angels cook?' I ask, glibly. 'Do they actually eat in Heaven? And what do you reckon they use? Gas or electricity?'

'You're trying to distract me.'

'Am I?'

'Obviously.' His eyes glint. 'I've discovered something about you, and now you're trying to put me off the scent.'

'Don't be daft.' I shift uncomfortably on my stool. 'All you know is I can cook a decent bourguignon.'

'Oh, I know more than that.'

My stomach churns, and I shift some more. I might have managed to back him into a corner earlier today, but I'm fully aware it won't take much for him to turn the tables.

'I had you tracked down, remember?' He takes a sip of wine. 'Which was bound to throw up a few facts.'

'Such as?' I hold my breath.

'Such as... I know you worked in a dive of a café, and lived in a slum of a shared house.'

That's it? Thank God. I let out the breath. 'I take it you spoke to The Walrus.'

He raises an eyebrow.

'The café owner,' I explain.

'Ah, him. No. I haven't personally experienced The Walrus. Alex went to see him.'

'Alex?'

'Another employee.' He puts down the glass and traces the stem, temporarily distracting me with his long, lithe fingers. 'The Walrus informed Alex you went by name Mary Smith.'

'There you go. I told you my name's Mary.'

'And I told you it's not.'

'But...'

'Because The Walrus said so.'

What? 'How did he know?'

'Ha!' He points one of those long, lithe fingers at me. 'It's not Mary, then.'

Shit. I've given myself away. I might as well throw in the towel.

'Apparently, you were desperate for cash-in-hand work.'

'So what?'

'That's how The Walrus knew.' He raises both eyebrows. 'I mean, what sort of person wants cash-in-hand in this day and age? Maybe someone living under an assumed identity?' He lifts his glass, waits for a reaction, receives nothing, and finally takes another mouthful of wine. 'Your ex-boss was left with a phone number and an offer of a reward. He texted Alex last night, when you finally returned to the café.'

Of course he did. The slimy, greasy bastard.

'But by the time Alex got there – along with a couple of others on my security team – you'd gone.'

'Security team?'

He wafts away the question. 'So, your ex-boss guided my men to your salubrious lodgings, but you'd already cleared out... almost as if you were scared of something.'

'I got thrown out.'

'Not according to your landlord.'

'I left before he booted me out.'

67

'In a hurry.'

'Look...'

'Do you remember anything about last night?'

I do. But I'm not about to admit the truth. Instead, I shake my head.

'Thought not.' He smiles. 'By the way, your landlord was very co-operative.'

'I bet he was. What did Alex give him?'

'Fifty quid. That was enough. He gave my men a description of you, including what you were wearing. They searched the surrounding areas.' He pauses. 'When they finally found you, you were rammed up against a wall.' As if suddenly energised, he leans forward. 'Tell me something. Why would a mugger attack someone who's obviously on the streets?'

'I wasn't obviously on the streets.'

'I beg to differ.'

I laugh. 'So, you've taken to playing Miss Marple?'

'I wouldn't have to play Miss Marple if I knew who you were.' The laugh disintegrates, and I'm drawn in by those deep chocolate eyes. He's perfectly serious now. 'There was a bit of a scuffle. Alex managed to see him off.'

'Good.'

'So, who was he?'

'I told you.'

'What are you hiding from?'

'None of your business.'

'So, you are hiding from something.'

I bite my lip. I've just let slip another fact, and now I'm on the back foot. To hell with treading on eggshells. I need to take charge of this conversation.

'Maybe I am. But so are you.' I nod to the bottle. 'Tell me. What is bothering you so much, you need to drown your sorrows?' There. That should do it.

He rubs his chin. 'Don't you ever give up?'

'Money troubles?'

'Please. Exactly what sort of person do you think I am?'

'I don't know. That's why I'm making assumptions.' And probably the wrong assumptions, because out of nowhere, I'm suddenly reminded of what Hal said about 'the boys'. They've already got enough.

'And you've assumed I'm a greedy, grasping relative?'

'Maybe...'

'And I want the ring for myself?'

'Don't you?'

'You see that painting above the fireplace?'

I lean to one side and squint at a landscape.

'It's worth at least ten of those rings. If I had money troubles, I wouldn't miss it.'

'Right.'

'The fact is, the ring belongs to Uncle Harry. It means a lot to him. I just want to...' Silencing himself, he rolls his eyes.

And I laugh again. 'Uncle?'

'Shit.' He gives me the most beautiful smile.

It sends a shiver right through me. And it's contagious too. With the tension between us quickly evaporating, I can't help smiling in return.

'Well,' he sighs, 'I think it's safe to say neither of us would last long at MI5. So much for being mysterious, eh?'

'I'm still better at it than you.'

'That's not saying much.'

Our gazes hold, and I sense the tiniest change. As if the shields are beginning to weaken, on both sides.

'So, where is Hal?' I ask. 'You can tell me that, at least.'

'Back home. Not a fan of hospitals.'

'I noticed. But where's home?'

'Can't say. Not until I know more about you.'

'Okay. So, how is he? And don't say he's fine again, because I know he's not. He was dehydrated, and probably had an infection...'

'Then you already know.'

'But there's more to it than that, Sebastian.'

Uttered with a hint of cheeky intimacy, I leave his name hanging in the air.

'Okay. I suppose there's no harm in telling you.' Gorgeous little crinkles appear at the corners of his eyes. 'He was diagnosed with dementia a couple of years ago. Obviously, it's been getting worse. There are times when he's fairly lucid, and times when he's not. We're getting more of the less lucid stuff these days.'

'I'm so sorry.'

'On top of the dehydration, he was a bit of a mess.'

'He won't remember me then.'

'Oh, but he does.' An eyebrow quirks. 'When I showed him the napkin, it jogged his memory. He rambled on and on about this beautiful angel who'd come to his rescue. He also remembered he'd given you the ring.'

'I'm only looking after it for him.'

And I should really let Sebastian know where it is. But, thanks to industrial quantities of gin, that's not currently an option.

'Is it safe?' he asks.

'Yes,' I half-squeak, desperately trying to poke a hole through an alcoholic dyke. Thankfully, I'm rewarded with a small trickle of something: vague memories of scraping at mud behind a gravestone.

'I don't suppose you're going to tell me where.'

'Not yet.' Because I'm still not entirely sure. And anyway, if I do tell him, he might just dump me back on the streets. 'After I've seen Hal.'

He purses his lips. 'If you tell me who you are, we might be able to discuss a visit.'

'Just call me Mary.'

'No way.'

'Why not?'

'Because it doesn't suit you. Besides, I had a great aunt called Mary. Total battle-axe.' He shakes his head. 'I can't go on like this, Mystery Woman.' Standing up, he disarms me with a twinkly smile and holds out a hand. 'Come with me.'

'Where to?'

'We're going to get you a new identity.'

'But...'

'Now.'

Nerves kicking in, I slip my hand into his and let him help me to my feet. The contact threatens to send me giddy, but I'm still disappointed when he releases my hand and saunters off down the hallway. I have no option but to follow in his wake, wondering what on earth's going on as I climb the staircase at the end.

'Welcome to my office,' he calls from ahead.

'Office?'

At the top of the stairs, I find myself inching over a threshold, taking in the fact that what Sebastian calls his 'office' is actually one of the most impressive spaces I've ever seen. Separated by a set of steps and an intricately designed iron banister, it's laid out on two levels. On the lower, there's a mahogany desk to my left, a huge leather sofa positioned in front of the banister, and floor-to-ceiling windows on both sides, giving out over the same idyllic landscape I admired from my bedroom. Straight ahead, on the upper level, a massive bookcase spans the entire length of the wall.

'Where are we?' I ask. 'What is this place?'

'I told you. My office.'

'I mean all of it. You mentioned lodges. Is it a hotel?'

'In a manner of speaking.'

'Why can't you just tell me?'

Slowly – and with supreme self-assurance – he closes the gap between us. 'For the very same reason I can't let you near my uncle.' Taking his time, he looks down at my lips, and then my cleavage. 'But let's not get distracted here. We've got a job to do.'

He turns away and takes the steps to the mezzanine level. At which point, I thank my lucky stars he brought an end to the proximity, seeing as it was about to turn my insides to mush.

Gathering my senses, I follow his footsteps, coming to a halt a couple of feet away from him. 'Jesus, how many books have you got?'

'No idea.'

'There must be hundreds.'

'Must be. Which is handy, seeing as I'm going to use them to choose you a name.'

A name? 'How?'

'Simple. I'll choose a book at random, and you'll be named after the author.' He pulls out a book and examines the cover. 'Bernard.'

'Can I pass on that one?'

'Certainly.' Casting the first book to the floor, he chooses another. 'Barbara. No.' He drops the second book and picks out a third. 'Ah, here we go. Eve Babitz. *Sex and Rage: Advice to Young Ladies Eager for a Good Time.*' He laughs. 'How apt.'

'Apt?'

'Oh, don't think I haven't noticed. Rustling up a fantastic meal? The perfect way to a man's heart. A tiny dress? The perfect way to another part of his anatomy.'

And now, I'm embarrassed. 'You think I'm trying to seduce you?'

'I don't just think. I know.' He holds out the book.

I take it. 'You've got it all wrong.' Seduction was the first tactic. It's certainly not my intention now.

'Eve,' he says, totally ignoring my denial. 'The first woman. Wearing nothing more than a few fig leaves.'

'Stop it.'

'Tempting Adam with a nice, juicy apple.'

'I said stop it.'

'Eve,' he muses. 'Evie. I like it.'

'So do I.' I hand back the book.

71

He returns it to the shelf. 'Then that's what we'll go with. Evie, the smouldering temptress.'

'Oh, for God's sake.' If he's determined to foist the role onto me, I might as well give it another go, whether my insides turn to mush or not. Moving closer, until I can virtually feel the warmth of his skin, I look up and hit him with my best doe-eyes.

'Definitely a good fit,' he breathes. 'But I still want your real name.'

'I can't give it to you.'

'Or maybe you won't.' Out of nowhere, he reaches up and traces a finger across my cheek. 'I'm no idiot, Evie. I know you want to stay. I know that's why you're trying to seduce me.'

'I'm not...'

He's so quick, I don't have time to react. Before I know what's going on, I'm drawn into his chest, and his arms are locked tight around me. Instantly, I'm alive with energy, all too keenly aware of his hard body, his power, his strength.

'Be careful,' he warns.

Switching his attention to my lips, he lowers his head a fraction. And there's something dangerous in his expression now; something a little frightening, but totally thrilling. It leaves me trembling for England... and silently willing him to kiss me stupid.

But those lips come no nearer.

Instead, they curve into a knowing smile.

'I don't deal well with temptation, Evie. You might want to remember that.'

Chapter Eight

A face emerges from the pitch, slowly taking on form and colour. My skin prickles and my heart pounds... because I know those eyes.

They're hard, hawk-like, unfeeling.

I open my mouth to scream, but manage nothing more than an incoherent groan. I try again and barely dent the silence.

'Evie?'

A voice penetrates the darkness. It beckons me back to consciousness.

'Wake up.'

Confusion gives way to understanding.

That's Sebastian's voice... and I'm Evie.

He's talking to me.

Struggling up on my elbows, I hear a click. Half-awake, I glance round the room, noting that the bedside lamp's switched on and my precious photograph's leaning against it. Flopping back, I lie perfectly still, waiting for my brain to catch up with reality. When it finally does, it tells me that the voice and the click weren't part of the dream. Sebastian must have come to check on me, perhaps because I called out in my sleep. He must have switched on the lamp and reunited me with my only possession. A totally unexpected act of kindness.

I'm far too groggy to muse over it for long. After drifting off again, the second time I wake, there's daylight peeping through the curtains, and I'm clear-headed enough to wince at the memory of the previous night's events. A failed seduction and a firm warning. A devious plan to gain the upper hand that left him wielding the balance of power, and me wallowing in embarrassment. No wonder I slunk off to my room as soon as he released me... and stayed there for the rest of the evening.

'Oh, God.'

I need to take the edge off my self-inflicted anxiety, and nothing but a good old soak can achieve that. Rising from the bed, I pad over to the en-suite and set about filling the bath. It takes an age, but the end result is definitely worth the wait. Slipping into the smooth embrace of warm water and luxurious bubbles, it doesn't take long for my body to relax. With a deep breath, I dunk my head underwater and think of those few, amazing moments in his arms. An all-to-brief taste of forbidden fruit, and yet another reckless breach of the rules; it's now my job to make sure it doesn't happen again.

Hair washed and body scrubbed, I emerge from the bath and return to the bedroom, where I pull a brush through my hair, don a bra and a pair of granny pants, and then browse the contents of the wardrobe. With Sebastian's warning still ringing in my ears, I pass over the skimpy black dresses and sort through the collection of drab new clothes, finally opting for a grey t-shirt and a pair of jeans.

A couple of minutes later, I'm alone in the kitchen, about to start fiddling with a menace of a coffee machine, when I spot a sticky label on the top. On it, a message written in a neat, confident hand. I pick up the sticker and gaze at it.

'Gone for a run. S.'

Surely he wouldn't have bothered with a note if he was still annoyed with me. I must be forgiven for behaving like a complete floozy.

'Thank God.'

Feeling a little more comfortable now, I give up on the coffee machine and help myself to a bottle of water from the fridge. Heading to the bi-folds, I'm surprised when one of the huge windows glides open at the slightest push.

'What?'

Either he's forgotten to lock it, or I'm being trusted with a little more freedom. And given he's rumbled my not-so-secret desire to stay, I'd say it's the second option. With my heart doing a little dance, I step onto the terrace, tip my head back and luxuriate in the sunlight.

And that's when it happens.

A curious interlude – probably brought on by a bout of giddy relief – during which I choose to forget all the rules and spend a few moments indulging in a rare bout of make-believe. Suddenly, and completely out of nowhere, I'm the princess in the tower; a willing captive to my own personal knight in shining armour who'll do anything to keep the dragons at bay.

'Oh, stop it,' I grumble, shaking the dream from my head. 'Get real.'

With no further ado, I set off to explore and quickly discover the terrace surrounds the entire flat. Taking my time, I stop at each side to take in the scenery. From the first, there's a huge lawn, cut in half by a gravel driveway that snakes round from the left, forking off in two directions before it dips beneath ground level – to a garage, perhaps. Next, I'm overlooking a car park: the second end point to the drive. Below me, just to the left, there's a deserted patio area. And in the distance, a lake and rolling forests. On the third side, I find myself gazing at a clutch of smaller buildings, probably the lodges Sebastian talked about.

And God knows why I haven't been transferred back out there. After all, I'm clean and sober now, and hardly likely to ruin any carpets. I take a sip of water, narrow my eyes, and wonder why he's opted to keep me close. After all, he has no real idea who I am or what sort of baggage I drag in my wake. It's a conundrum I've managed to overlook so far, thanks to the whirlwind of the last twenty-four hours. But it's still one I need to solve.

I've just begun to admire the view from the fourth side – a perfectly tended garden, complete with a well-established arbour – when I'm startled by a sudden clatter. It draws me back inside, where I come across Sebastian standing over the hob, a pan of water on the boil.

'Good morning,' I beam.

He turns and notes my outfit. 'What on earth are you wearing?'

'Clothes.'

'I can see that.'

'The ones Celine bought.'

'She bought those?' With a tut, he checks on something under the grill. 'I'll have a word with her.'

'No need.' I take a seat at the counter and put down my bottle. 'They'll do.'

'Guaranteed to stop any attempt at seduction in its tracks?'

'Yes, well...' My cheeks flush. 'Sorry about that.'

'Are you?' His eyes spark.

'Of course.' I gather my resolve. 'Let's just say it won't happen again.'

'Good. Coffee?'

'Please.'

While he pours a mug for me, I survey the countertop. A mobile. A box of eggs. White wine vinegar. A bag of flour. Butter. Muffins.

'What's going on here?'

'Returning a favour.' Picking out a couple of eggs, he breaks them into the water and gently swirls them with a spoon. 'Last night,' he says, inspecting the result, 'you wowed me with a magnificent beef bourguignon. So, this morning, you get eggs Benedict.' Abandoning the spoon, he returns to the grill, pulls out the pan and slides a halved, toasted muffin onto each plate.

And I'm thoroughly intrigued.

A creamy sauce joins the muffins.

'You made hollandaise?' I ask. 'From scratch?'

'Of course.' He sprinkles shredded ham over the sauce, then picks up the spoon again. One by one, he removes the eggs from the pan, drains them, and carefully places them on the muffins. After topping it all off with another spoonful of hollandaise, he raises his hands in triumph. 'Voilà.' He nudges a plate over to me. It's followed by a knife and fork. 'Dig in.'

I do as I'm told. And from the first mouthful, it's perfect. I don't even look up until I'm halfway through the plate.

'Bloody hell. Where did you learn to do this?'

'Like you, I'm a keen amateur.' As if he's waiting for a reaction, or maybe testing a theory, he watches me closely.

'I've fallen on my feet.' With a fake smile, I cut another slice of muffin. It seems I can't even enjoy breakfast without some sort of examination, which is enough to fire me up with an immediate and irresistible urge to address the new conundrum. I begin by pressing an obvious button. 'A kidnapper who can cook.'

'You haven't been kidnapped.' Apparently unbothered, he prods his egg. Yolk trickles over the muffin.

'Oh, yes. I remember.' And now for a little sarcasm. 'You tracked me down because of a ring. And brought me up here because of the state I was in. And until I produce said ring, you're just keeping me locked up.' I tap my fork against the top for emphasis. 'Right here in your own apartment.'

'But you haven't been kidnapped.'

'If it walks like a duck and quacks like a duck, then it is a chuffing duck.'

'Not in this case.'

Jesus. I'm getting no reaction at all. 'So, if it's not kidnapping, what is it?'

He shrugs.

Time to come to the point. 'And why am I not back in a lodge?'

I don't get an answer. The next thing I know, there's a buzzing sound and he's reaching for his mobile. I have just enough time to spot Celine's name before he answers.

'Yes?' He listens. 'Where is he?' A cloud descends over his features. 'No, don't do that. I'll come down.' Ending the call, he gets to his feet.

'What is it?'

'Nothing.' He slips the mobile into the back pocket of his jeans. 'Won't be long.' Clearly on a mission, he marches off down the hallway.

I wait a few seconds before following behind, watching the front door swing shut in his wake, and giving it a half-hearted kick when I find it locked. With nothing else to do, I retreat to the kitchen and begin clearing up. I'm still stacking the space-age dishwasher when I hear the door open again.

He's back.

But he doesn't join me in the kitchen.

Leaving the pots half loaded, I sneak down the hallway and stop at his bedroom door. Easing it open, I edge my way in.

'Sebastian?' I move towards the en-suite, drawn by the sound of running water. 'What's happened?'

He comes into view. Leaning over the sink, he's busy washing his hands. 'Nothing. Give me a few minutes.'

I can tell he means business. Saying nothing in return, I head back to the kitchen, ignore the dishwasher, and decide to crack the mystery of the coffee machine. I don't hear the front door open a second time; don't realise Celine's joined me until I turn, coffee pot in hand.

'Where is he?' Clearly ruffled, she stalks towards the counter.

'In his room.'

'Good. Hopefully, he'll stay there.'

I slam down the pot. 'Why?'

'Because you need to know what's going on.' All signs of irritation quickly disappear, schooled into submission by what seems to be her usual, impenetrable façade. 'Seb's just had a row with his brother.'

Brother? Another revelation. 'Okay.'

'The row was about you.'

Oh, I see. 'And his brother knew about me because?'

'I told him.'

I clench my fists. 'You had no right ...'

'It was my duty.'

'To cause trouble?'

'To step in.'

Okay. So, she's brazenly admitting to setting up an intervention. Fair enough. But why rub it in my face? 'I don't know why you're talking to me about it.'

'Because you're using him.'

'I beg your pardon?'

'Withholding information, giving yourself time to dig in your talons.' The face might be saying nothing now, but it's all there in her choice of words. Mata Hari's pissed off, big style. 'Some people might say you're just enjoying a few days of security, but I say you're after Seb's money.'

'Don't be ridiculous.'

'Ridiculous?' She studies me for a full thirty seconds, as if she's trying to read my deepest thoughts. And then they come, one by one: the almost-imperceptible signals that she's about to change tactic. A slight lowering of the eyelids, a twitch of the crimson lips, a general softening of everything. And finally, a cold-eyed smile. 'Okay. Let's assume you're not in it for the money.'

'Which would be true.'

'Let's assume you actually like Sebastian.'

Do I like him? Of course I do. But there's no harm in liking, is there?

She prowls round the counter, coming to stand right in front of me. 'If that is the case, then I need to fill you in on a few things.'

'Go ahead.' I steel myself.

'I don't blame you for liking him. I mean, he is very handsome, very charming when he's in the mood. And I realise there's a possibility he's attracted to you. You're pretty enough.'

I sense a flutter in my stomach, a rush of warmth in my chest.

'But there's nothing special about that,' she goes on. 'Not where Sebastian's concerned. Because he's an inveterate flirt, a womaniser, a playboy. It's well known he's had his choice of women over the years – beautiful women, rich women, famous women...'

'And?'

'Plenty fell for him.'

'So what?'

'They never stood a chance.'

The rush of warmth recedes, leaving nothing in its wake but an aching disappointment.

'Jesus.' A silly little fantasy's one thing, but aching disappointment? That's on a completely different level. And seeing as I've only just met the man, distinctly worrying too.

'Sorry to be the bearer of bad news.' Celine smiles, slyly. 'But there'll never be a happy ever after with Sebastian, because there's not a romantic bone in his body. So, if that's what you're hoping for, you'd better put the idea out of your head.'

'I don't have any hopes.' What a ridiculous lie. I must have hopes. That must be why I'm disappointed, because Celine's doing a grand job of dashing them to the floor. 'No need to worry.'

'Oh, but I can't help it.'

'I won't be staying much longer.'

'Every minute you stay, you're causing more damage.'

'What damage?'

'His brother.'

'That's all on you.'

'Oh, Max would have found out before long. He has a knack for that sort of thing. I just hastened the process.' She taps the counter. 'The thing is, I think I ought to let you in on a little secret, Evie.' She practically sneers my new name. 'Seb needs his brother. Always has and always will. But there's a little rift between them at the moment. You don't need to know the details.' She waves a hand. 'Suffice to say, with you on the scene, it's never going to heal. If you've got any sense of decency, you'll do the right thing: give him the ring and get out of his life.'

The sound of footsteps puts a much-needed end to our conversation. While Celine retreats from the counter, Sebastian joins us, notes Celine's presence, and heads straight to the fridge.

'What are you doing here?' He helps himself to a water.

'I came to see how you are.'

'I'm fine.'

He unscrews the top, and I catch sight of a graze on his right knuckle, the beginnings of a bruise, a trickle of blood.

'So you can go.' He takes a sip. 'But before you do, I've got a couple of questions.'

She folds her arms. 'Fire away.'

'How the fuck did he find out, and who the fuck let him in?'

Apparently unfazed by the swearing, not to mention the distinct undertone of irritation in his voice, she maintains her perfect composure. 'He found out because I told him. And I'm the one who let him in.'

'Why?' Noticing the blood, he puts down the glass, grabs a sheet of kitchen paper and dabs at his knuckle.

'Because you're not thinking straight. You're making mistakes.' She raises her chin in defiance. 'What else was I supposed to do? You wouldn't listen to me.'

'And you thought I'd listen to Max?'

'It was worth a try.' There's another tiny twitch of those lips. 'But enough of that. Let's just cut to the chase, shall we? We both know where this is coming from.'

'What are you on about?'

Her eyes glint. 'The letters.'

I practically see it happen: the blood draining from his face, the life from his eyes. Stone-like and rooted to the spot, he simply stares at her.

'You can shove them in a drawer and pretend they don't exist, but they're getting to you, Seb.' She slinks forwards. 'I mean, look at you. Bottling it all up, drinking yourself into oblivion, distracting yourself by locking up complete strangers...'

'That is not what's going on here.'

'You could have fooled me.'

'Back off.'

Delivered with a growl, it's a warning she'd do well to heed. With his shoulders hunched, and his teeth half-bared, Sebastian looks like a wild animal about to go in for the kill. If I were her, I'd be running a mile right now, but Celine seems to be made of harder stuff.

'You should tell Max about them,' she says calmly. 'He might be able to help.'

'Keep your nose out.'

'I can't. I'm your friend.'

'You're also my employee. And I should sack you right now.'

'But you won't.'

'I wouldn't bet on it.'

'Fine. Sack me, then. But a few words of wisdom first.' She raises a delicate finger at me. 'Get rid of her before Max tells the police.'

'If Max tells the police, he'll get me arrested, and you too. Just think of all that negative publicity.' He laughs. 'Get real, Celine. That's the last thing he wants. He's just like the old man.'

Long, piercing glares are exchanged. The air virtually crackles with mutual irritation. It's Sebastian who finally breaks the deadlock.

'I think we're done now.' He waves to the front door, inviting Celine to make her exit.

With a glance at me, she takes the hint.

As soon as the front door bangs, Sebastian heads for the sink, grabs another sheet of paper and dabs the back of his hand.

'What happened?' I ask.

'I punched a wall.' He turns on the tap and thrusts his hand into the flow.

'Why?'

'Because it was preferable to punching my brother.'

I watch him for a few seconds. 'That water's not cold enough.' Opening the freezer, I rummage through the contents and pull out a bag of ice. 'Here.' Leaning close, I turn off the tap and take his hand in mine. 'You'll have a nasty bruise.' I press the bag to his skin, holding it there while my senses flick to high alert. Only too aware of the warmth of his body and hint of his scent, my body soon threatens to betray me. Pulse accelerating, my hands begin to tremble. 'There.' I discard the ice, take the kitchen roll from him and quickly dab at the graze. 'The bleeding's stopped.'

He examines the wound. 'You're good at this.'

'Plenty of practice. When I was little, I used to rescue all sorts of creatures. Bees, butterflies, even the occasional bird.'

'And now you've taken to rescuing fully-grown men.'

I step back.

'Is that why you looked after Harry? An overwhelming instinct to nurture?'

I shrug. 'Couldn't just leave him. He was in trouble.'

Without warning, he moves closer and grasps my hand. 'Thank you,' he says. 'For what you did.'

'It was nothing.'

I try to pull away, but to no avail. I might have decided to keep my distance, but he's determined to keep fingers locked around mine. My pulse quickens again.

'It cost you your job.'

I frown. 'How do you know that?'

'The Walrus.'

'Of course.' So, he's feeling guilty. That's why he's treating me to a little luxury. 'You don't owe me because of that.'

'I know.'

I have no idea what to say next, largely because I'm already drifting away in those dark chocolate irises. After months spent in self-imposed isolation, it's an intoxicating overdose of intimacy. It must be at least thirty seconds before I manage to look away.

'I think you'll be fine now.' Tugging my hand from his, I discard the kitchen paper in the bin.

'I'll be even better after some coffee.' He grabs the pot and sets about working the machine.

'So, your brother's called Max?' I ask.

'Yes.'

'He sounds quite protective.'

'Too protective.'

'And he's older than you?'

'Yep.'

'Which is why he's protective?'

'That... and other things. Take a seat.'

I do as I'm told, waiting while the machine splutters and gurgles, and eventually fills the pot.

Coffee prepared, he pours out a couple of mugs and adds milk. 'What did Celine say to you?'

'Nothing really.' I've caused enough trouble for one day. But I'm still itching to state the obvious. 'She doesn't like me much.'

'She doesn't like you at all.' He slides a mug towards me. 'But she'll come round.'

I almost laugh. Getting Celine to like me – let alone accept my presence – isn't going to be a quick-and-easy task; which leaves me wondering exactly how long Sebastian's planning to keep me around. While we slip into another silence, I take a few sips of coffee, matching each one with a furtive peek at his gorgeous face, and decide to ask about that another time. For now, there's another burning issue I'd like to clear up.

'Can I ask you something?'

'Within reason.'

'Celine mentioned letters...'

'That's not within reason.'

'You can't blame me for being interested.'

'I suppose not.'

I waver under his gaze, finding no traces of irritation in his eyes. It's more the look of a man who's had about as much as he can take.

'We both have our boundaries, Evie.' Coffee in hand, he gets to his feet. 'Now, if you don't mind, I need to go downstairs for a while.'

'Of course.' I've gone too far again. I'm not surprised he's back to avoiding me.

'And if you need something to occupy your mind, I brought some books down from the library this morning.' He nods to a pile of novels on the coffee table. 'Try a bit of reading.'

***

I spend most of the day out on the rooftop, downing mugs of coffee and trying one book after another. Finally, I settle for *The Story of O*, but concentration doesn't come easy. Every few minutes, I put down the book and ponder what seems to be a growing problem.

No matter how much I want to get rid of it, the physical attraction isn't going anywhere. And that's not the end of it. Even though I only met Sebastian a few hours ago, I'm already in real danger of falling for him. Something that just can't happen – whether it's reciprocated or not – because it's bound to cause me nothing but pain. Whichever way I look at the situation, there's only one conclusion I can reach. I need to put an end to it – and quickly too.

At first, I'm hardly aware of the air growing cold. It's only when I feel the first few drops of rain that I look up at a newly cloudy sky. Putting an end to the thinking and reading, I take the book inside and revert to my favourite brand of distraction. By the time he re-appears, at just past five, I'm ready with a salmon risotto, a delicious side-salad and home-made ciabatta.

But Sebastian's in no mood for chatting. Avoiding all eye contact, he greets my small talk with monosyllabic answers. And when he's finished his meal, he sips at his wine and drifts off to God knows where. I've no idea what's troubling him now, but the time has certainly come to let him know my decision.

'I think I should tell you where the ring is.' My words sound hollow, but they draw him back to the present.

'I thought you weren't going to do that until I take you to see Harry.'

I shift on my stool. 'Slight change of plan. I'm causing you trouble. And that's the last thing I want, because I get the feeling you're a decent man...'

He holds up a hand. 'You don't know anything about me.'

'I know enough.'

'I disagree.'

I draw in a breath and press on. 'Regardless of how much I know about you, I'm going to tell you where it is. And then I'll be out of your hair.'

'No.'

'What do you mean no?'

'I mean...' He thinks for a moment. 'It's not that simple anymore.'

'How is it not that simple? We had a deal.'

'Slight change of plan.' A smile appears. He leans in. 'I want two things now... before I'll even consider letting you go.'

'Two?'

'Yes. Two.' The smile deepens. 'The location of the ring.'

'Obviously.'

'And your name.'

'My name?' What the hell's going on?

'Your real name. I'm afraid it's now a requirement.'

'A requirement?' For the life of me, I can't work out why he's changed his stance. 'Even if I tell you where the ring is?'

'Yes.'

'But why?' This can't be out of pure interest. Not anymore.

'Because.'

'But my name's worth nothing.'

'Once more, I disagree.'

'Then you get neither.'

'Then you stay here.' He raises one extremely self-satisfied eyebrow. 'And by the way, you should leave your door open tonight.'

'Why?'

'In case you have another bad dream.'

'Oh my God.' Half-formed memories return. 'It was you. You came in.' With the day's twists and turns, I'd totally forgotten.

'You were shouting. I left the light on for you.' He becomes serious. 'What were you dreaming about?'

I shake my head. No matter what I feel about this man, I haven't known him long enough to tell him the truth.

'I see.'

His eyes search mine, and I'm drawn back to that little reverie on the terrace. Suddenly, the idea of a knight in shining armour doesn't seem quite so ridiculous. After all, this isn't the first time he's probed me on my troubles.

'I'm not just here because of the ring, am I?'

'Information is power, Evie. And seeing as you're not about to share, neither am I.'

'Are you protecting me?'

'Protecting you? From what?'

There's a new determination in his eyes, and it's all the answer I need. He is protecting me. That's why he's keeping me close, using any excuse to stop me leaving. And it's costing him too. I only need to look at the bruised knuckles to remind me of that. But my answer comes with another pesky question. Why on earth go to such

84

lengths to guard a stranger? I can't believe it's just because I helped his uncle.

'Nothing to say?' He sighs. 'And you complain about me being mysterious.'

Chapter Nine

'So,' he says, 'what are you up to today?'

I push my empty cereal bowl to one side. 'This morning, I thought I'd teach myself a new language. Russian, probably. And then, this afternoon...' I tap the countertop. 'I can't decide whether to practise Morris dancing or learn how to walk on stilts.'

'I don't have any stilts.'

'Morris dancing it is, then.' I get up and wander over to a sofa, flopping down next to the pile of books. In all probability, I'll fill the hours exactly the same way I've done for the past three days.

Seventy-two hours – give or take – during which, we seem to have settled into a routine that already feels strangely normal. After breakfasting together, he disappears downstairs for a few hours, doing whatever he does. And in the meantime, I read, watch television, or cook. After he returns – at around five or six o'clock – we eat together and chat, filling the space between us with meaningless talk about books, films and food. At about nine o'clock, he withdraws to work in his office, leaving me to flick through television channels, or take a bath. At the end of each day, I'm always in bed by eleven, with the door left open... and my thoughts dominated by him.

'Might start with a bit of reading, though.'

'Tried any yet?' He leans back against the counter.

'Uh huh.'

'Anything taken your fancy?'

'Well...' I run a finger over the selection. 'They're all a bit weird.'

'How so?'

Shuffling them about, I read the titles. '*Bad Behaviour. The Story of O. The Unbearable Lightness of Being. House of Holes.*'

'And?' He folds his arms.

'They're all about sex.'

'Are they?'

'You know they are. You also know they're a bit weird.'

'Weird?'

'Yes. Weird. Tell me something. Did you, by any chance, choose these books for any particular reason?'

'No.' Clearly feigning offence, he frowns. 'I just pulled them out at random.'

'I don't believe you.'

'Why did I choose them, then?'

'To make me feel uncomfortable.'

'And why would I do that?'

'To make me talk.'

'Oh, come on now.' A distinctly naughty twinkle appears in his eyes. 'If I wanted to make you talk, I wouldn't use books.'

He's at it again, flirting outrageously. Something he's indulged in on an increasingly regular basis over the past couple of days. Not that I'm in any position to complain. With physical attraction running wild, and no choice but to be in close proximity to the man, all resolution to keep him at arm's length quickly withered like a neglected houseplant. Apart from wearing dowdy clothes, I've done bugger all to protect myself. No wonder the flirting's become a mutual habit.

'Idiot,' I mutter, knowing there's more to it than that.

Now all efforts to dig for information have been put on hold, we've finally reached a quiet comfort in each other's company. And I could be wrong, but I'm pretty sure there's a growing attachment too.

'You know what?' Reminding myself I am wrong – because he's a womanising, relationship-averse playboy – I flick through *House of Holes*. 'I think you're using these books. I think you're trying to tell me something about yourself.'

'An interesting theory. I wonder what I'm trying to say.'

'That you're a complete pervert.'

'Really? What's perverted about sex?'

Suddenly hot, I slam down the book.

'For your information...' He pushes away from the counter. 'I chose those books at random, possibly from the 'Books Max Lent Me' section.'

'Excuses.'

'Unlike me, he does read a lot. And he is a pervert.'

I blush, probably for the thousandth time. I should have known better than to drag the conversation down this particular path. 'Haven't you got work to do?'

'Always.'

'Go and do it then.'

'Yes, boss.'

With a mischievous grin, he disappears for the day.

***

MANDY LEE

The hours pass slowly. I catch up with the news, read another chapter of *The Story of O*, laze on a sun lounger, snooze for a while, drink a few coffees, and eventually make myself lunch. With the remnants of an omelette in front of me, I ponder the blue skies outside, and sigh.

Because I'm getting tired of it all. Because nothing can really stave off a growing dose of cabin fever. Not safety, not luxury, not even spending more time with the sexiest man alive. Increasingly restless, I want to know what he gets up to during the day. I want to know what's downstairs, what's outside, what's beyond those trees. Playing the princess in the tower is all well and good, but it's also mind-numbingly dull. A fact Sebastian's no doubt aware of. After all, it's probably central to his plan: bore me into submission, until I finally break down and spill every last detail about myself.

'No chance of that,' I whisper, getting to my feet. He may have decent reasons for upping the ante, but there's still no way I can reveal the truth.

At a loss for what to do next, I wander down the corridor, stopping outside his door to try the handle. Still open. Just like it was last night when I woke up at God knows what time, couldn't get back to sleep, and dared to venture out.

I think back to it now, the sight that greeted me when I slipped into his room: a soft light spilling from the bedside lamp; Sebastian lying on his front, one arm draped over the pillows; a silky sheet covering nothing but his legs, allowing me the opportunity to ogle a beautifully sculpted back and pert buttocks.

'Who's the pervert?' I grumble, annoyed at my own inability to deal with temptation. Because while I've woken twice now to find him sitting with me, gently coaxing me back from a nightmare, all I could do in return was leer at his naked body.

With a shake of the head, I resolve to behave properly from now on and wander further down the corridor. I'm fully intending to try his office, but don't get that far. Instead, I come to a halt by the front door, stunned to find it slightly ajar, swinging it open and inching my way out into a small, but immaculate lobby. Immediately, I'm drawn to the top of a flight of stairs.

I pause and listen out for signs of life.

But there's nothing.

'Okay...'

Stomach churning, I take the steps. A few seconds later, I'm standing on a deserted landing, noting a corridor leading off in each

88

direction; the usual marble floors and creamy walls; a series of mahogany doors, each one marked with a number.

'A hotel.' Just as I guessed. And pretty up-market, judging by the décor.

The next flight of steps sweeps round in a majestic arc, widening out before it gracefully delivers me to the ground floor. And that's when I falter, momentarily overwhelmed by the sight of windows stretching the entire height of two storeys, flooding what must be the main lobby with brilliant sunshine.

I squint, adjusting my eyes to the brightness, then turn my attention to other details: a massive chandelier overhead; an open doorway to the left; a marble desk and double doors to my right; a couple of leather sofas straight ahead. Hidden behind a newspaper, and clearly oblivious to my entrance, there's a man lounging on one of them. Thankfully, not Sebastian, judging by his shoes and trousers.

As quietly as I can, I pad towards the reception desk, and pause again. This time, I'm mesmerised by a series of portraits on the wall in front of me, more than slightly unnerved by the way I'm pinned down by every single pair of eyes. 'What are you doing?' they seem to ask. 'Go back upstairs, you fool. You're safe up there.'

But I'm far too intrigued to back off.

Instead, I focus on the desk, taking in a leather-bound book, a silver pen, and a tidy pile of black calling cards. Keen to uncover a clue to where I am, I pick up a card and study it. On one side, I find nothing more than three incomprehensible words inscribed in swirling silver writing: 'Nosce te ipsum.' On the other, a telephone number.

A rustling draws my attention back to the seating area. The newspaper's lowered now, revealing a dark-haired, grey-eyed man who, by the cut of his black suit and his languid self-assuredness, is another of these well-to-do types. In no particular rush, he lays the paper on the coffee table.

'Know thyself,' he says, the trace of a French accent lacing his voice.

'Pardon?'

'The card. It's Latin. It means "know thyself".'

'Does it?' I put it down.

'Quite pretentious, don't you think?'

'I don't know.' I glance at the portraits. 'Is that the name of this place?'

The man gets to his feet. Slim, lithe and handsome, he's about the same height as Sebastian, but maybe a little older. He comes to join me. 'This place doesn't have a name, but it's generally referred to as The Club.' He looks down at my feet. 'No shoes?'

Completely thrown, I follow his gaze. 'No. But I've got shoes... I just didn't... I didn't put them on...' God, I'm rambling.

'I've not seen you before. Are you new here?' Clearly entertained by the bare-footed, clueless woman in front of him, he offers a hand.

Automatically, I do the same. 'No. I mean yes.'

Firm, cold fingers enclose mine.

'Christophe Dupont. Pleased to meet you.'

'Evie.' I'm so befuddled by everything, it's a miracle I remember the latest alias.

'Evie?' He releases me. 'Are you a guest or a new member?'

'A guest. Sebastian's guest.'

'How strange.' His lips lift at the corners. 'Sebastian doesn't often have guests.'

'No?'

'And when he does, it's usually family.'

Not the typical behaviour of a playboy. 'Oh.'

'Perhaps I could get you a drink?' He motions to an open doorway. As if on cue, laughter erupts from what must be a bar.

'No, thank you. I'm fine.' Except I'm not. I'm feeling exposed, completely vulnerable. 'Is Sebastian around?'

'He went out with Celine. Over to the lodges, I think. I've heard he's having them redecorated.'

'Okay.'

With a nervous nod, I move past Christophe and take a look through the windows. They give out over the car park I've already seen from above. And beyond that, the driveway. I could be out of here within seconds, making my escape before Sebastian's any the wiser. Three days ago, I wouldn't have given it a second thought. But now...

'You're quite interested in the car park.' Christophe's voice comes from my side.

'I like a nice car.'

'Plenty of those here.'

Indeed. Plenty of very nice cars. And well-tended grass too. And a bar. *Of course...*

'This is a golf club.'

90

'Golf?' My companion bursts into laughter. 'Mon Dieu. Little balls and little holes. No. Not a golf club.'

Okay. 'What is it then?'

'You really don't know?'

'No.'

'He hasn't told you?'

'No.'

'I wonder why.' He narrows his eyes. 'Tell me something, Evie. How long have you been here?'

'Four days.'

'And this is the first time you've come downstairs?'

'Yes.'

'Curiouser and curiouser.'

'I must have been downstairs for a start...' I drift into silence, because I'm sounding distinctly weird now.

'You must have been downstairs?'

'Before I went upstairs.'

'Naturally. Unless you can fly.'

I'd better clear this up.

'I was drunk when I got here. So, I don't really remember... much.'

'Oh dear.' He frowns. 'May I ask you something, Evie?'

'Of course.'

'How did you meet Sebastian?'

'How?' I fumble through my brain, and plump for the obvious. 'At a posh nightclub. In London.' I just wish I could come up with a name, something to make my story a little more convincing, because it's obvious Christophe doesn't believe me.

'That's unusual.'

'Is it?' My brows furrow. 'How?' After all, I'm pretty sure it's a typical playboy's MO: go to posh nightclub, pick up woman, take her home.

'Like I said, his usual guests are family.'

'Oh.'

'In fact, Sebastian's become a bit of a recluse lately.'

'He has?'

'He's been to see his uncle, but apart from that, he rarely leaves the grounds.'

Suddenly, it all adds up. By his own admission, he hasn't been close to a woman in a long time. And he's cut himself off from his brother too. So, why wouldn't he isolate himself from everyone else? These must be some of those poor decisions Celine referred to.

'He probably fancied a bit of a change.' For no apparent reason, I gesture to the car park, and inwardly wince.

'Very strange.'

Feeling more uncomfortable by the second, I'm on the verge of a quick 'See you later' and a hasty retreat upstairs, when he decides to change tack.

'I still can't believe you don't know what this place is.'

It's enough to stamp out all thoughts of flight. I give a little shrug.

'I daresay Sebastian was planning to tell you in his own time.'

'Tell me what?' I'm going nowhere now, because he's got me hooked.

'I hope you're not a prude.'

'No, I'm not.' Although I am suddenly in possession of a distinct sense of foreboding. 'What is it?'

'I think it's best you see for yourself. Come. I'll give you a little tour.'

Like a mesmerised child trotting happily behind the Pied Piper, I follow him to the rear of the building. Passing through a set of doors to the left of the desk, we enter a curved corridor where Christophe comes to a halt, next to another set of mahogany doors.

'If you've led a sheltered life, you might want to brace yourself.' Warning issued, he pushes open the doors and waits for me to enter.

Cautious now, I descend a set of steps into a huge, circular space, surrounded by a series of windows. I take a few moments to examine the domed ceiling: seemingly decorated with classical frescos; a series of nude, writhing bodies. And then, I begin to make sense of what's below. To my left and right, huge sumptuous-looking beds encircle the entire room. In front of me, there's a raised area, bordered by couches. And right at the centre...

'What the...?' My heartbeat begins to race.

'The Circle.' Christophe comes to my side. 'It used to be a ballroom once upon a time, but it hosts a different type of dancing now.' He smiles at my expression. 'Communal coitus,' he explains, as if it's nothing out of the ordinary. 'This is a place for performing and observing. It's the star of the show, if you like. But there's so much more to The Club. Private rooms. Jacuzzis. Specialised areas.'

'It's a sex club,' I murmur, stating the glaringly obvious.

'A very expensive, elite sex club,' Christophe elaborates. Stepping up onto the central dais, he touches a large, free-standing wooden cross, set at an angle. 'You know what this is?'

'I think so.'

'A St Andrew's Cross.' He moves again.

'Right.' I follow him.

'And this is a spanking bench.'

He runs a palm over the leather seat, and I wonder why he feels the need to educate me. After all, he must know it's not putting me at my ease.

'Not sure what this is called.' He approaches what looks like a heavy-duty clothes rack. 'But you can dangle a person from it in a range of positions and treat them to various sensations ... all with their consent, of course.' And now, to the next piece of equipment. 'This is referred to as a licking chair.'

Suppressing the urge to let out a 'Yuk', I still can't prevent a disgusted grimace.

'And that's a spreader bench over there.'

'Okay.' I raise a hand. I've already heard enough. Stunned by it all, I can do little more than gawp at a second rack; this one displaying a range of manacles, chains and whips. 'Jesus. I thought I was staying in a hotel.'

'That's not too far from the truth. You can stay overnight, eat in the restaurant, relax in the grounds. These...' He waves a hand. 'Are the sundry, added extras.'

Falling silent, he gives me time to wander round and scrutinise one sundry, added extra after another. I run my hands over leather, wood and metalwork, my pulse clattering and clanging like faulty pipework. By the time I return to the heavy-duty clothes rack, I'm ready to scurry off and hide in a dark corner.

'Does it bother you?' Christophe asks.

My throat constricts. 'I don't know.'

An honest response. After all, I've only ever heard about places like this, and the people who frequent them. It's always been so distant from my world, it might as well have been fiction. But now it's right in front of me – an incontrovertible, absolute and concrete fact – I really don't know what to feel.

'Come.' Holding out a hand, he seems to sense I've seen enough of the Circle. 'I think you should see another side to The Club.'

Leaving the den of iniquity behind, I follow him gladly. Once outside the doors, instead of returning to the lobby, he gently encourages me to follow him round the curved corridor, stopping at the first door we come to on the left.

He knocks. 'These are usually empty at this time of day, but you can't be too careful.' Raising an eyebrow, he opens the door and leads me inside. 'This is for people who prefer privacy.'

It takes a few moments for my eyes to adjust to the gloom. I'm in a smaller space now, dimly lit by wall lights and maybe twenty feet by thirty. At the opposite side to the door, there's a window giving out over The Circle. A built-in wardrobe sits at the far end, complete with mirrored doors. To the left, there's a huge bed; and in between the two, another St Andrew's cross, a spanking bench, and some sort of weird leather hammock. After quickly taking it all in, I decide it's time to gather more information.

'So,' I venture. 'Sebastian owns this place?'

'Yes.'

I'm not sure I want the answer to the next question, but it still needs to be asked. 'And he's into this sort of thing?'

'Yes.'

'The Circle?'

'No. He's more of a one-on-one type of man, or so I've heard. Not an exhibitionist.'

Thank goodness for small mercies.

But still...

All the time I thought he was working, he must have been down here, availing himself of the facilities. And worse than that, while I thought we were getting close, he was obviously doing nothing more than sizing me up for a bout of kinky, no-strings coitus. It certainly explains all the flirting; not to mention the strange selection of books.

Christophe prowls the room. 'Forgive me, but you don't seem to know very much about your host.'

'No.' I don't know the first thing about him. Just like he said. And now, I feel like a fool.

'Seems he's been a little remiss.'

He certainly has. 'What can you tell me?'

'Plenty.' He stills.

Good. Because knowledge is power, and all that. I hold out a hand, palm upwards, inviting Christophe to share a little.

'Where would you like me to start?' he asks.

'What's his last name?' Seems like a decent place.

'Delaney. He's the youngest son of Phillip Delaney, owner of DelCorp.' He searches my face for a reaction. 'You have heard of DelCorp?'

94

'I...' There's something lurking in the recesses of my memory. 'Yes, but...'

'The biggest media and communications organisation in Europe?'

'Okay.' *Shit.*

'Television, newspapers, telecommunications.' He pauses. 'Your host is an extremely wealthy man.'

'Right.' I scan the equipment. An extremely wealthy man with an extremely deviant taste in sexual matters. I focus back on Christophe.

'You don't seem impressed.'

'Am I supposed to be?'

'Most women are.'

'I'm not most women.' And I have another question. 'Does Sebastian work at DelCorp?'

'No. He leaves all that to his brother. He was never really interested in the company. When he was younger, he was something of a playboy. Luxury yachts, private jets, expensive holidays. His father indulged him with a healthy allowance. But he dropped all that a few years ago, about the same time he got this place.' He runs a hand over the leather seat. 'I suppose you could say he moved on from the lifestyle, but couldn't quite give up the sex. He still manages to quench his thirst for women here. In fact, it's the perfect venture for him. Sex on demand. And his particular brand of sex at that.'

'Meaning?'

'The rough kind.'

'Rough?' There's a prickling at the nape of my neck. I'm about to make my escape, retreat to my castle in the sky and process this new information, when a deep, silky voice cuts across the silence.

'What's going on?'

Christophe looks over my shoulder. 'Oh. Hello, Seb. Good to see you.'

'I said, what's going on?'

I turn, slowly.

Sebastian's eyes flick from Christophe to me, then back again. My legs threaten to give way, and I quake inside, because I've never seen him like this before: all lean and mean, and seriously pissed off. He's nothing like the carefree man who left me this morning.

'I'm just giving your guest a quick tour,' Christophe explains. 'I bumped into her in the lobby. She seemed quite confused about where she was, so I've put her straight.'

MANDY LEE

'I think my guest has been leading you a merry dance. But thank you for your help.' Sebastian steps aside. 'I'll take over from here.' An insincere smile appears on his face. He waits in stony silence.

Frozen to the spot, I watch as Christophe takes his leave.

Closing the door behind him, Sebastian flicks a lock, and floors me with a question.

'How did you get out?'

Chapter Ten

The air crackles. My heart races and trips. My mouth's suddenly dry. I throw a glance at the spanking bench, sense a delicious twinge between my legs, and somehow manage to squeeze out a question.

'It wasn't you?'

'What wasn't me?'

'You didn't...' My lungs contract. I wrestle them back under control. 'You didn't leave the door open?'

'Clearly not.'

So, he had no intention of letting me out, no wish to reveal anything about the club. And given my reaction to his selection of reading matter, that's probably because he thinks I'm a complete prude.

'But it was open,' I babble, quickly taking in a rack of manacles. 'The front door was open. I thought you did it. I thought you trusted me.'

He moves closer, and I catch my breath in the face of this silent, simmering, utterly delectable man. He's effortlessly hot whatever he's doing, morning, noon and night. But when he's angry, the heat levels verge on volcanic. No sane female could bear it for long, and I certainly can't. Which is a huge surprise, considering what I've been through in the past. I look away, survey my surroundings, and wonder at the myriad of reactions kicking off in my body. Now the initial shock's worn off – and Christophe's out of the equation – I'm suddenly turned on by this room of kink.

'I don't trust you,' he says. 'Not that much. Not yet.' Giving me a short period of respite, he digs his mobile out of his jeans pocket, keys in a contact and speaks in a low growl. 'Where are you?' He listens to an answer. 'Apart from you, who else has keys to my apartment?' He listens again. 'Right. Get the lock changed. New keys for you and me. Not Celine.'

Celine. I just about manage to cling onto that thought as he ends the call, slips the phone back into his pocket and begins to study me. It makes absolute sense that she's the one who left the door open. She wanted me to see the truth about the club, wanted to give me the willies, good and proper... because she's determined to see me run.

Feeling distinctly uneasy, I eye the door.

'Don't even think about it,' he warns. 'You won't get far.'

'Okay,' I half squeak.

'What did you say to Christophe?'

I open my mouth, and close it again. What did I say to Christophe? And why the hell am I feeling so horny? For the life of me, I can't work it out. I'm surrounded by kinky contraptions, facing off with a man who – according to all evidence, and in spite of his earlier denial – must be a devotee of depraved sexual practices. Although I've never in my life gone down this route, out of nowhere, I'm champing at the bit, totally up for it, teetering on the edge of begging him to just take me now, any way he wants.

'Did you, by any chance, tell him you're being kept here against your will?'

I shake my head, furiously, and try not to fixate on his lips. But they're so soft, so full of promise...

'Why not?' he presses.

'I don't know.' Which is completely true. It didn't even cross my mind.

'And why didn't you run?'

'Why?' Because I'm safe here. Because he won't harm me. Because he intrigues me like no one else. Because I'm not wearing any shoes. But I say none of those things. Instead, I opt for a quick shrug.

'You had your chance, and you didn't take it. I wonder what's going on in that brain of yours.' He walks over to the window and looks out over The Circle. 'Okay. So, what did Christophe tell you?'

I'm breathing faster now. Even from behind, there's something new about his demeanour, something edgy – dangerous even – as if he's ready and primed to pounce. It knocks me completely off-balance.

'He... said...'

He turns slowly, shoulders taut. 'Get on with it.'

'He told me what this place is.' I wave a hand at the window. 'Not that I needed an explanation.' I can practically hear the wobble in my voice. 'You own a sex club.'

'What of it?' Leaning to one side, he flicks a switch. While a thick, black curtain sweeps across the window, shutting out the view of The Circle, he prowls back to me.

'What of it?' I swallow hard. 'You might have told me...'

'What difference does it make?'

Every difference. Because it proves beyond doubt he's a man who wouldn't know a relationship if it slapped him in the face.

'No answer?' His lips quirk.

But then again, why should I care? After all, I'm in no position for that sort of thing.

'I don't know what to say,' I admit. 'I'm in shock.'

'Which is why I kept you away from all this.' He folds his arms. 'What else did Christophe tell you?' As if he's limbering up for something, he stretches his neck to one side, then the other.

'Your name. Your full name.'

'Anything else?'

'He told me...' Oh, for God's sake. How can I think straight at a time like this? With the lust monster freed from a lengthy hibernation, it's causing all sorts of physical chaos... and firmly shoving any qualms about casual sex to one side. 'About your brother – about DelCorp.'

His dark eyes flash. He laughs quietly, moves closer. 'So now you think you know it all.'

'I know enough, Mr Delaney.' More than slightly annoyed by his supercilious tone, I'm suddenly determined to irritate him.

'I hope you don't think that gives you an advantage.'

'Of course it gives me an advantage.' But how does it give me an advantage? That's the question. Grappling for anything, I voice the first idiotic reason that comes to mind. 'There'll be no dumping me in a backstreet now.'

A hard smile appears. He moves closer still. 'Why not?'

'Because...' A host of heavenly tingles erupt in my core. 'I could just track you down, come crawling back to annoy you. Knowledge is power, and all that. I could go to the police with what I know.'

'But you wouldn't.' He studies me for a moment. 'If I had to take a guess, I'd say you're the type to steer clear of the police.'

I open my mouth to complain, but don't get very far. Lightning quick, he places an index finger on my lips.

And I shiver.

'And even if you did go to them,' he continues, sternly, 'I very much doubt they'd believe your story. You see, it's your word against mine, and I'm a Delaney. You wouldn't stand a chance.' Slightly, very slightly, he increases the pressure against my lips. 'Money is power, Evie. Money and connections.' He leans in. The air between us fizzles with some unseen force. 'Now, let's be honest, shall we? It doesn't matter that you know my name, or where I live. It makes absolutely no difference to your position.' He withdraws the finger.

And I take my chance. 'If it makes no difference, then why didn't you just tell me?'

'Leverage. Not to mention the fact that I was enjoying our little game.'

I blink in confusion. 'It was a game?'

'Of course. But now it's over.'

'Which means you don't need my name anymore.'

He brings his face to mine. 'I didn't say that.'

I don't know if it's the hunger in his eyes or the way he's standing, clearly primed and ready for action, but the lust monster takes it up a gear. He might still be demanding my real name, but I couldn't care less. All I know is I'm overheating and my brain's swirling, and there's an intense throbbing at the apex of my thighs. The scent of his skin, the raw masculinity looming over me, the absolute power ready to be unleashed: it all comes together in a wonderfully intoxicating brew that quickly transforms me into a wanton hussy. It's little wonder I can't help my next actions. Tipping my head back, I run my tongue over my lower lip.

'Trying to seduce me again, Evie?' he asks, his voice low and husky.

'Isn't it the other way round, Sebastian?' I smile, defiantly.

'Don't do that.'

'What?'

'Challenge me.'

'Why not?'

He stares at my mouth. 'I warned you,' he whispers. 'I'm not good with temptation.'

Excitement levels triple in an instant. He just needs another prod.

'I'm so scared.'

'You should be. Because if I kiss you, it won't stop there.'

'In all likelihood…' I gulp. 'I wouldn't want it to.'

'Is that so?'

'Probably.'

That does it. At the speed of light, I'm drawn into a tight embrace. Just as soft and warm as I thought they'd be, his lips cover mine. Before I know it, our tongues are entwined, igniting a passion that deepens so quickly, it's soon on the cusp of ferocity.

After an absolute age, he pulls back. 'Well?'

'Feel free,' I gasp, 'to carry on.'

It's an invitation he's keen to accept. Before I know it, he's delivering a second kiss: just as long as the first, but twice as intense; and executed with all the self-assurance of a world-renowned expert. It's not long before he moves on to the next stage of his offensive. Bringing his right hand to the back of my neck, he holds me firmly in place while his left hand presses my groin to his. It's enough to wipe my mind of all logical thought. Before long, there's an overwhelming rush of warmth throughout my core. By the time he's finished, I'm almost certain my legs are about to fold.

'A little heads-up.' He gives my left buttock a squeeze. 'We're doing this my way.'

'Which is?' I don't know why I'm even asking.

'Take a look around. Make an educated guess.'

I do as he suggests, raking over the spanking bench, the cross, the weird rack. My heartbeat falters.

'If you want to change your mind...' He skims a finger down my arm. 'This would be a good time.'

I have no idea why he'd want me to back out, but it's the last thing I intend to do, even though my brain seems have disconnected from my body, and my lungs have taken on a life of their own. I'm amazed I can even breathe, let alone force out an entire sentence.

'You pays your money, you takes your choice.' I tip my head back.

Immediately, he leans in and nips my earlobe.

I cry out in surprise.

'You think you hold all the cards, don't you?' Another nip. Another cry. 'It won't last long, Evie. I can assure you of that.'

Pressing his body against mine, he backs me up until I feel something behind me: a firm, padded surface.

'The St Andrew's Cross.' He brushes his lips across mine. 'My own personal favourite.'

I drag in a few unsteady breaths.

'My way,' he reminds me.

'Your way.' Which is rough, according to Christophe. And judging by the contents of this room, probably rooted in the world of BDSM. Four letters I've seen together plenty of times before. B for bondage. D for discipline or domination. All well and good. It's the final two letters that bother me, especially on the back of my recent reading material.

'I read some of *The Story of O* today.' And I'm thinking of whips, a woman stripped and used, flogged until she's raw, her cries for mercy ignored. 'Are you like that?'

'Like what?'

'Into... you know... sadomasochism?'

'Not my style.'

'Control, then? All that "I'm the master, don't look at me" crap.'

'I like to be in control, but a woman can look where she likes and say what she wants.' He cocks his head. 'Maybe I shouldn't have included that particular book.'

'You have read it then?'

'Yes.' His eyes flash. 'But I don't demean women. I do bondage, and pleasure.'

'But pain? Is there going to be pain?'

'Only if you want it.' He takes hold of my chin, kisses me, then nips at my bottom lip.

I jolt in surprise. 'What sort of pain?'

'The sort you can easily withstand.'

'I've never...'

'Then I won't.'

'But...'

'Then I will.' He watches me closely. 'For some people, believe it or not, it adds to the pleasure.'

'It does?'

He nods.

And I reel from yes to no, and back again.

'Okay.' I raise my chin. 'I'll give it a try.' *Oh Lord, what am I letting myself in for?* 'But I'll need a safeword,'

He laughs. 'You've done this before?'

'No.'

'Didn't think so.'

'But I've heard about it.'

'So you know how it works. If you don't like what I do, you say 'red', and I stop. Understand?'

A sensible little voice pipes up from the deepest, dustiest recesses of my brain, politely asking me why I'm letting myself in for this. Drowned out by lust and curiosity, it gets no answer.

'Yes.'

With a nod, he steps back and takes hold of my sweatshirt. 'Let's get rid of this offensive item. Hands up.'

In one swift movement, he lifts the sweatshirt over my head and throws it to the floor. And while he spends the next few seconds admiring my torso, my nerves decide to play up big style. Within seconds, I'm jittering like a washing machine on spin cycle. I'm about to retreat into full self-protection mode when he tugs down my right bra cup, leans in and begins to suck at the nipple. That does the trick. Nerves dismissed, I close my eyes and dig my fingers into his hair, overwhelmed by a flood of sensations that erupt from my groin and radiate outwards. I'm already wet through down below when he pulls away.

With a dark smile, he reaches round with both arms, unfastening my bra with such masterful ease, it's clear he's done this a million times. I hold my breath while he slowly draws the straps down my arms, colour under his gaze as he drops the bra, gasp and groan as he reaches out to brush a finger across my left nipple, trailing it around the areola, again and again. Finally, he moves the same finger down the centre of my torso and over my stomach, bringing it to the top of my jeans.

Every inch in control, he unfastens the zip, parts the fabric and gets onto his knees. And then, taking his time, he lowers the jeans over my hips, raising an eyebrow at the granny pants as the denim slowly crumples at my feet. As soon as I step out of them, he discards the jeans. Placing a big hand to the outside of each hip, he examines the pants again.

'What, in God's name, are these?'

'Celine bought them.'

'That woman.' He slips both index fingers into the waistband. 'She's definitely got a problem with you.'

'Or just a bad taste in knickers.'

He glances up, then moves into the final stage of the revelation, easing my knickers all the way to my feet and throwing them to one side with a disgusted sneer. Fixing his attention on my crotch, he blows out a quiet whistle.

'Nice.'

I cross my arms in front of myself. Immediately, he takes hold of my wrists and manoeuvres my arms back to my sides.

'No shame. You're a beautiful woman. Don't be embarrassed.' He stands again. 'Hands up.'

Sensing a glorious twinge between my thighs, I do as I'm told, watching as he closes the space between us, pressing his crotch against mine and urging me back against the leather. He wraps his fingers around my left wrist and moves my hand out to the side. Unable to tear my eyes from his face, I feel the cold touch of the metal on skin, hear a click as the cuff's fastened. He repeats the process with my right hand.

'I've got you now.' He places his hands over mine and makes eye contact. I see no warmth. It's as if he's withdrawn. 'What's your safeword?'

'Red.'

'Say that word, and I'll stop the pain.' He squeezes my right nipple, maintaining the tension until my legs weaken. 'But not the pleasure.' Leaving me bound in place, he walks away.

It takes a few seconds for my head to clear. 'Hang on.' I tug at the bindings. 'I thought a safeword was to stop everything.'

'Usually.' Coming to a halt, he turns and strips off his t-shirt.

I spend a few moments drinking it all in, the sight of his broad shoulders and perfect six-pack. 'Pain and pleasure.'

'Usually.' He rolls his shoulders, flexes his muscles and lowers his head. When he looks up again, everything about him seems to have hardened. And it turns me on big time.

'What's going on?'

'Slight change of plan.' Clearly satisfied with his efforts, he prowls back to me. 'My God, you're beautiful.' He touches a fingertip against my right shoulder and skims it across my collar bone. 'I've wanted to fuck you from the first moment I saw you.'

'The first moment you saw me, I was puking.'

'Ah, yes.' He suppresses a smile. 'Correction. I've wanted to fuck you from the first moment I saw you sober.' He traces the finger downwards, at an excruciatingly slow pace, over my breasts, across my nipples.

I drag in a ragged breath. 'You didn't answer my question. What's going on?'

'Isn't it obvious?' He unfastens his jeans.

'No. That's why I'm asking.'

'I'm about to get the truth out of you.' He draws the jeans over his hips.

'What?'

The jeans drop to the floor. He shrugs them off, leaving him in nothing but designer underpants. 'The truth,' he says nonchalantly.

'But you can't use sex like that.'

'I don't know if you've noticed, but you're all tied up. I can do what I like.'

'That's breaking the rules.'

'What rules?' Slowly, tantalisingly, as if he's putting on a show, he removes the pants, kicks them to one side, and straightens up. 'I'm not a fan of rules.'

'But ...'

'If you don't like what's going on, just say no. There's still time.'

I should say no, but I can't seem to. Largely because I'm fixated on his cock, which is definitely something to write home about. And to be perfectly honest, I don't want to say no, seeing as he's worked

Y

me up into a sexual lather and rendered me a horny black hole of lust. I want the pleasure ... and maybe a little bit of the pain. Which is why I clamp my lips together.

'Then we have an understanding.' He closes in on me. 'I'll pleasure you to within an inch of your life, fuck you halfway into next week, and you'll sing like a canary.'

'I wouldn't bet on it.'

'I'm not the betting type.'

'Sebastian...'

'You can call me Seb.' An eyebrow arches. 'Seeing as we're about to become very intimate.' It arches some more. 'Now, spread your legs. Time to see what you can take.'

As soon as I comply, he drops to his knees, attaching my ankles to the lower bindings, and spreading my legs further in the process. When he's done, he leans in, grabs me by the hips, and brings his mouth to my crotch. Immediately, I'm straining against the bonds, groaning quietly at the touch of his tongue against my clitoris. Swirling and pressing against the little nub of nerves, it quickly conjures up an exquisite warmth in my groin. Gradually working me up into a mess of anticipation, it goes on for an age, with no sign of a change of tack. I'm beginning to think this is the full extent of Mr Delaney's foreplay when his right hand leaves my hip, and a finger enters me.

As if it's in possession of its own personal roadmap to my nether regions, the finger homes in on precisely the right spot. With his tongue still swirling away at the nub, he begins to work me up from the inside too. In a split second, the warmth increases, spreading through muscle, sinew and nerve. It leaves me desperate to bring my legs together, especially when it's joined by an insistent pressure that quickly reaches breaking point, giving way to the kind of orgasm I never knew existed. Wave after wave of wicked contractions ripple through my core, a thousand tiny charges of electricity in their wake.

'Oh, god,' I cry, expecting him to bring me down.

But he doesn't. Instead, he waits for the ripples to calm before starting again, bringing me back to the edge and mercilessly tipping me over into a second climax.

'Now...' He leans back, withdraws the finger, and smiles in satisfaction. 'Give me your name.'

On the verge of hyperventilating, I blink down at him. 'Evie.'

'Wrong answer.'

'Mary.'

'Wrong again.'

'Sharon.'

'Don't push it.'

Closing in again, he returns his tongue to my clitoris. Using two fingers now, he slows the pace for the third assault, producing an end result that's all the more earth-shattering. With the pressure verging on unbearable, warmth becomes heat; a pulsating ball of energy that finally shatters into a thousand pieces.

'Name,' he demands again.

'Rita.'

I hear him tut before he returns to his mission. A lifetime later, I spin off into sexual oblivion; a sweaty, mindless, trembling wreck. When I finally manage to claw my way back to reality, I'm surprised to find him kneeling back on his haunches. Evidently, he's decided to give up. And I'm relieved... because I really couldn't have taken much more.

'Are you even human?' he asks.

'Very human,' I confirm. 'Maybe you're just not as good as you think you are.'

'Oh, I'm good.' He rises to his feet. 'Maybe we just need a different tactic.' His eyes harden in the gloom. 'Remember... you agreed to this.'

'To what?'

'If you want me to stop, just say the word.'

'What are you going on about now?'

I get no answer.

Without any further discussion, the fingers are back inside me, probing and stroking, pressing all the right buttons. But this time, to add to the mayhem, he leans in and takes my left nipple between his teeth. Blind-sided by a myriad of sensations, I moan incoherently, and brace myself for the pain. It's not long in coming. He bites hard, maintaining the tension while I swallow back the urge to scream.

'You like that?'

Do I? 'I think so.'

'Not good enough.' He repeats the process. 'What do you say now?'

'Yes.' I gulp, completely surprised by my own answer. 'I like that.'

'I wonder why.'

'I don't know.' Perhaps it's because this is a different kind of pain, the sort I can stop at any moment; a pain that consumes me and makes me forget. 'Anyway, it doesn't matter. What matters is why you like dishing it out.'

'I know exactly why I like dishing it out. It's all about control.' He brushes his lips across mine. 'Tell me something, Evie. Who's holding the cards now?'

'You.' I have no problem admitting it. After all, it's the truth.

'Say it again.'

'You.'

'Louder.'

'You,' I growl. 'You're the one in control. Happy now?'

'Almost.'

He moves to the other nipple, biting and sucking, mixing pleasure with pain until I'm no longer sure where one begins and the other ends. At last, I'm breaking into another sweat, and absolutely certain I've reached my limit.

'Red! Red, red, red!'

He stops.

'You shouldn't...' Lowering my head, I release a ragged laugh. 'You shouldn't have given me a way out. I've got you beaten.'

'Hardly.' He raises my face to his. 'It just means we go back to the pleasure. And there's no stopping that.' He dips down and releases my ankles. I'm fully expecting him to unbuckle my wrists. Instead, he takes a packet of condoms from his jeans pocket.

'I should have known.' I laugh again.

'Known what?'

'Condoms. You must go everywhere with them.'

'Nope.' He rips open the packet. 'I don't usually bother.'

'But you've got them now.'

'For you.' He drops the wrapper and rolls the condom onto his cock. 'I told you, Evie. I've wanted to fuck you for a few days now.' Job complete, he looks up. 'And I like to be prepared.'

'I bet you do.'

Receding behind a façade, he stretches his neck, flexes his shoulders, and fixes his eyes on mine. With all traces of humour despatched, he's serious now, and completely remote: nothing like the Sebastian I've come to know.

He closes in on me and places his hands over my wrists. 'A word of warning. I don't do gentle.'

'That's fine.' I smile sweetly, because I already know as much. And what's more, I don't particularly care. Thanks to his masterful attentions, I'm zinging with anticipation. I'll take it any way it comes.

Maintaining the eye contact, he nudges my legs apart, removes his right hand from my wrist, and guides himself in.

'Put your legs around my waist.'

As soon as I comply, he brings the same hand to my buttocks, holding me tight while he slides further in, allowing me time to get used to his size. Gauging my every reaction, he adjusts his position, probing further until he's completely buried in me. He pauses for a few seconds, then moves just a little, causing a hoard of shimmering sensations to spark in my core.

'Like that?'

'God, yes.'

There's a momentary crack in the veneer – the briefest ghost of a smile – before he withdraws to the tip and penetrates again. The shimmers increase exponentially.

'I thought this was going to be rough.'

'Just preparing the ground.' He withdraws again.

As he drives back in, my entire body threatens to liquefy. 'Holy shitty shit!'

His eyes flash with amusement. He blinks it away.

'And now, we're ready.'

His left hand tightens over my wrist, his right hand on my bottom. He withdraws for a second time, pauses, then begins to thrust hard. It's not long before muscles contract and spasm inside. But he gives me no respite. Instead, he carries on pounding into me, causing a second orgasm to follow on the heels of the first.

'Name.'

I manage nothing but a shake of the head.

'Name.'

'No.'

Keeping up a steady rhythm, he pounds some more, repeatedly demanding my name while I repeatedly refuse. I'm on the verge of a third orgasm when he finally gives up.

'Fuck it,' he growls.

Clearly going in for the end game, he ramps up the power and tempo. It doesn't take long for my body to be consumed by yet more contractions. But this time, as soon as I come, he gives a few final thrusts and reaches his own climax.

'Fuck.' He digs his head into my neck.

I have no idea how long we stay like this, both of us wrestling our breath back under control while our bodies cool. When he finally makes a move and unfastens the manacles, it's my full intention to wrap my arms around him and drag him in for a kiss. But as soon as my feet touch the floor, my knees buckle.

An arm closes round me, and I'm drawn onto his lap, where I spend the next few minutes swimming about in a warm fug. When I finally manage to crawl back to the real world, I turn my face to his.

'You didn't get what you wanted,' I murmur, satisfied that I've held out against all the odds.

He draws back, receding yet again, studying me as if I'm some sort of rare oddity.

'No.' He seems troubled. 'But it's only a matter of time.'

Chapter Eleven

By the next afternoon, I'm troubled too. Reclining on a lounger, an unread book next to me and my face turned to an azure sky, I just wish my mood could lift to match the weather. But there's no chance of that. With yesterday's events still bothering me, I'm a world away from contentment, raking back through what happened on a frustratingly endless loop.

I certainly got what I wanted – an exhilarating dose of shock and awe in its purest form. But at the end of the day, it was nothing more than gratification of the senses, which has never proved enough for me. The truth is, no matter what I wanted in the heat of the moment, it didn't miraculously transform me into a worldly-wise pleasure-seeker with zero interest in connection. While I'm only too aware this can only ever be a temporary dalliance, I still need some kind of intimacy.

And yesterday, I got nothing of the sort.

He might have told me to call him Seb, and he might have kissed me like a starving man; but every single time he strayed too close, he backed off at the speed of light. And his post-coital behaviour was no improvement. After dressing in silence and ordering his staff to clear the lobby, he simply led me back upstairs and abandoned me for the rest of the day. Fully intending to have it out with him on his return, I waited for as long as I could. But with exhaustion finally getting the better of me, I had no option but to crawl off to bed and slump into misery. I have no idea when he came in, what time he went out this morning... or even if he spent the night in the apartment at all. And now, there's only one conclusion I can reach. Having grabbed what he wanted, he's pushing me away. It's as simple as that.

'Bastard.'

Determined to distract myself from any more unpalatable thoughts, I pick up the book and flick it open. I've just about managed to plough my way through an entire paragraph when my attention's drawn by the sound of the front door.

'Shit.' He's back.

Stomach churning, I drop the book and head inside for a confrontation. Only to find Celine at the front door, hands on hips, glaring down at a middle-aged man who's busy fiddling with the lock. Immediately, all traces of trepidation disappear, because even

110

though she's clearly in a grump, I'd much rather face Celine than Sebastian.

'Why am I not getting a key?' she demands.

A second man steps through the open doorway. 'Seb's decision. Speak to him.'

'But I've always had a key. And anyway, why does he need to change the locks?'

'Like I said, it's Seb's decision.'

With a disgruntled huff, Celine marches into the lounge and swings to a halt in front of me. 'Is this your doing?'

'Is what my doing?'

'Changing the locks?'

'Nothing to do with me.' I crane my neck to look over her shoulder.

The middle-aged man is on his knees now, but it's the second man who's demanding my attention. Tall, fair-haired and dressed in an expensive suit, he's possibly in his mid-thirties, definitely built like the proverbial brick shithouse, and almost certainly not someone to be messed with.

'Who's that?'

'A locksmith.'

'The younger man.'

'None of your business.'

'Does he work here?'

'Like I said, none of your business.'

'Okay.' I fix my attention back on Celine. 'So, where's Sebastian then? Or is that none of my business too?'

She blinks. 'You don't know?'

'Haven't seen him all morning.'

'And he didn't tell you where he was going?' She smiles. 'Interesting.' All is not well in the penthouse, and she knows it. 'If you must know, he's gone to see his uncle. The frail old man who owns an expensive ring.'

I decide to ignore the dig. 'Do you know when he'll be back?'

'No idea.'

I head for the kitchen.

'Pining for him?'

Wrestling back the urge to tell her to piss off, I swivel round. In spite of all the niggles, I am pining for him. I just hope it's not obvious. 'Don't be silly.'

'After what happened yesterday?'

'Nothing happened yesterday.'

'Pull the other one. You were in that room for over an hour.'

'And?'

'What happened?'

She thinks she has a right to know? 'Nothing much. He was just giving me a tour.' And if she thought the whole 'discovering I'm staying above a sex club' thing would freak me out, I hope she's disappointed.

'Just a tour? I don't think so.' She prowls towards me, emerald eyes darkening by degrees, and delivers a statement that's anything but classy. 'I think he fucked you.'

'Oh, really?'

'Really. And you're blushing. That's all the confirmation I need.'

Damn my traitorous cheeks.

'But don't think it makes any difference,' she warns. 'Remember what I told you.'

I remember every word. Which is why I'm bristling now. It's a fact that shouldn't trouble me, but she was right. With Sebastian, there can never be a happy ever after, because he's nothing more than a playboy, a flirt, a womaniser.

'Oh.' Celine raises a finger. 'And one more thing before I go. If you do any harm to Sebastian, any harm at all... I'll kill you.'

I'm not really sure why I burst out laughing. It's possibly down to the nerves. Or it could be the sudden vision of a skinny, self-contained, elegantly attired woman trying to bash out my brains with a pair of Manolo Blahniks. But whatever causes it, the outburst certainly has a desirable effect. With no further ado, Celine makes a stormy exit, leaving me alone with a sweaty locksmith and an intimidating stranger.

'Hi,' I smile, approaching the stranger. Now I'm up close, I can see a scar above his left eye, as if a knife's cut straight through his eyebrow.

'Morning.' He extends a hand. 'Alex Thompson.'

'Evie.' I shake the offered hand, and realise I'd better get myself a new surname. 'You work here?'

'Seb's Head of Security.'

'Oh, right.'

'If you need anything, just let me know.'

'Will do.' With another smile, I withdraw to the living area.

It doesn't take long for the locksmith to finish his job. As soon as I'm left alone again, with Celine's words and Sebastian's behaviour threatening to consume me, I opt to pass the time in the kitchen, indulging in my own personal form of meditation.

At first, I play about with three versions of a savoury soufflé, taking a few mouthfuls of each before carefully concealing the leftovers in the bin. Next, I experiment with a steak tartare, eating the whole lot. Finally, I decide to knock together a basic Thai green curry. I'm searching through the cupboards for rice when I become aware I'm not alone. Rice in hand, I shut the cupboard door and take in a tiny, surprised breath.

There he is, leaning against the wall at the far end of the kitchen, arms crossed, watching me from beneath hooded lids. The very embodiment of a brooding sex god, it's enough to send a shiver down my spine, and several electric shocks through my groin. Hands trembling, I put down the bag of rice and try to remember what I'm doing.

'How long have you been there?' I ask.

'Not long.'

'I've made a curry.' I wave at the hob. 'Thai green.'

He nods.

Uncomfortably self-conscious, I fill a pan with boiling water, add the rice and set a timer. I'd love to ask what's going through his mind, but my earlier resolve to confront him seems to have shrivelled into inexistence. Instead, I opt for a touch of harmless conversation.

'Celine said you went to see Hal.'

'I did.'

'How is he?' I pick up a spoon.

'Not good.'

I pause, the spoon hovering mid-air. 'What do you mean?'

'Very weak.'

'Oh.' I hesitate. 'So, when can I visit him?'

'I thought that was off the table.'

'Was it?' Of course it was. Because I took it off the bloody table the last time we spoke about the ring. I stir the rice, put down the spoon and turn to meet his gaze, which is no easy task, especially when his expression seems to darken. It's as if he's about to tell me to sling my hook. 'I'd still like to see him though, if that's possible.'

The words hover between us, flighty, edged with nerves, just waiting for a gruff order to pack my bags and disappear. While I bite my lip and wait for the inevitable brush-off, he nudges himself away from the wall.

'You can see him when I know you're trustworthy.' He heads for the fridge. 'Glass of wine?'

Does that mean I'm staying? 'Please.'

Desperately trying to calm myself – which isn't easy, seeing as I'm now fighting the temptation to do a little dance – I reheat the curry and wait. It's not long before I feel him behind me, sense a thrum of want as he leans round to place a glass of wine on the counter.

'Thank you.'

'You're welcome.' Taking a seat, he places his own glass in front of himself, and watches me some more.

I dish out the rice, almost forgetting to be messy about it, thanks to a rise in anxiety levels. Rice presented in the most amateur fashion possible, I dollop a good amount of curry onto each plate. 'There you go. Enjoy.'

The cutlery's in a pile at the side of the counter. Reaching for it at the same time, our fingers touch. And suddenly, I'm thinking about two sweaty bodies, going at it like hyperactive rabbits. I glance up at his face, and immediately know the contact's had a similar effect on him. A moment's awkwardness quickly gives way to action, and we set about eating.

At the first forkful, his eyebrows rise in appreciation. By the third or fourth, I detect a hint of suspicion. 'This is good,' he announces at the halfway point. 'Bloody delicious.' When he's cleared away every last morsel, he lays down his knife and fork and takes a sip of wine.

'Penny for them,' I prompt. 'Is it Hal?'

He gives no answer.

'You can talk to me about it... if it is Hal.'

'It's not.'

I drop my fork and clench my fists. My previous anxiety seems to have abandoned ship, forced over the side by this moody, uncommunicative man. And with nothing left in its wake but annoyance, I'm beginning to spoil for a fight.

'Well,' I grumble, 'this is fun.'

He puts down the glass and looks out of the window.

'If you don't want me around, I'm quite prepared to go. I've already told you that. But if you're going to insist on me staying, I'd rather not feel like this.'

'Like what?'

Used? Abused? Unwanted? Disposable? 'Inconvenient.'

'Is that how you feel?'

'Are you completely stupid?'

I glare into his eyes, finding them devoid of all emotion. It's a discovery that only serves to fire me up even further, fuelling an absolute determination to get my way. If I am staying, I'm not prepared to put up with moodiness. I want to know where I stand.

'Are you actually going to tell me what's going on?'

He shrugs.

'Oh, for God's sake.' I'm on the verge of abject fury, but someone's got to address the giant elephant in the room, and it might as well be me. 'I don't know if it's slipped your mind, but we had sex yesterday.'

He opens his mouth.

'Sex,' I repeat, virtually hissing the word. 'And you've been avoiding me ever since.'

'Have I?'

'Yes. It's like you're withdrawing, going inside yourself.'

'Safest place to be.'

'What on earth is that supposed to mean?'

He shakes his head.

'For crying out loud. What's the problem? Was it disappointing? Is that it?'

'No.'

I laugh, sarcastically. 'But it must have been. Because you didn't get what you wanted. You said so yourself.'

'It wasn't disappointing. Not by any stretch of the imagination.'

He takes in a deep breath. 'It was a mistake.'

One word. Knife-sharp. It pierces me to the core and leaves anger on the back-foot.

'Okay.' I blink.

'It shouldn't have happened.'

'That's the thing about mistakes.'

'I took advantage...'

No, no, no. I'm not having that. 'You gave me the option to refuse.'

'It doesn't matter.'

'Knock it off. You didn't take advantage. I knew exactly what I was getting into. Let's be honest, shall we? You got what you were after, and now you can't wait to get rid of me.'

'Don't be ridiculous.'

'I'm not being ridiculous.'

'You're getting it wrong.'

Oh boy. That does it. I'm furious again. In fact, I'm seething. 'Stop lying,' I growl. 'I can see right through you, Sebastian Delaney. It's obvious. You don't like women hanging around after you've been at them.'

'Stop.'

'I tell you what. Just open that door, and I'll do the honours.'

'Really?' He gives me a hard smile. 'You'd give up all of this?'

I spring to my feet and shove back the stool. 'Exactly what are you insinuating?'

'Exactly what do you think I'm insinuating?'

'That I'm after your money, that I know a good thing when I see it, that I'm a cynical, hard-hearted, money-grabbing bitch.'

With consummate self-control, he gets up and stalks round to my side of the counter. He's soon close enough for me to spot the first signs of real reaction: a deepening crease between the brows, a twitch of the lips, a dark storm brewing in the depths of those eyes.

I falter for a split-second, then haul myself back on track.

'Maybe I should remind you that I didn't choose to come here. You locked me in...'

'You had your chance.'

'And I didn't take it, because I was actually beginning to like you.'

'Oh, come on...'

'Yes. I've always had bad taste in men. And anyway, none of that matters any more, because I've seen your true colours. It's all been ruined by sex... as ever.'

'Enough.'

Oh, he's using his favourite word.

'Don't you dare order me around. I am not an employee. I'm... I'm...' Very much in danger of losing my thread. That's what I am. What was I about to say? 'I'd like to leave.' *Yes, that's it.*

'Oh, really? Why?'

'Because the lap of luxury's all very nice, but it's not exactly pleasant when you have to share it with a foul-tempered git.'

'Two things,' he snarls, clearly battling back a temper flare-up of his own. 'The ring and your name.'

'For fuck's sake. You're impossible.' There's nothing else for it. I stomp off to my room. 'And you've made me say that word out loud,' I shout back at him. 'And I fucking hate it when I say that word out loud!'

Making sure to slam the door behind me, I flop onto the bed and spend the next few minutes fighting off the temptation to tear down the chandelier. When I've finally managed to calm myself, I check the time.

Just after half seven. Far too early to go to sleep. Briefly, I toy with the idea of returning to the lounge for my book. But seeing as I haven't yet heard footsteps or the tell-tale bang of a door – and I don't particularly fancy an embarrassing, post-strop appearance in front of Sebastian – I decide it's best to stay put. And so, with nothing else to do, I opt for a good, long soak in the bath.

It should be an opportunity to relax. Instead, as soon as I lean back into the bubbles, I return to stewing over Sebastian's behaviour. For some unknown reason, I need to pin down exactly why he's transformed from the mysterious, playful enigma I was growing to like, into a grumpy sod who blows hot and cold.

Sponging myself down, I remind myself that the 'fickle playboy dumps used goods' theory is still likely to be the best bet. But considering his behaviour over dinner, there's now another option to choose from: Sebastian Delaney's a royally screwed-up mess who doesn't have the faintest clue what he wants. Dipping my head in the water, I tell myself to go for the first explanation. After all, that would give me the perfect excuse to cut my losses and run.

'But then again...'

As the water cools around me, I can't help mulling a little more over the second option. When I'm thoroughly pruned and equally frustrated, I get out, dry off, and don my silky pyjamas. And then, I crawl onto the bed, shuffling under the luxurious covers with an absolute determination not to stew any more. But no matter how much I try to shove him out of my head, Mr Delaney resolutely refuses to budge. In fact, he's still in residence when my eyelids begin to droop, the last thought before I slip into unconsciousness... and it's his face that dominates my dreams.

Chapter Twelve

When I jolt awake, it's almost four in the morning. Restlessness drives me from my bed, back out into the living area. With no sign of Sebastian, I retrace my path down the corridor and stop outside his room, tentatively pushing at the door to peek inside. As ever, the bedside lamp is on.

But the covers are pristine.

'Stayed up, did you?'

Backing out into the corridor, I make my way to the winding staircase at the end. By the time I come to the top, I know exactly where he spent the night: the door's slightly ajar, a soft light spilling out from inside. Wondering what on earth I'm going to find, I cross the threshold and immediately freeze. With one arm draped behind his head, fingers touching the metal balustrade behind him, he's fast asleep on the sofa. On the table next to him, a half-finished bottle of whiskey and an empty glass tell the whole story. He's been drowning his sorrows again, whatever those sorrows might be.

I inch forwards, watching the gentle rise and fall of his chest, satisfying myself he's in a deep slumber before I pause to examine his face. With his soft loft lips parted, and a slight tremor to the eyelids, he's obviously dreaming. But there's a deep frown etched into his forehead, as if he's trying to understand those dreams. For a moment or two, I wonder if this is the real Sebastian Delaney, because I'm certainly not gazing down at the self-assured playboy or the dominating sex-god, or even the angry grump. In fact, what I'm staring at is a jumble of contradictions, a maddening puzzle that needs to be cracked.

Which is why I scan the room, briefly considering the possibility of a quick rummage, only to reject it. He's probably locked everything away. And that's when the idea occurs to me. A risky idea: probably all shades of wrong and bordering on immoral. But it's nothing worse than what he tried on me.

Five minutes later, slightly out of breath and jittering with nerves, I'm creeping towards him again, this time wielding the set of handcuffs I've just retrieved from his wardrobe. With extreme care, I lean over, attaching one of the cuffs to the balustrade railing and his left wrist. Smiling at the result, I place the silver key on his desk, take a seat in an armchair... and wait.

I'm on the verge of nodding off when I'm shocked back to my senses. A crash jolts me awake. I blink, and blink again, watching the scene come into focus, illuminated by dawn: an overturned table; the remains of a whiskey bottle glimmering in a pool of amber liquid on the floor. I raise my eyes to the sofa and find Sebastian sitting bolt upright with one arm extended back to the railing. Wild-eyed, he stares at the mess, glances back at the cuffs, then focusses on me.

'What the fuck?' he growls.

What the fuck, indeed? What the fuck was I thinking setting this up? It's a bonkers situation. Not to mention downright dangerous, judging by the unexpectedly feral creature in front of me. But what's done is done. I'll just have to weather the storm.

'Morning,' I beam, although I'm quaking inside.

'What going on?' He bares his teeth.

'Erm...' With my composure on the verge of running for the hills, it's all I can do to hold it in place. 'It looks like I found a set of handcuffs and decided to use them.'

'Don't try to be funny.'

'I'm not.'

'Where's the key?'

'Right here.' I pick it up from the occasional table, brandish it and put it down again.

'Get these things off me.'

'All in due course.'

'Now.'

'No.'

'Evie, I'm warning you...'

'Don't waste your breath. I'm the one in control now.'

The next few seconds pass in silence. Although he's completely still, I can see the trouble brewing in his eyes, and I'm hardly surprised when it finally erupts. Accompanied by a slew of vicious swearwords, he tugs violently at the handcuffs.

'Seb, no!' I spring up from the chair and hold out a hand. 'Be careful. You'll hurt yourself.'

He tugs even harder.

'Stop it, Seb! For God's sake!'

'I'll stop when you let me go.'

I touch him on the shoulder, and quickly retreat. It seems to do the job. With another growl, he gives up on the tugging and sinks back on the sofa, breathing deep and fast.

'Those are decent cuffs,' I tell him. 'You won't break them. And I'm not letting you go until I get what I want.'

'And precisely what is it that you want?'

'We'll come to that when I'm good and ready.'

I don't know why I glance at his crotch. To be perfectly honest, it is amongst the things I want. But I'm not stupid enough to want it now.

'Don't even think about that.' He slaps his hand over his manhood.

'Oh, I see. It's fine for you to use sex as a weapon, but not vice-versa?'

'I'm not in the mood.'

'Me neither. Calm down.'

Thankfully, he does as he's told. When his breathing's finally back under control, he gives up on protecting his groin and checks his pockets.

'Your mobile's on the desk,' I inform him. 'And don't bother shouting for help. I've been told this place is soundproofed.'

'Very funny.' He grimaces. 'They'll miss me downstairs.'

'So what? Celine doesn't have a key anymore. And if Alex turns up, I'll just tell him you've got man-flu. That should give me a few days.'

'A few days?' His eyes widen. 'You wouldn't...'

'Please don't underestimate me, Sebastian. When you kidnap a woman and hold her prisoner, have sex with her and then blow her out, you've got to expect some comeback.'

'Comeback.' He mulls over the word. 'So, that's what this is all about? You're punishing me.'

'Not punishing. Just digging for information.' And I really should get on with it. Clapping my hands, I consider the options. 'Now, where to start?'

I really should have planned the interrogation, because if I had, there wouldn't currently be a lull in conversation.

'Listen to me,' he says, utterly calm now. While I've wasted precious time raking through my head for a decent way in, he's clearly taken the opportunity to regroup. 'Whatever you're after, this isn't the way to get it.'

'Maybe it is, and maybe isn't.' I shrug. 'But there's only one way to find out.'

'Evie, come on...'

'And anyway, what's good for the goose, is good for the gander.'

He scowls at the shards of glass on the floor.

120

'Oh, and one more thing,' I add. 'There are no rules.'

He raises his gaze to mine. 'You're out of your depth.'

'I beg to differ.'

'What I did was in the heat of the moment, and I did it for a reason.'

'The same reason I'm doing this.'

'But you know who I am. You know what this place is. You've got all the information you need.'

'Not all the information I want.'

'Which is?'

'Why you're keeping me here, why you're so desperate for my name.'

He leans back against the sofa and gives me an insincere smile. 'And if I tell you, you'll let me go?'

'No.'

An eyebrow arches.

'Because there's more.'

'Such as?'

'Let's see.' Careful to keep out of arm's reach, I inch towards the sofa and hunker down. 'I'd like to know exactly why you decided to throw caution to the wind and have sex with me – because you must have known it would complicate matters. And I'd like to know exactly why it was a mistake, and why you're backing off. I suppose the essence of it is... I want to know why you're a mess.'

'What's it to you?'

'Just curious.'

'Curiosity killed the cat.'

'Good job I'm not a cat.'

'If you think I'm about to let you into my personal life, you're completely deluded.'

'And if you think I'm about to back off, you're way beyond that.' I let my words sink in before touching an index finger to my chest. 'Goose.' I point the same finger at him. 'Gander.'

He studies me closely, taking his time, evidently trying to work out just how determined I am. 'I'm not in the mood to give.' Apparently settling in for the duration, he stretches out his legs.

'Fair enough.' I get up. 'I'll just have to take.' I make my way to the desk and open the top drawer. 'Oh, it's unlocked.'

'Because you'll find nothing in there.'

Nevertheless, I riffle through the contents: a few pens, a couple of unused notepads, an old calculator. Giving up, I slam the drawer shut and turn to the next one down.

'Nothing in there either.'

'I'll be the judge of that.'

'Just leave it.'

I pause and cock my head, because there was something in his voice then: a faint note of panic. It's enough to convince me I'm about to find something juicy. I pull open the drawer. 'This looks more promising.'

'You have no right...'

Oh yes, something very juicy. 'Let me remind you of something, Mr Delaney. You have no moral authority here. You relinquished that when you locked me up.' I pick out a bunch of keys. 'Oh, look. I could make my escape.'

'As if you would.' He forces a caustic laugh. 'I think we've established you've no intention of leaving.'

'And just to be perfectly clear,' I counter, 'we've also established that's not because I'm interested in your money.' I drop the keys onto the desk. 'Because I'm not.'

'Not interested in money?'

'No. Because judging by the state of you, it definitely can't buy you happiness.'

A nice little dig. It earns me a full-on scowl.

'So what?' he growls. 'You're still staying.'

'For all you know, I might have changed my mind.'

'Yeah, right.'

'Now I've seen your true colours.'

'Sorry to disappoint.'

If his sarcasm was intended to hurt, it totally missed the mark... because it was accompanied by a flash of vulnerability in those dark eyes. I've just been gifted with the briefest glimpse of hidden wounds. Doubly determined to unearth the truth about this man, I return my attention to the drawer.

'Hello. What's this? A passport.' I take it out and study the photo page. An image of Sebastian, a few years younger, and... 'Oh, my word. Cyril Sebastian Delaney?' I look up. 'Cyril?'

He glares at me.

'No wonder you use your middle name.' I place the passport next to the keys, and delve further through the drawer. 'What else is in here?'

'Nothing.'

Which is blatantly untrue. Ignoring him, I sift through a pile of documents and finally come to a plain A4 envelope. I pull it out and weigh it in my hands.

'Bills,' he mutters.

But he's totally fixated on the envelope – far too fixated for his own good – which is why I empty the contents onto the desktop. There's no sign of a bill. Instead, I'm looking at a pile of short notes, each one printed in a large, black font on white paper.

I shuffle through them. 'What are these?'

'Nothing.'

Picking the first that comes to hand, I read it in silence. 'No address,' I muse. 'Just a weird message.' I read it out loud. *'Don't think you're safe.'*

'Leave it...'

I pick up another. 'Remember your time in the dark?' And now, a third. *'I'm back, Delaney.'*

'Stop.'

I read the next sheet. *'Fourteen days and fourteen nights, I listened to your cries.'* And the next. *'Let's bring back those memories. Poor little Sebastian.'* What are these about? As I sift through them again, the pieces of the puzzle suddenly slot into place. 'Oh, my God. These are the letters Celine mentioned. The ones you won't tell Max about.'

I look up... and freeze at the sight of him. The cocky, arrogant, self-assured man has gone. Shoulders slumped and staring into space, he suddenly seems like nothing more than a frightened little boy.

'What happened to you?' I ask.

He shakes his head.

'What are you so afraid of?'

'Just put them away.' Finally, he makes eye contact.

And I see a world of pain.

'Oh, God.' It's obvious I've just scratched at an open wound. This time, I really have gone too far. Floundering in regret, I'm slipping the papers back into their envelope when the realisation hits me: if these are the letters Celine mentioned, then this is why he's been drowning his sorrows. It's still affecting him now, which means that whatever happened to 'poor little Sebastian' must have been truly awful. 'I'm so sorry.' I tuck the envelope back into the drawer. 'I've been an idiot. I'll leave you alone. In fact, I... I'll go back to London.' My heart thumps against my ribcage, because that's the last thing I want to do.

The seconds pass. Locked into his gaze, I watch the pain ebb away. Slowly bringing himself back to the present, his eyes flicker.

'No,' he whispers at last. 'You're not going anywhere.'

I have no idea what to say in return. Instead, I stare at him, dumb struck. I can barely believe he wants me to stay after what I've just done.

He blows out a breath. 'There are too may locks in this place. I'm sick of them.'

Taking the hint, I grab the key from the table and approach him. Moments later, the handcuffs drop to the floor with a clatter. I straighten up and step back, half-expecting him to spring to his feet and make for the exit. But he doesn't. Instead, he slips onto the floor, leans back against the sofa and draws in his knees. Nursing his left wrist in his right hand, he lets his head slump.

I watch him in silence, wanting to close the space between us, to take him in my arms and comfort him against whatever demons are eating him alive. But I get the distinct feeling it wouldn't be welcome. With no alternative, I try a few choice words.

'That place you like,' I venture. 'That place inside yourself?'

Clearly exhausted, he looks up.

'It might be safe in there, but it's lonely too. Believe me. I know.'

He nods, slowly.

'It's where our secrets live, Seb. And they're not good companions.'

He glances out the window. 'Too many locks.'

Three little words. Uttered so quietly, they're almost lost in the stillness. It's a miracle I catch them.

I take a small step forward. 'We can open up, you know.'

His eyes return to mine, still wary.

'But we can't force it, can we? Because that sort of thing…' I wave a hand. 'It takes patience and trust.'

He gazes at me for an age.

Finally, he nods.

'On both sides, Evie. On both sides.'

Chapter Thirteen

It's just after three in the afternoon. Freshly showered, I'm hovering in reception, nervously watching Celine as she skims through a file.

'Is Sebastian around?' I ask. Because I haven't seen him since I left him this morning. After returning to bed, I rose from a fitful sleep an hour ago... and discovered the apartment deserted.

Saying nothing, Celine twiddles a silver pen.

'Is he around?'

Long, black eyelashes rise. 'He said you'd be down.'

'He did?' Confirmation it *was* Sebastian who left the front door unlocked. 'So, where is he?'

I wouldn't be surprised if he's come to his senses, made himself scarce and left the exit wide open in the hope I won't be here when he returns.

'He went for a run.'

'Oh.' Maybe not, then. 'Okay.'

I swivel round to the glass frontage. There's only one way to find out what's going on; and no point in putting it off. I need to find him, apologise properly for the mad interrogation, and carefully gauge his mood. Feeling distinctly nauseous, I gather my courage and head out to the front of the club.

As I descend the steps, I'm met by a soft breeze and a blue sky. Ahead of me, the car park's full, brimming over with just about every luxury vehicle I can imagine: Ferraris, Porsches, a couple of Bentleys, a Rolls-Royce – each one worth enough to permanently rescue a handful of people from the streets. With a disgusted shake of the head, I thread my way through the glittering excess and come to a halt at the edge of the gravel.

I've seen it before, this perfectly tended lawn. But somehow – between the last time I laid eyes on it from above, and now – it seems to have transformed into my own personal no-man's land. Faced with a nightmare landscape of total exposure, instinct tells me to withdraw.

But instinct can be wrong...

Taking a deep breath, I place one foot on the grass, squint at the distant lake, and fight back a sudden attack of the heebie-jeebies. After the last few days, it feels strange to be outside; strange to feel so vulnerable again. No wonder a familiar voice from somewhere deep inside warns me to take care.

'Stop it,' I whisper to myself. 'You're perfectly safe.' Doing my best to keep body and brain under control, I head out over the lawn. 'Safe.' I repeat the word as if it's a spell. 'Safe, safe, safe.'

But it doesn't stop me dithering halfway down the slope, or taking a moment to scan the treeline for the slightest hint of life. Seeing and hearing nothing of any note, I look back at the house.

'Jesus.'

It might be a den of iniquity, but it's also a thing of beauty. Glowing in the afternoon light like the ghost of a bygone age, its sleek, white structure gives off the unmistakable aura of elegance and wealth. It looks more like an upmarket hotel, or a peaceful country retreat. You'd never guess what goes on in there. And I really must be safe; staying in a place like this, protected by a man with God knows how much money.

'Security,' I remind myself, thinking of Alex and his team. Considering those high-end cars and their super-rich owners, it must be on a serious level.

A little calmer now, I walk on towards the lake, taking a seat on an iron bench at the water's edge and spending a few minutes soaking up the scenery, composing myself for the task ahead.

Before me, a stretch of water twinkles and glimmers in the sunlight. To the right, the lake veers off behind a bank of trees. To the left, a stretch of grass separates reeds from woodland. And about a hundred metres from where I'm sitting, there's a large boathouse. Deciding to take a closer look, I get up and circle the lake, appreciating more detail as it comes into view. With a balcony stretching all the way round the upper storey, the front of the boathouse sits right at the edge of the water. Painted a creamy white, it seems quite old, and definitely in need of some loving attention. Just to my right, a short jetty reaches out into smooth water. And next to it, an upturned rowing boat lounges on the grass.

As soon as I reach the boat, I notice a t-shirt, a pair of jogging bottoms and a towel discarded on the jetty. And then, I become aware of movement: a soft, rhythmic splashing. With my heart rate increasing, I squint out over the water and realise it's Sebastian. Fully immersed in a front crawl, he's aiming for the shore.

He doesn't notice me until he reaches the edge of the lake and treads water.

'Working out?' I call.

'Something like that.'

Smoothing back his hair, he rises like Poseidon, clearly stark naked, but thankfully waist-deep in water. I'm busy admiring the

126

taut muscles of his upper body when he heaves himself onto the jetty. I turn away and wonder why I'm so embarrassed. After all, it's nothing I haven't seen before. But it's also something I can't seem to resist.

While he turns away and towels himself down, I take a seat on the boat and treat myself to a few sneaky peeks at his pert buttocks before he slings the towel over his left shoulder, pulls on the joggers, and leans down to pick up the t-shirt. Bare-footed, he saunters towards me, biceps and six pack on full display. By the time he reaches the boat, I'm pretty sure my eyes have widened to the size of saucers, but I can't let lust get the better of me. I've come here for a reason.

'The front door was open again,' I tell him.

'How careless.'

He drapes the t-shirt over his right shoulder. His lips lift into a languid smile, and his eyes sparkle. It's the most beautiful sight I've ever witnessed.

'I assume it was you.'

'Of course it was me.'

'Hoping I'd disappear?'

'That's the last thing I want.' He gives his hair a quick dry. The result is gloriously ruffled. 'Trust.' He flattens down the mess. 'Thought I might give it a go.'

'And patience?' I venture.

'Not my strongest suit.' He runs the towel up and down his arms. 'But I've heard you *can* teach an old dog new tricks.' Done with the towelling, he examines his bruised wrist.

I wince. 'Does it hurt?'

'Just tender.'

'I really am sorry... for what I did.'

'We've both made mistakes.'

'But...'

I'm silenced by a raised hand. 'You handcuffed me to a railing and dug into my private life, but we both know what I did.'

Yes, we do. And the very thought of it sends a hot flush through my veins.

'I'm not going to lie, Evie. It got to me. I think that was pretty obvious.'

'It was.'

'But I've had a long run, a dip in a freezing cold lake, and a good think.'

'And?'

127

'*And...*' He turns his right arm, runs a finger over a tiny tattoo on the inside of his elbow, a pair of crossed swords. 'I've decided we should put those mistakes behind us.'

I can barely believe it. 'I'm forgiven?'

With a boyish grin, he hands me the towel. 'I'll forgive you if you forgive me.'

'Of course I forgive you.'

'Then we're good.'

Are we? I'd say there's a bit more explaining to do on my part. 'Look, Sebastian...' I'm about to inform him I don't usually indulge in restraining people against their will, but he gives me no chance.

'Call me Seb.' He slips on the t-shirt.

'Seb...'

'And no more apologies or explanations. We're moving on.'

'Yes, but...'

'As of now.'

Eyes lock. Smiles of understanding play between us, and a wonderful sense of peace settles over me, banishing all cares and worries from my mind. I have no idea how long I spend like this, luxuriating in his beautiful gaze, but my heart's on the verge of exploding by the time he reaches out.

'Come with me.'

I put my hand into his.

With no effort whatsoever, he pulls me up. 'Let me introduce you to my favourite place in the world.'

Without another word, he leads me to the side of the boathouse, pausing at a door to release me and retrieve a key from under a plant pot. Door opened, he ushers me inside, and up a set of wooden steps.

'Wow,' I breathe, emerging into a spacious living area.

There's a lounge to the front, complete with huge, comfy sofa and windows looking out over the lake. Next to me, a small kitchen area and a dining table. And between them, a corridor leading back to bedrooms, I presume. The beamed ceilings and wood-panelled walls are all a little worn around the edges, but it's charming, clean and bright, and infinitely more personal than the penthouse.

'This is gorgeous.'

'A bit tatty.' He stands at my side. 'I should redecorate.'

The words come out instinctively. 'Pastel blue for the walls.'

'Pastel blue?' he muses.

'Sorry. I'm not telling you what to do. It's just my favourite colour.'

He nods. 'Fancy a coffee?'

'Please.'

While he gets on with preparing drinks, I drape the towel over the back of a chair and investigate further, admiring the views, surveying a range of antique tables and lamps, and finally homing in on a sideboard that's practically littered with photographs. One, in particular, snags my attention. Obviously taken on the balcony outside, it's of a dark-haired boy – maybe four or five years old – sitting on a woman's lap, cosying up in a wicker chair. I pick it up.

'Me and my mother.' Mug in hand, Seb approaches. 'Guess who was holding the camera?'

I put down the photo and accept the offered drink. 'No idea.'

'Uncle Harry.'

'Really?'

'He used to visit a lot.'

'Oh.' I move on to a second photograph. Black and white this time, it's of the club, but the lodges and extensions are missing.

'That's from the thirties,' Seb explains.

'It's beautiful.' I lean in, examining a figure at the front steps.

'My great-grandfather. Sir Arthur Francombe. He built the place.'

'Sir? You come from money?'

'On my mother's side.'

'And you inherited all this?'

'Not exactly. My brother did.'

'*Max* owns it?'

'Not anymore.' He laughs at my incredulity. 'He sold it to me, at a very reasonable rate as it happens. When I bought it six years ago, it was a complete wreck. I had it renovated, adapted into what it is.'

'But why a sex club?'

'Why not?' he grins. 'My great-grandfather was a famed pleasure-seeker. It seemed appropriate.'

That's not the complete answer, and I know it. 'I'd say you've got to be into that sort of thing to run a kinky club.'

'You already know I'm into that sort of thing.'

My cheeks flush for all they're worth.

'I like it when you blush.' Taking my mug from me, he places it on the table.

'You do?'

'God, yes. It does things to me.'

What sort of things? That what I'm about to ask when I'm drawn into his arms and an accompanying maelstrom of lust. His eyes drift lazily to my lips. His left arm locks tight around me, his right hand comes to the back of my head, and his mouth covers mine. With immediate effect, I'm cast adrift in a mesmerising kiss, delivered Sebastian Delaney style: lava-hot, all guns blazing, demanding of absolute submission. When he finally releases me, I'm struggling for breath and almost certain my legs are about to fold.

But he gives me no respite. Instead, he grabs me by the hand and leads me to the back of the boathouse, into a bedroom. Totally blind-sided, I glance round at cool-white panelled walls. At the opposite side of the room, a set of French windows have been left open, and gossamer-thin curtains blow in a slight breeze. I quickly take in the view beyond – billowing trees and a hint of lake – before turning my attention to the king-sized bed, draped with luxurious, silk covers.

Say something, I urge myself, as he comes to stand in front of me.

'I... I thought last time was a mistake.'

He places a finger under my chin. 'I hate to admit it, but I have been known to get things wrong... on occasion.'

His smile threatens to turn my insides to pure liquid, and while his hands begin to explore, I take the opportunity to do the same. Touching him for the first time, I smooth my palms over his broad shoulders, down a perfectly sculpted back, and finally cup those hard buttocks.

'Enjoying that?'

'God, yes.'

Snaking an arm around my back, he leans in, trailing his lips over mine, across my left cheek and down my neck, dancing little kisses along the way. Before long, his hold tightens and the kisses become ever more forceful. We both know exactly where this is going. I just hope he's prepared.

'Do you keep condoms here?'

He laughs quietly. 'Actually, I squirrel them away all over the place. Ex-playboy, remember?'

And given his propensity to dominate, God knows what else he's squirreled away. But we're not going down that route today. Although I'm not averse to another kinky session, I'm also desperate to get a little closer to this man. If I let him take control, there'll be no chance of that.

I put a hand to his chest. 'Stop.'

'You don't want this?'

'Of course I do. But I want to try something different.'

'You don't like it my way?'

'I love it your way. But it's not what I want right now.' And it's definitely not what we need.

'So, what *do* you want?'

'Control.'

His brows crease. 'Oh, I don't know about that.' He dips his head to kiss me again.

'No.' I pull away. 'Trust me. It's a good thing to step out of your comfort zone.'

Because I'll get the chance to take things slowly and reel him in with a healthy dose of intimacy. And if, at any point, he begins to back off like a nervous fawn, I'll simply lure him in again.

As if he's calculating the dangers of my proposal, he eyes me for a few seconds. 'Fine,' he says at last. 'I'm always up for an experiment.'

It's not an experiment. It's a tactic. Adopted on the spur of the moment, but perfectly designed to open him up.

'We're going to take our time,' I tell him. 'And we're going to be gentle. Think you can manage that?'

'Certainly.'

'Good.' I smile triumphantly. 'Now, kiss me again.'

Drawing me back into his embrace, he does as he's told, taking his time, probing softly, engaging tongues in a lazy, languid slow dance that seems to go on forever. At some point, he brings a fingertip to the nape of my neck, touching lightly here, tickling there, teasing a whole host of sensations to life. It's a masterclass in tenderness that leaves my brain and body melting.

'I think I like this 'gentle' business,' he murmurs when he's done. 'You must have tried it before.'

'In the dim and distant past, with other lips. It never did anything for me. But with these lips...' He brushes a finger across my mouth. 'It's very moreish.'

Result. My fiendish plan is working. 'Glad to hear it,' I say, as calmly as possible. 'Now, what next?'

'How about –' He grabs the bottom of my t-shirt. 'We take this thing off?'

'No.' I clamp my hands over his. 'I'm in control, remember?'

'All the way?'

'All the way.' I give him a determined look and take a step back before lifting the shirt.

He watches closely, a smile teasing at his lips. 'I don't know what Celine was playing at, buying you this stuff.'

'Actually, I asked for it.' I sling the t-shirt into a corner, then kick off my trainers.

'I wonder why.' His eyes glimmer. 'Why would a beautiful woman like you want to hide away?'

Slipping out of my jeans, I bat away the question with a touch of self-deprecation. 'I'm not beautiful.'

'I'll be the judge of that.' He closes in, quickly wrapping his fingers around my left arm.

I shake myself from his grip. 'Slow down. Before you see any more of me, I want to see all of you.'

'You've already done that.'

'And I want to touch.'

'My God, you're demanding.'

'You have no idea. Arms up.'

With a wry grin, he complies, waiting for me to take the hem of his t-shirt and draw it over his head. Job done, I drop the shirt to the floor and trail my palms over every inch of bare flesh.

'You're absolute physical perfection, Mr Delaney. Ten out of ten for the body.'

'It's deserved.'

'Big head.' I sink to my knees.

'And what do you think you're doing now?'

'You'll see.'

I draw his joggers to the floor, pausing to admire his cock as it springs free.

'Somebody's eager,' I remark.

'He's been eager for the past half hour. Like what you see?'

'Very much.'

As soon as the joggers are despatched, I take his shaft in my left hand and lick at the glans, savouring a deliciously salty taste.

'Oh, Evie...'

Whispered with complete adoration, his words are enough to spur me on. Closing my mouth around the top of his penis, I begin to suck gently, occasionally tickling at the tip with my tongue. It's not long before I hear a groan and feel a hand on shoulders. Which is precisely when I tighten my grip, working my hand up and down in slow, rhythmic movements.

'That's so good.'

I'd tell him it's about to get better, but my mouth's otherwise engaged. Upping the tempo, I bring my right hand to his balls, adding a cheeky massage to the mix, and bringing him right to the edge before I ease off.

'No,' he grunts.

'Patience and trust,' I remind him, beginning the process again.

When I've worked him up into a complete mess for a second time, I release him.

'Do that much more, and you won't be in charge for long.'

'I'll be in charge for as long as I say.' I get to my feet. 'Now, take off my bra.'

Within seconds, he's tossing the bra to one side. Taking my left breast in his hand, he cups it for a moment, then skims a finger across my nipple, causing me to suck in a sharp breath.

'I have to say this, Evie.' Very slowly, he trails the same finger round and round the areola. 'You really do have the most incredible tits.' Joined by the thumb, his finger moves in on my nipple, and squeezes.

'Jesus,' I gasp, lapping up the sensations. Knowing he'll retake the reins if I don't act quickly, I reach for the next weapon in the armoury: a touch of humour. 'Actually, I'm not too keen on that word.'

'Tits?'

'Hideous.'

'Point taken. What should I call them, then?' Feigning innocence, he moves on to the right breast, swirling and skimming and tweaking the nipple. 'Breasts? Boobs? Bazookas?'

'This one,' I nod to my left breast, 'goes by the name of Brenda.'

'And this one?' He skims a wicked finger over my right nipple.

'Doris.'

'So, they've got names.' He raises an eyebrow. 'Now, that's unusual.' With a smile, he tweaks the nipple again.

'Stop.'

To my utter amazement, he does.

'My knickers.'

He glances down. 'They're adding insult to lingerie.'

'And they need to go.'

'Couldn't agree more.'

Eyes shimmering with amusement, he lowers himself to his knees, gives the knickers a look of complete disdain, and slips his index fingers into the waistband. It takes an age for him to draw them to my feet. And once they're gone, he spends another age brushing his palms over my legs, all the way down to my ankles and back up again. Halting at my thighs, he gazes longingly at my crotch.

'So, what do I call this?'

Mouth open, I'm suddenly flustered. In actual fact, I don't normally name my body parts, and I have no idea what to say. So, what *should* he call it? Without any prompting, some weird part of my brain makes the decision for me.

'Mavis,' I blurt.

'Hello Mavis.' He laughs. 'Now, I'm guessing Mavis enjoys the odd bingo session with Brenda and Doris. But does she like being kissed?'

'Probably,' I squeak. 'But make it gentle.'

He gives me a mock-scowl. 'As if I'd do it any other way.'

Leaning in, he plants a soft kiss on my hair and clasps a strong hand to my backside. Moments later, his tongue is at my clitoris, pressing here, swirling there, and generally causing havoc. I'm so distracted, I barely have time to react when he gets to his feet and manoeuvres me to the edge of the bed. Before I know it, I've toppled backwards, and I'm lying face-up with Seb on top of me, my arms pinned to the pillow. Kissing me senseless, he nudges my legs apart and positions himself between them.

'How did this happen?' I ask when I finally get the chance.

'How did what happen?'

'You've taken charge.'

'Have I?'

'You know you have.'

Yes, he does. And he's looking distinctly smug about it. 'It's not my fault. Blame Brenda and Doris, and Mavis. They're an axis of evil. Made me forget myself.'

'Excuses,' I grumble. 'I'm the one in charge.'

He brings the tip of his nose to mine. 'If you say so.'

'I do say so.' I nod to the space next to me.

With a huff, he takes the hint. Releasing my wrists, he repositions himself by my side.

'I'd like to take this slowly,' I tell him.

'Your wish is my command.'

With his head propped on his left hand, he raises his right arm and twiddles his fingers. Pursing his lips like a child at a sweet counter, he finally decides where to start. In no particular hurry, the fingers brush against my hips, tracing the contours again and again, before they set about a thorough exploration of my body. And while the next few minutes pass in lazy, mutual adoration, accompanied by long kisses and plenty of eye contact, I sense a new warmth rising in my heart. It's something I've never experienced before, and I have no idea what it is. But I'm in no mood for introspection.

Quickly brushing it aside, I move on top of Seb, straddling him, and dangle my hair in his face.

He takes a few strands and plays with them. 'I could get used to this.'

I grind slowly against his crotch. 'Ready to go?'

'Always, where you're concerned.'

'So, where do you generally do your squirrelling?'

'Right there.' He nods to the bedside cabinet. 'In the drawer.'

I lean over and help myself to a packet. Adjusting my position now, and only too aware that he's enjoying every second of my attentions, I remove the condom, place it over the tip of his cock and roll it down. With a smile playing on his lips, he brings his hands to my waist and urges me back over his crotch. I lower myself onto him, taking my time, easing him into me until I'm completely filled.

'Now, that feels good,' he whispers.

'Doesn't it just?'

I begin to move with patient, measured movements, stilling every now and then to keep things under control. But with Seb gazing up at me, his dark eyes brimming with promise, it doesn't take long for me to reach a climax. I'm not even halfway down when his grip tightens on my waist. Gritting his teeth, he suddenly becomes taut, the veins in his neck more defined.

'Jesus, Evie. You're going to send me mad.'

With that, he makes his move. In an instant, I'm hauled off him and rolled onto my back. I barely have time to react before he's on top of me again, nudging my legs further apart and bracing himself.

'Seb...'

I get no chance to complain. Bringing his face to mine, he delivers a long, tender kiss that's so exquisite, I'm completely engulfed in the moment. The next thing I know, I'm dragging myself back to reality, and he's buried deep inside.

'I think I've got it now.' He brushes his lips against mine. 'So, just relax and enjoy. This is going to be slow... and very, *very* gentle.'

True to his word, he takes his time withdrawing. After pausing at the tip, he enters again, inch by inch. And then, he repeats the process, over and over, creating an effect that's utterly spellbinding. I feel it all so keenly. A myriad of responses kick off in my body: tingles of sensation tripping across super-sensitized skin; heavenly tremors dancing through my core; an inexorable pressure rising deep inside. And it goes on until I really can't take any more.

'Faster,' I plead.

'Anything you say.'

Slipping his left hand under my buttocks, he increases the tempo. And I lift my hips to his, matching the rhythm with my own movements. Virtually pounding into me now, all sweaty and overheated, he closes his eyes.

'Look at me, Seb.'

He does as he's told. It's enough to tip me over the edge, sending a multitude of contractions spiralling through me. His own release follows moments later. With a few final thrusts, he stiffens under my hands and empties himself.

'Jesus. Fucking hell.' Collapsing on top of me, he holds me tight.

And while we both wrestle our bodies back under control, I spend the next minute or so smoothing his hair, relishing his warmth, luxuriating in the utter security of his embrace. At last, he lifts his head from my shoulder and studies me intently, as if he can't quite believe what he's seeing, as if I'm a puzzle he's trying to fathom.

'I hope you got what you wanted,' he whispers.

I can only smile.

Because I might be currently swimming about in a gloriously sexual fug, but a worrying notion just entered my mind. Despite all his words since we entered this room – and some of his actions – he never really relinquished control at all.

He just let me think he did.

My smile deepens, and I urge him down for a kiss.

Never mind, I tell myself. It's only a matter of time.

Chapter Fourteen

A buzzing stirs me from my nap.

'Bugger off, world.' Seb checks his mobile, quickly cancels the call, and abandons the phone on the bedside table. He stretches out an arm. 'Come here.'

I take full advantage of the invitation. Moving in close and resting my head on his shoulder, I'm soon gazing at a picture on the opposite wall: against a rich, gold background, two ornate silver birds fighting each other in mid-air.

I lift my head a little, admiring the way their tails fan out, catching the sunlight. 'Are they…'

'Phoenix cockerels. Ancient Chinese embroidery. Worth a complete bomb.'

'It's a lovely picture.'

'If you like that sort of thing.'

A quick glance at Seb tells me he doesn't particularly like that sort of thing.

'Uncle Harry gave it to my mother, years ago. It was a bit of an obsession with him…' The mobile buzzes again, cutting him off in mid-flow. He picks it up, glances at the screen, and silences the call again. 'Max,' he announces.

'Oh.' Enough said. I've no interest in Max. I'd rather talk about Hal. 'You know where it came from, don't you? Harry's obsession?'

He nods. 'That café you worked in. He talked about it a lot. And Cynthia… the nurse.'

We slip into silence, both of us gazing at the picture now. Seb's arm tightens round me.

'The ring was for her,' I murmur.

'It was.'

'I wonder where she went.' Out of nowhere, the worst-case scenario presents itself. 'Oh, my God. She might have died.'

'No.' An assertion delivered with absolute certainty.

'You know?'

He nods. 'Hal first mentioned her about three years ago, when the dementia was diagnosed. Max looked into it, and in typical Max fashion, he found her.'

I turn to face him. 'And?'

'We don't know what happened at the time, but she eventually moved to Suffolk, got married, had kids.'

'What?'

'She's still alive now. A happy grandmother, in fact. I daresay she forgot about Harry years ago.'

'But why on earth would she turn her back on him?' I can barely believe it. 'I mean, he was a handsome man. And I'm guessing he's always been kind...'

Seb smiles. 'Maybe she was into bad boys.'

'Bad boys are hard work.' And I should know.

'Good job I'm like Hal then.' He raises an eyebrow and looks back to the picture. 'Anyway, it doesn't really matter why she turned her back on him. Uncle Harry thought Cynthia was the love of his life... but she wasn't. And after that, no one ever measured up. The silly old sod should have moved on and left it all behind.'

'He's not a silly old sod.' I dig a finger into his side. 'He's a wonderful man.'

'Agreed. But a wonderful man who could have got married and had kids of his own. Instead, he wasted his life mooning over a woman he couldn't have.' The mobile buzzes again. He reaches for it. 'For fuck's sake, Celine. Leave me alone.'

'You'd better answer.'

He groans. 'If you say so.' Swiping a finger over the screen, he listens to an agitated voice. His eyes darken. 'Okay. Okay, I get it. I'm on my way.' Ending the call, he drops the phone onto his chest. 'Talk of the devil.' He sighs. 'Harry's been asking to see me.'

'Is that why Max called?'

'Probably. I'm sorry, I'm going to have to go.'

'Can I come too?'

'Not this time.' Before I can complain, he pulls me in and lands a chaste kiss on my forehead. 'It's not that I don't trust you. He's just not good today. It's best I go on my own.' He picks up the phone again, and squints at the screen. 'It's nearly seven now. I'll be back around ten. Wait for me here. That's an order.'

***

As soon as I'm showered and dressed, I make myself a coffee and collapse onto the sofa at the front window. Watching the sun dip behind the lake, I can't help mulling over the past few hours and where they've left me. The sex might not have gone entirely to plan, but after months in a cold wilderness, I'm high as a kite on sensual overload and totally re-energised. It's intoxicating, to say the least. And maybe that's why I close my eyes, allowing a brief daydream to

138

play out in my head: the lake in full sunlight; Seb teaching our son to row a boat while I watch from the shore.

'Stop it,' I grumble, dragging myself back to reality. Just because we've had two sessions now, it doesn't mean we're heading for a lifetime together. Far from it, in fact, because a full-on relationship's out of the question. At some point, I'll be forced to put an end to things. 'But maybe not yet...' Conjuring up a touch of wilful ignorance, I resolve to enjoy the fairy tale for a while longer. After all, it's doing no harm.

The click of a latch jolts me back from my thoughts.

Getting to my feet, I wait for Seb to appear, and quickly realise there's something wrong. Accompanying the sound of heavy footsteps, a set of heels clatter against the wood. I've barely had time to wonder what's going on when a stranger appears at the top of the staircase. Impeccably presented in a super-expensive black suit, he's tall, well-built, dark-haired and brown-eyed. And he's strikingly similar to Seb, the sort of man who'd have you tongue-tied if you didn't know better.

But I do.

'Max, I take it?'

'Correct.'

'I thought you were with your uncle.'

'You thought wrong.'

'Of course.' I give him a bright smile. 'Because you're here... conducting an ambush.'

He takes a step towards me, leaving space for Celine to appear in his wake.

'Correct again.'

I watch him for a moment, picking up on a distinct difference between the brothers. While it's always been easy to detect the warmth and vulnerability beneath Seb's veneer, I catch none of that with Max. Either he's in possession of a completely impenetrable shield, or there's nothing behind it but a hardened heart and steely determination. In silence, I vow not to let him intimidate me. As nonchalantly as I can, I make my way to the kitchen area, passing Max in the process, which only serves to set my nerves jangling because it's like skirting way too close to a dangerous dog.

'Drinks, anyone?' I ask chirpily.

'I see you've made yourself at home.'

'Yes.' Determined to show no sign of anxiety, I stiffen a little. 'Seb told me to.'

'Seb?' Possibly considering when to go for the jugular, he examines me from the other side of the counter. 'That's a little familiar.'

I fill the kettle.

'You can leave the drinks.'

Okay. So, Max Delaney wants to get straight down to business, and there's clearly no point arguing. Abandoning the kettle, I cross my arms and wait.

'I'm told you call yourself Evie.'

'I do.'

'Not your real name, of course.'

'No.'

He closes in on the counter. 'Does my brother know your real identity?'

What to say? Do I tell him the truth? Perhaps not. 'None of your business.'

He taps an index finger against the marble top. 'Let me tell you something, Evie – or whatever your name is – if I decide something's my business, then it is my business.'

'In your world, maybe.'

'In yours too.'

What an arrogant arse. 'Dream on.' Determined to wind him up, I smile again. He might be Seb's brother, but he still deserves to be taken down a peg or two. Emerging from my safe space, I head back to the sofa. 'I get it, Max. Celine's been pouring her poison into your ear. That's why you've lured Seb out of the way and come here... to do some damage.' I slump onto the cushions and watch his reflection in the darkened glass.

'I'm not the one doing the damage.'

'And I am?'

Rounding the end of the sofa, he comes to a halt directly in front of me, primed for a spot of top-notch intimidation. 'I'm a very busy man, Evie. So, let's just get down to business. I know how you ended up here. I know why Seb tracked you down. And I know exactly what happened when you were discovered.'

I can't help looking back at Celine. Her triumphant smile says it all. Having prepared her weapon of choice and aimed it in my direction, she's enjoying the fruits of her labour.

'I also know you're refusing to disclose your true identity,' Max continues, dragging my attention back to him. 'And my brother – for one reason or another – seems quite happy to put up with your nonsense.'

140

I raise my chin.

'However,' he says, 'I'm not happy to put up with it.'

'Shame.'

I get an icy smile for that.

'I'll give you one chance to tell me who you are.'

Deciding he needs to learn a lesson – that he's not entitled to anything he wants, especially my secrets – I simply hold his gaze.

'I told you she wouldn't talk,' Celine purrs, appearing behind him.

'You know me so well, Celine,' I purr back, eyes still fixed on Max.

'Don't I just?'

'Enough,' Max snaps.

I glance at Celine, momentarily enjoying the fact she's visibly chastised.

'I haven't come here to listen to a cat fight,' Max growls. 'What, exactly, do you want from my brother? If it's money you're after, I'm prepared to negotiate.'

'You can stick your money up your arse.'

He laughs. 'Money makes the world go round. And everybody's got a price.'

'Not me.'

'Even you.' He steps forward, a menacing figure now he's looming over me.

In a desperate effort to conceal the jitters, I fold my arms. 'I don't see the point of discussing anything with you. You've clearly made up your mind. You don't like me. That's pretty obvious. Why don't you just have me dragged out of here?'

'Because you'd only come crawling back.'

'But I don't know where we are.'

'I take it you know who we are.'

'The Delaneys. Such a lovely family.'

'You know nothing about my family.'

'I know you're Phillip Delaney's son.'

I hear a quiet growl, catch a hint of restrained fury in his eyes.

'So what?'

'Oh, come on.' My lips curl into a satisfied smile, because I seem to have stumbled on this man's Achilles heel, and I'm determined to use it. 'You're his heir. You've been groomed for the role. Your dad might not have bothered with Seb, but he's obviously been all over you. Like father, like son.'

His fists clench.

I stand up, and slowly list the attributes I'm pretty sure Delaney Senior passed onto his eldest. 'Ruthless. Cold-hearted. Power-hungry. Money-hungry. That's your father. Why wouldn't it be you?'

'You know nothing about me.'

'I know you're nothing like your brother. There's more to life than wealth and influence. You'll never understand that. But Seb does. And so do I.'

'Bollocks.' He laughs again. 'I know an opportunist when I see one.'

'I wouldn't make assumptions if I were you.'

As if he's about to pounce and tear me limb from limb, he bares his teeth. It's enough to wake up the fight or flight instinct and prompt me to take the second option. Holding my breath, I brush past him and return to the kitchen area, only to find he's followed me again.

'I don't make assumptions,' he says. 'You took a ring from an old man. And as yet, you haven't given it back. That tells me a lot.'

'Does it?'

'You're running from danger. That tells me a lot.'

Wondering how on earth he knows all this, I frown at the kettle

'You found yourself in the lap of luxury and smelt out my brother's wealth, so you decided to seduce him. That also tells me a lot.'

I look up. 'Sod off.'

'I take it you've been successful.'

The gall of the man. 'None of your business.'

'How much?'

'What?'

'How much? To make you go away?'

My stomach turns. 'I'm not going anywhere.'

'Fifty thousand.'

'I beg your pardon?' I can barely believe what I've just heard.

'Fifty. Thousand.' He repeats, slowly.

I shake my head.

'Okay. I'll double the offer.'

'You're disgusting.'

'And you're tempted.'

He couldn't be further from the truth. A hundred thousand pounds would easily set me up in a new life, but I'd be selling my soul to the devil. And anyway, I still have my pride. If I take the money and run, Seb will hate me for it. And no amount of cash is worth that.

'Keep your money.'

'It's not just money. It's security. And no need to sleep with my brother for it.'

'Shut up!' I snap. 'You're vile.' A cold-hearted monster who'll never know what love feels like. 'You just don't want to see your brother happy.'

'Oh, I'd love nothing more than to see my brother happy, but don't fool yourself. You're not the woman for the job.'

'You don't know the first thing about me.'

'And whose fault is that?' There's a new glimmer in his eyes: a sign, perhaps, of a change of plan. 'You need to understand me, Evie. My brother might not like me at the minute, but we've had disagreements in the past, and he always comes back.'

'This isn't a competition.'

'Quite right. Because that would imply you have a chance of winning.'

'And I suppose I don't.'

'Correct. I know my brother better than anyone.'

'I know him well enough.'

'I doubt that.'

'Doubt all you like.'

'You're not the only one withholding facts.'

'Meaning?'

'Meaning...' He smiles at my unease. 'There's plenty you don't know about Sebastian – things he'll keep to himself because you'd find them...' He pauses for a moment, taking his time to choose the right word. 'Unsavoury.'

If it's intended to unsettle me, it certainly does the trick. Knocked off balance, all I can is stare at my unwanted visitor, desperate to ask what he's going on about now. But I can't let this man know he's got the advantage. God knows what he'd do with it.

'You're just trying to scare me off,' I tell him, as calmly as possible. 'You're lying.'

'He's not,' Celine laughs. 'He's telling the truth. Where Seb's concerned, you've barely scratched the surface.'

Max checks his watch. 'I need to go.' He heads to the top of the stairs. 'If I were you,' he says, pausing by the banister, 'I'd listen to Celine.' He straightens his jacket. 'By the way, the money's off the table. You had your chance and blew it. Oh, and one last thing.' He pins me down with a harsh, unwavering glare. 'If you bring any trouble to my brother's door, I'll make you pay for it, big time. That's a promise.'

Watching him go, I hold in a breath and will myself not to crumble. But it's no easy task. Max Delaney might not have managed to pay me off, but his words have certainly fractured the dream. I wait until the door slams downstairs before I breathe again.

'He's means it.'

Great. Celine isn't done with me yet. And judging by her new, curiously gentle tone, I'd say she's trying a different tactic.

'I'm sure he does.' I sigh. 'So... the bad cop's done his bit. I suppose you're the good cop.'

'I suppose you're right.'

'Wonderful.'

I've been terrorised by a rabid billionaire, had the world ripped from under my feet, and now it's time for Celine to finish me off with a touch of unexpected kindness. It's all too much. No wonder I'm left clutching at one last, pathetic straw.

'Why do you hate me, Celine?' A doomed attempt to fish for sympathy.

'I don't hate you.'

'Oh, come on...'

'I dislike you. That's all. And I certainly don't trust you.' She takes a step forward. 'Max was telling the truth, you know. If you had the full picture about Seb, you wouldn't be quite so keen to stick around.' Her eyes soften. 'But for what it's worth, I don't share his assessment of you. I don't think you're an opportunist. How could you be? You just turned down a hundred thousand pounds.' She smiles. 'I think you do have feelings for Seb. And it's possible they're reciprocated. After all, he's never brought a woman down here before.'

'He hasn't?'

'No.' She speaks quietly now, slowly laying out the crux of the situation. 'The thing is, Evie, he doesn't need any more crap in his life. It'll destroy him. And I get the distinct impression you come with plenty of baggage.'

Yes. I do. Dangerous baggage.

'If you've got a heart – if you really do care for Seb – you should do the right thing.'

I close my eyes and acknowledge the inevitable. 'Leave.'

'Best all round really, because if you do cause trouble, Max will make you pay.' She gives me a few seconds to let the information sink in before moving on to practicalities. 'I know you've met

Christophe. He's at the club tonight. I'm sure he'd be only too willing to help. He might even find you somewhere to stay.'

***

By the time Celine's wraith-like figure drifts into the shadows, the first tears have already made their appearance – the inevitable result of an unwanted reality check.

I've been an idiot.

Taken my eye off the ball and wilfully buried an inconvenient truth.

Why else would Celine's final words have cut so deep? Why else would the tears be gathering in force? It's because I've been falling for him, secretly hoping for something more than a meaningless fling.

But there are too many shadows between us, and no way of getting rid of them. Whichever way I look at it, the fairy tale is at an end. It's time to turn my back on life and return to mere existence.

Chapter Fifteen

It's almost nine o'clock when I leave the boathouse. Under the light of a full moon, I half-run, half-stumble back up to the club. Within minutes, I'm standing in front of an open wardrobe, sorting through a hoard of clothes that don't belong to me. Alongside a few pairs of knickers, I select a couple of t-shirts, a sweatshirt, and a pair of jeans, slinging them onto the bed before I go in search of a coat and bag. Finding a waterproof jacket and an old gym bag amongst Seb's belongings, I return to my room, stuff the coat and clothes into the bag, tuck my precious photo into a side pocket, and head downstairs.

There's no sign of life in the lobby. To the left of me, the double doors to the bar are wide open. I stop near the threshold, not daring to enter, and spot Christophe a few feet away.

In the mid-conversation with Alex, he notes my presence, claps Alex on the back and comes to join me. 'Going somewhere?' He nods to the bag.

'I'm leaving.'

'Not working out with Sebastian?'

'Not really.'

'I did warn you.' He widens his eyes. 'Anyway, Celine mentioned you might need some help. Consider me at your service.'

Excellent. 'Could you take me into London? I know it's a lot to ask.'

'It's nothing.' He smiles. 'In fact, you're doing me a favour. Rescuing a damsel in distress is always good for the male ego.'

'Glad to hear it.' I force a smile in return. 'Can we leave now? It's just that Seb's out, and I want to be gone by the time he gets back.'

'But why the urgency?' He frowns. 'If you've decided to call it a day, I'm sure he won't stop you.'

I bite my lip.

'Ah.' A flicker of understanding passes through his eyes. 'He has been keeping you here against your will.'

'Not quite.'

'Not quite.' He glances up at a camera. 'This explains everything.' Taking me by the arm, he leads me over to the side of the lobby and lowers his voice. 'Security's been stepped up in recent days. It's been the talk of the club. More cameras, more guards, cars searched, in and out. I thought we must have had some high-profile new member – a government minister, that sort of thing.' He waves a hand. 'But now I think I understand.' He pauses, dramatically. 'It's to stop you leaving.'

'Me?'

Jesus. I've completely misread the situation. While I thought Sebastian was showing me trust, leaving the front door unlocked was nothing more than a ruse, designed to make me feel more like a guest than a prisoner. The truth is, he just expanded the prison walls, tucking them firmly out of sight.

'Couldn't I...' Oh, God. My next words are going to sound completely bizarre. 'Could I hide in your boot?'

Christophe laughs, quietly. 'When I said the cars are being searched, I meant thoroughly. Boots included.'

'So, how do I get out?' I wince at the note of desperation in my voice.

'Don't worry.' He places his hands on my shoulders. 'I have an idea. You give me the bag. I'll put it in my car. If they ask at the gates, I'll say the clothes belong to a lady friend.'

Right. 'But what do I do?'

'Stay calm. That's the first thing.' He gives me a gentle squeeze. 'I'm a nosy so-and-so, which means I pick up a lot of useful information. I've been chatting with Alex about security. You know Alex?'

I nod.

'He's concerned about a weak spot in the perimeter wall. Plans are afoot to sort it out, but yet to be addressed.' His grey eyes flicker. 'I understand it's just to the other side of the lake. Luckily, there's a full moon tonight, and not too much cloud. Go straight past the boathouse. On the other side, you'll find an opening in the trees. You can't miss it. Follow the path until you come to the wall. There used to be a gate there, but it's been bricked up. You'll know the spot. It's the only part of the perimeter not covered by CCTV.'

'But it's a wall.'

Christophe shrugs. 'It's only about eight feet high.'

The desperation increases. 'I can't get over that.'

'With a rope, you can.'

What? 'Where am I going to get a rope?'

'Evie.' He squeezes again. 'Please remember where you are. There's plenty of rope in this place. I'll get hold of some and wait for you on the other side of the wall. How strong are you?'

Jesus, how on earth do I know? 'Strong enough, I suppose.'

'Good. I'll knot the rope to give you footholds. You'll have to do the rest.' He takes the bag. 'Go.' He nods to the door. His voice becomes urgent. 'Now. Before Sebastian returns.'

I only need telling once. Knowing perfectly well he'll stop me in my tracks if he catches up with me, I move fast, pushing through the doors, skittering down the steps and across the car park, breaking into a run as soon as I reach the grass. Under a much-needed patch of cloud-cover, I've just about reached the water's edge when an engine starts up behind me. Seconds later, the clouds part, allowing a silvery moonlight to spill across the grounds.

'Bugger.'

It might ease my way to the perimeter wall, but I'm also visible to anyone back at the club. Turning to check on the situation, I catch sight of a car speeding off down the gravel driveway; another passing on its way in. My heart rate doubles. If that's Sebastian returning early from his visit, my escape plan could be in serious trouble.

With panic urging me on, I circle the edge of the lake and dip into the shadows behind the boathouse, sticking close to the tree line and tracking its progress until I eventually stumble over the promised gap: the beginning of a path that's grassed over in some places and bare mud in others; a mess of furrows and ridges, strewn with twigs and branches and clumps of moss.

Hoping the moonlight lasts long enough to see me to the other end, I take one last look back at a life that was never meant to be, catching sight of a lamp left on in the boathouse. Before I know it, there are tears in my eyes; the outward signs of a self-pity I can't afford to indulge. Wiping them away, I wrench myself from the dream, and delve into the woods.

I'm only a little way in when I trip on a branch. Veering forwards, I stagger to a halt and regain my balance, taking a moment to calm myself, scanning the ground and picking out the safest route before I begin again. But the calm doesn't last long. The further I penetrate, the faster my heart beats, bringing each breath more quickly than the last.

There's a crack... just to my right.

I freeze, listening to the hush of wind through leaves, the hoot of an owl, the flutter and clapping of wings.

And then, I search the shadows.

'No one there.' I move again.

Within moments, the path widens out into a clearing, confronting me with the unmistakable sight of the wall. A few more steps, this time over relatively even ground, and I'm right in front of it. With the brick section just to my right, I place my hands against cold stonework, wondering how on earth I'm ever going to scale this thing. I can see no footholds I'd trust, and as yet there's no sign of Christophe and his rope. I'm on the verge of giving up when I hear another crack.

This time, it's right behind me.

I turn and freeze again, noting the fact there's now a shadow lurking between the trunks. My breath hitches.

'What's going on?' a familiar voice demands. Deep and silky as ever, it's tinged with a distinct note of irritation.

'Seb?'

He moves forward, his face unreadable in the darkness. A sliver of moonlight catches his eyes. They're black as midnight.

'I just came out for a walk.' For no apparent reason, I point at the ground.

'I saw you leave the club. More of a run than a walk.'

'Bit of exercise...'

I have no chance to expand on the ridiculous explanation. The next thing I know, Christophe's car draws up at the other side of the wall: a perfect storm of bad timing.

'Shit,' I choke.

A door slams.

Say something, I urge myself. And for God's sake, do it calmly. 'You're back early.'

'I am. Harry was fine, by the way. Fast asleep. And Max was nowhere to be seen.'

'Oh.'

'And I think – although I can't be sure – I passed my brother's car on the way back.'

I remain silent.

'And then, I caught sight of you, running off round the lake.'

I start at the sound of another slam.

He moves closer. 'I've got to be honest with you, Evie. It all gave me a strange sense of foreboding.'

'Did it?'

'Mmm.' He reaches up, runs a finger down my cheek. 'And that's why I decided to follow you.'

'Oh.'

'Oh,' he mimics. Taking hold of my waist and drawing me in to his chest. 'Perhaps you might like to tell me the truth.'

At that precise moment, a length of rope tumbles over the wall.

In mock surprise, Sebastian releases me and takes a step back. 'Goodness me. What's this?' He takes hold of the rope and examines it closely. 'Soft cotton. Top grade. Just like we stock at the club. You're not planning on a spot of bondage, are you?'

I manage nothing but a pathetic squeak.

'Knotted too. Now, that can be very kinky, but also extremely uncomfortable if you don't know what you're doing. I wonder who we'll find at the other end.' He grabs the rope with both hands, and tugs hard.

'Merde! Don't pull so much!'

Giving me a quick, mischievous grin, Seb gathers the rope and throws it back over the wall.

'Evie?' Christophe calls.

'Guess again,' Seb calls back.

There's a brief silence before Christophe responds. 'Sebastian?'

'Yes, Christophe. It's me.'

The sound of a passing car briefly interrupts the exchange.

'Is Evie with you?'

'Maybe.'

'Is she alright?'

'Why wouldn't she be?'

'Well...'

'What's going on, Christophe?'

I hear muted curses, all in French. They're followed by a hasty explanation.

'This wasn't my idea. She came to me. She told me she was desperate to get away. She practically begged me for help.'

'But why the rope? Why the ridiculous escapade?'

'She wasn't sure you'd let her go. And I thought... what with security at the gates ...'

'Ah.' Seb's eyes flash. 'That explains it.' He calls again: 'I don't hold people against their will, Christophe.'

'What was that?'

'You heard me.' I'm gripped by the arm. 'Go and find someone else to rescue. You're not needed here.'

'I'm not leaving until I hear from Evie.'

I'm drawn in again, this time into a vice-like embrace. Immediately, the contact sends a myriad of mad sensations skittering through my body.

'We're going back to the club,' Seb whispers into my ear, 'and we're going to talk this through.' His lips brush against my cheek.

150

'In the meantime, I suggest you give Christophe what he wants. Because if you don't, he'll call the police ...'

'No.' A word spoken with too much haste. I pull back and fight off a shiver. 'It's alright, Christophe,' I shout, my voice on the edge of breaking. 'I made a mistake, that's all. Everything's okay.'

'Is it?'

'Yes!'

There's more grumbling and grouching – again in French. While Seb keeps his attention fixed solely on me, I decide I'm more comfortable staring at the wall. I listen to the tell-tale slam of a car door. It's not until the engine's fired up and Christophe's driven away, that Seb speaks again.

'I thought you were staying.'

I say nothing.

'Look at me.'

'No.'

I'm set free, but not for long. Big strong hands cup my cheeks, tilting my face to his. 'Whatever Max said, it's all lies.'

'How do you...?'

In a nanosecond, his mouth is on mine, kissing me with a fervour I've never known before. And I really must be a prize idiot, because I can't help kissing him back.

When he's finally taken his fill, he pulls away. 'I know my brother's been here. He can't help himself.'

'I suppose not.'

'He's filled your head with crap.'

'I don't know...'

'I do.' He chews at his bottom lip. 'And before you make any more bad decisions, I need to show you something.'

'Show me what?'

I get no answer. Instead, I'm released again, grabbed by the hand and guided back through the trees. At breakneck speed, and in complete silence, he leads me round the lake, across the lawn and up towards the club. By the time we reach the front steps, my mind's a restless whirlpool of questions and I'm totally out of breath. It's a relief when he finally pauses in the lobby. Less so when I realise why.

Leaning against the desk, with the gym bag at his feet and a stern expression plastered across his face, Christophe's waiting for us.

'I believe I'm owed an explanation.'

'You've had one,' Seb growls.

'But it doesn't make sense.'

151

'She made a mistake. Didn't you hear?'

'An hour ago, she was desperate to leave.'

'Fine.' Letting go of my hand, Seb motions in Christophe's direction. 'Explain yourself, Evie.'

'Explain myself?' I swallow. 'Okay. Right. Yes.' There's no doubt about it. This needs to be believable, because there's no way I can risk police involvement. And anyway, I'm desperate to see what Seb's got to show me. Summoning a brittle smile, I get on with it. 'I'm okay. It was just a misunderstanding. I overreacted. He's not holding me here against my will. I want to stay.' I scuttle over to Christophe, collect the bag, and scuttle back.

'So now you know,' Seb adds.

'But...'

'Back off, Christophe. Keep your nose out of my business.'

'Maybe you should tell Max the same thing.' A strange smile makes an appearance. 'He was here, you know.'

'And I wonder who called him.'

'Pas moi.'

With a dismissive grunt, Seb takes my free hand and urges me to the foot of the staircase.

'I don't go looking for trouble,' Christophe calls after him. 'In spite of what Max tells you... and Zachary too.'

I don't know why, but that brings Seb to a halt at the first step. Slowly – very slowly – he turns back. 'Drop it.'

'How can I?'

'Be very careful what you say next. You have a witness.'

A witness to what? That's what I'd like to ask. But this isn't the time to probe, not with two agitated alpha males engaging in a furious glaring contest. Instead, I fix my attention on Christophe. When he finally speaks, I'm no less flummoxed.

'I need to know you still believe in me.'

'Why?'

'Because I barely see you these days. Because we hardly talk. I can't even remember the last time you invited me upstairs.'

'And?'

'It's almost like you believe him.'

'I can think for myself.'

'We both know he poisoned Zach against me. I couldn't stand it if he got to you.'

'No chance of that. We don't even speak any more. That's the price I paid for having your back.'

'And I thank you for paying it, because it wasn't me who went to the press.'

'Enough!'

With that, Seb tightens his grip on my hand and virtually hauls me up the two flights of stairs to his apartment. As soon as the door's kicked open, I'm thrust inside.

'That way,' he half-snarls, pointing to the left and leaving me to make my own way to the kitchen counter.

I sling the bag onto the floor. 'I think you need to calm down.'

'I'm calm enough.'

'Seriously, I'm not talking to you while you're like this.'

'Fine.' Heading to the other side of the counter, he grimaces out of the window, takes a handful of deep breaths, and finally issues an edict. 'Stay away from Christophe.'

'Why?' I ask, because he's calm enough now to handle a little disagreement. 'He seems like a decent man.'

'Who knows what he's like?' he grumbles, staring at the floor.

'What do you mean?'

'Exactly what I say.'

'I don't get it. If he's such a thorn in your side, why do you let him come here?'

'Because.' He looks up, an obvious distaste in his features. But there's something else too. The slightest hint of unease. As if he doesn't quite believe his own feelings. 'It's complicated.'

'Try me. I'm not a moron.'

'Oh, I know that.' With a sigh of exasperation, he helps himself to a glass of wine.

'Were you lovers?'

'What?'

Oh, Jesus. Why did that come out of my mouth?

I shift from one foot to another. 'It's just that... he seems like... a bit like a spurned lover.'

Seb bursts into laughter. 'Just to be clear, I'm heterosexual.'

'Heterosexual. Right. Yes.'

The humour disappears. Keeping his eyes fixed on mine, he takes a sip of wine. 'I've known Christophe for years, since we were kids. He's a family friend. And there was a time when we were close.'

'So, what went wrong?'

Clearly unwilling to discuss the matter, he shakes his head.

'He mentioned the press.'

'He did.'

'And you defended him?'

153

'Nothing escapes you, does it? I have defended him, and maybe it was a mistake.'

'Because it caused the rift between you and Max?'

'Miss fucking Marple.' He raises his glass in a mock toast, then finishes off the wine. 'It's all in the past. There's no point dwelling on it. The thing is Christophe's got friends here, influential members I can't afford to lose. If he goes, others might follow. And that's why I keep him at the club.' With a shrug, he slams down the glass and changes the course of the conversation. 'I think it's time you told me about Max's little visit. What did he say to make you run?'

I hesitate.

'Evie?'

'Okay.' Silently urging myself to get on with it, I lean both hands on the counter. 'It wasn't just him. Celine was there too. She's the one who tipped him off.'

'Of course.'

'And I don't blame her, really. She's concerned about you. That's all. And so is Max.'

'You're defending them?'

I am, aren't I?

'What did they say? Come on.'

Oh, God. He's getting angry again.

'Right.' Bloody hell, what did they say? There's something about being put on the spot by a simmering Delaney that turns the brain to mush. 'Celine said you had enough crap in your life. She said I should leave you alone because I'm no good for you, and I'm causing damage.'

'Really?'

'Yes. And it's true.'

'I'll be the judge of that. What else?'

'Max said...'

'What?'

'He said...' Maybe I shouldn't mention the money, or the threat. 'No, Celine said...'

'Celine said what?'

'Oh, I don't know!' I straighten up. 'That you're not relationship material. There's not a romantic bone in your body. Basically, you just use women and dump them, and move on. Oh!' I clap a hand over my mouth. I'm getting it all wrong. She did say something like that, just not today.

'Oh?'

I squeeze my eyes shut, because my brain seems to have gone to pot.

'Let me tell you something, Evie.'

I open my eyes, stunned by a new tenderness in his voice.

'It's entirely possible that Celine knows fuck all about me.'

'Is it?'

'Yes. I might have been like that in the past, but it's entirely possible I've changed.' His lips twitch and his eyes glimmer. 'Because it's entirely possible I never met the right woman before.'

'The right woman?' Am I the right woman? I can hardly believe I am, but he's still smiling at me, and there's no other woman in the room.

'So ...' He cocks his head. 'Have we covered all the bases?'

Have we? Out of nowhere, my thoughts click into gear, reminding me of something I really should clear up. 'Not quite.' I hesitate, because this is going to be difficult. Sucking in a deep breath, I force out the words. 'Max told me there are things I don't know about you. He said they were ... unsavoury. And apparently, if I did know them, I wouldn't be so keen to stick around.' I bite my lip. 'Is that true?'

It seems like an age before he responds. And when he does, it's hardly reassuring.

'Probably.'

'Probably?' I stare at him, wishing I had the power to read his mind, because I'm fairly sure I'm not about to get a full and frank confession. 'So, what was he talking about?'

'You're not ready to hear.'

'But...'

'All in good time. Are we done now?'

'Almost.'

With a resigned sigh, he comes to my side of the counter. 'What else?'

'I'm still a prisoner.'

'And what makes you say that?'

'You've opened all the doors, but I still can't get out of the grounds. You've got people on the gates, checking cars.'

'To protect you.'

'Oh, please.'

'A little faith wouldn't go amiss.'

'I don't believe in anything that can't be proved.'

'Fair enough.' He holds out a hand. 'Like I said, there's something you need to see.'

155

***

He leads me back down the corridor, past the front door and up the staircase at the end. Halting just inside his office, I watch him walk over to his desk.

He unlocks a drawer on the left... and produces a gun.

I gawp at it.

'Don't worry. I'm not about to shoot you. I hate these things.' With a wry smile, he lays the gun on the desk. 'Give me a moment.' Pulling his mobile from his pocket, he makes a call. 'Come up to my study.' He places the phone on the desk – right next to the gun – and raises his eyes to mine. 'Alex is joining us. He won't be long.'

Not long at all, in fact. Less than two minutes later, he's hovering at my side. But it's more than enough time for me to slip into an abyss, reliving those last few seconds before I passed out, feeling nothing but the touch of metal against my forehead, hearing nothing but the sound of Crawley's voice.

'This is my Head of Security.'

'We've met.' I half-smile, relieved to be back in the present.

'He's the one who tracked you down in Bermondsey. And for your benefit, I'd like him to recap what was going on when he found you.'

Alex clears his throat and moves forward. 'Some bloke had her up against a wall.'

'A mugger?' Seb asks.

'Definitely not.' He glances from Seb to me, then back again. 'He was a bit of a handful, to be honest. Managed to fight off three of us and get away.' He motions to the gun. 'But he dropped that. Serious piece of kit. Not the sort of thing a mugger carries around.'

'So what?' Suspecting these men know more than they're letting on, I battle back a sudden attack of the shakes. 'It was some random nutter with a gun.'

'There was nothing random about it,' Seb counters, his gaze lingering on me. 'Tell her what you heard him say, Alex.'

'Are you sure?'

'Absolutely. She needs to hear the truth.'

With a reluctant nod, Alex does as he's told. 'Die, you fucking bitch.'

I remember them now, those four little words that accompanied me into unconsciousness. If Alex hadn't turned up, they would have been the last thing I ever heard. Even here, in the safety of Seb's

156

apartment, they're still threatening to squeeze the air from my lungs and drag me into oblivion. It's only Seb's voice that keeps me in place.

'Evie?'

'I'm fine.'

It's obvious he doesn't believe me. And I don't blame him.

'There's more,' he says.

'Fine.' I wave a hand. 'Go ahead.'

'You're sure?'

'Yes.'

'Okay.' He studies me for a moment. 'Alex, from the beginning, if you don't mind.'

I turn my attention to his Head of Security, trying my best not to fixate on the scar.

'Seb sent me to find you.' He addresses me directly. 'We had the napkin, so I went to the Phoenix and asked for Mary. The owner told me you'd been sacked. He said there was another man looking for you. He said this man had a photo, but no name. He left a phone number and offered a reward. I asked the owner to share the number, but he said he'd lost it.'

'Which was a lie?' Seb intervenes.

'I reckon so. Didn't think too much of it at the time. Just left my number, offered another reward and left.'

'And then you got the text.'

'I did.' He focusses back on me. 'That night you went back to the café, the owner texted me to let me know you'd shown up. We got there as soon as we could, but you'd already gone.' He pauses. 'We think the owner contacted the other man too. In fact, we think that other man was your attacker.'

I shake my head at the memory of Wallace's dodgy behaviour that night,

'Actually,' Seb adds, 'we know he was your attacker.'

'How?'

'Because it's not that difficult to put two and two together. It's obvious he was determined to track you down. And seeing as you left your lodgings in such a hurry, I'd say you were desperate to stay out of his way.'

Ready to offer up another pathetic denial, I open my mouth.

'Don't bother.' Seb raises a hand, silencing me before I can utter a word. 'I'm not finished yet.' Eyes fixed on mine, and filled with determination, he presses on. 'Alex has been back to The Phoenix since then. The Walrus denied making contact, but he did say this man had been round all the shops and cafés in the area. Alex got his number from a local shopkeeper. Needless to say, he didn't answer our calls. The phone's untraceable, by the way. Probably a burner. Probably at the bottom of the Thames.' Seb arches an eyebrow. 'So, there you have it.'

I turn away, half-listening while Seb gives Alex a quick dressing-down for not sorting out the hole in security. Issued with an order to get the CCTV shored up, the Head of Security makes an exit.

And I'm gently manoeuvred round to face Seb.

'This all started as nothing more than me tracing that ring,' he says, his hands on my arms. 'Bringing you back here was never part of the plan. But that all changed when Alex told me what happened. I had you brought here for your own safety. The lodge seemed a decent enough place, but then you caused a ruckus.'

'You should have left me down there.'

'If I'd been sober, I might have.'

'I knew it.'

'Yes. You were irritatingly right on that count.' He smiles. 'I don't normally make the best decisions when I've had a few, but that was a pretty good one. If I'd left you in the lodge, I wouldn't have met you. I wouldn't have had this stunningly beautiful, stunningly inebriated creature on my hands.' He runs a finger down my cheek. 'I was intrigued, to say the least. I wanted to know what sort of trouble you were in. So...' He brushes a thumb across my lips. 'After Celine sorted you out, I came to see you. Thought I might get some answers.'

'But you didn't?' God, I hope not.

'No. You were too busy telling me I don't know what it feels like to be afraid.'

'I did that?'

'At least ten times.' He laughs, quietly. 'Which intrigued me even more.' He becomes serious again. 'I don't want you to feel afraid, Evie. That's why there's extra security on the gates.'

'But he couldn't know where...'

Quickly, I silence myself. Because I've just confirmed it all with one brief, unguarded bout of anxiety. Now, Seb knows for sure that the man who turned up at The Phoenix was the man who attacked me.

'He might have stuck around,' he says. 'He could have seen Alex's car. Maybe he traced the plates.'

'How could he do that?'

158

'You tell me. Even though you were using an assumed identity and living cash-in-hand, he still managed to trace you to Bermondsey. And, by the way, I'd love to know how he did that.'

A stupid mistake with a bank card. But I can't let Seb know just how big this is. Instead, I just shrug.

'I want to find this man.' He tucks a strand of hair behind my ear. 'I want to get him out of your life.'

The tenderness in his eyes makes my throat constrict. 'You can't.'

'Don't underestimate my determination. I'm even prepared to go to Max for help.'

Seriously? 'But...'

'With Max on board, there'd be no limits.'

It makes no difference. He has no idea what he's up against.

'But if I'm going to help you, I'll need your real name. And I need to know what's going on.'

A tear trickles down my cheek. 'I can't tell you.'

'That's okay.' He nods. 'I get it. You don't want me to know what you're caught up in. Perhaps it's unsavoury.' A clear reference to his own secrets, he lets the words sink in. 'You think I wouldn't be so keen to stick around if I knew what it was... but you're wrong. My mistakes are in the past, and so are yours.' He draws me in tight and delivers a long, mesmerising kiss. 'And by the way,' he says when he's done. 'I do know what fear feels like. Believe me. I know it only too well.'

Chapter Sixteen

Wrapped in a luxuriously fluffy bathrobe, I lean against the balcony at the front of the boathouse and gaze out over the lake. It's a flat calm this morning, catching a hint of blue here, a ghost-like whisper of white there; the perfect, glassy surface winking in the sun.

I'd lose myself in the beauty of it all, if the last few hours weren't still demanding my full attention, casting me away in the memory of a magical interlude that somehow managed to undo the damage of Max and Celine's intervention. A late supper and a glass of wine. Cosy cuddles and inconsequential chat on the sofa. A long, slow session of glorious lovemaking in the bedroom, marked by tender kisses and gentle caresses. God knows what time we fell asleep in each other's arms, bathed in the soft glow of the bedside lamp, but it was late morning by the time we woke. It was only after another lazy session – during which he called the master of seduction out to play and mesmerised me with a bout of serious action – that we finally managed to part company with the bed.

'Evie?'

I sense his presence, a thrum of electricity rising like a tide, just before his chest makes contact with my back.

I lean against him. 'This is beautiful.'

'Isn't it just?' His hands close over mine.

'I can understand why it's your favourite place in the world.'

He scatters a handful of lazy, feather-light kisses across my neck. I'm on the verge of slipping into wordless pleasure when he pulls back.

'I used to stay here with my mother. It was her sanctuary.'

'Was?' I turn to face him.

'Was,' he confirms. 'She died a long time ago.'

And I feel like a fool. Although he's spoken about her before, he's never mentioned this before. But maybe I shouldn't have assumed she was still alive. 'I'm so sorry.'

'It's okay.' He plants a gentle kiss on my cheek. 'I'm a big boy now. I can deal with it. By the way, I just called Alex. The CCTV situation was rectified last night. He's organised extra patrols, and we've got some temporary security staff to boost the numbers.'

'So, it really is safe?' I turn back to the view.

'One hundred percent.' He rests his chin on my shoulder. 'Whoever this man is, on the off-chance he knows where you are, there's no way he's getting in.'

'Thank you.'

Words fade into a comfortable silence, making just enough space for the voice of reason to make itself heard. Accompanied by nothing more than a rustling of leaves, it pleads with me to give him something – anything – because I can't deny he's earned that much. Lowering my lids for a few seconds, I pick through the past and decide the earliest details are safe enough.

'I never knew my dad.'

I feel him tense. He squeezes my hands and moves closer, cocooning me against the world. It's all the reassurance I need. He knows I'm about to open up, and he'll let me do it on my own terms.

Looking out over the lake, I press on with a story I've never told, left buried so long it hardly seems to be mine. 'He left before I was born, but it doesn't matter. I had the best childhood I could possibly want. It made no difference that he wasn't around. My mum and my grandmother brought me up. I was happy. I had friends. I worked hard at school. I had a loving home.'

'But something went wrong along the way?' Seb prompts.

Plenty of things. A whole string of connected events. I settle on giving him the first. After all, it's safe enough.

'Mum died.' The words stick in my throat. Again, he squeezes my hands. It's enough to dislodge the rest. 'She had cancer. She died when I was thirteen. After that...' The word 'Oma' hovers on my lips. I swallow it back. 'After that, my grandmother looked after me. She was fantastic, so loving. It was because of her I didn't go to pieces.'

'And because you're a survivor.'

'It's in the blood.' I glance back, and that does it.

That strange warmth returns to my heart. And this time, it digs in for the long run, making it perfectly clear I've strayed into a new reality where everything's guided by a single, overwhelming force. Not ready to acknowledge it yet, I blink myself back to the moment and return to the job in hand.

'Mum was gone, but I couldn't give up. I carried on being the good girl, doing all the right things, because I wanted to please my grandmother. I wanted to make her proud. She's the one who...' No. Be careful. 'She loved to cook. I spent a lot of time in the kitchen with her. She taught me a lot. After Mum died, she distracted me with cooking, and it worked.' I lapse into silence, wishing I could give him more, resenting the tears that well in my eyes.

I've just about brushed them away when he wraps his arms around my waist and holds me tight. I lean my head back against his chest and place my hands over his, luxuriating in every little sensation.

'Is she still alive?' he asks.

'No.' A vision flashes through my brain: an unwelcome memory of thinning hair and fading blue irises, skin as delicate as tissue. 'She died when I was twenty.' Relieved to have shared a few scraps of information, I release a quiet breath.

'Tell me something,' he says, urging me round to face him. 'How does a girl who works hard at school, and loves cooking with her grandmother, end up homeless and destitute?'

How, indeed? Best to be vague. 'I made some poor choices.'

He doesn't probe further. Instead, he simply nods.

'I want to tell you more.' I bite my lip. 'I really do.'

'When you're good and ready. When you trust me. And talking of trust...' As if he's just entertained a brilliant idea, he breaks into a boyish smile. 'I wonder if you can swim?'

'Pardon?'

'I wonder... if you can swim.' His eyes sparkle.

'Yes, I can. But why would you want to know that?' I blink in disbelief. 'No. You're not suggesting...'

'Oh, but I am suggesting.' The smile morphs into a full-on, mischievous grin. 'Maybe you could look on it as an exercise, a way of developing said trust.'

My heart begins to beat madly, and it's nothing to do with the sexy body that's pressing against me. I glance back at the lake. 'I can't... I can't go in there.'

'Why not?' He draws back and takes hold of my hand.

'Because.'

'I think you'll find that's my line.' With no further ado, he half-drags me inside, through the bedroom, along the hallway to the top of the staircase.

'Seb!' I pull to a halt. 'I'm not going in that lake.'

'Why not? What's the problem?'

'I don't know.' Except, I do. I have no idea what's under the surface. 'It's scary.'

'Don't be daft.' With a laugh, he plants a quick kiss on my lips. 'There's nothing to fear but fear itself.'

'Hang on a minute.'

I've got plenty to say about his ridiculous quote, but I don't get the chance. Immediately, he's on the move again. And so am I. After stumbling down the stairs in his wake, and almost breaking my neck in the process, I'm guided out into bright sunshine.

'Seb, no!'

Within seconds, we're perilously close to the lake.

'You'll like it.'

'You reckon?' At the foot of the jetty, I dig in my heels.

He wheels round to face me, still smiling, but with the mischief now underscored by pure determination. 'Comfort zones. They're all well and good, but the problem is this. They stop you moving on.' He scans the lake. 'You can look on this as an exercise in trust, but it's also about facing your fears. You're coming in with me, and that's that.'

Out of nowhere, my brain's telling me to get on with it, because Seb might just have a point. In the meantime, my body continues to baulk and my mouth decides to throw out a final complaint.

'I haven't got a swimming costume.'

'Neither have I.' Leaving me where I am, he walks to the end of the jetty and strips off his t-shirt.

I gesture to the water. 'Isn't it dangerous?'

'Of course not.' He unfastens his zip and strips off his jeans. 'Come on, Evie. Get that robe off.'

'But what if someone sees me?'

'In the grounds of a sex club?' He laughs. 'Do you really think anyone's going to raise an eyebrow?'

Fair point. 'But...' Oh, Jesus Christ. Why on earth am I still fighting? 'Alright.' Quickly, before I can dither myself into a pathetic ball, I strip off the robe and let it drop to the ground.

'There you go. How difficult was that?' Without waiting for an answer, he executes a perfect dive.

Watching the ripples follow in his wake, I decide there's no way I'm doing that. Instead, I pick a point halfway down the jetty and sit on the edge, risking a few buttock-splinters in the process. While Seb emerges a few feet away, I dip my legs into the water. Much as I expected, it's freezing.

'Woman!' Seb calls, pointing at me. 'Water!' He aims the same finger downwards. 'Now!'

I gaze out over the surface; an opaque sheen concealing God knows what. 'I don't know...'

He swims back to me. 'You've come this far. One more little step.'

'Okay! Give me a count down.'

'Three. Two. One.'

I'm not sure what gives me the courage, but the next thing I know, I'm waist-deep in the lake and my teeth are chattering.

'What?' I squeal nervously. 'It's not deep?'

'Not here. Now, get swimming.' He swirls around and sets about a swift front crawl.

Digging my toes into soft mud, I waft my hands through water and decide to hell with it. I take the plunge, falling backwards, gasping as an icy cold envelops me. 'I'm getting hypothermia!'

'Just keep moving.'

'I am moving.'

I spin onto my front and attempt a timid breaststroke. Every now and then, I extend a leg downwards, exploring with my toes, feeling mud here, a stone there, an occasional clump of weed. After a minute or so, Seb beckons to me from a few feet away.

'Over here!'

With just his head and neck out of the water, he's clearly standing on the bottom. And seeing as I already fancy a rest, I head straight towards him. As soon as I'm close enough, he takes hold of me, rewarding me with a long, invigorating kiss. And while he does, I cling on tight, luxuriating in the contrast between the warmth of his skin and the arctic chill surrounding us. It's a delicious sensation. So delicious, I'm sorely disappointed when he sets me free and glides away on his back.

'There. Not so bad, is it?'

'No.' As if to mock my new confidence, something large and firm and slippery brushes against my right leg. 'What the...' It makes contact again. I squeal. 'Come back! Seb! Oh, my God. I felt something.'

Rolling onto his front, he returns to me in two strokes. 'Felt what?'

Another touch. 'Jesus! There's something alive in here.'

'No shit, Sherlock.' He laughs. 'Must be Jaws.'

'Jaws?'

'Our resident pike. There's a Mrs Jaws too.'

'What?'

'Calm down.' He catches me by the waist. 'They're both juveniles, and they actually help keep the water healthy. They eat the sticklebacks.'

'But they bite.'

'Very rarely, and usually only if you're wearing something shiny, which you're not. But this pair never bite. I promise. If they did, I certainly wouldn't let them anywhere near the old fella.'

With a quirk of the eyebrows, he disappears underwater, leaving me to swirl in circles, wondering if he's telling the truth; or if Mr and Mrs Jaws are, in, fact, eyeing me up for a quick snack. Before long, it's not the only concern on my mind. With the seconds ticking by, Seb still hasn't reappeared. I'm about to panic when he finally breaks the surface.

'For God's sake, Sebastian. I thought you'd drowned.'

'No chance of that.'

'But the weeds...'

'Will you stop worrying?' He swims over to me. 'It's a managed lake, Evie. Nothing's going to eat you. There's nothing to catch your feet on, nothing to drag you under.'

'There isn't?'

'No.' I feel a warm hand on my waist. 'I'd never put you in danger. Trust me on that. Now, slow your breathing.' He waits patiently, registering every lungful of air with a small nod, smiling his encouragement. 'That's better.' The hand slips away.

'There's really nothing?'

'No. Now chill out. Swim a bit. Think about how you feel.'

'How I feel?' I launch into another sedate breaststroke. 'Bloody freezing. That's how I feel.'

The next few minutes pass in silence. While Seb indulges in a deft front crawl, repeatedly surging away and closing in again, I concentrate on my strokes, scooping my hands through the water and leaving lazy circles in their wake. Before long, the chill seems to have done its job, rejuvenating every nerve and fibre in my body. With bright sunlight skating across the glassy surface and my body gradually warming, the water soon begins to feel like silk against my skin.

When we finally meet at the centre of the lake, I look up at the sky. It seems bluer, somehow. And crisper too.

'So?' he asks. 'How do you feel now?'

The answer surprises me. 'Alive.'

'Good.' His eyes glisten. He's clearly pleased. 'Shall I tell you why?'

'Go ahead.'

'It's because your heart's beating faster, because your body's releasing endorphins like there's no tomorrow. It's a natural high.'

'A high.' I laugh. 'I like it. No. I love it.'

Because for the first time in months – maybe years – I'm totally relaxed, released from fear and liberated by trust. And it's all down to this stunning man who swept me up out of the darkness and dragged me into the light.

'Job done.' Closing the gap between us, he gives me a quick peck on the lips. 'Now, let's get out before we both shrivel.'

**

After a long, leisurely shower together, I'm half-expecting more shenanigans. But, as soon as we're back in the bedroom, he becomes withdrawn. Dressing quickly, and making no eye contact whatsoever, he pauses in the doorway.

'I'll make us a coffee,' he says. 'When you're ready, there'll be something for you in the lounge.'

Ten minutes later, I'm looking down on him from the front of the boathouse. Sitting on the upturned boat, he's gazing out over the water, a mug of coffee languishing untouched at his feet. I glance at the table next to the sofa, where another mug sits alongside a tattered manila file.

I sit down, pick up the file and flip it open, only to discover it's crammed with aging newspaper clippings. Tipping them onto the cushions, I spread them out, discovering they're kept in no particular order. Curling at the edges and discoloured by time, some are carefully folded, others crumpled. I select one at random. It's from a broadsheet, dated about twenty-five years ago. There are no pictures, just reams of text introduced by a simple headline: 'Phillip Delaney's Son Found.' Immediately engrossed, I read through the article. And by the time I've finished, the bare bones of Seb's story are in place.

For a minute or so, I can do nothing more than stare at the text, trying to process the facts. A little boy snatched from the grounds of his uncle's house. A rejected ransom demand, followed by a two-week stand-off. The lucky break in the investigation. Boy found and returned to parents. Finally, I manage to shake myself back to life. After riffling through the rest of the articles – from a variety of newspapers and magazines – I take the time to read them all, every single one of them, pouring over grainy photographs of a four-year-old Seb, his anxious parents, a rambling, old house in the middle of nowhere.

'Jesus.' No wonder he got touchy every time I talked about kidnapping.

I get up to check on him.

He hasn't moved an inch. Still perched on the boat and gazing over the lake, he's waiting patiently for me to digest his past. Gathering the articles, I slip them back into the folder and take a moment to reflect. Encouraging the intimacy worked much faster than I anticipated. It opened him up and gave me the information I craved. But I don't feel the slightest hint of victory. Instead, I seem to be overwhelmed by sadness, and desperate to comfort a man who found the courage to share his demons.

Leaving the folder on the sofa, I head for the kitchen, prepare two fresh mugs of coffee and put together a quick snack. With everything ready – bread, butter, cheese and a selection of fruit – I carry the whole lot down the precarious staircase, even more precariously balanced on a tray.

As soon as the door shuts behind me, he turns.

'Thought you might be hungry,' I call.

He gets up from the boat. 'Ravenous.'

'Here you go then. Brunch.' Closing in on him, I offer the tray. 'It's not much.'

'It'll do nicely.'

He takes it from me, and we settle down together on dry grass, enjoying the perfect weather for a peaceful, impromptu picnic. And then, while we eat and drink in silence, I steal the occasional glance at the man sitting next to me. For someone who's just spilled his deepest secrets, he seems strangely calm.

'Thank you,' I murmur at last. 'For showing me.'

'You deserved it.' He picks up an apple and studies it intently. 'I wonder why.' He puts the apple down again.

'Why I deserved it?'

'Why I thought it was perfectly fine to lock you up in my apartment... after everything that happened to me.'

'Your apartment isn't a cellar.' I frown at a sudden realisation. It must be those memories of the dark that keep his bedside lamp forever switched on. 'And besides, I've never really been a prisoner.'

'Still....'

'What I did was worse. I definitely shouldn't have handcuffed you to those railings.' Because God knows what trauma it dragged up. 'Oh, my God.' In an instant, I'm hit by another realisation. 'Those letters. They're linked.'

He frowns at the tray. 'They come every month. A different post mark each time.'

'And they're from him?' We both know who I'm talking about. The man who locked him away.

'Can't think who else would send them.'

He picks at a blade of grass, clearly avoiding eye contact. And I can't really blame him. After all, I did something similar before we went for a swim. Somehow, it's easier to spill out your life story when you're staring at an inanimate object.

'He was released a few years ago. A reformed character, apparently.' He shakes his head. 'The letters only started last year. August, I think. I don't know why. Maybe he'd hit hard times. Maybe he blamed me, wanted to make me pay.'

'Bollocks,' I growl, suddenly furious on Seb's behalf.

He smiles, wryly. 'You seem to be swearing.'

'So bloody what?' I'm on a roll now. 'He's not a reformed character, Seb. He's harassing you. This is stalking. Bloody hell. Tell me you've been to the police about those letters.'

'Of course I have.' He pats my thigh and waits for me to calm. 'The police have got the originals. Trouble is, there's nothing to pin him down, no clear evidence linking the letters to him. No fingerprints. Nothing.'

'But the content...'

'Anyone who read the papers knows the details. Anyway, it doesn't matter. He's gone off-grid. Disappeared. The police can't trace him.' A heron takes off from the reeds nearby. He's momentarily distracted. 'The latest one came yesterday,' he says, watching the bird relocate at the opposite side of the lake. 'That's why I was upset. It was nothing to do with you.'

He turns to me now, eyes filled with dark echoes of the past. Despite the relaxed demeanour, it's clearly still painful for him to talk about what happened, and I'm not about to delve any deeper. But I still have one question to ask.

'Why didn't you tell Max?'

'We haven't been talking. You know that.' He cuts himself a lump of cheese and pops it into his mouth.

'Since when?'

'Last year.'

'That long?'

'Yes.'

'But why?'

'Family matters. Let's put it that way.' He swallows the cheese, takes a swig of coffee, and decides to give me more. 'Max has got a giant bee in his bonnet. I think he was born with it. Anyway ... even if we were getting on, I wouldn't tell him.' He notices my quizzical look. 'He'd over-react, blame the wrong person, take things too far.'

'Too far?' While Seb drinks more coffee, I mull over that final point. I don't know much about Max Delaney, but I'm pretty certain he's the ruthless type, which probably means he'd hunt this man to the ends of the earth and rip out his inner organs. 'Your brother sounds dangerous.'

Out of nowhere, Seb laughs. 'Not dangerous. Just a little domineering at times, and generally over-protective.'

Now I'm confused. 'What's so bad about that?'

'I don't need his protection anymore. I'm all grown up.'

'That's male pride speaking.'

'Maybe.' His eyes brighten. 'I suppose I should swallow it and wash it down with a swig of whiskey.'

'This why you've been drinking. The letters. They stirred up things you didn't want to think about. And on top of falling out with Max...'

'Hear that sound?' he interrupts, raising a finger.

'No.'

'It's the sound of the proverbial nail being hit on the proverbial head.' He touches the same finger against his brow. 'I'm not an idiot. I knew why I was drinking too much, but it didn't stop me wanting sweet oblivion.'

I lean over and cup his cheek. 'You've been destroying yourself, Seb. Giving him exactly what he wants.'

'And now I've stopped.'

He pulls away, leaving me to worry I've gone too far again. But it's soon evident he's preparing himself for another revelation.

'There was no abuse, you know.'

I nod. 'They said as much in the articles.' No evidence of sexual abuse, but no mention of the mental torture he must have suffered.

'My father never believed it though.' He sighs. 'After what happened, he always saw me as damaged goods. An embarrassment. He just threw money at me and hoped I'd go away.'

'That can't be true.'

'You've not met Phillip Delaney.' He picks at a clump of grass. 'Anyway, it worked. I didn't bother my father because I was far too busy living the playboy lifestyle. Good for blotting things out, but entirely overrated in many other ways.'

Given what I now know, I'm hardly surprised he was tempted by the good life, or that he reacted badly to those letters. By comparison, my own childhood was a breeze.

'Is this what Max was talking about?'

He gives me a quizzical look.

169

'"Unsavoury things?"' Because they don't seem unsavoury to me, and they certainly don't make me want to run a mile.

Deep in thought, Seb remains silent for a few seconds before he lands the blow. 'No. That's not what he was talking about.'

I shake my head in confusion.

'I won't lie to you. I'll tell you everything... when it's the right time. I promise.' As if his brain's just dragged up something he'd rather not recall, he frowns into space.

I touch his arm. 'Are you okay?'

'Yes.' With a smile, he looks up at the boathouse. 'Just thinking. Before you arrived, I hadn't been down here for a long time.' He pauses, looks back to me. 'When I was young, I used to spend a lot of time here with my mother. She brought me here after... after the kidnapping. I suppose she thought it might help me to talk about what happened.'

'Did it?'

'No.'

'I'm sure she understood.'

'How could she?' He glances round. 'She never knew the truth. I couldn't talk about it because I didn't remember. I still don't.'

The revelation throws me. I have no idea what to say. It's a good job he carries on talking.

'It's all a blank. A great, big, dirty hole. I'm told I didn't speak at all for the first few weeks. I suppose it was shock. They got me counselling, but it didn't do much good. Eventually, they just swept it all under the rug. But it's never gone away.' He pauses. 'Even though I can' remember it, it never goes away.' He tips his head back, and groans. 'God help me. Why am I telling you all this?'

I have no ready answer, but somewhere in the deepest recesses of my being, I hope it's because he's falling; that he's laying his cards on the table to pave the way for a future together.

'I don't know where you're from or what you've done,' he says. 'I don't have a clue what you're caught up in. I don't even know your real name. But I can talk to you. I mean really talk to you. Why is that?'

'Maybe I'm a witch,' I smile, because this is all getting a bit intense. It's time for a touch of levity. 'Maybe I've cast a spell on you.'

It seems to work. His lips curve upwards.

He leans over and plants a gentle kiss on my lips. 'There's no 'maybe' about it.'

Chapter Seventeen

I've been studying Christophe Dupont for a good five minutes now. Leaning against the bonnet of a silver Porsche and chatting amiably with the dangerous-looking blonde in front of him, he seems genuine enough on the surface. But looks can be deceiving.

'What are you?' I ask out loud.

An innocent man, cruelly misjudged? Or a scheming liar, pointlessly causing chaos left, right and centre? Although Max clearly thinks he's the latter, and Zach too – whoever he might be – Seb doesn't seem to have a clue what to believe. And as for me, I don't have enough evidence to form a judgement. With nothing more than instinct to go on, it's all pure conjecture and a complete waste of time. Which is why I finally give up on the Christophe conundrum, turn my face to the sky and wonder if we'll see the sun any time soon.

It's been three days now since the weather broke, leaving a heavy slab of grey to settle over the world. After two nights in blissful seclusion, and another day indulging solely in each other's company, it prompted Seb to bring our stay at the boathouse to an end. Back here at the club, we quickly settled into a new routine. And today's already following the customary pattern.

After the usual, steamy start to the day and a lazy breakfast in bed, I took a shower while Seb went for a run. Freshly showered himself, he's now flicking through the day's newspapers, prior to sharing a late lunch and slipping off to work. I'll be left to my own devices for the rest of the afternoon: a prospect that isn't so daunting now my options have been widened. Maybe I'll wander the grounds or dig into a book, or indulge in my favourite pastime in the kitchen. And then, this evening, we'll chat over dinner, snuggle up on the sofa in front of a film, and finally round it all off exactly where we started: tangled up in crumpled sheets, wrapped in each other's arms, drifting away in a wonderful post-coital haze.

But it's not all rosy perfection...

Every now and then, a dim and distant voice resurfaces – just like it's doing now – reminding me that nothing lasts forever, especially when it's built on fake foundations. There are no two ways about it. I need to tell Seb the truth, no matter the consequences.

'Get in there and get on with it,' I urge myself. But they're half-hearted words, easily discarded when a loud laugh draws my attention back to the car park.

Running a hand up and down her arm while he whispers sweet nothings in her ear, Christophe's closer to the woman now. Is he making a proposition, I wonder, or sharing memories of a secret tryst? I'll never know the answer, but it's enough to put an end to good intentions. Instead of preparing a confession, I'm back to dwelling on the subject of kink, something that's increasingly dominated my brain of late. We might have taken to sharing Seb's enormous bed and indulging exclusively in my kind of sex, but there's absolutely no question I'm beginning to hanker after his. It's ridiculous. As if some filthy sex gremlin has taken up residence in my head...

'Evie?' His voice jolts me from my reverie.

'Coming.'

Grateful for the interruption, I wander back inside, and can't help smiling at the sight of him. Reclined on the sofa, the very image of domesticity, he's currently wrestling with an uncooperative broadsheet.

'It's busy out there. The car park's full.'

'Yeah, I forgot to say...' He lays the paper on his knee and attempts to flatten it. 'There's a bit of a do today. I won't be able to spend the evening with you. Got a meal I can't get out of.'

'No worries.' I flop down next to him and pick up my book. After he cleared away my curious pile of reading matter and invited me to help myself to any book in his library, for some reason, I couldn't help but gravitate back to *The Story of O*. Opening it at the latest page, I skim over a couple of sentences and decide I'm not really in the mood. Instead, I turn to Seb. 'Anything interesting?'

'Just the usual misery.'

'One of Max's papers?'

'You mean one of my father's.' He grimaces. 'No. It's not. I prefer to get my news elsewhere. Look at this.' He leans over, showing me a page from the business section.

My eyes are drawn straight to a picture of the elder Delaney brother. 'Max? What's he up to?'

'Just bought a publishing company.'

'Really?'

'A long-held dream. By day, he works on world domination. By night, he's a secret bookworm.'

'I'd never have guessed.'

172

'He hides it well.' Closing the paper, he attempts to fold it. 'He's not all bad, you know.'

'I might need a little proof.'

With a tight smile, Seb switches his attention to the book in my hands. 'Why on earth are you still reading that thing?'

'I don't know, really.' I turn the book over. 'There's a lot I don't like about it.'

'Such as?'

'The way she's treated like an object.'

'For what it's worth, I don't like that either.'

'So, you have read it?'

'Possibly.' He taps the book. 'Come on, then. Tell me more.'

I chew at my lip and wonder what to say. 'I want to know what makes her tick, what she gets out of it.'

His eyes flash with interest, and I can't help wondering if we're moving on from discussing a book to negotiating sexual relations.

'And I suppose that's because of what we did...' I hesitate, a little embarrassed now. 'You know... downstairs.'

'You didn't get anything out of it?'

'I wouldn't say that.'

He gives me an 'is-that-so' sort of look.

'It was... exciting.'

'So, the vanilla stuff's not doing it for you anymore?'

'No, that's not what I mean.' I shake my head. 'It is doing it for me. In spades.'

'Excellent.' He drops the paper to the floor. 'Because I like to think I'm getting good at it.'

'You're extremely good at it.'

We gaze at each other like a pair of goofy teenagers, completely lost in the moment.

'But...' he says.

'But.' I swallow. My mouth seems to have dried up. 'I suppose a little variety might be nice.'

'Some say it's the spice of life.'

'And this is something you enjoy.' I smooth my palm over the book cover. 'All this BDSM stuff.'

'I wouldn't put it quite like that.'

I look up, questioning.

'All this BDSM stuff was something I needed.'

'But you don't need it anymore?'

'Things have changed.'

'So, you wouldn't want to...'

'I never said that.'

'Because I think I'd quite like to... explore. And I'm sure it wouldn't do any harm, now we know each other better. Now that I trust you.'

'But you don't trust me completely. If you did, I wouldn't be calling you Evie.'

'Point taken.' Any day now, I'll spill the beans, every single one of them. It's unavoidable, seeing as I'm determined to keep this man in my life. But, for now... 'I trust you enough for this sort of thing.' I wave the book.

He takes it from me. Very swiftly, it joins the newspaper. 'If we do try it my way again, it wouldn't remotely resemble anything in there.' He nods to the book. 'That's never been my idea of healthy sex.'

In an instant, I'm toppled backwards into the cushions, and Seb's on top of me, pinning my hands above my head. Gazing up at his gorgeous face, it's no wonder a whirlwind of sensation kicks off in my core.

He brushes his lips over mine. 'And to be perfectly honest with you, I don't even know what 'my way' is any more.'

'I'm sure we can work it out.'

'I'm sure we can.' His eyes darken. It's that same look he gave me downstairs. The look of the dominant. 'But there's one thing I do know. You'll need to submit to me, completely.'

'With pleasure.'

A smile plays on his lips, and the air between us begins to fizzle. I'm pretty sure he's about to suggest a quick visit to a special room when we're jolted from the moment by a furious knocking at the front door.

'Oh, fuck off,' he grumbles.

The knocking continues.

'You'd better get that.' I pout. 'Whoever it is, they're not about to give up.'

'Whoever it is, they're about to get an earful.' With a disgusted shake of the head, he hauls himself up and marches down the hallway.

Listening to a muffled conversation, I sit up, straighten my clothes and smooth my hair into place. Seconds later, Seb returns, accompanied by a distinctly flustered Celine.

'This had better be important.' He slumps back onto the sofa.

Celine takes a moment to inspect the room. 'It is.' With a glance at a half-finished bottle of wine on the counter-top, she folds her arms. 'Martin's gone and...'

'No.' Seb holds up a hand. 'I don't particularly care what our Head Chef's gone and done. The fact is, you're more than capable of sorting it out yourself, so don't bother me with kitchen things.'

'But...'

'More than capable,' he repeats. 'Sort it out. That's what I pay you to do.'

'But...'

'Sort it.'

Emitting a dainty little growl, Celine balls her hands and stares at the floor. I'm on the verge of thinking the discussion might be over when Seb speaks again.

'Actually...' Banishing all signs of irritation, he clasps his hands behind his head and leans back. 'While you're here, there's something I've been meaning to discuss, and we might as well do it now.'

'But this is more...'

'No, it's not. I've been thinking.'

Dragging her attention from the marble tiles, she scowls at her boss. 'Careful now. You'll do yourself an injury.'

'No, I won't. I've come to a conclusion.'

'Can't wait to hear it.'

'Good.' He pauses. 'Here it is, then.' Another pause. 'I'd be much, much happier if the women in my life could get along.'

'What?'

'You heard.'

'The women?' She gives me a quick, disdainful glance. Clearly, she can't quite believe what Seb's just said.

And I'm not surprised. I'm struggling too.

'Yes, the women,' he confirms. 'Plural.'

'You're not telling me...'

'I'm about to tell you a few things, Celine. So you'd better listen up.' He cracks a smile. 'For a start, that little check on the wine bottle didn't pass me by. You might be interested to know I've reined it in – just the odd glass here and there, the normal sort of thing. So, you can back off with the unwanted nagging.'

With a flourish, she slaps her hands on her hips.

'And now, to my second point. Behaving like a total bitch doesn't suit you. Perhaps you should knock it on the head.'

'Yes, well...' She points a manicured finger at me. 'When you bring a complete stranger into your life.'

'And trust them and shack up with them,' Seb adds.

'Shack up?' I turn to the man next to me. 'Is this shacking up?'

'Looks like it,' he mutters from the side of his mouth.

'But...'

'Oh, for God's sake,' Celine interrupts. 'Have your own little conversation later. It's my turn to say something.'

'So, it is,' Seb grins.

'You've lost it.'

'On the contrary. I've not lost it at all. In fact, I know exactly where 'it' is. And a lot of that happens to do with Evie, who – in spite of your meddling – is going to be staying.'

'For how long?'

'How long is a piece of string?'

'Be serious.'

'I am.'

'You don't know what she is.'

'Ah, but I know what she isn't.' He waves a finger. 'For example, I know she's not a drug addict or a psychopath, or a prostitute. She's not a criminal, either. And she's certainly no gold-digger.'

'I wouldn't bet on it.'

'I would. Evie's a decent, honest, upright person...'

'Who isn't even called Evie.'

'Who helped my uncle in his hour of need, which you should respect.'

Arms crossed now, Mata Hari taps a foot. 'So, where's the ring then? If she's so honest and upright, why hasn't she handed it over?'

'None of your business. And while we're at it, no more blabbing to Max.'

'I...'

'He's your pal. I get that. But I've known you longer. And I'm your employer.'

'But...'

'Understood?'

'I...' Those crimson lips curl into an elegant snarl. 'Understood.'

'Good. I'm glad we've got that straight.' With an unexpected burst of energy, Seb springs to his feet, straightens his t-shirt and fixes his attention on me. 'So, now it's your turn.'

'What?' That's it? No time to gloat?

Apparently not, because he's standing at Celine's side now, a hand on her back. It's enough to throw her into a state of complete confusion. And me too.

'Now let me tell you something about this woman,' he says. 'I know she's been pretty vile to you, but on the whole she's a good person. And when she's got her head screwed on the right way, a wise woman. And a good friend of long standing too.' He removes the hand. 'Now, I know you don't particularly like her...'

'It's not that,' I blurt. 'It's just ...' Oh, God. Do I admit the truth? Why the hell not? 'She scares the hell out of me.'

'I'm not surprised, but it's only because she's testing you.'

'Is she?'

He nods.

'But, why?'

'To see if you're worthy.'

I'm stumped. 'Worthy of what?'

'Me, of course.'

Delivered with an absolute conviction, his answer immediately robs me of breath. I have just enough time to catch a new, bone-shaking tenderness in his eyes before my vision blurs. It's entirely possible I'm about to pass out, and that will never do, which is why I drag in a huge lungful of air and silently give thanks I'm still sitting down.

'You okay?' he asks.

'Yes, of course.' I wave a hand. 'Carry on.'

Clearly entertained by my little turn, his eyes flash with amusement. 'Back to Celine.' He claps her on the shoulder. 'Believe it or not, she actually cares about me – sometimes a little too much – and I care about her too.'

I can barely believe what I see next. A smile materialises on Celine's lips. A quick, warm, apparently sincere smile that doesn't seem to fit her face. It leaves me feeling decidedly on edge.

'When I first met her, she was working at some seedy little dive in London. A very low-end sex club. And before you ask, we've never had sex. That's true, isn't it, Celine?'

'I wouldn't touch you with a barge pole.'

'Glad to hear it.' He performs a mock shiver of disgust. 'Anyway, after rescuing her from said dive, I eventually gave her a job here, not only because I saw her potential, but also because she's my friend and I'll always be in debt to her. She's been there for me at some sticky points. In fact, if you must know, she saved my life.'

'Literally.' Celine nods.

'The details aren't important. But it's a fact you need to know, Evie. So, there we have it. Hostilities will cease from this point onwards. Is that understood, ladies?'

After thinking it through for all of three seconds, Celine gives a curt, surprising answer. 'Yes.'

I can't help wondering if it's a ruse: if she's agreeing in front of his face and secretly planning my demise behind his back.

'Yes,' I echo. Because if that is the case, I can only benefit from playing along.

'Good.' Seb claps his hands.

'Can I talk to you about Martin now?' With her hands firmly back on her hips, it's obvious Celine means business.

'I thought you were dealing with that.'

'I would if I could. It's Mr Harrison's birthday meal tonight.'

'And?'

'Thirty covers.'

'And?'

'Martin's gone.'

'Gone where?'

'I don't know.' She wafts a hand. 'He's just gone.'

A big deal, apparently, seeing as all traces of humour have just disappeared from Seb's face.

'He turned up this morning,' she explains, 'over an hour late... and he looked pretty rough.'

'So what? He's worked with a hangover before.'

'This was more than just a hangover. He spent half an hour doing absolutely nothing. Then, he threw a knife at a wall and stormed out.'

After giving Celine a confused double-take, Seb offers up a solution. 'Put Tom in charge.'

'Tom didn't turn up at all.'

'Have you called him?'

'Not answering.'

He blinks in disbelief. 'No head chef and no sous chef. What the fuck's going on?'

'Do you really want to know?'

'Of course I do. That's why I'm asking.'

'For starters, as I've told you before, although they might be decent chefs, Martin's an unreliable prick and Tom's a gullible idiot. And what's more, I have it on good authority – and you're really not going to like this – they were both out with Christophe last night.'

'Christophe?' There's a distinct edge to his voice now.

178

It doesn't seem to affect Celine. 'DJ tells me he's been hanging around with them quite a bit recently. He hooks up with them round the back of the kitchens. Apparently, he's not above cadging the occasional cigarette.'

'And?'

'Martin likes the gee-gees, Tom likes what Martin likes, and Christophe's Christophe.' She pauses. 'He took them to the races last weekend.'

'It's a free country.'

'Martin took a serious hit.'

'That's Martin's problem.'

'But Christophe was there... encouraging them. Martin came back three grand down. That's serious money for a man like him. He's been in a total state about it all week.'

'And what do you want me to do about it?'

'I want you to see what's going on.'

'Which is?' The edge sharpens.

But hats off to Celine. She doesn't waver one bit. 'Christophe's working his way in with the staff.'

'Don't be ridiculous.'

'He's causing trouble any way he can.'

That certainly grabs my attention. Celine agrees with Max. And seeing as both also have Seb's best interests at heart, I can't believe their opinions stem from nothing. Unfortunately, Seb doesn't seem to share the same mindset.

'You're spending too much time with Max,' he grumbles.

'And you need to get your head out of your backside.'

After glaring at Celine for what feels like an age, he begins to pace up and down. 'Get agency staff. It's not ideal, but it'll have to do.'

'Don't you think I've tried? The agency chef was supposed to be here at one. Alex took a call at half past to say he'd broken down on the way. I booked another chef, but they won't be here until after three. We're cutting it too fine.'

'Just cancel the dinner then.'

'Are you kidding me? You don't cancel on James Harrison. And anyway...' She gestures to the front door. 'His guests are already arriving. You can't fob this lot off with a takeaway.'

'Fuck it.'

While Seb paces some more, I wrestle back a sudden burst of temptation.

'Can't DJ cope?' Seb asks. 'Or that other one?'

179

'The other one's called Nigel.' Celine scowls. 'And neither of them has enough experience to take the lead. You know that.'

'But they've got menus.'

'And that's all they've got. Martin keeps everything in his head.' As if to illustrate the point, she taps the side of her perfect black bob. 'I warned you this was going to be a problem.'

But it's not a problem. At least, not for me. Thirty covers, all probably pre-ordered: that's more like child's play in my world. Out of the blue, a rush of excitement nudges temptation into overdrive. And before I have a chance to think things through, the words are already out of my mouth.

'Perhaps I could help.'

The pacing stops. 'You're a bloody good cook, Evie.' Seb frowns. 'But this is something else.'

'I've, er...' I falter. 'I've worked in kitchens.'

His eyes narrow.

'Nothing major,' I add quickly. 'But I'm sure I can help. And we could google things. Just let me see the menu. We've got time to muddle through if we start now.'

His eyes narrow further. 'Are you mad?'

'Possibly. But it's worth a try.'

He stares at me.

'Okay,' he says at last. 'We'll give it a go.' He glances at Celine. 'All hands on deck, then.' He smiles uncertainly. 'Let's just hope we don't capsize.'

Chapter Eighteen

My skin prickles at the doorway. A familiar reaction to the unknown, it quickly disappears when my attention turns to the décor. Taking a couple of steps forward, I let my gaze rove across a thoroughly imposing space. With a lofty ceiling, polished marble floors and a huge set of bi-folds at the far end, it's luxurious and tasteful in every detail: from the chandeliers suspended above our heads, and the sumptuous array of leather armchairs and sofas; right down to the various, artfully positioned oil paintings, statuettes, lamps and vases. I've just begun to admire an opulent display of fresh, white roses when Seb appears at my side.

'Wow,' I breathe. 'Is there anything underwhelming about this place?'

'Not much, given the clientele.'

I glance at the strangers: a handful of members sitting around a single barrel-shaped table. Smart, elegant and clearly stinking rich, they seem completely oblivious to their exquisite surroundings.

'That's the restaurant in there.' Seb nods to an open doorway at the end of the bar. 'It's not big. We don't normally have many people eating here, but tonight's something different. We've got extra waiting staff arriving at six. Starters are due to be served at half seven.'

'Okay.'

My heartbeat quickens. It's the thrill of the challenge – a feeling I know only too well – but there's something else lurking just beneath the surface: a quiet excitement mixed with a dash of trepidation. I'm about to be reunited with my former existence. A tempting and dangerous prospect, all rolled into one.

'Come on, then.' Taking me by the hand, Seb leads me behind the bar and through the doorway, instantly transporting us from the glamour of a bygone age, into a sleek, ultra-modern future.

Released from his hold, I edge past him, blinking at the bright lights and whitewashed walls, mesmerised by smooth expanses of stainless steel and pristine glass. It takes a few seconds for the scene to come fully into focus. A spotlessly clean, top-of-the-range, professional kitchen – kitted out with just about anything a chef could ever want or need: spacious walk-in fridges and freezers; an array of ovens, hobs, hot plates, grills and griddles; a selection of water baths and deep fat fryers. I spend the next minute or so wandering round, drinking it all in, silently reconnecting with long-lost dreams.

'What do you think?' Seb asks.

'What do I think?' I pause by a dessert station and run my hands over the gleaming work surface. I'm in my own personal Wonderland and I could squeal with glee. But that would be a mistake. Instead, I give silent thanks to Christophe for whatever he did with the head chef and his lackey, then order myself to keep a lid on the mounting excitement, and a tight rein on instinct. 'It's... erm... lovely.'

'So it is.' He glances over my shoulder. 'And here's the team.'

I turn to find Celine emerging from an office at the rear of the room. She's joined by two young men dressed in chef's whites.

I smile at my soon-to-be workmates. Out of nowhere, my heart flutters and stalls, then beats again.

'This is DJ.' Seb motions to the man on his left. In his early twenties and as tall as Seb, he seems quite self-assured. I just hope his apparent confidence isn't misplaced. 'And, er... This is...' Seb waves a hand at the second man. Maybe a little younger than DJ, his pale skin still sports a handful of teenage spots.

'Nigel.' Taking control, Celine steps forward. 'They're both hard workers, but neither of them have been with us long. And they haven't racked up much experience. DJ was a chef de partie in his last job.'

'Which station?' I ask.

'Meat,' Celine replies. 'And Nigel was a pastry chef. Both worked in London restaurants. Nothing amazing. No Michelin stars.'

'Same as me,' I lie breezily.

At which point, the fluttering and stalling return. More forceful this time, they threaten to drag my lungs into chaos. 'Great,' I mutter. A touch of nerves is one thing – and entirely manageable too – but I can do without a full-on panic attack right now. Fortunately, the arrival of a third man distracts the group's attention while I avert disaster with a handful of deep breaths.

'And this is Derek.' Seb announces. 'Our foul-mouthed kitchen porter. Also known as the Prophet of Doom.'

Barely five feet tall, bald and wrinkly, and moving with all the ease of a malfunctioning robot, the Prophet of Doom looks like he should have retired at least five years ago. 'We're fucked,' he grumbles.

Y

'See?' Seb laughs. 'Fortunately, he also works like a Trojan. And that's why we keep him on.' He rubs his hands together. 'Right, then. Shall we look at the menus?'

DJ scurries to a workstation, retrieves a sheet of paper and hands it to his boss. In turn, Seb hands it to me.

'Oh,' I murmur, skimming it quickly. 'Okay.' It's all a bit basic and certainly lacking in imagination. But then again, given the situation, it's a godsend there's nothing too intricate. 'Yes. I think we can manage this.' I touch a hand to my chest. The deep breaths haven't done much good at all. I'm getting full-blown palpitations now.

'Are you okay?' Celine demands.

'Yes.' I gulp.

'It's half past two.' She nods to a clock on the wall. 'Time's pressing on. We've got thirty covers. All pre-ordered. Four vegetarians. The numbers are on the sheet.'

'And...' I gulp again. 'Has Martin left any instructions?'

'None whatsoever.'

'That's a pain.' My vision blurs. I blink a few times. 'Okay.' The sheet comes back into focus, and I somehow manage to do what normally comes as second nature: sorting out the order of importance. 'I'm sure we'll be fine.' I muster a nervous smile. 'What's been prepped?'

'I've done the beef,' DJ offers. 'It's good to go. Welsh Wagyu.'

The absolute best. 'Great. And you can cook to order?'

'Any way you like.'

Even with Wagyu? I certainly hope so. 'What have we got to go with it?'

'It just says seasonal vegetables.'

'Okay. Go and have a look in the fridge. Derek can help you.'

With a totally uncoordinated porter lurching in his wake, DJ retreats to the walk-in fridge at back of the kitchen.

'Nigel.' I turn to the spotty one. 'What have you managed to do?'

'Erm...' He scratches his head. 'I've been working on the mille-feuilles. They're nearly finished.'

'You obviously know your way around pastry. I reckon you can deal with the goats' cheese and onion tart for starters. When you've finished the mille-feuilles, knock up fifteen pastry cases. Blind bake them, and then...' Careful, I remind myself. Wisely, and slow. 'We'll... er... work it out from there.'

I'm feeling distinctly hot as Nigel retreats to his workstation. Hoping to God they haven't already picked up on the truth, I turn to

183

find Seb and Celine studying me closely, the first signs of suspicion appearing in their eyes. It's high time to get the pair of them out of the way.

'Seb?'

'Yes?'

'You told me you can make pasta.'

'Did I?' His eyes widen. 'I'm sure I didn't.'

'I'm sure you did. Go and make a batch. We've got an egg-yolk and ricotta ravioli starter.'

'Now, wait a minute!' He holds up a hand. 'That's way beyond my abilities.'

'I'm only asking you to prepare the pasta. Enough for twenty ravioli. You don't even need to roll it out. Just wrap it in cling film and leave it in the fridge. And then separate some eggs; duck eggs, if we've got any. We'll need about twenty yolks, just in case. Leave them in iced water.'

'But I'm a guest at dinner.' He points to the door.

'Which is bound to be a disaster if you don't play your part. Get stuck in. Ask Nigel where the ingredients are. You'll have time to shower and change later.' I wave him away.

One down. One to go. Feeling a little light-headed and increasingly short of breath, I swivel round to face Celine.

'No, no, no,' she complains. 'You're not using me.'

'Oh yes, I am. Potatoes. Enough for thirty. You need to get peeling.' I lead her to a workstation.

'No...' She totters to a halt. In her black designer dress and super-high heels, she's the proverbial fish out of water. And that's mainly because food and Celine just don't seem to go together. Given how skinny she is, I can barely imagine her preparing a sandwich, let alone a complete meal.

'Work here.' I slap a hand on the counter. 'I'm guessing there are more whites in the staff room. You can protect your dress with a chef's top. Find a peeler and get going. And leave the potatoes whole, in water.' Time for a little more deception. 'I'll find out what to do after that.'

She stares at the work surface. 'But I don't see any potatoes.'

'Ask Derek to get them.'

With a disgruntled sigh, she scurries off to the fridge, leaving me to duck inside the chef's office and close the door.

'Come on,' I whisper. 'You can do this.'

And maybe, I can. But seeing as my hands are shaking, my pulse has launched into a quick sprint and my lungs seem to have shrivelled to the size of lemons, it's going to be no easy task. Closing my eyes, I summon a vision of Oma and imagine what she would say. Almost immediately, I hear her voice. As if she's standing right next to me.

'You've been through much worse, little one. Just do your best... and don't give yourself away.'

I don't know where the words come from – whether they're really hers, or just the product of an overtaxed brain – but they seem to do the trick. Somehow, I manage to slow the breathing, calm the pulse and banish the shakes.

A minute or so later, after composing myself, I open the door and take a peek into the kitchen. Relieved to find everything under control – Nigel concentrating on his mille-feuilles, Celine glaring at a pile of potatoes, and Seb measuring out flour – I wait for the kitchen porter to make himself scarce before closing in on DJ.

'How about the Béarnaise?' I ask, lowering my voice. 'You okay with that?'

'I've only done it once. At college.' He produces his mobile. 'I can google it though.'

'No.' I touch his hand, a signal to put the phone away. 'I'll do that. I think you can make it as a foam. I'll find out how.' I check on Seb. He's busy rooting through cupboards now. 'In the meantime, get the cauliflower ready for the vegetarian main. It just says cauliflower three ways. I'm thinking a cauliflower steak.' I bite my lip. 'I've... er... seen it done on telly.'

DJ nods. 'On a purée?'

'Or maybe a nut butter. And how about tempura?'

'Seen that done on telly too?'

'Yes.' I laugh, nervously. 'I'm guessing you should just strip the cauli for now. We'll cut it into slices later, about an inch and a half thick... I think.' *Dial it down, woman. Dial it down.* 'And keep the leaves. We'll deep fry those, maybe.'

'I'll prep the butter while I'm at it.'

'Use cashews, if we've got any. And put some nice florets aside for the tempura. Can you prep the batter too?'

'Of course. What about the fish course?'

'Fillet the monkfish, if you get time. I'll put the agency chef onto poaching it. I'm sure they'll manage a beurre blanc. What about the vegetarian option?'

'Martin prepped something yesterday.'

'I'll track it down.'

185

Derek's orders come next. After discovering him lurking in the fridge, along with a vegetable terrine, I set him onto putting together a salad to accompany the starters. By the time I return to Nigel, he's finished the mille-feuilles and working on the pastry. Again, I move in close.

'You can make ice cream, I take it?'

'Yeah.'

'It's just vanilla. Enough for fourteen portions. That leaves the chocolate soufflé.' I note a bead of sweat on the spotty forehead. Obviously, a touch of reassurance is in order. 'Don't worry.' I glance round. 'I'm actually a soufflé genius.'

'You are?'

I nod. 'But keep it under your hat. I'll walk you through it later. Just get on with the ice cream for now.'

While my ad-hoc team concentrate on their tasks, I check out the vegetable terrine and decide it's good enough to use. Leaving it in the fridge for later, I grab a pen and paper from the office, write out a definitive plan of action – complete with timings and extra guidance – and hand the sheets to DJ and Nigel. And then, it's time to check on progress. Ice cream churning away. Pastry cases ready. Vegetables prepared. Nut butter and tempura batter finished. Fish nearly filleted. Using my notes, Nigel moves on to the tart filling. After a quick discussion with DJ about the Béarnaise, I return to Seb.

'Pasta's ready.' He juggles an egg between two halves of a shell. 'And that's the last egg. Time for me to go.' He gently drops the yolk into icy water and discards the rest. 'Sorry I can't help more, but I can't back out. Public relations and all that.'

'It's okay.'

'Besides, you're doing just fine.' He nods to Celine. 'And I think she's actually enjoying herself.'

I can't help laughing. 'We might be friends yet.'

'I hope so.'

He gives me a boyish smile causes my heart to trip.

'Go on,' I urge, resisting the urge to drag him into my arms and kiss him senseless. 'Go and do your job.'

As soon as he's made himself scarce, I check on Celine. Sporting an ill-fitting chef's jacket, and occasionally stopping to scowl at her fingernails, she's still daintily stripping potatoes of their skins. I help her finish off and send her on her way, leaving DJ to see to the finer details of the pommes Anna.

Y

At last, with Celine and Seb both out of the picture, I'm free to move into top gear. And, as ever, the challenge sends adrenaline pumping through my body. Rooting out a spare set of chef's whites, I prepare a simple filling for the ravioli: ricotta, a squeeze of lemon, a selection of herbs. A delicious pancetta and tomato sauce come next.

Just after four, the agency chef arrives and gets down to work on the fish course. An hour later, we hold a quick meeting to check on progress and divide up tasks for service. After distracting Derek with a few jobs, I make sure DJ's up to speed with creating the perfect Béarnaise foam, talk a decreasingly nervous Nigel through the process of cooking off cauliflower steaks, and finally put together the ravioli.

It's only then that I wander the kitchen, quietly tasting the work in progress and offering up further advice. With initial nerves banished, I'm functioning on well-honed instinct now, completely in my element and savouring every second. As if I've woken up from a long hibernation with senses on overdrive, it's a heady experience. And one that passes far too quickly. Before I know it, we've reached seven o'clock... and it's time to get down to the serious business.

While DJ concentrates on the mains, I set Nigel to plating up the starters, cook off the ravioli and join him at the pass to put the finishing touches to the dishes. With the temporary waiting staff playing their part, the ravioli and tarts soon disappear. After sending Nigel off to work on the cauliflower steaks, I turn my attention to the fish course. Pleased to discover the monkfish and beurre blanc are perfectly prepared, I help the agency chef to plate, alongside four helpings of vegetable terrine.

And then, it's time for the mains.

Thanks to DJ, the pommes Anna are ready to go. The agency chef gets down to cooking off the seasonal veg, while DJ pan fries the Wagyu to order and Nigel finishes off the cauliflower steaks. In the meantime, I deep fry the tempura and cauliflower leaves.

Half an hour later, we're ready to plate, pulling together as a team to get the job done, and moving on to desserts as soon as the last plate disappears. While DJ plates up the mille-feuilles, I work on the dreaded soufflés with Nigel.

'I'm crap at this,' he grumbles.

'But you're a fully trained chef. Just remember that. Have some confidence in yourself. You're doing great. Those mille-feuilles are amazing.'

'But soufflés...'

187

'It's all in the timing. Is the oven at one eighty?'

'Yes,' he squeaks.

'Excellent. Now do as I say.'

I run through the instructions, supervising him as he works, doling out any extra necessary reassurance, and then helping him to butter and fill the ramekins. Before long, we're taking his babies out of the oven. Each one risen to perfection, they're transported over to the pass, and finished off with a quenelle of ice cream, a few raspberries and a dusting of icing sugar.

With the last dish carried away, there's a collective sigh of relief; a brief hiatus, during which we simply stare at each other – dumbstruck, exhausted, but satisfied. I'm about to offer up my heartfelt praise and congratulations when Derek returns from emptying the bins and pips me to the post.

'Fuck me.' He props himself against a counter and rubs his head. 'We've only gone and done it.'

***

I retreat to the chef's office, make myself a cup of coffee and sink into a chair. Aching and worn out, I can do nothing but stare at an empty planner taped to the wall opposite, and the poster next to it – a semi-clad, huge-busted model reclining on a tropical beach.

'You've done this before.' Leaning against the door frame, Celine smiles at me.

Completely pleasant, and apparently sincere, it's the very same smile that unsettled me earlier.

'Pardon?'

'Working in a kitchen.' She drifts into the office. 'You've done it before.'

'I already told you that.'

'In what capacity?'

I fumble for something, anything. 'Just a skivvy.' It's all I can come up with.

'But you knew exactly what you were doing.'

'Did I?' I shrug. 'I just like cooking, that's all. And they trained me a bit.'

Celine's smile disappears. She's not convinced.

'I'm good at organising things,' I add, as if that's going to make any difference.

'You're a chef.' She walks over the poster and peers at it. 'Quite an experienced one, at that. And talented too.'

188

'Erm...' *Crap.* I've obviously gone too far. I should have made mistakes, let a dish go out late, or a little cold, or badly seasoned. But I didn't... because I couldn't resist temptation. I look down at my coffee. 'None of those dishes were anything special.' Abandoning the mug on a table next to me, I wipe the back of my hand over my forehead.

'The menu plan was nothing special.' In one swift movement, Celine tears down the poster. 'But the way you executed it? Every dish came out perfectly... and just a little different. The pasta sauce. The Béarnaise. The pommes Anna. The way that cauliflower was seasoned. Not to mention the soufflés.'

'That was all DJ and Nigel. They're better than you think.'

'Maybe they are, but that's beside the point.' She makes eyes contact. 'I've been watching you. Just the way you do the little things. It's so practised, so self-assured. And you didn't flap one bit.'

No. Because I was enjoying myself far too much.

'Pride comes before a fall. That's true in this case, isn't it? You just couldn't bring yourself to put out any old rubbish. And now you've been exposed.'

My heart begins to thud. Closing my eyes, I will my pulse under control. Yes, I have been exposed. Or more accurately, I've exposed myself. The carelessness that began with Hal seems to have run riot in Seb's company. And now, after months of hiding in the shadows, I've managed to lay myself bare.

'I'm right then. No denial.' Screwing up the poster, she tosses it into the bin. 'Head chef?'

We gaze at each other for ages – intrigue on her side, desperation on mine. I could always double down, I suppose; but I get the distinct impression it wouldn't be worth the effort.

'It's just a job. Why all the mystery?'

Because it's always wise to be mysterious when you're on the run, especially when you're a missing female chef with a strange name and a more-than-promising reputation.

'Please,' I beg. 'Not now.'

'It's high time the pair of you gave up the games.'

'There's no gameplaying on either side.'

'Really?'

'Really.' I hold her gaze for a few moments, hoping it's enough to drive the point home. 'Look. I know I need to be honest with him. And believe it or not, I actually want to be honest... because he's been so honest with me.'

'He has?' The intrigue returns. She moves closer. 'About what?'

'Everything.'

'Everything?'

I shrug, because I'm not entirely sure what she's fishing for now. 'He told me all about his father, and the kidnapping...'

'Oh, the kidnapping.' She frowns, almost as if that wasn't quite the answer she expected. 'What did he say?'

'He can't remember, so not much.'

'He can't remember?' The frown deepens.

'You didn't know?'

'No.' The word comes out on a breath. 'He's never spoken about it. Not to me. Not to Max. After they found him, he didn't even speak at all. In fact, he was mute for over a year.'

Which is news to me. I'm still trying to process the fact when she knocks me for six with another little nugget of information.

'Actually, it was Christophe who got him talking again.'

'Christophe?'

A black eyebrow arches. 'I know. It's hard to believe, but he spent more time with Seb than anyone. He coaxed him back out of his shell.'

'Then...' My mind flits back to the car park. 'He can't be that bad.'

'Oh, I wouldn't go that far. There's usually something else at play with Christophe: some weird, ulterior motive.' She's silent for a few seconds. Finally, her green eyes glimmer and the smile returns. 'I'm sorry for giving you a hard time, Evie. I misjudged you.'

That does it. An unexpected act of kindness. On top of the exhaustion, Celine's apology is enough to send me over the edge. Before I know it, my last defences have crumbled to dust... and I'm crying.

'Here.'

I look up to find her holding out a hand.

As soon as I'm on my feet, she takes me into her arms: a second unexpected act that leaves me blubbing like a child.

'This person who attacked you,' she says. 'I'm guessing he's the reason for all this secrecy.'

I nod against her shoulder.

'I'm sure he can be dealt with, whoever he is.'

If only it were that easy. 'Have you ever made mistakes?' I ask through the tears.

'God, yes.'

'And do they follow you around?'

'No. I dealt with them.'

'But what if you couldn't deal with them?' I draw back and look her straight in the eyes. 'What if you had absolutely no way of sorting them out? What if they were just too big?'

'I don't know what sort of mistake could be that bad. But I do know you can't live a lie. At some point, you're bound to trip up.' She cocks her head. 'I'd say you need to come clean. And you need to do it soon.'

Chapter Nineteen

With the kitchen cleaned down and the team dismissed, I discard my whites, take one final look around and switch off the lights. Courtesy of my new-found knowledge of the ground floor layout, I'm now aware I could by-pass the guests, leave by the back door and re-enter the club via the main entrance. But it's dark out there, and I'd quite like to see what's going on.

Pushing through the stainless-steel door into the bar, I find myself alone. There's not a soul around – not even staff. No sound but the quiet murmur of post-dinner conversation drifting in from the restaurant. Hearing Seb's unmistakable voice in the mix, I decide to leave him to his public relations exercise and head upstairs for a quick shower.

By the time I'm clean and dry, I'm wide awake, endorphins still flowing, my body quietly buzzing with a long-lost sense of fulfilment. Instead of climbing into bed, I pull on a silk robe and amble out into the lounge, fully intending to wind down with a spot of television.

But I'm not alone.

Apparently finished with socialising, he's standing at the windows now, gazing out into the darkness, apparently lost in thought. I come to a halt a few feet behind him, taking the opportunity to study him intently. So far, I've only seen him in jeans and casual clothes. But this black dinner suit – framing his broad shoulders and narrow hips to perfection – takes the man's sexiness to a new, totally ridiculous level.

'You scrub up well.'

'Don't I just?' He catches sight of my reflection and turns.

'How did the food go down?' I battle back a frisson of lust. Before we get on with the inevitable jiggery-pokery, I'd quite like a little feedback on my culinary efforts.

'It was a huge success.' Closing the space between us, he smiles, languidly. 'I've been asked to convey Mr Harrison's heart-felt compliments to the chef.'

'Chefs,' I correct him.

He raises an eyebrow.

'I'll pass them on to DJ and Nigel.'

'As you wish.' Fingers curl about my arm. 'But I think they were meant for you.'

Drawing me in to his chest, he brings his lips to mine and delivers a long, slow kiss that almost knocks me off my feet. When he's finally had enough, he pulls back and examines my face, as if he's seeing it for the first time.

'What?' I laugh, nervously.

'I was just thinking.' Releasing my arm, he touches a finger to my cheek, lets it drift down to my neck, and watches its lazy progress. 'You deserve a treat. A reward for grabbing victory from the jaws of defeat.'

'It wasn't just me. It...'

The finger comes to my lips, silencing me in mid-flow.

'Are you tired?'

'Not particularly.'

'Remember our little chat this morning?'

'Oh.' About his kind of sex. 'Yes.'

'Well, I'm in the mood to grant your wishes.'

'You are?'

My heartbeat accelerates and my breathing quickens. His kind of sex. Kinky, twisted, deviant sex. I've already had a taste of it – and actually asked for more – but now it's about to happen again, I can't seem to ward off a massive onslaught of nerves.

'Cold feet?'

'No. No, no, no.' I summon up a look of pure determination. 'Let's do it.'

'Yes,' he grins. 'Let's.'

Taking my hand, he locks his fingers around mine in a firm, commanding grip, and guides me out to the corridor. I'm fully expecting to be dragged downstairs – probably to one of those rooms surrounding the Circle – but we don't even make it as far as the front door. Instead, he swerves into his bedroom.

'In here?'

He kicks the door shut and leads me halfway to the bed.

'But you don't keep any kinky stuff up here.'

'And how would you know?'

My cheeks flush.

'Someone's been a nosey so-and-so.' With a quiet laugh, he squeezes my hand.

'Someone's had a lot of time on her hands,' I counter. 'What did you expect me to do?'

'Fair point. For your information, I helped myself to a spot of stock this afternoon.'

'Chicken or beef?'

'Very funny.' With a twinkle in his eyes, he touches the end of my nose. 'Club stock.' Releasing my hand, he heads for the wardrobe. 'Stay exactly where you are.'

'Isn't that misappropriation?' I call after him. 'Helping yourself to company assets?'

'Strictly speaking, yes. But who's going to notice?' He slides a door to one side, opens a drawer and begins to rummage.

With my curiosity in overdrive, I lean to one side, and then the other, desperate for a glimpse of the pilfered stock. 'So ... what have you got?'

'Oh, you know. This and that.' He turns, raising his right hand to brandish a set of leather cuffs, complete with accompanying silver chains. 'All brand new. I thought you'd prefer that. These are manacles.'

I manage a nod. A minor miracle, considering the fact my pulse is almost tachycardic.

'I've never kept anything like this up here before.' He prowls towards me.

'But you had those handcuffs,' I remind him, immediately wishing I hadn't. Some things are best forgotten.

'Max asked me to get those. That was just before we fell out. To be honest, I forgot about them.' He tosses the manacles onto the bed. 'Fact is, I've never had sex on that bed with anyone but you.'

'Oh.'

'Which leads me to the subject of my sort of sex – as you seem determined to call it.' Shrugging off his jacket, he lays it over the back of the armchair. 'Usually, my sort of sex consists of me keeping a woman at arm's length.' He unfastens the left cuff of his pristine white shirt. 'I dominate and she submits.' And now, the right cuff. 'I keep my distance, and so does she. It's never anything beyond the physical.' He loosens his tie. 'But let me tell you something very important, Evie.' Slowly, he unravels the knot, pulls the tie from his neck and throws it onto the chair. 'That's not for us.'

'No?'

'No.'

There's something new in his voice now: a low, caressing undertone that almost liquefies my bones. While he slowly unbuttons his shirt, I do my best to wrestle back some sort of control.

'Now,' he says. 'Time to lay down a few ground rules.' Unbuttoning complete, he shrugs off the shirt.

At the sight of his muscled torso, my heartbeat trembles. 'You dominate, and I submit?'

'Correct.' The shirt joins the jacket and tie. 'Those are the basics, but I have a few additions... on account of that book you've been glued to.'

'Uh huh?'

'In case you get any mad ideas, there'll be no ownership and no objectifying. Likewise, there'll be no branding.'

'Good.' I gulp.

'Although we might indulge in a touch of pain, here and there – all in the name of pleasure – there will be nothing that borders on the realms of sadism. I refuse to countenance any activity that might harm you.'

'Glad to hear it.'

'At no point will you address me as 'sir', or 'master'.'

'Wouldn't want to.'

'And finally, whenever we indulge in my type of sex, there will be no sharing.'

Sharing? Good grief. What? 'I wasn't even thinking...'

'I'm sure you weren't. Nevertheless, we need to set the parameters. I said no ownership, as in you're not some object to be passed around.' He frowns. 'However, I do see you as mine.'

'That's a little confusing.'

'Isn't it just?' He gives me a gloriously wonky smile. 'The thing is you're not a possession, but I do have to admit to... let's say, possessive tendencies where you're concerned.' He moves close, reaches down, unfastens the tie on my silk robe and slips his palms inside. 'This is about you and me, and no one else.'

'You mean... fidelity?'

'Absolutely.'

Shacking up and fidelity. Both referred to within the space of a single day. This all sounds distinctly like the relationship I'm yearning for.

'I trust it's all reciprocated.' He clamps his hands on my waist.

'Too right, it is.'

'Good. So, let's be clear. What we're about to do is a game, a little play acting, something to add a spice to our lovemaking. Nothing more.'

'Nothing more,' I confirm, feeling light-headed.

'Good. So, now we've got that straight... what's your safeword?'

Flummoxed, I rake through my brain. 'Red.'

He nods. 'Use it if you need to.'

With a quick squeeze of my waist, he releases me, returning to the drawer where he produces another set of manacles. I glance at the bed, taking in the sturdy slats of the headboard, and the equally sturdy slats of the footboard. So, that's two restraints for the hands... and two for the feet.

'Oh, Lord.'

Accompanied by a quiet jingle, the second pair of manacles land on the bed. I stare at them, swallow hard, and look back to Seb. Only to find him rolling his head from side to side, slowly flexing his shoulder muscles, transforming his entire stance right in front of me – just like he did that first time. I know exactly what's going on. He's getting ready to control, to dominate. And it sends a thrill right through me.

'Take off the robe.' Taking a seat in the armchair, he crosses his legs and places his hands on the arms.

Instinctively, I clutch at the silk.

He waves an index finger from side to side. 'Do as you're told, Evie. Take it off. And make it slow.'

He waits.

And I tremble. Out of nowhere, I'm feeling vulnerable... almost shy.

'This is what you wanted,' he reminds me. 'This is what you asked for.'

'It is, but...'

'Strip.'

I close my mouth, remind myself that this is what I asked for, and comply. Slowly peeling the robe from my body, I drop it to the floor, fighting back the urge to fold my arms again while he views me in silence, idly surveying every last inch of my body with a curious detachment.

'I'm going to give you what you want,' he says at last. 'But this isn't going to be like that first time.' Getting to his feet, he stalks towards me. 'It can't be.'

I could ask him why not. In fact, I probably should. But I don't seem to be capable of speech.

'This is what's going to happen.' He brushes a thumb across my left nipple. 'I take the reins, and you do exactly as you're told. You give yourself to me, completely. You open up like never before.'

Born of panic, a jittery breath escapes my lungs. If opening up like never before means surrendering my true identity, I can't go any further with this session, and I need to let him know. I'm about to speak when he presses an index finger to my lips.

196

'Relax,' he orders. 'I'm not after your secrets.' Taking my chin in his right hand, he brings his mouth to my left ear and nips at the lobe.

I start.

'On your knees,' he whispers, and promptly moves away.

In a daze now, I sink to my haunches and look up at him, watching him rid himself of belt and trousers. The designer underpants come next, removed in one fluid, self-confident action. Straightening up, he presents me with the perfect male specimen.

'Nice one, Cyril.' I lick my lips at the sight of his fully erect penis.

'Actually, the name's Seb.'

I can't help shimmering with anticipation as he closes in on me, playing the part of the dominant to a T. Coming to a halt, he smooths back my hair, gently moving a couple of errant strands out of the way.

'Take me in your mouth.'

Immediately, I push up onto my knees, eager to please him like never before. I lean in, wrap my fingers around his shaft and touch his glans with my tongue. After teasing with a few licks, I take him deep, leaving one hand on the shaft, while the other gently caresses his balls. Determined to give him a thoroughly memorable ride, I soon begin in earnest, sucking, laving, massaging him into such a frenzy he throws his head back, digs his fingers into my hair and rocks back and forth in time to my actions. I have no idea how long we spend like this, tangled up in the pleasure of give and take, but he's right on the edge when he suddenly urges me away.

'What?' Wiping my mouth, I blink up at him. 'I wanted to finish.'

'But I'm the one in charge.' He wrestles his breath back under control. 'That's why you're on your knees.' With no hint of humour whatsoever, he takes a step back and holds out his hands: a clear invitation to stand.

The moment I'm up, he draws me in to his chest and kisses me senseless, angling his head and deepening the kiss by small degrees, guiding the whole thing as if to remind me – yet again – that he's the one with the upper hand. When he's finally done, I'm fully expecting to be ordered onto the bed. Instead, he manoeuvres me in front of a mirrored wardrobe door, stands behind me, and slips his arms around my stomach.

'Look at yourself.'

I'd rather look at him, but it's clearly not up for debate.

'See how beautiful you are?'

'I'm not...'

197

He squeezes me tight. 'Don't disagree.'

'Or else?'

His eyes flash in the lamplight. In answer, he reaches up and tweaks my right nipple.

'Oh, God,' I moan. 'I think I can take that.'

'Not for half an hour without a break.' He tweaks again. 'Not while I do this at the same time.'

Keeping his fingers on my nipple, he slides his left hand down to my crotch, and immediately sets about rhythmically pressing the index finger against my clitoris. Stopping only to trace tiny circles around the nub before pressing again, he simultaneously tweaks my nipple, sometimes increasing the pressure, sometimes easing off. It's an unrelenting attack on the senses. I barely hear his voice when he speaks again.

'Five minutes down. Twenty-five to go.'

'What?'

The onslaught continues, and I'm soon on the edge. Apparently sensing the change in my body, he eases off, leaving me to recover before he begins to work me up again. Once, twice, three times, he does exactly the same... until I'm moaning and groaning, attempting to writhe in his vice-like hold.

'That must be half an hour,' I finally manage to gasp.

'More like fifteen minutes.'

What? Just halfway through? 'Oh, God. Okay. Point taken.'

'Excellent.' The finger stops. His arms return to my waist. 'Now, let's try again.' He smiles, darkly. 'See how beautiful you are?'

I study my reflection. Mussed hair. Drooping eyelids. Flushed skin. A sheen of sweat. I look like a half-drunk floozy. 'Not really.'

'You sure?' His hand returns to my clitoris.

'Okay!' I'll just have to give him what he wants. Any more of that, and I'll go permanently cross-eyed. 'You're right. I'm beautiful.'

'Like you mean it.'

'Jesus.'

Quickly, I survey my body. Still skinnier than usual after all those months of picking at scraps. Gangly. Gawky. Awkward. And nowhere near beautiful, in my humble opinion. If I'm to make this believable, I need some help.

'I'm beautiful,' I murmur, thinking of Oma now. She always said I had true beauty – inside and out – even if I couldn't see it myself. 'I'm beautiful,' I repeat, more forcefully than before, knowing the words are for her, not me.

'That's better.' Dropping the dominant persona, Seb gives me a warm, twinkly smile. 'You'd better believe it, Evie. Every last bit of you is beautiful.' His hands come to my breasts. 'These amazing things, for example.'

'Brenda and Doris,' I grin.

'Soft. Curvaceous. Firm. Sensitive. Absolute perfection.' Still caressing my left breast, he moves his right hand to my midriff. 'I love your stomach too. So smooth. Not too flat. Womanly.' He circles a finger round my belly button. 'And those legs. Perfectly formed. Strong, yet feminine.' The finger traces a slow, languid line to the apex of my thighs, swirling through my hair. 'And now to my favourite part.'

My breathing threatens to unravel.

'Mmm.' He raises his head. 'I'd like a better view of good old Mavis.' Releasing me, he collects a footstool from beside the armchair and settles it just to my right. 'Put your foot on that.'

With a little wobble, I do as I'm told. Another wobble leaves me wondering just how long I'll be able to keep my balance. It's a blessed relief when his left arm snakes around me again, steadying me back against a rock-hard chest.

'And now...' He takes my right hand in his, guides it down to my crotch, and keeps it there. 'We're done with the comedy names.' All humour disappears. 'Pleasure yourself.'

'What?'

'Do it.'

I bring the tip of my index finger to my clitoris and begin to swirl. At the same time, he extends his finger over mine, adding to the pressure.

'Look at me.'

I don't know if it's the smouldering eye contact or the touch of his hand, insistently guiding me towards a climax, but before long, muscles begin to twitch and dance. I lean back against him – heart pounding, pulse racing – and somewhere deep inside, a ball of heat flares and implodes. In an instant, I'm gone, convulsing and groaning through a tidal wave of contractions, held tight in his arms while he waits patiently for me to recover.

'Want to try something different?' he asks at last.

'Try what?'

'A surprise.' He trails a finger across my stomach.

And I quiver. Because there's something new in his voice now: a dark promise that makes me wonder just how kinky he wants to get.

As kinky as he likes, is the obvious answer. After all, I've got my safeword. 'Just don't ask me to pee on you.'

'As if,' he laughs. 'I'm not a complete weirdo. See that chest of drawers?' He nods to their reflection in the mirror.

'Yes.'

'I want you to stand in front of it, facing the wall.'

I look at him, uncertainly.

'I'm not going to hurt you.'

'I know that, but...' I waver for a moment. 'Oh, what the hell.'

Within seconds. I'm in front of the drawers. And he's behind me again, smoothing a palm over my right shoulder.

'Lean over,' he orders quietly. 'And brace yourself.'

'Brace myself? It's not spanking, is it?'

'Don't be daft.'

'Then, what?'

With a sigh, he turns me to face him.

'This.' Slowly, he raises his right hand.

He's holding what initially looks like an over-sized child's necklace. Bright purple and several inches long, it begins with a series of five spheres, gradually increasing from the size of a pea to something more like a small plum. At the opposite end – the end Seb's holding – there's some sort of circular grip.

'Are those what I think they are?'

'If you think they're anal beads, then yes.'

'And you want to put those in my...'

'Anus,' he says crisply.

My eyes widen.

'Don't worry. Top-grade silicone. Non-porous. And they're already lubricated.'

'But...'

He smiles, wryly. 'I take it you've never used them before.'

'Of course not.'

'Never had anal sex?'

'No.' And right now, I can barely believe we're having this conversation. 'What do they do? I mean, what's the point?'

'Some women say they increase the pleasure.'

'And they'll do that for me?'

'We'll have to wait and see. You can tell me all about it afterwards. Are you game?'

Three breaths later, I make my decision. Turning back to the chest, I lean over, place my hands on top and brace myself. Immediately, a warm palm comes to the base of my spine.

'Legs wider.'

Long, lithe fingers part my buttocks. Something cold touches against my anus.

'What the...'

'Relax.' Slowly, he inserts the beads, giving me time to adjust to each little increment in size. 'There. Any time you want them out, just say the word.' He runs a hand across my right buttock. 'Or just leave it to me. I know what I'm doing.'

'I hope so.' Straightening up, I swivel my hips, trying to accustom myself to the strange sensation.

'Now.' He swings me round, brings one hand to the back of my head, the other to the small of my back, and holds me firmly in place while he kisses my neck. Covering just about every inch of skin, he urges me backwards, releasing me only when I feel the touch of wood at the back of my legs. 'Lie down. On your back.'

I turn and crawl onto the bed. Rolling onto my back, I wait in delicious anticipation, taking the opportunity to admire his perfect torso – all sculpted muscles and taut sinew. Alongside the shifting beads, it's enough to ramp up the lust.

'Hands above your head.'

As soon as I comply, the beads shift, and a shiver of need kicks off in my core.

'So, I'm going to bind you to the bed.' Picking up a set of manacles, he briefly inspects them. 'And then I'm going to pleasure you to within an inch of your life.' With quick, deft movements, he unbuckles the cuffs. 'All you need to do is lie back and enjoy.' He looks up from under hooded lids. 'Patience on my part. Trust on yours.'

Coming to my left, he sits on the bed, taking the utmost care as he fastens a leather strap around my wrist. After attaching the chain to the headboard and adjusting the length, he gives me smuggest of smiles before moving to the other side of the bed, where he repeats the entire process with my right wrist.

'Comfortable?'

'Yes.'

'Excellent.' His eyes linger on mine, glistening with sinful intent. 'Spread your legs.'

Again, I do as I'm told.

It takes him a couple of minutes to bind my ankles, each cuff attached to the slats at the bottom of the bed. By the time he's finished, I'm left totally helpless, completely at his mercy... and thoroughly turned on by the whole experience.

'How do you feel?' he asks, eyes glimmering with triumph.

'Pretty frisky.'

'Thought so.' He joins me on the bed.

Kneeling between my legs, he leans over me and delicately skims a fingertip over my neck, down to my shoulders, across my sternum. Finally homing in on my breasts, he leans further in to take my right nipple in his mouth. I gasp at the touch of his warm tongue, moan quietly as he licks a circle around the areola, gasp again as he latches on and gently sucks, sending tingles through every nerve. After an age, he moves to my left nipple, paying homage in exactly the same way, and I'm half-tempted to thank him for not neglecting Brenda. But seeing as we're apparently done with the comedy names, and I'm not even sure I could string a sentence together at this point, I decide against it. Instead, I simply writhe and tug against the cuffs while he works me up into a mindless frenzy

At last, his lips begin to drift. Tracing a slow and steady path downwards, they sensitise my flesh wherever they touch, raining a stream of soft kisses onto my stomach before they withdraw. I don't have time to miss the contact. Immediately, he props himself up on one hand and trails a finger round my belly button, over and over again, in ever decreasing circles.

'Oh, Lord,' I groan, feeling the full effects.

'You like that?'

'Uh huh.'

He runs the same finger through my pubic hair, gently parting the folds of my labia and examining me in detail. But there's no embarrassment now. In fact, I'm lapping it all up – even more so when he takes the finger down to my opening, penetrates a little, trails moisture back to my clitoris, and begins to circle at a devilishly slow pace.

Bringing me right to the edge, he stops and waits, then begins to circle again. And I don't know if it's something to do with those beads, but before long I'm drunk on absolute pleasure, totally in awe of the man dishing it out, and teetering on the verge of opening up like never before. It's just as well he pauses again, inadvertently giving me time to wrestle a tiny scrap of sense from the chaos. If we carry on like this, I'll end up blurting out all my secrets. And I need to be level-headed and compos mentis for that... not strapped to a bed and out of my mind on lust.

'Red!' I blurt.

He cocks his head. 'What is it?'

'I can't?'

'Why not?'

'Because...' I need to give him the truth. 'I'm scared.'

He frowns. 'I'm not going to harm you.'

'I know. It's not you I'm scared of. It's me. I'm scared I'm going to say something I shouldn't.'

He moves from between my legs and comes to sit at my side. Smoothing my hair, he waits patiently for an explanation.

'I don't want to say things... just because you've driven me mad.'

'Trust me. That's not what I want either.'

'But that first time...'

'Things have changed. There'll be no torture. I want you to tell me on your terms, when you want to.'

'Then we can't carry on.'

'No?' He pouts, dramatically. 'Seems a shame to put an end to it.' He spends a few moments gazing into space. 'Actually, I might just have the perfect solution.' Getting up, he returns to the drawer and produces a thin strip of material.

'A blindfold?' My brows crease. 'I don't speak with my eyes.'

'Yes, you do. All the time. But it's not your eyes we're concerned about.' Again, he sits at my side. 'Open your mouth.'

'You want to gag me?'

'Why not?' He dangles the strip of material above my face. 'We can stop you blurting out your secrets and add to the kink at the same time. Two birds. One stone.'

I gaze at the one stone, think of the two birds, and decide Seb's got a point. It would indeed be a shame to put an end to it. I've nowhere near had enough.

'Go on, then.'

He leans over, places the strip in my mouth, and ties it at the back. 'How's that?'

I mumble something incoherent.

'I don't know if you realise...' He touches the end of my nose. 'But you've just robbed yourself of your safeword.'

'Gah?'

'But never mind. I suppose you can't have everything.'

In a complete flap, I watch him make another visit to the drawer of kink, and realise he's right. Not content with letting him splay me out like a spatchcock chicken, I've also given up my only means of control. There's no way I can stop him now.

Condom in hand, he returns to the bed and positions himself back between my legs. 'But there's no need to worry.' With practised moves, he pulls the condom from its packet, places it on the tip of his cock and rolls it down. 'I have complete control now – every dominant's dream – but I'm not about to do anything you might not like.' Muscles flexing, he leans over me; a powerful, looming presence that reduces me to a quivering mess of want. 'After all, I don't want to put you off.' With a quick quirk of the eyebrows, he places a hand to either side of my body, nudges against my opening, and enters.

The result is immediate... and completely overwhelming.

Muscles begin to quake and quiver. A ball of energy pulses in my core. Nerve endings light up like Oxford Street at Christmas. And Seb's enjoying every second of it. Grinning like the proverbial, creamed-up cat, he probes further, filling me completely before he alters his position.

'Keep your eyes on mine, especially when you come.' He withdraws to the tip before probing again, repeating the motion over and over, setting a steady, unrelenting rhythm that leaves my lungs floundering. 'Are those beads doing it for you?'

'Go, Geh!'

'I'll take that as a yes.' Increasing the tempo, he gazes into my eyes. 'Come on, Evie. Do it for me. Now.'

As if they've heard him, my muscles suddenly contract, clutching at his cock for all they're worth. I'm still struggling for breath when I feel his hand beneath my buttocks. In one swift movement, the beads are removed, and my orgasm seems to rewind, reset and double in intensity.

I hear a half-screamed, distinctly muffled 'Jeezus!'

'Eyes, Evie.'

Hardly aware of the broken rule, I force my lids to rise and find him temporarily stilled, totally focussed on me, an expression of complete satisfaction plastered all over his face. Obviously, he's getting a massive kick out of this. And clearly, he hasn't finished yet. After soaking up my orgasm, he begins to move again, gradually ratcheting up the tempo again until he's thrusting like a demon.

'Fuck!'

He stills for a moment, muscles taut, then thrusts a few last times, emptying himself inside me while I'm swept away on another wave of contractions.

'Fucking hell, Evie.'

Collapsing on top of me, he digs his face into my neck, gloriously overheated, boneless and sweaty. When he finally manages to stir, he withdraws, rolls onto his side and deals with the condom.

'There you go.' With every last hint of the dominant banished, he's back to being Seb. 'No spilt milk.' He removes the gag. 'You didn't utter one coherent word.'

'Thank God.'

'And now...' He gives me a bright smile and a quick kiss. 'I want a cuddle.' Pushing himself up, he sets about unfastening the bindings, one by one. When he's done, he lies on his back and holds out an arm. I shuffle into his embrace, lapping up the warmth of his body.

'So,' he murmurs. 'Was that what you wanted?'

'It was,' I murmur back. A truck load of kink, with Seb firmly in control. 'But... it was different this time.'

'It was.' He smiles. 'It seems your kind of sex is rubbing off on mine.'

Chapter Twenty

I should be riding a wave of euphoria. After all, I've found the perfect man and landed on my feet. But the doubts resurfaced in the early hours of this morning, dredged up by the return of an all-too-familiar nightmare. Leaning against the parapet and nursing a mug of coffee, I'm still thinking about it now: the face looming out of the shadows; those heartless, unforgiving eyes. It's a timely reminder I can't go on like this, because no matter how far I bury myself in fantasy, he's still out there, still searching for me. And every single time I break a rule – just like I did last night – I make it easier for him to track me down.

'Good morning.'

I pivot round at the sound of Seb's voice. Standing a couple of feet away, and wearing faded jeans and a black t-shirt, he's looking particularly delectable today.

'Been up long?' I ask, cheeks warming at the thought of what we got up to last night.

'An hour or so. I went for a run.'

'No swim?'

'Not this morning.' His eyes twinkle. 'Had a few things to do.'

'Such as?'

'A call to Martin.'

The in-house knife-throwing act. 'Oh?'

'He told me to fuck off.'

'Rude.'

'But understandable. I'd just sacked him.' He smiles brightly, and my heart races.

'Then you have no head chef, Mr Delaney.'

'No sous chef either. I sacked him too.'

Talk about shooting yourself in the foot. 'You'll have to close the restaurant.'

He takes the coffee from me and helps himself to a gulp. 'But DJ and that other one need a job.'

'That other one's called Nigel. And you're rich enough to pay them both for doing bugger all.'

'I'd rather pay them to work.' Carefully positioning the mug on the parapet, he grabs me by the waist. 'No need to encourage idle habits.' I'm drawn in for a long kiss. 'Anyway,' he says when he's done. 'I thought you might want to muck in a bit.'

'Pardon?'

'You enjoyed last night.'

'Yes, but it was a one-off.'

'Oh, I don't know about that.' Moving his hands to my buttocks, he gives them a squeeze.

And I'm suddenly wondering if he picked up on the clues and reached the same conclusion as Celine.

'Call me deluded, but I'm convinced you three can survive on your own for a while.' Releasing me, he heads back inside.

That's it? Decision made? 'A while?' Springing into action, I follow in his wake. 'Even with me, you're still a man down. You need a new chef.'

He waves a hand.

'Seb! Stop!'

He comes to a halt at the front door, which is precisely where I bowl into his back.

'Don't panic.' He turns and steadies me. 'On any normal day, there's no more than a handful of people eating here. Piece of piss.'

A handful? 'Then why have so many chefs? It doesn't make sense.'

'Ah, yes. About that.' He seems to think for a moment. 'Actually, I was planning on expanding the restaurant thing at some point. Didn't quite get round to it, mostly on account of Martin being a dick. But you're not a dick.'

Oh, God. Tell me he hasn't worked it out. 'I'm not a chef either.'

'Ah, but you've had experience in kitchens.'

'Yes, but...'

'Oh, come on, Evie. Just help me out. If you do, I'll reward you... big time.' A devilish grin appears, leaving me in no doubt about what form of reward's on offer.

'Okay.' *What? I'm agreeing?* 'Fine.' *Shit. I am.*

'Great.' With a quick peck on the lips, he opens the door. 'Better get busy. DJ and that other one are waiting for you.'

'Nigel,' I call after him, wondering how on earth I'm going to cope. A one-night stand with deceit was bad enough, but a regular relationship is bound to be seriously trying. 'And where are you going now?'

'Got a little project to see to.' Taking two steps at a time, he's already cleared the first flight of stairs.

'Project? What project?'

'Secret!'

With that, he disappears from view, leaving me to bristle over his unusually perky attitude and irritatingly secret project. But the brooding doesn't last long. As soon as I'm showered and dressed, my thoughts home in on the challenge ahead. I practically skip downstairs to the kitchen, where I'm relieved to discover DJ, Nigel and Derek have already made a start on preparation for lunchtime. After scanning the menu and making some much-needed tweaks, I don a fresh set of whites and join the fray. Before long – and for the second time in twenty-four hours – I'm swept up by the magical hurly-burly of a busy kitchen, quite unable to resist the temptation to take charge and guide the others at every turn. By the time service begins, we're ready for anything. Which is lucky, seeing as someone seems to have spread the word about Mr Harrison's meal, and more than a handful of guests decide to order lunch.

Two hours later, with more compliments delivered to the chefs and the clear-up completed, I hold an impromptu meeting with my team to discuss plans for the future. It's almost five o'clock, preparation for the evening service well under way, when I finally decide to hunt down Sebastian. If the covers are going to increase, I'll need to convince him to take on more staff.

**

I'm on my way through the lounge when I waver at the sight of Christophe Dupont. Leaning against the bar, he spots me and bows his head.

'Can I get you a drink?'

'I don't know...'

'I understand. You've been told to stay away.'

'No,' I lie, with a half-hearted smile. 'I'm just tired. That's all.' I motion to the kitchen, as if to explain.

'I won't keep you long.' He seems almost forlorn.

'Well...' A combination of sympathy and intrigue quickly get the better of me. In spite of what I've already heard, I still know barely anything about this man. It's probably worth risking a spot of first-hand contact in the interests of reaching my own conclusions. And anyway, we're not alone. With five or six other people sitting around, talking quietly, it's a case of safety in numbers. 'Okay.'

With a nod, Christophe orders the drinks and leads the way to a table. I sink into an armchair and accept a glass of wine.

'So, it's true then?' He takes a seat next to me. 'You're the one responsible for the amazing meal last night?'

'Me?' In an instant, the intrigue and sympathy disappear. Instead, I'm wondering if Monsieur Dupont suspects the truth, if he's trying to trip me up. 'No.' I force a laugh. 'Don't be silly.'

'But I hear today's lunch was also a distinct improvement on the normal fare.'

'I just helped out.' I manage a nonchalant shrug. 'It's the other two who made the difference. Honestly, they seem to be blooming without Martin breathing down their necks.' Wishing I'd passed on the drink, I put down the glass: an absolute necessity, seeing as my hands are shaking.

Christophe smiles. 'A little bird tells me that Martin and Tom have gone for good.'

'Your little birds work fast.'

'They certainly do. And they all agree it's about time Sebastian gave that pair their marching orders.'

A strange thing to say. 'I thought they were your friends.'

'I wouldn't go that far.'

'But you were out with them, the night before last.'

'We had a quick drink. Nothing more.' He leans in, lowering his voice. 'It might interest you to know that I hold no responsibility for the unfortunate outcome.'

And it might interest Christophe to know that I don't believe him. Given that Seb's hardly likely to confront him on the matter, I might as well give it a go. 'Are you sure?'

'Of what?'

'That you didn't ply them with booze?'

'Why would I?'

'I don't know. You tell me.'

His lips twitch. 'I have no motive for that sort of behaviour. The fact is Martin and Tom are more than capable of plying themselves with alcohol. I think they were celebrating. Martin told me he's bagged another job, one that pays much better than here.'

He's having a dig, and I decide to have one back. 'I suppose he needs it to fund the horses.'

'What Martin does with his money is entirely his own business.' The flinty eyes narrow. 'What does it matter anyway? Martin and Tom have gone... and now you're in charge.'

Great. He's back to his suspicions. 'I told you. I'm just helping.'

'Here's to more of your food.'

'It's not mine.'

'Of course not.' He raises his glass, takes a sip, and chuckles quietly. 'Sebastian should probably worry.'

'Why?'

'Because he'll have people coming here for dinner rather than sex.'

Almost of their own accord, my lips lift in amusement.

'Ah, finally. Would you look at that?' He motions to my face. 'You have a nice smile, Evie.'

Immediately, I quash it.

'Don't worry. I'm not coming on to you.' Suddenly conspiratorial, he leans in again. 'I just want to know you're okay.'

'Why?'

'Because I like to think of myself as your friend.'

'I'm fine.'

'And you're staying here because you want to?'

'Absolutely.'

'It's just that...' He chews at his lower lip. 'It was all a little strange. I mean, your aborted escape attempt.'

'A misunderstanding. That's all.'

'Right.' He seems to think.

'What is it?'

'It's just that I worry about Sebastian too.'

'Why?'

'Because he's changed so much.' He shakes his head, almost despairing. 'He used to come downstairs most evenings, used to socialise with the guests, partake in activities, but he hasn't done that for such a long time. Before you arrived, he even took to locking himself away in his apartment. And of course, he fell out with Max. It's all very concerning.'

Apparently sincere, he waits for my reaction. But Celine's words are still ringing in my ears, and I can't help wondering if there is something else at play. Although I'm sure there are better ways to uncover Christophe's motives, I don't stop to think about them. Instead, I blurt out the obvious question.

'Why should it bother you what Seb gets up to?'

'Because we have a long history. Because I care about him. Because...' He looks up at a chandelier. 'Because I've heard rumours, and I think he might have a problem with alcohol.'

'Really?' I could tell him Seb's hardly touched a drop in days now, and that when he does, it's always in moderation. But I don't know how far I can trust this man, which is why I opt for something vague. 'You don't need to worry. He doesn't have a problem.'

His gaze slips from the chandelier, passes over a couple at the next table, and finally comes to rest on me. 'Things might be going well at the moment,' he counters, 'but there is something you need to be aware of.'

'Is there?'

'Oh, yes. For the sake of self-preservation.' He pauses. 'Sebastian has what you might call an addictive personality. You should bear that in mind. In the long run, he's not the type to do anything in moderation.'

'Oh.' I'd love to dismiss Christophe's words out of hand, but it's impossible. After all, by his own admission, Seb doesn't deal well with temptation.

'But what do I know?' Christophe adds breezily. 'Maybe he's learning.'

'Maybe he is.' Feeling distinctly uncomfortable, I get up.

'If so, then I'm glad. Perhaps it's your influence.' He takes another lazy sip of whiskey. 'I just hope you're not his latest addiction.'

***

The next three days pass in a blur, accompanied by a new routine. Each morning, while Seb disappears off to work on his 'project', I head down to the kitchen where I'm kept busy between the hours of nine and four, developing menus, helping with lunchtime service, and overseeing preparation for dinner. It's only after running through the evening's tasks that I leave the others to it, returning upstairs for a much-needed assignation with Seb and his 'new' type of sex.

And that's when the real action begins.

By the end of the third night, I've been introduced to all manner of restraints, and bound in positions I never knew existed. But with everything delivered alongside tender kisses and absolute adoration, it no longer seems to matter that Seb's the one in control. After the long hours of hard work and constant decision-making, it's a blessed release to hand over the reins.

But it's not all perfection.

After my little chat with Christophe, I can't help searching for the tell-tale signs of addiction in Seb's behaviour, a mission that yields no real cause for concern. He doesn't touch a single drop of alcohol in days. And while he certainly can't do without me in bed, he's only too happy to give me my own space during working hours... which can only mean I'm not his latest go-to drug. It should be all the reassurance I need, but it doesn't stop me stewing over Christophe's words. In fact, I've spent half the night stewing over them when I wake on the fourth morning, woefully unrefreshed and seriously late for work. In a complete panic, I shower and dress in record time before practically hurtling downstairs.

'Sorry I'm late!' The stainless-steel door swings shut behind me.

Oblivious to everything, Nigel continues his preparation for today's sweets, while DJ simply shrugs. I aim for the staffroom and don my whites, reminding myself that I might have become the de facto head chef for now, but my colleagues are gaining in confidence by the day, and more than capable of coping without me. Half an hour later, I'm so caught up in slicing shallots, I hardly notice Celine's appearance at my side.

'Where's Seb?' she asks, getting straight down to business.

'No idea.' I continue chopping.

'He's not in the apartment.'

'Apparently, he's working on a project.'

'What project?'

My knife stops moving. I look up. 'I thought you'd know.'

'No.'

'It's not to do with the club then?'

She shakes her head. 'Tell me. Have you noticed anything different about him lately?'

'That's a strange question.'

'I know, but it's worth answering.'

I put down the knife and study Celine's features. There's something new in her eyes, something I've never seen before. I'm not quite sure what it is, but it's certainly unsettling.

'Well? she pushes.

'He just seems happier... relaxed. Laid back, almost.'

She checks on DJ and Nigel. 'Has he been drinking?'

'Not a drop.'

'And you've not seen him during the day?'

'No.' Suddenly, an alarm bell rings. Nobody knows where he's been, or what he's been up to. 'Surely, I'd know if he's been drinking...' I rally my senses and gather the facts. He's certainly been tired in the evenings, and always freshly showered by the time he presents himself to me. It's entirely possible he has been drinking, just earlier in the day, sobering up before our evening assignations, and using the shower to wash away the smell. 'Wouldn't I?'

I get no comfort from Celine's expression: a furrowed brow, lips firmed into a line, my own worries reflected in her eyes. 'I'll leave you to it,' she says, turning on her heels and heading for the bar.

I return to the chopping, setting a furious pace that renders the knife a blur. Several more shallots are dispatched before I slow down and eventually come to a complete halt. Gazing into space, I wonder if he really has been disappearing off for a secretive binge. Then I decide I'm being paranoid, giving far too much weight to what Christophe said because I'm exhausted and hardly thinking straight. Busy days in the kitchen and long nights in Seb's bed have seen to that.

'Alright, chef?' DJ asks.

I wipe a hand across my brow. 'I'm not a chef.'

'Yeah, right.' He laughs.

'And I'm fine.'

'You don't look it.'

'Just a bit tired.'

'Go and have a kip, then.'

'I can't.'

'Course you can. Have a bit of faith. We can cope.'

'I know.'

Gently prising the knife from my hand, DJ pats me on the back. 'Go and rest. And don't come back today.' With that, he takes me by the arm and guides me to the door.

Back in the apartment, I've only just shrugged off my chef's whites when there's a loud, insistent knock at the front door.

'Is he back yet?' Celine demands, as soon as I open it.

'No.'

'I need to look for something... in his study.'

'I'm not sure...'

'It won't take long. We're looking for a contract.'

Alex appears behind her, and a vague recollection comes into play. The missing CCTV contract. Surely, that must have been sorted by now. After all, it's been a few days since Alex came searching for it.

'It's quite urgent,' Celine insists.

And I'm almost certain she's lying. But there's no way I'm going to stop her, because I'm far too intrigued by what's going on.

'Okay.' I move back and let them in, following in their wake as they make their way to the end of the corridor and up the staircase. I'm almost at the top step when I hear Celine's voice.

'For God's sake.'

Quickening my pace, I enter the study and find her standing behind the desk, stock still, totally fixated on an open drawer.

'What is it?'

She looks up, eyeing me for a moment before she pulls a plastic bag from the drawer and drops it onto the desktop. 'Junk.'

'What?' With a frown, I edge forwards. 'I don't understand.'

'Oh, come on, Evie. You've been on the streets. You know what I mean.'

'No, I don't.' And it's time for a reminder. 'I haven't been on the streets.'

With a wave of a hand, she dismisses my statement. The same hand touches the bag. Her expression hardens. 'Heroin.'

I hear the word, but my brain can't seem to grasp its meaning. I glance from the bag to Celine's face. Her bright green irises sharpen, tiny shards of glass with a lethal edge.

'Are you involved?' she demands.

'What?'

'Did you get him back into this shit?'

'Back into it?'

'Did you?' she growls.

'What do you mean back into it?'

'Answer my question.'

'Why would I...?' It's impossible to finish the sentence. My lungs have suddenly halved in size, and my brain's turned to fudge.

'Maybe you're an addict too,' she goes on, her voice laden with threat. 'Maybe you couldn't go without your fix, so you lured him back into his old ways.'

'Old ways?' I close my eyes and feel myself sway. 'This is what Max was talking about. Unsavoury things.'

'It is.'

Fighting back an onslaught of tears, I search for one tiny shred of sense in all this madness, but find nothing. 'Jesus, I thought I knew him.'

A hand comes to my back.

I force my eyes open. 'This is nothing to do with me, Celine.'

'I know. I know.' Even through the blur, I hear the change in her voice. It's softer now, completely devoid of anger. 'I did tell you. He's not the man you think he is.'

I wipe my eyes and try to think. 'Surely I would have known.' A stupid thing to say. When it comes to covering up the truth, a real addict is a master of the art. I didn't know because Seb didn't want

214

me to. And now, it all makes sense. The absences, the fatigue, the secrecy.

'I'm so sorry.'

'You don't need to apologise.'

'No. But maybe I should explain.'

'I'd like that.'

'Alex, leave us, please.'

For the past couple of minutes, he's been hovering at her side. On her command, he does as he's told, and Celine makes a start.

'Seb should have told you about this way before now. God knows why he hasn't.' She pokes the bag. 'He spent three years of his life hooked on this crap.'

Three? 'He did?'

'He's been clean for six.'

'So, why would he ...?'

'I have no idea. But I'm guessing that's why he quit the drinking. He knows the dangers. Alcohol and heroin don't mix.'

A door slams downstairs. Jolted into silence, we stare at each other like a pair of stunned rabbits.

'He's back,' I breathe.

'And it's time for an intervention.' With renewed determination, she grabs the bag, storms past me and disappears down the stairs.

It takes a few seconds for me to gather my wits and scurry after her. I catch up just as she rounds the corner into the lounge.

'There you are,' she purrs.

'Yes, here I am.' Standing behind the counter, Seb helps himself to a mug of coffee. 'What's eating you now, Celine? You've got that look, like you're chewing a big, nasty wasp.'

'That's because I am chewing a big, nasty wasp.' She slams the bag onto the countertop.

Sebastian eyes it. 'Been shopping?'

'No. But you have.'

'Hardly likely.' He takes a sip of coffee. 'Can't remember the last time I even set foot inside a shop. One of the benefits of being filthy rich. Other people do that sort of thing for you.'

'And how about this sort of thing?' With a flourish, she lifts the bag and empties its contents across the top.

I listen to the clatter, glimpse a syringe, a packet of powder and a roll of foil. With a wince, I turn my attention to Seb. Suddenly devoid of all humour, he's staring at the collection of objects.

'What's going on?' Very slowly, he puts down the mug.

215

'That's what I'd like to know.' Celine cocks her head. 'Alex went sorting through the safe. He was looking for a contract, but guess what he found instead?'

'The bag, I suppose.'

'Correct.'

'And?'

'Don't try to play the innocent.'

His eyes flick to me, then back to Celine. He swallows. 'You've told Evie?'

'I had to.'

'But you had no right...'

'You were dragging your feet, Seb. It had to be done.'

'Really?' He shakes his head and points to the bag. 'That is not mine.'

'That's what I thought you'd say.'

'It's the truth, Celine.' His voice rises. 'It's not mine.'

'Prove it.'

'Prove it?' Giving me another glance, he comes out from behind the counter. 'You fucking prove it. It's not mine. And even if it was, why would I leave it there?'

'Hardly anyone goes in that safe, apart from you.'

'That's bollocks, and you know it. Alex goes in there, and so do you.' Verging on fury, he raises a finger. 'Even Martin had access.'

'Which is why I thought it best to double-check.' Totally unfazed by the snarling creature in front of her, Celine waves at the paraphernalia. 'This little lot isn't from the safe. It's from upstairs. We found it in your desk drawer.'

I'm expecting him to explode. Instead, he simply lowers the finger and gazes into space. In an instant, the anger's gone, crushed beneath the weight of confusion.

'I don't understand. How did it get there?'

'That's a question for you to answer.'

'But it's not mine.'

'So, why was it in your drawer?'

'I don't know.'

'You're using again.'

'Don't be stupid. Why would I do that?'

The next few seconds pass in silence. Occasionally looking at the bag, occasionally at me, Seb begins to struggle for breath.

'Okay,' Celine says, changing tack. 'Maybe you could tell us what you've been up to?'

'What do you mean?'

'During the day?'

He frowns. 'I've been at the boathouse.'

'Doing what?'

'It's secret.'

'I see.'

'No, you don't.'

'Yes, I do. You've been shooting up down there.'

In a split second, the accusation drags his fury back to the surface. 'Oh, fuck off, Celine!'

'You're back on drugs. That's why you stopped drinking.'

'I stopped drinking because of Evie. I am not back on this shit.' Again, he eyes the bag. 'It's been planted.'

'By whom?'

'I don't know.' He offers both arms. 'Do you see any tracks?'

She gives him a quick inspection. 'That doesn't prove anything.'

'You think I'm smoking it now?' He glares at her, eyes wide. 'Okay. Test me if you want to.'

'I will.'

'Good.'

'Fine. I'll order a kit. In the meantime, I suggest you explain yourself to your girlfriend. And good luck with that.' With a final glance at me, she heads for the hallway.

'Wait,' Seb calls. Moving quickly, he sweeps the objects back into the bag, marches over to Celine and thrusts the lot into her hands. 'I don't want it,' he snarls. 'And I certainly don't need it. It's not mine.'

With a curt nod, she makes her exit, leaving an ominous silence in her wake.

I watch him turn, eyes fixed on the floor, colour draining from his face as if he's dying right in front of me. Finally, he looks up. Wary. Tentative. Struggling to make the slightest bit of eye contact.

'It was planted,' he says quietly.

'It doesn't matter.' The fact is, I thought he was letting me into his life, but I didn't know a damn thing about the man.

He moves closer. 'I was going to tell you. I just needed the right time.'

I see the desperation in his eyes, but it makes no difference. This is far too close to past experience. I step away. 'Don't come near me.'

He reaches out. 'Please, Evie.'

'Don't.'

I'm hardly aware of what happens after that. One moment, I'm staggering down the marble staircase. The next, I'm hurtling

217

through the lobby and pushing past a pair of startled guests. Finally reaching the car park, I pause for a moment before leaving the crunch of gravel behind. On automatic pilot now – and cursing myself for every stupid mistake I've made in recent days – I march out across the lawn.

Chapter Twenty-One

A heron swoops over the water. A light breeze rustles through the trees. Seated on the upside-down boat, I look out over the glassy calm of the lake and wonder when this grim, temporary inertia will finally give way.

The man you fell for doesn't exist.

That's what I tell myself as the first droplets of rain break the surface.

Smoke and mirrors. That's all it was.

Delicate circles radiate outwards, tiny bursts of perfection.

Maybe history does repeat itself.

The raindrops gather in force, obliterating all signs of pattern beneath a hundred thousand pin pricks of silver-grey.

Maybe the world you ran away from isn't so different to this.

Finally, the spell breaks, collapsing like a dam, releasing a deluge of anger, a floodtide of hurt, a swirling mass of unwanted memories – all the aftershocks of previous deceptions. Knowing they're unstoppable, I lower my head and welcome in the chaos, letting it rip right through me and tear me apart, feeling it surge up from my chest and break into desperate sobs.

'But this time is different,' I murmur as soon as the torrent subsides. 'I know it is.'

And if I'm worth anything to him, he'll come and find me. He'll offer up the truth and beg for forgiveness. Which is why I simply wait, banishing the past and opening my mind to all possibilities. I have no idea how long I spend like this, but when I eventually hear him speak my name, I'm fully prepared to hear him out.

'Evie?'

I look up to find him standing in front of me, already soaking wet.

'I'm sorry.'

I nod.

'I get it. You think I'm lying. You think that was my stash.'

'No.' The answer comes with surprising ease. Despite the shock, I've somehow managed to recognise the truth. Even if he was using, there's no way he'd stow his little bag of goodies in the safe. 'I believe you. It was planted. You're not using. Not now, at any rate.' Gazing out at the lake, I add the rider. 'But you did. And that's the problem. Why didn't you tell me?'

219

When I get no answer, I turn back to him... and falter. With his normal veneer stripped away, there's no sign now of the super-confident ex-playboy. Instead, all I see is the shadow of a man, a tortured soul who's had enough. Eyes brimming with despair, as if he has no idea where he is or what he's supposed to be doing, he gazes blankly at the ground.

It's enough to spur me on. 'Seb?'

He raises his eyes.

'You need to talk.'

'I know.' He sticks his hands in his pockets and focusses on a clump of grass. 'I wanted to tell you, but it's not the easiest thing to admit. I was just waiting... for the right time.'

'When it comes to something like this, there is no right time.'

'Point taken.' He kicks at the clump. 'But I needed to be sure you wouldn't run for the hills.'

'No chance of that. Can't even get out of the grounds.'

'Still...'

'Still,' I repeat. 'I think you owe me an explanation.'

'I don't know how to explain it.'

'Just make a start. Say the first thing that comes into your mind.'

'I was young.' He takes in a jittery breath. 'I was spoiled, fucked-up and stupid.' Wiping raindrops from his face, he trails into silence.

'And?' I prompt.

'And...' He kicks again at the clump. 'I've been clean for six years.' As if the weight of the world is suddenly resting on them, his shoulders slump. 'But I'm still ashamed.' He gazes into space. 'I'm still disgusted by what I used to be. I couldn't bear it if you felt the same.'

Which is no surprise. After all, I've made it perfectly clear what I think about drugs, and that's probably why he's dragged his feet. Perhaps some reassurance is in order.

'I'm not disgusted.'

He looks up, eyes narrowed. 'You mean it?'

'Yes.'

'Good.' He breathes deeply now, evidently calming himself. 'Because I'll never be that man again. That's one promise I can keep.'

'And I trust your promise.'

'Most people don't.' He half-smiles. 'Once a junkie, always a junkie. That's what they say.'

'Then they need a good slap.' I raise my chin. 'Anyone can redeem themselves, including you. You got yourself clean and stayed clean. I admire that. But it's not the point, is it?'

'It isn't?'

Raindrops trickle down my back. With a little shiver, I shake my head. 'I thought I knew you.'

'You do.'

'Oh, come off it, Seb. You spent three years of your life hooked on heroin. That's a pretty big secret.' And yet, not quite so big as what I'm holding back. But there's no time to dwell on my own shortcomings. I'm still far too obsessed by his. 'You've made me feel like a complete idiot. Everyone knew about this, everyone apart from me. Max, Celine, Alex. Even Christophe...'

'Christophe?' He takes a step forward. 'When did you speak to him?'

Oh, Lord. I really shouldn't have mentioned Christophe Dupont, but what's done is done. 'A few days ago.'

'And what did he say?'

'He said...' *Do I tell him?* 'He said...' *Of course I do. There's no other option.* 'He called you an addict.'

'He what?'

The transformation's immediate. No more nervous repentant. He takes another step forward, anger sparking in his eyes, his entire body charged with tension.

'Seb?' A chill courses through my veins.

'You were supposed to stay away from him.'

'I know. I just...'

'Right. That's it.'

In a sudden rush, he grabs me by the hand and hauls me to my feet.

'What are you doing?'

'Sorting this out.'

I'm half expecting to be led to the boathouse. After all, it's the nearest refuge from the rain, and the perfect location for a row. But Seb seems to have other ideas. With my hand firmly clamped in his, he begins to drag me back to the club.

'Seb, please! We can do it here.'

'No, we can't.'

Stunned into silence, I let him haul me over the lawn. It's only when the sodden grass gives way to gravel that I tug against his grip.

'Seb, let me go.'

'Not on your life.' He veers to the left, away from the main entrance.

'Where are we going?'

He doesn't answer, doesn't stop until we've rounded the end of the east wing, crossed a patch of grass, re-joined the driveway just where the ground dips, and arrived at a huge, white garage door. In silence, he keys a code into a unit and waits for the door to lift, revealing three cars: two silver, one black. I'm led to the far end of the garage, where he keys another code into another unit, opens a metal cabinet fixed to the wall and picks out a key. Before I know it, I'm standing next to a gleaming, black Porsche... and the passenger door's already open.

'Get in.'

I stand my ground. 'Where are we going?'

'London.'

'No.' Panic flares. 'I can't.'

'You'll be perfectly safe.'

'I don't want to go.'

'Like you have a choice.'

'But I'm soaking wet.'

'I'll put the heater on.'

Before I can come up with any more objections, I'm manhandled into the car. Seconds later, he's sitting next to me. Starting the engine, he turns the heating to full blast and flips the car into gear. Before I know it, we're out of the garage and speeding down the driveway, sending wild sprays of gravel in our wake.

'Seatbelt,' he grates as we hurtle through a tunnel of trees.

Fumbling for the belt, I keep my eyes fixed on a set of gates up ahead.

'We're going to crash.'

'No, we're not.'

Just in time, the gates swing open, releasing us into the outside world. And then, I'm watching the world flash by in a high-speed slideshow of fields, hedgerows and trees, desperately trying to steady my nerves while Seb ignores all my pleas to slow down.

'Where are we?' I grumble at last.

He tightens his grip on the steering wheel and says nothing, which only serves to stoke the panic again. If he's refusing to tell me where we are, it's entirely possible he doesn't want me to find my way back.

'I'm being dumped.'

He glances at me.

'That's why you're taking me to London. You're annoyed I spoke to Christophe.'

'Am I?'

'You're annoyed I know the truth about you. You were never going to tell me, were you?'

'For crying out loud, Evie!' He slams a hand against the wheel. 'Is that what you think?'

'What do you expect me to think?'

'I have no idea.'

'For God's sake,' I mutter, staring past the windscreen wipers, and temporarily closing my mind to a world that seems to have flipped on its head. By the time I dare to return to reality and peek at my companion, he's clearly managed to restore some self-control.

'You're right on one count,' he says, a little calmer now. 'I am annoyed you talked to Christophe, but I'm not annoyed you know the truth. You needed to know. I just wish I could have told you on my own terms.' He chews at his lip. 'For future reference, you've been staying in Surrey. And I'm not dumping you. You don't get away from me that easily. We're visiting my brother's house.'

'Max?' As if the day couldn't get any worse. After discovering the man I've been falling for has a distinctly murky past, I'm now being dragged off to see his raving monster of a brother? 'Why?'

'Because...'

'Oh, don't start that again. Why are you suddenly so eager to see him?'

'Because it's time to build some bridges.'

***

With Seb still driving like a man possessed, I decide it's best not to distract him any further. Instead, I lapse into silence, cling to the seat and concentrate on the road ahead. Before long, we're on the M25, hurtling down the outside lane, overtaking car after car. It's a miracle we're not stopped by the police, and a relief when we finally leave the motorway behind and aim for central London.

With the suburbs giving way to built-up areas, and green fields replaced by brick and concrete, I feel my spirits sink even further. Edgeware, Brent Cross, Hampstead, Swiss Cottage. Each new sign brings me closer to the last place I want to be. I'm dreading catching sight of the Thames, and grateful when we change course at Primrose Hill Park. After a couple of turns, we slow down in an elegant Georgian crescent.

223

'We're here.' Pulling up outside a particularly impressive house on the right, Seb lowers his window and speaks into an intercom. 'I'm here to see my brother.' He turns his face to a camera.

A male voice speaks back. 'He's at work.'

'That's okay. I'll wait.'

The gates open, and we draw up onto a gravel drive.

I waste no time getting out and following Seb to the front door. Before he can even reach for the bell, the door opens to reveal a kindly, grey-haired woman who's clearly more than a little excited.

'Sebastian?' She claps her hands together.

'Mrs Keele.'

'Goodness me. It's been such a long time.' She touches his arm. 'I've missed you.'

'I've missed you too. What time's he home?'

'Never before seven.'

'Give him a call. Tell him I'm here. We'll wait upstairs.'

'But...'

'I'll take the rap, Mrs K.'

With a resigned smile, she ushers us in.

Given no time to properly take in my surroundings – but time enough to realise it's another sumptuous residence – I'm quickly guided up three flights of stairs. When we reach the top, Seb takes the lead, shepherding me through an open doorway to the right, straight into a predictably luxurious living space.

'Look...' Coming to a halt, I glance round, feeling every inch the intruder. 'If you're here to make up with Max, I don't think I should be around.'

'That's not the only reason we're here.' Saying nothing more, Seb walks away, heading towards a huge set of bi-fold doors at the rear of the house. Suddenly, he disappears to the left.

After taking a few moments to survey Max's lair, I follow on behind, surprised to find myself in a kitchen.

'What the ...' Fully equipped with high-end cabinets, marble tops, a central island and all mod cons, it's every foodie's dream. 'I didn't think media moguls cooked for themselves.'

'This one does.'

'Oh.' Completely in awe, I glance up at the lights and remind myself to stay on task. 'Why else are we here then, if it's not just to make up with Max?'

He grabs two mugs from a cupboard and begins to fiddle with a coffee machine. 'Because I need to earn your trust.'

'You've got my trust.'

'I'm not so sure about that.'

Taking a seat at the island, I watch him go in search of milk and wonder how on earth dragging me here is supposed to achieve his aim. I can only think he's banking on the evil brother pleading his case. But given the fact the evil brother doesn't like me one bit, that's the last thing I expect. In fact, the only thing I expect is a delighted Max – having found a splendidly convenient way to put me off for good – refusing point blank to corroborate anything Seb says.

'Here.'

I'm handed a mug of hot coffee. Sitting at the opposite side of the island, Seb proceeds to stare into space.

'We should talk,' I venture.

'I don't know where to begin.'

'But you did begin... back at the lake.'

'Yes.'

'So?'

'Let's just wait for Max.'

'Oh, for God's sake. I've had enough.'

In danger of completely losing my temper, I take my coffee to the living room, where I find Mrs Keele lighting a fire – probably on account of my still-bedraggled appearance. After she's gone, I stand in front of the blaze and dry out completely before distracting myself with a good look around. About half an hour later, during which time I've riffled through Max's extensive collection of books, admired his paintings and inspected the family photos, I finally drift back to the kitchen.

I've barely reclaimed my seat when Max Delaney makes his grand appearance. With no warning whatsoever, he's suddenly looming in the doorway, his cold gaze drifting from Seb to me, then back again. In absolute silence, he heads to an impressive-looking wine rack and picks out a bottle of red. After producing three wine glasses and sourcing a corkscrew, he makes a start on opening the bottle.

'To what do I owe the honour?' he asks, focussing on the task. Cork popped, he pours the first glass of wine and takes a slug. 'I suppose it's about the heroin.' He pours a second and hands it to me. 'Celine says you're using again.'

'Caffeine's my drug of choice these days.'

'And what about the whiskey?'

'A temporary blip. Things are better now.' Getting to his feet, Seb helps himself to a second mug of coffee, then leans back against the counter.

'As I understand it,' Max says, 'Celine found two secret stashes. One in the safe, the other in your study.'

'If I were using again, don't you think I'd be more imaginative with my hiding places?'

'You're being disingenuous.'

'And you're using big words. Some fucker's planting that shit, and you know it. They're either setting me up or hoping for a relapse.'

'You honestly expect me to believe that?'

I watch Seb lower his head, then turn to Max. Delaney the elder might still be giving me a nasty dose of the heebie-jeebies, but I'm suddenly itching to slap that supercilious look from his face.

'He's not using,' I inform him.

At first, I wonder if I've been heard. And then, if I'm just being ignored. I'm on the verge of repeating myself when Max delivers what must be the most unsettling, cold-eyed smile I've ever witnessed.

'And why should I listen to you?'

'Because I'm telling the truth.'

'Prove it.'

'I can't prove it. You've only got my word.'

'Well, then...'

That does it. Two simple words, delivered with utter and complete condescension; they're absolutely guaranteed to raise my hackles.

'Get over yourself.'

'Evie, no.'

I hear Seb's warning, but choose to ignore it. I'm standing up to Max Delaney, and that's that.

'You don't intimidate me, so you might as well drop the antagonism. It's a complete waste of time. I'm going nowhere. I don't particularly care what you think about me, Max, but I do care about your brother.' I wave a hand at a startled Seb. 'He's come back to you, just like you said he would. And he's here because he needs you. Because you're his brother, for God's sake. So why don't you just trust him?'

An equally startled Max takes another mouthful of wine. 'Finished?' he asks.

'Not yet.' I focus on Seb. 'Sebastian?'

226

'Oh, Lord. Naughty name.' He smiles, grimly.

'Don't turn this into a joke. I have no idea why you've decided it's time to make amends, but while you're at it, you can tell Max about the letters. Swallow that ridiculous pride and let him know the lot.'

The smile disintegrates. 'That's not what we're here for.'

'What letters?' Max intervenes.

'Jesus.' Stepping forward, Seb slams his mug on the counter. Droplets of coffee spill over the rim. 'I'm surprised Celine didn't tell you.'

'She doesn't tell me everything.'

'Thank God for small mercies.' For no apparent reason, he swipes a finger through the spillage. 'We'll talk about that later. Right now, we need to discuss Christophe.'

I'm still struggling to process the fact that I've just stood up to the rabid one – without any noticeable come-back – but I'm not so distracted, I fail to notice the change in Max. At the mere mention of Christophe Dupont, he's suddenly hawk-like.

'I thought he could do no wrong,' he says. 'What changed?'

'I don't know. He spoke to Evie.'

'He told me Seb has an addictive personality,' I add, only too willing to help. 'It's almost like he was preparing the ground.'

'Really?' There's a slight twitch of the lips, a small flicker in his eyes. Finally, he seems to regard me with a new-found respect. 'Interesting.' He pours a third glass of wine and nudges it towards his brother.

'I don't need it,' Seb grumbles.

'For what it's worth, I don't think you're an alcoholic.'

'Thank you.' Seb returns to his seat at the island. 'But I still don't need it.'

'I do.' Raising his own glass in a silent toast, Max swigs back another mouthful. 'So,' he goes on, 'I'm told you had the locks changed to the apartment.'

'Celine again?'

'Of course. According to her, only you and Alex had keys.'

'There were spares. Alex kept them in the safe.'

'And who had access to the safe?'

'Me, Celine, Alex. Martin, our ex-head-chef.'

'Martin?'

'Occasionally, they take cash in the bar and restaurant. That's where Martin stored the takings.'

Max thinks for a moment. 'Okay. We can rule out Celine. She was pretty pissed off about the keys. I don't think she even knew about the spares. How about this Martin character?'

'Very friendly with Christophe.'

'And Alex?'

Seb gives a shrug. 'He speaks to Christophe. Virtually everyone does. But he's been with me for years. He's trustworthy.'

'I hope so.' Max sighs, wearily. 'At any rate, it looks like Christophe's the prime suspect. He could have gained access to the safe via Martin and used the keys to plant the smack. I'm sorry to say this, brother, but I think the time's come for you to ban him from the club.'

'I don't see you sacking him from DelCorp.'

'Because I'm waiting for him to trip up.'

'Which is good enough reason to keep him at the club.'

'As you wish.'

'I do.'

With that particular subject exhausted, Max finishes off his wine. 'I need to think about how we deal with Christophe. In the meantime, perhaps you could tell me about those letters.'

Seb waves a hand. 'Later.'

'It's always later.'

'It is,' I agree. Both brothers look at me. And suddenly, I wish I could keep my big mouth shut, because I'm clearly expected to explain. Reaching for my wine, I knock back a couple of huge gulps, put the glass back on the counter, and decide to get on with it. 'I'm still waiting to hear the full story... of how Seb... you know... of how he came to use.'

'He's still not told you?' Max frowns.

'No.'

He studies me for a few seconds, then switches his focus to Seb. 'Poor show, Cyril. Want me to do the honours?'

It's Seb's turn to frown. Uncertainty flickers in his eyes. With a slight nod, he gets to his feet.

'I'll be out on the balcony,' he says, heading for the door.

As soon as he's gone, I turn to Max. With the heebie-jeebies banished, it's time to make my disapproval clear. 'I don't see why Seb can't tell me himself.'

Max raises an eyebrow. 'It's okay to tap out of a situation you can't handle. Don't take it as a sign of weakness. I'd say it's a sign of strength he wants you to know at all.' He picks up the bottle, refills my glass, and then his own. 'You know, I wasn't too keen on you at first, but I'm revising my opinion. I'm grateful for what you've done.'

'What have I done?'

'You've brought him back to me, made him re-think the Christophe situation. Credit where it's due. I understand he opened up to you about the kidnapping.'

'Is there anything you don't know?'

'Not much.' He smiles, and I wonder if I'm beginning to revise my own opinion. 'You, on the other hand, still have plenty to learn.' Absent-mindedly, he runs a finger up the stem of his wine glass. 'Do you think any less of him, knowing what you do?'

'I don't know.' If I'm honest, there was a moment – a split second – just after I learned the truth, when I did judge him... and found him wanting. Feeling decidedly guilty for it, I stare at Seb's untouched wine.

'It's all too easy to write off an addict,' Max says. 'To decide they're weak or selfish, or stupid. But I like to think they deserve more understanding than that. After all, the reasons for addiction are complicated. If you dig down beneath all that chaos, nine times out of ten, you're bound to find nothing more than a normal person who wants a normal life.' He pauses. 'Now... I happen to believe that anyone can be redeemed, and everyone deserves the chance. Given the right support, any individual can find their strength.'

Completely thrown by Max Delaney's show of humanity, I look up. 'And that's what Seb did?'

He nods.

But I still don't know how he first reached the depths. 'When did it all begin?'

'With the kidnapping. He was never quite the same after that. Not surprising, really.' He turns his glass. 'Our mother was his solace. You can imagine, it was particularly difficult for him when she died.'

'Of course.'

He leans back. 'Tell me something. What do you know about our father?'

I have no idea what their father's got to do with any of this. Regardless, I answer the question. 'Not much. Phillip Delaney. Owns DelCorp.'

'And a grade-A bastard. Trust me on that one.' He lets out a sigh and helps himself to another glug of wine. 'A couple of months after our mother died, he packed Seb off to boarding school.' He places the glass back on the countertop. 'If you ask me, he wanted him out of the way.'

'But...' I can barely believe what I'm hearing. 'Why?'

'Your guess is as good as mine. Needless to say, it didn't do Seb any good. He wasn't happy at school, used to beg me to bring him home, but I had my hands tied. Anyway, when he finally left, he was expected to join DelCorp, but he had no interest in the family business. Still doesn't.' He gets to his feet. 'And that's when it all started. The wild parties, the endless holidays, fast cars, fast women.'

'And your father funded that?'

'He did.'

'But why?'

'Because it was a convenient way to keep Seb at arm's length. He threw money at him and didn't care what happened.' He shrugs. 'Don't get me wrong. They had plenty of rows about the profligate lifestyle. My father never misses a chance to put anyone down.' He glances out of the window. 'And during one of those rows, he saw fit to tell Seb the truth about our mother.'

'The truth?'

A few seconds pass before Max explains. 'She killed herself.'

Jesus, that came out of nowhere. Hardly knowing what to say, I trot out the usual words. 'Oh, my God. I'm so sorry.'

'It's okay. It all happened a long time ago.' He shrugs again. 'She was an alcoholic. Driven to the bottle by my father, in fact. Finally, she got to the point where she couldn't take it anymore. Depression can do that to you.' He shakes his head. 'But Seb didn't see it that way, not in his teenage years. Instead, he convinced himself she'd abandoned him in his time of need. Inevitably, it sent him off the rails.'

'I'm not surprised.' My own mother fought tooth and nail to stay with me. Even when I lost her, I never lost my faith in her love. Without that, I might easily have gone down the same route.

'So, there you have it,' Max goes on. 'Seb was nineteen, hell bent on self-destruction, and hanging out with a bunch of layabout rich kids.' He sits down again. 'There are a lot of drugs in those circles, you know. I'm not surprised Seb fell into it. First it was dope, then cocaine. Then, the biggie.' He runs his fingers through his hair. 'He went mad for a while there. Lost friends, lost me, didn't even bother with Harry. It went on for three years. He doesn't remember much about it... but I do. It's not pleasant watching someone you love destroy themselves.'

230

'So... what stopped him?'

'The very real prospect of death. He overdosed. A careless mistake. It was Celine who found him.' He smiles again. 'Seb rescued Celine from a shitty situation, and she repaid the debt. If it wasn't for her, he'd be dead.'

'God.' No wonder she's so protective over him, and no wonder he's never sacked her. 'Was she ever into it?'

'No. Celine's demons lie elsewhere. Anyway...' The smile disappears, and he moves on with the story. 'When Seb got out of hospital, I put him through rehab at the boathouse. He had his own doctors, there were security guards making sure he didn't do a runner, and I made sure it never got into the press.' He drums his fingers on the counter. 'After that, he needed direction, something to occupy his mind. So, I sold him the main house and, hey presto, the club was born. It saved him in more ways than one. He had a business to focus on and ready access to the kind of activities that help you forget. It was what he needed at the time.'

'And now?'

'I'm not privy to that.' His eyebrows quirk. 'Perhaps you are?'

'Perhaps.' I take a moment to examine Max Delaney in more detail. Never judge a book by its cover. That's what Oma used to say. I should have learned my lesson by now. 'Why do I get the feeling you're not all bad?'

'Because it's the truth.' With a quiet laugh, he unfastens the cufflink of his right sleeve, rolls up the material, and lays his arm on the counter, palm upwards.

I find myself gazing at a small tattoo, just at the top of his inner forearm. 'Crossed swords. Seb's got the same thing.'

'We were fairly drunk when we had them done.' He runs a finger over the tattoo. 'That was a night and a half. But they remind us that we always look out for each other, and fight for each other. We may fall out from time to time, but it's only ever temporary. I'll always watch out for my brother... and anyone who brings him happiness.'

His face says it all. He means me. Barely able to believe it, I get up.

Max raises a finger. 'Before you go to Seb, a friendly word of advice.' His expression hardens. 'Be careful how you tread with Christophe. He has a track record of causing trouble.'

'But you don't have proof.'

'So far, he's been very clever... or lucky. Last year, we discovered we had a half-brother. Zach. He lives the quiet life down in

Cornwall. Wasn't too keen on being known as a Delaney, but someone tipped off the press. It caused Zach a lot of trouble.'

'And you think it was Christophe?'

He nods. 'But Seb doesn't share my suspicions. In fact, it was the root cause of our latest disagreement.'

'I see.'

'But thanks to you, I think he might be coming round to my way of thinking.'

'I'm glad.'

'Don't mention it to him yet. I want to keep the upper hand for a while longer, and Christophe has a habit of coming between me and my brother.'

'A habit?'

His lips twitch. 'Those undesirables who dragged my brother into the gutter? Guess who introduced him to them.'

Christophe? 'Surely he wouldn't have done it on purpose.'

He laughs, bitterly. 'I wouldn't put it past him.'

***

It's a mild evening out on the balcony. I stop for a moment at the threshold, taking in the sight of Seb. Just to the right of me, he's leaning against the balustrade, hands clasped in front of him. And he's busy contemplating the scene.

'Come and look at this,' he says, sensing my presence.

As soon as I join him, I'm in awe of the view: a vast swathe of London stretching out beneath us, from Docklands on the left to the Eye on the right.

'You've got the world at your feet, Evie.' I catch the hint of trepidation in his voice. 'But if you want to walk away, I understand.'

'I don't want to walk away.'

He turns to me, utterly serious now. 'Even though I'm damaged goods?' He takes my hand. 'A massive fuck-up with an addictive personality?'

I move closer. 'That's not who you really are.'

He takes me in his arms, deftly manoeuvring me so I'm backed against the balustrade. Pressing his crotch to mine, he plants a quick kiss on my lips.

'I'm going nowhere,' I tell him.

'Good. Because if you did try to walk away, you wouldn't get very far.'

'I wouldn't?'

'No. Because I'd have to come after you.' His embrace tightens. 'Like it or not, you're well and truly stuck with me.'

'My cross to bear.'

He delivers another kiss, much longer this time, and much deeper too. I have no idea how long it lasts, but by the time he's finished, I'm halfway to paradise.

'So,' he breathes. 'Now I've got to tell Max about those bloody letters. Thank you for that.'

'Any time.'

'I wouldn't be so flippant. You'll get your comeuppance.'

'Bring it on.'

'Alright.' He touches my chin. 'To begin with, you can spend an evening with my brother.'

'Oh.' Even though I've begun to make headway with Max, spending any length of time in his company isn't exactly a pleasant prospect, not yet. 'I don't think...'

He brings an index finger to my lips. 'Comeuppance,' he grins. 'Suck it up.'

Half an hour later, while Seb and Max cook dinner, I curl up on a sofa and indulge in a touch of eavesdropping. At first, the conversation doesn't flow easily, but by the time we sit down to eat, the brothers seem to have hit their stride. During the meal, they touch on their father's ailing health, the current state of play with Harry, and news of Zach's engagement. Afterwards, we retire to the lounge where we briefly cover the sticky subject of the letters. With Max declaring it 'something for another time', he spends a few minutes boring Seb with an update on his efforts to buy a publishing company before the discussion segues into sharing memories of happier times. It's then that I leave them to it. Withdrawing to a guest bedroom, I treat myself to a bath and stretch out on a luxuriously massive bed, musing over the fact that far from proving a 'comeuppance', my evening with the Delaney brothers seems to have been nothing less than a curiously pleasant experience.

It's nearly eleven o'clock when Seb finally appears. As soon as he shuts the door, I hear the scrape of a key.

'Seb?' I sit up. 'What's going on?'

'Max locked us in.'

'Pardon?' I scramble from the bed. 'Why?'

'Because I asked him to.'

He shrugs off his jeans, and I wonder if I've landed myself with a complete lunatic.

'Why?'

'Because...' He removes his t-shirt. 'I said I'd prove myself.' Leaning one hand against the wall, he strips off his socks. 'And that's what I'm about to do.' Slinging the socks onto a chair, he moves on to his pants.

'By locking us in?' I'm completely mesmerised by his newly revealed hard-on. It takes all my reserves of self-control to drag my eyes back to his face.

'Think about it.' He straightens up. 'How long have we been together now?'

'I don't know.'

'I mean, how many hours since we were at the lake?'

I do my best to calculate. It's not easy. I'm far too distracted by the sight of Seb flexing his shoulders. 'Not sure.'

'Five,' he says, closing in. 'And in all that time, apart from being with Max, I haven't left your side.'

'No.'

'No chance for a fix.'

'Seb...'

He raises a hand. 'No arguments. This is what's happening. We spend another few hours locked in here, and then you'll know for certain.'

'But...'

I get no chance to form a sentence. Swept up in his arms, I'm carried back to the bed and dropped onto the covers. I bounce – once, twice – and catch my breath.

'I want to prove myself to you.' He climbs onto the bed and straddles me.

'And you're doing it here?'

'Why not? It's the perfect location.' He pins my hands above my head. 'If we were at the club – or even the boathouse – you'd have to search everywhere.'

'I wouldn't...'

I'm silenced again, this time by a kiss.

'I'd make you,' he says when he's finished. 'And given the fact someone's been planting little surprises, I can't guarantee you'd find nothing.' He manoeuvres himself between my legs. 'But I can here.'

True enough. From what I already know about Max Delaney, there's no way he'd keep illegal substances on the premises.

'This is important to me, Evie. I don't want any doubt left in your mind. None whatsoever.'

And who am I to deny him the chance?

Chapter Twenty-Two

I've been watching him for a few minutes now, admiring that gloriously handsome face while he's still asleep. Thanks to my conversation with Max, I now know there's much more to admire in Seb than his looks.

Reaching out, I let a finger drift across his cheek, reminding myself of how he went through hell and fought hard for his own salvation, emerging a stronger man for it. Then I tell myself it's no surprise my feelings for him have intensified over the past few hours. There are no two ways about it, I decide. If I want this relationship to go anywhere, I need to open up... and soon.

Dwelling on that thought, I lean in and kiss him lightly on the lips.

His eyelids rise. 'Mmm.' He smiles. 'Morning.'

'Morning.'

'Why so serious?'

'Just relaxing my facial muscles.' I conjure a smile of my own, and check the clock on the bedside table. 'It's just after nine. Another two hours before we're free.'

'Excellent.'

He wiggles an eyebrow, and I know exactly what's on his mind – the very same thing that kept us awake well past midnight: a long, lazy, totally vanilla session; filled with soft caresses and reverent kisses, a slow-burning passion that left us both breathless and dazed. I'm still glowing at the memory of it all.

'So...' He stifles a yawn. 'You'd better tell me what you see.'

Deciding to play the fool, I glance around the room. 'Wardrobe, chair, curtains, chandelier.'

He gives me a gentle pinch.

'You Delaneys like your chandeliers.'

'I mean here.' He points to his head.

'The most gorgeous, sexy man I've ever met.'

He grins. 'Come on, Evie. You know what I'm talking about.'

'Okay.' I do. 'I see you.'

He slips a hand beneath my back and urges me over him. 'Which includes no shakes, and no sweating.'

'All the proof I need.' Propping myself up on my elbows, I brush my lips against his. 'Max could let us out right now.'

'He could. But I don't want him to.' He tightens his grip. 'And talking of Max, you were pretty impressive with him last night. I think he might be warming to you.'

I'm warming to him too, but I'll keep that quiet for now. 'That's a turn-up for the books.'

'It is.' He touches the end of my nose. 'However, I think he'd like you whole lot more if you coughed up the ring.'

'Oh, Jesus.' The ring. Not only buried in a churchyard, but also – until now – tucked away at the back of my mind. 'I suppose he mentioned it.'

'I suppose he did. I don't blame him, really. It means a lot to Harry... and it's worth a lot of money.'

Of course, I muse silently. The chandelier-loving Delaneys aren't likely to buy reasonably priced jewellery. 'How much?'

'One hundred and fifty.'

'Pounds?'

He suppresses a chuckle. 'Thousand.'

'Pardon?'

'One hundred and fifty thousand pounds.'

My mouth dries up. My eyes widen. 'You're kidding me.'

'No.'

I wriggle against his hold. 'Why didn't you tell me?'

'Because you said it was safe.'

Leaning on one elbow, I put my hand to my mouth. Suddenly, I feel extremely foolish... and incredibly sick.

'Evie?' He becomes serious. 'Where is it?'

I groan. 'In a cemetery.'

'A what?'

'A cemetery.' God, this sounds mad. 'I was drunk... panicking. I hid it behind a gravestone.'

'That doesn't sound particularly safe to me.'

'I did bury it.' As if that makes it any better.

'Bloody hell.' He closes his eyes. 'Which cemetery?'

'I'm not exactly sure.'

His eyes open again, and they're filled with disbelief. 'This just gets better.'

'Somewhere in Bermondsey.' I chew at my bottom lip. 'Near where Alex picked me up. If you took me back, I'd remember...' Possibly.

'And you're prepared to go?'

'I don't think I have a choice.'

'We'd better get this sorted.' Rolling me onto my back, he practically leaps from the bed, and heads straight to the door. 'Max!' he shouts, pounding the door with both fists. 'Wake up! It's urgent! You've got to let us out!'

***

With my forehead pressed against the window, I stare across the road, occasionally catching sight of a grubby neon phoenix between passing traffic. Almost lost in the clutter of shop fronts, and not yet illuminated, it's nothing more than a vague shadow, a ghostly marker of the spot where I drank tea with Hal. Drawing back from the glass, I realise it's the first time I've seen that sign in days. I can barely believe how much life has changed since then.

I feel a squeeze of my hand. 'You're sure he won't turn up?' Seb asks.

'Absolutely. Wallace is never up before noon.' Not even when he's short-staffed.

My gaze drifts along the High Street. It's a busy morning: plenty of people traipsing to and fro; most of them lugging shopping bags, some stopping to gawp at the Bentley I'm currently hiding in.

'What are we waiting for?' I ask.

'Who,' Seb corrects me. 'Alex is on his way. He'll take us back to the club as soon as we've rescued the ring.'

'Right.'

I blink into the traffic and wonder if this is a mistake. After all, failing to keep a low profile – breaking the cardinal rule.

'This is a bad idea,' I mutter.

'Everything's fine.' Leaning forward, Seb touches his brother's shoulder. 'He should be here by now.'

'Patience,' Max warns from the front seat. 'He's had further to come.' Another couple of minutes pass in strained silence before he speaks again. 'There you go,' he announces, opening his door. 'He's here.' Closely followed by our driver for the morning's journey – a muscle-bound security guard, apparently called Chesty – he's immediately out of the car.

Seb releases my hand. 'Come on.'

Moments later, we're standing on the pavement, watching a Jaguar pull up behind the Bentley. Emerging from the passenger side, Alex comes to join us. He nods a greeting to Max and Chesty, informs Seb he's arranged for the Porsche to be returned to the

238

club, then fixes his attention on me. Along with everyone else, he's waiting for me to make a start.

With anxiety levels already on the rise, I'm none too pleased about being the centre of attention, but there's nothing to be done about it. Willing myself to stay calm, I look up at a thick slab of grey sky, and search through blurred memories. I'm about to issue my first direction when a chirpy greeting causes me to swivel round.

'Morning.'

'Baz?' In complete disbelief, I stare into a pair of puffy, red-rimmed eyes. 'What the hell are you doing here?'

'A man's allowed to go shopping, ain't he?' His gaze flicks across the group of men. 'Run out of nuts.' He tugs his grimy t-shirt over his midriff. 'What's going on here then?'

'Who is this?' Max growls.

'Landlord.'

'Is that so?' In an instant, he lurches forward, grabbing Baz by the collar and ramming him against the window of a charity shop.

'Max!' I call. 'Go easy.'

Max shakes his head. 'Your attacker might have paid him a visit, which means he might have his number, not to mention a nice cash offer. Do we take him with us, Chesty?'

'Nah. He'll slow us down. Just grab his mobile and leave him in the Jag.'

'Fair enough.' Max tightens his grip on his hapless prey. 'Hand it over.'

'What?' Baz splutters.

'Give me your mobile.'

A strangled laugh escapes his lips. 'Behave, Mr Dandy.'

'Maybe I've not been clear enough.' He glances back at Chesty who, in turn, shifts his jacket to reveal a gun.

It's enough to put Baz firmly in his place.

'Now,' Max says calmly. 'Give. Me. Your. Mobile.'

'Fine.' With shaking hands, Baz retrieves a mobile from his jeans pocket. 'What's the problem?'

Ignoring the question, Max snatches the phone. 'You'll get this back when I'm done. What's the PIN?'

'Now, come on...'

'PIN,' Max growls.

Baz stutters out a four-digit number. 'But there ain't no attacker on there,' he complains.

'We'll see about that. In the meantime, you're going to sit in that car.' He waves at the Jaguar. 'And you're not going to do anything stupid.' With that, he leads Baz over to the Jaguar, installs him in the front passenger seat and spells out the situation to the driver.

I turn to Seb. 'Your brother's a bit full-on.'

'I did warn you.' His hand comes to the small of my back. 'I told Max the full story last night.' Which explains everything. 'We can't risk Baz calling your attacker.'

'And you can't hold people against their will.'

'Don't worry. Max is bound to smooth things over.'

'Money,' I sigh.

'Makes the world go round.' He nods to Baz. Now slouched in the front of the car, he's gazing into space like an abandoned puppy. 'Before long, he'll have all the nuts he can eat.'

Slamming the door shut, Max rejoins us and thrusts the mobile at Chesty. 'Take a look through his contacts when you get time.' He turns to me. 'Now, which way?'

'To the left. But...' I falter. 'I was on the other side.'

Immediately, Seb assumes the lead. Taking my hand, he guides me across the road. 'Take your time,' he says as we head north. 'And focus on the job.'

With Max, Chesty and Alex a few steps behind, we make our way along the High Street. I do my best to piece together the fragments of that night, but it's not easy. After spending days in the relative peace and quiet of the club, my senses are in overload: the constant rush of traffic claiming my ears; a ceaseless flow of faces and shop fronts distracting my eyes; aromas of fast food, cigarettes and rubbish bins clinging to my nostrils. It's a never-ending bombardment that leaves me wondering how I ever managed to survive the chaos. I'm just glad I've got Seb's hand to anchor me now.

I'm beginning to wonder if I'll ever be able to concentrate when I think of the off-licence. If I can locate it, I'll have a better idea of where to go. Buoyed by the idea, I press on. It's not long before I come to a halt in front of a smeared window.

Seb's fingers tighten around mine. 'What is it?'

'This is where I bought the gin.' I gesture to the bottles of spirits. 'I went that way.' I point along the road.

'Right. Come on.' I'm encouraged to move again.

A few minutes later, I'm standing at the entrance to a park.

'There.' I motion at a bench. 'I sat there.' And drank myself into a stupor.

Letting go of my hand, Seb looks around. 'Can't see a church.'

'No. But it's not far.'

This time, I need no encouragement. Completely determined, I move again, walking for what seems like an age, scanning the shops on both sides of the road, scouring for visual clues, but finding nothing familiar. I'm on the verge of panic, wondering if the church was nothing more than a gin-induced hallucination, when we reach a busy crossroad.

'Yes! There it is!'

A Victorian church nestled quietly at the other side of the road: set back from the High Street, protected by a stone wall, languishing in the company of a handful of gnarly trees. With its brickwork darkened by time, in the clear light of day it seems a little sad... a little neglected.

Pulling my hand from Seb's, I check the traffic and cross the road, leading the search party through a gateway into the graveyard.

'Which one?' Seb asks.

'Not sure.'

Struggling to remember anything, I spend the next few minutes wandering amongst gravestones – some still upright, some leaning wildly as if they've been at the gin too – scrutinising one moss-covered slab after another. I strain to read the faded inscriptions, but none of them jog my memory. And then, it comes to me, right out of the blue.

'Matthew.' A ghost in my life. My father. 'I've remembered,' I call to the others, excitement building now. 'Look for Matthew.'

There's a flurry of activity, and within the space of a minute, it's located: covered in moss, but with the name still visible – an inconspicuous stone at the rear of the yard.

'Matthew Longhorn,' Seb reads. 'Died in 1852. Good choice. Poor old Matthew's long forgotten. So, what now?'

'Round the back. I made a hole.'

I scurry round to the back of the gravestone, but Alex beats me to it. Crouching down, he scrapes away at the earth. A couple of inches down, he hits something, removes a final handful of soggy mud, and dislodges the box.

I laugh in relief. 'Oh, thank God.'

Alex hands the box to Seb, who quickly removes the ring and holds it up to the light.

'I think this is what you call a good day's work, Evie.'

'I still can't believe a ring can be worth that much.'

'It's mostly on account of this diamond.' He touches the centre stone. 'And the provenance. It belonged to Coco Chanel. Bought for her by the Prince of Wales.'

'Hal told me.' I gaze at the ring. 'But he said he couldn't prove it.'

'Oh, he did prove it,' Seb counters. 'He just forgot he'd proved it. Anyway, it's now a family heirloom, never to be sold.' He returns the ring to its grubby box. 'Now, let's get going.' Slipping the box into his pocket, he turns away to confer with his brother.

I scan my surroundings, feeling uneasy now, hardly able to believe the mission's gone without a hitch. While Seb and Max conduct their discussion a few feet away and Alex withdraws to check his phone, Chesty stands at the front wall, following the progress of a passing pedestrian. All is well, I tell myself, watching a blackbird land on a nearby gravestone. It eyes me for a few seconds before taking off again, flying off into the trees at the rear of the yard. I turn and watch its progress, lowering my gaze when I finally lose sight of it amongst the leaves.

And I blink.

Because there's a man lurking between the tree trunks. Dressed in a non-descript raincoat, with the hood pulled tight about his face, he raises his head.

'Seb?'

My pulse begins to race. Because I know that face. I know the dead-eyed smile trained in my direction. My brain tells me to run. But if I do, I'll leave protection behind. Instead, I grab hold of Seb's sleeve.

'What is it?' His voice seems to come from a thousand miles away.

'Him.' I sense a shiver in my bones. 'It's him.'

'Who?'

My lips part. My mouth's so dry I cough out the next word: 'Crawley. The man who... The one who...'

Eyes still fixed on the trees, and only vaguely aware of Seb urgently issuing orders, I blink again.

There's no one there.

Hands grasp my shoulders. Seb's face appears in front of mine. 'Alex and Chesty have gone after him.'

'We need to retreat,' Max snaps. 'Call your driver. Tell him to dump the idiot and get the car here, now!'

***

Less than five minutes later, I'm strapped into the back seat of the Jaguar, with Seb at my side.

'Are you sure it was him?' he asks.

242

'Yes.'

'But how did he know you were here?'

'There's a couple of possibilities,' Max intervenes from the front. 'Either your ex-landlord made a call before we took his phone, or your ex-employer spotted you.' His mobile rings. He answers. 'Where are you?' He listens for a moment, then ends the call. 'Back to the club,' he orders the driver. 'They lost him down by the river. Chesty's bringing Alex back after he's paid a couple of visits.'

'Baz and Wallace?' I ask.

'Baz and Wallace,' Max confirms.

While the car sinks into silence, Seb takes out the ring and inspects the diamond. Whatever he's thinking about, I leave him to it... because I've got thoughts of my own to deal with. Gazing out of the window, I realise it's begun to rain. A fitting backdrop for what's about to happen. Seeing nothing but a grey blur, I tell myself it's time to give up the truth, even if it means risking everything.

'I think we should lay the cards on the table.'

I turn from the window, surprised to hear my own decision voiced by Max.

'It can wait,' Seb tells him.

'No, it can't.' Max glances back at his brother. 'We need to know exactly what we're dealing with.'

Accompanied by the soft swish of the windscreen wipers, I sit up straight, mentally preparing myself to spill the beans, but I get no chance.

'Just tell her, Seb.'

Tell her? What's Max going on about now? 'Tell me what?' Out of nowhere, I have a sneaking suspicion that events are about to overtake me. 'Seb?'

Replacing the ring, he clicks the box shut and drops it into his lap. Seemingly resigned, he leans over and takes hold of my right wrist.

I try to pull back. 'What are you doing?'

Keeping a firm grip, he turns my arm and lightly touches the tattoo.

'Yara,' he murmurs, delivering the blow.

'What?'

I never knew it could do that to me. Never knew my own name could suck the lifeforce from every particle of my body. How do you know? That's what I want to ask. But words seem to have deserted me. Before I can gather my wits, he begins to answer the question.

'That's what the Y stands for.' He smiles. 'You gave yourself away.' He releases my arm.

And my brain kicks into action. 'When?' I demand.

'That first night... in the kitchen.'

I knew it. 'Celine.'

'No. DJ. He told me you knew your way round every bit of equipment in that kitchen. He said everything you did – even the way you chopped an onion – everything had the touch of a professional.'

I close my eyes as he carries on.

'So, I did a bit of digging. Didn't take long.'

There's a twinge in my stomach.

'Promising female chefs. First name beginning with Y. I found an online newspaper report about a young chef at a Michelin-starred restaurant in Manchester. Yara Richardson. Nice photo. Mystery solved... almost.'

'Almost.' I grumble. 'When did you find this out?'

'Somewhere between Mr Harrison's party and the apartment.'

Which explains his behaviour in the bedroom. Without me knowing, he's been in complete control for days now. He must have loved every second of it.

'Last night,' he goes on, 'I told Max everything I knew. He had Chesty look into you.'

Feeling nauseous, I listen vaguely to what Max says next.

'You were in a relationship with the owner of the restaurant, living with him, in fact... until he died.'

My breathing quickens.

'Miles Crawley. I've read the post-mortem report. Shared the findings with Seb this morning while you were in the shower. Crawley had a fall and cracked his skull on a table. According to toxicology, he was drunk and high as a kite. High levels of amphetamines and cocaine. No sign of foul play.'

Eyes still closed, I see the blood, feel the shock, reacquaint myself with absolute fear.

'Did you know he had CCTV in that room?' Seb asks.

I look up. 'Not at the time.'

'No sound on it,' he explains. 'Crawley had his back to the camera, and you didn't say much. Apparently, it's impossible to tell what was going on, but it caught Crawley's death. You had no part in it. Death by misadventure.'

'I know.' A quick visit to an internet café had given me all the details.

244

'And yet, you disappeared.'

The car begins to swirl. 'I did.'

'Officially, you're a missing person.' He leans in. 'Tell me what's going on, Yara.'

If I was about to pass out, the second use of my given name drags me back from the edge. Suddenly, I'm not shocked, or horrified. Instead, I'm caught in the grips of a visceral, all-consuming anger. 'Don't call me that!'

'But it's your name.'

'And I don't want it. I don't want to be that person anymore.' Determined to wrestle back control and put these men in their place, I raise my chin. 'I'm Evie now.' And I need to clear something up. My next words are aimed at Max. 'So, you read the post-mortem report,' I growl. 'Tell me something, Max. How the hell did you manage to get your hands on that?'

He doesn't reply.

'Just tell me, Max. It's fucking important.'

That does it. There's nothing like an unexpected swearword, delivered with absolute fury, to jolt a man into action. 'Chesty's contact in the Met.'

'No.'

That's all I can say. Out of nowhere, the anger disappears, leaving nothing but a curious detachment in its wake. As if I'm not really here, I'm a remote witness now, idly watching the worst possible scenario play out in front of my eyes.

'His contact got in touch with Manchester and spoke to an investigating officer.' Max glances back at me. 'It seems Miles Crawley has a brother in the force up there.'

'I know.'

Seb touches my arm. I turn to him, but he's blurred. I must be crying.

'Evie?' I hear his concern.

'You weren't to know.' The words come quietly, almost of their own accord. 'It's his brother who's after me.' I feel a tear trickle down my cheek. 'And now he knows exactly where I am.'

Chapter Twenty-Three

'Who are you?'

That's what they all seem to ask – each and every one of those strange portraits hanging in the club lobby. I've been studying them for a few minutes now, idly passing the time before I'm told what to do next.

'Not quite sure,' I whisper.

Certainly not the loved-up heroine of a sickly-sweet romance with the perfect, happy ending. It doesn't matter that I'm living in the lap of luxury, or that I fell head over heels for the gorgeous hero and somehow managed to capture his heart. None of that makes any difference anymore.

Because I'm the hapless fool who broke all the rules.

'Evie?'

I hear Seb's voice, turn to where he's spent the past few minutes in conversation with Max and Celine, and my heart trips... pointlessly.

I could have spent the rest of my days with this man. But now I've come crashing back to earth, I know there's no way I can ever lay down roots. To put it quite simply, my past won't let me.

'Are you okay?' Seb approaches.

'Fine.' Except I'm not. Because there are some mistakes that stalk you for ever, like a bitter ex, laser-focused on retaliation. And I'm not prepared to expose him to any more of this. 'What's going on?' I watch Max and Celine disappear into the bar.

'We're closing the club.'

'Why?'

'Because...' He takes my hand. 'It's necessary.'

'Necessary?' Here we go. He'll do everything he can to solve the problem, not realising it's a problem that can't be solved.

'Necessary,' he repeats. 'I'm locking this place down until we've got a handle on the situation. Now, come with me.'

There's no point arguing. Hell hath no determination like an Alpha Male in protective mode. In silence, I let him lead me upstairs to the apartment and out onto the terrace. Before I know it, I'm standing at the parapet, with Seb by my side.

Leaning back against the stonework, he folds his arms. 'Now would be a good time.'

'Would it?' I falter, momentarily entertaining the idea of making a run for it. But it's hardly worth the effort. After all, I wouldn't get very far.

'I've been patient. I've waited for you to tell me on your own terms, but we've run out of time. I need you to tell me everything. Now.'

'It's... difficult.'

'Believe me, I know all about difficult.'

'Of course.' I laugh. 'But you had your brother tell me your secrets. I don't have that particular luxury.'

'No, you don't. And you don't have a choice either. I need to know it all.'

I run my hands over my face.

'Whatever it is,' he murmurs, 'I don't care.'

'That's easy enough to say.'

'Very easy. In fact, I'll say it again. I. Don't. Care.'

'Jesus.'

'Turn around.'

'What?'

'I said, turn around.'

'Fine.' I do as I'm told.

Moments later, his chest is against my back. Held tight in his arms, I'm wedged between his hard body and the stone parapet.

'What do you see?' he asks against my ear.

'What do you mean?'

'Exactly what I say. What do you see?'

'Grass.'

'And?'

'The lake. Clouds.' Thick, grey clouds that are threatening more rain at any minute.

'Okay, let's do this a different way. I'll tell you what I see.' His grip tightens. 'I see a house over there, at the far side of the lake. A home. For us. In fact, I see it so clearly, I've got an architect coming over next week. We're going to discuss plans with him. You and me.'

Confirmation that Seb wants everything I want. But I can't let him go on.

'No. You don't need to do that.'

'Yes, I do. I can't have you living above the business. And on that subject, I'm thinking of closing the club.' He brushes his lips against my neck. 'Think about it. No more Christophe. I could cut him off completely.'

Which would be ideal.

'What would you do with this place?'

'Turn it into a hotel... with a decent restaurant.'

'I can't...'

'Evie.' His voice softens. 'Don't even try to back out on me. Because of you, I have a future. And whether you like it or not, that future includes you. If you back out on me now, it all falls to pieces.' He pauses. 'I fall to pieces.'

I'm just glad he can't see my face. It must be blindingly obvious I'm anything but happy about his declaration. I could always tell him why – that there's no point building anything if I'm involved, because the only possible outcome is destruction – but I already know he'd dismiss my worries out of hand. And that's why I make my decision. Left with no other option, at some point over the next few hours, I'll need to disappear from his life. But before then, I'll to offer up the rest of my story. It might just help him understand.

A raindrop touches my forehead. 'We should go in.'

'Not until you've told me everything.'

Another raindrop. 'But we'll get wet.'

'Then I suggest you make a start.'

There'll be no more argument. That's perfectly clear. He's had enough of waiting.

'But I don't know where to start.'

'Try the boyfriend.'

I concentrate on the lake. The rain's coming down heavily over the water, and it's clearly moving this way. The air turns cold as I begin to speak. And the words don't come easily, not to begin with.

'It was my second job after college... my dream job. A Michelin-starred restaurant.' I can still see it now. Ultra-modern, ultra-stylish. The place to be seen. 'Miles owned it. He came to speak to me on my first night. A few days later, he asked me out.'

It begins to rain in earnest, and I shiver, registering every single prick of icy water.

'Go on,' Seb prompts.

'He was good-looking, popular... funny.' I shiver again, this time at the memory of those first dates, and my total inability to see past the beguiling façade. 'Three weeks after we met, I moved in with him. At first, everything was fine. It took me a while to realise what he was really like.'

'Which was?'

'Secretive, moody, controlling. Chaotic too. Sometimes, he'd sleep halfway through the day. Sometimes, he'd disappear for days. And when he showed up again, he'd never tell me where he'd been.'

With Seb's hold relaxing, I manoeuvre myself round to face him.

'That was all down to the drugs. I know that now. He was into everything, Seb. Cannabis. Cocaine. It was a few months before I knew about the heroin.' I shake my head. 'I never touched any of it.'

'I know you didn't. And if you think this is going the same way, you're nowhere near the mark.'

I manage a nod.

'And I still need to know what's putting the fear of God into you.'

'Okay.' I take in an unsteady breath. 'There were other things that bothered me about Miles. He had all these phones, lots of phones.' Jesus, this sounds ridiculous. 'And weird friends. Business associates who never discussed business in front of me.' I lower my head. 'I knew something was wrong, but I was too stupid to work it out...'

'Hold it right there.' Putting a finger under my chin, he raises my face back to his. 'You're anything but stupid.' He wipes the raindrops from my face. 'Sometimes, we just blind ourselves to the truth.' He reassures me with a smile. 'I take it you eventually found out what he was up to?'

'I did. Someone put me straight. A journalist.' I can still see her face now. Young. Earnest. Full of life. 'She told me the restaurant was his respectable face. Behind it all, Miles was renting all sorts of places, employing all sorts of people. He was laundering money.'

'Drug money.' He glances out at the lake, eyes darkening by the second.

'But he wasn't working on his own. This is the thing. He was just a part of something bigger... an organisation.'

'So why didn't you just walk away?'

'I started to think about it – to plan it – but he must have realised something was wrong.' I glance up at the sky. 'One day, he told me... he said he wasn't sure what he'd do if I ever left him. He tried to make it sound like a joke, but it wasn't a joke. It was a threat. And then ...' I close my eyes. Somehow, telling the story has managed to bring everything into focus like never before. And this, by far, is the hardest part.

'Evie?' Gently prompting me, he squeezes my arm.

'The journalist who warned me about Miles...' The tears are flowing now, and I can barely go on. 'Anna Wilson. Manchester. Google her. Now.'

With a small nod, he takes his phone from his pocket, taps in the name, and spends a minute or so reading through an article.

'Heroin overdose?' He looks up, brows furrowed.

249

'She didn't use.'

I watch the realisation hit him.

'I told her everything I knew. I thought it might just get him out of my life.' I feel it rising up inside – that same blind, flailing anger I always feel when I think of her. 'But I was stupid. And she was stupid. We were both stupid for thinking we could ever make a scrap of difference. Miles had me followed. He found out what was going on, and he...'

'You think Miles killed her?'

'I know who killed her.' I struggle to compose myself. 'It was Stefan.'

'The brother?'

'The policeman.' Untouched by addiction, and twice as ruthless. 'It was useful having a brother in the force. Stefan covered for Miles and kept him safe, well away from suspicion. He made plenty of money out of it too.' I pause for a few moments, just long enough to steady myself completely. 'Miles came home one night and told me he knew I'd spoken to Anna. He told me she was dead. He said Stefan was going to kill me, just like he'd killed her. He said he was on his way.' I smile, grimly. 'Miles was an evil piece of work, but I don't think he was up to it, really. I suppose that's why he got so drunk. He was already high.' I shrug. 'He did a lot of ranting, a lot of pacing up and down. And then he fell.' Out of nowhere, the tears regroup with a vengeance.

'And so, you ran.' Seb blows out a breath. 'No wonder you lived cash in hand. But I don't get it. How did he find you?'

I wipe away the tears. 'I took some money out of my bank account when Wallace sacked me. I knew I shouldn't, but I was desperate. Crawley must have tracked my card. I'm guessing he paid someone at the bank to let him know when I used it. And then, he turned up in Bermondsey.' I wave a hand. 'You know the rest.'

'I know you were sacked for helping my uncle. If you hadn't done that, Crawley would never have found you.'

'That doesn't mean it's your responsibility to sort him out.'

'I'm just musing over the irony.' He runs a palm up and down my arm. 'And while you might think it's not my responsibility, I'm still going to deal with him.'

'No. You can't. They didn't operate alone, Seb. I told you that. There were others. There are others. And they'll all want me dead.'

'Not necessarily.' He cocks his head. 'It's entirely possible the Crawley brothers kept the situation to themselves.'

'But...'

'Think about it. Those business associates of theirs wouldn't have been too pleased about the lapse in security.' His arms tighten around me. 'My mind's made up. Once this place is secure, I'll go after Stefan Crawley.'

'And do what?'

'Whatever it takes.' He takes my face in his hands. 'You don't need to be scared anymore. I'm going to sort it out.'

'But...'

'No. No more arguments.' He kisses my forehead, draws back and studies me. 'It all makes sense now. That first night you came here, you were terrified. I don't think I've ever seen anyone so afraid in my entire life.' His lips twitch. 'Do you remember telling me about your grandmother?' He smiles at my shock. 'Obviously not.' The smile deepens. 'Oma. Escaped from East Germany all on her own. She was one brave woman, just like you. She overcame fear, and you're going to do the same.'

'I will.'

Putting a hand to his cheek, I drink him in, memorising every little detail of his features. This man I've known for a matter of weeks – this amazing, wonderful man who's seen right to the heart of me, protected me and saved me – he's already had far too much trouble in his life. There's no way I can involve him any further in this mess, no way I can put him in so much danger. In spite of all his efforts to reassure me, my decision's final.

'Thank you for telling me.' He brushes his lips against mine. 'Now, come on. Let's go and get dry.'

'Yes. Let's.'

Feeling every inch a Judas, I smile and slip my hand into his.

***

While Seb goes downstairs to share the new information with his brother, I take a quick shower and change into fresh clothes. Less than ten minutes later, I'm making coffee when Seb returns, accompanied not only by Max, but Chesty too. Grabbing a couple of extra mugs, I finish off the drinks.

'Did you catch up with Baz?' I hand Chesty a mug.

'No. He's done a runner.'

'Then we don't know if it was him who tipped off Crawley.'

'I don't see who else it could have been.' He takes a tentative sip and pulls a face. 'Don't worry. I'll track the bastard down.'

251

'And what about Wallace?' The only other possible rat. 'He might have seen me.'

'He wasn't in.'

'That's for later.' Max nudges the sugar pot towards Chesty. 'We've got other priorities right now. Chesty's Met contact knows he works for me. We'll find out what he said on that call to Manchester, just in case it leads Crawley here. I don't think it will, but we'll cover all the bases.'

It doesn't make me feel any safer. 'What if Crawley got a registration number?'

'Then he probably got mine.' Watching Chesty spoon sugar into his mug, Max grimaces. 'He'll have seen you get out of my Bentley.'

'And if he turns up at your house?'

'He'll have a surprise. In the meantime, we're making sure this place is safe. The clientele are being asked to leave, security's been put on high alert, and I'm bringing in a few extra hands.' He focusses on his brother. 'And yes, before you ask, they will be armed. Talking of which, where's Crawley's gun?'

'What do you want that for?' Seb demands.

'He could have lifted it from the police store,' Chesty explains, stirring his newly sweetened coffee. 'In which case, it might come in useful.'

'How?'

'Getting him banged up.'

Seb sighs. 'Alright. Upstairs. Desk drawer.'

After a quick gulp of coffee, Chesty disappears down the hallway. At which point, Max's mobile buzzes. He answers, listens and ends the call.

'Celine,' he tells Seb. 'You're needed downstairs. You've got a problem.'

'What sort of problem?'

'A couple of members who want to know what's going on. They're not listening to her.'

'For fuck's sake.' I'm offered a quick, apologetic shrug. 'Play nice while I'm gone, Peregrine.'

'Naturally.'

As soon as his brother's gone, Max turns to me. 'We need to be quick.' He puts down his coffee.

And I do the same. Although I'd love to ask him about the whole 'Peregrine' thing, I'm momentarily distracted by Chesty reappearing in the background. Totally engrossed in the gun, he's like a child with a new toy.

'The money's still on the table.'

My attention snaps back to Max. 'I don't want your money.' Still riled by his fickle, double-dealing ways, I give him a damn good glare. 'But no need to worry, Max. I'm leaving anyway.'

I'm expecting a nonchalant 'okay then'. Instead, he sticks his hands in his trouser pockets and knocks me for six.

'Tell me something, Evie. Do you love my brother?'

'Pardon?'

Out of nowhere, my heartbeat stalls. 'I... er...'

'You don't know?'

Of course I know. I do love him, and it's burning me up from the inside out, stripping away my armour and leaving me right on the edge of irreversible damage. 'Just take me back to London.'

Withdrawing from Max's presence, I slump onto a sofa. It's no surprise when he follows me.

'Why?'

'Because I need to disappear.'

'I don't understand.'

'You don't have to.'

He takes a seat opposite.

'Just take me back to London, and I'll be out of Seb's life.'

Crossing his legs, he spreads his arms across the back of the sofa, taking up the pose of the ruthless business mogul. 'No.'

'What?'

'You heard.'

'But you want me gone.'

'What gave you that idea?'

Jesus. This man can be just as mystifying as his brother. 'You offered me money.'

'It was a test.' He raises a finger. 'Which you passed, by the way.'

'I don't care about your tests. I can't stay.'

'Why not?'

'You know why not. I'm trouble.'

'We can deal with Crawley.'

'You can't. You know what he's involved in.'

'Uh huh.'

'Organised crime, Max. If you think you can deal with that, you must be thick, or deluded, or both.'

He winks at Chesty. 'I think she'll do.'

'Totes.' Chesty winks back.

'Cut it out,' I snarl. 'Both of you. This isn't a joke. I'm trouble. Big trouble. A whole Pandora's Box worth of trouble. Just open me up and watch me destroy everything.'

Max rolls his eyes, then slowly, languidly, begins to clap. 'Bravo! Nice image.'

'Fuck the image, Max. It's the truth.'

'Lord above. You're getting very sweary. Okay, Yara Richardson...'

'That's not my name.'

'It's on your birth certificate.'

'So?'

'So...' He arches an arrogant eyebrow. 'Here are a few things you need to know. Number one. I agree with Seb. The Crawley brothers were working alone. If those big, scary crime lords were involved, you'd already be dead. And so would Stefan Crawley. The fact is, his brother made a mistake letting you into his life, and then tried to cover it up. There's no way he'd confess his sins to his bosses. Those kinds of people don't take too kindly to fuck-ups.' He checks on Chesty. Oblivious to the conversation, he's still examining the gun.

'This is all guesswork, Max.'

'If it's going to make you feel any better, I'll have Chesty find out for sure.'

'If...'

'Where was I?' Max cuts in. 'Oh, yes. Number two. You are in love with my brother. I've seen and heard enough to know that.'

'What would you know about love?'

'Plenty,' he grins. 'I've read about it. Which brings me to number three.' He gets up. 'My brother's in love with you.'

Vaguely aware that time seems to have stopped, I gaze into space, opening and closing my mouth like Mrs Jaws on acid. Even though Seb's already made his feelings perfectly clear – albeit, without using the magic word – I seem to have gone into denial. And now, to hear those feelings confirmed by a semi-friendly third party... it's unsettling, to say the least.

'In love,' Max persists. 'It's as obvious as the nose on Chesty's ugly face. He'd do anything for you. Seb, that is. Not Chesty. And that means I'm honour-bound to do the same.'

'There's no fucking honour in it,' Chesty mutters.

I look up to find him holding the gun in front of his anything-but-ugly face. Fiddling complete, he's now busy admiring it.

'Actually,' Max says breezily, 'Chesty's right. My motives are completely selfish. After all, if my brother's happy, I'm happy. And I like being happy. After all, I am human.'

'Hadn't noticed.' Chesty lowers the gun.

'Oh, I can prove it.' With a grin, Max focusses back on me.

I shift, uneasily.

'Which brings me to the final thing you need to hear.' The grin disappears. 'You're not on your own anymore. Pending further developments, you're now an honorary member of the Delaney clan. And much like the Mafia, there's no escape. Sorry to have to tell you this, but Seb's not about to let you go, and I'm not about to magic you away. In fact, if you do try anything silly, you can count on me to help Seb find you.'

'But why?'

'Because when something's worth fighting for, the Delaneys never give up.' He gives me a warm, friendly, almost brotherly smile. 'Do we have an understanding?'

I think so.

But it's hard to tell.

Because there's still something going on in my brain, some sort of change I haven't yet had time to process. Spurred into action by Mr Delaney's words, despair seems to have packed its bags, ready to make way for an old friend I haven't seen in months. Hope.

'I suppose so,' I mutter without nearly enough conviction.

'Not good enough.'

'Fine.' I huff. 'We do.'

'Good.' Max re-adjusts his jacket. 'By the way, Celine's bringing you a handbag.'

'Pardon?'

'A handbag. You'll need it. And a mobile too. Fuck knows why Seb hasn't got you one.' He shrugs. 'Is that thing suitable, Chesty?'

'It'll do.'

'Excellent.' Max checks his mobile. 'My brother's no coward. He'd go head-to-head with anyone in a fist fight, and he'd gladly lay out Stefan Crawley if he got the chance. But he draws the line at firearms. I'm hoping you're made of different stuff.'

'But... I thought... I thought you needed it.'

'Nah,' Chesty grins. 'This is for you.'

He holds up the gun, and I stare at it. Carried around in Crawley's pocket, the weapon that nearly put an end to my existence.

'Why would I want that?'

'In case there's a chink in the armour.' He clicks out the magazine. 'It's possible your ex-boss called Crawley. It's possible your ex-landlord called him. But it's also possible there's a mole on board. It's wise to be prepared for any possibility.'

'Any possibility,' Max repeats, slipping the phone into his jacket pocket. 'I need you to be ready to protect yourself.' His gaze comes to rest on me. 'And my brother. So, up you get.'

'What?'

'Up.' He motions for me to stand. 'Time for the lesson, Chesty. A very quick lesson.'

'Right, boss.' Holding the gun on the flat of his palm, Chesty approaches and waits for me to get to my feet. 'Now this is a handy piece of kit. Here's the safety catch.' He points to the catch, then deftly takes the gun in his right hand and demonstrates. 'Flick it on. Flick it off. Nice and quiet. There you go. Hold it.' He offers up the lump of sleek, black metal. 'Familiarise yourself.'

Reluctantly, I take it.

'Now aim.'

I raise the gun, levelling it at a vase on the windowsill.

'Steady yourself. Legs slightly apart. Use both hands. Left hand on your right wrist.'

Adopting the stance, I raise my left hand.

'Good. Now, flick the safety and squeeze the trigger.'

I hesitate.

'Go on. Squeeze. It's not loaded.'

Shaking with nerves, I do as I'm told, wincing at the sound of a click.

'Again.'

I follow the order, a little less nervous this time. While Max withdraws to the hallway and hovers near the front door, Chesty shows me how to load and unload the magazine.

'Get as much practice as you can.' He glances after Max. 'Obviously, don't practice when it's loaded. But when you're not practising, keep it loaded at all times. Safety on. Got it?'

I nod.

'By the way, when you're aiming this thing at a man, go for the chest. Nice big target. You're bound to do some harm. But be fucking careful with it.'

'Language,' Max warns, returning from the hallway. 'Celine just texted. Seb's on his way back up. Go and hide the gun.'

I scurry off to my bedroom and store the offending article at the back of the wardrobe, covering it with a t-shirt. When I return,

Chesty and Max are reclining on opposite sofas, innocently sipping at lukewarm drinks.

'When the handbag arrives,' Max says, 'tuck it down at the bottom. Put some girly stuff over the top. Make-up. Tampons. That sort of thing.'

'But I don't have any girly stuff.' Rescuing my own coffee, I take up position next to Chesty.

'Don't worry. Celine's providing it. And one more thing. Bring it with you. And the mobile.'

'Where?'

'Harry's not good. It's likely you'll be seeing him over the next few days. I'm willing to bet Seb won't leave you here.' He smiles again, glancing towards the hallway at the sound of steps. 'Not this time.'

Chapter Twenty-Four

Less than twenty-four hours later, Max's prediction comes true. A short phone call during breakfast brings the news that Hal's deteriorating. Within half an hour, we're back in the Jaguar – overnight bags in the boot, the handbag of doom at my feet – and we've already left the grounds.

'How bad is it?' I ask, tucking my hand under Seb's. After the rush to get ready, it's my first chance to gain more detail.

'Another mini-stroke last night.' He gazes out of the window. 'He's weak. Might not remember you. Might not even recognise me.'

'I'm so sorry.'

He nods. 'You must have been through this.'

'Twice.'

He squeezes my hand, and we both know there's nothing more to be said. The next few minutes pass in silence, until country lanes finally give way to the M25.

Shaking himself back to life, Seb speaks to Alex. 'What have we got in terms of security?'

'Five from the club, including me and Dave.' He nods briefly to the stranger in the front passenger seat before returning his concentration to the road. 'Max is putting another five in place.'

'Is that enough?'

'Should be. The grounds aren't extensive. Everything's covered.'

'We'll be safe then.'

Accompanied by a squeeze of my hand, those last words are meant for me. But while I'm grateful for the reassurance, it doesn't seem to have much effect. No matter how hard I try to shove Crawley out of my mind, he steadfastly refuses to go. In fact, every single time I try to think of anyone else, he simply jostles for attention and thrusts himself back into prime position, leaving me tangled up in thoughts that never seem to settle in any one place. In the end, I close my eyes against a world of grey tarmac and impatient traffic, and desperately try to empty my brain of everything.

I've made very little progress by the time the Jaguar slows. Eyes open again, I discover we're back to minor country roads and picturesque English fields. It's not long before we turn into a gravel drive and come to a halt before a set of iron gates. Ushered through by security guards, we finally pull up in front of a stone portico.

I get out of the car and take a moment to admire Hal's beautiful home. Three storeys of biscuit-brown stonework, topped by a gabled roof and intricate, oversized brick chimneys. Simple, rustic and grand, it's clearly a one-off work of art.

'Wow!' Turning slowly, I take in a pristine lawn and woods beyond. It's almost impossible to match this idyllic scene with the confused, old man I met at The Phoenix.

'Wow, indeed.' Seb comes to my side. 'This is a Lutyens house.'

'Lutyens?'

'Famous architect. Don't know if you've noticed, but Delaneys don't do bog-standard. Uncle Harry, in particular. He was an art dealer. Always had an eye for beauty. Talking of which.' He produces the ring box from his jacket pocket. 'Do me a favour. Put this in your handbag.'

I take the box and lay it on top of a whole load of 'lady stuff' helpfully provided by Celine. And then, because I'm sure I won't need the contents any time soon, I give the handbag to Alex. 'If you're taking the luggage up, could you leave this in our room?'

'My usual suite,' Seb adds, studying the three high-end cars parked further down the drive, alongside an ancient, battered Land Rover. 'I hope you're ready for this, Evie. The whole family are here.'

'It's to be expected.'

'That includes my father.'

'Oh.' I'm touched by a sense of anxiety.

'Whatever he says to you, just ignore it. And remember, me and Max are nothing like him. And neither is Zach.'

'Zach's here?'

'Yup.' He waves a hand at the Land Rover. 'That's his pitiful excuse for a car. There's a fourth brother too.' As if it's of no particular consequence, he leads me up the steps into the house, giving me no time at all to ask about the mysterious extra sibling.

A surprisingly airy entrance hall awaits us, along with a distinctly serious-looking Max.

'Any change?' Seb asks him.

'Not really.'

'He should back be in hospital.'

'You know his wishes.' Holding out an A4 manilla envelope, Max approaches. 'Besides, he's got two nurses waiting on him. The family doctor visits every day, and his housekeeper won't leave him alone.' He slaps the envelope against Seb's chest. 'Time to do the business.'

'Really? Does it have to be now?'

'You know the rules.'

'Fine.' Clearly disgruntled, Seb grabs the envelope and empties the contents onto a side table. A pen slips out, followed by a single sheet of paper. 'Evie, you need to sign this.'

'Me?' Thoroughly intrigued, I join him. 'What is it?'

'An NDA.' He stares at the sheet. 'If you don't sign, you don't stay. It's as simple as that.' He picks up the pen and offers it to me. 'My father insists. I'm sorry.'

'It's okay.' I take the pen. 'I've no problem with a non-disclosure, but I'm signing it as Evie.' I hesitate. 'I'll need a surname.'

'Smith,' Max intervenes.

I raise an eyebrow at him. 'Are you sure?'

'Absolutely.'

'Fair enough.' I sign at the bottom of the sheet. 'Evie Smith.' With a flourish, I present the sheet and pen to Max. 'Not my legal name, so I'm not sure how it can be legally binding.'

'It can be arranged.' Max folds the sheet and tucks it into his jacket pocket. 'The old man's with Harry at the minute. We get to visit after lunch.' He motions to an open doorway. 'We're all eating together.'

'Count me out.' Seb grimaces. 'That's not why I'm here.'

'Me neither, but it's not optional.'

Trailing behind Seb and Max, I enter the dining room, quickly taking in the centrepiece – a huge, mahogany table laid out with a handful of settings at the far end – before my attention's drawn to a set of French windows on the right. Flooding the room with bright sunlight, and giving up the briefest glimpse of a suited figure outside, they've been left wide open. I'm straining to get a better view of the stranger when Seb's hand comes to my back.

'Let's do the introductions.'

I'm urged forwards.

'Zach,' he announces.

I find my hand in a vice-like grip, and look up into a pair of blue irises. A similar height to Seb and Max, he's in possession of a slightly different, more muscular build. And with his ruffled blond hair and distinctly rugged appearance, he's disgustingly handsome. Seeing as it seems to be a Delaney trait, I'd be more surprised if it was any other way.

'Pleased to meet you,' I smile.

'Likewise.' He puts an arm around his companion's waist. 'And this is Amy. My fiancée.'

It's impossible not to notice the uneven ridge of skin running almost the full length of her face, from just next to her right eye down to the middle of her cheek. But it makes no difference to the fact that she's absolutely stunning.

'And this,' Seb goes on, 'is Evie. My girlfriend.'

My heartbeat flutters. And this time there's nothing pointless about it. To hear him call me his girlfriend is nothing less than confirmation it's all moving in the right direction. Since my little talk with Max, I've somehow managed to accept my new-found status as an honorary Delaney. I've also adopted their mantra. When something's worth fighting for, the Delaneys never give up. And I'll be damned if I ever give up on Seb.

'Pleased to meet you both.' Trying not to float off into giddiness, I decide to engage Amy in conversation while Seb, Max and Zach exchange pleasantries. I'm still wondering how to make a start when I catch sight of that suited figure again. 'What?' My mouth falls open.

Seemingly unaware of my presence, Christophe Dupont inhales deeply on a cigarette and scowls into the sun.

I nudge Seb. 'What's he doing here?'

He follows the direction of my gaze. 'Fourth brother.'

'Pardon?'

That's two huge secrets within a week, and this one's even harder to process than the first. If Seb told me the sky was green, and the grass red, I'd be more inclined to believe him. Although I've only witnessed them together on a couple of occasions, I've never detected any sign of brotherly connection.

'Half-brother, to be precise.' He begins to turn away.

In complete shock, I grab his sleeve. 'Excuse me? Why didn't you tell me before?'

'Because you hadn't signed the NDA.' He smiles.

'That's what it was about?'

'Yes. And now you're legally bound to keep it under your hat, just like the rest of us.'

'Why?'

The smile turns sour. 'Because Daddy Dearest doesn't want it known that he fathered a child with a prostitute.'

'A prostitute?' I gawp at Christophe.

He flicks the half-finished cigarette into a bush and steps inside. 'Good to see you again, Evie.'

My gaze swings from Christophe to Seb, and back again. 'Brothers?'

MANDY LEE

Christophe laughs. 'Oh dear, Sebastian. You let the cat out of the bag. You know it's against Delaney law.' He narrows his eyes at me. 'Unless…'

'She's signed.' Sebastian looks away.

And I can't wait to get him on his own, because I need to drill down to the bottom of this bizarre situation. Whatever's gone on in the past, it's clear there's no love lost between Christophe and everyone else in the room. Even Zach can't hide his distaste.

'Ah, here they are,' a brittle voice announces from somewhere behind me. 'All my sons.'

Conversation stutters to a halt. And I get my first sight of Phillip Delaney. Standing in the doorway to the hall – tall, grey-haired and bordering on emaciated – even though he's trapped in a body that's clearly bleeding strength, he still carries the unmistakable aura of power.

'I've said my goodbyes.' He scans the gathering, still sharp-eyed despite the frailty. 'Rest assured your uncle will last a little longer. We have time to eat together.' Aided by a walking stick, and moving like a decrepit spider, he shuffles to the head of the table. 'One last meal with the dysfunctional fruit of my loins, and then I'll leave.'

I want to look away, but I can't. For some reason, I'm mesmerised by the points of resemblance between father and sons. For a start, there's the slightly aquiline nose and firm chin shared by all of them. And then, the dark irises inherited by all but Zach. Finally, although the old man's now a shadow of his former self, it's clear he once possessed a commanding physical presence, just like all his offspring.

'Will you not stay longer, Papa?' Christophe steals into position on his father's left.

'No, I will not. And what are you doing here?'

'Uncle Harry asked to see me.'

Phillip Delaney's lips rise into a cold smile. 'Uncle Harry doesn't know his own mind half the time. By now, he'll have forgotten what he's asked for. You should have ignored the request.' Delivered with venom, his words have the ring of the absolute.

But they don't seem to daunt Max. 'I organised it,' he says. 'Harry asked a few times. It wasn't my place to deny him. And Christophe is family.'

'Sometimes I worry about you, Max.' The old man's eyebrows rise. 'Please don't tell me you've decided to become honourable. That's the sort of behaviour I'd expect from Sebastian. Sit down. All of you.'

262

He lays his stick on the floor and sits down, flanked by Max on the right and Christophe on the left. While he sets about surveying the platters of cold food on the table, I'm urged into place between Seb and Max, watching as Amy takes a seat at the opposite side of the table, Zach at her side. As soon as we're all in position, the father examines his sons, one by one. Finally, he settles his full concentration on Amy.

I have no idea what she really thinks of this foul creature, but if she holds him in any disregard, she manages to cover it up with style. 'Nice to meet you again, Mr Delaney,' she beams.

'Still with her, I see.' Although he's glaring straight into Amy's eyes, his comment is squarely levelled at Zach. When he gets no response, he takes in a weary breath. 'I said you're still with her.'

'I heard you.' Zach snakes a protective arm across the back of Amy's chair. 'But I'd prefer it if you didn't talk about my fiancée as if she wasn't in the room. I'd like you to treat her with more respect.' Gruff and straight to the point, as soon as he's finished, he helps himself to a bread roll.

'Fiancée?' A rattling cough evolves deep in the old man's lungs. 'I hope you've drawn up a pre-nup.'

'No need.'

'There's every need. Once I'm gone, you'll be a very wealthy man.'

'Makes no difference.'

'If that's what you think, you're a fool. Never trust a woman. Especially when...'

'When what?' Zach drops the bread onto his side plate.

'When she's got nothing to her name.'

'She's got plenty to her name, Phil.'

'Don't call me that.'

Scowling at the roll, Zach shakes his head. 'Thanks for the advice. I'm sure it's well meant.' His gaze shifts lazily from the plate to his father. 'But feel free... to stick it up your arse.'

A hush descends across the room. The pit bull's eyes darken. His bony fists clench. I'm convinced he's about to erupt in anger. Instead, he simply smiles.

'You're an even bigger idiot than I thought you were.'

'Thank you.' Zach smiles back.

'But I'll overlook your attitude.'

'How kind.'

'After all, you're a Delaney now.'

'The name's Reynolds.'

'But you're still my son, whether you like it or not. And as such, you'll receive your inheritance.'

'Trust me, Phil, I don't need it. And I certainly don't want it. If there's any space left in your rectum, you know what to do.' Evidently done with the conversation, Zach glances round the table. 'Don't know about you lot, but I'm fucking starving. Shall we eat?'

Accompanied by murmurs of assent, the guests help themselves to food, filling the next few minutes with nothing more than small talk. I'm beginning to think we'll be spared any further awkward conversation when I look up from my salad to find Phillip Delaney gracing me with his attention.

'Who is this?' he demands.

'Evie.' Under the table, Seb slips a hand onto my thigh. 'My girlfriend.'

'That's not your style.'

'People change.'

'Rubbish.' He coughs again. 'Evie who?'

'Smith.'

'Smith? Another gold-digger, Sebastian?'

'Anything but.'

'Come on, boy. You and Max have a particular talent for attracting them.'

'And a particular talent for rejecting them,' Seb counters. 'Evie has no interest in money.'

'Deluded as ever.' He focusses back on me. 'Any woman who shows an interest in my sons has an interest in money.' His gaze sends a shiver down my spine. 'Do you have your own source of wealth, Miss Smith?'

'No.'

'Then I rest my case.'

I'm about to inform the old man he's a rude, presumptive idiot when another voice joins the fray.

'Seb's telling the truth.'

My jaw drops... because Max Delaney seems to be fighting my corner.

'Evie's no gold-digger,' he goes on, the transformation from devil to angel complete. 'I've had the pleasure of meeting her a few times now, and I've come to the conclusion she's a decent woman. In fact, if it weren't for Evie, we wouldn't have Harry back.'

'I find that hard to believe.' With a snort of derision, Phillip Delaney picks up his fork and prods a slice of ham. 'Perhaps you should fill me in on this little story, Sebastian.'

Humouring his father, Seb recounts the tale of how I rescued Hal, took him to hospital, promised to safeguard the ring and left a note for his family. Abandoning the fork, Phillip Delaney listens to it all with no discernible interest.

'And she returned the ring?' he asks.

'She did,' Seb confirms.

'Queen sacrifice.'

'What?'

'If you'd ever bothered to learn the game of chess, Sebastian, you'd know the move. A grand sacrifice, designed to win the game.' His eyes flick from Seb to me. 'Perhaps she saw it as an investment, a risk worth taking. She gives back the ring only to set herself up for much greater riches.'

'What an interesting theory.' Seb squeezes my thigh. 'There's only one problem with it.'

'Which is?'

'It's complete bollocks.'

Zach laughs out loud. Amy almost chokes on a sandwich. And to my left, I hear Max suppress a groan.

'Perhaps you should show a little more respect for both of the ladies at this table,' Seb goes on. 'I know it's difficult for you, but give it a try.'

'I see no point.'

'Because you always search for the worst in everybody.'

'Because the worst is always there. Everyone can be bought.'

'You heard what Max said. Evie doesn't have your interest in money.'

'What nonsense. There isn't a man or woman on this earth who has no interest in money. There are merely different levels of interest.' Leaning forward, Delaney Senior places an emaciated hand on the table, as if he's holding down his point. 'For some people, it's the roof over their head or the food in their child's mouth. For some it's a new car, a bigger house, a holiday abroad. To others, it's luxury and power. Money really does make the world go round, Sebastian. And anyone who tells you otherwise, is a liar.' Supremely pleased with his little lecture, he sits back. 'Haven't you told her yet?'

'Told her what?'

'How much you stand to inherit?'

'No. Because, like Zach, I don't care for your money.'

'Of course you do. Because, unlike Zach, you're used to it. It's one habit you'll never kick.'

'We'll see.'

'I'm sure we will... when twenty million lands in your bank account.'

'Twenty?' Out of nowhere, my body refuses to function. I see nothing... hear nothing but a ridiculously surprised voice at the back of my head. 'Yes, you knew he was wealthy,' it whispers. 'But this wealthy?'

'Miss Smith.' Phillip Delaney's crackling words drag me back to the moment. 'You seem a little taken aback. Do you still profess no interest?'

I blink at Seb. Still holding my thigh, he's staring resolutely into space, jaw twitching, lips clamped firmly together.

'I don't really know...' I falter. 'I don't know why anyone would need twenty million pounds, not when you think of all the suffering in the world.'

'Oh, spare me the sob stories.' I'm dismissed with a tut. 'The world will never change.'

'Really?' After what I've witnessed over the past few months, his contempt is enough to ignite my temper and send my mouth on a mild rampage. 'It could. If people like you were willing to share your riches.'

'Why should we share them?'

'Because they're made off the back of other people's sweat.'

He laughs. 'If I were you, Miss Smith, I'd keep my naïve opinions to myself.'

'Really?'

I check on my fellow diners. With his attention now fixed on his father, Seb looks ready to spring up and engage in a bout of fisticuffs. And while Max regards me with something suspiciously like respect, Zach and Amy smile and nod their approval. It's only Christophe who seems oblivious to it all. Engrossed in his meal, he might as well be anywhere else but here.

'You might not like what she says,' Sebastian growls, 'but Evie's entitled to a point of view.'

'Of course she is.' Delaney Senior slaps his lips. 'But the fact remains, you'll soon be an extremely rich man. So, if you do decide to do anything stupid – like that idiot over there...' He gestures to Zach. 'Make her sign a pre-nup first.' He helps himself to a mouthful of water. 'I assume she knows about your past.'

'I know everything about his past,' I tell him, laying both hands on the table and tightening my fists.

'I'm assured it's all over now, but I can't help wondering. After all, you know what they say. Once an addict, always an addict.'

'You're wrong.'

'But it's in the bloodline, Miss Smith. On his mother's side.'

'Don't bring her into this,' Seb warns. Releasing my thigh, he moves his left hand over my fist and gently rubs his thumb against my skin. It's a much-needed act of reassurance.

'I'll bring whoever I like into any conversation,' the old man presses on. 'The truth is, Sebastian, you have far too much of your mother in you. I could tell that as soon as you were born. You inherited her weakness.' He eyes his youngest son with all the warmth of an iceberg. 'Nothing like Max.'

'Max, Max, Max,' Christophe grumbles into his food.

'What was that?'

Christophe looks up. 'Oh, excuse me, Papa. Did I speak aloud?'

'You know you did. And if you have a problem with Max, I suggest you spit it out.'

With the pit bull lured in a different direction, I relax my hands. Immediately, Seb threads his fingers through mine and gives me a warming smile. He leans in, evidently about to say something when Christophe speaks again.

'I'm very sorry, Papa. But I believe your faith in Max is quite misplaced. You trust him far too much, give him more responsibility than he can handle. He makes mistakes...'

'I'm not aware of any.'

'Phillips,' Christophe sneers.

'What about it?'

'A shitty little publishing house that's doomed to haemorrhage money. Anyone with an ounce of business sense can see it.'

'And you're suggesting I don't know what I'm doing?'

'Goodness me, no.' Christophe laughs. 'I'm suggesting Max is pulling the wool over your eyes.'

Both men turn to Max.

Halfway through cutting himself a piece of quiche, he looks up.

'Perhaps you'd like to tell us,' Christophe goes on, 'how you convinced Papa to go along with your hair-brained plan?'

Slowly, and very deliberately, Max puts down his cutlery. 'I don't need to justify myself.'

'Because you can't.'

'Because everyone knows why I'm buying it. We need a foothold in every part of the media.'

'Oh, yes. I forgot.' Christophe waves a hand. 'To shore up the power. But what does Phillips publish?' With a smug grin, he looks around the table. 'Silly detective stories. Boring historical novels. And don't forget those pathetic, slushy romances. Come on, Max. Where's the power in that?'

'Be quiet,' Phillip Delaney barks. 'Whatever time I've got left, I don't intend to waste a single second of it listening to your twaddle. In fact, let's make this simple. After today, I never want to see your idiotic face again.'

Christophe Dupont opens his mouth to complain. Immediately, he's silenced by a raised hand.

'Don't worry. You'll get your money. And you can do what you like with it. Gamble the whole lot away, for all I care. And yes, I do know about that.'

'Lies,' Christophe hisses.

'Enough!' Delaney roars.

Another cough rattles from his lungs. Red-faced and apparently done for the time being, he picks up his fork and returns to prodding his food. I'm expecting the meal to resume, but no one follows suit. Like Seb, Amy and Zach, I haven't touched a thing for a couple of minutes now. It seems a distinct lack of appetite has spread around the table. Even Christophe's taken to doing nothing more than staring blankly into space.

'Still no woman in your life, Max?' the old man asks. 'Don't you think it's time to sow your seed? You've had enough women throwing themselves at you. I'm beginning to wonder.' He waits for a reply. 'Well?'

Snapping back to life, Christophe's eyes gleam with mischief. 'He wants to know if you're gay.'

'I don't have time.' Max gives his father a tight, controlled smile.

'Time to be gay?' Christophe laughs. 'Does it take a lot of time to be gay?'

'Time for relationships,' Max counters, keeping the smile firmly in place.

'Then make time,' his father orders. 'And find someone appropriate.' He quickly inspects Amy, then me. It's obvious neither of us are deemed anywhere near appropriate. 'Once you've married and produced an heir, you can do what the hell you like. That's the way it goes.' Suddenly exhausted, he slams down his fork, and sits back. 'What on earth must you think of this family, Miss Smith?'

Caught off guard, I have no idea why he's addressing me again. He's not even looking at me.

268

'Two bastards.' He points at Christophe. 'That one sired by a French whore to entrap me. A feckless, money-grabbing thorn in my cancerous side. And that one...' The finger moves to Zach. 'I had a soft spot for his mother. That's the only reason I put up with his stupidity.' Next, he picks out Sebastian. 'And now, we come to the sons of wedlock, the product of my time with a self-pitying alcoholic. Sebastian. The idle layabout. A former heroin addict and a sexual deviant to boot.'

'Pot,' Zach mutters. 'Kettle.'

'Oh, do be quiet. I despair...' Another cough interrupts him mid-flow. After clearing his lungs, he presses on. 'At least I have Max. The only one with enough brain cells to take on DelCorp. Nowhere near perfect, of course, but at least I can trust him.'

Christophe snorts quietly.

And out of nowhere, I hear my own voice, brazenly carrying my thoughts into the open. 'You seem to have a low opinion of your sons, Mr Delaney.' I blink, swallow, blink again. I can barely believe I'm saying this. 'Why don't you just cut them all out of your will?'

'And make my disappointment public?' The pit bull chuckles. 'If I disinherit my sons, Miss Smith, I make them a laughingstock. And no one laughs at a Delaney. If you invite derision...'

'Oh, for fuck's sake.' In a sudden flourish of movement, Seb pushes back his chair and gets to his feet.

'What are you doing?' his father demands, clearly stunned by the interruption.

'I've had enough of your twaddle.' He holds out a hand to me. 'Come on, Evie. Let's go. We're here to see Harry.'

Chapter Twenty-Five

'Where's our suite?' I draw to a halt at the top of the stairs.

'I'll show you later.'

'No. Now.' I squeeze his hand. 'I need to give Hal the ring.'

'Fair enough.' He leads me down a gloomy corridor, through an open doorway on the right into what seems to be a sitting room. Graced with various pieces of antique furniture – including an armchair, a sofa and a coffee table – it's just as tasteful as the rest of the house.

'Bedroom and bathroom.' He waves to a second doorway. 'And there's your bag.' Left on an occasional table next to the window.

I head over to it and retrieve the ring box.

'I'm sorry you had to witness that.'

I turn back to find him gazing at a painting above the fireplace. 'You don't need to apologise.'

'My father's a piece of shit.'

An understatement, if ever I've heard one. 'It's hardly your fault.'

'But it's embarrassing.'

'It also explains a lot.' Although the past half an hour's been thoroughly unpleasant, it's also given me a new perspective on things.

'It does?'

'Of course.' I close the gap between us. 'He wrote you off from birth. It must have had an effect on you.' And Christophe too, but I'm not about to get into that. 'On top of all the other stuff ...' Trailing into silence, I tell myself not to bring up his mother's death, or the kidnapping. A few minutes with his father have left him teetering on the edge, and I've already thrown enough into the mix. The last thing I want is push him any further. 'I suppose what I'm saying is... I'm not surprised you went off the rails. And for what it's worth, I think it's him. Your father. I think he's at the root of it all.'

'I've only got myself to blame for the choices I made. I don't make excuses and I don't want sympathy.'

'That's just as well, because you're not getting any.'

'Good.'

I touch his cheek. 'But I think you should give yourself a break.'

At first, he does nothing. Just stares at me, eyes flickering. And then, he takes my hand. 'Okay.' He kisses my palm. 'I'll give it a try.'

With that, he guides me back out into the corridor. In absolute silence, we walk further in the gloom, passing a procession of oil paintings and side tables, until we finally reach a closed door at the end.

'Wait here.' He grips the doorknob. 'I'll see what he's like.'

A couple of minutes later, I'm beckoned inside the room. Flooded with a pearly, afternoon light, it's eerily peaceful, like something out of a dream. I blink the scene into focus and take in a sharp breath at the sight of Hal. Lying still under silky covers, and propped up on a mound of pillows, he's already a shadow of the man I met in Bermondsey.

'Here she is, Uncle Harry.' Seb urges me to the bedside.

The old man stirs. 'Here's who?'

'Mary.'

He squints at the ceiling. 'Mary?'

'Hal.' I sit on the side of the bed. 'Hello again.'

He turns his head to me, confusion flickering across his face before realisation takes hold. 'My wonderful lady.' He takes my hand, skin cold to the touch, fingers almost weightless. 'So pretty, so kind. My friend. My lovely friend from The Phoenix.'

'That's me.' I smile.

'You make such nice tea.'

'I don't know about that.'

'I do.' He grins. 'Terrible biscuits though.'

'I'll let you into a secret, Hal. I didn't make them.'

'Relieved to hear it.' He draws in a weary breath. It's clear the effort's already taking its toll.

'Hal, I've brought you something.' I offer up the box.

An eyebrow twitches. 'What's this?'

I flick the lid and reveal the ring.

'Nice.' Gazing at it like a long-lost friend, he brushes a finger over the diamond.

'You left it with me,' I remind him. 'To keep it safe.'

'I did. But you should keep it.'

'I can't.'

'Make an old man happy. Put it to good use. It's an engagement ring, you know.'

'Is it?' Out of the blue, the idea of marriage seems to have been dragged into the room, and I'm not entirely sure what to do with it. 'Okay.'

'Look after it. And him too.' He nods to Seb.

'I will.'

'And you look after her, Sebastian.'

'I will.' He takes a seat at the opposite side of the bed. 'I promise.'

'There you go. I know love when I see it.'

Another mention of that pesky little word. It reminds me that Max was totally right about my feelings for Seb. But I still can't quite believe the sentiment's requited. Perhaps that's why I'm startled when I look up to find him studying me like a man about to take his vows. It's enough to mesmerise me on the spot. Returning every single emotion with interest, I can almost see the words 'I do' on the tip of his lips when Hal speaks again.

'What time is it?'

With a resigned smile, Seb leans in. 'Just after one.'

'I should get up.'

'No. Stay where you are. You're not well.'

'Not well? Goodness me.'

'You've had a stroke.'

'Have I?'

'Yes.'

'But I feel perfectly fine.' He glances round the room. 'And I can't stay here. I need to find her.'

We both know who he's talking about. Endlessly bouncing between past and present, he's thinking of Cynthia again.

'Another day,' Seb tells him.

'No.' Suddenly agitated, Hal struggles to sit up. 'Today.' He grasps Seb's hand. 'You don't understand. I have to find her.'

'And you will. But first, you need to rest.'

'He's right,' I intervene. 'You'll need all your energy if you're coming back to The Phoenix. I'll have the tea and biscuits ready.'

'Tea and biscuits?'

'I promise.'

That seems to do the trick. With a slight nod, he relaxes back into the pillows.

'There,' Seb whispers. 'You've got that to look forward to. Now rest.'

A long, calming silence settles over the room. While Seb smooths his uncle's hair and Hal seems to drift, I can't help thinking of Oma and Mum. From first-hand experience, I know how it feels to watch a loved one fade away in front of your eyes, to witness the slow, inevitable demise of a person who once held your world together.

'Where's your mother?' Hal mutters.

A timely reminder I'm not the only one who's already experienced loss. I focus back on Seb and watch his eyes flicker.

'She's...' He shakes his head. 'She's at home.'

'Is she well?'

'Yes.' His voice cracks. 'She is.'

'She was never the same, you know. Not after that terrible business. Always so sad.' He yawns. 'And you were never the same too.'

'I'm fine now, Harry. I'm over it.' He places a hand on his uncle's arm.

'No, you're not.' Eyes open again, a tear trickles down Hal's cheek. 'I blame myself for what happened.'

'It wasn't your fault.'

'I shouldn't have let you go off like that.'

'It wasn't your fault.'

'I was responsible.'

'But you weren't to know.'

The old man sighs. 'I've made so many mistakes.'

'Everyone makes mistakes, Harry. The trick is not to let them get to you.'

'Ah, it's that easy.' With a quiet laugh, the old man closes his eyes again.

Silently, I will him to sleep, to get some respite from the endless suffering, but he's clearly not finished yet.

'You made me a promise, Sebastian.'

'I did.'

'I hope you'll keep it.'

'I will.'

'Good.' Delicate crows' feet appear at the corners of Hal's eyes. 'You're a good boy, Sebastian. Always were a good boy. Perhaps a little lost at times.'

'I used to be.' He gives his uncle's arm a gentle squeeze. 'But I'm not lost now. In fact, I know exactly where I am.' He looks up, locking his gaze firmly onto mine. 'Don't you worry, Harry. I've found my compass.' His eyes glimmer. His lips rise into a beautiful smile. 'And I'll never lose it again.'

**

Half an hour later, as soon as Max joins us, I decide to withdraw and give the family some space to themselves. Leaving the old man with a kiss on the forehead, I return the ring to the handbag, ignore the gun, and head off for a quiet walk in the grounds.

273

MANDY LEE

At the back of the house – set in the middle of another immaculate lawn and surrounded by beautifully groomed hedges and shrubs – I come across a long, rectangular pond. I also come across Amy. Sitting at the far end, with her bare feet dangling in the water, she seems to be miles away... until I'm close enough to interrupt her.

'You okay?'

'Fine. Just thinking about Hal. Come and join me.' She pats the space next to her. 'You won't believe the size of the fish in here.'

I take off my trainers and sit down. 'I hope they're not pike.' Dipping my feet in the water, I catch a flash of gold in the gloom.

'Koi carp. Perfectly friendly.' She leans back. 'Zach's gone to see his uncle. I hope it goes well.'

'Has he met him before?'

'A couple of times.'

The carp approach and recede. I wiggle my feet. Amy wiggles hers.

'We've got to go back tonight.'

'That's a shame.'

'Can't be avoided. Zach's running a surfing retreat tomorrow.'

'Sounds interesting.'

'It's for veterans. He can't let them down.' She wiggles her feet again. 'So... I'm dying to ask. How long have you two been together?'

'Not sure,' I reply with absolute sincerity, since I have no idea when sleeping together and sharing the same living space morphed into something else. 'How long have you been with Zach?'

'About a year. Feels like longer.'

'He's quite a character.'

'You have no idea.' She laughs. 'I hope you'll come to the wedding.'

'When is it?'

'October.'

'If I'm still around.'

'Oh, you will be. If you ask me, Sebastian Delaney's smitten.'

'I don't know about that.'

'Trust me.' She beams. 'I'm right. Pack for Cornish weather. Plenty of t-shirts, but don't forget the raincoat.' As if it's a done deal, she raises her eyebrows. 'Anyway, change of subject. You'll be pleased to hear that Darth Vader's gone back to the Death Star.'

'Darth Vader?'

'Zach's nickname for daddy dearest. He's a big Star Wars fan.'

274

'Oh.'

'And Christophe's gone too. He spent all of five minutes with Harry. Apparently, that was enough.'

'Really?' I watch an inquisitive carp nudge at my big toe, and decide I'd like to improve my knowledge of the family's designated black sheep. 'I don't know much about Christophe.'

'I don't think anybody does.' Amy turns her face to the sky.

'How did you meet him?'

'Oh.' She pulls a mildly disgusted face. 'It was just after I got with Zach. Christophe turned up in Newquay, completely out of the blue. He told Zach he'd heard a rumour about a fourth Delaney brother and decided to track him down. When it was all confirmed, someone tipped off the press.'

'Christophe?'

She smiles. 'I didn't say that.'

'But you think it?'

'Maybe.' Leaning forward, she watches another carp approach her feet. 'That's the thing about Christophe. He operates in the shadows, just like these lovely fish. No one can ever prove a thing. Let's just say the press exposure caused a lot of trouble. Zach thinks it was Christophe. Max too.'

'But not Seb.'

'Hence the great falling out.' Clearly wondering if she's said too much, she bites her lip. 'Is this just between you and me?'

I nod. 'Seb hasn't told me much. And to be honest, I need all the information I can get.'

'But I only know what Max tells me.'

'That'll do.'

'As long as none of this gets back to Seb.'

'It won't.'

'Okay.' She gazes at me for a few seconds. 'According to Max, Seb and Christophe used to be really close. Seb's given Christophe the benefit of the doubt for years.' She picks at a clump of moss. 'Did you know Christophe was with Seb when he was taken?'

'No.'

'The way Max tells it, Christophe took his time getting back to the house, then guided the search party in completely the wrong direction. Max always thought he did it on purpose. And from everything I've seen and heard, I tend to agree. Christophe enjoys causing chaos. And he doesn't care about the consequences.'

'But...' Christophe was the one who got Seb talking again. Which begs the question: why contribute to your brother's possible demise, only to put him back together again in the aftermath? Could it be a sign of guilt? 'There must be a reason for it.'

'Maybe. But I wouldn't feel sorry for him.'

'I don't.' After all, I've had enough warnings. 'It's just so sad... when your own father can't stand you.'

'Phillip Delaney can't stand anyone apart from himself.' Amy gets to her feet. 'He wasn't exactly the perfect father to Seb and Max, but they don't go around merrily shitting on other people's lives.' She narrows her eyes. 'You know what's ironic in all of this?'

'Not really.' I join her.

'The old man doesn't want anything to do with him, but it's Christophe who takes after him the most.'

'Not Max?'

'Definitely not Max.' She laughs. 'Which is a miracle, isn't it? I mean, all of them could have gone to the dark side.'

'I wonder why they didn't.'

She squints at a passing heron. 'Zach never had anything to do with his dad. His mum brought him up, and made a damn good job of it. But with Seb and Max... I think it was all down to Uncle Harry.'

I glance over at the house. 'Thank God for Hal, then.'

'Hear, hear,' Amy smiles. 'He actually made them human.'

***

I'm back in familiar surroundings. A place I've not dreamt about for a long time. It's all so vivid, so real. The haphazard shelves, crammed with dry ingredients and jars; the oak table at the centre of the room, smothered in flour; the sideboard cluttered with tins and packets. It's all exactly as it used to be, right down to the ancient fridge and the Belfast sink, chipped at one corner.

And there she is, cradling a bowl under her bosom, stirring briskly with a wooden spoon.

'Oma?'

The spoon moves so fast, I can barely see it. 'Remember what I taught you, little one. Right ingredients, right amounts, right order.' She lifts the spoon. 'When you've got all that sorted, put some love into it. You can't go wrong.'

'No.' I smile. 'You can't.'

A second voice comes out of nowhere. 'Super biscuits.'

Sitting at the end of the table, Hal holds up a freshly made cookie.

'Beautiful.' He bites into it and chews happily.

I'm about to offer him a cup of tea, but the scene begins to disintegrate. Shapes fall apart. Colour and light bleed into an inky gloom. My throat constricts, readying itself for a choked scream that never comes.

'Evie?'

Reeled back to consciousness, I open my eyes to find Seb sitting at my side. Clearly drained, he runs his fingers through ruffled hair.

'Did you get much sleep? he asks.

'Enough.' After a quiet dinner with Seb and Max, and another visit to Hal, I left the brothers to their vigil and opted for an early night. 'How is he?'

He puts a hand on my shoulder. His bleak expression says it all.

'Oh, Seb. I'm so sorry.' I push myself up.

'Passed away in his sleep. Just after three. We sat with him for a while.'

I brush a palm over his forearm. 'At least you were both with him when he went.'

'And we've got you to thank for that.'

Knowing exactly what he needs, I open my arms and welcome him in for a long embrace, holding him tight, giving him all the understanding I can. And the next thing I know, I'm feeling it again, as keenly as if she's only just passed – the raw, visceral anger that consumed me during those few minutes I sat with Oma.

Stunned, I blink up into the sunlight.

Somewhere along the way, I must have consigned the memory to oblivion. I must have rewritten my own story and told myself I'd simply accepted her passing.

But that's not the truth.

In those silent minutes following her death, in the depths of my twisted, grieving mind, I decided she'd abandoned me. After what happened to Mum, it must have proved too much. It's certainly the reason why I backed off from old friends and avoided love. I was keeping clear of trust and connection in all its forms. And when I finally relented – making the biggest mistake of my life with Miles Crawley – no wonder I doubled down and cocooned myself in loneliness for almost a year.

'I understand,' I murmur.

With a slight nod, Seb straightens up, leaving me to gaze into those chocolate irises, completely in awe of this amazing man who's known his own struggles with trust and loss; a man who carefully built up his own defences, only to let them crumble right in front of my eyes. Against all the odds, he's finally managed to crack me open. And I know it now, with absolute conviction. I can place my heart firmly in his hands... and he'll keep it safe.

'We're just waiting,' he says. 'For the doctor.'

'I know.'

'Max is staying another night. If it's okay with you, I'd like to stay too. I want to... I don't know, remember him before it all disappears.'

'You're not keeping the house?'

'It doesn't suit any of us. Not in the right location.'

'Such a shame to lose it.'

'I know. But sometimes...' His eyes flicker. 'Sometimes, you've just got to let go.'

I reach up, gently wipe a tear from his cheek.

Trapping my hand in his, he holds it tight. 'Come on, lazy bones. Time to get up. I'm in need of some fresh air.'

***

Within minutes, I'm washed and dressed. Downstairs, we make our way out to the terrace at the rear of the house. Standing at the far end, and completely oblivious to our presence, Max is busy scanning the garden.

'Peregrine!' Seb calls.

Max turns.

Caught off guard, he seems so vulnerable, so unlike the Max I've known so far, I'm overcome by what I can only think is daftness. Before I know it, I've closed the distance between us, given him a hug, a peck on the cheek, and left him utterly perplexed.

I draw back, quickly.

'Er... thank you.' He collects himself.

'I'm sorry,' I mutter. 'About Harry.'

'Thank you.' At the squawk of a bird, he turns back to the lawn.

Seb comes to his side. 'The bastard heron?'

'The one and only.'

For the next minute or so, the two brothers follow the progress of a large, grey bird. Prowling along the edge of the pond, attention fixed on the water, it seems intent on a bite to eat.

'We need to go through the will,' Seb says.

'The solicitor's due at ten, but first things first.' Still watching the bird, Max motions to the pond. 'Harry wouldn't want that fucker helping itself to the carp.'

278

Together, they spend another couple of minutes tracking the evil heron. It's Max who finally breaks the silence.

'He never faced facts, you know. Never put the past to bed.' He cocks his head. 'Don't make the same mistake, brother.'

Seb gets no chance to reply. With a sudden screech, the bird lurches closer to the water.

'Bastard!' Max growls, striding out over the grass. 'Fuck off! There's nothing here for you!'

In spite of the morning's sadness, I can't help laughing at the sight of the billionaire mogul in hot pursuit of an angry heron. Waving his arms in the air, he skirts the edge of the pond, reeling off a seemingly endless supply of choice expletives.

Putting an end to the laughter, Seb touches my arm. 'Harry loved those fish. And Max is right.' He takes my hand and leads me to the end of the terrace. 'Let's take a walk.'

'Where?'

'You'll see.'

Without another word, he guides me down a set of steps, aiming for a stone wall to the right. At the other side of a rickety gate, an enclosed garden awaits. Filled with nothing but tranquillity and roses. I'd love to stop and take it all in, but Seb keeps going, marching us on to a second gate at the far side. Faltering for a moment, he glances back at me before leading the way into a meadow.

'Wow.' I drink in the view.

Bathed in morning sun, with wildflowers growing in abandon, fields in the distance and a coppice to the left, it's a picture-perfect scene. And yet again, like a man possessed, Seb doesn't pause to admire it.

'This is all part of the grounds,' he explains, urging me towards the coppice. 'It all belongs to Harry.'

In silence now, we enter the wood, following a narrow path that's flanked by huge shrubs and ancient oak trees. At last, we come to a clearing. Letting go of my hand, Seb comes to a halt and stares at a low, wooden fence, just visible beyond the trees. It's clearly neglected, rotting away in places, falling apart.

I say nothing. There's no need to speak because I can hear his breathing. Growing more ragged by the second, it tells me everything I need to know. Engrossed in thought, eyes fixed on the fence, he doesn't move.

'The road's just over there,' he says at last, finally breaking the spell. 'We were making a den. Me and Christophe.' Lowering his head, he kicks at a log. 'That's all I remember.'

Leaves rustle in a sudden breeze. Somewhere in the distance, a dog barks. I hardly know what to say.

'Is this the first time you've been back?'

He nods.

I move forward and touch his arm.

'He said it was my fault. Whenever he was mad at me... he'd say I brought it on myself.'

'Your father?'

'Yes. My father.' He grimaces. 'He said I should have run. I should have fought. He said I was taken because I was weak, because I was a silly little boy who trusted strangers.'

If I disliked Phillip Delaney before, I'm close to hating him now. He had no right to fill his son's head with lies. 'That's rubbish, and you know it.'

'Yes, well...' He takes a moment to survey the scene. 'You were right, you know. What you said earlier.' His gaze flicks to me. 'He's at the root of it all. He wrote me off and made me doubt myself.' His jaw tightens. 'And he killed my mother too.'

'Seb...'

He closes his eyes. 'He drove her to kill herself. Just take my word for it. You know, for years I thought she'd abandoned me.'

'No.' I step forward and hold out a hand. 'Don't say that. It's not true. She didn't abandon you.' Just like Oma didn't abandon me. 'She loved you. She just... couldn't stay.'

He stares at my hand, then takes it in his, smoothing his thumb over my knuckles. 'It's not just those few days I've been hiding from.' He glances back at the fence. 'It's him.'

'And now it's time to move on,' I tell him quietly. 'Hal's the father you never had, the real influence in your life. He's the one you should think about now, the one you should honour.'

Finally, he cracks a smile. 'You have this scary tendency to be right, Evie.' He looks up at the sky, and the smile grows deeper. 'Well then, Uncle Harry – wherever you are – I'm going to do exactly as this lady says.' He tightens his hold on my hand. 'And I'm going to keep that promise too.'

The promise Hal mentioned. Somehow, it managed to slip clear out of my head. 'Which is?' I prompt.

'The real reason I tracked you down.' He leans in and plants a chaste kiss on my forehead. 'Not for the ring.'

Y

'No?'

'No. Your kindness made a real impression on Harry. When I showed him the napkin, it all came back to him. He couldn't remember your name, but he made me promise to find you and give you a life.' His eyes glimmer.

And my heart glows.

'That's why I needed to know who you were, and what you were caught up in.'

I can barely believe what I'm hearing. 'That's the truth?'

'Yep.' Letting go of my hand, he cups my face. 'But things changed, didn't they?'

'They certainly did.'

'I'm still going to give you a life, Evie. But I want a promise from you in return.' He gazes into my eyes for what seems like an eternity. 'Just make sure I'll always be part of it.'

Chapter Twenty-Six

After the doctor pays a visit and the nurses take their leave, the undertakers finally arrive and go about their business. Once they've overseen their uncle's send-off, the two brothers spend the rest of the morning in Hal's study, sifting through paperwork and talking to the solicitor. Eager not to get in the way, I explore the garden and sit by the pond, making myself useful in the only way I can: by occasionally shooing off an irritatingly persistent heron.

Eventually, the housekeeper beckons me in for lunch. After which, I'm invited to pass the afternoon in the library with Seb and Max, digging through a pile of old photograph albums. Rigorously organised by date, the first images are all in black and white. Alongside other members of the family, there's Hal as a baby, a wide-eyed boy, a handsome teen and a striking young man. Before long, we stumble across a single picture of Cynthia. Sitting on a park bench, wearing her nurse's uniform and laughing into the camera, she's as beautiful as everything else in Hal's life; but her appearance heralds a distinct change. From then on, with the photos slipping into colour – whoever he's with and whatever he's doing – Hal's eyes have lost their sparkle.

As soon as the last album's been perused, a firm silence descends over the room. Business matters complete and reminiscences shared, it's time for the men to return to their own thoughts. And I'm happy to leave them to it.

Making myself scarce for a second time, I wander through the house now, admiring Hal's taste in décor and furnishing, before finally withdrawing to our guest suite. After a quick session familiarising myself with the new mobile – and finding Max's number already stored on it – I decide a quick nap is in order. But sleep doesn't come easy. Gazing up at the canopy of the four-poster, I'm kept awake by ghosts of the past. I think of Hal, giving up on love after one failed relationship; and Seb, tormented by a difficult childhood and an even more difficult father. And then, quite inevitably, I muse over the two amazing women who couldn't stay. Closing my eyes, I try to summon their faces from the depths of memory. I'm almost there when Seb rouses me.

'Dinner in an hour.' Obviously weary, he sits on the side of the bed. 'I'm going to take a bath. Sorry you've been alone so much.'

'It's okay. I've been fine. You and Max needed some time together.'

'It's done us good.' Absent-mindedly, he trails a finger across the back of my hand. 'Where's the ring?'

I nod to the sitting room. 'Back in the handbag.'

'Good.' He gets to his feet. 'Might need it later.'

He drifts off to the bathroom, leaving me completely stunned.

'Holy shit,' I breathe.

Surely, he doesn't mean what I think he means? Surely, he's not about to propose... not the day after his uncle passed away? I sit up straight, my heart racing, and decide there's a more likely reason for Seb needing the ring. After all, it might be an important part of Hal's estate, mentioned in the will and left to someone else. But then again, if Seb does mean what I think he means, we can't possibly do this now, especially with Crawley still on the scene.

It's a thought that drags me straight back to Bermondsey, and a niggling question that's never been answered. Although everyone else seems satisfied, I'm not convinced it was my hapless landlord who tipped off Crawley. If he'd already seen me and made the call, he would have needed to feign surprise when he joined us – and Baz could never feign anything. There are no two ways about it. I need to tick Wallace off my list of suspects. And I might just have a way to do it.

Springing to my feet, I head straight to the sitting room and come to a halt by the occasional table, looking round. With the sun dipping down to the horizon, shadows are beginning to deepen now: a prelude to night – the best time for unwanted guests to creep in unnoticed. It's enough to give me the shivers, even though the grounds must be crawling with security guards. Hoping a little light might despatch the anxiety, I switch on a lamp ... then freeze at the creak of a floorboard.

'It's nothing,' I assure myself. Nothing but the sad sighs of a house descending into mourning. 'Get on with it.'

Retrieving the new mobile, I set about googling The Phoenix Café. It doesn't take long to dig up a number. I give it a try, unable to believe my luck when Chet finally answers. Wallace isn't there, he tells me. But he's only too happy to give me his contact details, even waiting while I search for a pen and paper. A minute later, I'm trembling with nerves as my erstwhile boss answers.

'Who is it?'

I almost introduce myself as Evie, remembering the correct alias just in time. 'Mary.'

There's a silence.

'Mary,' I repeat. 'Used to work for you. Got the sack.'

That earns me a thick chortle.

'Don't tell me you want your job back,' Wallace slurs.

'And don't tell me you're drunk again.'

'Why wouldn't I be? Got my reward, and I'm pissing it up the wall. Lovely weather.'

'Glad to hear it. Where are you?'

'Wouldn't you like to know?'

'Horse and Garter?'

'Get bent.' There's another chortle. 'Mallorca. Five star, all-inclusive. Fucking mint.'

'I bet it is.' And it begs a very pertinent question. 'How long have you been there, Wallace?'

'What's it to you?'

'Nothing much. Just wondering ...'

'Three days.'

'Okay.' I bite my thumbnail.

'Is that all?' Wallace asks. There's a tinkle of music in the background. 'You're interrupting my Sex on the Beach.'

'Just one more thing.'

'Make it quick, babe.'

'How much did he pay you?'

'For what?'

'Don't mess about. That night at The Phoenix, you texted someone. You got a reward for letting them know I was there. How much?'

'Why do you want to know?'

'That's my business. How much?'

'Two grand.'

'I'll give you the same.'

He laughs. 'You ain't got a pot to piss in, Treacle.'

'That's where you're wrong,' I hit back. 'I've fallen on my feet, Wallace. And I've currently got a lovely pot to piss in.' I give him a few seconds to process the information. 'Want another two grand in your bank? Maybe three?' I wince at my own audacity. Although I'm now officially the girlfriend of a multi-millionaire, I have absolutely no idea if I'll ever have money of my own. But hey, ho. After what Wallace did to me, an empty promise is just desserts.

'Go on,' he says.

'Two people came to see you about me. I'm guessing one of them had a photograph, maybe even a name.'

He doesn't speak.

'Wallace. What have you got to lose?'

'Nothing.'

'Then tell me what happened.'

'Alright. The first one asked for Mary. The second one had the photo. Didn't mention a name. Said you were probably going by an alias. Said he was a relative.'

'You got a phone number from both?'

'Correct.'

'And that night I came back... you called them both?'

He coughs. 'Correct.'

'Has anyone else been in contact since then?'

'Just the first bloke.'

'The first one?'

My disbelief's all too evident. He's talking about the man who asked for Mary... the man with the serviette.

'Yeah. That one. He gave me a grand for the tip-off. Offered another grand for the second bloke's number.'

Crawley's number. 'But you'd lost it...'

'Had it stored on my mobile.'

'And you gave it to him?'

I hold my breath. One... two... three...

'Course I did, Treacle. Five star don't come cheap.'

The breath escapes, forced out of my lungs by a hammer-like realisation. Chesty was right. There is a mole on board. And now, I need confirmation.

'Describe this first bloke to me.'

I hear a thick growl at the other end of the line. 'Fuck's sake.'

'Just do it, Wallace.'

'Alright. Tall. Blond hair. Black suit.'

Not enough. 'Scar?'

'Yeah... over his eye.'

'Shit.' Ending the call, I sling the mobile back into the bag and wrap my arms around myself. 'Alex.'

Not the Walrus. And certainly not Baz. He picked up the number from Wallace and lied to Seb. Alex is the one who tipped off Crawley about the trip to Bermondsey. And now he's out there, part of the team guarding the house.

'Yeah, that's the one.' The voice comes out of nowhere. I know it only too well.

I turn... and freeze.

Because there's a man silhouetted in the doorway.

285

Slightly shorter than Seb – and distinctly stockier – he steps forward into the light and pushes back his hoodie. His eyes come into focus: stone-cold and razor-sharp.

And I do nothing.

Completely fixated on Stefan Crawley's face, I'm paralysed by shock. Even my heart and lungs seem to have stopped working.

Holding a gun in one hand and a plastic bag in the other, he moves further forward. 'Alex Thompson,' he says, in that thick Mancunian accent of his. 'One of Mr Delaney's crew.' He places the bag on the table, next to mine. 'Right up to his ears in debt, and more than happy to sell his soul to the devil. He's organised a little diversion tonight. An intruder in the grounds. They're all out there now, even the big bro.' He waves the gun at the window. 'Apart from a couple of staff downstairs, it's just you and me, cock.' And now, to the en-suite. 'And him, of course. Poor, little rich kid. Got plans for that one.'

Somehow, even though my veins are filled with ice and my limbs with lead, I manage to coax a few jittering words from my mouth. 'Whatever you're planning, Stefan, it... it won't work. You'll... you'll never get out.'

'That's where you're wrong, Yara.' He smiles, cruelly. 'I always plan ahead. Got an escape route, so it's all good. Take a pew.'

I glance at the sofa, then the handbag.

'Might as well get comfy while we wait.'

'I'll stand.' Because it gives me a better chance of reaching the bag and its precious contents.

'Suit yourself.'

With a shrug, he begins to wander the room, idly contemplating furniture and ornaments while I take the opportunity to assess the situation. I might be trembling now, but at least the heart and lungs are functioning again. It's all moving in the right direction, I tell myself. Which means I'll soon be thinking straight and cobbling a plan together.

'What he up to in there?' Crawley picks up a framed photograph. 'I mean, how long does it take a rich kid to get clean?' He peers at the picture and quickly puts it down. 'Don't like being kept waiting, me.' With a quiet whistle, he brushes a finger across a lampshade. 'But then again, I suppose it's more time to enjoy the situation.'

He flashes me another smile, this one so deadly it puts an end to hope. In an instant, I see the truth. There's no way I can get to that bag in time, no way I'll ever distract Crawley enough to raise a gun at him before he does the same to me; because in spite of all his apparent nonchalance, he's totally focussed on his task.

'You can't kill him,' I mutter, sensing the beginnings of panic. There may be no hope for me, but at least I can still plead for Seb's life.

'Is that so?' Crawley cocks his head.

'It's me you want.'

'But you've told him everything. And I don't like loose ends.'

The panic flares. 'He's not the only one...' I slap a hand to my mouth, horrified at what I've just said. It was only meant to make him think twice, not to put others in danger.

Crawley laughs. 'Never could keep your gob shut, could you?' The mirth disappears. 'No need to worry, though. Alex told me everything. I've already got my list. When I'm done here, I'll deal with Max and Chesty. Then it's off to that kinky club you've been holed up in. Some woman called Celine. Alex said it's not gone further than that. Thank fuck.' He glances round the room. 'Can't spend all chuffing night killing people. There's more to life than death.' Suddenly distracted by the painting above it – an image of a nameless Georgian lady in a flowing white gown – he walks over to the fireplace. 'Now, that's proper mint, that is.' He inspects the picture closely. 'She looks a bit like you. Nice frock too. You know what? If you'd dressed like that, you'd have been a damn sight easier to find.' With a chuckle, he returns his attention to me. 'Speaking of which, Yara. What in fuck's name made you use that bank card?'

Stupidity. That's the answer. But Crawley doesn't deserve the truth. 'Desperation.'

'Exactly what I'd been waiting for. One silly, little cock-up.'

One huge, moronic cock-up. Made in spite of the fact I knew this man's capabilities, it bought me nothing more than a bottle of gin and a bag of crisps. 'Stefan...' Closing my eyes for a moment, I remind myself it bought me so much more than that. While my breathing shallows and the trembles increase, my brain decides it's time for some pointless pleading. 'You don't need to do this.'

'Oh, you know that's not true, Yara.' His eyes flash in the lamplight. His tone softens, almost as if he's addressing a child. 'I've got two – shall we say – very compelling reasons for doing this.' He holds up a single finger. 'Reason number one. Revenge. And number two.' A second finger joins the first. 'That mess you left when you took off.' With a tut, he lowers the hand. 'My business associates don't like that sort of thing. They have standards, see.' He sighs dramatically. 'I'm sick and tired of worrying the shit's gonna hit the fan. Can't risk that, can I? Too much to live for.'

I hear the scrape of a door latch. My stomach lurches.

And, in an instant, the situation switches up a gear.

'Come here.'

I'm grabbed by the arm, dragged over to an alcove next to the curtains.

Withdrawing behind me, Crawley forces the gun into my back. 'Don't let me down, Yara.'

Watching the door to the en-suite swing open, I think about yelling a warning, but I'm pretty sure Seb wouldn't heed it.

'Did I hear voices?' Clearly relaxed, and back in his jeans and t-shirt, he wanders over to the sofa, smooths back his damp hair and turns to me. Immediately, the smile disappears. 'Evie? What's wrong?'

I sense a movement behind me.

Seb's eyes narrow.

'It was Alex,' I tell him, my voice uneven. 'Alex let him in. I'm so sorry.'

He spends a few seconds staring at Crawley before his gaze locks onto mine. 'You don't need to apologise,' he says. 'It's not your fault.'

I catch the tenderness in his eyes, feel a sudden rupture in my chest. 'Seb...' Was that my heart, I wonder? Did it really just crack into a thousand tiny, irretrievable pieces? 'I need you to know...'

'Enough,' Crawley intervenes. 'Let's get down to business.' Releasing my arm, he pushes me to one side, takes a step forward and aims the gun directly at Seb. 'I take it you know who I am.'

'I do.'

'Good. Then we'll press on. Sit down, Mr Delaney.'

Taking a seat on the edge of the sofa, Seb fixes his attention firmly on the gun.

'Sound.' Crawley surveys the set-up. 'Perfect, in fact.'

'For what?' Seb demands.

'Revenge, of course.' He pauses, dramatically. 'It's a form of justice, you know. Eye for an eye, and all that malarkey. Always served best when it's in balance with the original offence.'

'There was no original offence,' Seb counters. 'Evie didn't kill your brother.'

'Not directly. I'll give you that.' Crawley touches the gun to his lips. 'But if she'd never got with our kid – and if she hadn't ratted on him – none of this would have happened, see.' He lowers the gun.

'But she did get with him. And she did rat. And then, we get the perfect, fucking storm. Booze, drugs, her... and the edge of a fucking rug.' He shakes his head in disbelief. 'What a stupid fucking way to go.'

'Fucking stupid, indeed.'

'Watch it.'

The two men study each other: a growing irritation on Crawley's side; an arctic distaste on Seb's. The stand-off seems to go on for minutes. Giving my anxiety enough time to spike like never before, it's only broken by a distant call from the grounds.

With a quick glance at the window, Crawley picks up the plastic bag and dumps it on the coffee table in front of Seb. 'They'll be a while yet. You might not believe it, Yara, but I loved my brother. Can't tell you how hard it hit me. Losing someone you love is the worst thing in the world. Seeing them dead. Knowing it's final.' His lips lift into a twisted smile. 'It's an experience I never want to repeat... and one I'm going to share with you.'

'Just shoot me, then,' Seb growls. 'Get it over with.'

The smile morphs into a snarl. It's quickly directed at Seb. 'You're a fucking muppet, you are. Didn't you hear what I said? An eye for an eye. Now, empty the bag... and be careful about it.'

Ignoring the command, Seb looks up at me.

And his eyes speak volumes through the silence, cramming a few, precious seconds with all the tenderness and love of an entire lifetime. It's almost too much to bear, but I can't let him down. Keeping my gaze locked firmly onto his, I let him know I feel exactly the same. Given half a chance, I'd be by his side until we're old and grey, sharing every single moment with the man I love. Losing myself in a glorious web of mutual adoration, I wish we could stay like this forever.

But Crawley has other ideas.

'I think that's enough,' he grates. 'Empty the fucking bag.'

Immediately, Seb does as he's told. I catch sight of a small foil packet, a syringe, a lighter, a spoon, a tie.

'Your favourite treat, Delaney.'

'I don't use any more.' Ignoring the paraphernalia, Seb leans back.

'Clean for six years, according to Alex. You deserve a medal. But once a junkie, always a junkie.'

'A bit of a generalisation.'

'Stop wasting time. Get on with it. I'm sure you remember what to do.'

'Vaguely.'

He surveys the collection of objects in front of him. His jaw clenches, his eyes flicker and something new washes over him. Wiping away all traces of the man I've come to know, it leaves nothing in its wake but a husk. Apparently giving himself up to fate, he leans forward and picks up the tie.

'A little birdy tells me you've got enough there for an overdose.'

Seb nods.

'And that's exactly what I want.' Clearly fascinated by the situation, Crawley steps forward. 'I want you to bite the dust in a drug-addled haze, just like our kid. And I want it to be all over the papers, so the world knows you were a weak piece of shit. I want shame to be your epitaph, just like it was his.' He pauses, mid-snarl, and waves the gun at me. 'And I want her to witness it all.'

I don't know how I've managed to hold them back so far, but it's only now that tears make an appearance. Welling in my eyes and trickling down my cheeks, they take me right to the edge of oblivion.

'I assume you've got something to offer in return,' Seb murmurs. 'Because I'm going to need a damn good reason for putting this shit in my veins.'

'Oh, I've got something very good to offer,' Crawley tells him. 'A very simple choice, in fact. Either you shoot up... or I shoot her.'

'Don't listen to him,' I growl, dragging myself back to the moment. 'You don't need to do this. He's going to shoot me anyway.'

'Am I?' Crawley demands. 'Did I say I'd kill you?'

'No.' Wiping my eyes, I turn to face him. 'But there's no way you're going to let me live.'

'You reckon?' With a savage twinkle in his eyes, Crawley focuses back on Seb. 'It's true I need to tie up a few loose ends. And I think that's understandable, given the circumstances.' His voice lowers. 'But if you do this one thing for me, Sebastian, I promise I'll spare her. I'll tuck her away somewhere nice and quiet, so she can spend the rest of her days reliving this moment.'

Seb grimaces at the barrel of gun. 'Give me your word you won't kill her.'

'You have it.'

The trembles increase. I inch forward. 'He's lying.'

'Maybe.' With a shrug, Seb takes one end of the tie in his mouth. Clamping it tight with his teeth, he wraps the other end around his left arm, makes a knot and pulls tight.

'Don't.'

Satisfied with the knot, he releases the tie. 'It's the only chance I've got to save you. And remember, you've still got Max. He'll find you in the end.'

'But he's going to kill Max too.'

'I'd like to see him try.'

'Seb, please...'

'Leave it, Evie. My mind's made up. Just do me one last favour.'

I shake my head. I have no idea what sort of favour anyone could want at a time like this.

'Get me the ring.' He picks up the spoon.

'Why?'

'Because I'm going to use it to pay for your safety. If he finds the right buyer, he'll get at least a hundred grand.'

'But he won't keep his promise.'

'He will.' Seb's eyes find mine. They're hardened now. Utterly determined. 'Just get that thing out of your bag and let him have it.'

My eyes widen and my lips part. Because judging by the look on his face, he knows an uber-expensive ring isn't the only useful item stowed away in the bag. As if to confirm my suspicions, he gives me a slow nod. And hope drags itself back to life – just like a Phoenix, fire-worn and blackened by soot. Giving him a nod in return, I will my body into action and begin to close in on the table.

'Wait.' Raising a hand, Crawley stops me in my tracks. 'Let's see the bauble in a minute, after we've got things rolling. Start cooking, Mr Delaney.'

I give up on the mission. Seeing as Crawley's picked the ideal position – allowing him to keep a firm eye on me and the gun trained on his first prospective victim – it's impossible to move any further. Instead, I return my gaze to Seb.

'Don't watch,' he whispers.

'Seb...' My throat constricts. The tears flow with renewed force.

'I'm begging you, Evie.' He looks down at the items strewn in front of him. 'I don't want you to see this. Look away, now.'

I clamp my lips shut and do as he asks. Wiping my eyes, I focus my attention on the painting above the fireplace. And over the next few seconds, while I look past the elegant Georgian lady to the perfect landscape beyond – the rolling hills and peaceful woodlands, offering up a promise of heaven – I hear nothing more than the rustle of foil and the flick of a lighter. Silently, I will Seb to understand the truth. There's no shame or weakness in what he's doing now, because a sacrifice like this can only ever come from strength.

'Oh, this is a thing of beauty,' Crawley observes, revelling in the cruelty of it all. 'He certainly knows what he's doing. It's like watching an artist. There it goes. All of it, if you please. No tricks.'

I hear the clatter of a dropped syringe.

'Good lad.'

It's then that I dare to turn back, only to realise Seb's already feeling the effects. Leaning to one side and struggling to remove the ligature, he's dragging in one deep breath after another.

'The ring,' he gasps, dropping the tie. 'Show him the ring.'

'Oh yeah.' Crawley waves the gun. 'Be a good girl and do the honours.' Leaving me to it, he wanders over to Seb, grabs him by the hair and yanks his head back. 'Nothing more to say, Delaney? Not very chatty now, are we?'

Which means I'm running out of time.

On automatic pilot now, I head for the table and slip both hands into the bag. My left hand tightens around the ring box. The right digs further, past the make-up, the mobile, the tampons and tissues... and finally touches metal.

'Remember that bulldog Miles got me?' Crawley joins me at the table. 'Fucking thing shat everywhere.'

'It did.' Before it disappeared.

'I'm no good at keeping pets, me.'

A coded message, if I've ever heard one. He is going to kill me. Just like he probably killed that poor dog. It's exactly what I need. One final, little push.

'Here.' I produce the ring box, present it to him with a shaking hand, and drop it.

Glancing off the table, it lands on the floor.

And I've just given myself a few seconds' worth of distraction.

With my right hand still concealed in the bag, I take my one and only chance. Fumbling for the safety catch, I draw it back, pull the gun from the bag and aim it squarely at Crawley's chest.

'What the...'

He gets no further.

In an instant, the air explodes. A vicious rebound sends me staggering backwards until I somehow manage to steady myself. With shock waves still ringing in my ears, I drop the gun and re-focus.

'Shit.' On a sharp inhale, I realise Crawley's on the floor. 'I did it.'

I hit my target.

But he's still alive. Sprawled on his back, a crimson stain spreading across his top. And he's reaching for his own gun.

292

Y

I step forward and kick it away, leaving him to look up at me, stunned features twisted by hatred and pain. A trickle of blood appears at the corner of his mouth. His lips move.

'Bitch.' It's all he manages before his eyes glass over.

He's dead.

But I feel no triumph in the moment.

'Fuck,' I breathe. 'I've killed him.'

Chapter Twenty-Seven

There's no time to think. Seb's on his knees now, steadying himself against the sofa.

Stumbling over to him, I drop to the floor and place a hand on his back.

'Good shot,' he rasps.

'No talking. Save your energy. Just stay still and hold on.'

Within seconds, I'm back at the table, fishing the mobile out of my bag and trying to steady my heartbeat. I cast a glance at the gun, the crumpled body on the floor, the slick of blood. But there's no time to dwell on what I've done. If I don't act fast, Seb's likely to join Crawley in his fate. I'm about to key in 999 when I hear the thunder of heavy footsteps.

The door bursts open.

Closely followed by Chesty, and another man I've never seen before, Max hoves into view.

'He's overdosed,' I blurt. 'Heroin.'

Max takes in the scene. 'Chesty, you know what to do.'

Enough said. While Chesty disappears back down the hallway, Max grabs the mobile from my hands. Cancelling the call, he thrusts the phone into his pocket.

'What are you doing?'

'I'll deal with this.'

'But he needs an ambulance.'

'No, he doesn't.' He kneels at Seb's side and shoots off an order to the second man. 'Get Chris back here.'

'Who the hell is Chris?' I demand.

'Family doctor. Soul of discretion.'

'Discretion? Is that all that matters to you?'

'It matters to Seb too. And for your information, Chris and Chesty are more than capable of dealing with this.' Slipping an arm behind Seb's neck, he gently raises his head. 'Open your eyes, Cyril.'

'Fuck off.'

'Do it.'

With a massive effort, Seb complies.

'Now, keep them open,' Max orders. 'How much?'

'Not sure.' He blinks. 'Into the muscle though.'

'Good man.'

'Good man?' I step forward. 'What do you mean, good man?'

'Calm down.' Although he hasn't broken eye contact with Seb, Max is speaking to me now. 'I'm guessing he didn't take it willingly.'

'Of course not.'

'Then he did the right thing.' He smooths a palm over Seb's forehead. 'It's slower in the muscle. Gives us more time.'

'For what?'

'You'll see.'

'Jesus, Max. I hope you know what you're doing.'

Dropping to my knees for a second time, I place a hand on Seb's shoulder and study his face. Within the last few seconds, his skin has turned a deathly grey. It sends a chill right through my bones: the effect of fear at its abject worst. The sort of fear that can't be tamed or leashed or taken in hand... because I'm not afraid for myself.

'I take it that's Crawley.'

I look up to find Max studying the corpse. 'Yes.'

'How did he get in?'

'Alex.'

'What?'

'Alex Thompson. Crawley told me himself.'

'That bastard,' he growls. 'When I get my hands on him...'

'You won't,' I counter. 'He'll be long gone by now. Just concentrate on your brother.'

With a quick nod, Max does as he's told. 'Shit. He's drifting. Wake up, Cyril. Keep your eyes open.' He rubs his knuckles across Seb's chest.

It's a vicious action, but it seems to do the trick.

Seb's eyelids flicker and rise again. 'That hurts.'

'It's supposed to. Come on. Let's get you comfy.' Manoeuvring him round, Max sits his brother up straight – back against the sofa, legs stretched out in front of him – then shuffles back to his side. 'It's a good job I doubted you.'

'You did?'

'Yes.' He smiles. 'I've got Naloxone.'

'Why?' Seb frowns.

'Better safe than sorry.'

'You're fucking anal. Do you know that?'

'Yes.' He taps Seb's cheek. 'And you should be grateful. Chesty's fully trained, we've got enough doses to get you through, and Chris is on his way back as we speak.'

Seb gives his brother a weary nod. His breathing's shallow now; his skin even more ashen. 'I'll be fine.' He turns his head to me. 'Deliverance is on its way.' It's all he can manage.

'Deliverance?' I look to Max for help.

'Naloxone,' he explains. 'Reverses the reaction. Should keep him going until the heroin's out of his system.' He's distracted by the arrival of Chesty.

Wielding what looks like a medical bag, the big man gets straight down to business. Waving Max out of the way, he kneels at Seb's side, rummages through the bag, pulls out a package and rips it open. 'Talk to him,' he orders gruffly. 'I mean you, Evie. Keep him awake.' With that, he gets on with the job of preparing the first injection.

Focussing back to Seb, I say the only thing that comes to mind. 'You can't die.'

His lips twitch. 'I'm trying not to.'

'Because... I love you.'

There. That's done it. Declaration made, I've committed myself.

'Well,' he sighs. 'That's a bloody good reason to stay alive.'

I take his hand in mine. Distinctly clammy to the touch, his skin seems to be losing its customary warmth. Watching the light begin to fade from his eyes, I'm vaguely aware of Chesty administering the injection.

'Thank God,' Seb grumbles, shifting a little on the floor.

Struggling to find his pulse, Chesty orders him to stay still.

'Do as you're told,' I add, with a squeeze of his hand.

'Yes, boss.'

While the next couple of minutes drag their heels, and I spend every second watching him closely, waiting for the slightest sign of improvement.

Finally, he looks over to the window. 'Is Crawley dead?'

'Yes.'

'Good. I knew you could do it.'

'You knew?' Somewhere at the back of my head, I hear an echo of Seb's voice: *Get that thing out of your bag, and let him have it.* 'You knew about the gun.'

'I did.' He smiles.

'How?'

'Ah,' he grins. 'Had a quick snoop this morning. While you were out in the garden. Wanted a look at the ring. Found out my girlfriend's a bad ass.'

296

'I'm not a bad ass,' I tell him, relieved he's already getting his breath back. 'And anyway, I thought you didn't like guns.'

'I don't. But like Max said, better safe than sorry.' He raises an eyebrow. 'Thank God for sneaky brothers, eh? And women with balls. I couldn't have done what you did.'

'I'm not exactly proud.' Far from it, in fact.

As if drawn by some grim, magnetic force, I turn to gaze at Crawley's body. Try as I might, I just can't work out who pulled that trigger and snuffed out a life. Because it certainly wasn't the innocent little girl who rescued bees and butterflies, and even the occasional bird. Somewhere along the way, I must have become a monster. But if I had, then surely I wouldn't be so troubled right now. I certainly wouldn't be listening to that persistent voice at the back of my head, niggling from the depths of my conscience, promising nothing but guilt and regret for the rest of my days.

'Jesus.' He may well be dead, but Crawley's still going to make me suffer.

'Evie.' Seb wraps his fingers around mine. 'You had no choice. He was a piece of shit. Don't even think about it.'

Easy enough for him to say. 'I killed him, Seb. He might have been a piece of shit, but I killed a man – a policeman, for God's sake.' And no one does that sort of thing without consequence. Conscience aside, there are bound to be other repercussions. 'I'll go to prison.'

'No, you won't.' With his fingers clamped to Seb's wrist, Chesty grimaces. 'Not if I can help it.' He focusses on Seb. 'How are you feeling?'

'Hanging in there.'

'Good. It's working, but you're going to need more. This dose won't last.' He raises his voice. 'Where's that fucking doctor?'

'Language.' Standing by the window now, with a mobile clamped to his ear, Max scowls at his head of security.

'Fuck that.' His head of security scowls back. 'This man needs proper monitoring.'

'Relax.' Max ends the call. 'He'll be here in ten.' He waves a hand at Crawley. 'In the meantime, what are we going to do about that?'

'I know a decent cleaner.' Chesty puts a palm to Seb's forehead. 'The sort that doesn't bother with dusters.'

'And what about the staff?' Max nods to the door. 'How are we going to make sure they don't talk?'

'The usual way.' Evidently satisfied, Chesty leans back. 'Money.' He rummages through the bag again. 'Don't worry. I'll see to all that when I'm done here. Right now, we need to get this one into bed.'

'In a minute,' Seb mutters, drawing my attention back to him. 'This is going to take some time. You should go back to the club.'

'I can't.'

'You can.' His eyes flicker with renewed life. 'The drug's doing its job. I can feel it. And now Crawley's gone, there's no danger.'

'But...'

'Please.' Deadly serious now, he holds my gaze. 'I don't like you seeing me like this. Go home and wait for me there. We'll talk this through when I'm in a fit state. I promise.'

I nod, uncertainly.

'And one more thing.' He takes in a deep breath. 'Leave the ring with me.'

***

I hear a distant mobile. Then Celine's voice – so faint from inside the apartment, I can barely make out what she's saying. Tugging a blanket tight around my shoulders, I look up at the sky and watch the first signs of dawn, telling myself it can't come soon enough after the long hours of turmoil, dominated by worries over Seb and flashbacks to Crawley's demise. My thoughts did nothing but toss and turn all night. And now – as if things aren't bad enough – they seem to have homed in on Christophe Dupont.

Wondering how on earth he's managed to wheedle his way in, I gaze down at his Porsche and think of that first time I emerged from the penthouse to find him waiting for me in the lobby – something he must have organised with Alex, because I'm sure Celine didn't leave that door open. And then, I think of how he jumped at the chance to help me escape from The Club, only to fall flat on his face when Seb intervened. Finally, I muse over the ridiculous kitchen debacle: an unforeseen emergency, caused by two hung-over, disgruntled chefs.

With the evidence mounting up, I can't help agreeing with Celine's theory. It was Christophe who engineered it all. But unlike Celine, I can't bring myself to believe he simply did it to cause chaos. In fact, the more I mull over it, the more convinced I become that he's been trying to remove me from Seb's world, even to the point of exposing my past and putting lives in danger. And he's done it all from behind a carefully constructed smoke screen, hiding every last scrap of hard evidence.

'But why?'

That's the question.

With his family providing the most convenient target, maybe it's just in his nature to hate and destroy. Or maybe, it's something more...

'You should come in now.' Mobile in hand, Celine joins me.

'In a minute.' I motion to the car park. 'What's he doing here?'

She cranes her neck. 'Christophe? No idea.' She touches my arm. 'Forget him. You need some rest.'

'So do you. You've stayed up all night with me.'

'Can't sleep.'

'Neither can I.' During my one aborted attempt, I did nothing but brood and fidget.

'That was Max.' She gives the mobile a little wave. 'Seb's improving quickly.'

'Good.'

'One less thing to worry about.'

'One less?' I study her face. 'You're not... You're not worried about me?'

'Of course I am.' She smiles. 'Because you're in shock.'

'Am I?'

'Obviously. And being out here isn't going to help.' She runs a hand over my back. 'If you're thinking about Crawley again...'

'Crawley.' The mere mention of his name drags me straight back to those few, awful minutes. As if under a spell, the real world recedes, leaving me with nothing but the scent of sulphur, a vision of blood, and the memory of light fading in vengeful eyes.

'You had to do it, Evie.'

'I know, but...'

I'm stopped in my tracks by an eruption of sobs. Bursting with all the frustration and despair of the past few years, they tear through me with astonishing force, stripping away all self-control and reducing me to a blubbering mess. I'd make a run for it if I could – tuck myself away in some dark corner until it all blows over – but I can barely move because Celine's skinny arms are wrapped around me now, and they're surprisingly strong.

'It's okay,' she soothes. 'It's all okay.'

I really ought to tell her it's not, but my voice isn't yet obeying my brain. It takes a good couple of minutes for the sobs to die down and finally transform into the occasional gulp for air.

'I understand what you're going through,' she says. 'Trust me.'

Frowning at her words, I pull back.

'Now, shall we go in?'

I glance round, and shiver.

'You're perfectly safe.'

'I know. But...' It's still difficult to believe Crawley was acting on his own. I've spent so long looking over my shoulder, it's not going to be easy to adjust. 'Will I ever be free?'

'No.' With a delicate sigh, Celine becomes serious. 'You're with Seb now. You're practically a Delaney. And there's no true freedom in that family.' Noting my confusion, she puts a hand on my shoulder. 'What I mean is, there'll always be threats – because of the money – so there'll always be security.' She shrugs. 'But you're a strong woman. You'll get used to it.' The hand's withdrawn. 'And talking of security, the club's an absolute fortress at the minute. Max has sent in reinforcements.' The smile returns. 'So, what do you say? Shall we?' She gestures to the open bi-folds.

And finally, I relent.

Half an hour later – after a quick coffee, a shower and a change of clothes – I'm sitting in the club kitchen, attempting to distract myself with a spot of menu planning. But it's all in vain. I've barely managed a handful of new ideas for lunch before my attention begins to wander.

Shrouded in absolute silence, I survey the room. With the darkest of shadows banished for the time being, dawn's already done its job, leaving bright sunlight to stream in through high windows, casting a silvery glow across tiled walls, immaculate floors and stainless-steel worktops. Taking time to examine every little detail of my surroundings, I sit back and wonder at a long-lost sense of calm that seems to have settled over my world. I'm not sure if it's pure fantasy or the weird workings of an over-taxed brain, but out of nowhere, I feel as if I'm blessed with brand new eyes, seeing everything – and everyone – with a clarity I've never known before.

'Thought you might be here.'

Celine's voice rouses me.

'Max and Seb are back.' She holds out a hand. 'They've just drawn up at the front.'

Abandoning the menus, I spring to my feet and follow in her wake, pulse racing as we scurry through a silent, gloomy bar. By the time we reach the lobby, they're already inside, standing next to the desk, deep in conversation.

'Seb?'

Still dressed in last night's outfit, he begins to head in my direction. 'Evie? Are you okay?'

I get no chance to answer. At the sound of a whistle, he draws to a halt and swings round.

'You certainly look rough.' Standing in the doorway to the east wing, Christophe Dupont laughs quietly. 'Heavy night?'

'What are you doing here?' Seb demands.

'I stayed in my room.' With a shrug, Christophe steps forward. Wearing joggers and a t-shirt, he's wide awake and thoroughly chirpy.

'The club's not open.'

'Max told me Harry passed away.'

'He did.'

'So, I wanted to be here with my brothers.'

'Go home,' Max intervenes.

Christophe turns to him, eyes flashing with pure distaste. 'But I'm family.'

'You,' Max sneers, 'have no idea what 'family' means. Go. Home.'

Surveying us all, Christophe seems to decide he's on a hiding to nothing. Without another word, he swerves round and disappears down the hallway.

'I should beat the shit out of him,' Max grumbles.

'Don't start,' Seb grumbles back, pressing a finger to his forehead. 'I'm not in the mood.'

'But it's obvious...'

'It's Alex who's missing.'

'And Alex was in Christophe's pocket.'

'I'd like to see you prove it.'

With no reply from Max, Seb looks up. 'Let's think about this logically, shall we?' He sighs deeply, as though he's had enough. 'It was Alex who contacted Crawley, Alex who planted the junk on Crawley's behalf, and Alex who got him into Hal's place...'

'But you thought it was Christophe.' The words fly out of my mouth before I can stop them. 'A couple of days ago,' I remind him. 'You thought Christophe planted the drugs.'

'I know.' He sighs again. 'But now I've had a chance to think, it doesn't make sense.'

Only it would, if Alex were in Christophe's pocket. I'm about to say as much when I catch a warning from Max – the slightest touch on my arm.

'We'll talk about this later,' he says.

'No,' Seb counters. 'We won't talk about it at all. I know you can't stand him, Max, but he's our brother. You can't go flinging accusations about when there's no real proof and no real motive.' He winces. 'I don't want any more arguments.'

'Relax. You won't get any from me.'

'Good. Because I'm exhausted. I've got a banging headache and I need a shower.' Looking back to me, he finally manages a smile. 'I'm going down to the boathouse. Give me half an hour to spruce up.' He brushes a finger across my cheek. 'And then, we need to talk.'

I watch him go, feeling sick as he descends the steps and walks out over the car park.

'He's not about to dump you,' Max announces.

'What?' I swivel round to face him.

'He's tired. That's all. A bit thrown by what happened last night. But apart from that, he's fine... unlike you.'

'I'm fine too.'

'No, you're not.' He chews at his lower lip. 'What you did took some guts. You saved my brother's life, and I'll be forever in your debt for that.' His eyes flash. 'But I know it's costing you.'

I grimace. 'You think you know everything, don't you?'

'No need for sarcasm. Seb's worried about you.'

'He doesn't have to worry.'

'Yes, he does. And so do I. Just so you know, as of now, there's no trace of Stefan Crawley's earthly remains. And for future reference, Chesty knows an excellent counsellor, someone who can be trusted to keep secrets. If it's needed, you will make use of their services. Is that understood?'

'Yes.' I bristle.

'Good.'

I glance at the doorway to the east corridor.

'There's something else.' He waits for a moment. 'Come on, Evie. Tell me what's on your mind.'

As quickly as it appeared, the bristling subsides. Max Delaney might be irritatingly astute, but he's just offered up the perfect opportunity to try out my theories. And there's no way I'm going to pass.

'It's just... I've been thinking too.' I glance through the glass frontage. Seb's already half-way across the lawn. 'And like you, I don't buy it. No matter what trouble Alex was in, I can't believe he'd go to those lengths on his own.'

Clearly intrigued, Max moves towards me.

'I don't know why he'd want to put us all in danger, but I do know Christophe was involved in what happened last night.'

The intrigue increases. 'Evidence?'

I hold up a hand. 'Circumstantial.' There's no point creating false hope. 'It's just a feeling, really... because other things have happened.' Gathering my thoughts and fighting back a wave of fatigue, I tell him all about my first meeting with Christophe and the aborted escape attempt. 'And I suppose you heard what happened with the kitchen?'

'Yes.'

'So, you know about Christophe's involvement there? The big night out? The gambling?'

He nods.

'I think Christophe planned it all. Celine does too.' Something he's bound to be aware of. 'She thinks he did it to mess things up for Seb. But I can't help wondering...' I hesitate.

'Go on.'

Suddenly, it seems a ridiculous idea, but I still need to air it. 'If Christophe was in contact with Crawley, then he'd have known all about my past. He might have done it to lure me back into a kitchen, so I'd give myself away. I mean, it sounds mad ...'

'Not to me,' Max interrupts. 'Not when you know how Christophe's mind operates. And if that was the plan, then it was a success.'

'To a point,' I counter. 'Because I didn't leave.'

'Thank God.' He greets my shock with a broad smile. 'Yes. You'd better believe it. You're getting the nice Max from now on.'

'That is progress.' Pushing the surprise to one side, I press on. 'The way I see it, Christophe's trying to destroy Seb. In fact, I'm sure he wants to rob him of any chance of happiness. That's why he wanted to get rid of me.' I have no idea why, but my brain homes in on a collection of notes... and the cogs begin to whir. 'And those letters,' I murmur, absently. 'Maybe it was Christophe who sent them.'

Max cocks his head.

'I mean, it's possible, isn't it? He might have done it to unsettle Seb, to drive him to self-destruct.' I trail into silence, because I'm beginning to sound like a lunatic conspiracy theorist on acid.

But Max doesn't seem to share my misgivings. 'Then, it was another success,' he says. 'After all, that's why Seb took to the bottle.'

'But it failed. Because I turned up.' I narrow my eyes at Max. 'I told him, you know. When we had that little chat in the bar, Christophe was going on about Seb's drinking, and I told him... I told him Seb didn't have a problem with the booze.'

Max raises an eyebrow.

'That's when the heroin appeared, right after he warned me about addiction, right after he prepared the ground.' The cogs whir some more, churning out a new possibility. 'What if Christophe was upping the game because Seb wasn't drowning his sorrows?'

'It's possible.'

'And what if he banked on me freaking me out in the process? What if he thought it might drive me away?' I gaze into space. 'I don't agree with Seb. I'm certain Crawley had nothing to do with the heroin at the club. I mean, he was in full-on bragging mode last night, and he didn't even mention it.'

'Did he mention Christophe?'

'No, but I don't think Christophe had any direct contact with him. I think it was all done through Alex.'

Clamping his lips tight shut, Max wanders off to the portraits and spends a minute or so apparently studying one face after another. 'Occam's Razor,' he says at last.

'Pardon?'

'The simplest answer is usually right.' Running his fingers through his hair, he returns to me. 'Christophe's behind it all. The letters, the kitchen, the heroin, even what happened last night. Christophe's the one who's been pulling the strings, but staying well out of the way so no one can point a finger. The trouble is, there's no proof.'

'Only...' I chew at my lip, because my brain seems to be coughing up something vaguely helpful. 'Stefan was useless with money. He just blew it. Never put anything away.'

'You're sure of that?'

'Yes. He borrowed from Miles all the time. I don't think he had enough money to pay Alex, at least not enough for Alex to risk everything. Only Christophe has those sorts of funds.'

'Agreed.' Grim-faced, Max stares at the marble floor. 'But still no proof. Unfortunately, I can't gain access to Christophe's bank account. And even if I could, I'm pretty sure he'd have it covered.' He raises his head. 'You need to understand something. I'm with you on everything, because it makes sense. It's all part of the pattern. Christophe has been trying to destroy Seb. He's been doing it for years. He had a damn good try with Zach too.'

'And you?'

'Not yet. He's never managed to get close enough. But I expect he'll have a go at some point. After all, I'm his main target.'

'You are?'

'Yes.' He grimaces. 'Christophe thinks I've stolen his inheritance. I'll tell you all about it another time. But for now, we don't bring this up with Seb.'

'Then how do we make him see sense?'

'He's already beginning to see it. Didn't you notice the hesitation? That little hint of doubt in his voice?'

'You think he's coming round?'

'I know he is. But let's not push this any further. It can't end well. I've only just got my brother back and I don't want to lose him again.' He smiles again, and there's a new warmth in his eyes. 'There's another thing you need to understand. Seb's more like his uncle than any of us. Maybe a little too caring, and always ready to give the benefit of the doubt. If he's dragging his heels over seeing the truth about Christophe, that's just who he is.'

And I'm glad of it. 'It's just ...'

'You're worried about keeping Christophe at the club.'

Jesus. Can this man actually read my mind? 'Of course.'

'There's no need. Take it from me. Seb's wary now, and that's a positive development. He'll be keeping an eye on Christophe, and Christophe's bound to give himself away.'

'Right.'

'Oh.' He holds up a finger. 'And about those letters... I'm already working on them.'

'You are?'

'What else would an interfering, older brother do?' With a grin, he lowers the finger. 'Seb tells me they've stopped, but I know they're still getting to him. I'll sort it out. That's a promise.'

A promise he'll make good on. I'm sure of it. Which is why I silently give thanks to have the all-powerful Max Delaney working on my side. After all, if I'm going to tackle Seb's demons, I'll need all the help I can get.

'Not a word, though,' Max warns.

'No.'

'Just concentrate on being in love.' Waving a dismissive hand, he pulls a mock-disgusted face. 'Now, go to him. If you need me, I'll be staying in my room.'

'Your room?' I almost choke. 'You've got a room here?'

'Naturally.' A mischievous twinkle flits through his eyes. 'I'm only human.'

Chapter Twenty-Eight

I can't reach the boathouse quickly enough. With my heartbeat in overdrive, I practically sprint across the lawn, only slowing when I reach the lake. Skirting the edge, I finally arrive at the boathouse and immediately tug open the door. After mounting the steps two at a time, I come to a halt at the top, grab the banister and steady my breath.

'Seb?'

As soon as I call, he emerges from the bedroom, towel in hand. Hair damp and wonderfully ruffled, he drops the towel on the kitchen top and closes the gap between us. Wrapping his arms around me, he pulls me in to his chest, giving me a few moments to listen to his precious heartbeat, now returned to its usual strength.

I pull back and lock eyes with him. 'How are you feeling?'

'Tired.' He frowns. 'And you?'

'Okay.'

'Really?'

'Of course.' Maybe a little too uncertain, I look down. A moment later, there's a finger under my chin and my face is raised to his.

'No more hiding,' he says.

'No,' I smile. 'But I'm fine. Honestly. I'm more bothered about you, after... you know...' Unwilling to put a name to the act, I drift into silence.

His frown deepens. 'I had to do it. You understand that, don't you? I had no choice.'

I nod.

'And it won't happen again, if that's what you're worrying about.'

'Of course not.'

'It felt sordid, Evie.' I watch his eyes flicker at the memory of it all. 'Disgusting. I hated every single second.'

'I understand.'

'I'll never relapse. Never.'

'And I trust you.' I brush a finger against his cheek. 'I just want to know you're alright.'

'I am.' He captures my hand and kisses it.

That glorious warmth revives in my heart. A thousand shimmers spark to life in my core.

'You're a brave man,' I tell him.

'And you're a brave woman.'

307

'For taking you on?' I give him a cheeky smile.

'For what you did last night.'

The smile disappears. 'I killed a man.'

'And as far as I'm concerned, he got what he deserved.' He kisses my hand again. 'But things like this can get to people. Has Max talked to you about counselling?'

'Yes.'

'Good. If you need it, I want to know.' He looks deep into my eyes, waiting for my assent.

I give it to him with a nod.

'And apart from the counsellor, we keep this to ourselves,' he goes on. 'Only me, you, Max, Celine and Chesty know what happened, and that's the way it stays. The fewer people in the picture, the better... because if this ever gets out, I'll be taking the rap.'

'No.'

'Yes,' he counters firmly. 'And you'll just have to deal with it.' Determination etched across his face, he waits again.

'Fine,' I sigh. There's no point arguing. I know better than to waste my time. 'Have it your way.'

'I will.' Moving both hands to my backside, he presses his crotch to mine. 'Now, let's change the subject, shall we?'

'If we must.'

'We must.' He grinds against me. 'Because I seem to have a hazy recollection of something you said at Harry's.'

'Really?' Somehow, a dose of serious crotch action seems to have done the trick. With irritation banished, I'm ready to discuss more enjoyable matters.

'Yes. I believe you told me you love me.'

'I can take it back, if you like.'

'Certainly not.' His eyes twinkle. 'Because I love you too.'

'Oh.' It's all I can say. Although I've suspected as much – and Max has roundly proclaimed it to be a fact – I'm still shocked to hear the words on Seb's lips.

'Oh?' He leans in.

'Oh,' I repeat.

Words are still beyond me. But actions aren't. Pulling him in for a long, simmering, über-passionate kiss, I tangle my fingers through his hair and keep him in place while I lead every single second of it.

'Understood?' I breathe when I'm done.

'Understood,' he breathes back. 'I take it this means we'll have no more escape attempts.'

'None at all.'

'Excellent news. All that hard slog wasn't for nothing, then.'

'What hard slog?'

'Take a look around.' He stands back and waves a hand.

Turning slowly on the spot, I do as I'm told... and gasp in surprise. Because it's only now I notice the whole place has been freshly painted in a perfect pastel blue.

'This is the project?'

'It certainly is.'

'It's beautiful.'

'Thank God for that.' Taking me by the hand, he leads me to the back of the boathouse, and into the main bedroom. 'Did in here, too. Painted it all myself.'

The same colour as the living area. The colour I suggested. 'You didn't have to.'

'I wanted to.'

'But you're rich enough to hire a decorator.'

'Apparently so,' he grins. 'However, I wanted to give it the personal touch. Just for you.'

My heart skips several beats.

'Don't look too closely, though. Bit of a bodge job. Might have to get someone in to put it right.'

'Oh, I don't know.' I squint at a stray blob of blue on the skirting board. 'I think you've done a grand job.'

'Liar.'

We laugh together. And I turn to him, swept away in his gaze, completely overwhelmed by adoration.

'This is our place now.' He lets go of my hand. 'Our sanctuary.'

'And I love it.'

'Somewhere to retreat to. Somewhere to indulge in lots and lots of filthy sex. Talking of which.' Taking the hem of my t-shirt, he begins to lift it.

'Seb?'

'Yes?' Urging me to raise my arms, he pulls the t-shirt over my head and drops it.

'I thought you were tired.'

He reaches round to unhook my bra. 'Not that tired.'

'But shouldn't you be taking it easy today?'

'Can't.' With a rueful shake of the head, he draws the straps down my arms. 'Because I'm in love.'

'You're also recovering.'

'From a totally heroic act.' He slings the bra into a corner. 'I was willing to give my life for you last night. I believe that earns me a reward.'

Taking in a deep, satisfied breath, he surveys me; then brings a hand to my back, holding me in place while he smooths a palm across my neck and down my sternum. Homing in on my left breast, he slowly massages the nipple to a peak. I'm half expecting him to move on to my right breast when I sense the change. It happens so quickly I can barely keep up. He stalls. Eyes darken. Clamping his lips together, he backs away.

'What is it?' I ask.

'Old habits die hard.'

With his gaze levelled on mine, he's completely serious now. It leaves me wondering if he's had a sudden, unexpected change of mind. I'm beginning to feel the chill of rejection when he strips off his own t-shirt.

'Seb?'

His jeans quickly follow suit. Then he sinks to his knees, naked in front of me, head lowered.

I have no idea what's going on. 'Seb? What's wrong?'

'Nothing.'

'But...'

'Wait.' Evidently preparing himself for something momentous, he looks up. Completely earnest, stripped of all armour, he begins to speak. 'You've turned my world upside-down, Evie. That's not an overstatement. It's a fact.' He takes my hand. 'You dragged me out of my safe space and brought me back to life. You made me change for the better, but there's still one last change to make.' He pauses. 'And I'm the one who needs to make it.'

'I don't understand.'

'I'm talking about control.' He takes in a breath. 'The truth is I've always used it to keep my distance.' With a shake of the head, he decides to clarify matters. 'I'm talking about sex now.'

'Oh.'

'I never dropped the control, not even when you introduced me to your little axis of evil.'

'Ah,' I smile, happy to reassure him. 'I know. I believe it's called 'topping out'.'

An eyebrow arches.

'Don't worry, Seb. I had you rumbled.'

'I'm sure you did.' He gazes up at me and finally gets to the point. 'I don't want it anymore. I don't want the control or the power play. And I certainly don't want the deception. I want to give it all up… because it's the last thing between us, the last bit of the shield. Tell me you understand.'

'I do.'

'Thank God.' He sighs. 'I want you to get right to the heart of me, Evie, and I want to get right to the heart of you. And as far as I know, this is where we do it.' He nods to the bed. 'When we're naked. When we join…'

'It's okay.' Releasing his hand, I smooth his hair. 'I get it.'

'Good.' Clearly relieved, he smiles again. 'Because this is me on my knees, offering myself up to you, body and soul.'

And I couldn't be happier.

'From now on,' he says, 'we don't do it my way. And we don't do it your way. We do it our way.'

'Which is?'

'I have no idea.' He unfastens my jeans, draws them down, and encourages me to step out of them. 'I suppose we work it out together.'

'I'm up for that.'

Slipping both index fingers into the waist band of my knickers, he takes his time removing them. Then, he rises to his knees, grabs me by the hips, and leans in to kiss my crotch.

'But I hope it doesn't mean…' With his tongue teasing at my clitoris, a rising tide of pleasure threatens to empty my brain.

'You were saying?'

'I was saying…' What was I saying? Oh, yes. 'I hope this doesn't mean…' His tongue finds the most sensitive part of the nub. 'Oh, God… no more kink.'

He pulls back. 'Didn't say that.' Urging my legs a little further apart, he trails tiny, delicate kisses down the front of my thighs.

'Good. Because I like it.'

'So do I.'

'And it's got to be said…' Although he might not like it. 'I quite like the dominant Seb.'

'You do?'

'Yes.' His hands leave my hips. 'Because he's actually quite sexy.' Palms move lightly over my stomach. My lungs contract. 'Very sexy.'

'I see.' Shooting me a knowing look, he gets to his feet and sweeps me into his arms.

A few seconds later, I'm lying on the bed with the perfect male specimen looming over me, utterly glorious in all his naked perfection.

'Looks like I've created a monster,' he grins.

'Well done, Dr Frankenstein,' I grin back, taking the opportunity to admire every inch of him: from the ruffled hair and the gorgeous face, right down to those magnificently sculpted legs. 'So, we can still do it, then? You know, the dominant stuff?'

'Don't see why not.' Suddenly panther-like, he crawls onto the bed. 'As long as you realise it's nothing more than an act, whenever you want him, I'll bring out the dominant Seb.' He straddles me. 'But you need to ask for him.' He lowers his crotch to mine, setting off a frisson of excitement. 'We can do it all, Evie. The kinky stuff, the dominant stuff, the intimate, gentle stuff.' Taking my hands, he raises them to the pillow. 'I say we mix it all up and see what happens.' He touches his lips to my neck. 'But no real control.'

Immediately, I lose myself in the softness of his skin, the warmth of his body, the sheer strength of the man. It's a wonder I have enough presence of mind to ask my next question. 'I hate to say this, but aren't you being a bit controlling now?'

He pulls back. 'Just taking the lead. There's a difference, you know. If you want something else, feel free to change the script.' He leans in for a kiss. 'I believe it's called give and take.'

'Oh,' I breathe, already drifting off into sexual oblivion. 'That.'

'Yes. That.' He smiles against my lips. 'Anything you want. It's yours.'

'Anything?'

'Anything.'

'Okay.' I grin. 'Right now, I want you inside me.'

He raises his head. 'Your wish. My command.'

Leaning over, he helps himself to a condom from the bedside drawer, then nudges my legs apart and settles between them. Packet opened, he slips the condom over his already-erect penis and positions his body over mine, propping himself up on one elbow.

'Ready?'

'God, yes.' I run my hands over his shoulders.

Watching me intently, he guides himself in, probing as far as he can until he's buried to the hilt. And then, we still. Eyes locked, both of us lost in a wordless bubble of intimacy, we spend an age like this, offering ourselves up to each other, body and soul.

'I love you,' I murmur.

'I love you too.'

With that, he begins to move, slowly at first, steadily increasing the pace until I'm on fire with lust and gripped by an irresistible urge to take him up on a promise.

'Give me some of that dominant,' I rasp.

'On his way.'

The transformation's immediate. Suddenly intent on getting what he wants, he takes my hair in his left fist and pins my head to the pillow. After kissing my neck with a vengeance, and virtually devouring me in the process, he releases my hair and orders me to return my hands above my head.

'Stay like that,' he growls, moving his attention to my left breast. Dispensing with gentleness, he latches on and sucks hard, pausing only to grate his teeth across tender flesh.

With a groan of delight, I lower a hand to his left arm. Immediately, he captures it, pinning it back to the bed with a force that takes my breath away.

'Do as you're told.'

Still thrusting into me at a rate of knots, he brings his face to mine and stares at my lips for all of five seconds before dishing out a long, commanding kiss. The fire soon threatens to flare and implode. But just when I think I'm about to climax, he comes to a sudden halt and waits for the impending orgasm to recede. As soon as he's satisfied I'm back from the edge, the action begins again. And within seconds, I'm at the mercy of twitching nerves and fluttering muscles. Again, he stops. Again, he waits.

And so, it continues... repeatedly.

Pinned down by the strength and weight of his body, I'm quickly gasping for breath and sweating for England. But I'm also floating away on a tide of ecstasy, pleasured beyond belief by this particular trick of the dominant's trade. It's not the first time he's delayed my orgasm – and I'm sure it won't be the last – but he's doing it for me now, not for himself. The moment I want him to stop, he will. Because there's no real control anymore. I can feel it.

But it's always wise to test a theory.

Which is why I bring my hands from the pillow and push against him. Immediately, he gives way, rolling effortlessly until he's flat on his back and I'm the one on top. Leaning over him, with my hair falling across his face, I place my hands on his chest and ride him at my own pace, taking him deep, lapping up every single, exquisite sensation.

And before long, he's moving too, steadying me with his hands on my hips, never once breaking eye contact as the pleasure takes

313

us higher. Between us, we settle on a new rhythm, the two of us moving in absolute harmony, neither of us wrestling for the upper hand, because neither of us want or need it.

It's me who comes first, so consumed by contractions I'm only vaguely aware of his grip tightening against my skin, his body tensing for release, his cock twitching and pulsing inside me. When I finally return to the world, I can do nothing more than collapse at his side.

'I think this might be our new type of sex,' I muse.

'I think you're right.' He deals with the condom.

'Kink and intimacy. The perfect combination.'

'Like chocolate soufflé and vanilla ice cream.' With a smile, he pulls me into his embrace. 'A basic recipe, elevated by a few delicious tweaks.'

'Just take two bodies indulging in dubiously twisted activities.'

'Add two souls circling ever closer.' He kisses my forehead. 'And you've got a Michelin-starred creation.'

'Something above and beyond?'

He raises an eyebrow. 'No doubt about it.'

***

It's almost three in the afternoon by the time I wake from a much-needed sleep. Finding myself alone in bed, I yawn and stretch, and look out through the open French doors. Which is where I find him, leaning against the balcony, dressed only in his jeans, probably lost in thought as he gazes out over the lake.

I take a moment to admire the man I love – the man who snapped me up from the depths of despair and gave me everything I could ever need. And in that moment, I realise it's way past time to voice my gratitude. Suddenly gripped by the need to do it, I get up, pull on a robe, and join him under a cloudless sky.

'It's a beautiful day.' Sensing my presence, he turns and opens his arms, inviting me in for a long, cosy cuddle.

I snuggle into his warmth. 'You're looking much better for a rest.'

'I'm feeling much better.'

'Good.' I spend a few seconds lost in his embrace, silently telling myself I'm the luckiest woman in the world. And then, I remember there's a job to do. 'Thank you,' I murmur.

'For what?' His lips twitch. 'The insanely amazing sex?'

'Well, that,' I smile, determined not to be swayed off-course. 'And various other things.' Brushing a hand over his cheek, I cast my mind back to the dark days. It's enough to send a chill through my veins and banish the smile. 'When you brought me back here, I was dead inside. I had no hope. Nothing to enjoy, nothing to look forward to, no one to share it with.' I close my eyes, desperate to find the next words. It isn't easy. 'I spent months in Bermondsey.' A series of images flash through my mind: a sparse bedroom and a single lightbulb; cold, grey streets filled with strangers; a downtrodden café. 'And in all that time, Hal was the only person I ever got remotely close to.' Eyelids rise. 'It was hell... and I honestly couldn't see an end to it. So, what I want to say is... what I need to say is... Thank you for rescuing me and bringing me back to life.'

There's a breath of relief on my part.

An understanding smile on his.

'You're welcome.' He moves a strand of hair from my face. 'But you're not the only one who's been rescued.'

'No?'

'No.' The smile deepens. 'I might have been brought up in the lap of luxury, but before I met you, I was nothing more than a shadow.' His eyes flicker. 'For the first time in my life, I don't feel lost, I don't feel aimless, and I certainly don't need to block anything out.' He cups my cheek. 'And it's all because of you, Mystery Woman. So, thank you too... for dragging me back to life.'

His words are sealed with an utterly perfect kiss.

'I'm never going to let you go,' he says when he's done.

'I think I can deal with that.'

'Excellent... because I've got a couple of propositions for you.'

My stomach flutters. 'I like propositions.'

'You might not like the first.' Apparently steeling himself, he wavers for a moment before throwing me a curveball. 'I want you to take charge of our new restaurant.'

'What?'

'The hotel needs a damn good restaurant.'

'Yes, but...'

'I'd be an idiot not to put it in your capable hands.'

'But...'

'And you'd be an idiot not to take it.'

'Well...'

'Time to come out of the shadows, Evie.'

'I know.' I spend a good thirty seconds gazing over his shoulder, chewing at my top lip and telling myself I should grab the opportunity, because this is everything I've ever dreamed of. 'But...' It seems the anxiety of the last few months isn't quite finished with me. I still haven't managed to put fear on a leash. 'I don't know if I'm ready.'

He tips his face to mine. 'I understand. You're worried. After all, it's bound to be a huge success.'

I nod.

'And that means you'll be noticed. So... I've asked Max to sort out a few things.'

'Such as?'

'Removing everything about Yara Richardson from the internet.'

'He can do that?'

'Have you met my brother?' He laughs. 'Seriously, though, we thought you might appreciate it.'

I nod again.

'Apart from that, we thought it best to keep everything above board. A simple change of name by deed poll, if that's okay with you.'

I can't help wondering if a completely new identity might be better.

'Then we can set up a bank account for you, a passport and a driving licence...'

'I could still be traced,' I interrupt, ashamed to sound so ungrateful.

'You could be, but nobody's coming after you.'

'No.' I glance out over the lake, reminding myself that Stefan said as much.

'But...' he adds ominously. 'When you eventually make your name as a chef – which is inevitable, by the way – you will have people digging into your past.'

'Don't be daft.'

'I'm not being daft.' His eyebrows arch. 'Think about it. A talented chef and a Delaney to boot. It's going to happen. And when it does, we can't risk anything suspicious coming to light.'

'A name change is suspicious.'

'If anyone ever asks...' He kisses my forehead. 'You tell them you wanted a new beginning after Manchester. After all, we can't cover up what happened there.'

'No.' He's right. Even the all-powerful Delaneys can't erase police records and a coroner's report. All of which exonerate me, and rightly so. 'Okay,' I half-whisper. 'Go ahead with the deed poll, the bank account and the passport.' Because it is time to start easing myself out of the shadows. 'But I need time to think about the restaurant.'

He opens his mouth to speak.

I hold up a hand. 'Just so you know, I'll probably say yes. But I'm not ready to commit. Not yet.'

To my surprise, he shrugs. 'No worries. I can wait.'

'I didn't think patience was your strong suit.'

'Let's just say it's a work in progress.' The next few seconds pass in silent, mutual adoration before he speaks again. 'If it makes you feel any better, you'll have plenty of protection. As we speak, Chesty's reviewing the security situation. He's appointing a new Head, vetting the current team, sorting out bodyguards ...'

'Bodyguards?'

'A necessity, I'm afraid.' He gives me an apologetic look. 'After all, you're a Delaney now.'

'Actually,' I grin, 'I think you'll find I'm an Almost-Smith.'

'Double-barrelled, eh?'

'Very posh.'

He studies me for a moment or two. A twinkle appears in his eyes. 'No,' he says. 'It doesn't suit you.'

'Oh?'

'And that brings me to my second proposition. Another damn good reason to keep things on the straight and narrow. As far as I'm concerned, a wedding needs to be legally binding.'

'Wedding?' The flutters return.

'Wedding,' he repeats. Reaching into his back pocket, he produces the ring box and opens it with a flourish. 'This little piece of jewellery has saved us both, in more ways than one.' He takes out the ring, clicks the box shut and places it on the balustrade. 'Evie Almost-Smith...' He drops to his knees and looks up, his beautiful eyes gleaming in the sunlight. 'Do me the honour of marrying me... and changing your name, again.'

Stunned by the moment, I gaze at the ring.

'Say you'll marry me, Evie. If you don't, I'll go mad.'

'We can't have that.' I hold out a jittering left hand. 'I will marry you, Sebastian Delaney.'

Slipping the ring onto my finger, he takes a moment to admire it before getting to his feet. 'Come here, future wife.'

I'm drawn back into his arms. Where I belong.

'Kiss me, future husband.'

'With pleasure.'

It's the kiss to end all kisses. An utterly tender dance between lips and tongues that goes on for an eternity. Closing the space between us for once and for all, it seals the deal with an absolute surplus of give and take. When our lips finally part, I'm incapable of speech. I can only watch in silence as Seb turns his face to the sky.

'I hope you're listening, Uncle Harry.' He smiles into the brightness. 'Because this was all your doing.' A flicker of sadness crosses his eyes. 'I'm sorry you never found your happy ending. But thank you.' His gaze returns to mine. 'Thank you – from me and Evie – for helping us to find ours.'

Chapter Twenty-Nine

Epilogue
One Year Later

Celine looks up from her file. 'What are you doing down here?'

'Looking for Seb.' Clutching the banister – mainly because I can't see my feet – I finally reach the bottom of the staircase.

'You should be resting.'

'I'm pregnant, Celine. Not ill.'

'So says the woman who spent months throwing up.'

'Haven't thrown up in a while now.' Although I do feel distinctly nauseous after Max's phone call. 'Where is he?'

'If you mean that fusspot fiancé of yours, he's down there.' Making absolutely no effort to hide her irritation, she waves towards the east wing. 'Checking the building work, again.'

And we both know why. So determined to give me the perfect wedding, he's kept a sharp eye on every step of the renovation, eager to have it all done on time and to extremely exacting standards. Unfortunately, he's also made a complete nuisance of himself in the process.

'You might like to remind him the wedding's still three months away, which is more than enough time to get the work finished.' She slams the file shut. 'And while you're at it, you can tell him to stop worrying over the house. It's not as if you haven't already got a perfectly decent home for the little one.'

I couldn't agree more. The penthouse is already set up with a nursery. And with the family house on course to be finished well before he – or she – begins to crawl, let alone toddle, I see no problems on the horizon. Unfortunately, Seb doesn't seem to share my laid-back attitude to the impending arrival of the newest Delaney.

'I'll have a strong word with him.'

'Good. Because he's getting on my nerves. If he doesn't calm down, I swear I'll do him physical damage.'

'I'll inform him of the danger.' Prior to popping into the kitchen for an update on progress.

Quietly working towards the time when I'm ready to take the reins, I've steadily increased my involvement in the restaurant over the past few months. But an unexpectedly swift pregnancy put a spanner in the works. I'm just thankful for the current hiatus. With the restaurant temporarily closed, and DJ and Nigel working on new recipes and skills, it's been a gift to be able to slow down.

'It's very real,' Celine calls after me as I waddle to the open doorway.

With a laugh, I wave a hand, and press on into the corridor.

It doesn't take long to find Seb. Standing in the middle of Christophe's old room – now stripped of all fixtures and fittings – he's busy staring at a space where the exterior wall used to be. With the ceiling propped up by huge, metal jacks, dust hanging in the air, and bits of plastic sheeting flapping in a breeze, I can almost believe I've wandered into a post-apocalyptic hellhole.

'It's a mess,' he announces, apparently sensing my presence.

I approach and touch his back. He slips an arm around me.

'It won't be for long. The bi-folds are going in tomorrow, aren't they?'

He nods, grimly.

'Just think how fast they worked on the ballroom. I looked in on it earlier. They're doing a fantastic job.' Now The Circle's disappeared – along with every other trace of the building's previous life – the ballroom's already restored to its former glory, with final decoration in full swing.

'It just feels like it'll never be finished.'

'The Project Manager says otherwise. And so does Celine. Everyone wants you to stop fussing.'

'Including you?'

'Including me.'

With a nod, he stares into space. It's obvious there's something else on his mind.

'What is it?'

He draws me in for an awkward cuddle. 'Just thinking about... you know... what happened in here.' The night Christophe finally outed himself. 'What he did to Max.'

'Don't feel guilty about it. Max is fine now. Ella too.' In fact, after the first hectic weeks of their relationship, the pair of them have managed to put all the drama behind them. Just like Zach and Amy, they're now entirely focussed on being in love.

'Still,' Seb grumbles. 'If I'd chucked Christophe out of the club...'

'He would have found another way to interfere. I'm just glad Max got here in time.' Because I dread to think what would have happened if he hadn't. 'And I'm glad Christophe finally exposed himself.'

Because it opened Seb's eyes to the truth about his half-brother at last: a truth that came directly from the horse's mouth. Once he'd been caught red-handed, Christophe couldn't resist the temptation to crow about his accomplishments. And by his own admission, he'd done his level best to destroy his brothers' happiness, alerting the press to Zach's existence, pulling the strings with Alex Thompson and bringing Stefan Crawley back into my life, without a care for the consequences. It was only when he turned on Max, stalking his girlfriend and luring her back to the club, that he finally tripped himself up.

'Anyway...' I sigh. 'It's done now.' With Christophe on remand and a guilty plea entered, it means the trial – when it eventually happens – should be relatively quick and painless.

'So it is.' Seb guides me to the doorway. 'Last piece of the puzzle solved.'

Not quite. That's what I'd like to say. But it's best to keep silent for now. Instead, I wait for him to close the door before I offer up the news. 'Max called.' I give him a breezy smile. 'It's all on for next week. He's lined up the golf pro. You've got to meet him in London though.'

'Oh, I don't know about that.' He touches my stomach. 'It's all getting a bit close.'

'Two weeks,' I remind him.

'And next week, it'll be one week.' He folds his arms. 'Why can't he come down here?'

'Busy man. And he's the best there is. You need to grab him while you can.'

'Golf.' Seb grimaces. 'Whose idea was a fucking golf course?'

'It's good for business,' I remind him, brushing an imaginary speck of dust from his shoulder. 'Just go up to London, ask him what he can offer, and tell him what's on the table.'

'Fine. But you're not coming.'

'I am.' A damn good glare lets him know I'm not about to change my mind. 'Ella's taking me to Hamleys.'

A pleasurable shopping trip in enjoyable company, cooing over fluffy toys and spending ridiculous amounts of money. It's definitely the first item on the itinerary, and I'm thoroughly looking forward to it.

I just wish I could say the same about the second.

***

Over the rim of a mug of coffee, Max Delaney raises an eyebrow. Alongside myself, and a man in a dirty anorak sitting a couple of tables away, we're the only punters in the place.

'Ready for this?' Max asks.

'Not really.' At the thought of what we're about to do, my stomach executes a little somersault. 'I'm just glad we're doing it together.'

'Strength in numbers.' He takes a sip of coffee.

Musing over how much the Rottweiler from Hell has changed over the past few months, I do the same. Not only is he now a loyal and trusting friend, he's also an excellent ally in a battle that's about to reach its climax.

'How was Hamleys?' he asks, clearly in need of a little distraction.

'Great,' I smile, happy to provide it. 'We pretty much cleared out the soft toy section.' And that was mostly down to Ella. 'I could be wrong, but I think your girlfriend's getting quite broody.'

'Is she now? That's interesting.'

'How's it going then?'

'With what?'

'Ella, of course.'

'Ah.' He smiles to himself. 'It's all good. Wonderful, in fact.'

Which is glaringly obvious to anyone with half a brain. After finding his perfect woman, Delaney the elder has finally come into his own. Distinctly laid back and always in a ridiculously good mood, by his own admission, he's evolved into a loved-up fool.

'So... when, exactly, are you going to propose?'

He puts down his mug, totally serious now. I'm about to apologise for being a nosey so-and-so when he breaks into a grin.

'As soon as the building work's finished at the club.' His eyes flash with barely concealed delight. 'I want to do it where we first met. On the front steps.'

Resisting the urge to execute a fist-pump, I nod.

'Do you think she'll say yes?' he asks.

'I know she'll say yes.' Largely because it was one of our topics of discussion this morning.

'Seb suggested your wedding day, but I'm not sure. It's not the done thing, is it?'

'I don't see a problem.'

'Really?'

'Really.'

'Excellent. Not a word to Ella though.'

'As if I would.' I take another sip of coffee and decide it's time to address the elephant in the room. 'Is that him?' I nod to the anorak-clad stranger. He's sitting with his back to us, head slumped.

'Yes. That's him.'

'What's he like?'

'Couldn't scare a mouse.'

'Still...'

'What?'

'I don't know.'

'You're getting cold feet.'

'Of course I am.' I chew at my bottom lip. 'It's just that Seb's come so far. I don't want to set him back.'

'It won't set him back.' Max checks his mobile. 'Trust me. He's about to be a dad. He knows it's time to sort out his shit. I just hope he's not in too much of a bad mood when he gets here. Being dragged down to Bermondsey after two hours with a golf pro, it's enough to try any man's patience.'

'Yes. Well...'

Whatever I was about to say flies straight out of my head. There's a sudden tightening of my stomach, which is nothing new. It's been going on all morning. But this time, it's accompanied by an intense ache at the small of my back.

Max frowns. 'Is my nephew kickboxing again?'

'Sort of.' I gasp. Out of nowhere, the ache transforms into pain. 'And for the last time...' I take a couple of deep breaths. The pain dies away. 'You don't know it's a boy.'

'And for the last time,' he smiles, 'I do. I'm omniscient. If you recall, I even predicted you'd be barefoot and pregnant within a year.'

'Because Seb told you we'd decided to go for it.' I run a hand over my huge stomach. 'A bit mad, but there you go. We didn't really expect it to happen so quickly.'

'Maybe the pair of you should have paid more attention to sex education lessons?'

'Maybe.' I chuckle. 'But we couldn't be happier.'

The doorbell jingles.

And I freeze.

'Business time.' Suddenly über-serious, Max turns to the door and waves a hand.

I've just about managed to un-freeze when Seb appears at my side. Surprisingly breezy after his morning meeting, he puts a hand on my shoulder.

'What's going on?' he asks.

'Sit down, and you'll find out.' Max nods to the spare chair.

With a quick glance at the stranger, Seb pulls out the chair and joins us. 'I assume we're here because one of you has gone completely mad and decided to buy this place.' He gives me a questioning look.

'No,' I answer firmly. 'It's already under new ownership.'

'And closed, according to the sign on the door.'

'Max paid the owner. The staff are out back, having a cup of tea.'

Suspicion takes hold. 'Why?'

'Because we needed the place to ourselves.'

'And again. Why?' The breeziness disappears.

'Because...' I falter. What sounded like a good idea last week, suddenly feels like the height of lunacy. But lunacy or not, I've reached the point of no return. 'We're here because this is neutral ground. And I thought it was appropriate... because it's where I met Hal.' Watching the clouds gather in his eyes, I falter again. 'All he ever wanted was for you to be happy.' I feel sick now, and I'm not entirely sure it's down to the fast-approaching endgame. That weird, aching sensation is back.

'I am happy.'

'But...' My mouth dries up. I look to Max for help.

Immediately, he takes the reins. 'You know as well as I do that nobody's truly happy until they've faced their demons.'

'Good job I've faced mine, then.'

'Not all of them.' Blow delivered, Max leans back and offers up the evidence. 'I happen to know this poor, heavily pregnant woman shares a bed with a man who won't switch off the bedside lamp.'

I open my mouth to intervene, but Max holds up a hand.

'She tells me it's not a problem. But that's not the point, is it?' Leaning forward, he places an index finger on the tabletop and fixes his attention on Seb. 'Unfortunately, I haven't got all day, so I'll cut to the quick. Forgive me for being blunt, but the point is this. You keep that light on because you're afraid of waking up in the dark. And you're afraid of that because it reminds you of the cellar. The fact is, you've still got a bogeyman in your head, brother. I know it, and Evie knows it too. So we've brought you here to let you know he's outstayed his welcome.' Clearly on a roll, he turns to the figure behind us and barks an order. 'Over here.'

324

On cue, the stranger rises to his feet. Slight of build, with thinning hair and vapid eyes, he shuffles towards our table, coming to a halt little more than a foot away.

'Raymond Barnes,' Max explains. 'Your final demon.'

My full attention darts to Seb, catching the tail end of a defensive scowl that quickly gives way to shock. Eyes wide, he shakes his head.

'You,' he breathes.

Barnes remains silent.

And the seconds tick by... until Max takes over again.

'A hundred pounds. That's all it took to bring him here today. Needless to say, it cost a damn sight more to track him down.' He checks on his brother. 'These days, Mr Barnes lives on the streets of Nottingham. That's why he went off the radar.' He looks back to Barnes. 'It's a sad story, really. A petty criminal who decided to try his hand at the big time and fell flat on his face. But that was just the beginning of the misery for Raymond. While he was in prison, his wife divorced him, which left him with nothing to come out to. No home, no job, no benefits. So now, he spends his days begging and drinking his own bodyweight in cheap cider. In fact, at the grand old age of sixty-one, it's a fucking miracle he's still alive.' He lets the information sink in. 'So this is your bogeyman, Seb. A nobody. A failure. A shell of a man.' He folds his arms. 'Mr Barnes, would you tell us something before you go? Did you, by any chance, send any letters to my brother?'

'What?' The vapid eyes narrow.

'You heard me. Did you send any letters?'

'Why would I do that?' He shuffles from one foot to the other.

'I don't know. Punishment, perhaps? Because you blame him for your misery.'

Other than more shuffling, there's no reaction.

'Well?' Max demands. 'Do you blame him?'

'Never give him a thought.'

'Of course you don't.' The Rottweiler returns, eyes flashing with murderous intent. 'Because you have no conscience, Mr Barnes. Because you're a piece of shit. And as such, you deserve everything you get.' He waves a hand. 'Now fuck off. You've served your purpose. My man's outside with the rest of your payment.'

Without another word, Raymond Barnes disappears from view.

The tinkle of the doorbell marks his exit, but it doesn't break the spell that seems to have settled over our table. While Max watches his brother and I fidget uncomfortably, waiting for an explosion that fails to materialise, Seb does nothing more than stare at a sugar bowl.

After a minute or so, Max gets to his feet and puts a hand on Seb's shoulder. 'I'll leave you two alone.'

I listen to his footsteps, a second tinkle of the bell.

Seb continues to stare at the bowl.

'Are you angry?' I ask, my heart rattling against my rib cage.

'No.' An answer so quiet, I almost miss it. 'I just need some time... to process.' Slowly returning to the moment, he looks up. 'I take it this was my brother's idea.'

'It was.'

He reaches for Max's unfinished coffee and takes a gulp.

'I know you don't like him interfering, but he wouldn't have done it without my say-so. And I wanted you to meet Barnes because you needed closure.'

'I understand.'

'You do?'

'Yes.' He puts down the mug. All signs of tension disappear. 'I'm okay,' he assures me. 'Honestly. It's just...' He leans back. 'I'd built him up in my head, Evie, and he never looked anything like that.'

Relieved this really was a good idea, I touch his arm. 'Like what?'

'I don't know. Broken.' He spends a few moments staring into space before he speaks again. 'It was Christophe, wasn't it? He sent those letters.'

'I think so. There's been nothing since he went to prison.'

'That's it, then...'

His eyes meet mine and for the next few seconds, we indulge in one of our favourite pastimes: drifting away in each other's gaze, soaking up the warmth like a pair of flowers idling in the sun.

'You know,' he says. 'It's going to be a hard habit to break.'

'What is?'

'Sleeping with the lamp on.'

'You don't have to...'

'I do.' He takes my hand in his. 'I don't want to be afraid of anything anymore.'

'Fear's not an easy thing to shake off.'

'But that doesn't make it impossible.' An eyebrow quirks. 'In fact, I happen to know a heavily pregnant woman who's making a pretty decent job of it.'

'She's still got a way to go,' I remind him.

'But she'll get there in the end, just like I will.' He treats me to one of his gloriously lopsided smiles. 'All it takes is patience and trust.'

'On both sides.' I'm about to float away for a second time when pain returns to my back. 'Oh, God,' I groan, finally facing the obvious. 'I think it's starting.'

'What is?'

'What do you think?'

He shifts closer. 'The baby?'

The pain spikes. Squeezing my eyes shut, I will myself not to scream.

'Evie? Is it the baby?'

'Yes,' I growl. 'Of course it's the sodding baby. Fucking hell!' Now, that's not good. Labour's only just begun and I'm already irritated beyond belief, running out of patience, and swearing to boot. No more of that, I decide, just as the contraction deepens. 'Oh, fuck!' I squeal. 'Shit, fuck, bugger, arse.'

'Right. That's it.' In an instant, Seb's on his feet. 'You need to get to a hospital.'

'No.' I hold up a hand. 'It's okay. Nothing to worry about. Plenty of time. Just call for the car.'

I'm urged up from the chair. The room sways precariously before settling back into place. The next thing I know, the pain's subsided and I'm gazing at a patch of Victorian brickwork.

'Ha!' I laugh. 'Now, that's fitting.'

'What is?' A hand comes to my back.

Gathering my senses, I turn to the man I love. 'New life.' I nod to the image of the phoenix.

He slips an arm around my back. 'So it is,' he smiles, smoothing his free hand over my stomach. 'New life for us all.'

Books by Mandy Lee

The *You Don't Know Me* Trilogy

You Don't Know Me (Book One)

Maya Scotton, a young artist with a severe case of painter's block, is in need of money. When she takes on an office job at a construction company, she finds herself firmly in the sights of the owner, Daniel Foster – a dangerously attractive man with a dark past and particular tastes in bed.

Although she tries to resist him, Maya soon finds herself embroiled in a steamy relationship with Dan. And while he slowly encourages her to paint again, she begins to peel back his layers. At last, when she believes that she's finally come to understand his ways, he has one final secret to reveal... and it's a secret that threatens to blow them apart.

True Colours (Book Two)

Reeling from the shock of discovering Dan's true identity, Maya struggles to make the right decision. But she's incapable of resisting the man she loves, and soon finds herself drawn back into his world – a world of intensely sexual passion.

While his love and support help her to confront her fears and blossom as an artist, what she needs more than anything is the ability to trust. Determined to discover the truth and build a future with Dan, she makes it her mission to find out what transformed him into the man he is now.

However, the shadows of the past won't leave them alone. And when those shadows converge, the consequences are far more dangerous than anyone could have predicted.

Shut Your Eyes (Book Three)

'I'd like to tell him we're never through with the past, that it's with us forever, sometimes out of sight, sometimes in full view, always unchangeable. We can only ever learn from it... and manage the consequences.'

Spending time apart from the man she loves, Maya's forced to survive in a world where nothing is what it seems. With her faith tested to the limit, a trip to New York sets off a train of events that will reunite her with Dan, but threaten to destroy everything they've worked so hard for.

Now, neither of them can hide from the past. If their love is to survive, they need to deal with the threats and face the truth.

The *X, Y, Z* Trilogy

X (Book One)

As her life spirals into crisis, Ella Fairbrother takes a risk. Visiting an elite sex club, she accepts a proposal from a man known only as 'X'. He wants her to wear a blindfold in the bedroom – to protect his anonymity – and in return, she'll experience pleasure that's off the charts.

A simple enough arrangement.

But it's soon complicated by Max Delaney, the new owner of the publishing house where Ella works. Enigmatic, ruthless and devastatingly handsome, he's a man who's used to getting exactly what he wants. And right now, he wants Ella.

Addicted to her mystery lover's touch, but plagued by questions over his true identity, Ella finds herself increasingly attracted to Max. So, what to believe about Mr Delaney? Rumours and gossip, or the claims of the man himself?

In a world where no one is quite what they seem, where should you place your trust?

Y (Book Two)

Haunted by the past and forced to live under an alias, Evie has spent months in limbo, keeping the world at arm's length. But when fate intervenes, setting off a disastrous chain of events that nearly end her life, she finds herself thrown into the path of Sebastian Delaney – a super-wealthy, dangerously handsome man with demons of his own.

Unable to resist temptation, they quickly embark on a steamy sexual relationship. But with so many secrets lurking in the shadows, will they ever be able to open up to each other? Or will the past consume them both?

Y is the second book in the X, Y, Z trilogy.

Z (Book Three)

— Coming in 2023

Robbed of her dream career in dance and forced to spend months in recovery after an accident, Amy Freelove is finally ready to live again. But when a chance meeting propels her into an intense relationship with a handsome surfer — the supremely confident Zach Reynolds — her future threatens to spiral into new chaos.

Still struggling to put together the missing pieces of Zach's colourful past, she's soon blind-sided by a bombshell neither of them expected: Zach is the son of Phillip Delaney, an all-powerful media magnate with a fearsome reputation.

Exposed to new dangers, and with life changing at lightning speed, will Amy find the confidence to fit in with Zach's glamorous new world? Or will her lover's biggest secret — dragged up by a blaze of unwanted publicity — manage to destroy them both?

Z is the third book in the *X, Y, Z* trilogy.

Printed in Great Britain
by Amazon

21810504R00192